Principles and Practice of Group Accounts: A European Perspective

Principles and Practice of Group Accounts: A European Perspective

Aileen Pierce
and
Niamh Brennan

Australia • Canada • Mexico • Singapore • Spain • United Kingdom • United States

Principles and Practice of Group Accounts: A European Perspective

For more information, contact Thomson Learning, High Holborn House, 50–51 Bedford Row, London WC1R 4LR or visit us on the World Wide Web at: http://www.thomsonlearning.co.uk

---

British Library Cataloguing-in-Publication Data
A catalogue record for this book is available from the British Library

---

ISBN 1-86152-928-7

First edition published by Thomson Learning, 2003

Typeset by Saxon Graphics Ltd, Derby
Printed in Great Britain by TJ International, Padstow, Cornwall

Contents

Foreword

The objective of the International Accounting Standards Board is to produce a single set of high-quality global standards. In doing so, we intend to look at national standards throughout the world and select the best as the global standard. Many national standard setters have already committed themselves to this objective so that no matter where a transaction occurs, be it in Dublin, Dusseldorf, Dunedin or Denver the accounting will be the same – at present there could well be four means of accounting for the same transaction.

For major companies, the group accounts are the statements to which most attention is paid. Worldwide, however, there are disputes about the way in which such accounts are compiled. Consolidation involves theories about the composition of the group itself. Arguments abound internationally over whether control of the operating and financial policies or of the Board should take precedence over ownership of 50% + 1 of the voting equity. Issues are raised about accounting for joint ventures which are not subsidiaries but operations involving joint control. Even more difficult questions arise over special purpose entities and what this book terms 'quasi-subsidiaries'. When should these corporate vehicles be consolidated? Will the control concept always work, or should we resort to a risks and benefits model? Given that the Enron disaster involved many of these special purpose entities this is clearly a pressing problem for standard setters worldwide.

This book looks at all of these major issues. It considers the differences between merger and acquisition accounting, an issue at the heart of an international debate on whether merger accounting should be prohibited. It discusses accounting for goodwill, again an area of controversy. But this book does more, it tells how business combinations should be put together – the adjustments to be made to ensure that only transactions external to the group are shown. In essence, it also deals with the nuts and bolts of consolidated accounts.

This book, therefore, serves several purposes. It puts consolidations in the context of the European regulatory framework, it discusses the structure and concepts of group accounting and then comprehensively deals with the mechanics of preparation of the consolidated balance sheet and profit and loss account.

A few of the issues discussed in the book may, by 2005, have new accounting requirements differing from those described in the following pages. Nevertheless it is important for the reader to understand the present situation and the reason for potential future actions of the IASB and national standard setters. Much of this book will remain unchanged no matter what the IASB decides. It is a clear route map for the construction of consolidated accounts – the foundation stone of a group's reporting to its owners and possible investors.

I congratulate Dr Pierce and Professor Brennan for giving the readers the benefit of their experience in teaching courses in group accounts over many years. Their students have been privileged.

Sir David Tweedie

Preface and acknowledgements

Preparation of group accounts is an area of immense difficulty for students. When we were accountancy students in the 1970s one of our recommended texts was a wonderful book *Consolidated Accounts* by Barry S. Topple. This book has been out of print for many years. No book on group accounts since then has (in our opinion) adequately dealt with the techniques for preparing group or consolidated accounts. Our primary objective in writing this book is to provide students with detailed guidance on the mechanics of preparing group accounts similar to that provided by Barry Topple many years ago. The book teaches consolidation primarily from a double entry book-keeping perspective of accounting, and it contains considerable technical detail. In that sense, it is computational and practical in nature. Accounting regulation has, however, expanded since the 1970s when Barry Topple's book was published. As a result, our book contains a significant amount of regulatory material, in addition to practical 'how to' guidance.

This book is long because it is comprehensive and extensive in its coverage of all topics related to group accounts. In addition to detailed technical coverage, it has a Europe-wide focus, with examples from published accounts of over 60 companies from 11 European countries. The book has five parts: Part 1 contains an introductory background chapter to group accounts. Parts 2 and 3 deal with the detailed mechanics of preparing group accounts, the consolidated balance sheet and consolidated profit and loss account, respectively. Part 4 deals with the regulatory framework. The book concludes with Part 5 which contains sundry other topics such as the treatment of foreign subsidiaries, consolidated cash flow statements, quasi subsidiaries and segmental reporting.

The book is primarily written with advanced accounting students (postgraduates or students of the professional accountancy bodies) in mind. However, parts 1, 2 and 3 are eminently suitable for final year undergraduate students. It may also be a useful reference book for practitioners.

Part 4 dealing with the regulatory framework sets out the professional accounting requirements in Financial Reporting Standards (FRSs) currently applying to UK and Irish companies, and those in the International Accounting Standards (IASs) of the International Accounting Standards Board. Accounting standards are in almost all respects the same in Ireland and the UK and the phrase *UK GAAP* is used to refer to these standards. The term *IAS GAAP* is used to refer to regulations in IASs. Legal regulations in any specific jurisdiction are not covered in Part 4 as these vary somewhat from European country to country. However, the requirements of the Fourth and Seventh Directives (which have been incorporated into legislation in EU member states) are referred to where relevant.

In June 2002 the EU adopted the International Accounting Standards (IAS) Regulation, whereby all EU listed companies will be required to comply with IASs by the year 2005.[1] This book addresses the significant impact of this EU regulation on the preparation of group accounts by identifying the similarities and differences between UK GAAP and IASs. In this manner, the changes to be made by UK companies to comply with IASs are highlighted.

Chapters start by setting out the learning objectives for the chapter, and end with a chapter summary and learning outcomes. In the majority of chapters, three distinct types of problem material then follow: ① multiple choice questions, ② self-assessment exercises and ③ examination-style questions. Solutions to the multiple choice questions are included in Appendix 1 in the book. Solutions to the self-assessment exercises are to be found in a companion website to the book at *www.thomsonlearning.co.uk/accountingandfinance/piercebrennan*. Solutions to the examination-style questions are available to the lecturers, at the same site. We acknowledge with thanks the permission of the Association of Chartered Certified Accountants, the Chartered Institute of Management Accountants, the Institute of Certified Public Accountants in Ireland, the Institute of Chartered Accountants in England and Wales, the Institute of Chartered Accountants in Ireland, and University College Dublin (UCD) for permission to reproduce questions from their past examination papers.

Given the aim and focus of the book to be a practical 'how to' guide, detailed worked examples are included throughout the text to illustrate the topics discussed in each chapter. These examples use an incremental, building block approach, building on students' knowledge by moving from simple to more advanced examples. In these examples, a standard approach to naming companies is adopted as follows: *Parent*, *Subsidiary* and *Associate*. No plc/Ltd (or international equivalent) is shown as part of the name. In a number of examples (particularly in Parts 4 and 5 of the book), we have adapted material from Peter Holgate's (and others) "Accounting solutions" column in *Accountancy* (the monthly magazine of the Institute of Chartered Accountants in England and Wales). We are grateful to Peter for his permission to use this material. The currency used throughout the book (other than in the exhibits from published accounts) is Euro, and years are shown as 20X0, 20X1, etc.

In relation to the chapters dealing with regulatory material (Parts 4 and 5), exhibits from published accounts from many European countries are reproduced to illustrate application of the regulations in practice. Exhibits were mainly taken from the top 50 UK listed companies and the top 50 European listed companies. Many of the European company accounts follow International Accounting Standards (IASs) but in some instances the company follows local or US GAAP (this has generally been pointed out in the text where relevant). Although not explicitly following IASs, these exhibits are included in the book because they illustrate issues discussed in the IAS regulation section of some chapters.

A number of willing assistants provided us with invaluable support in completing this book. Eithne Egan and Catherine Allen of the Department of Accountancy, UCD provided word processing expertise, especially in helping to reproduce exhibits from published accounts. Barry Smith obtained published accounts for the 100 companies from which we selected exhibits. He extracted examples and categorised these by topic, from which we

1 European Commission (2000). *EU Financial Reporting Strategy: The Way Forward*, European Commission (COM (200) 359), Brussels; Also available from www.europa.eu.int/comm/internal_market.

were able to select material for reproduction in the book. Two of our former students, Declan Maunsell and Dáibhí O'Leary, assisted us by reading and checking early draft material. Dáibhí, in particular, helped us with reading the proofs – a labour-intensive exercise which he carried out with his usual high professional standards and good humour.

We thank our Commissioning Editor, Pat Bond, for his encouragement and support, and our production editor, Paula McMahon, for her patience in dealing with our many corrections on the page proofs. We also acknowledge the assistance of Helen Baxter, our copy editor. Despite our best efforts at checking everything, and our many debates on some of the more obtuse technical issues, there may remain some errors, for which we apologise. We would greatly appreciate being made aware of any such errors discovered by readers.

We are delighted that Sir David Tweedie, Chairman of the International Accounting Standards Board, has provided the foreword to this book and we are grateful to him for his helpful insights and observations. Given the focus of the book on IAS GAAP as well as UK GAAP, we can think of no one more expert or appropriate to write the foreword.

Our respective families were both tolerant and supportive during the writing of this book, which strictly speaking commenced in 1991, but which required our special attention over the past two and a half years. We are blessed to have such forbearance and encouragement.

Last but not least, we thank our Master of Accounting students at UCD who since the 1980s have suffered to be taught a course on group accounts by one or other author. Over the years, they have provided critical feedback on the material which finally is captured in this book, particularly the contents of Parts 2 and 3. For their tolerance and insights we are particularly appreciative. We take heart from the knowledge that they have survived the experience to qualify as chartered accountants and put what they learnt at UCD into practice in the preparation and interpretation of group accounts for their clients or employers.

Aileen Pierce and Niamh Brennan
December 2002

Abbreviations

The following abbreviations have been used throughout the text, except in examples reproduced from company accounts.

ACCA	Association of Chartered Certified Accountants
ASB	Accounting Standards Board
ASC	Accounting Standards Committee
CIMA	Chartered Institute of Management Accountants
EC	European Commission
EEC	European Economic Community
ED	Exposure draft
EPS	Earnings per share
ESOT	Employee Share Ownership Trust
EU	European Union
FRC	Financial Reporting Council
FRRP	Financial Reporting Review Panel
FRS	Financial Reporting Standard
GAAP	Generally Accepted Accounting Principles
IAS	International Accounting Standard
IAS GAAP	Term used to refer to the adoption of accounting standards of the IASC/IASB
IASB	International Accounting Standards Board
IASC	International Accounting Standards Committee
ICAI	Institute of Chartered Accountants in Ireland
IFRIC	International Financial Reporting Interpretations Committee
IFRS	International Financial Reporting Standard
IOSCO	International Organization of Securities Commissions
JANE	Joint Arrangements that are Not Entities

PAYE	Pay As You Earn taxation
SEC	Securities and Exchange Commission
SIC	Standing Interpretations Committee
SSAP	Statement of standard accounting practice
STRGL	Statement of total recognised gains and losses
UITF	Urgent Issues Task Force
UK	United Kingdom
UK GAAP	Term used to refer to the professional accounting standards applying to UK and Irish companies
US	United States
VAT	Value added tax

List of exhibits from published accounts – by type of exhibit

Part One

Background

1

Business combinations and introduction to group accounts

Learning objectives

After studying this chapter you should be able to:

- differentiate between group accounts and consolidated accounts
- appreciate the various methods of combining businesses
- outline how investments are accounted for in individual accounts of parent companies
- understand different types of group structure
- appreciate the conceptual background underlying the preparation of group accounts

Introduction

The purpose of this chapter is to introduce the concepts, terminology and objectives of group accounts. Various methods of investing in other companies and of combining businesses are considered. Following this, the methods of accounting for such investments in the investor's accounts are described. Three basic group structures are then outlined. Regulations governing group accounts are briefly introduced and some of the terminology in these regulations is considered. The chapter concludes by examining the rationale behind group accounts and some of the concepts underlying alternative methods of preparing group accounts.

Group accounts

If a company invests in another company, all that appears in the accounts of the investor company is the original cost of the investment which is shown in the balance sheet and dividends received (if any) appear in the profit and loss account. This provides very limited information about the investment. If the investee pays no dividends, no information is available on the performance of the investment. If the investee is increasing in value, this will not be reflected in the individual accounts of the investor as the investment is generally shown at cost in the investor's balance sheet.

Group or consolidated financial statements show the financial position and results of a group of companies as if the group were a single entity. A group consists of a parent company (also referred to as a 'holding' company) and its subsidiaries. It may also include investments in associated companies and other investments such as joint ventures. Group financial statements are prepared by the holding company in addition to its own individual company financial statements.

Group financial statements normally comprise a consolidated balance sheet, a consolidated profit and loss account and usually a consolidated cash flow statement. Under United Kingdom (UK) and Irish regulations, the annual report of a group will also include the individual balance sheet of the parent company, but not the individual profit and loss account – this does not have to be shown provided the accounts disclose separately the amount of the parent company's profit or loss that is included in the group consolidated profit and loss account.

In the consolidated balance sheet, the holding company's asset, *Investment in subsidiaries*, is replaced by the underlying assets and liabilities of the subsidiaries. In the consolidated profit and loss account, *Income from financial assets in subsidiaries* (i.e., investment income from subsidiaries) is replaced by the underlying revenues and expenses of the subsidiaries. The purpose of consolidated financial statements is to report the financial position and results of a group controlled by the parent to its shareholders.

Group accounts are prepared when one company controls another. Otherwise, when a company owns shares in another company, it includes the investment in its balance sheet at cost and includes dividend income in its profit and loss account when received or receivable. However, where a company has a substantial shareholding in another company without having a controlling interest, including the investment at cost may not provide shareholders with useful or sufficient information about the investment. Equity accounting was introduced to deal with such situations. Investments where the holding company's investment is substantial but not a controlling interest and where the holding company exercises significant influence are referred to as 'associated' or 'related' companies.

Group accounts versus consolidated accounts

In practice, the terms 'group' accounts/financial statements and 'consolidated' accounts/financial statements are used interchangeably, but technically speaking they are not exactly the same. Consolidated financial statements are one form of group accounts and group accounts are normally presented in consolidated form. Consolidated accounts present the information contained in the separate accounts of the parent and its subsidiaries as if they were the accounts of a single entity.

However, 'group accounts' is a wider term comprising the accounts (not just the consolidated accounts) of all companies in a group. For example, a holding company may prepare consolidated financial statements to include some of its subsidiaries, with separate statements for others.

In addition, group accounts may include entities (subsidiaries) that are consolidated and non-consolidated entities such as associates, joint ventures, joint arrangements etc. These non-consolidated entities will be included in group accounts using methods of accounting other than full consolidation, such as the equity method, the gross equity method, proportional consolidation, etc.

Methods of combining businesses and investing in other entities

Businesses can combine in a number of ways: by absorption, amalgamation or by acquisition of shares. These alternative methods of business combination are summarised in Table 1.1.

Table 1.1 Types of business combination

Type of combination	*Company A*	*Company B*	*New company*
Absorption			
Company A takes over assets and liabilities of Company B. Company B ceases to exist.	No change	Liquidation	No formation
Amalgamation			
AB formed to take over assets and liabilities of Company A and Company B. Company A and Company B cease to exist.	Liquidation	Liquidation	Formation
Acquisition of shares			
New holding company			
AB formed to acquire shares in Company A and in Company B	No change	No change	Formation
Share exchange			
Company A acquires shares of Company B and issues its own shares as consideration	No change	No change	No formation

Absorption

Absorption is where the various assets (and sometimes liabilities) of a business are acquired by another business. The first business ceases to exist. These assets (and liabilities) are included with the acquiring company's own assets (and liabilities). Any difference between the amount paid for the net assets and the value of those assets is recorded as goodwill (which may be positive or negative depending on whether the amount paid is higher or lower than the value of the assets).

Amalgamation

Amalgamation is where the various assets (and sometimes liabilities) of two or more businesses are acquired by a newly formed business and the original businesses cease to exist. As with absorption, the assets (and liabilities) acquired are included with the acquiring company's own assets (and liabilities). Any difference between the amount paid for the net assets and the value of those assets is recorded as goodwill (which may be positive or, less likely, negative).

Acquisition of shares

Acquisitions of companies occur when one company acquires shares in another company. The two companies continue to exist independently. The only change in the acquired company caused by its shares being acquired by new owners is in its share register. These shares acquired may be paid for by:

- cash
- issuing shares
- issuing loan stock
- a combination of all three.

Shares may be acquired by a new holding company or by an existing company. Shares may be acquired in exchange for issuing shares in the acquiring company to the shareholders of the acquired company. In this case, the shareholders of the acquired company continue to have an interest (albeit indirectly through the parent company) and, in addition, they now have a shareholding in the acquiring company. When shares are acquired for cash the relationship of the previous shareholders with the acquired company ceases.

Where more than 50% of the ordinary share capital of a company is acquired, the acquiring company is deemed to have control of the company acquired. (In practice, however, the definition of a subsidiary is usually more complex.) The acquired company (generally referred to as *Subsidiary* in this book) becomes a subsidiary of the acquiring company (generally referred to as *Parent* in this book).

The parent company's individual company accounts will include an asset *Investment in subsidiaries* in the balance sheet, usually within *Financial fixed assets*. This asset represents the cost of shares acquired by Parent in Subsidiary. The profit and loss account of Parent will only include dividends received and/or receivable from Subsidiary.

The information in the parent company's accounts has long been seen as inadequate:

- in reflecting the investors' interests in subsidiaries controlled by their company
- in reporting the income earned by subsidiaries on capital employed therein.

Thus, there is a need for consolidated accounts to provide full information on the group of companies comprising the parent or holding company and its subsidiaries. The consolidated accounts combine the net assets at the year-end and income of all group companies for the period.

Accounting for subsidiaries in individual parent company accounts

The purchase of shares in a subsidiary is reported by the parent company in its individual company (rather than consolidated) balance sheet. In addition, the parent's share of dividends declared and paid/payable by the subsidiary are reported in the individual profit and loss account of the parent company.

Parent company balance sheet

When Parent purchases shares in Subsidiary, the purchase is recorded at cost in the balance sheet. Such an acquisition of shares is usually intended to be held for the long term. Consequently, the cost is recorded as part of *Fixed assets*, and under the sub-heading *Financial assets*.

Example 1.1 illustrates this treatment. In this case, the transaction has no effect on the 'financed by' section of Parent's balance sheet. Only the assets are affected, net current assets reducing by the amount of the cash payment (€200) to purchase the shares in Subsidiary. The cost of the shares in Subsidiary is shown as part of *Fixed assets*, under a separate heading *Financial assets*.

Example 1.1 Accounting for the purchase of shares in Subsidiary by paying cash: Parent's balance sheet

Example

Parent acquired 80% of Subsidiary in return for a payment of cash of €200. Parent's balance sheet before the transaction is as follows:

	Before purchase Parent
	€
Fixed assets	
Tangible assets	870
Net current assets	625
	1,495
Share capital (€1 shares)	700
Reserves	795
	1,495

Required

Show the balance sheet of Parent after purchase of Subsidiary.

Solution

	Adjustment	After purchase Parent
	€	€
Fixed assets		
Tangible assets		870
Financial assets	+200	200
		1,070
Net current assets	–200	425
		1,495
Share capital		700
Reserves		795
		1,495

In Example 1.2, the same information is assumed as in Example 1.1 except that, instead of paying €200 in cash, 160 ordinary €1 shares were issued at a value of €1.25 each. In this case, the transaction does affect the 'financed by' section of Parent's balance sheet. The share capital and the share premium amounts increase. These increases are matched by the cost of the shares in Subsidiary which is shown as part of *Fixed assets*, under a separate heading *Financial assets*.

Example 1.2 Accounting for the purchase of shares in Subsidiary by issuing shares in Parent: Parent's balance sheet

Example

Parent acquired 80% of Subsidiary in return for issuing 160 €1 shares at an issue price of €1.25 each.

	Before purchase Parent
	€
Fixed assets	
Tangible assets	870
Net current assets	625
	1,495
Share capital (€1 shares)	700
Reserves	795
	1,495

Required

Show the balance sheet of Parent after purchase of Subsidiary.

Solution

	Adjustment	After purchase Parent
	€	€
Fixed assets		
Tangible assets		870
Financial assets	+200	200
		1,070
Net current assets		625
		1,695
Share capital	+160	860
Share premium	+40	40
Reserves		795
		1,695

Parent company profit and loss account

When the subsidiary pays a dividend, the parent's share of this dividend is credited in its individual profit and loss account as part of *Income from financial assets* (the debit side of the entry is in *Bank and cash* in the balance sheet). Dividends proposed by the subsidiary can also be included in *Income from financial assets* as dividends receivable (the related asset is included in *Debtors* in the balance sheet).

Group structures

Group structures are introduced briefly in this chapter. Detailed consideration of group structures is outlined and explained in Chapter 6 in Part 2 of this book, which deals with consolidated balance sheets.

There is an infinite variety of structures comprising a parent and its subsidiaries in a group of companies. In practice, a group of companies can form a complex network of holdings.

Three simple examples of alternative forms or structures are now discussed and these are illustrated in Example 1.3.

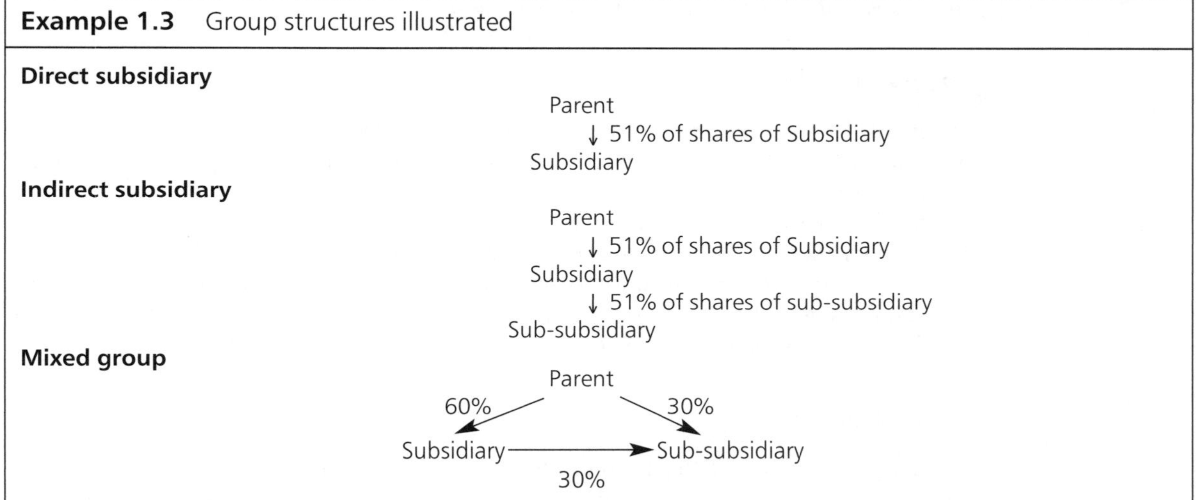

It is essential for students to identify and be clear on the group structure at the start of the year and to identify any changes to the group during the year (e.g., subsidiaries acquired or disposals of previously held subsidiaries). The starting point in completing examination questions should be to set out in diagrammatic form the group structure (such as is done in Example 1.3).

Group accounts are prepared when one company 'controls' another. There is a distinction between the proportion of share capital over which the parent exercises control and the effective rate of ownership.

To determine whether a Subsidiary relationship exists, the proportion over which the parent exercises control is identified. This is the aggregate of the holdings of the parent and the *whole* of each subsidiary's holding (without deduction for any minority) in a potential subsidiary. Where control is exercised over more than 50% of the voting share capital of the company, a parent–subsidiary relationship is assumed to exist (but not necessarily so – see definitions later in this chapter and further discussion of what constitutes a subsidiary relationship in Chapter 14).

The effective rate of ownership used to determine the group share and the minority interest for consolidated accounts purposes allows for minority interests in the shareholdings. Thus, the percentage shareholding for determining whether control is exercised and for determining the effective percentage ownership may be different – differing by the minority interest which is not deducted in determining effective ownership. The effective ownership of a subsidiary may be less than 50% – in some cases substantially less than 50%.

Direct subsidiary

There are many ways for a parent or holding company (referred to throughout this book as Parent) to acquire an interest in a subsidiary (referred to throughout this book as Subsidiary). A direct subsidiary arises where the parent controls the subsidiary through its own shareholding (rather than through another subsidiary). A simple example of this is where Parent owns more than 50% of the ordinary share capital of Subsidiary. Following this, Subsidiary is a direct subsidiary of Parent.

Indirect subsidiary

When a subsidiary of Parent has its own subsidiary (Sub-subsidiary), Sub-subsidiary is automatically a subsidiary of Parent. A group structure comprising a parent, a subsidiary and a sub-subsidiary is called a vertical group.

The effective interest of Parent in Sub-subsidiary may be less than 50%. For example, if Parent owns 60% of Subsidiary and Subsidiary owns 60% of Sub-subsidiary, then the effective interest of Parent in Sub-subsidiary is 36% ($60\%_{\text{Parent}} \times 60\%_{\text{Subsidiary}} = 36\%$). However, because Parent controls Subsidiary and Subsidiary controls Sub-subsidiary, Sub-subsidiary is also controlled by Parent.

Mixed group

Sometimes a sub-subsidiary is controlled through a combination of direct ownership of shares by Parent and indirect holding through shares owned by Subsidiary. If the combined percentage of ordinary share capital controlled in Sub-subsidiary is more than 50%, the investment is deemed to be an investment in a subsidiary (even if the group's effective interest in the ordinary share capital of Sub-subsidiary is less than 50%).

This is illustrated in Example 1.3. Parent owns 60% of Subsidiary and Subsidiary owns 30% of the share capital of Sub-subsidiary. Subsidiary is a subsidiary of Parent but Sub-subsidiary is not a subsidiary of Subsidiary. However, Parent also owns 30% of Sub-subsidiary. Consequently, Sub-subsidiary is a subsidiary of Parent because the *combined* holding of Parent and Subsidiary is more than 50%. Parent controls Sub-subsidiary through control of 60% of the shares in Sub-subsidiary. The group's effective interest in Sub-subsidiary is only 48% (i.e., $30\%_{\text{Parent}} + [60\% \times 30\%_{\text{Subsidiary}}]$).

Regulations governing group accounts

There are four sources of regulations that influence the preparation of group accounts. These are:

1 Legal regulations of the country of incorporation of the parent company.
2 EU regulations, notably the Fourth Directive on company accounts and the Seventh Directive on group accounts which will have been promulgated in individual EU countries through legislation.

3 Professional accounting requirements of the country of incorporation of the parent company.
4 International accounting regulations.

In the case of listed groups, stock exchange regulations will also apply, but these regulations have a relatively minor impact on published group accounts.

The detailed regulations applying to group accounts are outlined and explained in Part 4 of this book, which deals with the regulatory framework for group accounts. Legal regulations are not discussed as these will vary from jurisdiction to jurisdiction. The Seventh Directive is mentioned only where necessary. Thus, Part 4 concentrates on professional accounting standards under:

- UK generally accepted accounting principles (GAAP) – UK GAAP
- international accounting standards as set out in standards of the International Accounting Standards Board (IASB – formerly the International Accounting Standards Committee (IASC)) – IAS GAAP.

Definitions

Legislation dealing with group accounts uses a number of basic terms which are introduced here. They are discussed in more detail in Part 4 which explains the regulations concerning group accounts. In the context of group accounts, the terms undertaking, parent undertaking, subsidiary undertaking, associates and minority interest appear throughout this book. Consequently, brief descriptions of what these terms represent are included in this introductory chapter.

Undertaking

An *undertaking* is a body corporate or partnership or an unincorporated association carrying on a trade or business, with or without a view to profit (section 259 (1) UK Companies Act 1985).

Parent undertaking

The definition of *parent undertaking* in legislation is complex and is discussed in detail in Chapter 14. At this juncture it is sufficient to say that a parent undertaking is an undertaking that has one or more subsidiary undertakings.

Subsidiary undertaking

The EU Seventh Directive changed the definition of a subsidiary for the purpose of consolidated financial statements from one based strictly on the form of the shareholding relationship between the companies to one which reflected the substance of the commercial relationship. In particular, the focus is now on whether the reporting company actually, in fact, exercises control – referred to as *de facto* control.

The definition of a *subsidiary undertaking* is contained in Articles 1, 2 and 3 of the Seventh Directive. The definition is somewhat legalistic and is summarised (rather than quoted verbatim) here, as follows:

An undertaking is deemed to be a subsidiary of another if, and only if, the other (i.e., the parent):

(1.A) – holds a majority of voting rights; or
(1.B) – is a member, and has the right to appoint or remove a majority of members of its board; or
(1.C) – has the right to exercise dominant influence over it
  (i) by provisions in memorandum or articles; or
  (ii) through a control contract;
(1.D) – is a member of, and
  (i) controls through the exercise of voting rights a majority of its board;
  (ii) controls a majority of voting rights;
(2) – has a participating interest, and
  (i) actually exercises a dominant influence; or
  (ii) both are managed on a unified basis;
(3) – is a subsidiary of any subsidiary undertaking.

Example 1.4 illustrates the application of this definition, showing that the exercise of control through the exercise of voting rights, rather than the absolute percentage of shares held, is the critical determinant of control.

Example 1.4 Percentage shareholdings and percentage shares carrying voting rights

Example
Subsidiary has the following share capital structure:
10,000 A voting ordinary shares
10,000 B non-voting ordinary shares

Both classes of share have the same dividend rights.

Consider the following possible shareholdings:
(i) Parent owns 6,000 A ordinary shares
(ii) Parent owns 10,000 B ordinary shares and 4,000 A ordinary shares

Required
Discuss the implications of the two possible shareholdings for the status of the investment.

Solution
(i) Parent would own 30% of the total shares in Subsidiary (6,000/20,000). This would suggest that the investment should be treated as an associated company investment (assuming other conditions relating to associated company status were satisfied). However, as Parent owns 60% of the voting shares (6,000/10,000), it does, in fact, control Subsidiary and should account for the investment as a subsidiary.
(ii) Parent would own 70% of the ordinary shares in Subsidiary ((10,000 + 4,000)/20,000). Although it may appear that a 70% ownership of the ordinary shares should convey a subsidiary company status, close attention to the holding of the *voting* shares reveals that Parent holds only 40% of them. Thus, Subsidiary would not be a subsidiary of Parent and may not even be an associate.

Although there is a presumption of associated company status when the investor's share of the voting shares is 20% or above (see brief explanation below), there is no guarantee that this would give the investor the required significant influence. This would depend on other factors such as who holds the other shares in Subsidiary. For example, if another company owns the remaining 60% of Subsidiary, it would be a subsidiary of the other company as it would be under that other company's control. Many commentators believe that in these circumstances a 40% shareholding would not be able to exert significant influence and thus would not constitute an interest in an associated company.

Associates

Associates are considered in more detail in Chapters 7, 11 and 15. At this stage in the book, it is sufficient to state that associates are those entities in which the investor has a participating interest enabling the exercise of significant influence. Generally speaking, equity holdings of more than 20% and less than 50% are presumed to be investments in associates.

Minority interest

Minority interest is the interest in net assets of a subsidiary attributable to shares held by those other than the parent undertaking and its subsidiaries.

Concepts underlying group accounts

Shareholders of a holding company do not automatically receive copies of subsidiary company accounts as they are not shareholders of those companies. Even if they did receive the individual accounts of companies in a group, such accounts do not meet the needs of holding company shareholders who are interested in information concerning the financial position of a group of enterprises. Consolidated financial statements are designed to give effect to the economic substance of the intra-group relationships, rather than the strict legal form of the corporate relationships.

The traditional approach to preparing group accounts focuses on providing information for the equity investors of the parent undertaking. As the dominant shareholders in the subsidiary, the interests of the minority shareholders are seen as secondary. This approach is sometimes referred to as the parent company concept. Under the parent company concept, there is an assumption that the parent company has the power to exercise control (rather than *actually* exercising control).

Consolidation is the process whereby the individual accounts of a parent company and each of its subsidiaries are combined and presented as if they were those of a single entity without regard for the legal boundaries between the companies in the group. It essentially involves aggregating the amounts shown in each of the individual accounts, on a line-by-line basis, and making appropriate adjustments to achieve consistency of measurement and to eliminate double counting.

It is important to appreciate that it is the individual companies in a group that are the legal entities. Double entries are made to record transactions in the accounts of those legal entities. Consolidated accounts, while legally required, are not prepared from a comprehensive double-entry system. Rather, they come from an amalgamation of parent and subsidiary final accounts.

Concepts of control

Control is defined by the various regulations governing group accounts. Control is important in determining whether a particular investment is classified as a subsidiary and thus whether the investment is required to be consolidated in group accounts.

As we saw earlier, the percentage holdings to assess whether control exists and percentages relating to the effective interest of Parent in Subsidiary can differ. Thus, the percentages applied in calculations for consolidation purposes will differ from those percentages that determine whether a controlling interest is held. Part 2 of this book explains and illustrates the use of effective interests when preparing consolidated balance sheets.

As already explained, the definition of subsidiary undertaking was changed by the Seventh Directive. Two concepts of control underlie the definitions in the Seventh Directive.

Legal control concept

In the UK and Ireland, before enactment of the Seventh Directive, the legal definition of control was based on ownership of more than 50% of equity (rather than voting) shares. In addition, control of composition of board of directors would have resulted in a parent–subsidiary relationship.

In countries such as the US and Australia, legal control is defined as the ownership of a majority of shares with voting rights (sometimes called the *de jure* approach). Ownership may be held directly or indirectly through other subsidiaries.

The legal concept of control is evident in the Seventh Directive's definition of subsidiary undertaking, in that holding a majority of voting shares gives rise to a parent–subsidiary relationship, as does control of the composition of the board of directors. However, the Seventh Directive's definition is much broader and also encompasses the economic concept of control.

Economic concept of control

Under the economic (or entity) concept of control (also called *de facto* concept of control) practised in Germany, control is judged by reference to the economic reality of the relationship between the parties. Thus, if legally independent entities are managed under a mutually agreed system of central management, a group is deemed to exist irrespective of shareholdings. The entities comprising a group of companies, and forming an economic unit, are considered together in determining whether control can be exercised or not.

The original definition of a subsidiary included in the Seventh Directive was based on the German economic concept of control. After objection by some member states, the original directive was modified to allow the legal concept of control as the principal criterion but the Directive also accommodates the German concept.

A third concept is the proprietary concept which is referred to briefly in the following section.

Methods of accounting for investments

Investments in other companies (e.g., shares, debentures, etc.) can be accounted for at cost or by using one of a number of consolidation approaches. Each of these is now discussed briefly. The methods are described in more detail in the relevant chapters later in the book.

Cost method

Under the cost method of accounting for investments, in the investing company's own individual accounts, the asset *Investments* is recorded at cost in the balance sheet. Dividends are recorded in the profit and loss account when received or receivable (as described earlier).

Under the cost method, no consolidated accounts are prepared. Prior to the mid-20th century, there were no legal or professional accounting requirements to prepare group accounts. Most companies would have accounted for *all* their investments using the cost method. That is, the asset/investment is recorded and reported at its original cost.

This approach, however, is not considered adequately to reflect performance or value for significant investments. Nowadays, this method of accounting for investments is only suitable for holdings that are classified as *simple* investments – generally holdings of less than 20% – although there are some limited circumstances when investments in subsidiaries might be accounted for in this way.

Methods of consolidation

There are a number of methods of incorporating the activities of investments in group accounts, including:

- acquisition method (the most common method)
- merger method
- equity method
- gross equity method
- proportional consolidation.

These methods are briefly introduced in this section and are explained in detail in Parts 2 and 3 of the book.

The acquisition method is also called the 'purchase method' (particularly in the US) and 'capital consolidation' (in European countries such as Germany). This is the traditional and most widely used method of consolidating the accounts of parent companies and their subsidiaries.

The merger method is also called the 'pooling of interests' method (particularly in the US) and the 'uniting of interests' method (IAS GAAP). Regulations indicate that this method should only be used in rare or exceptional instances, where the business combination meets strict criteria. However, in practice, the merger method is more frequently found than would be suggested by the words 'rare' or 'exceptional' referred to in regulations.

These two methods are briefly described here and are dealt with in more detail in later chapters. The acquisition method is the method primarily used throughout this book, especially in Parts 2 and 3. The merger method is considered in Chapters 9 and 16.

Acquisition method

The holding company's *Investment in subsidiary* is replaced by the underlying net assets of the subsidiary. Thus, consolidated accounts are an extension of the parent company accounts. *All* assets and liabilities of subsidiaries are brought into the consolidated accounts to reflect the fact that these are under the control of the holding company.

Minority shareholders are regarded as outsiders and, consequently, minority interest in net assets of subsidiaries is disclosed in the group balance sheet as a separate item, shown outside shareholders' funds. Minority interest is not treated as a liability since minority shareholders are not entitled to payment of the amount disclosed in the consolidated accounts as their interest. It is included after shareholders' funds to indicate its role in financing some of the net assets of the group.

Equally, the consolidated profit and loss account includes *all* revenues and expenses of the group, with the minority's share of profit shown as a separate deduction in the consolidated profit and loss account.

The acquisition method is the traditional method of accounting for investments in subsidiaries. Part 2 of this book (Chapters 2 to 6 in particular) explains how the consolidated balance sheet is constructed using this method of accounting. Part 3 (Chapters 10 to 12) explains the techniques involved in preparing consolidated profit and loss accounts applying acquisition accounting principles.

Merger method

Under the merger method, parent and subsidiaries are combined as if the parent–subsidiary relationship had always existed, even before the combination. The resulting consolidated balance sheet and consolidated profit and loss account are very different from those prepared following acquisition accounting principles. This method may, under restrictive circumstances, be used instead of the acquisition method and is discussed in more detail in Chapters 9 and 16.

Equity method

The equity method of accounting is defined in FRS 2 and FRS 9 and this definition is reproduced in Chapters 7, 11 and 15. In effect, it involves reporting the investment in the investee in the group accounts as a single-line entry in the consolidated balance sheet and consolidated profit and loss account. It reports the group's share of the (i) results and (ii) net assets of the investee (plus any unamortised goodwill on the acquisition). This is equivalent to showing the investment at original cost plus the group share of post-acquisition retained reserves of the investee. This method of accounting is primarily used to account for investments in associates and joint ventures, but there are also limited circumstances where it might apply to investments in subsidiaries.

The 'one-line' equity method does not always give an adequate indication of the extent to which the holding company's business is conducted through the investee (such as an associate). For example, the group's share in a highly geared joint venture investment might look small, whereas its scale of operation might be significantly larger than that of the holding company itself.

The practical application of the equity method of accounting is explained in detail in Chapter 7 (balance sheet) and Chapter 11 (profit and loss account). The regulations governing the equity method of accounting are dealt with in detail in Chapter 15.

Gross equity method

To provide additional information where a substantial proportion of the group's activities is conducted through an equity accounted entity, the gross equity method is sometimes used. While similar to the 'one-line' equity method, the gross (or 'expanded') equity method gets around the problem of the equity method highlighted earlier. Under the gross equity method, the figure for *Investment in investee* is analysed separately into the group's share of investee company assets and liabilities and the profit and loss account analyses turnover separately.

The gross equity method is the method recommended by FRS 9 to account for investments in joint ventures. The computations and the regulations required under the gross equity method of accounting are set out in more detail in Chapter 15.

Proportional consolidation

In proportional consolidation, only that proportion of the net assets of the subsidiary belonging to the parent company is brought into the consolidation. The group share of assets, liabilities and profits are included in group amounts (not separately disclosed). Only the assets and liabilities of proprietors are recorded (i.e., only the group share of assets and liabilities is included and only the group share of intra-group gains/losses is eliminated). Thus, no minority interest is recognised under this method. This method of consolidation is based on the proprietary concept of control. This concept caters for companies that are not controlled by any one company.

This method is appropriate where there is no legal dominance and no single parent company. It can cater for enterprises belonging to more than one group. However, it is the recommended method of accounting for non-corporate joint ventures in FRS 9. This method is disallowed by the Seventh Directive in respect of subsidiaries. Proportional consolidation is considered further in Chapter 15 and using simple data, four of the five methods discussed here, i.e., the acquisition method, the equity method, the gross equity method and proportional consolidation, are compared.

Limitations of consolidated accounts

Aggregated information

Consolidated accounts focus on the information needs of equity shareholders of the parent undertaking. They are less useful for other stakeholders such as creditors, lenders, tax authorities and employees because information is in aggregate and is not analysed undertaking by undertaking. However, it is acknowledged that most of these interest groups will have access to individual accounts of the companies concerning them and published in accordance with the requirements of the Fourth Directive.

The aggregated nature of the data means that 'average' group performance is reported in consolidated accounts. No distinction is made between profitable and loss-making subsidiaries. For example, it is possible that in the consolidated profit and loss account, losses made by some poorly performing group companies will be cloaked by profits of others. Similarly, in relation to the consolidated balance sheet, financial difficulties and potential insolvencies of subsidiaries may be hidden. It is important to recognise that a group is not a legal entity and that the assets of the group may not be available to satisfy the liabilities of the group. Only the assets of a legal entity can be used to pay the liabilities of that entity.

To some extent, segmental analysis provides some further analysis of the aggregated amounts reported in consolidated financial statements. This is discussed in Chapter 20.

Other limitations

Additional limitations of consolidation include:

- consolidated accounts are subject to the same criticisms as single-entity financial reports. For example, they do not reflect current values. They are backward looking and many valuable assets, such as intellectual capital, are excluded
- ratio analysis of consolidated accounts is difficult due to aggregation of information.
- the requirement for group companies to follow the same accounting policies notwithstanding, there may nonetheless be some residual differences in valuation/classification policies in the group that may distort consolidated results.

Summary

This chapter has introduced some of the basic principles and terminology relating to group accounts. The remainder of this book considers all of these in more detail. The mechanics of the calculations involved in preparing consolidated balance sheets are explained and illustrated in Part 2, while the consolidated profit and loss account techniques and computations are dealt with in Part 3. The regulatory framework, including regulations under UK and Irish generally accepted accounting principles (referred to throughout the book as UK GAAP) and regulations under international accounting standards (referred to throughout the book as IAS GAAP) is covered in Part 4. The book concludes with sundry other aspects of group accounts in Part 5, including foreign currency considerations and consolidated cash flow statements.

Learning outcomes

After studying this chapter you should have learnt:

- the difference between group accounts and consolidated accounts
- to appreciate the various methods of combining businesses
- how investments are accounted for in individual accounts of parent companies
- to distinguish between different types of group structure
- to appreciate the conceptual background underlying the preparation of group accounts.

Multiple choice questions

Solutions to these questions are prepared under UK GAAP and are presented in Appendix 1.

1.1 Red

Which of the following companies would *not* be a subsidiary undertaking of **Red**?

(a) Black
Red holds 60% of the voting rights of Black.

(b) Blue
Red is a member of Blue and has the right to appoint directors holding a majority of the voting rights at meetings of the board of directors on substantially all matters.

(c) White
Red has the right to exercise a dominant influence over White by virtue of a control contract.

(d) Green
Red has a participating interest in Green but does not exercise a dominant influence.

1.2 Sam

Sam has a share capital of €10,000 split into 2,000 A ordinary shares of €1 each and 8,000 B ordinary shares of €1 each. Each A ordinary share has ten votes and each B ordinary share has one vote. Each class of shares has the same rights to dividends and on liquidation. Tom owns 1,500 A ordinary shares in Sam. Dick owns 6,000 B ordinary shares in Sam.

All three companies conduct similar activities and there is no special relationship between the companies other than that already stated. The shareholdings in Sam are held as long-term investments and are the only shareholdings of Tom and Dick.

Sam is a subsidiary of:

(a) Neither Tom nor Dick
(b) Tom only
(c) Dick only
(d) Both Tom and Dick

1.3 Reddie, Ret and Asy

Reddie has 10,000 A equity shares and 50,000 B equity shares. The only difference between the two classes of shares is in voting rights. Each A equity share has eight votes and each B equity share has one vote. **Ret** owns 9,000 A shares and **Asy** owns 45,000 B shares. There is no other connection between the three companies.

Is Reddie a subsidiary of:

	Ret	Asy
(a)	No	No
(b)	No	Yes
(c)	Yes	Yes
(d)	Yes	No

1.4 Alice, Betty and Carol

Alice owns 90% of **Betty**. Betty owns 70% of **Carol**. Carol owns 30% of Dawn and 60% of Eve. Eve owns 30% of Dawn.

The following are subsidiaries of Alice:

(a) Betty
(b) Betty and Carol
(c) Betty, Carol and Eve
(d) Betty, Carol, Dawn and Eve

1.5 Jack, Packie and Kevin

Jack owns 90% of **Packie** and 30% of **Kevin**. Packie owns 25% of Kevin and 60% of Paul. Paul owns 40% of Roy.

Which of the following should be accounted for as subsidiaries of Jack:

(a) Packie
(b) Packie and Kevin
(c) Packie, Kevin and Paul
(d) Packie, Kevin, Paul and Roy

1.6 Anna, Bella and Emma

Anna owns 80% of **Bella** and 15% of **Emma**. Bella owns 80% of Camilla and 40% of Emma. Camilla owns 60% of Dora.

The subsidiaries of Anna are:

(a) Bella
(b) Bella and Camilla
(c) Bella, Camilla and Dora
(d) Bella, Camilla, Dora and Emma

1.7 Ash, Beech and Cedar

Ash owns 80% of **Beech**. Beech owns 55% of **Cedar** and 70% of Oak. Cedar owns 30% of Elm and Oak owns 40% of Elm.

The following companies are subsidiaries of Ash:

(a) Beech
(b) Beech and Oak
(c) Beech, Oak and Cedar
(d) Beech, Oak, Cedar, and Elm

1.8 Alan, Brian and Colin

Alan owns 70% of **Brian** and 25% of **Colin**. Brian owns 30% of Colin and 10% of David. Colin owns 50% of David and 30% of Eric.

The subsidiaries of Alan are:

(a) Brian
(b) Brian and Colin
(c) Brian, Colin and David
(d) Brian, Colin, David and Eric

1.9 Orchard, Plum and Damson

Orchard purchases 60% of **Plum**. Orchard already owns 30% of **Damson** and Damson owns 40% of Pear. Plum owns 80% of Cherry and 25% of Pear.

The following companies are subsidiaries of Orchard:

(a) Plum only
(b) Plum and Cherry only
(c) Plum, Cherry and Damson only
(d) Plum, Cherry, Damson and Pear

1.10 Ovett, Elliott and Moorcroft

Ovett acquires the following during the year ended 30 June 20X6:

(1) The separable net assets of **Elliott**, a sole trader
(2) 100% of the share capital of **Moorcroft**, a limited company.

Purchased goodwill may arise in the *individual* accounts of Ovett in respect of:

(a) Elliott and Moorcroft
(b) Elliott only
(c) Moorcroft only
(d) Neither Elliott nor Moorcroft

1.11 Garden, Flower and Hedge

During the year ended 31 December 20X4 **Garden** made the following acquisitions:

(i) The entire share capital of **Flower**, a limited company
(ii) The separable net assets of **Hedge**, a sole trader.

Purchased goodwill may arise in the *individual* accounts of Garden in respect of:

(a) Hedge only
(b) Hedge and Flower
(c) Flower only
(d) Neither Hedge nor Flower

Examination-style questions

1.1 Early days of group accounting

In the early days of group accounting (up to about 1929), the consolidation and equity methods were regarded as alternative accounting treatments for investments in subsidiaries and for the profits/losses generated by them. Since then, the consolidation method has prevailed in this field.

You are required:

(a) to outline the similarities, and differences, between the two methods;

(b) to explain the conventional present-day uses of the two methods; and

(c) to argue for or against the general use of the equity method, in accounting for investments in subsidiaries.

1.2 Treatment of minority interests

'Three different approaches can be recognised in the treatment of minority interests. These have become known as the three concepts of consolidation: the parent company concept, the entity concept and the proprietary concept.'

You are required to explain the three concepts of consolidation, namely the parent company concept, the entity concept and the proprietary concept.

Part Two

Consolidated balance sheet

2

Consolidated balance sheet: basic working accounts

Learning objectives

After studying this chapter you should be able to:

- prepare a simple consolidated balance sheet
- identify minority interest in the group's net assets
- deal with the subsidiary's preference share capital when preparing the consolidated balance sheet
- prepare a simple set of consolidated balance sheet working T accounts

Introduction

As explained in Chapter 1, consolidation is the process whereby the individual accounts of a parent undertaking and of each of its subsidiary undertakings are combined and presented as if they were those of a single entity without regard for the legal boundaries between the companies in the group.

Consolidation essentially involves aggregating the amounts shown in each of the individual accounts, on a line-by-line basis, and making appropriate adjustments to achieve consistency of measurement and to eliminate double counting.

In preparing the consolidated balance sheet, the asset *Investment in subsidiary* in the parent undertaking's balance sheet is replaced with the net assets of the subsidiary undertaking. The asset *Investment in subsidiary* in the parent undertaking's balance sheet is usually recorded at the original cost of the investment. The *net assets* of the subsidiary comprise all its assets less all current and long-term liabilities. Initially in the examples in this chapter, it is assumed that the parent has acquired 100% of the shares in the subsidiary.

At the date of acquisition, it is reasonable to assume that the net assets of the subsidiary bear some relationship to the cost to the parent of its 100% stake in the subsidiary. However, it would be unusual for the book value of the net assets of the subsidiary to exactly equal the cost to the parent of acquiring the stake, i.e., 100% of the share capital. The difference between the cost of investment and the net assets at the date of acquisition is *goodwill*.

Example 2.1 provides a basic illustration of how goodwill is calculated. As shown by this example, when preparing the consolidated balance sheet at the date of acquisition, *Investment in subsidiary* on the parent's balance sheet (which is shown at cost of €100,000) is replaced with the various fixed assets, current assets and liabilities of the subsidiary (i.e., €90,000) and by the asset goodwill (i.e., €10,000). Goodwill is the difference between cost of the investment and the amount of net assets of the subsidiary.

Example 2.1 Calculating goodwill

Parent undertaking's balance sheet	
Investment at cost	€100,000
Balance sheet of subsidiary at acquisition	
Net assets	
Fixed assets	
Current assets	
Current liabilities	
Long-term liabilities	€(90,000)
Goodwill	€10,000

It should be noted here that because of the balance sheet equation (whereby assets minus liabilities equals owners' equity), net assets at any date can be identified either (i) directly (by adding all assets and taking away all liabilities) or (ii) indirectly (by focusing on shareholders' funds). Thus, net assets *at any date* can be determined:

- by adding assets and subtracting liabilities; or
- by adding share capital and reserves.

In the context of calculating goodwill at acquisition, *cost* of the investment is compared with the parent undertaking's share of the *net assets* of the subsidiary. The share capital of the subsidiary plus the reserves of the subsidiary at acquisition are used to represent the book value of the net assets of the subsidiary when preparing consolidated balance sheets. This approach is followed as it is more expedient than trying to establish the book amounts of assets and liabilities directly.

Where a parent controls less than 100% of the shares of the subsidiary there is a minority interest in the net assets of the subsidiary. The term *Minority interest* refers to the percentage of the subsidiary owned (and financed) by shareholders other than the parent's shareholders. The consolidated balance sheet includes the combined net assets of the group without any deduction for the share of the subsidiary's net assets not owned by the parent undertaking. It records the entire net assets *controlled* by the group and therefore includes all of the net assets of the subsidiary (in addition to those of the parent). The amount of net assets financed by the minority (those shareholders of the subsidiary outside the group) is indicated in the consolidated balance sheet by the caption *Minority interest*, which is included after shareholders' equity.

Consolidation at a subsequent date to the date of acquisition

Consolidation is often carried out at a date after acquisition. Preparation of a consolidated balance sheet would still require replacing *Investment in subsidiary* with the net assets of the subsidiary undertaking. However, the net assets at the current balance sheet date are different from the net assets acquired at the date of acquisition. The change in net assets after acquisition is reflected in reserves.

This is illustrated in Example 2.2. Net assets have increased by €10,000 (from €19,000 to €29,000) and this is represented by an equivalent change in reserves.

Example 2.2 Consolidation after date of acquisition

Example

Investment at cost	€20,000
Net assets at acquisition	€19,000
Net assets at balance sheet date	€29,000

Required

Prepare the consolidated balance sheet at (i) the date of acquisition and (ii) the current balance sheet date.

Solution

Consolidated balance sheet	**At acquisition**	**At balance sheet date**
	€	€
'Debits'		
Net assets of subsidiary	19,000	29,000
Goodwill	1,000	1,000
	20,000	30,000
'Credits'		
Financing of investment	20,000	20,000
Increase in group reserves	—	10,000
	20,000	30,000

The change in subsidiary reserves since acquisition (i.e., the increase in net assets from €19,000 to €29,000) is described as *post-acquisition reserves*. Only post-acquisition reserves of the subsidiary are included in group reserves in the consolidated balance sheet, along with the parent undertaking's reserves.

In both Examples 2.1 and 2.2, positive goodwill arose because the consideration paid for the investment exceeded the value of the net assets acquired. Positive goodwill is included within fixed assets in the consolidated balance sheet until it is written off (by amortisation through the profit and loss account or otherwise (such write-offs are discussed in detail in Chapter 17)). Less frequently, consideration paid can be less than the value of net assets acquired. This gives rise to *negative* goodwill. Negative goodwill is something of an anomaly. Although it is a *credit* balance in the consolidation workings, it is not a liability. Again, the treatment of negative goodwill under current UK and IAS GAAP will be discussed in Chapter 17. For the purposes of Part 2 of this book, where negative goodwill arises, it should be entered as a 'negative' asset in the consolidated balance sheet, within fixed assets.

Simple examples of consolidated balance sheet preparation

We will now look at some simple examples to illustrate the preparation of a consolidated balance sheet. In all cases, Parent is the parent undertaking and Subsidiary is the subsidiary undertaking.

In Example 2.3, Parent acquired 100% of Subsidiary at the date of Subsidiary's incorporation, at par (i.e., the shares in Subsidiary were acquired at their nominal or face value of

€40,000). A consolidated balance sheet is to be prepared at a date subsequent to acquisition (and incorporation). This means that:

- since the acquisition occurred at the date of incorporation of Subsidiary, there are no pre-acquisition reserves
- net assets of €40,000 (represented by share capital) were acquired for €40,000, so there is no goodwill
- net assets are currently included in Subsidiary's books at €200,000 (compared with their value at incorporation of €40,000)
- the increase in the net assets since acquisition is reflected in post-acquisition reserves (i.e., Subsidiary's reserves increased from zero at acquisition to €160,000 at the balance sheet date).

Example 2.3 Simple example 1 – no goodwill

Example

Balance sheet at 31.12.20X1	**Parent**	**Subsidiary**
	€	€
Sundry net assets	120,000	200,000
Investment in Subsidiary	40,000	—
	160,000	200,000
Share capital	80,000	40,000
Revenue reserves	80,000	160,000
	160,000	200,000

Required

Prepare the consolidated balance sheet at 31.12.20X1.

Solution

Consolidated balance sheet	€
Sundry net assets	320,000
Share capital	80,000
Consolidated revenue reserves	240,000
	320,000

Note that:

- Sundry net assets in the consolidated balance sheet include net assets of *both* Parent and Subsidiary.
- These group net assets at the balance sheet date are financed by *Parent's* share capital and *group* reserves.
- Group share capital is the share capital of *Parent* alone.
- Group reserves include Parent's reserves (€80,000) and the *group share of post-acquisition reserves* of Subsidiary (100% × €160,000).

Example 2.4 differs from Example 2.3 in that Parent paid more than the value of the net assets for its shares in Subsidiary. Example 2.4 assumes the same data as Example 2.3, except that Parent acquired 100% of Subsidiary at the date of incorporation for €50,000 (rather than €40,000 as in Example 2.3). As shown in Example 2.4, this means that:

- net assets of €40,000 were acquired for €50,000.
- goodwill at acquisition therefore amounts to €10,000.

Example 2.4 Simple example 2 – goodwill

Example

Balance sheet at 31.12.20X1	**Parent**	**Subsidiary**
	€	€
Sundry net assets	110,000	200,000
Investment in Subsidiary	50,000	—
	160,000	200,000
Share capital	80,000	40,000
Revenue reserves	80,000	160,000
	160,000	200,000

Required

Prepare the consolidated balance sheet at 31.12.20X1.

Solution

Consolidated balance sheet	€
Sundry net assets	310,000
Goodwill	10,000
	320,000
Share capital	80,000
Consolidated revenue reserves	240,000
	320,000

The similarities with Example 2.3 are as follows:

- net assets are currently included in Subsidiary's books at €200,000 (compared with their value at incorporation of €40,000)
- the increase in net assets since incorporation is reflected in Subsidiary's reserves.

Note that group reserves include Parent's reserves (€80,000) and the *group share of post-acquisition reserves* of Subsidiary (100% × €160,000).

In Example 2.5, Parent acquired 100% of Subsidiary some time after incorporation for €70,000. Reserves of Subsidiary at the date of acquisition amounted to €20,000. This means that:

- net assets of €60,000 (share capital of €40,000 plus reserves of €20,000 at acquisition) were acquired for €70,000
- goodwill at acquisition therefore amounts to €10,000
- net assets are currently included in Subsidiary's books at €200,000 (compared with €20,000 at the date of acquisition)
- the increase in net assets since acquisition is reflected in Subsidiary's reserves.

Example 2.5 Simple example 3 – acquisition subsequent to date of incorporation of Subsidiary

Example

Balance sheet at 31.12.20X1	**Parent**	**Subsidiary**
	€	€
Sundry net assets	90,000	200,000
Investment in Subsidiary	70,000	—
	160,000	200,000
Share capital	80,000	40,000
Revenue reserves	80,000	160,000
	160,000	200,000

Required

Prepare the consolidated balance sheet at 31.12.20X1.

Solution

Consolidated balance sheet	€
Sundry net assets	290,000
Goodwill	10,000
	300,000
Share capital	80,000
Consolidated revenue reserves	220,000
	300,000

Note that group reserves include Parent's reserves (€80,000) and the *group share of post-acquisition reserves* of Subsidiary (100% × €140,000$_{€160,000-€20,000}$).

Example 2.6 introduces a minority interest to the consolidated balance sheet preparation. In this example, Parent acquired 80% of Subsidiary (not 100% as in the previous three examples) some time after incorporation for €56,000. Reserves of Subsidiary at the date of acquisition amounted to €20,000. This means that:

- net assets of Subsidiary were €60,000 at the date of acquisition (share capital of €40,000 plus reserves of €20,000)
- the group acquired 80% of the net assets of €60,000 (i.e., €48,000) at a cost of €56,000
- goodwill at acquisition therefore amounts to €8,000 (€56,000 minus €48,000)
- net assets are currently included in Subsidiary's books at €200,000
- the minority is financing 20% of these net assets (i.e., €40,000)
- the increase in the net assets (from €60,000 at acquisition to €200,000 at the balance sheet date) is in post-acquisition reserves
- the group includes its share of these post-acquisition reserves (80% × €140,000) in consolidated reserves on the balance sheet.

Example 2.6 Simple example 4 – minority interest

Example

Balance sheet at 31.12.20X1	**Parent**	**Subsidiary**
	€	€
Sundry net assets	104,000	200,000
Investment in Subsidiary	56,000	—
	160,000	200,000
Share capital	80,000	40,000
Revenue reserves	80,000	160,000
	160,000	200,000

Required

Prepare the consolidated balance sheet at 31.12.20X1.

Solution

Consolidated balance sheet	€
Sundry net assets	304,000
Goodwill	8,000
	312,000
Share capital	80,000
Consolidated revenue reserves	192,000
Shareholders' funds	272,000
Minority interest	40,000
	312,000

Note that:

- group reserves include Parent's reserves (€80,000) and the *group share of post-acquisition reserves* of Subsidiary (80% × €140,000 = €112,000)
- minority interest represents the amount of net assets of Subsidiary financed by shareholders other than the parent undertaking (20% × €200,000).

Impact of preference share capital on minority interest

Generally speaking, voting power, and thus control, is vested in ordinary or equity share capital. However, for a variety of reasons, many companies also part-finance their activities by issuing preference shares. These shares are usually limited in the amount of dividend to which they are entitled in any given year and while they rank behind debenture holders, lenders and creditors for repayment when the company is liquidated, they rank before ordinary shareholders in such a situation.

In the context of preparing group accounts, holdings of preference shares are dealt with very similarly to holdings of ordinary or equity shares. That is, to the extent that the group holds any such shares, their cost is offset against the nominal value of the shares held, to establish if goodwill (positive or negative) arises. Holders of preference shares are not entitled to any share of amounts remaining in reserves. They are only entitled to the specified annual dividend. To the extent that preference shares in a subsidiary are held by outside shareholders, the amount of such shares is included in minority interest in the consolidated balance sheet.

Example 2.7 illustrates the calculation of minority interest in a subsidiary where its net assets are financed both by equity and preference shareholders.

Example 2.7 Preference shareholdings and minority interest

Example

Parent owns 80% of the ordinary shares and 25% of the preference shares of Subsidiary. The following balances represent the net assets of Subsidiary at 31.12.20X3:

	€000
Ordinary share capital	300
Preference share capital	100
Share premium	80
Revaluation reserve	220
Profit and loss account	200
Net assets of Subsidiary	900

Required

Calculate the minority interest in Subsidiary at 31.12.20X3.

Solution	€000
Net assets at 31.12.20X3	900
Less: financed by preference shareholders	(100)
Financed by ordinary shareholders	800
Minority interest in equity-financed net assets (20% × 800)	160
Minority interest in preference shares (75% × 100)	75
Minority interest in Subsidiary's net assets	235

Working accounts

In the four simple examples just completed (Examples 2.3 to 2.6), there was no need to use a formal structure for the calculations involved in preparing the consolidated balance sheets. However, as group structures become more complicated, and as more adjustments become necessary, mental arithmetic becomes more difficult. A formal and structured approach to the consolidation workings facilitates accuracy.

Ledger accounts (or *T accounts*) are used in this book to present the consolidation workings. These ledger accounts are not part of the double entry system of any individual company (and therefore can be referred to as *memorandum* accounts). The starting points for all ledger accounts in the consolidation workings are the amounts taken from the balance sheets of group companies. The consolidation workings use *T accounts* to combine related figures from group entity balance sheets before recording consolidation adjustments. These adjustments are then recorded in the memorandum *T accounts*. Consolidation adjustments, however, require double entries within the workings, whereas the balances transferred from a group entity balance sheet only require a single entry.

There are three basic T accounts which appear in every set of consolidated balance sheet workings. These are:

1 *cost of control* or *adjustment* account
2 *consolidated reserves* account
3 *minority interest* account.

The following outline T accounts indicate the source of the basic entries and the meaning of the resulting balance in each account.

Cost of control account

This account is used to calculate goodwill arising on acquisition. Goodwill is the difference between the cost of the investment and the group share of the net assets acquired in the subsidiary. The balance on the cost of control account is goodwill. Positive or negative goodwill will arise depending on whether the investment cost more or less than the value of the net assets acquired. The entries in this account are illustrated as follows:

Cost of control/adjustment account

Cost of investment in subsidiary ①	Net assets taken over: represented by group share of: – share capital of subsidiary ② – pre-acquisition reserves of subsidiary ③

① This amount is taken from the parent undertaking's balance sheet.
② This amount is taken from the subsidiary undertaking's balance sheet (it is an allocation within the consolidation workings of the subsidiary's share capital [remember to include both preference and ordinary share capital where appropriate]; the minority is credited with its share of the subsidiary's share capital within the minority interest account).
③ This is an allocation of the subsidiary undertaking's revenue and other reserves from within the consolidation workings.

Thus, the cost of the investment (on the debit side of the T account) is compared with the group's share of the net assets of the subsidiary (on the credit side of the T account). The difference between the two sides is goodwill on acquisition. To the extent that this goodwill is not written off (either by amortisation through the consolidated profit and loss account or against consolidated reserves), it is included as an intangible fixed asset in the consolidated balance sheet.

Consolidated revenue reserves account

This account is used to bring together the reserves of all group entities and to transfer (out) amounts relating to pre-acquisition activity (group share only) and amounts attributable to the minority. The balance on this account in a simple case will equal the balance in the parent's revenue reserves plus the group share of post-acquisition reserves of the subsidiary. This balance is then included in the consolidated balance sheet.

Consolidated revenue reserves

Minority share of subsidiary's reserves ②	Parent's revenue reserves balance ①
Group share of pre-acquisition reserves ②	Subsidiary's revenue reserves balance ①

① These amounts are taken from the parent and subsidiary undertakings' balance sheets.
② These are double entries within the consolidation working accounts.

The same approach can be adopted, in separate T accounts, for other reserves (e.g., share premium or revaluation reserves) in order to calculate the amount to be included on the consolidated balance sheet for the relevant consolidated reserve.

Minority interest account

This account is used to identify the amount of subsidiary net assets that is financed by the minority (i.e., subsidiary shareholders from outside the group, shareholders other than the parent company). As net assets can be represented by the sum of share capital and reserves, minority interest is calculated by adding together the minority share of those two categories of shareholders' funds.

Minority interest

	Minority share of: share capital of subsidiary ① reserves of subsidiary ②

① This amount is taken from the subsidiary undertaking's balance sheet (it is an allocation of the subsidiary undertaking's balance sheet amount, the majority of the subsidiary undertaking's ordinary share capital has already been credited to cost of control account. Some, all or none of the subsidiary's preference share capital will be credited to the minority interest account, depending on whether some, all or none of the preference shares are held outside the group).

② This is an allocation of the subsidiary undertaking's revenue and other reserves from within the consolidation workings (some of the subsidiary undertaking's reserves has already been credited to cost of control and the minority is now being credited with its share of the year-end balance).

Important points

The three working accounts described are:

- not part of any individual company's nominal ledger
- memorandum workings only
- not continuous, they must be prepared each time a consolidated balance sheet is required.

The T account framework used in this book is not the only approach used in consolidated balance sheet preparation. For example, a spreadsheet approach is also often used. However, the T account approach is chosen because it is consistent with the traditional double entry approach to accounts preparation and it encourages consideration of the dual aspect of all consolidation adjustments.

Summary

This chapter introduced simple consolidated balance sheets. Basic working accounts, in the form of traditional ledger T accounts, were also introduced and the entries contained therein explained. The structure for the consolidated balance sheet workings introduced in this chapter will be used throughout Part 2 of this book.

Learning outcomes

After studying this chapter you should have learnt:

- how to prepare a simple consolidated balance sheet
- how to identify minority interest in the group's net assets
- how to deal with the subsidiary's preference share capital when preparing the consolidated balance sheet
- how to prepare a simple set of consolidated balance sheet working T accounts.

Multiple choice questions

Solutions to these questions are presented in Appendix 1.

2.1 Parent and Baby

Parent acquired 70% of the ordinary shares of **Baby** for €100,000 on 31 December 20X1. At that date the net assets of Baby were €110,000.

The goodwill arising upon the acquisition of Baby is:

(a) €10,000 positive
(b) €23,000 positive
(c) €40,000 positive
(d) €10,000 negative

2.2 Rugby and Soccer

Rugby acquired 60% of the ordinary shares and 50% of the preference shares of **Soccer** for €100,000 on 31 December 20X1. An extract from Soccer's balance sheet as at 31 December 20X1 is as follows:

	€
Net assets	150,000
Financed by	
Ordinary shares	100,000
Preference shares	40,000
Retained profit	10,000
	150,000

The positive goodwill arising upon the acquisition of Soccer is:

(a) €10,000
(b) €14,000
(c) €34,000
(d) €40,000

Data for questions 2.3 and 2.4

Heather acquired all 200,000 of **Pearl**'s ordinary shares. The consideration comprised €1.50 cash for each Pearl share and one Heather share (market value €5) for every two Pearl shares. Heather did not previously own any of Pearl's equity.

Immediately before the combination, their summarised balance sheets were as follows:

	Heather €000	Pearl €000
Sundry net assets (at fair value)	900	800
Share capital (in shares of €1)	500	200
Profit and loss account	400	600
	900	800

2.3 Heather and Pearl (a)

The value of Heather's reserves and of the Heather Group's consolidated reserves immediately after this business combination are:

	Heather	Heather Group
(a)	€400,000	€1,000,000
(b)	€400,000	€1,200,000
(c)	€800,000	€800,000
(d)	€800,000	€1,000,000

2.4 Heather and Pearl (b)

The value of Heather Group's consolidated sundry net assets and of its share capital is:

	Sundry net assets	Share capital
(a)	€1,400,000	€500,000
(b)	€1,400,000	€600,000
(c)	€1,700,000	€700,000
(d)	€1,700,000	€800,000

2.5 Megalith and Pebble

On 1 January 20X1 **Megalith** acquired 80% of the issued share capital of **Pebble** for €3m. Pebble's net assets had a book value of €2.5m on acquisition and its reserves then stood at €2m.

As at 31 December 20X1, the summarised balance sheets of Megalith and Pebble are as follows:

	Megalith €000	Pebble €000
Net assets	109,000	4,000
Share capital	50,000	500
Reserves	59,000	3,500
	109,000	4,000

Assuming goodwill on acquisition is to be fully written off by the year-end, what is the figure for consolidated reserves to be shown in the Megalith Group balance sheet as at 31 December 20X1?

(a) €59.2m
(b) €59.5m
(c) €60.2m
(d) €61.3m

2.6 Aardvark and Bobbin

Aardvark acquired 75% of the ordinary shares of **Bobbin** on 31 December 20X1. The consideration consisted of 10,000 of its own €1 ordinary shares and €80,000 in cash. At the acquisition date the net assets of Bobbin were €100,000. The market value of each share in Aardvark at that date is €4.

Goodwill arising on consolidation is:

(a) €5,000
(b) €10,000
(c) €20,000
(d) €45,000

2.7 Monster and Minnow

Monster acquired all of the share capital of **Minnow** on 31 December 20X1 by issuing 80,000 of its own shares. The *financed by* section of Monster's consolidated balance sheet prior to the acquisition is shown below. The fair value of a Monster share is €3. No goodwill arose upon the acquisition.

	€
Share capital (€1 shares)	1,000,000
Share premium	50,000
Group retained profits	nil

The consolidated shareholders' funds of Monster Group on 31 December 20X1 comprise:

	Share capital	**Share premium**
(a)	€920,000	€50,000
(b)	€1,000,000	€80,000
(c)	€1,080,000	€160,000
(d)	€1,080,000	€210,000

2.8 Rasher, Sausage and Burger

Rasher owns 80% of the ordinary share capital of both **Sausage** and **Burger**. Balance sheet extracts for Rasher, Sausage and Burger as at 31 December 20X1 are as follows:

	Rasher	**Sausage**	**Burger**
	€000	**€000**	**€000**
€1 ordinary shares	10,000	10,000	10,000
Reserves	12,000	15,000	(15,000)

Minority interest in the consolidated balance sheet of Rasher as at 31 December 20X1 is:

€000

(a) 4,000
(b) 5,000
(c) 7,000
(d) 8,400

2.9 Newbridge and Sheffield

Newbridge acquired 80% of the ordinary share capital and 30% of the preference share capital of **Sheffield** many years ago. Balance sheet extracts of Sheffield at 31 December 20X1 are as follows:

	€000
€1 Preference shares	1,000
€1 Ordinary shares	8,000
Retained profits	2,000

Minority interest in the consolidated balance sheet of Newbridge as at 31 December 20X1 is:

€000

(a) 2,000
(b) 2,200
(c) 2,300
(d) 2,700

2.10 Koala and Bear

Koala acquired 60% of the ordinary share capital of **Bear** on 31 December 20X1. At that date Koala's reserves were €10,000 and Bear's reserves were €15,000. At 31 December 20X4 Koala's reserves were €40,000 and Bear's reserves were €25,000.

The consolidated group reserves (ignoring goodwill) as at 31 December 20X4 are:

(a) €55,000
(b) €40,000
(c) €46,000
(d) €65,000

2.11 Lion, Tiger and Cub

Lion acquired 80% of the ordinary share capital of **Tiger** and 60% of the ordinary share capital of **Cub** a number of years ago. At the acquisition date, the retained reserves of Tiger were €10,000 and the retained reserves of Cub showed an accumulated loss of €5,000.

Extracts from the balance sheets of the companies as at 31 December 20X1 are as follows:

	Lion	**Tiger**	**Cub**
	€000	**€000**	**€000**
€1 ordinary shares	50,000	40,000	30,000
Reserves	20,000	15,000	10,000

The consolidated group reserves (ignoring goodwill) as at 31 December 20X1 are:
(a) €33 million
(b) €39 million
(c) €45 million
(d) €50 million

2.12 Christmas and Tree

Christmas acquired 90% of the ordinary share capital of **Tree** on 1 January 20X3. At that date Christmas's reserves were €30,000 and Tree's reserves were €15,000. At 31 December 20X4 Christmas's reserves were €60,000 and Tree's reserves were €25,000. Goodwill of €5,000 arose upon the acquisition. This is to be amortised over five years.

The consolidated group reserves as at 31 December 20X4 are:
(a) €60,000
(b) €67,000
(c) €69,000
(d) €70,000

Self-assessment exercises

Solutions to these self-assessment exercises can be found at:
www.thomsonlearning.co.uk/accountingandfinance/piercebrennan

2.1 Tony and Gerry

The following are the balance sheets of a parent company and its subsidiary undertaking at 30 June 20X7:

Balance sheets at 30 June 20X7

	Tony	Gerry
	€	€
Fixed assets	20,000	50,000
Investment in Gerry	71,000	—
Net current assets	35,000	50,000
	126,000	100,000
Share capital	100,000	80,000
General reserve	15,000	12,500
Profit and loss account	11,000	7,500
	126,000	100,000

Tony acquired 80% of Gerry on 30 June 20X4, when the following balances were included in Gerry's balance sheet:

General reserve	€5,000
Revenue reserve	€2,500

Required

You are required to prepare the consolidated balance sheet of Tony and group at 30 June 20X7.

2.2 Tom and Joe

The summarised balance sheets of **Tom** and **Joe** as at 30 September 20X7 are as follows:

	Tom	**Joe**
	€000	**€000**
Investment in Joe at cost	130	—
Sundry assets	140	290
	270	290
Ordinary shares €1 each	50	100
Revenue reserves	73	46
Debentures	50	80
Creditors	97	64
	270	290

Tom acquired 75% of Joe when Joe's revenue reserves were €60,000. Joe has not declared any dividends since then.

Goodwill has been written off in full by 30 September 20X7.

Required

Prepare the consolidated balance sheet of Tom as at 30 September 20X7.

Examination-style question

2.1 Tomato and Slicer

Tomato acquired 75% of the ordinary shares and 50% of the preference shares in **Slicer** on 1 January 20X1 for €800,000 at which date Slicer had retained profits of €100,000.

The draft balance sheets of the companies as at 31 December 20X8 are as follows:

	Tomato	**Slicer**
	€000	**€000**
Fixed assets		
Tangible assets	2,000	700
Investment in Slicer	800	—
	2,800	700
Current assets		
Stock	1,500	400
Debtors	1,200	300
Bank	600	100
	3,300	800
	6,100	1,500
Ordinary share capital	3,000	600
Preference share capital	—	100
	3,000	700
Retained profits	1,200	300
	4,200	1,000
Current liabilities		
Creditors	1,200	300
Taxation	400	200
Proposed dividends	300	—
	1,900	500
	6,100	1,500

Goodwill on acquisition is amortised over ten years.

Required

Prepare the consolidated balance sheet of Tomato at 31 December 20X8.

3

Consolidated balance sheet: consolidation adjustments

Learning objectives

After studying this chapter you should be able to:

- eliminate any debenture or loan stock in a subsidiary held by the parent or another subsidiary
- eliminate any accrued interest on inter-company loans against the related receivable (debtor) balance
- eliminate inter-company current or trading account balances
- identify and deal with goods and cash-in-transit
- calculate and eliminate any unrealised profit on stock and fixed assets remaining in the group, from inter-company sales
- make appropriate adjustments when the fair value of net assets is different from the book value at acquisition

Introduction

The objective of the consolidated balance sheet is to show:

- total net assets employed in the group
- total obligations to parties outside the group
- interests of parent company shareholders in group net assets
- interests of outsiders in the same net assets.

Transactions between group companies, while legitimately recorded in the books of the individual company involved in the transaction (and therefore correctly included in year-end amounts), must not be reflected in the group balance sheet. This is because such transactions are not considered to be realised as far as the group is concerned because they have not taken place between group companies and independent third parties. These transactions are described as *inter-company transactions*.

Amounts outstanding between group companies at the end of the year are included in the individual balance sheets of the parent and its subsidiaries. However, these assets and liabilities should not be included in the consolidated balance sheet as assets and liabilities. As the balances in the individual company accounts reflect two sides of the same transaction, they should cancel each other out when viewed from the perspective of the group. That is, an asset representing a sum receivable in one group company should exactly match a liability representing a sum payable by another group company.

There are four categories of inter-company transactions dealt with in this chapter:

- debenture and loan stock
- current account balances
- stocks and unrealised profits
- inter-company sale of fixed assets.

Another significant category of inter-company transaction is subsidiaries' dividends (Chapter 4).

A related topic, although not an inter-company item, is the recognition of *fair value* of net assets at acquisition where fair value differs from book value. Consolidation adjustments arising from such recognition are also dealt with in this chapter.

Debentures and loan stock

Capital can be raised by subsidiaries using debenture or loan stock. To the extent that the parent undertaking contributes some or all of that loan capital, an inter-company balance exists. The amount advanced by the parent undertaking is an asset in its balance sheet and the total loan or debenture stock is a liability on the subsidiary undertaking's balance sheet. In addition, where interest is unpaid at the year-end, there are related receivable and accrual balances on the individual company balance sheets (see later).

Inter-company debenture and loan balances

When preparing the consolidated balance sheet, the inter-company elements related to outstanding loans are cancelled within the consolidation working accounts. The parent's share of the subsidiary's loan should be cancelled in the cost of control account against the related financial fixed asset amount from the parent undertaking's balance sheet (*Investment in subsidiary's debentures* or *Advances to subsidiary*). That is, the investment (asset) in the subsidiary's loan stock is transferred from the parent's balance sheet to the debit side of the cost of control account. The parent's share of the subsidiary's loan (liability) is transferred from the subsidiary's balance sheet to the credit side of the cost of control account. To the extent that there is a difference between these two amounts, it is included in consolidation goodwill.

The remaining loan liability from the subsidiary's balance sheet is included in the consolidated balance sheet as a group liability. It is important to remember that this liability is *not* part of minority interest. This treatment is illustrated in Example 3.1.

Example 3.1 Inter-company debentures

Example

	€
Debentures in Subsidiary balance sheet	100,000
Held by Parent	40,000
Held by outsiders	60,000

Required
Set out the debenture elimination account in the consolidation workings.

Solution

Debenture elimination account

	€		€
Cost of control	40,000	Balance sheet of Subsidiary	100,000
Consolidated balance sheet	60,000		
	100,000		100,000

The remaining €60,000 is included in the consolidated balance sheet as a liability (*not* as part of minority interest).

Inter-company debenture and loan interest

When group entities provide other group entities with loan capital a further inter-company transaction arises in relation to interest payments on the loan. The lending company records interest income while the borrower records interest expense. Assets and liabilities are included in individual entity balance sheets to the extent that interest payments remain outstanding at the year-end. Such inter-company interest should be cancelled through an interest elimination account in the consolidation workings, as illustrated in Example 3.2.

Example 3.2 Inter-company debenture interest

Example

Interest accrued in Subsidiary	€10,000
Loan capital held by Parent	40%
Loan capital held by outsiders	60%

Required
Show how the interest accrued in Subsidiary's balance sheet is dealt with in the consolidation workings.

Interest elimination account

	€		€
Balance sheet of Parent	4,000	Balance sheet of Subsidiary	10,000
Consolidated balance sheet	6,000		
	10,000		10,000

The remaining liability of €6,000 is included in the consolidated balance sheet as a liability (*not* as part of minority interest).

Current accounts

Trading activities between group companies are normal. Because of the special relationship between group entities, these transactions are often recorded separately in accounts labelled *current account* rather than through accounts within the debtors' and creditors' ledgers. Current account balances reflect the position with regard to inter-company indebtedness at any point in time. Because the same transactions are recorded by the entities involved (albeit from a different perspective), it is reasonable to assume that their balances should be equal at a specific point in time. However, due to the dynamic nature of business and the artificiality of financial year-end dates (and consequent accounts' cut-off dates) differences can exist between current account balances. These differences are caused by items in transit, disagreements between the parties, or inter-company transactions for which an invoice has not been received (e.g., the month-end statement from the parent might initiate recording of management fees by the subsidiary).

In order to prepare the consolidated balance sheet, current account balances must be eliminated and, to achieve this, current account balances must agree (i.e., be equal in amount). Where the related balances disagree, they must first be brought into agreement. In addition, cash or goods in transit must be included within group assets. While they are in transit they are excluded from both parent and subsidiary cash and stock balances and, therefore, they are not included in the group total.

To bring inter-company account balances into agreement, the following steps must be taken:

- record goods or cash-in-transit (or any other incompletely recorded transaction)
- cancel the revised current account balances against each other.

Example 3.3 illustrates the cancellation of inter-company account balances along with recording cash-in-transit in the consolidation workings. As the example shows, the current accounts between Parent and Subsidiary$_2$ cancel and do not cause a problem. However, there is a difference of €11,300 in the current accounts between Parent and Subsidiary$_1$. The example also states that there is cash-in-transit of €11,300. This is clearly the cause of the difference in the current accounts between Parent and Subsidiary$_1$. When the consolidation adjustment is completed, this group cash is recorded and the current accounts agree.

Example 3.3 Cancelling inter-company balances

Example

Parent has two subsidiaries, $Subsidiary_1$ and $Subsidiary_2$. Intra-group balances are included in current accounts at the following amounts at the year-end:

			€
Parent	Current account:	$Subsidiary_1$	45,600 Cr
		$Subsidiary_2$	28,900 Cr
$Subsidiary_1$	Current account:	Parent	56,900 Dr
$Subsidiary_2$	Current account:	Parent	28,900 Dr

A cheque drawn by Parent for €11,300, was not received by $Subsidiary_1$ until after the year-end.

Required

(i) Explain how the cheque drawn by Parent and the inter-company accounts are dealt with in the consolidated balance sheet.

(ii) Show the ledger account dealing with the inter-company accounts in the consolidated balance sheet workings.

Solution

(i)
- include €11,300 in consolidated balance sheet cash
- reduce creditors of Parent by €74,500 (€45,600 + €28,900)
- reduce debtors of $Subsidiary_1$ and $Subsidiary_2$ by €56,900 and €28,900, respectively.

Double entry

	€	€
Dr Cash	11,300	
Dr Creditors	74,500	
Cr Debtors		85,800

(ii) *Consolidation workings*

Inter-company accounts

	€		€
Current accounts		Current accounts	
$Subsidiary_1$	56,900	Parent	45,600
$Subsidiary_2$	28,900	Parent	28,900
		Cash-in-transit	11,300
	85,800		85,800

Cash-in-transit

	€		
Inter-company accounts	11,300		

By bringing current account balances into agreement, two purposes are achieved. First, the cancellation of inter-company account balances is facilitated. Second, the completeness of group cash and stock assets is ensured.

Unrealised profit: inter-company sales of goods

Sales of goods between group companies are often for an amount which provides a profit to the selling entity. Where these inter-company sales are subsequently sold to customers outside the group, the purchasing entity (within the group) records its profit on the transaction in its profit and loss account. The group profit on the transaction comprises the profit recorded on the original intra-group transaction plus the subsequent profit recorded when the goods are sold outside the group. However, if the purchasing entity has not sold the goods outside the group by the year-end, the goods are included as stock in the balance sheet of the purchasing entity (within the group) at cost to that entity (assuming there is no need to reduce carrying amount to a lower net realisable value). Consequently, two problems arise when preparing the consolidated balance sheet:

- cost to the purchasing entity exceeds cost to the group
- the profit recorded by the selling company is not *realised* from the perspective of the group.

Group stock must be recorded at the lower of cost and net realisable value *to the group* and any unrealised profit must be eliminated. Two questions arise when dealing with these consolidation adjustments:

- what amount of unrealised profit should be eliminated?
- how should the adjustment be treated?

Amount of unrealised profit to be eliminated

There are two possible approaches to the amount of unrealised profit to be adjusted for:

- eliminate the entire unrealised profit
- eliminate group share only.

There is no difference between these two alternatives when the unrealised profit has been recorded by the parent. Similarly, where the unrealised profit has been recorded by a wholly owned subsidiary, there is again no difference between the two alternatives. However, if the profit was recorded by a subsidiary with a minority interest, a different amount of unrealised profit would be eliminated under the two alternatives.

In the UK, FRS 2 *Accounting for Subsidiary Undertakings* requires that the entire unrealised profit be eliminated regardless of which company recorded the profit in the first instance and regardless of the proportion of that entity owned by the group (paragraph 39).

Treatment of adjustment

Given that the entire unrealised profit is eliminated, there are also two approaches to eliminating that amount. It can be charged either against:

- group reserves
- or group and minority, where appropriate.

It would only be appropriate to charge the minority where the profit was recorded in the subsidiary *and* the subsidiary has a minority.

FRS 2 also settles this debate by requiring the second approach. Paragraph 39 of the standard requires:

> The elimination of profits or losses relating to intra-group transactions should be set against the interests held by the group and the minority interest in respective proportion to their holdings in the undertaking whose individual financial statements recorded the eliminated profits or losses.

Application of these two principles ((i) entire unrealised profit should be eliminated and (ii) profit should be eliminated against the group and the minority) is illustrated in Example 3.4.

Example 3.4 Unrealised profit in stock

Example

- Parent owns 80% of Subsidiary.
- Subsidiary sold goods to Parent for €12,000.
- Profit margin is 25%.
- $^1/_3$ of the goods were in stock at the year-end.

Required

Show the double entry required to record the elimination of unrealised profit in year-end group stock.

Solution

	€	€
Dr Consolidated reserves [(€12,000 × $^1/_3$ × 25%)[1] × 80%[2]]	800	
Dr Minority interest [(€12,000 × $^1/_3$ × 25%)[1] × 20%[2]]	200	
Cr Stock[1]		1,000

[1] Entire unrealised profit
[2] Eliminated in proportion

Example 3.5 uses one set of circumstances with two different assumptions regarding which entity initially recorded the unrealised profit. This example aims to clarify the difference between situations where the parent records the unrealised profit and where a subsidiary with a minority records the profit.

Example 3.5 Inter-company sale of goods and unrealised profit

Example

Parent owns 80% of Subsidiary.

Assumption 1

- Parent sold €100,000 worth of goods to Subsidiary, profit €20,000
- Subsidiary had €25,000 of these goods in stock at balance sheet date

Assumption 2

- As above, but Subsidiary sold the goods to Parent

The draft consolidated revenue reserves account (before dealing with unrealised profit in stock) is as follows:

Consolidation workings

Revenue reserves account

	€000		€000
Cost of control	160	Parent	1,500
Minority interest	80	Subsidiary	400
Consolidated balance sheet	1,660		
	1,900		1,900

Required

For each of the two assumptions, show the double entry to record the elimination of inter-company profit, and show the relevant T accounts in the consolidated balance sheet workings.

Solution

- All unrealised profit in year-end stock is eliminated from consolidated balance sheet total for stock.

Assumption 1 (Parent made profit on inter-company sale)
Dr Revenue reserves account €5,000
Cr Stock €5,000

Revenue reserves account

	€000		€000
Cost of control	160	Parent	1,500
Minority interest	80	Subsidiary	400
Unrealised profit in stock	5		
Consolidated balance sheet	1,655		
	1,900		1,900

Assumption 2 (Subsidiary made profit on inter-company sale)

	Dr	Cr
Dr Revenue reserves account (80% × €5,000)	€4,000	
Dr Minority interest (20% × €5,000)	€1,000	
Cr Stock		€5,000

Revenue reserves account

	€000		€000
Cost of control	160	Parent	1,500
Minority interest	80	Subsidiary	400
Unrealised profit in stock	4		
Consolidated balance sheet	1,656		
	1,900		1,900

Minority interest

	€000		€000
Unrealised profit	1	Minority share:	
		Subsidiary's share capital	X
		Subsidiary's reserves	80

Unrealised profit: inter-company sales of fixed assets

The principles for dealing with inter-company sales of fixed assets are the same as those used for inter-company sales of goods. As before, a problem arises where one group entity transfers a fixed asset to another group entity at an amount other than its written down value in the selling entity's books.

In the context of preparing the consolidated balance sheet this means that:

- the profit or loss on disposal is unrealised from the perspective of the group
- where depreciation has been provided on the transfer price, that depreciation is not based on the cost to the group (or valuation, where a policy of valuation is adopted).

Four adjustments may have to be made to restore the carrying amount of fixed assets to that which would have prevailed had the inter-company transfer not taken place:

1. *Asset*: the asset must be adjusted back to the original cost to the group.
2. *Profit or loss on disposal*: an adjustment to remove the entire profit or loss on disposal of the asset must be made in the consolidated workings. This adjustment is charged against consolidated revenue reserves and minority interest, as appropriate.

3 *Depreciation*: the depreciation charge for the year must be adjusted to what it would have been, based on cost to the group (or valuation). As with unrealised profit, the depreciation adjustment is charged against the consolidated reserves and minority interest, as appropriate.
4 *Aggregate depreciation*: the balance on this account should be the aggregate depreciation that would have arisen had all depreciation calculations been based on the original cost of the fixed asset.

Similar to inter-company sales of goods, it is important to identify which company (Parent or Subsidiary) sold the fixed asset and recorded the profit or loss and which company records the depreciation. By correctly identifying the location of the disposal and subsequent depreciation, accurate consolidation adjustment is facilitated.

Examples 3.6 and 3.7 illustrate the adjustments required.

Example 3.6 Inter-company sale of fixed assets (1)

Example

Parent owns 60% of Subsidiary. Parent purchased an asset costing €10,000 on 1.1.20X1, which it transferred to Subsidiary for €12,500 on the same day. The rate of depreciation is 10% straight line.

Required

Show the adjustments in the consolidation workings for the year ended 31.12.20X1.

Solution	**Books**	**Should be**	**Adjustment**
	€	€	€
Asset	12,500	10,000	2,500
Depreciation charge	1,250	1,000	250
Profit on disposal	2,500	Nil	2,500
Aggregate depreciation	1,250	1,000	250

	Dr	**Cr**
	€	€
Dr Consolidated revenue reserves	2,500	
Cr Fixed asset		2,500
Being reversal of unrealised profit		
Dr Aggregate depreciation	250	
Cr Consolidated revenue reserves [60% × €250]		150
Cr Minority interest [40% × €250]		100
Being depreciation adjustment on consolidation		

Example 3.7 Inter-company sale of fixed assets (2)

Example

	€
Parent owned an asset which originally cost	20,000
Aggregate depreciation at 1.1.20X1	8,000
Net book value at 1.1.20X1	12,000

Parent owns 100% of Subsidiary and transferred the asset to Subsidiary on 1.1.20X1 for €15,000. The rate of depreciation is 20% straight line.

Required

Show the consolidation adjustments required in respect of this transaction in the accounts to 31.12.20X1.

Solution	**Books**	**Should be**	**Adjustment**
	€	€	€
Asset	15,000	20,000	5,000
Depreciation	3,000	4,000	1,000
Profit or loss on disposal	3,000	Nil	3,000
Aggregate depreciation	3,000	12,000	9,000

	€	€
Dr Fixed asset	5,000	
Dr Revenue reserves: Depreciation	1,000	
Dr Revenue reserves: Profit on disposal	3,000	
Cr Aggregate depreciation		9,000

Fair value adjustments: revaluation of fixed assets

The underlying net assets of an acquired subsidiary will normally be revalued on acquisition. The EU Seventh Directive requires that identifiable assets and liabilities of an acquired company should be included in the consolidated balance sheet at their *fair values* at the date of acquisition. According to both FRS 7 *Fair Values in Acquisition Accounting* and FRS 10 *Goodwill and Intangible Assets*, goodwill is the difference between the fair value of the purchase consideration and the fair value of the net assets acquired. Chapter 17 discusses the concept of fair value and details the regulatory framework relating to goodwill calculations and disclosure. In this part of the book, it is sufficient to know that fair values of the net assets of a subsidiary at acquisition may differ from their book values and to understand how to deal with such differences in preparing the consolidated balance sheet.

Although fair values must be recognised for group accounts purposes, they do not have to be recorded in the individual subsidiary accounts. These two alternative situations are now discussed separately.

Fair values included in individual accounts of subsidiary

The subsidiary may have recorded fair values in its own accounts. In these circumstances, the related reserves (e.g., revaluation surplus) are treated as pre-acquisition reserves when preparing the consolidated balance sheet. The assets included in the subsidiary's balance sheet are already restated to fair value.

Fair values not included in individual accounts of subsidiary

Where fair values of a subsidiary's net assets differ from book values at acquisition and the fair values are *not* recorded in the individual accounts of the subsidiary, a consolidation adjustment is required. The adjustment represents a revaluation surplus or deficit at acquisition. Consequently, revaluation to fair value is regarded as a pre-acquisition adjustment in the consolidated balance sheet workings.

Fair value of stock differs at acquisition

Fair value adjustments at acquisition sometimes arise in the context of assets that are consumed (charged as expenses) in the post-acquisition period, before the date of the consolidated balance sheet currently being prepared. Consequently, the fair value adjustment affects the goodwill calculation and consolidated reserves, but it does not affect minority interest.

To reflect the impact on goodwill calculations, the group's share of the fair value adjustment is transferred from post-acquisition profits to pre-acquisition profits when preparing the consolidated balance sheet. The adjustment does not affect minority interest because the asset to which the adjustment relates is not included in the subsidiary's net assets at the balance sheet date. Example 3.8 illustrates the impact of fair value adjustments relating to stock at acquisition.

Example 3.8 Fair value of stock different from book value at acquisition

Example

The summarised balance sheets of Parent and Subsidiary as at 31.12.20X5 are as follows:

	Parent	Subsidiary
	€000	€000
Investment in Subsidiary	8,200	—
Other net assets	10,050	11,000
	18,250	11,000
Share capital in €1 shares	6,000	7,500
Profit and loss account	12,250	3,500
	18,250	11,000

Notes

1 Parent acquired 6 million shares in Subsidiary on 1.1.20X2 when the balance on Subsidiary's profit and loss account was €1.25m.

2 At 1.1.20X2 the fair value of the net assets of Subsidiary exceeded their balance sheet carrying values by €300,000. This excess was entirely due to stock, which had been sold by the first year-end after acquisition.

3 All other net assets on Subsidiary's balance sheet at the date of acquisition had fair values equal to their book values.

4 Goodwill on acquisition is amortised over five years, including a full year's charge in the year of acquisition.

Required

Prepare the consolidated balance sheet of Parent Group at 31.12.20X5.

Solution

Cost of control

	€000		€000
Investment at cost	8,200	Share capital (80% × €7.5m)	6,000
		Profit and loss account (80% × €1.25m)	1,000
		Fair value adjustment (80% × €0.3m)	240
		Goodwill c/d	960
	8,200		8,200
Goodwill b/d	960	Profit and loss account ([960 ÷ 5] × 4)	768
		Consolidated balance sheet	192
	960		960

Consolidated profit and loss account

	€000		€000
Cost of control	1,000	Parent	12,250
Cost of control (fair value adjustment)	240	Subsidiary	3,500
Minority interest (20% × €3,500)	700		
Goodwill amortised	768		
Consolidated balance sheet	13,042		
	15,750		15,750

Minority interest

	€000		€000
		Ordinary share capital (20% × €7.5m)	1,500
Consolidated balance sheet	2,200	Profit and loss account	700
	2,200		2,200

Consolidated balance sheet	**€000**
Sundry net assets (€10,050 + €11,000)	21,050
Goodwill	192
	21,242
Ordinary share capital	6,000
Revenue reserves	13,042
	19,042
Minority interest	2,200
	21,242

In Example 3.8, the fair value of stock is greater than its book value at the date of acquisition. This stock is sold within 12 months of acquisition and is therefore not included in Subsidiary's net assets at the consolidated balance sheet date. Consequently, the difference between fair value and book value of stock at acquisition has no impact on minority interest at 31 December 20X5. Its only impact is on goodwill calculations and group reserves at that date. In effect, a transfer between pre- and post-acquisition profits has taken place. Had the stock been included in the subsidiary's accounts at its fair value at the date of acquisition, accumulated profits at that date would have been higher by €300,000 [(€1.25m + €0.3m) = €1.55m] and post-acquisition profits would have been €300,000 lower at the current year-end (€1.95m rather than €2.25m $_{[€3.5m - €1.25m]}$).

Fair value of tangible fixed assets differs at acquisition

Revaluation reserves (surplus or deficit) arising from fair value adjustments at acquisition should be apportioned between the group (through the cost of control account) and the minority (through the minority interests account), when the affected asset remains on the subsidiary's balance sheet at the consolidated balance sheet date. Where the revaluation relates to a tangible fixed asset and it is not recorded in the subsidiary's books, an adjustment to accumulated depreciation and to the depreciation charge is also required in the consolidation workings. Great care needs to be taken to calculate correctly the depreciation charge and related adjustment. Similar to the treatment of unrealised intra-group stock profit, the minority must bear their share of the depreciation adjustment.

Table 3.1 summarises the procedure for incorporating fair values of the subsidiary's fixed assets into the consolidated balance sheet, where those values have not been incorporated into the subsidiary's own accounts. Table 3.1 assumes a revaluation upwards. The entries would be reversed for a downward revaluation.

Table 3.1 Procedure for incorporating fair values of tangible fixed assets at acquisition

Incorporating fair values in accounts for consolidation purposes (where not already in subsidiary's accounts) involves the following:

- → Increase asset values
- → Apportion capital reserve on revaluation between:
  - **a** Cost of control account (group share of pre-acquisition capital reserve)
  - **b** Minority interest account (minority share of capital reserve)
- → Charge additional depreciation on increased value of asset from date of acquisition to the date of consolidated accounts preparation
- → Charge group with its share of increased depreciation
- → Charge minority with their share of increased depreciation

Double entry to record revaluation of fixed assets at acquisition – fair values included in consolidated accounts only

		Amount of adjustment
Dr	Fixed assets	Revaluation surplus
Cr	Cost of control	Group share of revaluation surplus
Cr	Minority interest	Minority share of revaluation surplus
Dr	Consolidated profit and loss account	Group share of depreciation adjustment
Dr	Minority interest	Minority share of depreciation adjustment
Cr	Aggregate depreciation	Cumulative depreciation adjustment to balance sheet date

Example 3.9 illustrates the treatment of fair value adjustments to a tangible fixed asset where the subsidiary has not incorporated fair values at acquisition in its accounts. The difference between this example and Example 3.8 is the nature of the asset which is subject to the adjustment. Example 3.8 focused on the subsidiary's stock at the date of acquisition, whereas Example 3.9 deals with land *which remains in the subsidiary's balance sheet at the current year-end.*

Example 3.9 Fair value of land different from book value at acquisition

Example

All details in this example are the same as in Example 3.8, except for note 2.

The summarised balance sheets of Parent and Subsidiary as at 31.12.20X5 are as follows:

	Parent	Subsidiary
	€000	€000
Investment in Subsidiary	8,200	–
Other net assets	10,050	11,000
	18,250	11,000
Share capital in €1 shares	6,000	7,500
Profit and loss account	12,250	3,500
	18,250	11,000

Notes

1 Parent acquired 6 million shares in Subsidiary on 1.1.20X2 when the balance on Subsidiary's profit and loss account was €1.25m.

2 At 1.1.20X2 the fair value of land owned by Subsidiary exceeded its balance sheet carrying value by €300,000. This land remains on the balance sheet, at cost, at 31.12.20X5.

3 All other net assets on Subsidiary's balance sheet at the date of acquisition had fair values equal to their book values.

4 Goodwill on acquisition is amortised over five years, including a full year's charge in the year of acquisition.

Required

Prepare the consolidated balance sheet of Parent Group at 31.12.20X5.

Solution

Cost of control

	€000		€000
Investment at cost	8,200	Share capital (80% × €7.5m)	6,000
		Profit and loss account (80% × €1.25m)	1,000
		Revaluation surplus (80% × €0.3m)	240
		Goodwill c/d	960
	8,200		8,200
Goodwill b/d	960	Profit and loss account ([960 ÷ 5] × 4)	768
		Consolidated balance sheet	192
	960		960

Consolidated profit and loss account

	€000		€000
Cost of control	1,000	Parent	12,250
Minority interest (20% × €3,500)	700	Subsidiary	3,500
Goodwill amortised	768		
Consolidated balance sheet	13,282		
	15,750		15,750

Minority interest

	€000		€000
		Ordinary share capital (20% × €7.5m)	1,500
		Profit and loss account	700
Consolidated balance sheet	2,260	Revaluation surplus (20% × €0.3m)	60
	2,260		2,260

continued overleaf

Example 3.9 Continued

Consolidated balance sheet	**€000**
Sundry net assets (€10,050 + €11,000+ €300)	21,350
Goodwill	192
	21,542
Ordinary share capital	6,000
Revenue reserves	13,282
	19,282
Minority interest	2,260
	21,542

In Example 3.9, Subsidiary's net assets at acquisition are €0.3m higher than their book value, just as they were in Example 3.8. However, there is one significant difference between the two examples. The minority is credited with their share of this surplus in Example 3.9 because the asset remains on the subsidiary's balance sheet and will be included at its fair value in the consolidated balance sheet at 31 December 20X5. Goodwill is the same amount in both examples, but group reserves are different. The group's share of post-acquisition reserves of Subsidiary is based on €2.25m (€3.5m – €1.25m) in Example 3.9, whereas it was based on €1.95m in Example 3.8.

Summary

This chapter explained how transactions between group entities can lead to assets and liabilities in their individual balance sheets which should not be included in the consolidated balance sheet. Such inter-company balances may not initially agree in amount and therefore will not immediately cancel against each other. The adjustment required to ensure such inter-company balances agree was also explained and illustrated. In addition, adjustments required where fair values of subsidiaries' net assets differ from their book values at acquisition were explained and illustrated. The basic principles detailed in this chapter provide the foundation for the more challenging inter-company transaction, dividends, dealt with in Chapter 4.

Learning outcomes

After studying this chapter you should have learnt:

- how to eliminate any debenture or loan stock in a subsidiary held by the parent or another subsidiary
- how to eliminate any accrued interest on inter-company loans against the related receivable (debtor) balance
- how to eliminate inter-company current or trading account balances
- how to identify and deal with goods and cash-in-transit
- how to calculate and eliminate any unrealised profit on stock and fixed assets remaining in the group, from inter-company sales
- how to make appropriate adjustments when the fair value of net assets is different from the book value at acquisition.

Multiple choice questions

Solutions to these questions are presented in Appendix 1.

3.1 Heron, Sparrow and Swift

Heron owns 80% of **Sparrow** and 75% of **Swift**. Sparrow has made a long-term loan of €500,000 to Swift. In the financial statements of Heron group, the loan will appear:

(a) as a fixed asset investment in the balance sheet of the parent company and nowhere in the consolidated balance sheet
(b) as a fixed asset investment in the balance sheet of the parent company and as a fixed asset investment in the consolidated balance sheet
(c) nowhere in the balance sheet of the parent company and as a fixed asset investment in the consolidated balance sheet
(d) nowhere in the balance sheet of the parent company and nowhere in the consolidated balance sheet

3.2 Bright and Cool

Bright purchased 70% of the ordinary share capital of **Cool** in 20X1. Cool regularly supplies goods to Bright at cost plus 50%. At 31 December 20X5, the stocks of Bright included goods supplied by Cool for €60,000.

In preparing the consolidated financial statements of Bright for the year ended 31 December 20X5, the stock of goods supplied by Cool will be valued at:

(a) €40,000
(b) €46,000
(c) €54,000
(d) €60,000

3.3 Clock and Watch

On 1 January 20X3 **Clock** acquired the entire share capital of **Watch**. During January 20X3 Clock transferred plant and machinery to Watch and recorded the transaction by means of the following journal entry:

		Dr	Cr
31 January 20X3	Current account: Watch	€50,000	
	Plant and machinery at cost		€30,000
	Profit and loss account		€20,000
	Being transfer of plant purchased in January 20X1 to Watch at agreed price		

Both companies provide for a full year's depreciation on plant and machinery owned at the year-end at 10% per annum on cost.

The final draft balance sheets of Clock and Watch at 31 December 20X3 include the following:

	Clock	Watch
	€	€
Plant and machinery at cost	356,200	187,000
Accumulated depreciation thereon	119,700	78,870

The amounts in the consolidated balance sheet of Clock at 31 December 20X3, will be:

	Plant and machinery (at cost)	Accumulated depreciation
(a)	€523,200	€196,570
(b)	€523,200	€198,570
(c)	€543,200	€196,570
(d)	€543,200	€198,570

3.4 Bee and Wasp

Bee acquired 90% of the ordinary shares of **Wasp** for €100,000 on 31 December 20X1. The book values and fair values of the assets and liabilities of Wasp at the acquisition date are shown below. An external valuer agreed the fair values.

	Book value	Fair value
	€	€
Land and buildings	12,000	40,000
Vehicles	26,000	23,000
Stock	35,000	30,000
Debtors	27,000	27,000
Creditors	10,000	10,000

The goodwill arising upon the acquisition of Wasp is:

(a) €1,000 positive
(b) €19,000 positive
(c) €100,000 positive
(d) €1,000 negative

3.5 Amp and Bulb

Amp has owned 75% of the share capital of **Bulb** for many years. On 1 October 20X3, Amp transferred a machine purchased in June 20X1 for €100,000 to Bulb for €95,000. Both companies charge a full year's depreciation on all machinery owned at the end of each financial year, at a rate of 10% straight line. Neither company charges depreciation in the year of disposal.

The balance sheets of the two companies at 31 March 20X4 included fixed assets at the following net book amounts:

Amp €1,565,000
Bulb € 872,000

The consolidated balance sheet of Amp at 31 March 20X4 should disclose fixed assets at:

(a) €2,421,500
(b) €2,437,000
(c) €2,441,500
(d) €2,442,000

3.6 Holmes and Watson

Holmes purchased a short-term investment on credit terms from its 100% subsidiary **Watson** on 1 December 20X9 for €100,000. The book value as at that date was €80,000. The transaction was recorded by Watson's accounting system but not by Holmes'.

Stock costing €50,000 was purchased by Watson and sold to Holmes for €60,000 in December 20X9. As at 31 December 20X9 it remained unsold. Both companies recorded this transaction in full.

If Holmes' net assets are €80,000 and Watson's are €50,000 (excluding receivable for the short-term investment), according to their draft balance sheets, at what value should consolidated net assets be stated?

(a) €220,000
(b) €130,000
(c) €200,000
(d) €140,000

Self-assessment exercises

Solutions to these self-assessment exercises can be found at:
www.thomsonlearning.co.uk/accountingandfinance/piercebrennan

3.1 Jack and Box

The following are the balance sheets as on 31 March 20X7 of Jack and Box:

	Jack	Box
	€	€
Property	25,400	10,100
Plant and machinery	14,200	8,180
Fixtures and fittings	3,200	1,020
Motor vehicles	3,160	2,100
Investment in subsidiary company	80,000	—
Stock	34,140	32,100
Trade debtors	16,800	48,050
Prepayments	1,200	5,050
Cash at bank	1,470	38,200
Cash in hand	30	900
	179,600	145,700
Issued share capital	100,000	50,000
Capital reserve	10,000	20,500
Retained earnings	21,600	40,000
Trade creditors	44,500	34,000
Accrued expenses	3,500	1,200
	179,600	145,700

You are given the following additional information:

1 The share capital of Box is in shares of €1 each fully paid and Jack owns 40,000 of the shares in issue.
2 Jack acquired the shares in Box with effect from 1 April 20X1, when Box had capital reserves of €10,000 and retained earnings of €30,000.
3 Goodwill is to be amortised over eight years from the date of acquisition.
4 Trade debtors of Jack include €2,800 due by Box, but in the books of Box the amount due was €2,100, the difference being due to goods in transit.

Note: Inter-company transfers of goods take place at cost.

Required

Prepare the consolidated balance sheet of Jack and group at 31 March 20X7.

3.2 Potato and Peeler

Potato acquired 75% of the ordinary shares and 50% of the preference shares in **Peeler** on 1 January 20X1 for €800,000, at which date Peeler had retained profits of €100,000.

The draft balance sheets of the companies as at 31 December 20X8 were as follows:

	Potato €000	Peeler €000
Fixed assets		
Tangible assets	2,000	700
Investment in Peeler	800	—
	2,800	700
Current assets		
Stock	1,500	400
Debtors	1,200	300
Bank	600	100
	3,300	800
	6,100	1,500
Ordinary share capital	3,000	600
Preference share capital	—	100
	3,000	700
Retained profits	1,200	300
	4,200	1,000
Current liabilities		
Creditors	1,200	300
Taxation	400	200
Proposed dividends	300	—
	1,900	500
	6,100	1,500

You are given the following additional information:

1. The debtors of Potato include €200,000 due from Peeler while the creditors of Peeler include €50,000 due to Potato. Stock, invoiced by Potato to Peeler for €100,000 in December 20X8, was not received by Peeler until January 20X9, while cash sent by Peeler to Potato in December 20X8 was not received by Potato until January 20X9.
2. Potato sells goods to Peeler at cost plus $33\frac{1}{3}$%.
3. Excluding any goods in transit, the stocks of Peeler at 31 December 20X8 included goods invoiced to it by Potato for €160,000.
4. Group policy is to write goodwill off over five years.

Required

Prepare the consolidated balance sheet of Potato at 31 December 20X8.

Examination-style questions

3.1 Pete and Poach

The balance sheets of **Pete** and **Poach** as at 31 December 20X9 were as follows:

	Pete €	Poach €
Fixed assets	91,920	42,800
Investment in Poach (at cost)	160,000	—
Stocks	68,280	64,200
Debtors	36,000	106,200
Bank	3,000	78,200
	359,200	291,400

	Pete	Poach
	€	€
Share capital	200,000	100,000
Capital reserve	20,000	41,000
Revenue reserves	43,200	80,000
Creditors	96,000	70,400
	359,200	291,400

You are given the following information:

1 The share capital of Poach is in shares of €1 each fully paid, of which Pete owns 80,000.
2 Pete acquired its shares in Poach on 1 January 20X6 when Poach had capital reserves of €20,000 and revenue reserves of €60,000.
3 Goodwill is to be amortised over eight years.
4 Debtors of Pete include €5,600 due by Poach. In the books of Poach the amount due was €4,000; the difference arose from goods in transit. Pete invoiced these goods to Poach at cost plus $33\frac{1}{3}$%.

Required

Prepare the consolidated balance sheet of Pete and its subsidiary as at 31 December 20X9.

3.2 Darby and Joan

The summarised balances extracted from the accounting records of **Darby** and **Joan** at 31 March 20X4 are as follows:

	Darby	Joan
	€	€
Land and buildings	447,500	230,950
Plant and machinery	600,500	—
Fixtures and fittings	54,500	41,000
Investment at cost	367,500	—
Stock and work in progress	526,610	163,290
Debtors	241,920	129,680
Cash and bank	88,200	4,725
Creditors	(95,480)	(86,645)
	2,231,250	483,000
Capital and reserves:		
€1 ordinary shares	1,750,000	—
75 cent ordinary shares	—	420,000
Other reserves	350,000	—
Profit and loss account	131,250	63,000
	2,231,250	483,000

Additional information:

1 Darby bought 420,000 shares in Joan for €367,500 on 1 April 20X1 when there was a credit balance of €35,000 on Joan's profit and loss account.
2 On 29 March 20X4, Darby dispatched and invoiced goods for €12,500 to Joan which were not recorded by Joan until 3 April 20X4. A mark-up of 25% on cost is added by Darby on all sales to Joan. Joan already had goods of €10,400 in stock at 31 March 20X4 which had been bought from Darby.
3 Darby received a remittance of €8,000 on 2 April 20X4 which had been sent by Joan on 29 March 20X4.
4 Included in Darby's debtors is a balance of €25,500 owed by Joan.
5 Included in Joan's creditors is €5,000 due to Darby.
6 Goodwill is written off over five years through the consolidated profit and loss account.

Required

Prepare the consolidated balance sheet of Darby group at 31 March 20X4.

4

Consolidated balance sheet: inter-company dividends

Learning objectives

After studying this chapter you should be able to:

- adjust for the subsidiary's proposed dividends when preparing the consolidated balance sheet workings, regardless of whether the parent has accrued the dividend or not
- use two different approaches to facilitate the cancellation of inter-company dividends, depending on the assumption that neither company or both companies recorded the proposed dividend
- deal with proposed preference dividends within the subsidiary's liabilities
- make any necessary adjustments relating to dividends received by the parent out of pre-acquisition profits of the subsidiary

Introduction

Dividends paid and proposed by subsidiary companies are received or receivable by the parent. In the context of the group, these transactions are inter-company and any balances outstanding at the year-end must be eliminated when the balance sheets of group companies are combined into the consolidated balance sheet. This chapter deals with three different issues relating to inter-company dividends:

- proposed dividends
- preference dividends
- dividends out of pre-acquisition profits.

Proposed dividends

Dividends paid by a subsidiary and received by a parent do not generally cause problems when preparing the consolidated balance sheet. As these transactions are completed by the year-end (and presuming they are recorded correctly by all affected group companies), there is no remaining inter-company amount in the individual balance sheets of parent or subsidiary.

Dividends proposed by subsidiary undertakings are receivable (in part, possibly) by the parent. The payable and receivable balances in the balance sheets should cancel when preparing the consolidated balance sheet. However, dividend balances may not cancel because one of the companies has not yet recorded a proposed dividend. It is more likely that the parent will not have recorded a dividend receivable from its subsidiary when the subsidiary has recognised the proposed dividend than vice versa.

To facilitate cancellation of the related dividend payable and receivable balances, the records of the parent and the subsidiary must be consistent. That is, either both entities must have recorded the dividend or neither entity should have recorded the dividend. Where the entries relating to subsidiary dividends are inconsistent, one of two possible approaches can be adopted:

- *complete* the entries relating to proposed dividends to ensure that both parent and subsidiary have recorded the two sides of the transaction; or
- *reverse* any entries relating to the dividends proposed in both parent and subsidiary accounts.

The most appropriate (or indeed, the easiest!) treatment is determined by how the parent and subsidiary have dealt with (or not dealt with, as the case may be) the proposed dividends in their individual accounts. The choices and issues will become clear in the following discussion. Example 4.1 later in this chapter also helps to clarify the intricacies of dealing with proposed dividends of subsidiaries when preparing the consolidated balance sheet.

Treatment of proposed dividends – completing the entries

The approach taken depends on whether or not credit for the dividend receivable has been taken by the parent. Three possible situations may arise:

1. If credit for the dividend receivable *has not* been taken by the parent, the following steps should be taken:
   - As part of the consolidation workings, the parent should accrue its share of the subsidiary dividend as follows:

     Dr Dividends receivable
     Cr Revenue reserves.

   - A dividend elimination account should be opened in the consolidation workings.
   - Proposed dividends from the balance sheet of the subsidiary should be transferred to the credit side of the dividend elimination account.
   - Dividends receivable should be transferred from the (adjusted) balance sheet of the parent to the debit side of the dividend elimination account.
   - The balance remaining on the dividend elimination account represents dividend payable to the minority. This is included in short-term liabilities (*Creditors: amounts due within one year*) in the consolidated balance sheet.
2. If credit for the dividend *has* been taken by the parent, the dividend elimination account in the consolidated balance sheet workings is used to cancel the receivable balance (in the parent's balance sheet) and the payable balance (in the subsidiary's balance sheet). The remaining balance in the dividend elimination account is the dividend payable to the minority, which should be shown in *Creditors: amounts due within one year* in the consolidated balance sheet.
3. If a subsidiary dividend is declared but has not been provided for in the subsidiary accounts, it would be very inefficient to *complete the entries* relating to that dividend.

In effect, because neither parent nor subsidiary has recorded the dividend, the starting position is equivalent to that arrived at after *reversing the entries*. This situation is dealt with below.

Treatment of proposed dividends – reversing the entries

As with *completing the entries* for proposed dividends, the approach taken to *reversing the entries* depends on whether or not credit has been taken by the parent for its share of dividend receivable from the subsidiary. Two situations may arise:

1 If credit for the dividend receivable *has not* been taken by the parent, the entries in the subsidiary's books are reversed. Given that there is no entry relating to this dividend in the parent's records, there is no question of reversing entries in the parent's balance sheet. The double entry to reverse the entries in the subsidiary's books is as follows:

   Dr Proposed dividends
   Cr Revenue reserves

   The adjusted subsidiary revenue reserves are included in the consolidated revenue reserves account in the consolidated workings. The minority's share of the subsidiary's reserves is then based on the subsidiary's grossed-up revenue reserves (i.e., after adding back its proposed dividend). This amount is included in (credited to) the minority interest account. The *minority's share of the proposed dividend* must subsequently be calculated and disclosed separately from the remaining long-term minority interest. This is achieved by transferring the minority share of the subsidiary's proposed dividend out of minority interest account and into proposed dividend (to be included as part of *Creditors: amounts due within one year* in the consolidated balance sheet).

2 If credit *has* been taken by the parent for dividends receivable from the subsidiary, the entries in both sets of records will have to be reversed. (It should be noted here that completion of entries is more efficient in these circumstances.) The double entries are as follows:

   Dr Parent revenue reserve
   Cr Dividend receivable in parent balance sheet

   Dr Proposed dividends in subsidiary balance sheet
   Cr Subsidiary revenue reserve

   Again, it must be remembered to transfer the minority interest in the proposed dividend of the subsidiary out of minority interest account (in the consolidated balance sheet workings) to *Creditors: amounts due within one year* in the consolidated balance sheet.

Dividend declared by subsidiary but not provided for

If a subsidiary dividend is declared but has not been provided for in the subsidiary accounts, the dividend should be ignored except for the minority interest in that dividend. (It is assumed here that the parent undertaking has not recorded the dividend as receivable in its books.) This is the most efficient and effective way of dealing with the situation where neither company has recorded the dividend. The dividend payable to the minority shareholders must be transferred out of minority interest and into short-term liabilities

(*Creditors: amounts due within one year*), using the following double entry within the consolidation workings:

Dr Minority interest
Cr Proposed dividends

Worked example

Example 4.1 illustrates the two approaches to dealing with proposed dividends of a subsidiary undertaking when the subsidiary has provided for the dividend payable, but the parent has not recorded the dividend receivable.

Example 4.1 Treatment of proposed dividends

Example

	Parent	**Subsidiary**
	€000	**€000**
Net assets	100	40
Investment in Subsidiary	25	—
	125	40
Share capital	60	30
Reserves	65	10
	125	40

- Parent acquired 80% of Subsidiary when Subsidiary revenue reserves were €5,000.
- Parent has proposed, but not yet recorded, a dividend of €20,000 for the year.
- Subsidiary has proposed a dividend of €10,000, which is recorded in Subsidiary's books but not in those of Parent.

Required
Prepare the consolidated balance sheet using both *Completing the entries* and *Reversing the entries* approaches to dealing with proposed dividends in the consolidation workings.

Solution

- Before the dividends of Subsidiary are dealt with, those of Parent must be provided for by the following double entry:

	€000	**€000**
Dr Consolidated revenue reserves	20	
Cr Creditors: amounts due within one year		20

- As Subsidiary's dividends are recorded by Subsidiary and not recorded by Parent, the entries have to be completed in Parent's books *or* reversed in Subsidiary's books to ensure that both companies treat the transaction consistently.

Solution 1 Completing the entries for proposed dividend of Subsidiary

	€000	**€000**
Dr Dividend elimination account	8	
Cr Consolidated reserves		8
To record dividend receivable by Parent		
Dr Net assets	10	
Cr Dividend elimination account		10
Transfer proposed dividend of Subsidiary to dividend elimination account		

continued overleaf

Example 4.1 Continued

Cost of control

	€000		€000
Cost of investment	25	Share capital (80% × 30)	24
Negative goodwill	3	Revenue reserve (80% × 5)	4
	28		28

Consolidated revenue reserves

	€000		€000
Proposed dividend (of Parent)	20	Parent	65
Cost of control (80% × 5)	4	Subsidiary	10
Minority interest (20% × 10)	2	Dividend elimination	8
Consolidated balance sheet	57		—
	83		83

Minority interest

	€000		€000
		Ordinary share capital (20% × 30)	6
Consolidated balance sheet	8	Revenue reserves (20% × 10)	2
	8		8

Dividend elimination account

	€000		€000
Dividend receivable: Parent	8	Dividend payable: Subsidiary	10
Consolidated balance sheet	2		—
	10		10

Consolidated balance sheet	**€000**	**€000**
Net assets ($100_{\text{Parent}} + 40_{\text{Subsidiary}} + 10_{\text{Subsidiary's proposed dividend}}$)		150
Negative goodwill *		(3)
Proposed dividends		
Group	20	
Minority	2	(22)
		125
Share capital		60
Revenue reserves		57
		117
Minority interest		8
		125

* Negative goodwill is treated the same as positive goodwill in the consolidated balance sheet. (see Chapter 17.)

Solution 2 Reversing the entries for proposed dividend of Subsidiary

	€000	€000
Dr Proposed dividend account	10	
Cr Revenue reserves of Subsidiary		10
To reverse dividend payable by Subsidiary		
Dr Minority interest	2	
Cr Proposed dividends		2

Being transfer of minority share of proposed dividend of Subsidiary to Creditors: amounts due within one year

Notes

- Cost of control account is identical to that for *completing the entries* (Solution 1).
- There is no dividend elimination account where *reversing the entries* approach is adopted.

Consolidated revenue reserves

	€000		€000
Proposed dividend (of Parent)	20	Parent	65
Cost of control (80% × 5)	4	Subsidiary (10 + $10_{\text{dividend reversal}}$)	20
Minority interest (20% × [10 + $10_{\text{dividend reversal}}$])	4		
Consolidated balance sheet	57		
	85		85

Minority interest

	€000		€000
Current liabilities (20% × 10)	2	Ordinary share capital (20% × 30)	6
Consolidated balance sheet	8	Revenue reserves (20% × 20)	4
	10		10

Consolidated balance sheet is identical to that for *completing the entries* (Solution 1).

Students consistently find the treatment of dividends proposed by subsidiaries very challenging. However, if the situation to be dealt with is clearly identified (e.g., proposed in subsidiary and receivable in parent; or proposed in subsidiary and not recorded by parent), the accounting treatment is systematic and not overly difficult. The approach recommended in this chapter is summarised in Table 4.1.

Table 4.1 Proposed dividends of subsidiary: accounting treatment summarised

- Recorded in *both* parent and subsidiary
  Use dividend elimination account
- Recorded in subsidiary only, i.e., *not* recorded in parent
  - either *complete the entries* (i.e., use a dividend elimination account)–
  - or *reverse the entries* (i.e., treat the dividend as if it was never provided for by the subsidiary)
- Neither company has recorded the proposed dividend of the subsidiary
  Equivalent to having already reversed the entries

Preference dividends

Preference shareholders are entitled to their dividends before ordinary shareholders can receive any dividend. Preference dividends may or may not represent inter-company items. It depends on whether or not the parent company holds any of the subsidiary's preference shares. Where the parent does not hold any preference shares, all proposed preference dividends of the subsidiary are liabilities of the group. To the extent that the parent holds preference shares, the subsidiary's proposed preference dividends are inter-company items which require similar adjustments to those outlined earlier. Where preference dividends have been paid by the subsidiary, consolidation adjustment is unnecessary as subsidiary profits (and bank balances) have been reduced and parent revenue reserves (and bank balances) include any relevant dividends received from the subsidiary.

Preference dividends recorded by both subsidiary and parent

Where preference dividends are included in proposed dividends (dividends payable) in the balance sheet of the subsidiary and in dividends receivable in the parent's balance sheet, the dividend receivable asset in the parent is offset against the dividend payable liability in the subsidiary using the dividend elimination account. Any balance of dividend payable by the subsidiary is dividend due to the minority and is properly included in *Creditors: amounts due within one year* in the consolidated balance sheet.

Preference dividends not accrued by parent

Where preference dividends are included in proposed dividends in the balance sheet of the subsidiary and are *not* accrued in the balance sheet of the parent, a choice must be made between *completing the entries* in the parent's books and *reversing the entries* in the subsidiary's books. Whichever approach is adopted, care must be taken to ensure that preference dividends are dealt with *before* allocating ordinary dividends and remaining subsidiary reserves.

As indicated earlier, *completing the entries* involves:

- accruing the dividend receivable in the parent's books (Dr Dividend receivable; Cr Revenue reserves)
- offsetting the dividend receivable (from the parent's amended balance sheet) against the dividend payable (from the subsidiary's balance sheet) in the dividend elimination account in consolidated workings
- the balance on the dividend elimination account is the dividend payable to the minority (include in *Creditors: amounts due within one year* in the consolidated balance sheet).

Reversing the entries involves:

- reversing the entries for proposed dividends in the subsidiary's books
- allocating the grossed-up subsidiary reserves between group and minority, ensuring that the different (and priority) entitlement of preference shareholders is reflected in the allocation
- identifying the amount (within minority interest) of proposed dividend payable to the minority and transferring that out of minority interest to short-term liabilities (include in *Creditors: amounts due within one year* in the consolidated balance sheet).

Preference dividends not recorded

Where the preference dividend is not provided for in the subsidiary's balance sheet (although declared, or it has not been declared but it is cumulative), it should be provided for in the consolidated workings before allocating the subsidiary reserves between cost of control, minority interest and consolidated reserves. Example 4.2 illustrates the effect of unprovided preference dividends on the allocation of subsidiary reserves in the consolidated balance sheet workings.

Example 4.2 Preference dividends proposed (1)

Example

Parent owns 75% of 40,000 €1 shares of Subsidiary and €6,000 of its €10,000 7% preference shares. All these shares were acquired at Subsidiary's incorporation.

At the current balance sheet date: Parent revenue reserves are €60,000
Subsidiary revenue reserves are €22,700.

The directors of the subsidiary agreed to provide for the preference dividend and for a 10% ordinary dividend at the year-end.

The directors of Parent agreed to provide for a 20% ordinary dividend on 100,000 €1 ordinary shares of the company.

The revenue reserve amounts given *do not* include any adjustments for these dividends.

Required

Prepare (1) consolidated revenue reserves
(2) minority interest accounts in the consolidation workings.

Solution

Consolidated revenue reserves

	€		€
Proposed dividend: Parent	20,000	Parent	60,000
Minority interest (W1)	5,780	Subsidiary	22,700
Consolidated balance sheet	56,920		
	82,700		82,700

Minority interest

	€		€
To current liabilities		Ordinary share capital	10,000
Preference dividend proposed	280	Preference share capital	4,000
Ordinary dividend proposed		Revenue reserves (W1)	5,780
(40,000 × 10% × 25%)	1,000		
Consolidated balance sheet	18,500		
	19,780		19,780

Working 1 Minority interest in Subsidiary's revenue reserves

	€
Balance in Subsidiary reserves	22,700
Preference dividend (7% × €10,000)	(700)
Equity interest	22,000
Minority share (25% × €22,000)	5,500
Minority share of preference dividend (40% × 700)	280
	5,780

Example 4.3 illustrates the effect of proposed dividends (including preference dividends) recorded by the subsidiary where the parent has not recorded dividends receivable. The choice between *completing the entries* and *reversing the entries* in this situation is open. There is no benefit, in terms of greater efficiency, in choosing one approach over the other. Each approach involves similar effort. Solution 1 adopts the *completing the entries* approach, while Solution 2 adopts the *reversing the entries* approach. The only working

accounts that are different between the two approaches are consolidated revenue reserves and minority interest and therefore, they are the only workings included in Solution 2.

Example 4.3 Preference dividends proposed (2)

Example

		Parent	Subsidiary
		€	€
Shares in Subsidiary:	Ordinary	68,000	—
	Preference	10,700	—
Sundry net assets		79,300	132,600
		158,000	132,600
Ordinary share capital		80,000	60,000
Preference share capital		—	40,000
Revenue reserves		62,000	25,000
Proposed dividends:	Ordinary	16,000	6,000
	Preference	—	1,600
		158,000	132,600

Parent acquired 80% of Subsidiary's ordinary share capital and 25% of its preference share capital when Subsidiary's revenue reserves were €10,000.

Parent takes credit for dividends when they are received in cash.

Required

Prepare the consolidated balance sheet workings, using both *Completing the entries* and *Reversing the entries* approaches to dealing with proposed dividends in the consolidation workings.

Solution 1 Completing the entries approach

Cost of control

	€		€
Cost: Ordinary	68,000	Ordinary share capital	48,000
Preference	10,700	Preference share capital	10,000
		Revenue reserves (10,000 × 80%)	8,000
		Goodwill	12,700
	78,700		78,700

Consolidated revenue reserves

	€		€
Cost of control (10,000 × 80%)	8,000	Parent reserves	62,000
Minority interest (25,000 × 20%)	5,000	Subsidiary reserves	25,000
		Dividend elimination	*5,200
Consolidated balance sheet	79,200		
	92,200		92,200

Minority interest

	€		€
		Ordinary share capital	12,000
		Preference share capital	30,000
Consolidated balance sheet	47,000	Revenue reserves	5,000
	47,000		47,000

Dividend elimination account**

	€		€
Dividend receivable: Parent	*5,200	Dividend payable: Subsidiary	7,600
Consolidated balance sheet	2,400		
	7,600		7,600

*Dividend receivable by Parent: (80% × $6{,}000_{ordinary}$) + (25% × $1{,}600_{preference}$)
**Includes ordinary and preference dividends

Consolidated balance sheet	€	€
Sundry net assets (€79,300 + €132,600)		211,900
Goodwill		12,700
Proposed dividends		
Minority (ordinary and preference dividends)	2,400	
Group	16,000	(18,400)
		206,200
Ordinary share capital		80,000
Revenue reserves		79,200
		159,200
Minority interest		47,000
		206,200

Solution 2 Reversing the entries approach

Notes

- Cost of control account is identical to that in Solution 1, *completing the entries* approach.
- There is no dividend elimination account where *reversing the entries* approach is adopted.
- The consolidated balance sheet is identical to that in Solution 1, *completing the entries* approach.
- The only accounts that differ (in detail) from Solution 1 are consolidated revenue reserves and minority interest.

Consolidated revenue reserves

		€		€
Cost of control (10,000 × 80%)		8,000	Parent reserves	62,000
Minority interest			Subsidiary reserves	
	32,600		(25,000 + $6{,}000_{ordinary\ dividend}$	
	(1,600) × 75%	1,200	+ $1{,}600_{preference\ dividend}$)	32,600
	31,000 × 20%	6,200		
Consolidated balance sheet		79,200		
		94,600		94,600

Minority interest

	€		€
Current liabilities		Ordinary share capital	12,000
Ordinary dividends (6000 × 20%)	1,200	Preference share capital	30,000
Preference dividends (1,600 × 75%)	1,200	Revenue reserves	7,400
Consolidated balance sheet	47,000		
	49,400		49,400

Dividends out of pre-acquisition profits

A dividend declared out of pre-acquisition profits is a distribution of the assets which existed at the date of acquisition. This dividend is not normally treated as distributable in the hands of the parent and therefore should not be credited to the profit and loss account when received. The dividend should be offset (credited) against the cost of the investment in the subsidiary as it is considered to be a return *of* investment rather than a return *on* investment.

Pre-acquisition dividends can also cause problems when identifying pre-acquisition profits of the subsidiary for the purpose of calculating goodwill. A useful rule of thumb involves matching 'like with like'. This means that when the cost of the investment is stated before pre-acquisition dividend (gross), the group share of subsidiary reserves credited to the cost of control account should be based on subsidiary reserves *before* pre-acquisition dividend is deducted. Equally correct is the approach where the 'net' cost is matched with the group share of subsidiary pre-acquisition reserves *after* pre-acquisition dividend.

Example 4.4 is a simple illustration of matching 'like with like'. Where a share is purchased *cum* dividend, this means that the purchaser of the shares is entitled to receive the dividend declared at or around the time of purchase. The reverse is the case where shares are purchased *ex* dividend. In such cases, the vendor of the shares (rather than the purchaser) is entitled to the dividend.

Example 4.4 Pre-acquisition dividends (1)

Example

Parent purchased 100% of Subsidiary's ordinary share capital *cum* dividend for €100. Subsidiary's share capital was €50 and revenue reserves at the date of acquisition were €50. Subsequently, Subsidiary declared a dividend of €20.

Required

Explain how the pre-acquisition dividend should be dealt with in the consolidated balance sheet workings and show the cost of control account using:

(i) the *gross* and

(ii) the *net* approach to dealing with pre-acquisition dividends.

Solution

The €20 dividend is pre-acquisition and should be credited against the cost of the investment in the individual accounts of the parent.

In the consolidation workings:

- If the cost is included in cost of control account *net* of dividend, pre-acquisition reserves credited to that account must also be *net* of dividend.
- If the cost is included in cost of control account *gross* of dividend, pre-acquisition reserves credited to that account must also be *gross* of dividend.

Cost of control

	Gross	Net		Gross	Net
	€	€		€	€
Cost	100	100	Share capital	50	50
Pre-acquisition dividend	—	(20)	Revenue reserves	50	30 (50–20)
			Goodwill	—	—
	100	80		100	80

Example 4.5 provides another illustration of how the gross cost approach compares with the net cost approach, when preparing the cost of control account in the consolidation workings. In addition, it illustrates the situation where, although the subsidiary has declared dividends at the date of acquisition, the parent buys shares *ex div*. In this situation, gross cost is the same as net cost and the parent's share of pre-acquisition reserves acquired is based on the subsidiary's reserves after the dividend.

Example 4.5 Pre-acquisition dividends (2)

Example

The following summarised balance sheet is provided (at the date of acquisition) for Subsidiary, the wholly owned subsidiary of Parent.

	€
Net assets	125,000
Proposed dividends	(5,000)
	120,000
Share capital	100,000
Revenue reserves	20,000
	120,000

Required

Assuming two alternative situations:
(1) Parent purchased 100% of Subsidiary *ex div* for €150,000.
(2) Parent purchased 100% of Subsidiary *cum div* for €150,000.
Show the cost of control account using:
  (i) the *gross* and
  (ii) the *net* approach to dealing with pre-acquisition dividends.

Solution (1) Shares acquired *ex div*

Where shares in Subsidiary are acquired *ex div*, there is no pre-acquisition dividend received by Parent to deal with. Consequently, there is no difference between the *gross* and the *net* approaches to preparing the cost of control account.

Cost of control

	€		€
Cost	150	Share capital	100
		Revenue reserves	20
		Goodwill	30
	150		150

Solution (2) Shares acquired *cum div*

Cost of control

	(i) Gross	(ii) Net		(i) Gross	(ii) Net
Cost	150		Share capital	100	100
Cost less pre-acquisition dividend		145 (150 – 5)	Revenue reserves	25	20 (25 – 5)
			Goodwill	25	25
	150	145		150	145

Dividends out of pre-acquisition profits: possible situations

A number of different situations arise in the context of recording pre-acquisition dividends of a subsidiary. They include:

- pre-acquisition dividend is paid by the subsidiary and credited by the parent against the cost of investment. In this case, consolidation adjustment is not necessary as parent's treatment of transaction is correct
- pre-acquisition dividend is proposed by subsidiary, taken as receivable by parent and credited to cost of investment. Again, no adjustment is necessary. The net cost to the group (recorded by the parent) is compared with the subsidiary reserves after pre-acquisition dividends (net)
- pre-acquisition dividend (either paid or proposed by the subsidiary) is credited by the parent to the profit and loss account. This treatment is incorrect and adjustment is required as follows to take the pre-acquisition dividend out of the profit and loss account and to credit it to reduce the cost of the investment in the subsidiary:

  Dr Profit and loss account
  Cr Cost of investment

- pre-acquisition dividend is proposed by the subsidiary but is not treated as receivable by the parent. The best way to deal with this situation is to reverse the subsidiary's proposed dividend. Then, gross cost can be compared with the group's share of net assets of subsidiary before providing for the dividend ('gross of pre-acquisition dividend').

Example 4.6 shows the correct approach to dealing with pre-acquisition dividends.

Example 4.6 Pre-acquisition dividends (3)

Example

Parent acquired 80% of Subsidiary for €70 *cum* dividend on 31.12.20X6, on which day Subsidiary paid a total dividend of €10.

Balance sheets of Parent and Subsidiary *after* recording the above transactions were as follows:

	Parent	Subsidiary
	€	€
Net assets	278	70
Investment in Subsidiary	70	—
	348	70
Share capital	200	50
Revenue reserves	108	20
Proposed dividends	40	—
	348	70

Parent credited its share of Subsidiary's dividend to revenue reserves, through its profit and loss account.

Required

Prepare the consolidated balance sheet of Parent and group and show all working accounts.

Solution

- Parent should not credit pre-acquisition dividend to its profit and loss account but should offset it against cost of investment.
- However, Parent has already credited the dividend (€8 $_{€10 \times 80\%}$) to reserves. Therefore, adjustment is necessary.
- Once the cost (net of pre-acquisition dividend) is matched in the cost of control account with Subsidiary's pre-acquisition reserves (net of pre-acquisition dividend), the correct goodwill figure will result.

Cost of control

	€		€
Cost (€70 – €8)	62	Share capital (80% × €50)	40
		Revenue reserves (80% × €20)	16
		Goodwill	6
	62		62

Consolidated revenue reserves

	€		€
Minority interest (20% × €20)	4	Parent (€108 – €8)	100
Cost of control (80% × €20)	16	Subsidiary	20
Consolidated balance sheet	100		
	120		120

Minority interest

	€		€
		Share capital (20% × 50)	10
Consolidated balance sheet	14	Revenue reserves (20% × 20)	4
	14		14

Consolidated balance sheet	€
Goodwill	6
Net assets (€278 + €70)	348
Proposed dividends	(40)
	314
Share capital	200
Revenue reserves	100
Shareholders' funds	300
Minority interest	14
	314

Calculating pre-acquisition dividends: mid-year acquisition

The implications of mid-year acquisitions for the preparation of consolidated balance sheets are dealt with in detail in Chapter 5. However, the particular case of a mid-year acquisition with pre-acquisition dividends arising from an interim dividend is discussed here.

Example 4.7 illustrates the issue involved. Parent acquires its shares in Subsidiary nine months into the current year. The interim dividend has already been paid by Subsidiary and none of that dividend accrues to Parent. The entire final dividend accrues to Parent, despite the shares in Subsidiary having been acquired only three months before the year-end. Moreover, although the two dividend payments are made at six-monthly intervals, the final proposed dividend is a different amount to the interim dividend paid. The example illustrates three different ways of identifying how much of Parent's dividends receivable could be categorised as pre-acquisition dividend.

Example 4.7 Pre-acquisition dividends (4): mid-year acquisition

Example

The current year of Subsidiary runs to 31.12.20X2. Its profits for this period amount to €1.2m. It paid an interim dividend of €240,000 on 30.6.20X2 and has proposed a final dividend of €360,000. The entire share capital of Subsidiary was acquired by Parent on 1.10.20X2.

Required

How much of the final dividend of €360,000 should be considered by Parent to be pre-acquisition?

Solution

There are three possible ways of calculating pre-acquisition dividends in this situation.

	€	€
Solution 1		
Final dividend relates to last six months profits		
Pre-acquisition dividend is therefore 50% × €360,000 (3 months' pre-acquisition and 3 months' post-acquisition)		180,000
Solution 2		
Total dividend for year is aggregated		
Total dividend for the year (€240,000 + €360,000)	600,000	
Post-acquisition dividend (3/12 × €600,000) time apportioned	150,000	
Parent receives 100% of final dividend	360,000	
Less: Time-apportioned post-acquisition dividend	(150,000)	
Pre-acquisition element of the final dividend		210,000
Solution 3		
Pre-acquisition dividend is final dividend not earned in post-acquisition period		
Final dividend	360,000	
Less: Post-acquisition profits (3/12 × €1.2m) time apportioned	(300,000)	
Pre-acquisition element of the final dividend		60,000

Solution 1 to Example 4.7 reflects the argument that the interim dividend relates to the first six months of the year and the final dividend to the last six months. Following this logic, 50% of the final dividend (€180,000) would be considered pre-acquisition by Parent when it receives the dividend after the year-end.

It can also be argued that the interim and final dividends should be considered in aggregate, rather than in isolation. Thus, the total dividend for the year amounts to €600,000, of which Parent will receive €360,000. On a time-apportioned basis, the post-acquisition dividend is €150,000 (3/12 × €600,000). Thus, the pre-acquisition element of the final dividend is €210,000 (€360,000 – €150,000). This calculation is illustrated in Solution 2 to Example 4.7.

The final possibility, illustrated in Solution 3 to Example 4.7, is that pre-acquisition dividend is that amount which cannot have been paid out of post-acquisition profits. In this case, post-acquisition profits (on a time-apportioned basis) are €300,000 (3/12 × €1.2m). Therefore the pre-acquisition element in the final dividend is €60,000 (€360,000 – €300,000).

If Subsidiary paid the interim dividend based on the first six months' performance, then Solution 1 would probably be justified. However, this is rarely the case and many companies view the interim and final dividends as a total distribution relating to the entire year. In such circumstances, Solution 2 is the best approach. Solution 3 is difficult to justify apart from the pragmatic beneficial outcome, where it minimises the amount of dividend identified as pre-acquisition. The approach indicated under Solution 2 to Example 4.7 is used in this book unless the particular circumstances in a question or example clearly suggest that an alternative approach would be preferable.

Summary

This chapter has explained and illustrated the adjustments required in consolidated balance sheet workings for three different categories of dividend. Because dividends paid or payable by subsidiaries are received or receivable by the parent, dividends of subsidiaries are inter-company items. Subsidiaries' proposed dividends in general were dealt with initially. Two different approaches to dealing with such dividends were illustrated: *completing the entries* and *reversing the entries*. Preference dividends were then discussed. Depending on whether or not the parent holds any preference shares of its subsidiaries, these dividends may or may not be inter-company. The priority status of such dividends was discussed and the techniques already explained for dealing with proposed dividends, in general, were applied in the context of preference dividends. Finally, pre-acquisition dividends were discussed and the related adjustments required in consolidation balance sheet workings were illustrated.

Learning outcomes

After studying this chapter you should have learnt:

- how to adjust for the subsidiary's proposed dividends when preparing the consolidated balance sheet workings, regardless of whether the parent has accrued the dividend or not
- how to use two different approaches to facilitate the cancellation of inter-company dividends, depending on the assumption that neither company or both companies recorded the proposed dividend
- how to deal with proposed preference dividends within the subsidiary's liabilities
- how to make any necessary adjustments relating to the dividends received by the parent out of pre-acquisition profits of the subsidiary.

Multiple choice questions

Solutions to these questions are presented in Appendix 1.

4.1 Parrot and Hornbill

Summarised draft balance sheets of **Parrot** and its subsidiary **Hornbill** as at 31 December 20X9:

	Parrot		Hornbill	
	20X9	**20X8**	**20X9**	**20X8**
	€000	**€000**	**€000**	**€000**
Investment in 50,000 shares in Hornbill (at cost)	160	—	—	—
Dividend receivable	—	—	—	—
Dividend payable	(100)	(80)	(12)	—
Sundry net assets	440	480	252	180
	500	400	240	180
Capital and reserves				
Ordinary €1 shares	200	200	60	60
Reserves	300	200	180	120
	500	400	240	180

- Parrot made its investment in Hornbill on 1 January 20X9. It has no other long-term investments.
- Goodwill on acquisition of Hornbill is amortised over five years.
- The book value of Hornbill's assets represented their fair values on acquisition.

The consolidated reserves of the Parrot Group as at 31 December 20X9 are:

(a) €350,000
(b) €360,000
(c) €348,000
(d) €358,000

4.2 Vane and Wimsey

Vane acquired 90% of the issued share capital of **Wimsey** on 1 July 20X8 for €125,000. During the year ended 31 December 20X8, Wimsey paid an interim dividend of €20,000 on 1 June 20X8 and proposed a final dividend of €40,000.

What is the amount to be shown in Vane's own balance sheet in respect of the investment in Wimsey?

(a) €125,000
(b) €116,000
(c) €112,000
(d) €105,000

4.3 Mozart and Schubert

On 1 January 20X2, **Mozart** bought 55% of the issued share capital of **Schubert**, a company incorporated on 1 January 20X1. There was no goodwill on this acquisition.

On 1 February 20X2, Schubert declared and subsequently paid a dividend of €2,000 in respect of the year ended 31 December 20X1.

At 31 December 20X2, Mozart had a balance on profit and loss account of €45,000 excluding this dividend.

The profit and loss account of Schubert comprised:

		€
Profit after tax	20X1	15,000
	20X2	7,000
		22,000
Dividend paid 1 February 20X2		(2,000)
Balance at 31 December 20X2		20,000

Under the acquisition method of accounting, the consolidated profit and loss account balance of Mozart on 31 December 20X2 was:

(a) €47,750
(b) €48,850
(c) €52,000
(d) €56,000

4.4 Pansey and Snowdrop

Pansey acquired 80% of the share capital of **Snowdrop** on 31 October 20X7. Snowdrop paid an interim dividend of €150,000 on 1 October 20X7 and its profit and loss account for the year ended 31 March 20X8 includes a proposed final dividend of €300,000.

The profit and loss account of Pansey for the year ended 31 March 20X8 should include dividends received and receivable from investments in Snowdrop of:

(a) €100,000
(b) €150,000
(c) €187,500
(d) €240,000

Self-assessment exercise

Solution to this self-assessment exercise can be found at:
www.thomsonlearning.co.uk/accountingandfinance/piercebrennan

4.1 Monitor and Screen

The balance sheets of **Monitor** and **Screen** as at 31 December 20X8 were as follows:

	Note	Monitor €000	Screen €000
Fixed assets			
Tangible assets		4,500	5,000
Financial assets	1	4,500	1,000
		9,000	6,000
Current assets			
Stocks		3,900	2,900
Debtors		5,600	3,800
Cash at bank		900	500
		10,400	7,200
Creditors: Amounts due within one year	2	(6,100)	(3,800)
		4,300	3,400
Total assets less current liabilities		13,300	9,400
Creditors: Amounts due after more than one year	3	2,000	1,000
Share capital and reserves			
Issued share capital	4	8,000	5,000
Capital reserve		2,000	2,000
Profit and loss account		1,300	1,400
		11,300	8,400
		13,300	9,400

Notes

1 *Financial assets:*

	Monitor €000	Screen €000
3,000,000 €1 ordinary shares in Screen	3,800	—
500,000 €1 preference shares in Screen	490	—
€200,000 5% loan stock in Screen	200	—
Trade investments	10	1,000
	4,500	1,000

Monitor acquired its shares in Screen in 20X4 when Screen had capital reserves of €400,000 and retained profits of €200,000.

continued overleaf

	Monitor €000	Screen €000
2 *Creditors: Amounts due within one year:*		
Proposed dividends		
Preference	10	4
Ordinary	30	20
	40	24
Trade creditors	6,060	3,776
	6,100	3,800

Monitor has not accrued dividends receivable in its own accounts.

3 *Creditors: Amounts due after more than one year:*		
5% loan stock	2,000	1,000
4 *Issued share capital:*		
Ordinary shares of €1 each	6,000	4,000
Preference shares of €1 each	2,000	1,000
	8,000	5,000

5 Goodwill is fully written off at the balance sheet date.

Required

Prepare the consolidated balance sheet of Monitor and its subsidiary as at 31 December 20X8.

Examination-style questions

4.1 Esk and Dee

The balance sheets of **Esk** and its subsidiary **Dee** as at 31 March 20X7 are summarised as follows:

	Esk		Dee	
	€	€	€	€
Property at valuation		—		95,000
Plant, machinery and vehicles, at cost	203,200		134,300	
Less: Aggregate depreciation	120,400		69,300	
		82,800		65,000
Investment in subsidiary company – Dee		210,000		—
Stock		22,100		18,500
Debtors		35,530		23,200
Current account – Esk		—		26,700
Dividend receivable		2,870		—
Cash at bank		7,200		1,500
		360,500		229,900
Share capital (authorised, issued and fully paid)	€			€
Ordinary shares of €1		80,000		40,000
Profit and loss account		158,600		91,400
7% debentures		—		50,000
Creditors		26,860		25,770
Taxation		25,000		12,000
Current account – Dee		24,500		—
Bank overdraft		39,900		7,450
Dividend payable		5,640		3,280
		360,500		229,900

Esk bought 35,000 shares in Dee on 30 June 20X4, when the balance on the profit and loss account of Dee was €30,000. No goodwill amortisation is required as goodwill is assumed to have an indefinite life and annual impairment reviews confirm its ongoing value.

On 30 March 20X7 Dee dispatched goods to Esk and on the same day invoiced them at a price of €2,200. Esk did not receive the goods until 4 April and has not taken the transaction into its accounts at 31 March. Included in the stock of Esk at 31 March 20X7 are goods purchased from Dee for €3,800. The mark-up on cost made by Dee on its sales to Esk is 20%. At 31 March 20X6 neither company held any stock purchased from the other.

On 28 March 20X7 Esk purchased a vehicle from Dee for €1,100 and entered this price as the cost in its balance sheet. The vehicle had originally cost €2,800 and had been written down to €500 at the date of this sale. Dee charged a full year's depreciation prior to disposal and Esk did not charge depreciation on this vehicle in the year ended 31 March 20X7.

Required

Prepare the consolidated balance sheet of Esk and its subsidiary, Dee, as at 31 March 20X7.

4.2 Astor and Ritz

The accounts of **Astor** and **Ritz** for the year ended 31 March 20X8 are summarised as follows:

Profit and loss accounts for the year ended 31 March 20X8

	Astor	Ritz
	€	€
Profits after tax (including, in the case of Astor, dividends from Ritz, amounting to €19,500)	49,375	17,800
Balances brought forward at 1 April 20X7	75,500	33,500
	124,875	51,300
Deduct: Dividends paid and payable	45,000	27,000
	79,875	24,300

Balance sheets as on 31 March 20X8

		Astor	Ritz
		€	€
Net assets: Subsidiary company	Ritz shares	240,750	—
	Dividend receivable	18,000	—
Other assets, less liabilities, amounts set aside for corporation tax based on the profits of the year to date and proposed dividends (Astor €40,000; Ritz €24,000)		371,125	324,300
		629,875	324,300
Capital and reserves:			
Ordinary shares of €1 each		400,000	240,000
5% cumulative preference shares of €1 each		100,000	60,000
Capital reserve		50,000	—
Profit and loss account		79,875	24,300
		629,875	324,300

You are given the following information:

1. Astor bought 180,000 ordinary shares at €1.25 a share and 30,000 preference shares at par in Ritz on 30 September 20X6. The balance sheet of Ritz as on 31 March 20X6 showed a credit balance on profit and loss account of €13,000.
2. In the year ended 31 March 20X7 Ritz made a profit of €59,500 after providing for taxation. Out of this profit there was declared for the year an ordinary dividend of 15% and a preference dividend of 5%. Astor had credited the appropriate part of the dividends against the cost of the shares acquired in Ritz.
3. The dividends on the preference shares in Astor and Ritz were paid on 31 March in each year.
4. The profits of each company are deemed to accrue evenly throughout each accounting period.

Required

Prepare the consolidated balance sheet of Astor and group as at 31 March 20X8.

5

Mid-year and piecemeal acquisitions

Learning objectives

After studying this chapter you should be able to:

- deal with an acquisition at a time in the reporting period other than the first day
- identify pre-acquisition reserves of a subsidiary when the parent company's investment takes place in stages

Introduction

In the earlier chapters of this book, acquisitions were assumed, for simplicity, to take place at the end of the accounting period (or the beginning, which is the same thing!). Moreover, the percentage holding of the parent was assumed to have been acquired in a single purchase transaction. These two simplifying assumptions are relaxed in this chapter as we consider the impact on preparation of the consolidated balance sheet of acquisitions (i) *during* the accounting period and (ii) acquisitions by the parent of more than one tranche of shares in the subsidiary. When shares are acquired in stages, this is referred to as *piecemeal acquisition*.

Acquisition of subsidiary during accounting period (mid-year acquisition)

In practice, acquisition of subsidiaries takes place during an accounting period more often than at the beginning or end of the period. These are sometimes referred to as *mid-year* acquisitions. Because it is necessary to identify net assets at the date of acquisition in order to calculate goodwill, mid-year acquisitions are more challenging than those completed at the year-end. In addition to accumulated earnings of the acquired subsidiary up to the end of the preceding full accounting period, profits for the period during which the acquisition takes place must be apportioned between those arising before acquisition and those arising after acquisition to calculate net assets at the date of acquisition.

They should be apportioned on the basis of the facts, time, or fairness and reasonableness. For example, if trading is cyclical it may be that 50% of the profits are earned in the last three months of the year. If this is true, then apportionment of profits in the year of acquisition must accommodate this cyclical trading pattern. If, by way of contrast, profits are generated evenly throughout the year, apportionment on a time basis is fair and reasonable. A further complication may arise where the cyclical trading pattern affects sales in a different proportion to the effect on profitability. For example, although (say) 50% of sales occur in the first three months of the year, it is possible that only (say) 33% of profits are generated in that time period.

Example 5.1 illustrates apportionment of the acquired subsidiary's profit by time in the year of acquisition. The acquisition takes place nine months into the financial year. Profits are assumed to accrue evenly. Calculation of pre- and post-acquisition profits are therefore apportioned on a time basis.

Example 5.1 Mid-year acquisition: time apportionment of profits

Example

Parent acquired 90% of Subsidiary on 30.9.20X4. Consolidated accounts are to be prepared on 31.12.20X4. Assume profit accrues evenly throughout the year.

	Parent		Subsidiary	
	€	€	€	€
Investment in Subsidiary		100		—
Net assets		250		100
		350		100
Share capital		200		50
Profit brought forward at 1.1.20X4	120		40	
Profit for 20X4	30	150	10	50
		350		100

Required

Prepare the cost of control account in the consolidated balance sheet workings.

Solution

Cost of control account

	€		€	€
Cost of investment	100.00	Share capital (90% × €50)		45.00
			€	
		Revenue reserve	40.0	
		Profit to 30.9.20X4	7.5	
		Group share (90%)	47.5	42.75
		Goodwill		12.25
	100.00			100.00

Disposals can also take place mid-year. Under acquisition accounting, profits up to the date of disposal are included in the consolidated profit and loss account. Profits or losses on disposal are based on proceeds less the carrying amount of the disposed subsidiary. The carrying amount includes group's share of post-acquisition retained profits up to the date of disposal. Where disposal takes place mid-year, an apportionment of the subsidiary's profits in the year of disposal is required. Disposals are explained and illustrated in detail in Chapter 12.

Piecemeal acquisition of shares in subsidiary

Piecemeal acquisition occurs when the parent acquires its holding in a subsidiary by means of a series of share purchases at different times. During the period between the first purchase of shares and the last acquisition, the underlying value of the subsidiary is likely to change both because of the change in trading profits (or losses) retained and because of other movements in the fair value of net assets. The accounting problem which this creates is how to establish the fair value of net assets acquired and, therefore, how to measure pre-acquisition reserves. Three situations might arise in the context of piecemeal acquisitions:

- existing stake in subsidiary might be increased
- simple investment becomes a subsidiary
- associate becomes a subsidiary.

There are a number of possible ways of calculating pre-acquisition reserves where control is achieved in stages. The approach adopted is determined to some extent by which of these three situations prevails. In particular, where an existing stake in a subsidiary is increased, the accounting treatment is relatively straightforward (see next section).

Where an associate becomes a subsidiary, the approach to calculating pre-acquisition reserves is more debatable. The accounting practice adopted for identifying pre-acquisition reserves in this situation is discussed a little later in this chapter. If a simple investment becomes a subsidiary, the scope for debate depends on whether there are two or more stages in the graduation of the investment from simple investment to subsidiary status. In a two-stage acquisition ((i) acquire a simple investment; (ii) simple investment becomes a subsidiary), a single purchase transaction by the parent changes its relationship with the investee from a simple investment to a subsidiary. Where there are more than two stages, the investment is likely to be classified as an associate at an intermediate stage between being a simple investment and becoming a subsidiary.

When the starting point for piecemeal acquisition is an investment where the parent does not already control the investee, eventual control might be achieved either where a simple investment becomes a subsidiary or where an associated undertaking becomes a subsidiary. These two situations are discussed later in the chapter.

Where control already exists

When a parent has an investment in a subsidiary and purchases an additional block of shares, the reserves attaching to the additional purchase must be treated as pre-acquisition when the next consolidated accounts are prepared. This calculation is independent of earlier calculations of goodwill for share purchases that led to control in the first instance.

The original majority percentage holding (say 60%) is applied to the subsidiary's reserves at the date control is originally achieved. The additional percentage acquired (say 5%) is applied to the subsidiary's reserves at the date the additional shares are acquired. Pre-acquisition reserves amount to the combined total of these two amounts. To calculate goodwill, the cost of the investment (i.e., the combined cost of 60% and 5%) is compared with 65% of the subsidiary's equity share capital plus the pre-acquisition reserves as calculated at the two stages (i.e., based on the amounts in reserves when (i) the 60% and (ii) the 5% stakes were acquired).

Simple investment becomes a subsidiary

It is only at the end of the accounting period during which control is obtained that the subsidiary must be consolidated into the group accounts. There are two possible methods for calculating pre-acquisition reserves:

- *single computation* at the date when control is achieved
- *step-by-step* method.

With the single computation approach, pre-acquisition reserves are calculated by reference to the total proportion of shares held when control is first obtained. Under the step-by-step approach, pre-acquisition reserves are calculated retrospectively by reference to the proportion of reserves at the date of each purchase. In order to apply this method:

- the subsidiary's balance on reserves at the date of each purchase of shares must be identified
- the proportion of reserves acquired with each share purchase must be calculated.

Traditionally, the intention of the acquiring company was the deciding factor between the two methods. Multiple purchases of small quantities of shares over an extended period of time were assumed to indicate absence of intent to acquire control. Consequently, the first method was used. When a more aggressive purchasing pattern was evident, the intention of the purchasing company to acquire control was assumed. In this case, the step-by-step method was used.

Example 5.2 illustrates the effect of the two approaches to calculating pre-acquisition reserves. The step-by-step method in this example produces lower pre-acquisition profit and therefore higher distributable profits for the group. Consequently, the step-by-step method is preferred when the subsidiary is profitable, because lower amounts of reserves are classified as pre-acquisition and are thus treated as non-distributable.

Example 5.2 Piecemeal acquisition: single computation and step-by-step approaches compared

Example

Subsidiary has 100,000 €1 ordinary shares. Parent acquired its interest in Subsidiary as follows:

Date	No. of shares	% acquired	Cumulative %	Subsidiary revenue reserves (€)
1.1.20X1	10,000	10	10	20,000
30.6.20X1	20,000	20	30	40,000
1.3.20X2	15,000	15	45	60,000
30.6.20X2	25,000	25	70	80,000
	70,000			

Required

Calculate how much of Subsidiary's revenue reserves are pre-acquisition to the group.

Solution

(i) If the assumed intention were *not* to acquire control, the *single computation at date of control* method of calculating pre-acquisition reserves is used i.e., 70% × €80,000 = €56,000.

(ii) If the assumed intention *were* to acquire control, the *step-by-step* method is used to calculate pre-acquisition reserves, as follows:

	€
10% × €20,000	2,000
20% × €40,000	8,000
15% × €60,000	9,000
25% × €80,000	20,000
	39,000

Legislation implementing the Seventh Directive in the EU effectively requires the '*single computation* at the date control is achieved' approach to calculating pre-acquisition reserves for the purpose of calculating goodwill. In the UK, this requirement is amplified in FRS 2 *Accounting for Subsidiary Undertakings*. In the *Explanation* section, FRS 2 (paragraph 88) states (emphasis added):

> Where a subsidiary undertaking is acquired in stages, its net identifiable assets and liabilities are to be included in the consolidation at their fair values *on the date it becomes a subsidiary undertaking*, rather than at the date of the earlier purchases.

Therefore, where an acquisition occurs through two or more purchases of shares, the effect of this requirement is that the goodwill calculation is performed only on the date control passes. That is, pre-acquisition reserves are calculated by reference to the net assets at the date control is achieved without any reference to the net assets on previous dates when holdings in the same entity were acquired.

Example 5.3 illustrates the impact FRS 2 had when it was introduced in 1992. In this example, the parent acquired its controlling interest in two stages. Prior to FRS 2, such activity could have been interpreted as justifying the step-by-step approach to calculating pre-acquisition reserves. Since FRS 2 was introduced, the step-by step approach is prohibited in situations similar to this example.

Example 5.3 Piecemeal acquisition: influence of FRS 2 on pre-acquisition profit caculation

Example

Parent acquired Subsidiary in two stages: 15% on 31.12.20X2 for €300,000 and a further 50% on 31.12.20X3 for €2 million. The initial 15% was recorded as a trade investment at cost by Parent. The fair values of Subsidiary's net assets at the two relevant dates were as follows:

	31.12.X2	**31.12.X3**
	€000	**€000**
Fixed assets	1,000	2,000
Other net assets	600	1,000
	1,600	3,000
Share capital	500	500
Reserves	1,100	2,500
	1,600	3,000

Required

(i) Indicate how these two investments are dealt with in the group accounts of Parent.

(ii) In your answer, indicate the implications of the two different methods of calculating pre-acquisition profits on a piecemeal acquisition.

Solution

(i) The first acquisition on 31.12.20X2 at a cost of €300,000 is recorded as a simple investment in fixed assets. The second acquisition on 31.12.20X3 causes the investment to be classified as a subsidiary, as Parent now holds 65% of the ordinary shares of Subsidiary. Consequently, full consolidation of Subsidiary is required and goodwill is calculated based on fair value of net assets in Subsidiary on 31.12.20X3.

(ii) *The two methods of calculating pre-acquisition profits*

(a) Prior to FRS 2, pre-acquisition reserves relating to the acquisition on 31.12.20X3 would have been calculated using the *step-by-step* method, assuming that Parent's intention was to obtain control of Subsidiary.

	€000	€000
Cost (€300 + €2,000)		2,300
Acquired: 15% × €1,600$_{\text{net assets at acquisition}}$	240	
50% × €3,000$_{\text{net assets at acquisition}}$	1,500	(1,740)
Goodwill		560

(b) FRS 2 now requires pre-acquisition reserves to be calculated as follows:

	€000
Cost (€300 + €2,000)	2,300
Acquired: 65% × €3,000$_{\text{net assets when becoming subsidiary}}$	(1,950)
Goodwill	350

Thus, under FRS 2, pre-acquisition profits are higher and goodwill is lower where the subsidiary (acquired in stages) is profitable.

Associate becomes a subsidiary

Example 5.3 illustrated the case of graduation from a simple investment to a subsidiary in one single transaction. An exception to the *single computation* approach occurs where, prior to becoming a subsidiary, earlier purchases of shares resulted in a significant long-term investment that is classified as an associated undertaking. As we will see in Chapter 7, such an investment is accounted for under the equity method, which requires that:

- the investor's share of the associate's net assets is calculated based on the fair value of those net assets at the date of becoming an associate
- goodwill is the difference between the cost of the investment in the associate and the investor's share of the associate's net assets at fair value
- subsequent changes in the associate's net assets are reflected in the investor's consolidated reserves.

On further purchases of shares that result in an associate becoming a subsidiary, the *single computation* approach required under the Seventh Directive and FRS 2 would cause two problems:

- profits already included in the investor's consolidated retained earnings (and therefore, treated as post-acquisition and distributable) would form part of the calculation of goodwill on acquisition of the subsidiary (being treated as pre-acquisition under the single computation approach)
- since the aggregate cost of shares in the subsidiary is a mixture of earlier and new costs, but fair value of subsidiary net assets would be measured at the single more recent date, the resulting goodwill may be negative. This would in part represent a revaluation of net assets between the dates of becoming an associate and a subsidiary.

The solution offered by FRS 2 to relieve the possible tension between its requirements and those of equity accounting is that this situation may represent special circumstances where compliance with legislation would be misleading and thus the true and fair override is invoked (FRS 2, paragraph 89). Specifically, FRS 2 suggests it will be appropriate to calculate goodwill on a piecemeal basis taking, for each parcel of shares acquired, the cost of the parcel compared with the related share of net assets at fair value when acquired.

Example 5.4 is based on the same data as provided in Example 5.2. In the context of the discussion in this section, Example 5.4 concludes that pre-acquisition reserves amount to €41,000. This compares with €56,000 calculated under the single computation approach and €39,000 calculated under a strict step-by-step approach as indicated in Example 5.2.

Example 5.4 Piecemeal acquisition: associate to subsidiary

Example

Details are as for Example 5.2.

Required

Discuss the implications for the calculation of pre-acquisition reserves of subsidiary, of associate undertaking status being achieved in advance of control being finally obtained.

Solution

- Once a shareholding in excess of 20% is acquired, the investor is assumed to exert significant influence over the management and policy formulation of the investee.
- Significant shareholdings (between 20% and 50%) are classified as associates under FRS 9 *Associates and Joint Ventures* (subject to criteria).
- Associates are accounted for using the equity method of accounting.
- Under the equity method of accounting, goodwill is calculated when the investment is acquired, using the investee's reserves (at the date the investment qualifies as an associate) as pre-acquisition reserves in the calculation of net assets acquired.
- In this example, associate status is achieved once the cumulative shareholding reaches 30% and the investment continues to be classified as an associate when the stake is increased to 45%.
- It is only when the final investment is made that the investee is classified as a subsidiary.
- The investing group's share of all subsequent reserves of the investee are treated as post-acquisition and are included in consolidated distributable reserves.
- Pre-acquisition reserves in the context of including the investment as a subsidiary are calculated as follows, using a combination of *single calculation* (for initial 10% and subsequent 20% stakes) and *step-by-step* approaches:

	€
30% × €40,000	12,000
15% × €60,000	9,000
25% × €80,000	20,000
	41,000

It is useful to have a rule of thumb to assist in consistent application of the accounting technique set out in this section. The following general rule can be used to identify pre-acquisition reserves in a piecemeal acquisition:

- ignore share purchases that keep the company's share below 20% (i.e., until associated undertaking status is reached)
- treat all shares purchased up to the purchase which brought ownership above 20% as a single purchase
- use the step-by-step method thereafter.

Example 5.5 applies this rule of thumb.

Example 5.5 Piecemeal acquisition: application of rule of thumb

Example

Parent acquired shares in Subsidiary, which has 100,000 €1 ordinary shares in issue, on three separate dates:

Date	No. of shares	% acquired	Cumulative %	Cost	Subsidiary revenue reserves
				€	€
1.2.20X0	10,000	10	10	16,000	40,000
1.11.20X0	25,000	25	35	42,000	60,000
1.4.20X1	20,000	20	55	40,000	80,000
	55,000				

Required

Calculate the pre-acquisition reserves of Subsidiary.

Solution

With the second purchase, the investment becomes an associate (greater than 20% ownership). Consequently, the reserves at that date are treated as pre-acquisition with regard to the 35% stake, and reserves at the later date (when the additional 20% is acquired) are treated as pre-acquisition with regard to the later stake.

Thus, pre-acquisition reserves are as follows:

	€
35% × €60,000	21,000
20% × €80,000	16,000
	37,000

Note: Had the *single computation* been applied, pre-acquisition reserves would have been €44,000 (55% of €80,000).

Summary

In this chapter, the issues involved in preparing the consolidated balance sheet when acquisitions take place at a date other than the year-end, and where a controlling interest is acquired through a number of separate purchase transactions, have been discussed. The two self-assessment questions that follow allow students to test their grasp of the principles discussed and illustrated in this chapter before moving on to the next topic relating to the preparation of consolidated balance sheets. In the next chapter, we will see how more complex group structures (e.g., where a subsidiary has its own subsidiary) are dealt with in consolidation workings.

Learning outcomes

After studying this chapter you should have learnt:

- how to deal with an acquisition at a time in the reporting period other than the first day
- how to identify pre-acquisition reserves of a subsidiary when the parent company's investment takes place in stages.

Multiple choice questions

Solutions to these questions are presented in Appendix 1.

5.1 Red and Black

Red acquired voting shares in **Black** as follows:

Date	% of voting shares acquired	Reserves of Black (per balance sheet)
1/7/20X0	10	€100,000
1/4/20X2	25	€150,000
1/7/20X3	25	€240,000

At 1 July 20X3 the fair value of the net assets of Black exceeded their book value by €25,000 and the surplus was not reflected in the accounts of Black.

The amount to be treated as pre-acquisition in respect of Black in the cost of control account in the consolidated workings is:

(a) €107,500
(b) €102,500
(c) €159,000
(d) €118,750

5.2 Robin and Hood

Robin purchased 75% of the share capital of **Hood** on 1 September 20X2. The profit and loss account of Hood for the year ended 31 December 20X2, includes the following:

	€000
Dividend – interim (paid 31 July 20X2)	200
Dividend – final proposed	400

The amount included in the individual profit and loss account of Robin for the year ended 31 December 20X2, as dividends received and receivable from investment in subsidiary company is:

(a) €100,000
(b) €150,000
(c) €200,000
(d) €300,000

5.3 Doncaster and Wentworth

Doncaster acquired 75,000 equity shares in **Wentworth** on 1 January 20X8. Wentworth has 120,000 equity shares in total and made a profit after tax of €500,000 in the year ended 31 March 20X8. A final dividend of €200,000 was proposed, bringing the total dividend for the year up to €300,000. The interim dividend was paid in November 20X7.

What is the resulting credit for dividend receivable in Doncaster's own profit and loss account?

(a) €31,250
(b) €37,500
(c) €46,875
(d) €50,000

Self-assessment exercises

Solutions to these self-assessment exercises can be found at:
www.thomsonlearning.co.uk/accountingandfinance/piercebrennan

5.1 Piecemeal and mid-year acquisition: increasing stake of existing subsidiary – Teeny and Tiny

The summarised balance sheets of Teeny and its subsidiary Tiny as at 30 June 20X5 are as follows:

		Teeny €000	Tiny €000
Investment in Tiny		16,400	—
Other net assets		20,100	22,000
		36,500	22,000
Share capital in €1 shares		12,000	15,000
Profit and loss account:	Carried forward	20,000	5,500
	Current year	4,500	1,500
		36,500	22,000

Notes:

1 The investments in Tiny were made as follows:

	€000
9 million €1 shares on 31 December 20X1 (when profit and loss account of Tiny had a balance of €2.5m)	11,500
3 million €1 shares on 31 December 20X4	4,900
	16,400

2 At 31 December 20X4 the fair value of the net assets of Tiny exceeded their balance sheet carrying values by €600,000. This excess was entirely due to stock, which had been sold by the year-end.

3 At 31 December 20X1, the fair value of the net assets of Tiny exceeded their balance sheet value by €400,000. None of the assets which were the subject of fair value adjustments at the original date of acquisition remained in the financial statements of Tiny at 30 June 20X5.

4 Goodwill on acquisition is amortised over five years, including a full year's charge in the year of acquisition.

Required

Prepare the consolidated balance sheet of Teeny Group at 30 June 20X5.

(*Source*: Robins P., 1995, 'Consolidating accounts: accounting for acquisitions – Part 2,' adapted, *ACCA Students' Newsletter*, July, pp.38–42 and p.51.)

5.2 Piecemeal and mid-year acquisition: simple investment becomes subsidiary – Teeny and Tiny

Assume the same details as 5.1 above, except the piecemeal acquisition of shares in Tiny took place as follows:

	€000
1.5 million €1 shares on 31 December 20X1 (when profit and loss account of Tiny had a balance of €2.5m)	1,750
10.5 million €1 shares on 31 December 20X4	14,650
	16,400

Required

Prepare the consolidated balance sheet of Teeny Group at 30 June 20X5.

(*Source*: Robins P., 1995. 'Consolidating accounts: accounting for acquisitions – Part 2,' *ACCA Students' Newsletter*, July, pp. 38–42 and p.51.)

5.3 Piecemeal and mid-year acquisition: associate becomes subsidiary – Teeny and Tiny

Assume, again, the same details as 5.1 above, except the piecemeal acquisition of shares in Tiny took place as follows:

	€000
6 million €1 shares on 31 December 20X1 (when profit and loss account of Tiny had a balance of €2.5m)	7,400
6 million €1 shares on 31 December 20X4	9,000
	16,400

Required

Prepare the consolidated balance sheet of Teeny Group at 30 June 20X5.

(*Source*: Robins P., 1995. 'Consolidating accounts: accounting for acquisitions – Part 2,' adapted, *ACCA Students' Newsletter*, July, pp.38–42 and p.51.)

Examination-style questions

5.1 Trunk, Arms and Legs

The summarised balance sheets of **Trunk** and its subsidiary companies, **Arms** and **Legs**, as on 31 March 20X7, were as follows:

		Trunk	Arms	Legs
		€	€	€
Plant and machinery, at cost		30,000	2,000	15,000
Depreciation		(8,000)	(500)	(3,000)
		22,000	1,500	12,000
Freehold land, at cost		50,000	—	—
		72,000	1,500	12,000
Subsidiary companies:	Shares, at cost	39,500	—	—
	Amounts due	17,300	—	6,000
Stocks, at cost		32,500	16,000	9,000
Debtors		11,000	13,000	6,000
Bank balance		16,000	17,000	—
		188,300	47,500	33,000
Share capital: Ordinary shares of €1 each		50,000	25,000	20,000
6% preference shares of €1 each		—	6,000	—
7½% preference shares of €1 each		—	—	10,000
General reserve		55,000	—	—
Profit and loss account		45,300	1,000	(10,000)
		150,300	32,000	20,000
Inter-company balance		—	13,500	8,500
Creditors		24,000	640	4,000
Taxation		14,000	1,000	—
Preference dividend		—	360	—
Bank overdraft		—	—	500
		188,300	47,500	33,000

The following information is relevant:

1 Trunk acquired shares in its subsidiary companies at cost as follows:

Company	No. of shares	Date of acquisition	€
Arms	5,000	ordinary shares on incorporation	5,000
	3,000	preference shares on incorporation	3,000
	10,000	ordinary shares on 1 April 20X4	14,000
	2,000	preference shares on 1 April 20X4	2,500
Legs	20,000	ordinary shares on 1 April 20X2	15,000

2 On 1 April 20X4 there was a debit balance of €1,000 on the profit and loss account of Arms and on 1 April 20X2 there was a nil balance on that of Legs.

3 Inter-company balances as on 31 March 20X7 were:

Trunk:	Debtors –	Arms	€7,800;	Legs	€9,500
Arms:	Creditors –	Trunk	€7,500;	Legs	€6,000
Legs:	Debtors –	Arms	€6,000;		
	Creditors –	Trunk	€8,500.		

4 No preference dividends have been paid by Legs for two years.

5 A remittance of €1,000 from Trunk to Legs was not recorded by the latter company until after the books had been closed.

6 Included in the stocks of Trunk are goods costing that company €10,000, sold by Arms in February 20X7 at cost plus 25%.

Required

Prepare the consolidated balance sheet of Trunk, and its subsidiary companies, as at 31 March 20X7.

5.2 Arrow, Bow and Target

You are supplied with the following trial balances of **Arrow** and its subsidiaries, **Bow** and **Target**, as at 31 December 20X3.

	Arrow	**Bow**	**Target**
	€	**€**	**€**
Cash	164,000	22,000	54,000
Debtors	208,000	82,000	286,000
Stock	482,000	140,000	156,000
Investment – Bow	300,000	—	—
Investment – Target	350,000	—	—
Other investments	370,000	—	—
Fixed assets	750,000	116,000	198,000
Accumulated depreciation	(192,000)	(14,000)	(42,000)
Cost of sales	1,640,000	600,000	700,000
Operating expenses	120,000	70,000	80,000
	4,192,000	1,016,000	1,432,000
Creditors	92,000	66,000	48,000
Sales	1,920,000	550,000	1,140,000
Gain on sales of assets	18,000	—	—
Dividend income	36,000	—	—
Share capital – €20 shares	1,000,000	400,000	200,000
Revenue reserves:	1,126,000	—	24,000
Contingency reserve (note 6)	—	—	20,000
	4,192,000	1,016,000	1,432,000

You are informed that:

1 Bow was formed by Arrow on 1 January 20X3. To secure additional capital, 25% of the issued capital was sold at par on the stock market. Arrow acquired the remaining share capital at par for cash.

2 On 1 July 20X3 Arrow acquired from stockholders 8,000 shares of Target's issued share capital for €350,000. A condensed trial balance of Target at 1 July 20X3 was as follows:

	Dr	**Cr**
	€	**€**
Current assets	330,000	—
Fixed assets (net)	120,000	—
Current liabilities	—	90,000
Issued share capital	—	200,000
Revenue reserves	—	72,000
Sales	—	400,000
Cost of sales	280,000	—
Operating expenses	32,000	—
	762,000	762,000

continued overleaf

3 The following inter-company sales of certain products were made in 20X3

	Sales	Gross profit on sales	Included in purchaser's stock on 31.12.20X3 at lower of cost or market value
	€		€
Arrow to Target	80,000	20%	30,000
Bow to Target	60,000	10%	20,000
Target to Arrow	120,000	30%	40,000
	260,000		90,000

In valuing Arrow's stock at the lower of cost or market value, the stock purchased from Target was written down by €3,800.

4 On 2 January 20X3 Arrow sold a machine to Bow. The machine was purchased on 1 January 20X1 and was being depreciated by the straight-line method over ten years. Bow computes depreciation by the same method, based on the remaining useful life. Details of the sale are as follows:

	€
Cost of machine	50,000
Accumulated depreciation	10,000
Net book value	40,000
Sales price	48,000
Gain on sale	8,000

5 Dividends were paid on the following dates in 20X3:

	Arrow	Target
	€	€
30 June	44,000	12,000
31 December	52,000	28,000*
	96,000	40,000

*from revenue reserves

6 At the year-end Target provided €20,000 for a loss in connection with a law suit that had been pending since 20X1.

Required

Prepare the consolidated balance sheet as at 31 December 20X3.

6

Indirect holdings

Learning objectives

After studying this chapter you should be able to:

- illustrate complex group structures graphically
- distinguish between *controlling* and *effective* ownership interests
- calculate effective interests in a particular subsidiary where the ownership structure is complex
- identify the appropriate date from which subsidiaries in a complex group should be consolidated
- prepare the consolidated balance sheet for complex groups using the T account workings learnt in previous chapters

Introduction

In earlier chapters, direct control of individual subsidiaries was used to illustrate the basic principles of consolidation. However, in practice, investing companies often control subsidiaries through a combination of direct and indirect investment. This has been discussed already (Chapter 1).

An indirect subsidiary relationship arises where a subsidiary has a subsidiary (or subsidiaries) of its own. The parent, therefore, controls both the subsidiary and the sub-subsidiary. In addition, where the combined holdings of the parent and subsidiaries enable the parent to control another entity, a subsidiary relationship exists between the parent and that other entity (referred to in Chapter 1 as a mixed group). In this chapter, *complex group structure* refers to the situation where a parent has more than one subsidiary. The subsidiaries can be controlled directly by the parent, indirectly through ownership interests in a direct subsidiary, or through a combination of direct and indirect investment. The techniques for preparing consolidated balance sheets where group structures are more complex than those dealt with in earlier chapters are set out in this chapter.

Complex group structures

Complex group structures dealt with in this chapter include groups with more than one direct subsidiary (fellow subsidiaries), groups with subsidiaries of subsidiaries (vertical groups) and groups with subsidiaries where control is exercised through a combination of direct and indirect investment by the parent (mixed groups).

Fellow subsidiaries

Where the parent has more than one direct subsidiary, the direct subsidiaries are referred to as *fellow* subsidiaries. The relationship is depicted in Example 6.1.

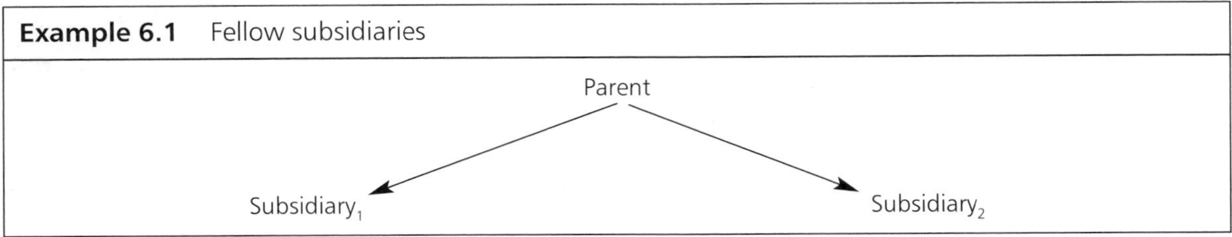

Example 6.1 Fellow subsidiaries

When preparing consolidated balance sheets, the group structure depicted in Example 6.1 is treated identically to the single subsidiary situation. However, there are two amounts involved for cost of investment, pre-acquisition reserves, minority interest, etc., when completing the consolidation workings. The entries for both subsidiaries may be made through one set of T accounts (i.e., one cost of control, one minority interest and one revenue reserves account), resulting in aggregate goodwill, consolidated reserves and minority interest figures.

Sub-subsidiaries – vertical group

The definition of subsidiary undertakings, which came from the Seventh Directive and is now included in company law throughout the EU, was set out in Chapter 1. Under this definition, a subsidiary relationship can arise when a subsidiary of the parent has its own subsidiary. This second subsidiary (sub-subsidiary) is also a subsidiary of the ultimate parent. The relationship is illustrated in Example 6.2.

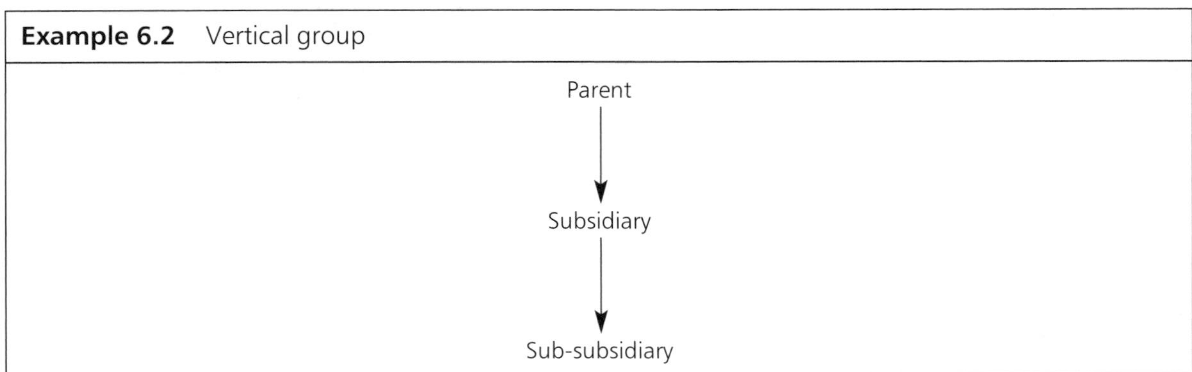

Example 6.2 Vertical group

Where Subsidiary is wholly owned by Parent, preparing the consolidated balance sheet is no more difficult than if there were two separate direct subsidiaries. The entries in the consolidated balance sheet working accounts are the same as when consolidating two fellow subsidiaries.

Where Subsidiary is not wholly owned, there are two possible methods for completing the consolidated balance sheet workings: (i) the *two-stage* approach and (ii) the *single-stage* approach. These are discussed later in this chapter.

Mixed groups

A mixed group is a group in which the interest of the parent in a sub-subsidiary arises from a combination of a direct and an indirect interest. The parent can control the sub-subsidiary through a combination of a direct holding (less than a controlling interest) in the sub-subsidiary and an indirect holding (through a subsidiary and also less than a controlling interest) in the sub-subsidiary. Through a combination of the two holdings, the parent controls the sub-subsidiary. Panel A in Example 6.3 illustrates one possible combination of holdings which can lead to the parent controlling the sub-subsidiary.

A mixed group can also arise where, in addition to controlling the sub-subsidiary through control of the subsidiary, the parent has a direct holding in a sub-subsidiary. The mixed group structure in this situation incorporates a vertical group, in addition to a direct investment by the parent in the sub-subsidiary.

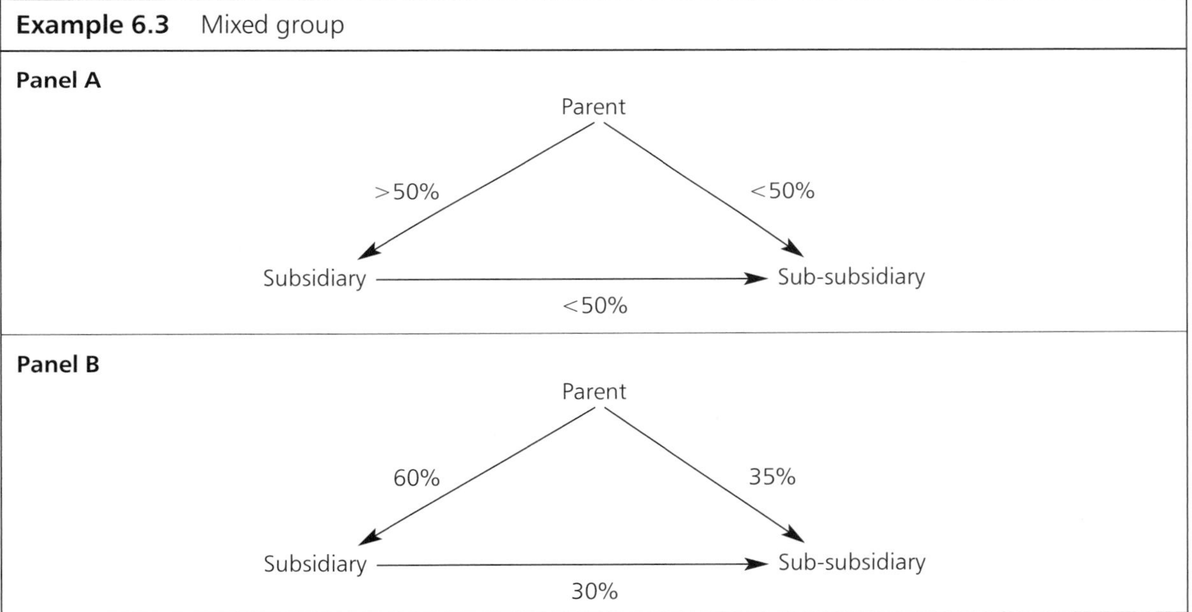

Calculating shareholdings

Controlling interests

To establish whether or not control exists, the absolute value of the shareholding (called *controlling interests*) in each company is taken into consideration. Consider Panel B of Example 6.3. Parent owns 60% of the shares in Subsidiary and 35% of the shares in Sub-subsidiary and Subsidiary owns 30% of the shares in Sub-subsidiary. Parent therefore controls both Subsidiary and Sub-subsidiary. Parent controls both its own direct 35% interest in Sub-subsidiary and, because it controls Subsidiary, it controls the 30% owned by Subsidiary. Therefore, Parent controls 65% of Sub-subsidiary. Controlling interests are calculated to determine where control lies. To complete the consolidation workings, *effective interests* must be calculated.

Effective interests

While the controlling interests of 60% in Subsidiary and 65% in Sub-subsidiary determine that both Subsidiary and Sub-subsidiary are subsidiaries, these percentages are not used when preparing the consolidation workings. Composite percentages (called *effective interests*) are calculated for consolidation purposes to allow for the minority interest of Subsidiary shareholders in their company's investment in Sub-subsidiary. Example 6.4 illustrates the calculations involved for a simple mixed group.

In Example 6.4, Parent has a direct holding (80%) in Subsidiary and the minority interest in this case is referred to as a *direct* minority interest (20%). Parent has a direct holding (40%) in Sub-subsidiary and also an indirect holding through its holding in Subsidiary (80% × 35% = 28%). Consequently, Parent's effective interest in Sub-subsidiary is only 68% (40% + 28%), although its controlling interest is 75% (40% + 35%).

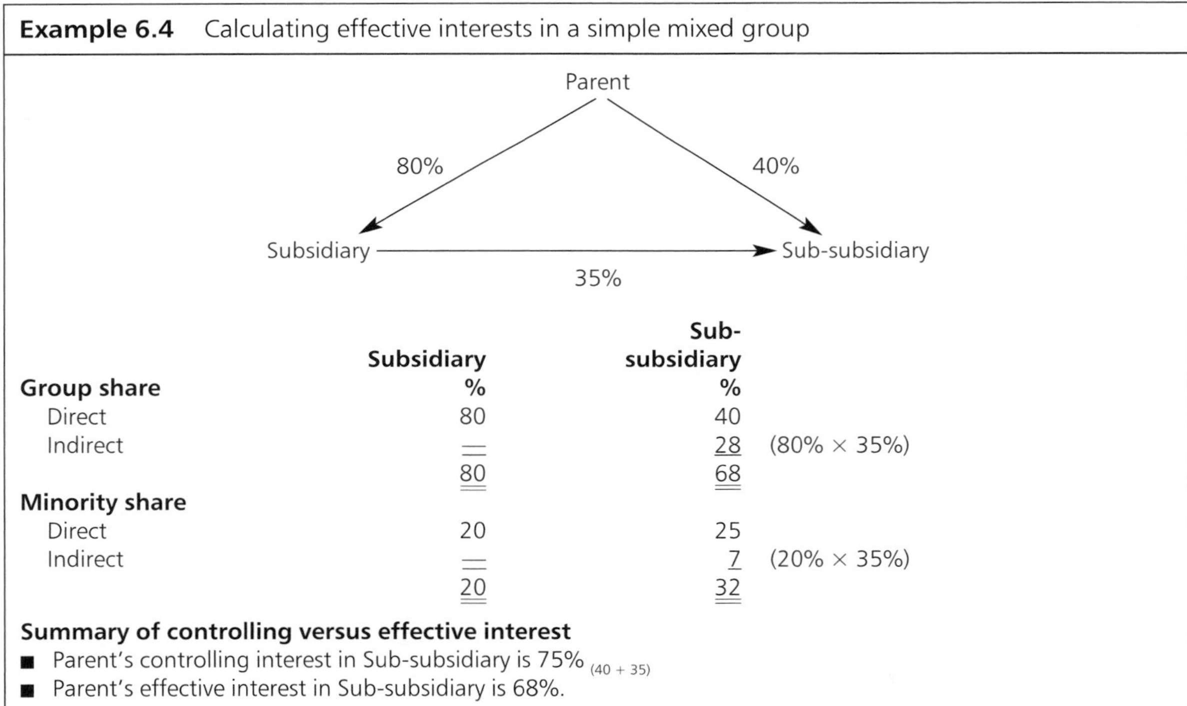

Example 6.4 Calculating effective interests in a simple mixed group

	Subsidiary	Sub-subsidiary	
	%	%	
Group share			
Direct	80	40	
Indirect	—	28	(80% × 35%)
	80	68	
Minority share			
Direct	20	25	
Indirect	—	7	(20% × 35%)
	20	32	

Summary of controlling versus effective interest

- Parent's controlling interest in Sub-subsidiary is 75% (40 + 35)
- Parent's effective interest in Sub-subsidiary is 68%.

Similarly, there is a direct minority interest in Sub-subsidiary (100% – (40% + 35%) = 25%). In addition, there is an *indirect* minority interest in the sub-subsidiary. This arises because of the *direct minority interest in Subsidiary* and Subsidiary's *direct investment* in Sub-subsidiary. The indirect minority interest in Sub-subsidiary is the direct minority in Subsidiary's *share* of Subsidiary's investment in Sub-subsidiary, i.e., 20% × 35% = 7%. Thus, the total minority interest in Sub-subsidiary is 32% (25% + 7%).

The calculations illustrated in Example 6.4 assume the use of the *single-stage* consolidation approach which is discussed in detail later in the chapter. It is also useful to remember that the sum of group interest and minority interest must always equal 100%. This is illustrated in Example 6.4, where total interest in Subsidiary is 100% (80% + 20%) and total interest in Sub-subsidiary is also 100% (68% + 32%).

As stated earlier, mixed groups can also incorporate vertical groups within their structure. Example 6.5 illustrates such a mixed group, which we describe as a vertical mixed group. The difference between such a group and the simple mixed group illustrated in Example 6.4 is that the subsidiary holds a controlling interest in the sub-subsidiary in the vertical mixed group. Consequently, the parent controls the sub-subsidiary independently of its own direct shareholding in that sub-subsidiary. The direct holding simply increases the parent's majority stake in the sub-subsidiary.

Example 6.5 Calculating effective interests in a vertical mixed group

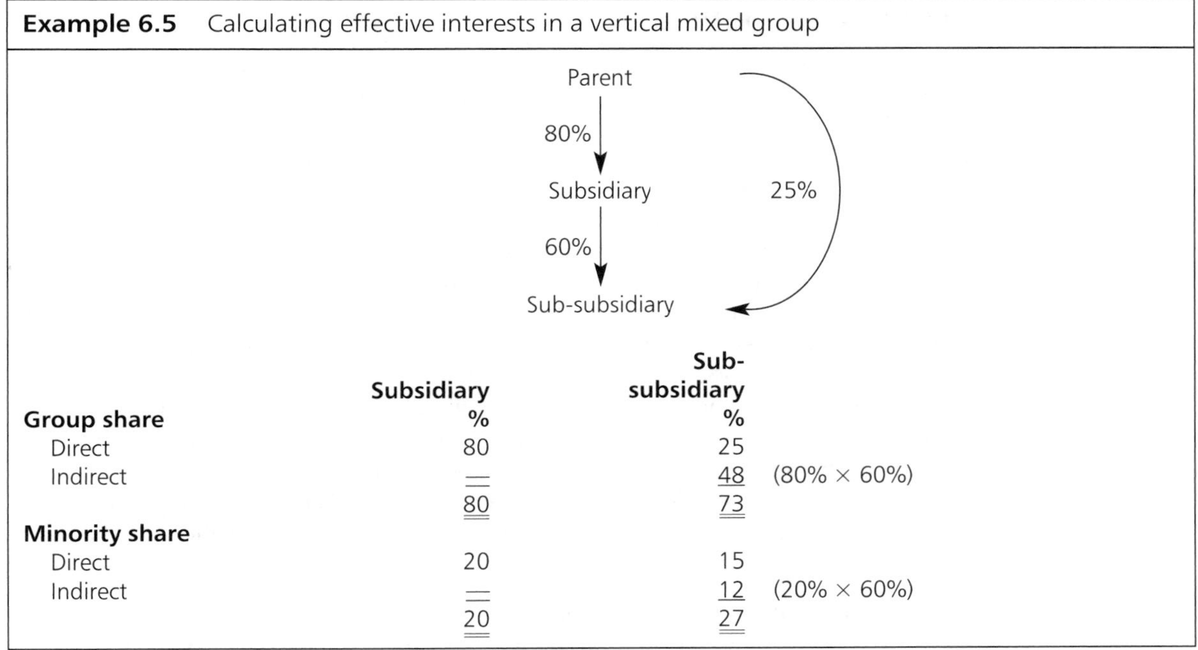

	Subsidiary	Sub-subsidiary	
Group share	%	%	
Direct	80	25	
Indirect	—	48	(80% × 60%)
	80	73	
Minority share			
Direct	20	15	
Indirect	—	12	(20% × 60%)
	20	27	

As before, the group has a direct interest in both Subsidiary and in Sub-subsidiary of 80% and 25%, respectively. It also has an indirect interest in Sub-subsidiary of 48% (80% × 60%). Therefore, the effective interest of the group in Sub-subsidiary is 73% (25% + 48%). The direct minority interest is 20% in Subsidiary and 15% in Sub-subsidiary, while the indirect minority interest in Sub-subsidiary is 12% (20% × 60%).

It is important to bear in mind that while effective interests are used in the consolidated balance sheet computations, controlling interests determine where control lies. That is, it is possible to have a situation where an investor controls an investee, despite the effective interest being less than 50% (see Example 6.8).

Consolidation technique for mixed groups

Traditionally, there were two methods of preparing consolidation workings where there are indirect subsidiaries (i.e., sub-subsidiaries). The different methods give different results. The consolidated balance sheet can be prepared using the *two-stage* or the *single-stage* (indirect) method.

Two-stage method

Under the two-stage approach, the parent produces the consolidated accounts by preparing a sub-consolidation for the subsidiary and the sub-subsidiaries first. It then completes the consolidation by consolidating the subsidiary group accounts with its own accounts. As this effectively duplicates the work involved in an examination situation, this method is not recommended in this book.

Single-stage method

Under the more commonly used *indirect* method, the parent prepares the consolidated accounts in a single set of consolidated working accounts, without first preparing consolidated accounts of the sub-group (the subsidiary and sub-subsidiaries). The descriptor *indirect* comes from the practice of including the composite percentages (equivalent to the effective interest discussed earlier) for net assets acquired (in cost of control) and for minority interests in the sub-subsidiary.

Using the three main consolidation working accounts, Example 6.6 sets out the entries required to complete the balance sheet consolidation workings where the parent has an indirect interest in a sub-subsidiary. The balancing amount in each account represents the consolidated balance sheet entry and is shaded for emphasis in Example 6.6. The entries are similar to examples in previous chapters, except for the treatment of the cost of investment from the subsidiary's balance sheet (the relevant entries are highlighted by italics for emphasis in Example 6.6). The issues involved in accounting for the cost of investment included in the subsidiary's balance sheet are discussed in detail in the following section. In addition, it should be noted that what is described as *group* share and *minority* share in relation to the sub-subsidiary refers to their respective *effective* interests in the sub-subsidiary.

Example 6.6 Indirect method – the three working accounts

Cost of control account

Full cost of investment by parent in subsidiary	X	Group share of subsidiary's share capital	X
		Group share of subsidiary's pre-acquisition reserves	X
Parent's share of subsidiary's cost of investment in sub-subsidiary	X	Group share of sub-subsidiary's share capital	X
		Group share of sub-subsidiary's pre-acquisition reserves	X
Bal c/d negative goodwill	X	Bal c/d positive goodwill	X
	X		X

Consolidated revenue reserves

Subsidiary		Parent's revenue reserves	X
Group share of pre-acquisition revenue reserves	X	Subsidiary's revenue reserves	X
Minority share of revenue reserves	X	Sub-subsidiary's revenue reserves	X
Sub-subsidiary			
Group share of pre-acquisition revenue reserves	X		
Minority share (direct and indirect) of revenue reserves	X		
Consolidated balance sheet	X		
	X		X

Minority interest

		Minority share of subsidiary's share capital	X
		Minority share of subsidiary's reserves	X
Direct minority share of subsidiary's cost of investment in sub-subsidiary (see following section)	X	Minority share (direct and indirect) of sub-subsidiary's share capital	X
Consolidated balance sheet	X	Minority share (direct and indirect) of sub-subsidiary's reserves	X
	X		X

Cost of investment

The most significant variation on the calculations already explained in earlier chapters is the treatment of the cost of the subsidiary's investment in the sub-subsidiary. Up to now, the only cost of investment dealt with in the cost of control account was the cost of the parent's investment in the subsidiary. The entire amount of this cost was transferred from the balance sheet of the parent to the debit side of the cost of control account. This cost was then compared with the group's share of the net assets of the subsidiary at acquisition to calculate goodwill. No cost of investment was entered in the minority interest account because, in that account, we were only interested in calculating the minority share of the net assets of the direct subsidiary at the year-end. Cost to the minority was not recorded in any of the group balance sheets.

In vertical and mixed groups, the cost of the subsidiary's investment in the sub-subsidiary is a cost that is borne partly by the group and partly by the minority. It is borne by the group to the extent that the parent has a majority share in the subsidiary, and by the minority to the extent that there are minority shareholders in the subsidiary. Because this cost is recorded on the subsidiary's balance sheet, it must be eliminated on consolidation. It is transferred from the balance sheet of the subsidiary and allocated between the cost of control account (group share) and the minority interest account (minority share). The group and minority shares referred to here are their shares in the net assets of the *subsidiary* and *not* their share of the net assets of the *sub-subsidiary*. It is important to distinguish between the treatment in the cost of control and minority interest accounts of:

- the parent's cost of investment (and related net assets) in the subsidiary; and
- the subsidiary's cost of investment (and related net assets) in the sub-subsidiary.

Example 6.7 compares the treatment of cost and net asset amounts for the subsidiary and the sub-subsidiary in a vertical group. The same principles apply in the context of a mixed group.

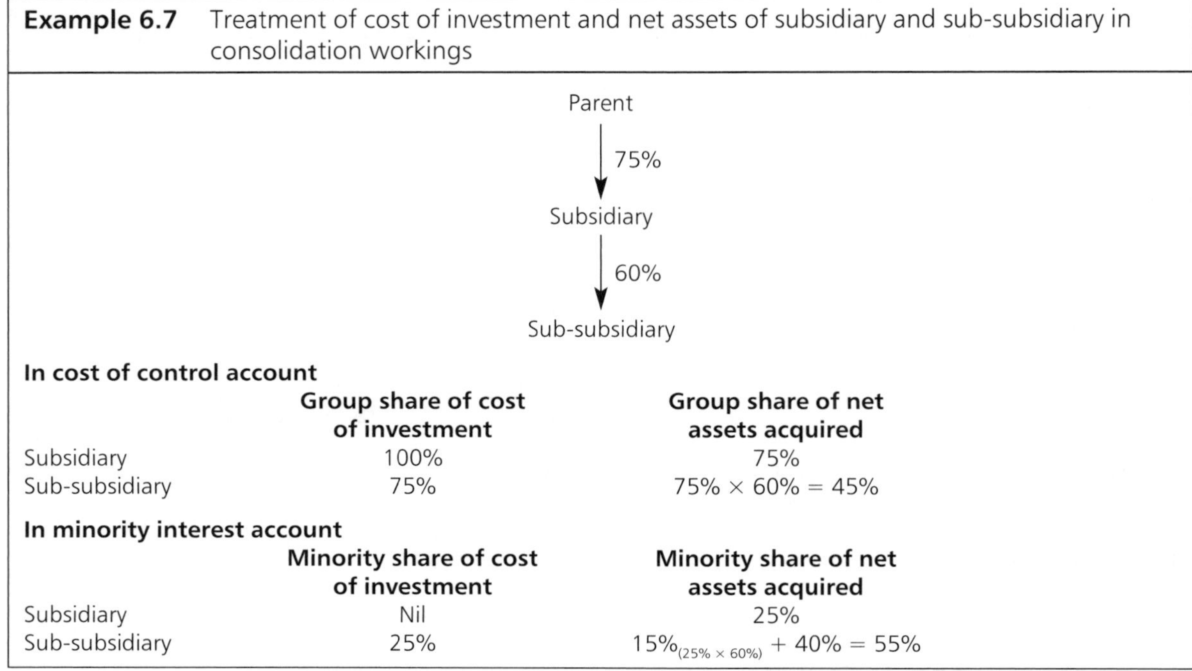

Example 6.7 Treatment of cost of investment and net assets of subsidiary and sub-subsidiary in consolidation workings

Parent
↓ 75%
Subsidiary
↓ 60%
Sub-subsidiary

In cost of control account

	Group share of cost of investment	**Group share of net assets acquired**
Subsidiary	100%	75%
Sub-subsidiary	75%	75% × 60% = 45%

In minority interest account

	Minority share of cost of investment	**Minority share of net assets acquired**
Subsidiary	Nil	25%
Sub-subsidiary	25%	$15\%_{(25\% \times 60\%)} + 40\% = 55\%$

Example 6.8 combines Examples 6.6 and 6.7. It elaborates on Example 6.6 by applying the shareholdings in Example 6.7 to the outline accounts in Example 6.6. It is interesting to note in Example 6.8 that, although the parent controls the sub-subsidiary, its share of the sub-subsidiary's net assets is less than 50%.

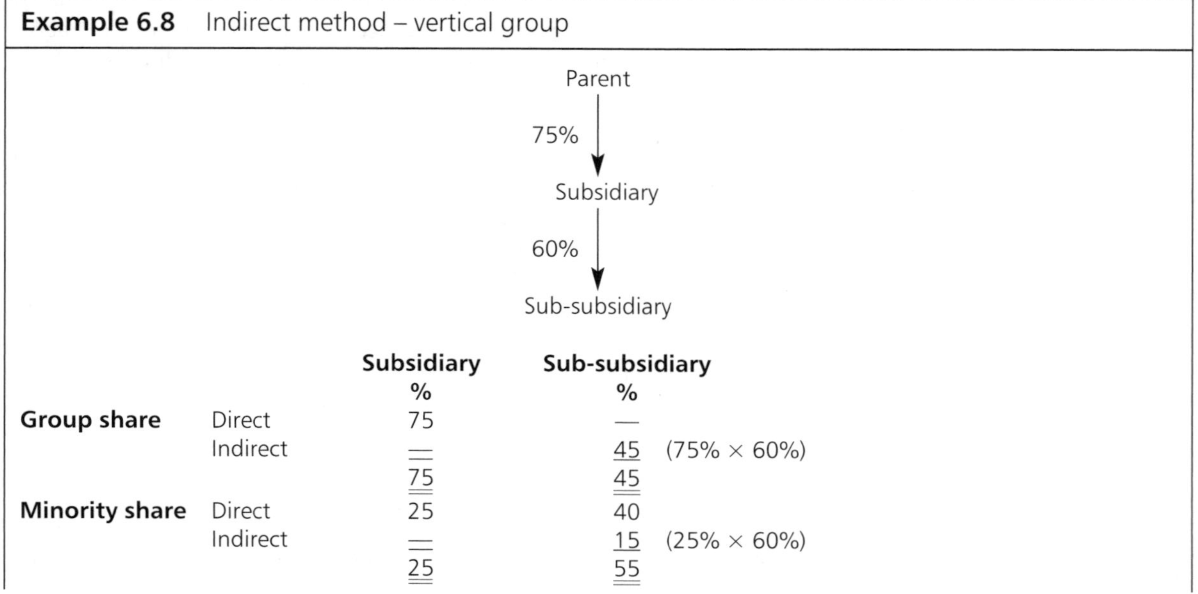

Example 6.8 Indirect method – vertical group

Parent
75% ↓
Subsidiary
60% ↓
Sub-subsidiary

		Subsidiary	**Sub-subsidiary**	
		%	**%**	
Group share	Direct	75	—	
	Indirect	—	45	(75% × 60%)
		75	45	
Minority share	Direct	25	40	
	Indirect	—	15	(25% × 60%)
		25	55	

Cost of control account

Full cost of investment by Parent in Subsidiary (from Parent's balance sheet)	X	Group share of share capital of Subsidiary (75%)	X
Parent's share of Subsidiary's cost of investment in Sub-subsidiary (75%)	X	Group share of pre-acquisition reserves of Subsidiary (75%)	X
		Group share of share capital of Sub-subsidiary (45%)	X
		Group share of pre-acquisition reserves of Sub-subsidiary (45%)	X
Bal c/d: Negative goodwill	X	Bal c/d: Positive goodwill	X

Consolidated revenue reserves

Subsidiary		Parent's revenue reserves	X
Group share of pre-acquisition revenue reserves (75%)	X	Subsidiary's revenue reserves	X
Minority share of revenue reserves (25%)	X	Sub-subsidiary's revenue reserves	X
Sub-subsidiary			
Group share of pre-acquisition revenue reserves (45%)	X		
Minority share of revenue reserves (55%)	X		
Consolidated balance sheet	X		
	X		X

Minority interest

Direct minority share of Subsidiary's cost of investment in Sub-subsidiary (25%)	X	Minority share of Subsidiary's share capital (25%)	X
		Minority share of Subsidiary's reserves (25%)	X
		Minority share of Sub-subsidiary's share capital (55%)	X
Consolidated balance sheet	X	Minority share of Sub-subsidiary's reserves (55%)	X
	X		X

Example 6.9 provides a more detailed worked example, where the technique outlined in Example 6.8 is applied. In this example, the effective interest of the group in Sub-subsidiary is 50%. Sub-subsidiary is a subsidiary of Parent because Parent controls $66^2/_3$% of Sub-subsidiary through its control of Subsidiary.

Example 6.9 Detailed worked example of indirect method

Example

The balance sheets of Parent, Subsidiary and Sub-subsidiary at 31.12.20X4 are as follows. Group shareholdings were acquired when Subsidiary and Sub-subsidiary revenue reserves were €1,400 and €450, respectively.

	Parent	Subsidiary	Sub-subsidiary
	€	€	€
6,000 shares in Subsidiary	8,000	—	—
2,000 shares in Sub-subsidiary	—	3,100	—
Net assets	10,000	6,900	4,200
	18,000	10,000	4,200
Share capital	12,000	8,000	3,000
Revenue reserves	6,000	2,000	1,200
	18,000	10,000	4,200

Required

You are required to show the:

(1) group structure

(2) cost of control, revenue reserves and minority interests consolidation working accounts.

Solution (1) Group structure

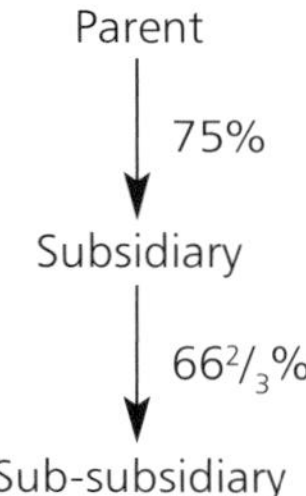

		Subsidiary	Sub-subsidiary	
		%	%	
Group share	Direct	75	—	
	Indirect	—	50.00	(75% × 66⅔%)
		75	50.00	
Minority share	Direct	25	33.33	
	Indirect	—	16.67	(25% × 66⅔%)
		25	50.00	

Solution (2) Balance sheet working accounts

Cost of control account

	€		€
Full cost of investment by Parent in Subsidiary	8,000	Share capital: Subsidiary $_{75\% \times €8,000}$	6,000
Parent's share of Subsidiary's cost of investment in Sub-subsidiary $_{75\% \times €3,100}$	2,325	Revenue reserves: Subsidiary $_{75\% \times €1,400}$	1,050
		Share capital: Sub-subsidiary $_{50\% \times €3,000}$	1,500
		Revenue reserves: Sub-subsidiary $_{50\% \times €450}$	225
		Bal c/d: Goodwill	1,550
	10,325		10,325

Consolidated revenue reserves

	€		€
Cost of control account:		Parent revenue reserves	6,000
Group share pre-acquisition revenue reserves Subsidiary$_{75\% \times €1,400}$	1,050	Subsidiary revenue reserves	2,000
Minority interest account:			
Subsidiary revenue reserves $_{25\% \times €2,000}$	500	Sub-subsidiary revenue reserves	1,200
Cost of control account:			
Group share pre-acquisition revenue reserves: Sub-subsidiary$_{50\% \times €450}$	225		
Minority interest account:			
Sub-subsidiary revenue reserves $_{50\% \times €1,200}$	600		
Bal c/d: Consolidated balance sheet	6,825		
	9,200		9,200

Minority interest

	€		€
Minority share of Subsidiary's cost of investment in Sub-subsidiary$_{25\% \times €3,100}$	775	Minority share of Subsidiary's share capital$_{25\% \times €8,000}$	2,000
		Minority share of Subsidiary's reserves$_{25\% \times €2,000}$	500
		Minority share of Sub-subsidiary's share capital$_{50\% \times €3,000}$	1,500
Bal c/d: Consolidated balance sheet	3,825	Minority share of Sub-subsidiary's reserves$_{50\% \times €1,200}$	600
	4,600		4,600

Acquisitions at different dates

Another complication with mixed and vertical groups is that the dates of acquisition of the subsidiary and the sub-subsidiary rarely coincide. This causes problems when trying to identify pre-acquisition reserves. The problem is highlighted in Example 6.10.

Example 6.10 Vertical and mixed groups and acquisitions at different dates

Example

Subsidiary acquired Sub-subsidiary	1.1.20X0
Parent acquired Subsidiary	30.6.20X4
Sub-subsidiary reserves at 1.1.20X0	€2,000
Subsidiary reserves at 30.6.20X4	€1,500
Sub-subsidiary reserves at 30.6.20X4	€3,500

Required

What reserves should be treated as pre-acquisition reserves in respect of Sub-subsidiary when preparing the consolidated balance sheet of Parent and group?

Solution

Sub-subsidiary only becomes a subsidiary of Parent when Subsidiary becomes a subsidiary, i.e., on 30.6.20X4. In the context of preparing consolidated accounts of Parent and group, it is the date that each company becomes a subsidiary of Parent that is important in determining which amounts should be treated as pre-acquisition. In this case, Sub-subsidiary's reserves at 30.6.20X4 (€3,500) are pre-acquisition as regards Parent.

The effective date of acquisition of the sub-subsidiary must be identified with care in order to calculate pre-acquisition reserves (and therefore, goodwill amounts) accurately. Two different situations can arise with respect to the relative acquisition dates. Either:

- the sub-subsidiary is acquired by the subsidiary *before* the parent acquires its interest in the subsidiary; or
- the sub-subsidiary is acquired by the subsidiary *after* the parent acquires its interest in the subsidiary.

Earlier acquisition of sub-subsidiary by subsidiary

Where the subsidiary acquires its controlling interest in the sub-subsidiary *before* the parent acquires control of the subsidiary, the sub-subsidiary becomes a member of the parent's group from the date the parent acquires control of the subsidiary. Consequently, profits earned by the sub-subsidiary after the date the parent acquires control of the subsidiary are regarded as post-acquisition by the parent and all profits earned by both the subsidiary and the sub-subsidiary before that date are pre-acquisition from the parent group's perspective. This is because the consolidated balance sheet is prepared from the parent's perspective. Example 6.10 illustrates this point.

In a more detailed example (Example 6.11), Parent acquires its interest in Subsidiary *after* Subsidiary had acquired its interest in Sub-subsidiary. The major issues illustrated by this example are (i) the treatment of the cost of the investment in the sub-subsidiary and (ii) the identification of Sub-subsidiary's pre-acquisition reserves.

Example 6.11 Earlier acquisition of sub-subsidiary by subsidiary

Example

This example assumes the same details as in Example 6.9, except that Parent acquired its investment in Subsidiary on 30.6.20X3 when revenue reserves were €1,600 and Subsidiary acquired $66^2/_3$% of Sub-subsidiary on 1.1.20X2 when Sub-subsidiary revenue reserves were €450. Sub-subsidiary's reserves were €800 on 30.6.20X3 when Parent acquired its investment in Subsidiary.

Required

Show the:

(1) group structure

(2) cost of control, revenue reserves and minority interests consolidation working accounts to record these acquisitions.

Solution (1) Group structure

Group structure is identical to that in Example 6.9.

Solution (2) Consolidation workings

Cost of control

	€		€
Full cost of investment by Parent in Subsidiary	8,000	Subsidiary's share capital $_{75\% \times €8,000}$	6,000
Parent's share of Subsidiary's cost of investment in Sub-subsidiary$_{75\% \times €3,000}$	2,325	Revenue reserves: Subsidiary$_{75\% \times €1,600}$	1,200
		Sub-subsidiary's share capital$_{50\% \times €3,000}$	1,500
		Revenue reserves: Sub-subsidiary$_{50\% \times €800}$	400
		Bal c/d: Positive goodwill	1,225
	10,325		10,325

Consolidated revenue reserves

	€		€
Cost of control account:			
Group share pre-acquisition revenue reserves of Subsidiary$_{75\% \times €1,500}$	1,200	Parent revenue reserves	6,000
Minority interest account:			
Subsidiary revenue reserves$_{25\% \times €2,000}$	500	Subsidiary revenue reserves	2,000
Cost of control account:		Sub-subsidiary revenue reserves	1,200
Group share pre-acquisition revenue reserves of Sub-subsidiary$_{50\% \times €800}$	400		
Minority interest account:			
Sub-subsidiary revenue reserves$_{50\% \times €1,200}$	600		
Consolidated balance sheet	6,500		
	9,200		9,200

Minority interest account is identical to that in Example 6.9.

The treatment of the cost of the investment in Sub-subsidiary has been discussed at length earlier in the chapter. As already explained, the cost (from Subsidiary's balance sheet) is apportioned between cost of control account and minority interest account in the proportion of Parent's interest in Subsidiary and the direct minority's interest in Subsidiary, respectively.

The pre-acquisition reserves of Sub-subsidiary are determined by reference to the date Sub-subsidiary became part of the Parent group, i.e., 30 June 20X3. The fact that Sub-subsidiary is a subsidiary of Subsidiary from 1 January 20X2 is irrelevant from Parent's group perspective. Consequently, the only working accounts affected by the changes in pre-acquisition profits (by comparison with Example 6.9) are cost of control and consolidated revenue reserves. Because the minority interest account quantifies the minority's share of net assets of Subsidiary and Sub-subsidiary at the balance sheet date, that account is exactly the same for Example 6.11 as it was for Example 6.9.

As a self-study exercise, students should now prepare the consolidated balance sheet for Examples 6.9 and 6.11.

Later acquisition of sub-subsidiary by subsidiary

Where Subsidiary acquires its controlling interest in Sub-subsidiary *after* Parent acquires control of Subsidiary, Sub-subsidiary becomes a subsidiary of Parent on the same date as it becomes a subsidiary of Subsidiary. Therefore, the reserves which are identified as pre-acquisition with respect to Sub-subsidiary's immediate parent (Subsidiary), are also pre-acquisition with respect to the ultimate parent (Parent). Similarly, profits of Sub-subsidiary considered to be post-acquisition as far as Subsidiary is concerned are also post-acquisition as regards Parent. Example 6.12 provides a detailed illustration.

Example 6.12 Later acquisition of sub-subsidiary by subsidiary

Example

The balance sheets of Parent, Subsidiary and Sub-subsidiary at 31.12.20X4 are as follows. Subsidiary acquired its shares in Sub-subsidiary on 1.1.20X4 when Subsidiary and Sub-subsidiary revenue reserves were €30 and €25, respectively. Parent acquired 75% of Subsidiary on 1.1.20X1 when Subsidiary revenue reserves were €20.

	Parent	Subsidiary	Sub-subsidiary
	€	€	€
60 shares in Subsidiary	105	—	—
48 shares in Sub-subsidiary	—	80	—
Net assets	77	55	100
	182	135	100
Share capital	120	80	60
Revenue reserves	62	55	40
	182	135	100

Required

You are required to show the:

(1) group structure

(2) cost of control, revenue reserves and minority interests consolidation working accounts to record these acquisitions.

Solution (1) Group structure

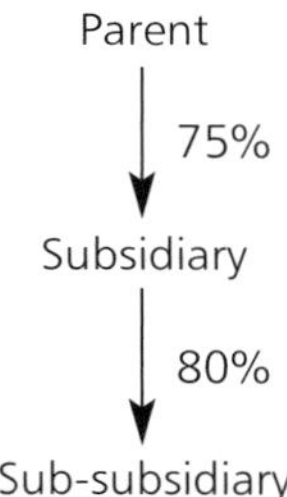

		Subsidiary	Sub-subsidiary	
		%	%	
Group share	Direct	75	—	
	Indirect	—	60	(75% × 80%)
		75	60	
Minority share	Direct	25	20	
	Indirect	—	20	(25% × 80%)
		25	40	

Solution (2) Consolidation workings

Cost of control account

	€		€
Full cost of investment by Parent in Subsidiary	105	Subsidiary's share capital$_{75\% \times €80}$	60
Parent's share of Subsidiary's cost of investment in Sub-subsidiary$_{75\% \times €80}$	60	Sub-subsidiary's share capital$_{60\% \times €60}$	36
		Revenue reserves: Subsidiary$_{75\% \times €20}$	15
		Sub-subsidiary$_{60\% \times €25}$	15
		Bal c/d: Goodwill	39
	165		165

Consolidated revenue reserves

	€		€
Group share pre-acquisition revenue reserves of $Subsidiary_{75\% \times €20}$	15.00	Parent revenue reserves	62.00
Minority interest in $Subsidiary_{25\% \times €55}$	13.75	Subsidiary revenue reserves	55.00
Group share pre-acquisition revenue reserves of $Sub\text{-}subsidiary_{60\% \times €25}$	15.00	Sub-subsidiary revenue reserves	40.00
Minority interest in $Sub\text{-}subsidiary_{40\% \times €40}$	16.00		
Bal c/d: Consolidated balance sheet	97.25		
	157.00		157.00

Minority interest

	€		€
Minority share of Subsidiary's cost of investment in $Sub\text{-}subsidiary_{25\% \times €80}$	20.00	Minority share of Subsidiary's share $capital_{25\% \times €80}$	20.00
		Minority share of Subsidiary's $reserves_{25\% \times €55}$	13.75
		Minority share of Sub-subsidiary's share $capital_{40\% \times €60}$	24.00
Bal c/d: Consolidated balance sheet	53.75	Minority share of Sub-subsidiary's $reserves_{40\% \times €40}$	16.00
	73.75		73.75

In Example 6.12, Parent acquired its interest in Subsidiary before Subsidiary acquired its shares in Sub-subsidiary. Consequently, Sub-subsidiary becomes a member of the Parent group on the same date it became a subsidiary of Subsidiary (i.e., 1 January 20X4). It is easier in this situation to identify the correct pre-acquisition reserves for both subsidiaries than it was in Example 6.11. The relevant amounts are the reserves on the actual date each subsidiary was acquired by its immediate parent (i.e., Subsidiary – 20X1 – €20; Sub-subsidiary – 20X4 – €25).

Summary

This chapter explained how more complex group structures are dealt with when preparing consolidated balance sheets. In particular, the indirect approach to dealing with vertical and mixed groups was explained and illustrated. A further complication in the context of vertical and mixed groups was also considered, i.e., the impact of sub-subsidiaries being acquired on different dates to the date the parent acquires its subsidiary.

Learning outcomes

After studying this chapter you should have learnt:

- how to illustrate group structures graphically
- how to distinguish between *controlling* and *effective* ownership interests
- how to calculate effective interests in a particular subsidiary where the ownership structure is complex
- how to identify the appropriate date from which subsidiaries in a complex group should be consolidated
- how to prepare the consolidated balance sheet for complex groups using the T account workings learnt in previous chapters.

Multiple choice questions

Solutions to these questions are presented in Appendix 1.

6.1 Alleline, Tarr and William

Consider the following group structure:

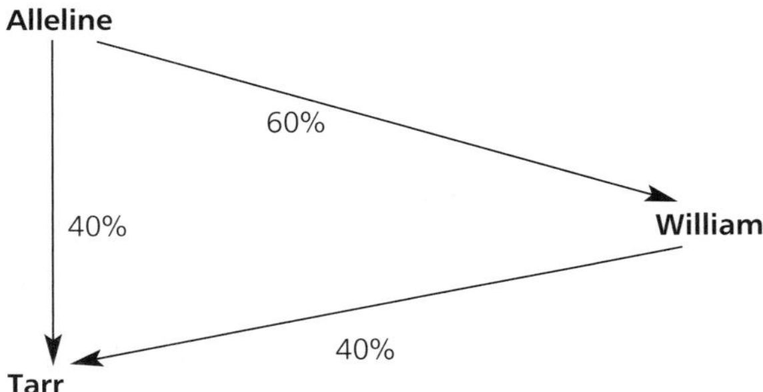

The following proportion of Tarr will be shown as a minority interest in Alleline's group accounts:

(a) nil
(b) 20%
(c) 36%
(d) 60%

6.2 Fish, Cod and Trout

Fish purchased 80% of the share capital of **Cod** in 20X0 for €360,000. Cod acquired 80% of the shares in **Trout** in 20X1 for €100,000 which represented exactly 80% of the fair value of the separable net assets of Trout at that date. At 31 December 20X3, the capital and reserves of Cod and Trout (including fair value adjustments in the case of Trout) were as follows:

	Cod	**Trout**
	€000	**€000**
Ordinary shares of €1 each	200	80
Reserves	400	120

The amount disclosed as *minority interests* in the consolidated balance sheet of Fish at 31 December 20X3, is:

(a) €140,000
(b) €160,000
(c) €172,000
(d) €192,000

6.3 Wig, Hair and Bald

For many years the structure of the **Wig** group has been as follows:
Wig owns 70% of **Hair** (cost €200,000) and 50% of **Bald** (cost €30,000). Hair owns 10% of Bald (cost €20,000). At 31 December 20X1 their respective balance sheets showed the following total net assets:

Wig	€500,000
Hair	€100,000
Bald	€200,000

The amount to be included in the consolidated balance sheet of the Wig group at 31 December 20X1, for *minority interests* is:

(a) €110,000
(b) €116,000
(c) €130,000
(d) €184,000

6.4 Gandalf, Frodo and Sam

Gandalf acquired 80% of the share capital of **Frodo** on the day it was incorporated, several years ago. On the same day, Frodo acquired 75% of the share capital of **Sam**, also incorporated that day. There were no other inter-company investments and these proportions have been maintained ever since.

Summarised balance sheets as at 30 June 20X9 follow:

	Gandalf	**Frodo**	**Sam**
	€000	**€000**	**€000**
Sundry net assets	2,200	925	700
Investment in subsidiary at cost	800	375	—
	3,000	1,300	700
Ordinary share capital	2,000	1,000	500
Profit and loss account	1,000	300	200
	3,000	1,300	700

The *minority interests* amount in the consolidated balance sheet of Gandalf and group at 30 June 20X9 is:

(a) €365,000
(b) €435,000
(c) €465,000
(d) €540,000

6.5 Grape, Wine and Vinegar

The following are extracts from draft balance sheets of three group companies:

	Grape	**Wine**	**Vinegar**
	€000	**€000**	**€000**
Investments, at cost			
80,000 shares in Wine	120	—	—
60,000 shares in Vinegar	—	110	—
Sundry net assets	155	160	215
	275	270	215
Capital and reserves			
Ordinary shares (€1 each)	80	100	100
Reserves	195	170	115
	275	270	215

When **Grape** acquired its shareholding in **Wine**, Wine's reserves stood at €70,000. When Wine acquired its shares in **Vinegar**, Vinegar's reserves stood at €50,000.

What is the figure for minority interest to be disclosed in the consolidated balance sheet?

(a) € 93,800
(b) €140,000
(c) €143,800
(d) €165,800

6.6 Yeast, Beer and Bread

The following are extracts from draft balance sheets of companies within the **Yeast** Group:

	Yeast	**Beer**	**Bread**
	€000	**€000**	**€000**
Ordinary €1 shares	500	50	120
Investments			
6,000 €1 shares in Bread	100	—	—
60,000 €1 shares in Bread	—	130	—
40,000 €1 shares in Beer	120	—	—

The minority interest in the Yeast group is:

(a) 20% in Beer; Bread is not a subsidiary
(b) 20% in Beer and 55% in Bread
(c) 20% in Beer and 50% in Bread
(d) 20% in Beer and 45% in Bread

6.7 Milk, Cream and Butter

Milk bought 60% of the equity shares of **Cream** on 1 April 20X9 and 20% of the equity shares of **Butter** on 1 October 20X9. Cream had purchased 70% of the shares of Butter on 1 January 20X9 when Butter's reserves were €72,000. In the year ended 31 December 20X9 Butter made profits of €36,000.

What amount for Butter's pre-acquisition profits will be credited to the Milk Group cost of control account for the year ended 31 December 20X9?

(a) €53,820
(b) €57,780
(c) €77,400
(d) €81,180

6.8 Chicken, Egg and Mayonnaise

Chicken bought 80% of the shares of **Egg** on 1 April 20X9 and 30% of the shares of **Mayonnaise** on 1 October 20X9. Egg had bought 40% of the shares of Mayonnaise on 1 January 20X9. Mayonnaise made profits of €100,000 in the year ended 31 December 20X9 and its reserves at 1 January 20X9 were €300,000.

What amount for Mayonnaise's pre-acquisition reserves will be credited to the Chicken Group cost of control account for the year ended 31 December 20X9?

(a) €375,000
(b) €242,500
(c) €232,500
(d) €216,500

Self-assessment exercises

Solutions to these self-assessment exercises can be found at:
www.thomsonlearning.co.uk/accountingandfinance/piercebrennan

6.1 Tic, Tac and Toe

The individual balance sheets of **Tic**, **Tac** and **Toe** at 31 December 20X4 are as follows:

	Tic	**Tac**	**Toe**
	€m	**€m**	**€m**
Investments	28	5.9	—
Other net assets	22	30.1	20
	50	36.0	20
Ordinary share capital in shares of €1 each	30	20.0	10
Revenue reserves	20	16.0	10
	50	36.0	20

- Tic owns 16m of Tac's shares. They were acquired for €22m on 30 June 20X2 when revenue reserves of Tac amounted to €6m and revenue reserves of Toe amounted to €4.5m.
- Tic owns 3.5m of Toe's shares. They were acquired for €6m on 31 December 20X2 when revenue reserves of Toe amounted to €5m.
- Tac owns 4m of Toe's shares. They were acquired for €5.9m on 31 December 20X1 when revenue reserves of Toe amounted to €4m.

Required

Show the group structure based on the information given and prepare the consolidated balance sheet for the Tic group at 31 December 20X4.

(*Source*: Robins P., 1995. 'Consolidated accounts: how to account for sub-subsidiaries and mixed groups,' adapted, *ACCA Students' Newsletter*, March, pp.36–40.)

6.2 Petal, Rose and Stem

The draft balance sheets of **Petal**, **Rose** and **Stem**, as at 31 December 20X6, are as follows:

Balance sheets as at 31 December 20X6

	Petal	Rose	Stem
	€000	€000	€000
Tangible fixed assets	100	100	50
Investments at cost			
80,000 shares in Rose	180	—	—
32,000 shares in Stem	—	100	—
Current assets	375	215	140
Creditors: Amounts falling due within one year	(130)	(121)	(80)
	525	294	110
Ordinary shares of €1 each	200	100	40
Share premium	150	60	–
Revaluation reserve	30	50	–
Profit and loss account			
Brought forward 1 January 20X6	90	50	50
Retained profit for the year	55	34	20
	525	294	110

The following additional information has been ascertained:

1. Goodwill on consolidation is to be written off over four years from the date of acquisition, with a full year's charge in the year of acquisition.
2. Petal purchased 80,000 shares in Rose, on 1 January 20X4, when the balance sheet of Rose included the following balances:

	€
Share premium	60,000
Revaluation reserve	10,000
Profit and loss account	20,000

3. Rose purchased 32,000 shares in Stem on 1 July 20X6. The balance sheet values of the net assets of Stem were agreed to represent their fair values.
4. Inter-company current account balances at 31 December 20X6, were as follows:

Petal Creditors included €15,000 owing to Rose. This was after including a cheque for €7,000 which had been sent to Rose, on 23 December 20X6, but which had not been received or recorded by Rose until 6 January 20X7.

Rose Debtors included €20,000 due from Stem. Goods sent to Stem on 24 December 20X6, valued at €5,000, had not been received or recorded by Stem until 8 January 20X7.

Apart from the items detailed above, inter-company balances were in agreement and there were no other inter-company balances. There are no material amounts of goods purchased from other group companies included in stocks.

Required

Prepare the consolidated balance sheet of the Petal group as at 31 December 20X6.

Examination-style questions

6.1 X, Y and Z Group

A new company, **Z**, was incorporated on 1 October 20X7 and started operations on that day. It became a subsidiary of **Y** on 1 April 20X8, when Y obtained 60% of the ordinary shares of **Z** for €25,520.

X was Y's holding company, having purchased 80% of Y's ordinary shares on 1 June 20X7 for €53,600. Subsequent to Z becoming a member of the group, X purchased 25% of Z's ordinary shares on 1 July 20X8 for €12,200. The following are the summarised balance sheets of the three companies as at 30 September 20X8, their accounting year end:

	X	Y	Z
	€	€	€
Net assets (including for X and Y investment in subsidiaries)	200,000	77,000	42,400
Ordinary share capital	100,000	60,000	36,000
Profit and loss account			
Balance at 1.10.20X7*	60,000	(9,000)	—
Profit for year ended 30.9.20X8	40,000	26,000	6,400
	100,000	17,000	6,400
	200,000	77,000	42,400

*You also discover that Y had made a loss of €18,000 during the year ended 30 September 20X7.

Required

Prepare a summary consolidated balance sheet of the XYZ Group as at 30 September 20X8.

6.2 W, G and C Group

The following is a summary of the balances in the books of **W** and **G** and **C** as at 31 December 20X2:

	W	G	C
	€	€	€
Fixed assets, at cost	271,000	143,400	46,500
Provision for depreciation of fixed assets	(70,000)	(40,000)	(12,000)
60,000 ordinary shares in G at cost	104,000	—	—
30,000 ordinary shares in C at cost	—	40,200	—
€6,000 5% Debentures of G	6,000	—	—
Current assets	108,600	56,600	21,900
Creditors	(68,400)	(27,800)	(18,750)
Debenture interest accrued	—	(500)	—
Proposed dividends	(30,000)	(11,000)	—
	321,200	160,900	37,650
Ordinary shares of €1 each	250,000	80,000	30,000
6% cumulative preference shares of €1 each	—	25,000	—
Profit and loss accounts	71,200	45,900	7,650
5% debentures	—	10,000	—
	321,200	160,900	37,650

W acquired the shares in G, *cum* dividend, on 31 December 20X0 and G acquired the shares in C on 31 December 20X1.

The balances on the profit and loss account of G and C are made up as follows:

	G	C
	€	€
Balance on 31 December 20X0	34,800	5,550
Profit for 20X1	4,100	1,200
Balance on 31 December 20X1	38,900	6,750
Profit for 20X2	18,000	900
	56,900	7,650
Less: Proposed dividends	11,000	—
	45,900	7,650

The balance on the profit and loss account of G on 31 December 20X0 is after providing for the dividend on the preference shares (€1,500) and a proposed ordinary dividend (€6,400), both of which were subsequently paid. The dividend received by W from G had been credited to the profit and loss account of W. No dividends were declared or paid by G in respect of 20X1. No entry had been made in the books of W in respect of debenture interest due from, or dividends for 20X2 proposed to be distributed by, G.

The stock of G, valued at cost, included €12,780 in respect of goods purchased from W in 20X2. The cost of these goods to W was €8,520.

Required

Prepare the summarised consolidated balance sheet at 31 December 20X2.

6.3 Fog, Mist and Vapour

The following is a summary of the balances in the books of **Fog**, **Mist** and **Vapour** on 31 December 20X5:

	Fog	**Mist**	**Vapour**
	€	**€**	**€**
Fixed assets, at cost	134,000	94,200	30,600
Provision for depreciation of fixed assets	(48,000)	(27,000)	(8,000)
45,000 ordinary shares in Mist at cost	81,000	—	—
20,000 ordinary shares in Vapour at cost	—	28,600	—
€5,000 5% debentures of Mist	5,000	—	—
Current assets	82,800	45,900	15,400
	254,800	141,700	38,000
Authorised and issued share capital			
Ordinary shares of €1 each fully paid	140,000	60,000	20,000
6% cumulative preference shares of €1 each fully paid	—	15,000	—
Profit and loss account	52,300	31,600	5,250
5% debentures	—	8,000	—
Debenture interest accrued	—	400	—
Proposed dividends	16,800	6,900	—
Creditors	45,700	19,800	12,750
	254,800	141,700	38,000

Fog acquired the shares in Mist, *cum* dividend, on 31 December 20X4, and Mist acquired the shares in Vapour on 31 December 20X3.

The balances on the profit and loss accounts of Mist and Vapour are made up as follows:

	Mist	**Vapour**
	€	**€**
Balances at 31 December 20X3	22,600	2,450
Profit after tax 20X4	9,600	2,000
	32,200	4,450
Less: Proposed dividends (20X4)	5,700	—
Balances at 31 December 20X4	26,500	4,450
Profit after tax 20X5	12,000	800
	38,500	5,250
Less: Proposed dividends (20X5)	6,900	—
	31,600	5,250

The provision for dividends, €5,700, in the profit and loss account of Mist for the year 20X4 represents the dividends on the preference shares (€900) and the proposed ordinary dividend (€4,800), both of which were subsequently paid. The dividend received by Fog from Mist has been credited to the profit and loss account of Fog. No entries have been made in the books of Fog in respect of debenture interest due from Mist, or for the holding company's share of the proposed dividends of Mist 20X5.

Required

Prepare the consolidated balance sheet as at 31 December 20X5.
(Ignore taxation.)

7

Equity accounting

Learning objectives

After studying this chapter you should be able to:

- understand what is meant by equity accounting
- distinguish between equity accounting and full consolidation in the context of the consolidated balance sheet
- understand the difference between *gross* equity accounting and equity accounting
- calculate the group's effective interest in an associate in a complex group situation
- calculate the amount to be included in the consolidated balance sheet when equity accounting is used to measure an investment
- adjust for unrealised profits related to equity accounted entities

Introduction

The rationale for preparing consolidated balance sheets is that the balance sheet of the parent undertaking (which shows the investment in the subsidiary at cost) does not give shareholders sufficient information about an undertaking which the parent is able to *control*. Therefore, the consolidated balance sheet replaces the asset *Investment in subsidiary* with the underlying net assets of the subsidiary and minority interest in those net assets. This method of consolidation is known as *line-by-line consolidation* or *full consolidation*.

Traditionally, investments in companies not satisfying the criteria for recognition as subsidiaries were carried at cost in the balance sheet. Dividend income was the only revenue from these investments included in the profit and loss account. During the 1960s there was an increasing tendency for groups to conduct significant parts of their business through investments, where they exercised significant influence without controlling the investee. Such investments became known as *associates* in the UK. The investor is partly accountable for the activities of the investment because of the degree of influence it can exercise over the affairs of the investee. Consequently, it was increasingly recognised that some intermediate measure between cost-based accounting and full consolidation was required for many significant investments. It was recognised that inclusion of dividends in the profit and loss account was inadequate as a measure of the return on many of these investments. It was also considered manipulable, given the extent of influence exerted by the investor. The investor could dictate the amount and timing of dividend payments. Moreover, since many such investments were held for the long term, and shareholders' equity was building up in these companies, the cost of the investment was considered to give an increasingly unrealistic measure of the underlying value of the investment.

The intermediate form of accounting (between cost based and full consolidation) introduced in the 1960s was the *equity* method of accounting. It was first used by the Royal Dutch Shell group in 1964. Equity accounting involves using a modified form of consolidation where the interest of the investor is significant, but control cannot be exercised. A holding of at least 20% of equity shares, but no more than 50%, is usually presumed to enable significant influence to be exerted. Under equity accounting, the investor's share of the investee's net assets is included as a single-line item in the consolidated balance sheet. By contrast, in full consolidation, all assets and liabilities of the subsidiary are included in each consolidated balance sheet item. Consolidated reserves are credited with the group's share of the increase in the investee's net assets (since acquisition) and the consolidated profit and loss account includes the group's share of (i) the investee's profits or losses before taxation and (ii) taxation for the year.

Equity accounting was first introduced as a requirement in the UK and Ireland in 1971 when SSAP 1 *Accounting for Associated Companies* was published. Some difficulties were anticipated when the Fourth Directive was introduced in the early 1980s because the Directive prohibited the inclusion of unrealised profit in the profit and loss account. However, the first significant use made of the *true and fair override* was to permit the continued use of equity accounting for investments classified as associated companies under SSAP 1. Nonetheless, the term *equity basis of accounting* was not used or defined in SSAP 1. It has since been defined in both FRS 2 *Accounting for Subsidiary Undertakings* and FRS 9 *Associates and Joint Ventures*.

The regulatory framework underlying equity accounting will be dealt with in greater detail in Chapter 15. However, a certain amount of background and relevant definitions are introduced in this chapter to provide the context for the equity accounting techniques explained and illustrated therein.

Definitions

The equity method of accounting was first introduced to deal with investments categorised as associated companies. Both the equity method of accounting and associates are defined in this section. In addition, two related definitions are provided: joint venture and gross equity method of accounting.

Equity method of accounting

The definitions included in both FRS 2 and FRS 9 are very descriptive. The later definition included in FRS 9 is more detailed than that in FRS 2, although it is clearly based on the FRS 2 definition. FRS 2 (paragraph 8) defines the equity method of accounting as:

> A method of accounting for an investment that brings into the consolidated profit and loss account the investor's share of the investment undertaking's results and that records the investment in the consolidated balance sheet at the investor's share of the investment undertaking's net assets including any goodwill arising to the extent that it has not previously been written off.

FRS 9 (paragraph 4) defines the equity method as:

> A method of accounting that brings an investment into its investor's financial statements initially at its cost, identifying any goodwill arising. The carrying amount of the investment is adjusted in each period by the investor's share of the results of its investee less any amortisation or write-off for goodwill, the investor's share of any relevant gains or losses, and any other changes in the investee's net assets including distributions to its owners, for example by

> dividend. The investor's share of its investee's results is recognised in its profit and loss account. The investor's cash flow statement includes the cash flows between the investor and its investee, for example relating to dividends and loans.

These two definitions give an insight into what is involved in applying the equity method. The mechanics of applying the method are explained in a later section of this chapter, after an overview of full consolidation and how it compares with the equity basis is provided in the next section. In addition, a sample of the variety of investment situations that might lead to categorisation as an associated undertaking is also discussed further on in this chapter.

Associate

Associated companies were defined in SSAP 1 (paragraph 13) as companies (other than subsidiaries) in which:

(a) the interest of the investing group or company is effectively that of a partner in a joint venture or consortium and the investing group or company is in a position to exercise significant influence over the company in which the investment is made; or
(b) the interest of the investing group or company is for the long term and is substantial and, having regard to the disposition of the other shareholdings, the investing group or company is in a position to exercise significant influence over the company in which the investment is made.

More recently, FRS 9 (paragraph 4) defines an associate as:

> An entity (other than a subsidiary) in which another entity (the investor) has a participating interest and over whose operating and financial policies the investor exercises a significant influence.

There is scope for debate on the significance of the explicit exclusion of subsidiaries in the latter definition. Very simply interpreted, the definition merely excludes subsidiaries of the reporting entity. The investor clearly exercises significant influence when it controls a subsidiary. However, the option of using equity accounting in this situation is eliminated as more rigorous full consolidation is already required for subsidiaries. Explicit exclusion of subsidiaries in the definitions of associates could also mean that if a company is already a subsidiary of another parent then, despite a shareholding in excess of 20% by the reporting entity, it cannot exert significant influence over the investee.

FRS 9 also defines *participating interest* and *significant influence*. These definitions are dealt with in detail in Chapter 15 within the regulatory framework section of this book.

Joint ventures

From the early 1970s a joint venture was recognised from an accounting point of view to be a mechanism for shared participation in business, where the investor has significant influence without having control. FRS 9 (paragraph 4) defines a joint venture as:

> An entity in which the reporting entity holds an interest on a long-term basis and is jointly controlled by the reporting entity and one or more other venturers under a contractual arrangement.

Gross equity method

Under SSAP 1, joint ventures were accounted for using the equity method of accounting, although some joint ventures were accounted for using proportional consolidation.

A variation of the equity method, the gross equity method, was introduced by FRS 9 for use when reporting interests in joint ventures. The FRS (paragraph 4) defines gross equity method as:

> A form of equity method under which the investor's share of aggregate gross assets and liabilities underlying the net amount included for the investment is shown on the face of the balance sheet and, in the profit and loss account, the investor's share of the investee's turnover is noted.

The gross equity method and proportional consolidation are further discussed in Chapter 15.

Equity method of accounting explained

Comparison with full consolidation

It is useful at this point to illustrate the differences in the consolidated balance sheet between using full consolidation and the equity method of accounting for a given investment. Example 7.1 illustrates these differences. Example 7.2 then uses the same details to illustrate the differences between the equity method and gross equity method of accounting.

Example 7.1 Comparison between full consolidation and equity method of accounting

Example

The balance sheets of Investor and Investee at 31.12.20X9 are as follows:

	Investor €000	Investee €000
Tangible fixed assets	14,500	10,000
Investment in Investee	10,750	—
Dividends receivable	600	—
Dividend payable	(2,000)	(800)
Other current assets	12,650	8,800
Other current liabilities	(4,000)	(3,000)
	32,500	15,000
Share capital (in €1 shares)	20,000	12,000
Reserves	12,500	3,000
	32,500	15,000

Investor acquired 9 million shares in Investee on 31.12.20X3 when Investee's reserves were €1 million. Goodwill on consolidation is amortised over a ten-year period starting in the year ended 31.12.20X4.

Required

Prepare the consolidated balance sheet, assuming:

(1) investment in Investee is to be fully consolidated and

(2) the equity method is used.

Note: Full consolidation is normally appropriate where a majority of equity shares is owned by Investor. The equity method is used in this example for illustrative purposes.

continued overleaf

Example 7.1 Continued

Solution

Group structure

Investor —— 75% ——► Investee

	Full €000	Equity €000
Tangible fixed assets	24,500	14,500
Goodwill on consolidation (W_1)	400	—
Investment in Investee (W_2)	—	11,650
Dividends receivable	—	600
Dividend payable: Investor	(2,000)	(2,000)
Minority (W_3)	(200)	—
Other current assets	21,450	12,650
Other current liabilities	(7,000)	(4,000)
	37,150	33,400
Share capital (in €1 shares)	20,000	20,000
Reserves (W_4)	13,400	13,400
	33,400	33,400
Minority interest (W_5)	3,750	—
	37,150	33,400

Workings

W_1 Goodwill

	Full €000	Equity €000
Investment at cost	10,750	10,750
Share of net assets at acquisition date (75% × €13m)	(9,750)	(9,750)
Goodwill on acquisition	1,000	1,000
Amount amortised ($^6/_{10}$)	(600)	(600)
	400	400*

* Included in investment carrying value under equity method (see W_2).

W_2 Investment under equity method

	€000
Share of net assets at balance sheet date (75% × €15m)	11,250
Unamortised goodwill (W_1)	400
	11,650

W_3 Dividend payable to minority: Full consolidation only

	€000
Dividends payable by Investee	800
Less: dividend receivable by Investor (75%)	(600)
	200

W_4 Consolidated reserves

	Full €000	Equity €000
Investor	12,500	12,500
Share of Investee's post-acquisition reserves (75% × [€3m – €1m])	1,500	1,500
Goodwill written off (W_1)	(600)	(600)
	13,400	13,400

W_5 Minority interest

	€000
Minority share of Investee's net assets at year-end (25% × €15m)	3,750

The following additional notes to Example 7.1 should help clarify points of detail that might otherwise be confusing:

- equity accounting includes only the *group share* of the net assets of Investee in the balance sheet, therefore there is no minority interest
- full consolidation includes 100% of Investee's assets and liabilities on a line-by-line basis (except any inter-company balances related to transactions with Investor). Therefore, minority interest of 25% of Investee's net assets must be shown in the consolidated balance sheet
- in full consolidation, dividend receivable by Investor is offset against dividend payable by Investee, any remaining balance being included as dividend due to minority in the consolidated balance sheet
- under equity accounting, inter-company balances do *not* cancel, because assets and liabilities of Investee are not shown in group debtors and creditors
- dividends receivable by Investor are included in the consolidated balance sheet when using equity accounting (there is no inter-company liability – for dividends payable by Investee – included in the consolidated balance sheet against which to cancel the receivable in Investor's assets)
- consolidated reserves are the same under both methods.

Gross equity method

The gross equity method is the same as the equity method, except that the investor's share of the total assets and of the total liabilities underlying the net equity amounts are analysed and disclosed on the face of the consolidated balance sheet.

If Investee in Example 7.1 had been consolidated using the *gross equity* method, rather than the *equity* method, presentation in the consolidated balance sheet would be as shown in Example 7.2.

Example 7.2 Gross equity method illustrated

Example

Details are as for Example 7.1, except assume that Investee is a joint venture.

Required

Show the consolidated balance sheet presentation of 'Investment in Investee' assuming, in turn, that the *equity* and the *gross equity* methods are used to account for the investment in the consolidated balance sheet.

Solution	**Equity €000**	**Gross equity €000**
Within fixed assets		
Share of gross assets (75% × €18.8m)		14,100
Unamortised goodwill (W_1 in Example 7.1)		400
		14,500
Share of gross liabilities (75% × €3.8m)		(2,850)
Share of net assets (W_2 in Example 7.1)	11,650	11,650

The gross equity method changes the balance sheet presentation, by elaborating on the amounts included under the equity method. There is no difference between the two methods in terms of accounting treatment. The difference is only one of detailed disclosure and presentation. Therefore, the equity method and the accounting treatment of associates (rather than joint ventures) will be the focus for the remainder of this chapter.

Calculating group share of associate

In order to qualify as an associate, and to justify the investing group accounting for the investment using equity accounting, the investor must be able to show that it exercises significant influence over the operating and financial policies of the investee. For simplicity in this chapter, the exercise of significant influence is presumed where an investor holds more than 20% of the equity shares. Holdings of less than 20% are presumed to be simple investments. These are included in the consolidated accounts exactly as they are treated in the individual accounts of the investor.

To calculate the proportion over which the investor has influence, the aggregate of the holdings of the parent and the *whole* of each subsidiary's holding (without deduction for any minority) in a potential associate is taken into account. However, the effective rate used to determine how much of the associate's net assets and profits to include in the consolidated accounts allows for minority interests in the shareholdings (see Chapter 6 for a similar discussion on controlling versus effective interests in the context of subsidiaries). The distinction between the proportion of the investee influenced by the parent and the effective rate of ownership is illustrated in Examples 7.3, 7.4 and 7.5.

A number of hypothetical situations are presented to illustrate the complexity of identifying whether a particular investment is classified as an associate under the more simplistic criterion of equity shareholdings between 20% and 50%.

Example 7.3 illustrates a situation where Parent has two subsidiaries. Each of these subsidiaries has a shareholding in a fourth company. Neither shareholding in isolation would suggest that the company is an associate. However, Parent controls 27% (12% and 15%) of Investee, which provides *prima facie* evidence that Parent exercises significant influence over Investee. When the equity method is applied, the minority interests in both subsidiaries must be acknowledged in calculating the group share (or the effective interest). Consequently, the proportion of Investee's net assets and profits to be included in the consolidated accounts is 18% [(75% × 12%) + (60% × 15%)].

Example 7.3 Classification of investment (1)

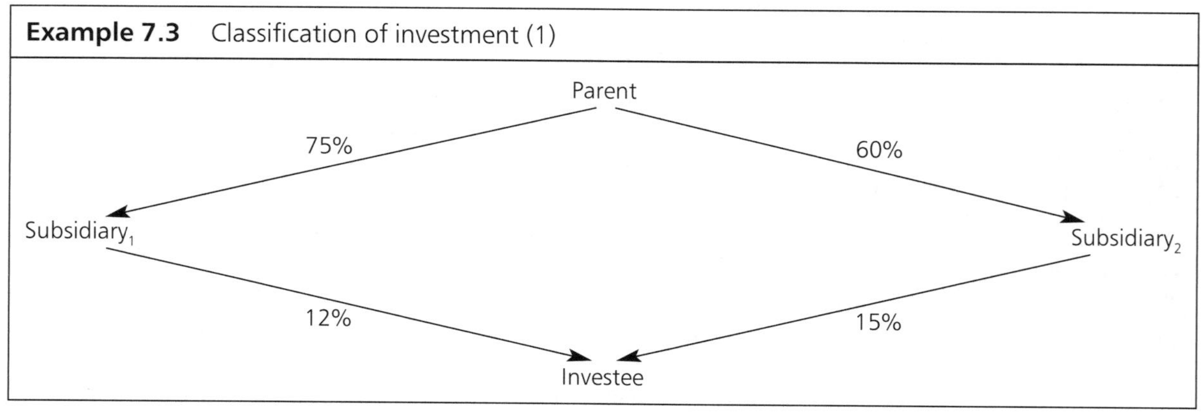

Classification of the investment in Investee is also the issue in Examples 7.4 and 7.5. Parent has a 100% subsidiary and a 30% associate in Example 7.4. Although Associate is presumed to have a significant influence over Investee and Parent is assumed to have significant influence over Associate, these two shareholdings are not sufficient for Parent to exercise significant influence over Investee. Parent controls 15% of Investee through its wholly owned subsidiary, but this percentage is below the 20% threshold for significant influence. Consequently, Investee's treatment in Parent's accounts is determined by its treatment in Associate's accounts. Associate can use equity accounting to record its investment in Investee and Parent equity accounts for Associate. Consequently, 9% (30% × 30%) of the profits of Investee are included in Parent's consolidated accounts.

Subsidiary controls 15% of Investee. It is therefore presumed that Subsidiary has no significant influence over Investee and must treat it as a simple investment recording the investment at cost and only recording dividends received and receivable in the profit and loss account. Arising from the relationship between Subsidiary and Investee, Parent also includes in its consolidated accounts the 15% dividends received by Subsidiary.

In conclusion, in Example 7.4, Parent's consolidated balance sheet would include a 9% stake in Investee accounted for using the equity method of accounting and a 15% stake accounted for as a simple investment.

Example 7.4 Classification of investment (2)

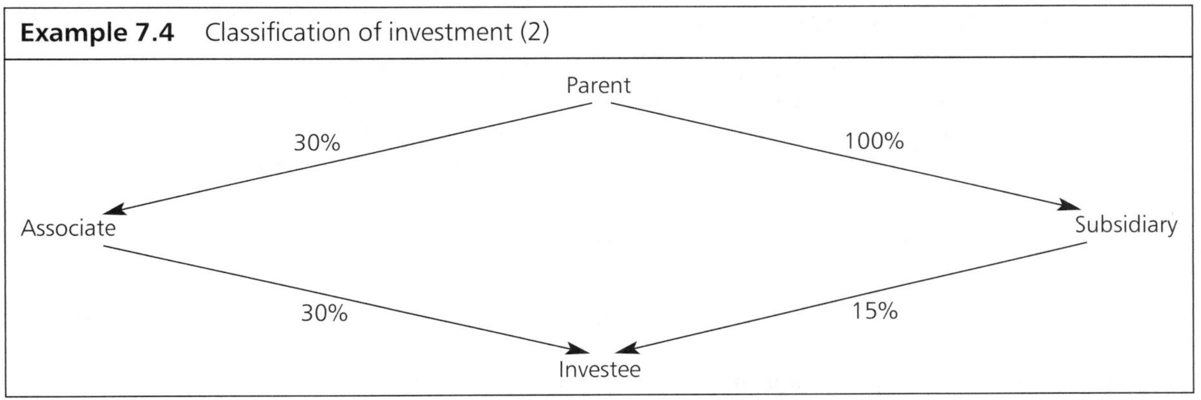

In Example 7.5, each of the two subsidiaries has two subsidiaries of its own. Each of these four sub-subsidiaries has a 6% interest in Investee. Because Parent controls each of the 6% holdings through its four sub-subsidiaries, it effectively controls 24% of Investee. Thus, Investee is an associate of Parent.

Individually Subsidiary$_1$ and Subsidiary$_2$ only control 12% each of Investee. Investee would therefore not be an associate of Subsidiary$_1$ or Subsidiary$_2$. Investee would be accounted for as a simple investment in their respective balance sheets. In the consolidated balance sheet of Parent group, Parent would include the group share of Investee's net assets [4 × (80% × 80% × 6%)], which is an effective interest of 15.36%, as an associated undertaking within financial fixed assets.

Example 7.5 Classification of investment (3)

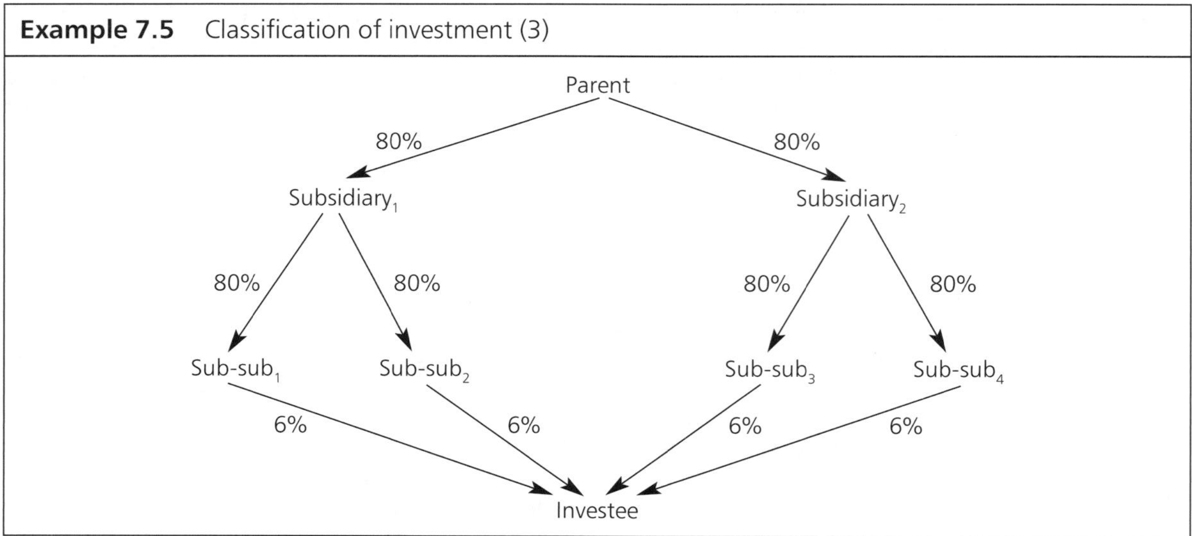

Equity accounting technique

On the date of acquisition of an investment which is to be equity accounted (for simplicity we will refer to this as Associate from now on in this chapter), the amount recorded in Parent's individual balance sheet and in its consolidated balance sheet will be the same. However, in the consolidated balance sheet the amount will be analysed as:

- group's share of net assets; plus
- unamortised goodwill.

That is, cost at the date of acquisition is analysed (for consolidated balance sheet purposes) into its components – group share of net assets and goodwill.

Example 7.6 illustrates how the investment at cost on Parent's balance sheet is equal to the group's share of net assets of Associate plus unamortised goodwill at the date of acquisition.

Example 7.6 Balance sheet presentation of associate at acquisition

Example

Investor acquired 25% of shares of Associate with net assets of €600, for €200.

Required

Show how the investment in Associate would be presented in the individual balance sheet of Investor and in the consolidated balance sheet.

Solution

Investing company balance sheet	€
Investment at cost	200

Consolidated balance sheet	€
Investment in Associate	
Fair value of net assets (25% × €600)	150
Unamortised goodwill (W_1)	50
	200

W_1 Goodwill	€
Investment in Associate at cost	200
Fair value of net assets at acquisition (25% × €600)	150
Goodwill	50

As time passes, Associate generates post-acquisition retained reserves (or suffers post-acquisition retained losses). Consequently, the value of the group's share of Associate's net assets changes. In addition, Parent will amortise any related goodwill arising on acquisition. These two effects will cause the value at which the investment is initially recorded under equity accounting to change.

To record entities under equity accounting using the double entry approach adopted for preparing the consolidated balance sheet in previous chapters, a T account is opened for *Investment in associate* in the consolidation workings. *Investment at cost* is transferred from Parent's balance sheet to the debit side of the T account. Subsequent entries to implement the equity method are all double entries *within* the consolidation workings. These are:

- group's share of post-acquisition retained earnings of Associate are debited to *Investment in associate* account and credited to group revenue reserves
- group's share of post-acquisition changes in other reserves of Associate (e.g., revaluation surpluses) are debited to *Investment in associate* account and credited to appropriate group reserve account
- goodwill amortised is credited to *Investment in associate* account and debited to group reserves.

Example 7.7 takes Example 7.6 forward one year in time. By that date, Associate has retained post-acquisition profit of €200. In addition, the group amortises €10 of the goodwill which arose on acquisition of Associate. Group reserves are adjusted by the group's share of this retained profit (€50) less the goodwill written off (€10).

Example 7.7 Balance sheet presentation of associate: one year post-acquisition

Example

Investor originally acquired 25% of shares of Associate for €200 when net assets were €600. One year later, net assets of Associate have increased to €800. Goodwill of €10 is charged against current year consolidated profits.

Required

Show how investment in Associate is presented in the consolidated balance sheet and show the related T account in the consolidated balance sheet workings.

Solution

Consolidated balance sheet presentation	€
Investment in Associate	
Fair value of net assets (25% × €800)	200
Unamortised goodwill ($€50_{\text{W1 in Example 7.6}}$ − €10)	40
	240

Consolidated balance sheet workings

Investment in Associate

	€		€
Investment at cost	200	Goodwill amortised	10
Group share of post-acquisition $\text{profits}_{25\% \times €200}$	50	Consolidated balance sheet	240
	250		250

A more comprehensive example incorporating investment in Associate into the consolidated balance sheet using the equity method is provided in Example 7.8.

Example 7.8 Equity accounting for investment in associate

Example

The following balance sheets were prepared for Parent group and its investee, Associate:

Balance sheet as at 31.12.20X9

	Parent group	Associate
Fixed assets:	€000	€000
Tangible assets	4,000	800
Investment in Associate at cost	500	—
	4,500	800
Current assets	5,000	2,000
Creditors due within one year	(3,000)	(1,040)
Net current assets	2,000	960
	6,500	1,760
Ordinary share capital	2,000	1,000
Profit and loss account	4,500	760
	6,500	1,760

Parent bought 25% of the ordinary shares in Associate in 20X6 for €500,000 when Associate had retained profits of €400,000. Parent appoints one-quarter of the directors to the board of Associate. Goodwill is amortised over five years.

Required

Prepare the consolidated balance sheet of Parent group, assuming equity accounting is used to record investment in Associate.

Solution

Consolidated balance sheet as at 31.12.X9

	€000	€000
Tangible assets		4,000
Investment in Associate (W_2)		470
		4,470
Current assets	5,000	
Creditors due in one year	(3,000)	
Net current assets		2,000
		6,470
Share capital		2,000
Profit and loss account (W_3)		4,470
		6,470

Workings

W_1 **Goodwill on acquisition**	€000
Cost	500
Net assets acquired:	
Ordinary share capital (25% × €1m)	(250)
Reserves (25% × €0.4m)	(100)
Goodwill	150
Less amortised (4/5: 20X6 – 20X9))	(120)
Unamortised at 31.12.20X9	30

Note: Alternatively, a *memorandum* cost of control T account could be used to calculate goodwill.

W_2 **Investment in Associate**	€000
Share of net assets (25% × €1.76m)	440
Goodwill (W_1)	30
	470

Note: Alternatively, a T account working could be presented with debit entries for cost of investment (€500,000) and 25% of post-acquisition profits ($90{,}000_{W3}$), and a credit entry for amortised goodwill ($120{,}000_{W1}$). This approach will generate the same €470,000 year-end balance.

W_3 **Retained profit at 31.12.20X9**	€000
Parent	4,500
Associate [25% × (€0.76m – €0.4m)]	90
Goodwill written off (W_1)	(120)
	4,470

Treatment of intra-group trading

Intra-group transactions between the group and entities accounted for under the equity method are commonplace. Unlike full consolidation, year-end balances associated with these transactions are not eliminated where the equity method is used to account for an investment. This is because the assets and liabilities of the equity accounted entities are not included with the separate categories of assets and liabilities in the consolidated balance sheet. Consequently, dividends receivable from an associate and included as an asset in the parent's balance sheet are also included in the consolidated balance sheet. There is no corresponding liability against which to offset this asset because the group's share of the associate's *net* assets is included only as a single-line item in the consolidated balance sheet. However, profits related to transactions between the group and its equity accounted entities which are not realised as far as the group is concerned must be provided for when preparing the consolidated balance sheet.

Under full consolidation, intra-group profits and losses are eliminated in full in the consolidated financial statements. Where the profit is recorded in a subsidiary that is not wholly owned, the minority is charged with its share of the unrealised profit. The rationale behind these adjustments, and the techniques involved, are explained in Chapter 3.

UK regulation (FRS 9) requires that a similar adjustment should apply for transactions between a group member and an associate or joint venture. Where the associate is equity accounted, the group's share of any unrealised profit or loss should be eliminated. It is necessary to look back to the exposure draft which preceded FRS 9 (ED 50) to find explicit guidance on how this adjustment should be implemented. ED 50 recommended that the adjustment in the balance sheet should be made against the asset which was the subject of the transaction if it is held by the group (e.g., stock or fixed asset) or else against the carrying amount for the associate if the asset is held by the associate.

Example 7.9 illustrates the contrast between the treatment required when an inter-company transaction gives rise to a profit in a subsidiary and the treatment required where the transaction is with an entity that is equity accounted.

Example 7.9 Treatment of inter-company sale of stock with subsidiaries and associates

Example

Parent sells goods at a profit of €200. The goods are unsold at the year-end and are included in the buyer's balance sheet as stock.

Required

Explain the treatment of the unrealised profit in the consolidated balance sheet of Parent and group, where the buyer is:

(i) a 51% owned subsidiary (ii) a 50% owned associate.

Solution

Parent to Subsidiary: inter-company stock

(i)
- The entire unrealised profit of €200 is eliminated.
- Stock on the consolidated balance sheet is reduced by €200.
- Because Parent recorded the profit in the first instance, the provision for unrealised profit is charged fully against group reserves.

Parent to Associate: inter-company stock

(ii)
- 50% of the profit (€100) is eliminated.
- Since Associate's stock is not included in the total group stock, it would be incorrect to adjust group stock in this case. A proportion of the stock is included in the consolidated balance sheet within the group's share of Associate's net assets. Thus, the provision for unrealised profit is charged against *Investment in associate.*
- The profit eliminated is taken from group profits in the consolidated profit and loss account (rather than from group share of associated company profit*).

* The eliminated profit would have been taken from the group's share of Associate's profit, had the associate made the profit in the first instance.

Example 7.10 illustrates the treatment of unrealised profit arising from a transaction between a parent and an associate, where different assumptions are made regarding which entity recorded the profit.

Example 7.10 Inter-company sale of stock to associates

Example

(i) Parent buys goods from Associate (40% owned) for €200. Profit of €100 is recorded by Associate and the goods are unsold at the year-end.
(ii) Alternatively, consider the situation with the same details, but Parent sells the goods to Associate.

Required

Explain the treatment of the unrealised profit in the consolidated balance sheet of Parent and group.

Solution

In both cases the group's share of the unrealised profit of €100 is eliminated, i.e., €40.

(i) Profit is recorded by Associate, stock is in Parent's balance sheet:
   - Stock on the consolidated balance sheet is reduced by €40.
   - Consolidated revenue reserves are reduced (through the group share of Associate's profit) by €40.

(ii) Profit is recorded by Parent, stock in Associate's balance sheet:
   - Investment in Associate is reduced by €40.
   - Consolidated revenue reserves are reduced by €40.

Investing company does not prepare consolidated accounts

So far in this chapter, application of the equity method of accounting was assumed to take place within the consolidated balance sheet. Where an investor has no subsidiaries, or is otherwise exempt from preparing consolidated accounts (see Chapter 14), using the equity method of accounting in its own individual accounts can cause legal problems. This is because the group's share of the associate's retained earnings would be classified as unrealised. FRS 9 requires that the relevant information should be shown in a separate set of accounts or by adding the information in supplementary form to the investor's own balance sheet.

Summary

This chapter explained and illustrated the equity method of accounting. This is an intermediate form of accounting for investments, between cost basis and full consolidation. This chapter only considered balance sheet effects of equity accounting. Equity accounting also has profit and loss account implications. These are considered in Chapter 11. The accounting regulations governing equity accounting (FRS 9 in the UK and IAS 28 under IAS GAAP) address many regulatory and other technical issues which have not been discussed in this chapter. These are dealt with in detail in Chapter 15.

Learning outcomes

After studying this chapter you should have learnt:

- what is meant by equity accounting
- how to distinguish between equity accounting and full consolidation in the context of the consolidated balance sheet

- the difference between *gross* equity accounting and equity accounting
- how to calculate the group's effective interest in an associate in a complex group situation
- how to calculate the amount to be included in the consolidated balance sheet when equity accounting is used to measure an investment
- how to adjust for unrealised profits related to equity accounting entities.

Multiple choice questions

Solutions to these questions are presented in Appendix 1.

7.1 Eagle and Hawk

Eagle acquired 25% of the ordinary share capital of **Hawk** for €640,000 eight years ago, when the profit and loss account of Hawk stood at €720,000. Eagle appointed two directors to the board of Hawk and the investment is regarded as long term. Group policy is to amortise goodwill over five years. Both companies prepare accounts to 31 December each year. The summarised balance sheet of Hawk on 31 December 20X4 is as follows:

	€000
Sundry net assets	2,390
Capital and reserves	
Called-up share capital	800
Share premium	450
Profit and loss account	1,140
	2,390

Hawk has made no new issues of shares, neither has there been any movement in the share premium account, since Eagle acquired its holding.

At what amount will the investment in Hawk be shown in the consolidated balance sheet of Eagle as on 31 December 20X4?

(a) €745,000
(b) €640,000
(c) €597,500
(d) €560,625

7.2 Blue, Black and Red

Blue acquired 80% of ordinary shares of **Black** when the reserves of Black were €150,000 and 40% of the ordinary shares of **Red** when its net assets were €100,000. At 31 May 20X3 the following information is extracted from the financial statements of the companies:

		€
Blue	Reserves	450,000
Black	Reserves	250,000
Red	Net assets	150,000

Assuming no goodwill has been written off by the balance sheet date and that share capital of Red is unchanged since acquisition, the figure for reserves in the consolidated balance sheet as at 31 May 20X3 would be:

(a) €450,000
(b) €530,000
(c) €550,000
(d) €850,000

7.3 Laurent

David owns 90% of the equity of Patrick, which owns 70% of the equity of George. David also owns 30% of the equity of Andrew.

All four companies own equity voting shares in **Laurent** as follows:

	% held
David	15
Patrick	10
George	8
Andrew	12

When deciding whether Laurent is an associate of David's in accordance with FRS 9 *Associates and Joint Ventures*, what is the relevant percentage shareholding?

(a) 29.04%
(b) 32.64%
(c) 33.00%
(d) 45.00%

7.4 Darcy and Wickham

Darcy acquired 49% of the ordinary share capital in **Wickham** for €250,000 some years ago when the retained losses of Wickham stood at €100,000. The goodwill on this investment is fully written off by the current balance sheet date. Darcy appoints a director to Wickham's board and considers the investment to be long term.

The summarised balance sheet of Wickham as at 31 December 20X9 is:

	€000
Net assets	200
Capital and reserves	
Called up share capital	400
Profit and loss account	(200)
	200

There has been no change in Wickham's share capital since Darcy's investment.

At what amount will the investment in Wickham be shown in the Darcy group's draft consolidated balance sheet as at 31 December 20X9, before making any provision for diminution in value?

(a) €49,000
(b) €98,000
(c) €201,000
(d) €250,000

7.5 Fagan and Dodger

Fagan owns 30% of **Dodger** along with other investments in subsidiaries. As at 31 January 20X9, Dodger's balance sheet is summarised as follows:

	€000
Purchased intangibles	100
Sundry net assets	300
	400
Share capital	50
Retained profits	350
	400

Fagan paid €200,000 for its shares in Dodger at a time when Dodger's net assets were €160,000 in total at fair value. By the current year-end, all consolidation goodwill is fully written off. There has been no change in Dodger's share capital since Fagan's investment.

At what amount will Fagan's investment in Dodger be stated in its group financial statements?

(a) €48,000
(b) €90,000
(c) €120,000
(d) €200,000

7.6 Alex and Peter

On 1 September 20X2 **Alex** acquired 30% of the ordinary shares of **Peter** (cost €110,000) when the issued capital of Peter was €200,000 and its reserves were €100,000. At 31 August 20X5 the net assets of Peter are €600,000. Premium on acquisition is amortised over five years. Alex has two subsidiary undertakings. In the consolidated balance sheet as at 31 August 20X5 the investment in Peter would be shown as:

(a) €180,000
(b) €188,000
(c) €192,000
(d) €200,000

7.7 Wine and Port

Wine acquired 30% of the share capital of **Port** on 1 January 20X5 and thereby gained a significant influence over Port. The consideration was €1,000,000 and the fair value of the separable net assets of Port on 1 January 20X5 was €3,000,000. During the year ended 31 December 20X5, Port made a profit after tax of €200,000 and declared a total dividend for the year of €80,000. Wine follows a policy of amortising all goodwill arising on consolidation over a period of 20 years.

The investment in Port is carried in the consolidated balance sheet of Wine on 31 December 20X5 at:

(a) € 936,000
(b) €1,000,000
(c) €1,031,000
(d) €1,036,000

Self-assessment exercise

Solution to this self-assessment exercise can be found at:
www.thomsonlearning.co.uk/accountingandfinance/piercebrennan

7.1 Champion Group

You are given the following information relating to the **Champion Group**:

1 On 1 January 20X4, **Champion** acquired 80% of the ordinary share capital of **Winner**. This latter company already owned 75% of the ordinary share capital of **Trier** which it acquired on 1 September 20X3.

On 1 July 20X7, Champion acquired 30% of the ordinary share capital of **Ship**.

2 The following information is available with respect to the retained profits of these four companies:

Date	Champion €000	Winner €000	Trier €000	Ship €000
1 September 20X3	1,820	1,200	820	218
1 January 20X4	1,947	1,450	940	244
1 July 20X7	2,464	1,526	1,123	300

3 Summarised balance sheets at 31 December 20X9:

	Champion €000	Winner €000	Trier €000	Ship €000
Land	750	400	850	140
Equipment	1,045	345	250	110
Investment in Winner (at cost)	2,500	—	—	—
Investment in Ship (at cost)	240	—	—	—
Investment in Trier (at cost)	—	1,500	—	—
Stock	644	423	241	146
Debtors	921	647	407	198
Bank	713	232	353	68
	6,813	3,547	2,101	662
Creditors	843	1,047	311	142
Loan (long-term)	1,000	—	—	—
Ordinary share capital	2,000	750	500	100
Retained profits	2,970	1,750	1,290	420
	6,813	3,547	2,101	662

4 At the relevant dates of acquisition the fair values of the net assets of Winner, Trier and Ship closely approximated their balance sheet values with the exception of the land held by Winner which had a market value €350,000 in excess of its balance sheet value. This land is still held by Winner.

5 The following inter-company transactions took place during 20X9:

	Sold by	Sold to	Sales value €000	Original cost €000
January 20X9	Champion	Trier	380	200
June 20X9*	Trier	Winner	250	150

*Only in this case were the goods received (by Winner) still held at 31 December 20X9.

6 There are no inter-company balances in debtors or creditors at the year-end.

7 During 20X7 Winner transferred a machine to Champion for €500,000. At the time of this transfer the machine's written down value in Winner's books was €400,000 (cost €800,000, aggregate depreciation €400,000, useful life eight years and depreciation rate of 12½% per annum straight line). The total useful life is estimated to be unchanged.

It is group policy to provide a full year's depreciation on assets in the year of purchase and none in the year of disposal.

8 Accounting policies:

(a) Goodwill on consolidation is calculated as the parent company's share of any goodwill arising on group acquisitions.

(b) Goodwill arising on consolidation is written off over eight years on a straight-line basis, including a full year in the year of acquisition.

(c) Intra-group profits earned by subsidiaries are eliminated, where appropriate, proportionately against the majority and minority interests in the group.

Required

Prepare the consolidated balance sheet for the Champion Group at 31 December 20X9.

Examination-style questions

7.1 Ripe, Sour and Tart

The following information relates to the balance sheets of **Ripe**, its subsidiary **Sour** and an associated company **Tart** at 31 July 20X1.

	Ripe €000	**Sour €000**	**Tart €000**
Tangible fixed assets	16,400	14,500	—
Financial fixed assets	—	—	5,000
Shares in Sour (at cost)	13,200	—	—
Shares in Tart (at cost)	3,000	—	—
	32,600	14,500	5,000
Current assets			
Stock	2,612	2,010	—
Debtors	2,036	1,196	—
Cash at bank and in hand	882	114	—
	5,530	3,320	—
Creditors: Amounts falling due within one year	(2,502)	(1,360)	—
Net current assets	3,028	1,960	—
Total assets less current liabilities	35,628	16,460	5,000
Creditors: Amounts falling due after more than one year	(5,350)	(1,470)	—
	30,278	14,990	5,000
Capital and reserves			
Ordinary €1 shares	20,000	8,000	5,000
5% preference €1 shares	—	4,000	—
Share premium account	4,950	350	—
Profit and loss account	5,328	2,640	—
	30,278	14,990	5,000

The following information is relevant for the preparation of the Ripe group balance sheet:

(a) Ripe owns 80% of the ordinary shares, and 30% of the 5% preference €1 shares of Sour:
   (i) The preference shares of Sour were originally issued on 1 August 20X0 at par.
   (ii) Ripe paid €13.2 million for the ordinary shares and the 5% preference shares on 1 August 20X0 when Sour's profit and loss account was €3 million (credit balance).
   (iii) The share premium account of Sour comprises the original premiums on the issue of the ordinary shares.

(b) The fair values of the net assets of Sour were not materially different from their book values at the time of its acquisition by Ripe.

(c) Sour has already paid its dividends for the current financial year and no other dividends are proposed. The company paid an ordinary dividend of 1 cent per share and the 5% preference dividend. Ripe has included the dividends received in its profit and loss account. The auditors of Ripe observed that the payment of the dividends by Sour was out of pre-acquisition profits and that this has contributed to a diminution in the value of the holding company's investment. They feel that Ripe should account for the dividends accordingly.

(d) Sour sold an item of stock to Ripe on 1 August 20X0. Ripe has treated this item correctly as plant and machinery in its financial statements. The item was sold at cost plus 20% and is included in the fixed assets of Ripe at cost of €2.4 million. A full year's depreciation of 20% per annum has been charged on this amount in the financial statements of Ripe (€480,000). Ripe has not fully paid the cost of the fixed asset to Sour by the end of the current year. There is an amount of €0.5 million outstanding.

(e) Ripe bought 30% of the shares of Tart on 31 July 20X1. Tart is an investment company whose only asset is a portfolio of investments with a book value of €5 million. The market value of these investments on 31 July 20X1 was €9 million.

(f) Goodwill arising on acquisition is to be amortised through the profit and loss account over six years. Goodwill is charged pro rata in the year of acquisition.

Required

(i) Prepare the consolidated balance sheet for the Ripe Group as at 31 July 20X1.

(ii) Assuming Ripe continues to hold its investment in Tart until at least 31 July 20X4, indicate how the investment would be dealt with in the consolidated accounts for the year ended on that date.

7.2 Barrow, Nore and Slaney

Barrow, a medium sized company, purchased two investments on 1 April 20X1, as follows:

(i) the entire share capital of **Nore**

(ii) 40% of the share capital of **Slaney**.

Barrow makes up its financial statements to 31 March each year. The terms of the acquisitions were:

Nore

The total consideration was based on a price earnings (PE) multiple of 12 applied to the reported profit of €4 million of Nore for the year to 31 March 20X1. The consideration was settled by Barrow issuing €28 million 8% debentures (at par) and the balance by a new issue of €1 ordinary shares, based on a market value of €2.50 each.

Slaney

The value of Slaney at 1 April 20X1 was mutually agreed between Barrow and the vendor to be €56.25 million. Barrow purchased its share (40%) of this amount by issuing 9 million €1 ordinary shares (market value of €2.50 each) to the vendor.

Barrow has not recorded the acquisition of these investments or the issuing of the consideration. The summarised draft balance sheets of the three companies at 31 March 20X2 are as follows:

Summarised balance sheets at 31 March 20X2

	Barrow		Nore		Slaney	
	€000	€000	€000	€000	€000	€000
Fixed assets						
Tangible assets		51,390		40,500		31,590
Current assets						
Stocks	14,460		10,800		27,960	
Trade and other debtors	16,800		7,590		6,930	
Cash	—		5,115		60	
	31,260		23,505		34,950	
Creditors: Amounts falling due within one year						
Trade and other creditors	19,680		7,905		21,150	
Bank overdraft	2,310		—		—	
Taxation	8,460		3,600		1,140	
Proposed dividends	6,000		—		—	
	(36,450)		(11,505)		(22,290)	
Net current (liabilities)/assets		(5,190)		12,000		12,660
Total assets less current liabilities		46,200		52,500		44,250
Capital and reserves						
Ordinary shares €1 each		15,000		30,000		37,500
Profit and loss account		31,200		22,500		6,750
		46,200		52,500		44,250

The following information is relevant:

1 The book values of the net assets of Barrow and Slaney at the date of acquisition were considered to be a reasonable approximation to their fair values.
2 Included in Nore's tangible fixed assets is land with a fair value of €2 million greater than its carrying amount at the date of acquisition. The fair value is not incorporated in Nore's draft balance sheet.
3 In March 20X2 Barrow sold goods to Nore at a price of €1,875,000. This included a mark-up on cost of 25%. Nore has not yet sold any of these goods, but it paid for them on 28 March 20X2. Barrow had not received this payment at the balance sheet date. This has been the only intra-group trading.
4 The profits of Nore and Slaney for the year to 31 March 20X2 were €12 million and €3 million, respectively. No dividends have been paid by any of the entities during the year.
5 Interest on the debentures issued on 1 April 20X1 has been fully reflected in the year-end balance sheet.
6 Goodwill is to be amortised on a straight-line basis over ten years.

Required

(a) Prepare the journal entries to record the acquisition of Nore and Slaney in the accounting records of Barrow as at 1 April 20X1. Show your workings.

(b) Prepare the consolidated balance sheet of Barrow Group as at 31 March 20X2.

8

Bonus and rights issues

Learning objectives

After studying this chapter you should be able to:

- deal with bonus issues of shares out of the subsidiary's *pre*-acquisition reserves when calculating goodwill
- deal with bonus issues of shares out of the subsidiary's *post*-acquisition reserves when preparing the consolidated balance sheet
- understand the impact of a rights issue in the subsidiary on the preparation of consolidated balance sheets

Introduction

When preparing consolidated balance sheets, the fair value of any consideration paid is compared with the fair value of net assets acquired to calculate goodwill on acquisition. So far in this book, the simplifying assumption has been made in the vast majority of questions and examples, that fair value of assets and their book value equate. Fair value of net assets acquired has been identified by reference to share capital and reserves of subsidiaries at acquisition. Consequently, book values of share capital and reserves at acquisition are used to quantify net assets at acquisition. Where the subsidiary makes a bonus issue or issues rights to its existing shareholders, care has to be taken to ensure that appropriate amounts for share capital and reserves are used to measure net assets at acquisition.

Bonus issue by subsidiary out of pre-acquisition reserves

A bonus issue arises when a company issues shares to its existing shareholders for no consideration. When a subsidiary makes a bonus issue of shares out of pre-acquisition reserves there is no effect on the value of goodwill at acquisition. The bonus issue can affect the absolute amounts of share capital and reserves used in calculating goodwill, but the aggregate of the two amounts is unchanged. The company has merely issued shares from existing reserves. The increase in share capital is matched by an equal reduction in reserves at acquisition. Nonetheless, care must be taken to ensure that consistent amounts are included in consolidation workings and that correct matching of pre- and post-bonus issue share capital and reserves is made. This means that goodwill is calculated by taking:

- share capital and reserves as they were at the date of acquisition; or
- new share capital (after bonus issue) and reserves as decreased by bonus issue.

Example 8.1 illustrates the effect of a bonus issue from pre-acquisition reserves on the components of the net assets at acquisition calculation. (Remember that net assets at acquisition are represented by the subsidiary's share capital and pre-acquisition reserves.) Both share capital and reserves should be (1) before the bonus issue or (2) after the bonus issue. So long as consistent amounts are used, the total for share capital and reserves will be correct at €3.5 million.

Example 8.1 Bonus issue out of pre-acquisition reserves (1)

Example

A subsidiary company with 1 million €1 ordinary shares, issued one bonus share for each ordinary share held on the first day following acquisition.

Reserves at the date of acquisition amounted to €2.5million.

Required

Calculate net assets at acquisition using amounts (i) before the bonus issue and (ii) after the bonus issue.

Solution

	(i) Before bonus	(ii) After bonus	
	€000	€000	
Share capital	1,000	2,000	1,000+1,000
Reserves	2,500	1,500	2,500–1,000
Net assets	3,500	3,500	

Example 8.2 provides a similar illustration to that in Example 8.1, except that the entries in the cost of control account in the consolidated balance sheet workings are provided in Example 8.2.

Example 8.2 Bonus issue out of pre-acquisition reserves (2)

Example

Parent acquired 100% of Subsidiary for €280 when Subsidiary's pre-acquisition reserves were €200. One month later Subsidiary made a 1-for-1 bonus issue out of pre-acquisition profits. After the bonus issue, Subsidiary's share capital is €100 in shares of €1 each.

Required

Prepare the cost of control account to calculate goodwill on acquisition using amounts (i) before the bonus issue and (ii) after the bonus issue.

Solution

- Share capital after the one-for-one bonus issue is €100, therefore share capital before the bonus issue was €50.
- If reserves before the bonus issue were €200, reserves after the bonus issue are €150.

Cost of control account

	(i) Pre-bonus	(ii) Post-bonus		(i) Pre-bonus	(ii) Post-bonus
	€	€		€	€
Cost of investment	280	280	Share capital	50	100
			Reserves	200	150
			Bal c/d: Goodwill	30	30
	280	280		280	280

A more detailed example is provided in Example 8.3, where all three consolidation working accounts are presented. Goodwill, consolidated revenue reserves and minority interest are the same regardless of whether pre-or post-bonus amounts are used, provided that the matching is done consistently.

Example 8.3 Bonus issue out of pre-acquisition reserves (3)

Example

Parent acquired 3.2 million shares in Subsidiary on 1.1.20X1 when Subsidiary revenue reserves were €1.5million. On 30.6.20X1, Subsidiary made a bonus issue of 1-for-4 out of pre-acquisition profits (the share capital of Subsidiary increased from 4 million to 5 million shares). The balance sheets of Parent and Subsidiary at 31.12.20X1 are as follows:

	Parent €000	**Subsidiary €000**
Shares in Subsidiary (4 million €1 shares)	6,500	—
Net assets	8,500	8,000
	15,000	8,000
Share capital in shares of €1 each	8,000	5,000
Revenue reserves	7,000	3,000
	15,000	8,000

Required

Show the cost of control, revenue reserves and minority interest accounts in the consolidation working accounts, using amounts (i) before the bonus issue and (ii) after the bonus issue.

Solution

Group structure

Parent —80%→ Subsidiary

Cost of control account

	(i) Pre-bonus €000	**(ii) Post-bonus €000**		**(i) Pre-bonus €000**	**(ii) Post-bonus €000**
Cost of investment	6,500	6,500	Share capital$_{80\% \times 4m/5m}$	3,200	4,000
			Revenue reserves $_{80\% \times 1.5m}$	1,200	
			Revenue reserves $_{80\% \times (1.5m-1m)}$		400
			Bal. c/d: Goodwill	2,100	2,100
	6,500	6,500		6,500	6,500

Consolidated revenue reserves

	(i) Pre-bonus €000	**(ii) Post-bonus €000**		**(i) Pre-bonus €000**	**(ii) Post-bonus €000**
Cost of control$_{80\% \times 1.5m/0.5m}$	1,200	400	Parent	7,000	7,000
Minority interest$_{20\% \times 4m/3m}$	800	600	Subsidiary	3,000	3,000
Consolidated balance sheet	9,000	9,000	Bonus	1,000	—
	11,000	10,000		11,000	10,000

continued overleaf

Example 8.3 Continued

Minority interest

	(i) Pre-bonus €000	(ii) Post-bonus €000		(i) Pre-bonus €000	(ii) Post-bonus €000
Consolidated balance sheet	1,600	1,600	Ordinary share capital 20% × 4m/5m	800	1,000
			Revenue reserves 20% × 4m/3m	800	600
	1,600	1,600		1,600	1,600

Bonus issue by subsidiary out of post-acquisition reserves

When a subsidiary makes a bonus issue of shares out of post-acquisition reserves, the bonus issue does not interfere with the calculations for goodwill at acquisition. Such a bonus issue does, however, reduce distributable group reserves. Again, care is required to ensure that such bonus issues are correctly treated. Where the bonus issue has been recorded by the subsidiary, share capital in the subsidiary's balance sheet comprises share capital relevant to calculating net assets at acquisition and, in addition, bonus shares that are irrelevant when calculating net assets at acquisition. The group's share of these bonus shares must be treated as a group capital reserve in the consolidated balance sheet.

If revenue reserves *before* the bonus issue are included in the subsidiary's balance sheet, the group share of the bonus issue needs to be transferred from group distributable profits to a capital reserve in the consolidated workings. Example 8.4 illustrates the treatment of a bonus issue out of post-acquisition reserves in the consolidated balance sheet workings.

Example 8.4 Bonus issue out of post-acquisition profit

Example

Details as for Example 8.3, except that on 31.12.20X1 Subsidiary made a bonus issue of 1-for-4 out of post-acquisition profits (share capital increased to 5 million shares).

Required

Show the cost of control, consolidated revenue reserves, consolidated capital reserve and minority interest accounts in the consolidation workings.

Solution

Cost of control account

	€000		€000
Cost of investment	6,500	Share capital 80% × 4m	3,200
		Revenue reserves 80% × 1.5m	1,200
		Goodwill	2,100
	6,500		6,500

Consolidated revenue reserves

	€000		€000
Cost of control 80% × 1.5m	1,200	Parent	7,000
Minority interest 20% × 3m	600	Subsidiary	3,000
Consolidated balance sheet	8,200		
	10,000		10,000

Consolidated capital reserves

	€000		€000
Consolidated balance sheet	800	Group share of bonus issue shares 80% × 1m	800

Minority interest

	€000		€000
Consolidated balance sheet	1,600	Ordinary share capital (20% × 4m) + (20% × 1m)	1,000
		Revenue reserves 20% × 3m	600
	1,600		1,600

The following points should be noted in relation to Example 8.4:

- share capital and pre-acquisition reserves *before* the bonus issue are used in the cost of control account
- minority interest reflects the minority share of Subsidiary's net assets at the year-end. This is calculated by reference to both share capital and reserves *after* the bonus issue
- consolidated revenue reserves must exclude the reserves which have been converted into bonus shares and are, therefore, now non-distributable
- the group's share of the bonus shares (80% x €1m = €800,000) must be included in the consolidated balance sheet as a capital reserve.

Rights issues

A rights issue arises when a company offers shares to its existing shareholders for consideration, which is usually less than the current market price for the shares.

All rights taken up

Where a subsidiary makes a rights issue subsequent to its acquisition by a controlling entity and *all the rights are taken up* by all shareholders, there is no effect on goodwill as calculated before the rights issue. From the group's perspective, the cost of the shares taken up in the rights issue is matched by their par value and associated share premium in the cost of control account. This leaves the original goodwill amount unaltered. There is no change in the respective percentage interests of the group and the minority.

When preparing the consolidated balance sheet workings, the cost of the shares in the subsidiary, including the cost of shares issued following the rights offer, is debited to the cost of control account. The group's share of net assets of the subsidiary, which is credited to the cost of control account, comprises the following:

- group share of subsidiary's share capital (including the rights shares)
- group share of subsidiary's share premium (balance at date of acquisition plus amount of premium arising on rights shares)
- group share of all other reserves at acquisition.

Proportion of rights taken up

Where a subsidiary makes a rights issue subsequent to acquisition and *only a proportion of the rights is taken up*, this can cause a change in the respective group and minority holdings. It is then necessary to calculate the change in the percentage shareholding held by the parent. The group share of the subsidiary can increase or decrease as result of an under-subscribed rights issue, depending on whether the group or minority shareholders acquired the higher proportion of the shares on offer to them. For example, if Parent owns 80% of Subsidiary and does not take up the full rights issue entitlement (while all other shareholders take up a higher proportion of the rights issue than Parent), Parent's percentage ownership of Subsidiary falls and there is a corresponding increase in the minority interest. Where Parent takes up a higher proportion than other shareholders, the position is reversed.

The treatment of the rights issue in the consolidated balance sheet workings depends on whether the parent takes more than, or less than, the proportion of rights shares taken up by other shareholders:

- if the group percentage holding in the subsidiary increases as a consequence of the rights issue, this is equivalent to a piecemeal acquisition
- if the percentage holding in the subsidiary decreases as a consequence of the rights issue, this is equivalent to a disposal of part of the group's holding to the minority shareholders.

Particular care is required when dealing with these situations in the consolidated workings. It is difficult to be definitive because the approach to be adopted depends on how the information relating to the rights issue and the subsidiary's shareholders' funds is presented. However, the following guidelines are useful, but they should not be applied without first assessing their appropriateness.

Piecemeal acquisition where control is increased following rights issue

The double entry in the consolidation balance sheet workings to record the acquisition is:

Dr Cost of control account
(with total cost, including cost of shares acquired in rights issue)

Cr Cost of control account
(with group's share of ordinary share capital (new percentage)
+ group's share of share premium on rights issue
+ group's original share of revenue reserves at the date of initial acquisition (old percentage)
+ the additional percentage of revenue reserves at the date of the rights issue.

Example 8.5 illustrates the treatment of an increased stake following a rights issue in the consolidated balance sheet workings.

Example 8.5 Control increased following rights issue

Example
Parent acquired 75% of the share capital of Subsidiary for €100,000. Subsidiary had 100,000 ordinary €1 shares in issue. Subsequently, Subsidiary made a 1-for-2 rights issue which increased its share capital to 150,000 shares. The share premium on the rights issue was €50,000. The group acquired more than its rights entitlement and the group's interest in Subsidiary increased to 80%. The additional cost of the rights shares was €90,000. Revenue reserves at the date of the original acquisition were €10,000 and at the date of the rights issue were €40,000.

Required
Show the cost of control account to calculate goodwill on acquisition.

Solution
Group structure

75% pre-rights
80% post-rights
Parent ——————→ Subsidiary

Cost of control account

	€			€
Cost of investment €100,000 + € 90,000	190,000	Share capital 80% × €150,000		120,000
		Share premium 80% × €50,000		40,000
		Revenue reserves	75% × €10,000 = 7,500	
			5% × €40,000 = 2,000	9,500
		Goodwill		20,500
	190,000			190,000

Piecemeal acquisitions are dealt with more fully in Chapter 5.

Part-disposal where control is reduced following rights issue

Where the group loses control of part of a shareholding previously held following a rights issue, the related net assets have to be transferred to the minority interest. This means that the minority interest is credited with a higher proportion of the subsidiary's net assets at the end of the year than it would have been before the rights issue. This transfer to minority interest includes two elements:

1 an amount that was formerly part of the group's share of net assets at acquisition
2 an amount relating to the group's share of post-acquisition retained earnings to which the group no longer has access.

The first element increases group goodwill while the second represents a loss on disposal. The group no longer has access to that amount of the subsidiary's post-acquisition reserves transferred to the minority and it received no consideration for the effective disposal.

Disposal of subsidiaries is dealt with in greater detail in Chapter 12.

Summary

This chapter explained and illustrated the effect of bonus and rights issues by subsidiaries on the preparation of consolidated balance sheets. Bonus issues are relatively easier, as the proportions held by the group and the minority remain unchanged as a result of the bonus issue. While care is required to ensure the correct amounts from the subsidiary's accounts are used to represent net assets at acquisition, questions with bonus issues are useful to test your understanding of consolidation principles in the context of the balance sheet. Rights issues are more complex because they introduce the complexities of piecemeal acquisitions and disposal of subsidiaries.

Learning outcomes

After studying this chapter you should have learnt:

- how to deal with bonus issues of shares out of the subsidiary's *pre*-acquisition reserves when calculating goodwill
- how to deal with bonus issues of shares out of the subsidiary's *post*-acquisition reserves when preparing the consolidated balance sheet
- how a rights issue in the subsidiary impacts on the preparation of consolidated balance sheets.

Self-assessment exercise

The Solution to this self-assessment exercise can be found at:
www.thomsonlearning.co.uk/accountingandfinance/piercebrennan

8.1 Luke and Warm

Luke acquired 60,000 €1 ordinary shares in **Warm** on 31 December 20X1. The summarised balance sheets of Luke and Warm on that date were:

	Luke	**Warm**
	€	**€**
Fixed assets	253,000	128,000
Investment in Warm at cost:		
60,000 shares of €1 each	100,000	—
Stock	30,000	10,000
Bills receivable (including €700 from Warm)*	2,000	—
Debtors and balances at bank	20,000	17,000
	405,000	155,000
Issued and paid up share capital		
600,000 shares of 50 cent each	300,000	—
80,000 shares of €1 each	—	80,000
Capital reserve	—	34,000
Revenue reserve	20,000	10,000
Profit and loss account	50,000	10,000
Bills payable (including €1,000 to Luke)	—	3,500
Creditors	35,000	17,500
	405,000	155,000

*Note on balance sheet of Luke:

There is a contingent liability for bills receivable discounted of €1,200.

You are given the following information:

1 On 1 January 20X2 Warm used part of its capital reserve to make a bonus issue of one share for every four shares held and used the balance of the reserve to write down its fixed assets to their fair value for consolidation purposes.

2 Stock of Luke includes €4,800 for goods at invoice price bought from Warm. When invoicing goods to Luke, Warm adds 20% to cost.

Required

Prepare the summarised consolidated balance sheet of Luke and group as on 31 December 20X1.

Examination-style questions

8.1 Definition, Scotty and Kingtop

Definition acquired 60% of the ordinary share capital of **Scotty** on 30 June 20X0, on which date the retained profits of Scotty were €1.5m.

On 1 January 20X1, Scotty made a 1 for 4 rights issue. The issue was fully subscribed with Definition taking up its full share of the rights issue.

On 1 January 20X2, Definition acquired 25% of the ordinary share capital of **Kingtop**. On that date Kingtop's retained profits were €1.86m.

On 28 December 20X3, Definition recorded a credit sale of €500,000 to Scotty. The items sold had cost Definition €200,000. Scotty had not recorded the purchase of these items by 31 December 20X3.

At the respective dates of acquisition of Scotty and Kingtop by Definition, the book value of both companies' assets closely approximated their fair value with the following exceptions:

(a) Stock held by Scotty had a fair value of €400,000 in excess of its book value. This stock was sold during 20X0.

(b) The transport fleet of Scotty had a fair value of €1,750,000. The book value was €1,250,000. All vehicles in the fleet at the date of acquisition are still owned by Scotty. They are depreciated at 20% per annum using the straight-line method.

No adjustment has been made to the books of Scotty to reflect these fair valuations.

Goodwill on consolidation is amortised on a straight-line basis over four years. A full year's amortisation is charged in the year of acquisition.

The summarised balance sheets at 31 December 20X3 were as follows:

	Definition	Scotty	Kingtop
	€000	€000	€000
Tangible fixed assets	26,427	4,916	3,135
Investment in Scotty (at cost)	3,500	—	—
Investment in Kingtop (at cost)	750	—	—
Trade debtors	12,105	2,108	1,907
Stock	14,629	3,417	2,112
Bank	384	122	143
	57,795	10,563	7,297
Trade creditors	10,196	1,947	1,633
Tax payable	1,054	236	204
Long-term loans	20,000	2,500	2,000
Ordinary share capital	10,000	2,500	500
Share premium*	—	500	—
Retained profits	16,545	2,880	2,960
	57,795	10,563	7,297

*Relates to Scotty's rights issue on 1 January 20X1.

Required

Prepare the consolidated balance sheet at 31 December 20X3 for the shareholders of Definition.

8.2 Rowan, Spruce and Pine

Rowan, a manufacturing company, holds a number of long-term investments, including:

1 €1 ordinary shares in **Spruce**

On 1 May 20X3 Rowan had acquired 1.8m of the 3m shares in issue at that date, at a cost of €4,268,000. Subsequently, in October 20X3, Spruce distributed a previously declared 1 for 5 bonus issue from pre-acquisition reserves, by utilising the share premium account. On 31 March 20X4 Spruce made a 1 for 9 rights issue at €1.25 per share. Rowan took up its full entitlement (and no more than that) at a cost of €300,000 and all other rights in Spruce's shares were fully exercised.

At the date on which Rowan acquired its initial holding (1 May 20X3), the reserves of Spruce had comprised:

	€000
Share premium account	670
Other reserves	Nil
Profit and loss account	70 (debit balance)

The book values of Spruce's assets at the date of acquisition were the same as their fair values with the exceptions that:

(a) the fair values of land and buildings were €500,000 and €610,000 respectively, compared with their book values which were €300,000 and €410,000 respectively. The fair values were not recorded in the accounts. Spruce depreciates buildings at the rate of 5% per annum straight line, including a full year in the year of acquisition

(b) certain items of stock with a book value of €562,000 had a fair value of €742,000. The whole of this stock had been sold by 31 December 20X4.

2 €1 ordinary shares in **Pine** (cost €1,684,000)

Rowan had acquired a 30% holding of the equity shares on 31 March 20X4 and treats Pine as an associated undertaking. At 1 January 20X4, the capital and reserves of Pine had consisted of:

	€000
Ordinary share capital (called up and fully paid)	2,200
Revaluation reserve	730
Other reserves	140
Profit and loss account	230

Pine's profits for the year ended 31 December 20X4 were earned evenly throughout the period. All Pine's reserve increases came from profits.

Balance sheets at 31 December 20X4

	Rowan		Spruce		Pine	
	€000	€000	€000	€000	€000	€000
Fixed assets						
Intangible						
Development costs		—		—		72
Tangible						
Land and buildings	1,926		854		1,900	
Plant and machinery	4,727	6,653	4,236	5,090	2,047	3,947
Investments						
Shares in group company	4,568		—		—	
Loan to group company	630		—		—	
Shares in related company	1,684		—		—	
Loan to related company	340		—		—	
Other investments	208	7,430	127	127	229	229
		14,083		5,217		4,248

	Rowan		Spruce		Pine	
	€000	**€000**	**€000**	**€000**	**€000**	**€000**
Current assets						
Stocks	2,432		1,605		1,866	
Debtors						
Trade debtors	3,868		2,570		2,192	
Amounts owed by group company	737		—		—	
Amounts owed by related company	208		—		—	
Bank and cash	104		92		100	
	7,349		4,267		4,158	
Creditors: Amounts falling due within one year	(5,706)		(3,717)		(3,275)	
Net current assets		1,643		550		883
Total assets less current liabilities		15,726		5,767		5,131
Creditors: Amounts falling due after more than one year						
Debenture loans	5,000		—		—	
Convertible loan stock	—		—		900	
Trade and other creditors	1,362	(6,362)	630	(630)	340	(1,240)
Provisions for liabilities and charges						
Deferred taxation		(877)		(337)		(271)
		8,487		4,800		3,620
Capital and reserves						
Called-up share capital		6,500		4,000		2,200
Share premium account		820		170		—
Revaluation reserve		—		—		730
Other reserves		306		110		220
Profit and loss account		861		520		470
		8,487		4,800		3,620

Additional information:

1. The called-up share capital of each of the companies consists of ordinary shares of €1 each.
2. Goodwill on consolidation is amortised at the rate of 20% per annum on a straight-line basis, with a full year's write-off in the year in which the acquisition takes place. This policy applies to both subsidiary and associated companies.
3. The amount owed by Spruce for goods and services supplied by Rowan, €737,000, is included in trade creditors within Creditors: amounts falling due within one year.
4. Amounts owed by Pine for goods and services supplied by Rowan, €148,000, are included in trade creditors and proposed dividends, €60,000, are included in other creditors within Creditors: amounts falling due within one year.
5. Rowan has advanced loans of €630,000 to Spruce and €340,000 to Pine. These sums are shown under Creditors: amounts falling due after more than one year.
6. At 31 December 20X4, the closing stock of Spruce included goods bought from Rowan for €860,000, which includes a mark-up of one-third on cost.

Required

Prepare the consolidated balance sheet of Rowan and group for the year ended 31 December 20X4.

9

Merger accounting

Learning objectives

After studying this chapter you should be able to:

- appreciate the rationale for merger accounting
- compare and contrast merger and acquisition methods of consolidation
- apply the merger method of accounting for business combinations

Introduction

A business combination is the bringing together of two or more separate entities into one economic entity. As described in Chapter 1, businesses can combine by one acquiring the separate assets and liabilities of another, causing that other to cease to exist (absorption). In such combinations, only one business remains and, consequently, group accounts are not an issue. Businesses can also combine through the purchase of shares in another, resulting in control over the net assets and operations of that other. Where control over another company is acquired, the individual accounts of the parent are inadequate to reflect the results and financial position of the economic entity. Consequently, group accounts are required.

There are two methods of preparing group accounts:

1. *acquisition* or *purchase* method
2. *merger*, *pooling of interests* or *uniting of interests* method.

The traditional and most frequently used method is the acquisition method. This method is used in the techniques illustrated in Chapters 2 to 8 and 10 to 12. Under accounting and legal regulations, merger accounting can only be used in restricted circumstances. In fact, its legality in some countries is uncertain. Consequently, this method is used infrequently in practice.

This chapter provides some background on merger accounting and shows how the technique is applied. Consolidated balance sheets, based on acquisition and merger accounting, are also compared and the rationale behind merger accounting is discussed.

Overview

The main criticism of the traditional acquisition method of accounting is that pre-acquisition reserves are not distributable to shareholders. Where two companies come together (rather than an acquisition of one by the other) by, for example, an exchange of shares, there has been no change in the members of the group. It is argued that the non-distributability of reserves in such a situation is inequitable. Merger accounting is defined in Chapter 16 and the criteria to be met by the combining entities for the combination to be accounted for as a merger are discussed in detail in that chapter.

In merger accounting, financial statements are aggregated and presented as if the combining companies had always been together. The full year's results of the combining companies are included in the group profit and loss account regardless of the date of acquisition and corresponding amounts for the previous year are presented on the same basis. Thus, the merger method is attractive to companies because distributable reserves are usually higher.

Under the merger method of accounting:

- assets and liabilities are recorded in group accounts at their book values in the subsidiary undertaking's financial statements
- in the year of acquisition, income and expenditure of the undertaking acquired should be included in the group accounts for the entire period, including the pre-acquisition period
- in the year of acquisition, corresponding amounts should be shown as if the undertaking had been consolidated throughout that year
- nominal value of shares acquired should be set off against the sum of (i) shares issued and (ii) the fair value of any other consideration (any difference arising is dealt with as a reserve adjustment).

Rationale for merger accounting

Merger accounting is justified where there has been no substantial change in the ownership or in the nature of the combining businesses as a result of the combination. It is usually only justifiable where shares are issued as consideration for shares acquired. The intent of mergers is the bringing together of two entities into a larger organisation, with little or no change in overall group structure or resources. Very limited non-equity consideration is tolerated in most share purchases accounted for using merger accounting. It is argued that it is as if the two companies had always been part of the same team. Thus, the intention, spirit and substance of the merger are keys to determining whether a given business combination should be accounted for using the acquisition method or the merger method of accounting.

The rationale behind merger accounting is that if two entities join together to form a larger group with no alteration in overall resources, then there is no logical reason to carry out a revaluation of either company's net assets or to calculate a fair value of the consideration paid by one company to the other.

Merger accounting has a number of advantages over acquisition accounting. Costly and time-consuming fair valuation exercises do not have to be carried out which makes it a simpler exercise compared with the acquisition method. In addition, merger accounting avoids the knock-on consequences arising from increased depreciation and amortisation charges. It also reduces or eliminates the problem of dealing with goodwill.

Conversely, however, combining profit and loss accounts is considered to create 'instant' earnings. Over the years, there have been abuses of merger accounting and accounting regulations have attempted to prevent this by prescribing in detail the limited circumstances in which merger accounting is permitted.

Acquisition and merger accounting methods compared

The main differences between acquisition and merger accounting are:

- the acquired company's net assets are included, on acquisition, in the consolidated accounts at fair values in acquisition accounting but not in merger accounting. Thus, increased depreciation charges are likely to arise under acquisition accounting
- most revenue reserves of the combining companies are distributable if received as dividends by the parent using merger accounting. Pre-acquisition reserves received as dividends from subsidiaries are not distributable by parent undertakings under acquisition accounting
- results of acquired companies are included for the full year in the year of acquisition in merger accounting. Under the acquisition method, results are included from the date of acquisition only
- there is no goodwill in merger accounting. Where there is a difference in the nominal value of the shares issued and acquired, an adjustment to reserves is necessary under the merger method
- share premium is not usually recorded on the shares issued as part of the consideration under merger accounting. Shares issued are usually recorded at their nominal value.

These differences are summarised in Table 9.1.

Table 9.1 Differences between acquisition and merger accounting

	Acquisition	*Merger*
• Assets and liabilities at acquisition	Fair value	Book value
• Depreciation	Likely to be higher	As before the combination
• Goodwill	Difference between fair values of consideration and net assets acquired	None
• Consolidation difference	None (other than goodwill)	Difference between nominal value of shares issued and acquired
• Pre-acquisition profit of subsidiary	Not distributable	Distributable
• Subsidiary results in year of acquisition	From date of acquisition	For whole year
• Share capital	Parent undertaking	Parent undertaking
• Share premium on shares issued as consideration	Difference between fair value and par value of shares	Usually none
• Corresponding figures	No restatement	Restate for merger

Example 9.1 illustrates the differences between the two methods. In this example, the same number of shares is issued and acquired. Consequently, under the merger method, there is no adjustment on consolidation.

Example 9.1 Merger and acquisition accounting compared – share for share exchange

Example

Parent acquired all 80 shares of Subsidiary by issuing 80 of its own shares. Both Parent and Subsidiary shares are worth €3 each. Balance sheets of Parent and Subsidiary immediately before the acquisition were as follows:

	Parent	**Subsidiary**
	€	**€**
Net assets	150	110
Share capital (shares of €1 each)	100	80
Share premium	—	—
Revenue reserves	50	30
	150	110

You are to assume the book value of Subsidiary's net assets is equal to its fair value.

Required

Show:

(a) Parent's individual company balance sheet after the combination under (i) the acquisition method and (ii) the merger method of accounting.

(b) Parent group's consolidated balance sheet after the combination under (i) the acquisition method and (ii) the merger method of accounting.

Solution

(a) Parent's own balance sheet

	(i) Acquisition method	**(ii) Merger method**
	€	**€**
Net assets	150	150
Investment in Subsidiary	240	80
	390	230
Share capital (shares of €1 each)	180	180
Share premium	160	—
Revenue reserves	50	50
	390	230

(b) Consolidated accounts of Parent group on date of combination

	(i) Acquisition method	**(ii) Merger method**
	€	**€**
Net assets	260	260
Goodwill (240–(80+30))	130	—
	390	260
Share capital (shares of €1 each)	180	180
Share premium	160	—
Revenue reserves	50	80
	390	260

In Example 9.1, under the acquisition method, the investment is recorded in the parent's individual accounts at cost of €240 (80 shares at €3 each). Under the merger method, shares issued in consideration and the investment are recorded at par value of €80. In group accounts, consolidated revenue reserves are those of the parent company under acquisition accounting. Post-acquisition revenue reserves of the subsidiary are normally included, but there are no post-acquisition reserves in this example. Under merger accounting, consolidated revenue reserves are the aggregate of those of the combining companies. Whether the subsidiary's reserves relate to pre- or post-acquisition activity is irrelevant under the merger method. There is no goodwill in the consolidated accounts prepared under merger accounting. Goodwill in acquisition accounting is the fair value of the consideration paid less fair value of the net assets acquired. Since any shares issued to effect the merger are recorded at nominal value under merger accounting, no share premium arises.

Technique

The technique involved in preparing group accounts using the merger method is briefly explained in this section.

The technique involved in merger accounting is basically an exercise in straightforward arithmetic (subject to making adjustments to align accounting policies). Example 9.1 has already illustrated this using a very simple scenario. However, when the number of shares issued is different from the number of shares acquired, some adjustments are required.

In Example 9.2, there is a difference in the number of shares issued and acquired, resulting in a consolidating adjustment. The nominal value of the shares issued is greater than the nominal value of shares acquired. Under merger accounting, where this happens, it is necessary to make an adjustment against reserves.

Example 9.2 Merger and acquisition accounting compared – nominal values of shares differ

Example

Use the data in Example 9.1, but assume that Parent issued 100 shares valued at €2.40 each to acquire Subsidiary's 80 shares worth €3 each.

Required

Show:

(a) Parent's individual company balance sheet after the combination under (i) the acquisition method and (ii) the merger method of accounting.

(b) Parent group's consolidated balance sheet after the combination under (i) the acquisition method and (ii) the merger method of accounting.

Solution

(a) Parent's own balance sheet

	(i) Acquisition method	(ii) Merger method
	€	€
Net assets	150	150
Investment in Subsidiary	240	100
	390	250
Share capital (shares of €1 each)	200	200
Share premium	140	—
Revenue reserves	50	50
	390	250

(b) Consolidated accounts of Parent group

	(i) Acquisition method	(ii) Merger method
	€	€
Net assets	260	260
Goodwill (240–(80+30))	130	—
	390	260
Share capital	200	200
Share premium	140	—
Revenue reserves	50	60*
	390	260

$*50_{\text{Parent}} + 30_{\text{Subsidiary}} - 20_{\text{difference between nominal value of shares issued and that of shares acquired}}$

Example 9.3 is a more comprehensive example of the merger method which illustrates three situations:

- the nominal value of the shares issued is greater than the shares acquired
- the nominal value of the shares issued is less than the shares acquired
- there is additional consideration other than equity shares.

Example 9.3 Merger and acquisition accounting compared – comprehensive example

Example

Individual pre-acquisition accounts of Parent and Subsidiary	Parent	Subsidiary
	€	€
Net assets (book value = fair value)	5,200	3,200
Share capital (shares of €1 each)	4,000	2,000
Revenue reserves	1,200	1,200
	5,200	3,200

Parent acquires all Subsidiary's shares.

Required

Prepare consolidated balance sheets using (i) the acquisition method and (ii) merger method assuming Subsidiary is valued at €4,000 (i.e., each share is valued at €2) and:

(a) 3 Parent shares were issued for every 2 Subsidiary shares
(b) 1 Parent share was issued for every 2 Subsidiary shares
(c) Parent paid 25 cent per share to Subsidiary as well as a 1-for-1 share exchange.

Solution

(i) Consolidated accounts using the acquisition method	(a)	(b)	(c)
	€	€	€
Net assets (5,200 + 3,200)	8,400	8,400	
$(5{,}200 + 3{,}200 - 500_{\text{cash [25 cent} \times 2{,}000]})$			7,900
Goodwill (fair value of consideration paid – fair value of assets acquired) $(4{,}000_{\text{consideration}} - 3{,}200_{\text{assets acquired}})$	800	800	800
	9,200	9,200	8,700

continued overleaf

Example 9.3 Continued

	(a)	(b)	(c)
	€	€	€
Share capital: 4,000 + (3/2 × 2,000)	7,000		
4,000 + (1/2 × 2,000)		5,000	
4,000 + (1/1 × 2,000)			6,000
Share premium: $4{,}000_{\text{fair value}} - 3{,}000_{\text{nominal value}}$	1,000		
$4{,}000_{\text{fair value}} - 1{,}000_{\text{nominal value}}$		3,000	
$4{,}000_{\text{fair value}} - (2{,}000_{\text{nominal value}} + 500_{\text{cash}})$			1,500
Revenue reserves: Parent only	1,200	1,200	1,200
	9,200	9,200	8,700

(ii) Consolidated accounts using the merger method	(a)	(b)	(c)
	€	€	€
Net assets (5,200 + 3,200)	8,400	8,400	
$(5{,}200 + 3{,}200 - 500_{\text{cash [25 cent} \times 2{,}000]})$			7,900
Share capital: 4,000 + (3/2 × 2,000)	7,000		
4,000 + (1/2 × 2,000)		5,000	
4,000 + (1/1 × 2,000)			6,000
Revenue reserves: $1{,}200_{\text{Parent}} + 1{,}200_{\text{Subsidiary}} - 1{,}000$[1]	1,400		
$1{,}200_{\text{Parent}} + 1{,}200_{\text{Subsidiary}}$		2,400	
$1{,}200_{\text{Parent}} + 1{,}200_{\text{Subsidiary}} - 500$[2]			1,900
Capital reserve[3]		1,000	
	8,400	8,400	7,900

[1] Shares issued 3,000 – shares acquired 2,000 = 1,000 reduction in group reserves.
[2] Shares issued 2,000 + cash 500 – shares acquired 2,000 = 500 reduction in group reserves.
[3] Shares issued 1,000 – shares acquired 2,000 = 1,000 increase in group reserves.

Summary

This chapter briefly considered the rationale behind and techniques involved in merger accounting. The merger method of accounting was compared with the more traditional acquisition method. Using simple examples, the merger accounting technique for preparing the consolidated balance sheet was explained and illustrated.

Learning outcomes

After studying this chapter you should have learnt:

- the rationale for merger accounting
- the difference between merger and acquisition accounting methods
- how to apply the merger method of accounting for simple balance sheets.

Multiple choice questions

Solutions to these questions are presented in Appendix 1.

9.1 Using merger accounting

If, when accounting for a business combination using merger accounting, the amount of *Investment in subsidiary* in the parent's balance sheet is less than the nominal value of the shares held in that subsidiary, the difference should be treated as:

(a) Goodwill arising on consolidation
(b) A credit to the profit and loss account
(c) A movement on consolidation reserves
(d) A share premium

9.2 The merger method

Where a business combination is consolidated using the merger method, an excess of the carrying value of the investment in the subsidiary over the nominal value of the shares held in that subsidiary should be treated on consolidation as:

(a) An intangible fixed asset
(b) A reduction in reserves
(c) A reserve arising on consolidation
(d) A share premium

9.3 Merger accounting

In merger accounting, the combining companies' assets are included in the consolidated balance sheet at:

(a) Market value at date of merger
(b) Carrying values in the combining companies' accounts
(c) Fair value
(d) Net replacement cost

9.4 Art Bog and Bacall

Art Bog made an offer to acquire all two million equity shares of **Bacall** and succeeded in buying 1,910,000 shares. A share exchange was arranged so that Bacall shareholders who accepted the offer received one €1 ordinary share in Art Bog for every two shares held in Bacall. The market value of Art Bog's shares was then €2.80. Art Bog had no previous investment in Bacall.

Which of the following journal entries describes how Art Bog would normally record the purchase of its investment in Bacall in its own books, using merger accounting?

		Dr	**Cr**
		€000	**€000**
(a)	Investment in Bacall	2,674	
	Ordinary share capital		955
	Merger reserve		1,719
(b)	Investment in Bacall	2,674	
	Ordinary share capital		955
	Share premium account		1,719
(c)	Investment in Bacall	955	
	Ordinary share capital		955
(d)	Investment in Bacall	1,910	
	Ordinary share capital		1,910

9.5 John Group

	John	Ann
Summarised balance sheets at 31 December 20X8	€000	€000
Investment in 90,000 shares in Ann at cost	90	—
Sundry net assets	400	500
	490	500
Ordinary €1 shares	200	100
Reserves	290	400
	490	500

John invested in **Ann** some years ago when Ann's reserves were €100,000. There have been no changes in Ann's issued share capital since then. Goodwill is fully amortised by 31 December 20X8. Assume nominal value of shares issued was equal to nominal value of shares acquired.

What are the John Group's consolidated reserves under the acquisition and merger methods?

	Acquisition	Merger
(a)	€560,000	€650,000
(b)	€650,000	€650,000
(c)	€590,000	€690,000
(d)	€690,000	€690,000

9.6 Nigel and Georgia

Nigel merged with **Georgia** by buying all its issued share capital on 1 July 20X9 to form the Strangeways Group. Both companies' accounting periods ended on 31 December 20X9. Details of dividends paid in the year are as follows:

		Nigel	Georgia
1.4.20X9	Interim	€100,000	€50,000
1.10.20X9	Final	€220,000	€180,000

Under the merger method, what will be shown in the Strangeways Group's consolidated profit and loss account as the total of dividends paid in the year?

(a) €320,000
(b) €330,000
(c) €370,000
(d) €550,000

9.7 Copse and Wood

The summarised balance sheets for **Copse** and **Wood** as on 31 December 20X6 are as follows:

	Copse	Wood
	€000	€000
Sundry net assets	5,000	3,500
Share capital – €1 ordinary	2,000	1,000
Profit and loss account	3,000	2,500
	5,000	3,500

On l January 20X7 Copse acquired the entire issued share capital of Wood by issuing its own shares as consideration. Shareholders in Wood received two €1 ordinary shares in Copse for every one €1 ordinary share held. The quoted market prices per share of Copse and Wood on 1 January 20X7 were 260p and 530p, respectively.

What is the balance on the profit and loss account in the consolidated balance sheet of Copse on 1 January 20X7, assuming that merger accounting is applied?

(a) €3,000,000
(b) €4,200,000
(c) €4,500,000
(d) €5,500,000

Self-assessment exercises

Solutions to these self-assessment exercises can be found at:
www.thomsonlearning.co.uk/accountingandfinance/piercebrennan

9.1 Harold and Sivex

On 1 January 20X6 **Harold** acquired all the ordinary share capital of **Sivex** for €250,000. In the negotiations the freehold property of Sivex was valued at €160,000.

The consideration of €250,000 was satisfied by the issue of 100,000 ordinary shares of Harold at market value of €2.50 each to the former shareholders in Sivex. No other transactions took place on 1 January 20X6.

Balance sheets as at 31 December 20X5

	Harold	Sivex
	€	€
Freehold property at cost	800,000	60,000
Current assets		
Cash	—	79,000
Other	70,000	—
	870,000	139,000
Ordinary shares of €1 each	250,000	70,000
Capital reserves	60,000	5,000
Revenue reserves	5,000	64,000
	315,000	139,000
Bank term loan	400,000	—
Current liability	155,000	—
	870,000	139,000

Required

Show the consolidated balance sheet of Harold and Sivex at 1 January 20X6 assuming that the combination is accounted for using:

(a) the acquisition method
(b) the merger method.

9.2 Mergacquis and Sambon

On 1 January 20X6 **Mergacquis** acquired 90% of the ordinary share capital of **Sambon** for €180,000. It was agreed that the freehold property of Sambon was undervalued by €50,000 gross. The consideration of €180,000 was satisfied by the issue of 100,000 ordinary shares of Mergacquis at market value of €1.80 each to the former shareholders in Sambon. No other transactions took place on 1 January 20X6.

Balance sheets as at 31 December 20X5

	Mergacquis	Sambon
	€	€
Freehold property at cost	810,000	70,000
Current assets		
Stock	120,000	—
Debtors	80,000	—
Cash	—	99,000
	1,010,000	169,000
Ordinary shares €1 each	300,000	80,000
Capital reserves	80,000	15,000
Revenue reserves	125,000	54,000
	505,000	149,000
Bank term loan	350,000	—
Current liabilities	155,000	20,000
	1,010,000	169,000

Required

Show the consolidated balance sheet of Mergacquis and Sambon at 1 January 20X6 assuming that the combination is accounted for using:

(a) the acquisition method

(b) the merger method.

Examination-style question

9.1 Hurley and Sliothar (1)

On 1 July 20X2 **Hurley** acquired all the issued share capital of **Sliothar** in exchange for shares in Hurley. The shares in both companies have a nominal value of €1 each and a market value at 1 July 20X2 of €5.50 for a €1 Hurley share and €2.80 for a €1 Sliothar share. One ordinary share in Hurley was issued in exchange for every two ordinary shares in Sliothar.

The draft accounts of the two companies at 31 December 20X2 are now presented. These draft accounts do not include any record of the acquisition by Hurley.

Profit and loss accounts for the year ended 31 December 20X2

	Hurley	**Sliothar**
	€	**€**
Profit before depreciation	454,648	349,656
Depreciation on plant and machinery	73,032	32,028
Trading profit	381,616	317,628
Profit on sale of investments	—	110,772
Profit before tax	381,616	428,400
Taxation	95,404	119,952
Profit after tax	286,212	308,448
Balance b/fwd	520,812	358,020
Balance c/fwd	807,024	666,468

Balance sheets as at 31 December 20X2

	Hurley	**Sliothar**
	€	**€**
Freehold premises	1,326,000	459,000
Plant and machinery at cost	522,444	253,572
Aggregate depreciation	(220,932)	(134,028)
Net current assets	199,512	699,924
	1,827,024	1,278,468
Ordinary share capital	1,020,000	612,000
Retained earnings	807,024	666,468
	1,827,024	1,278,468

Additional information:

1. There were no additions or disposals to Sliothar's tangible fixed assets during 20X2.
2. Quoted investments which were included in Sliothar's net assets at 1 July 20X2 at their cost of €112,200 were disposed of before the year-end. Their market value at 1 July 20X2 was €255,000.
3. Included in the Sliothar tax charge is €25,000 charged on the disposal profit.
4. The market values at 1 July 20X2 of Sliothar's premises and plant and machinery were €663,000 and €240,000 respectively. The expected remaining useful life of the plant at that date was four years.
5. Goodwill is amortised over ten years, including a full year's amortisation in the year of acquisition.

Required

Prepare the consolidated balance sheet at 31 December 20X2 on the basis that:

(i) merger accounting is applied

(ii) acquisition accounting is applied.

(Note: Hurley and Sliothar (2) is included as Examination-style question 16.2 in Chapter 16.)

Part Three

Consolidated profit and loss account

10

Consolidated profit and loss account: preparation

Learning objectives

After studying this chapter you should be able to:

- prepare a detailed consolidated profit and loss account from data on individual group companies
- set out your workings for the consolidated profit and loss account in a columnar format
- incorporate adjustments for unrealised profit, fair value depreciation and goodwill into the columnar workings
- calculate minority interest in subsidiaries' profits for the reporting period
- cancel inter-company dividends in the columnar workings

Introduction

The consolidated profit and loss account includes the combined profits and losses of all group companies for the accounting period. It provides a detailed analysis of group revenues and expenses under the prescribed headings selected from the EU Fourth Directive options available under national legislation. The pro-forma consolidated profit and loss accounts included in Examples 13.1 and 13.2 in Chapter 13 provide an overview of the detailed captions used in the consolidated profit and loss account. It would also be useful at this stage to refer to some annual reports of listed companies to see examples of consolidated profit and loss accounts as they are presented to shareholders.

Because the entire profits and/or losses of all subsidiaries are included in the group totals in the consolidated profit and loss account, a one line deduction is made for the interests of minority shareholders in these profits. Minority interest in profits of subsidiaries must take account of the minority entitlement of preference shareholders before allocating the remaining profits based on the entitlement of ordinary shareholders.

Underlying principles

The consolidated profit and loss account is prepared on the basis that the group is the reporting entity. However, accounting records are not maintained on a group basis. Individual companies within the group are legally required to keep proper records and to report profits or losses and financial position to their owners. These individual accounts form the basis for preparing consolidated accounts. In earlier chapters we saw how individual balance sheets of the parent and subsidiaries are combined to produce a single balance sheet for the economic entity, the group. In this chapter, we introduce techniques for preparing the group (or consolidated) profit and loss account using individual profit and loss accounts of the parent and its subsidiaries as the starting point. As in Chapters 2 to 8, the acquisition method of accounting is the consolidation approach adopted in this chapter.

Consolidation adjustments

Similar to preparing consolidated balance sheets, a number of consolidating adjustments are required when preparing consolidated profit and loss accounts. Because the group is the reporting entity, intra-group transactions included in individual company profit and loss accounts must be adjusted for in the consolidation workings. Common intra-group transactions for which adjustment is made include:

- dividends received or receivable by the parent from subsidiaries must be excluded from group income as the profit from which they have been appropriated is included in that income by the process of consolidation
- turnover must be adjusted for inter-company sales to avoid double counting
- inter-company purchases must be eliminated from group cost of sales
- unrealised profit on inter-company sales of goods or fixed assets must be eliminated
- depreciation adjustments must be made for additional or reduced depreciation charges in individual accounts based on transfer prices between group companies.

Group retained profit at the period end includes:

- profit or loss retained by the group for the year; plus
- accumulated retained earnings brought forward from the previous period.

Accumulated retained earnings brought forward include retained earnings of the parent plus the group's share of subsidiaries' post-acquisition retained earnings, plus or minus aggregate consolidation adjustments and goodwill amortisation to the beginning of the period.

The year-end total should agree with the balance on the consolidated revenue reserves (or profit and loss) account in the consolidated balance sheet workings.

Consolidated profit and loss account workings

As with the consolidated balance sheet, it is important to adopt a systematic approach to preparing the consolidated profit and loss account. The group structure should be identified initially, as should any changes to the group during the year (e.g., subsidiaries acquired or disposals of previously held subsidiaries). Under the acquisition method of preparing group accounts (see Chapter 9 for the merger method), profits of subsidiaries acquired during the year (disposed of during the year) should only be included in the consolidated profit and loss account for the year from the date of acquisition (to the date of disposal).

The basic approach to preparing the consolidated profit and loss account involves adding together amounts for all group companies on a line-by-line basis. For example, group turnover is made up of the turnover of all group companies (parent and all subsidiaries). Group expenses comprise costs for all group companies for the period. The basic working schedule for the consolidated profit and loss account is a columnar spreadsheet, although additional workings are normally required to provide the numbers to feed into the spreadsheet (e.g., adjustments for unrealised profit and for inter-company dividends). The steps involved in preparing the consolidated profit and loss account are summarised in Table 10.1.

Table 10.1 Steps in preparing the consolidated profit and loss account

1. Establish group structure
2. Head up columnar workings, with one column for the parent company and one for each subsidiary, in addition to an adjustment column (see Example 10.1). Amounts in the total column will be the figures in the final consolidated profit and loss account
3. Transfer amounts from the individual profit and loss accounts of group companies to the columnar working schedule, remembering to include pro rata amounts for acquisitions and disposals during the year
4. Make adjustments for inter-company amounts
5. Adjust combined depreciation charges for effects of fair value adjustments at acquisition
6. Adjust combined depreciation charges for effects of inter-company transfers of tangible fixed assets
7. Enter amount for amortised goodwill through the adjustment column and the appropriate expense caption total
8. Group profit before tax should be the total of amounts in parent and subsidiaries' columns plus or minus the total in the adjustment column
9. Calculate group tax charge and subtract this from group profit before tax
10. Calculate minority interest in group profit or loss for the year. The profit or loss remaining, after minority interest has been subtracted, is attributable to the shareholders of the group (i.e., the parent's shareholders)
11. Parent's dividends (both paid and proposed) are deducted from the profit attributable to group shareholders
12. Group's share of each subsidiary's dividends is subtracted from the subsidiary's column and added into the adjustment column
13. Calculate and subtract group transfers to reserves
14. Profit retained for the year (arrived at after step 13) is transferred to revenue reserves

Example 10.1 illustrates the columnar working schedule recommended in this book, for a sample of profit and loss account captions. Amounts in the *Total* column are the consolidated profit and loss account amounts.

Example 10.1 Columnar profit and loss account working schedule

	Parent	Subsidiary	Adjustment	Total
	€000	€000	€000	€000
Sales	X	X	(X)	X
Cost of sales	(X)	(X)	X	(X)
Gross profit	X	X	(X)	X
Distribution costs	(X)	(X)	X/(X)	(X)
Administration expenses	(X)	(X)	X/(X)	(X)
Other operating expenses	(X)	(X)	X/(X)	(X)
Other operating income	X	X	(X)	X
Operating profit	X	X	(X)	X

Detailed guidance on calculations

The following paragraphs set out guidelines, under specified profit and loss account captions, for calculating amounts to be included in the consolidated profit and loss account.

Turnover

Group turnover is the sum of parent and subsidiary company amounts, less total inter-company sales. Only post-acquisition turnover of subsidiaries acquired during the year should be included in group turnover. Turnover should only be included up to the date of disposal for subsidiaries disposed of during the year.

Cost of sales

Group cost of sales is the sum of parent and subsidiary company amounts with the following adjustments:

- deduct purchases from other group companies (inter-company purchases)
- adjust for any unrealised profit in stock purchased from other group companies.

Only post-acquisition cost of sales of subsidiaries acquired during the year should be included in group cost of sales. Cost of sales should only be included up to the date of disposal for subsidiaries disposed of during the year.

Example 10.2 illustrates how sales and cost of sales adjustments are made in the profit and loss account workings. The inter-company cost of sales adjustment depends on whether the goods bought from another group company have been sold externally to the group, are in stock, or a combination exists. By making three different assumptions relating to the year-end status of these goods, a variety of cost of goods sold adjustments is illustrated in Example 10.2.

Example 10.2 Inter-company cost of sales adjustments

Example

Sales and cost of sales of Parent were €2 million and €1 million, respectively. Those of Subsidiary were €700,000 and €450,000, respectively. Subsidiary sold goods to Parent during the year. These goods cost €150,000 and were sold to Parent for €200,000.

Assume: (a) All goods bought by Parent from Subsidiary are sold.
(b) All goods bought by Parent are still in stock at year-end.
(c) 20% of goods bought by Parent (€40,000) are still in stock at year-end.

Required

For each of the three scenarios presented with respect to inter-company stock, explain, and illustrate by extracts from the columnar consolidated profit and loss account workings, the effect of inter-company sales of stock on the consolidated profit and loss account.

Solution (a)

- Turnover of Parent includes sales revenue for all external sales.
- Turnover of Subsidiary includes €200,000 in relation to inter-company sales.
- These goods have been sold outside the group by the year-end and the related revenue is included in Parent's turnover.
- Therefore, to avoid double counting, the adjustment to turnover is €(200,000).
- Cost of sales of Parent includes €200,000 in relation to inter-company purchases.
- The cost to the group of these goods (€150,000) is already included in Subsidiary's cost of sales.
- Therefore, to avoid double counting, the cost of sales adjustment is €200,000.

Consolidated profit and loss account working schedule

	Parent		Subsidiary		Adjustment	Total
	€000		€000		€000	€000
Turnover	2,000		700	incl 200	(200)	2,500
Cost of sales	(1,000)	incl 200	(450)	incl 150	200	(1,250)
Gross profit	1,000		250		Zero	1,250

Solution (b)

- Turnover of Subsidiary includes €200,000 in relation to inter-company sales which have not yet been sold outside the group. Therefore, the adjustment to turnover is €(200,000).
- Cost of sales of Parent includes zero in relation to the goods bought from Subsidiary (€200,000$_{\text{purchases}}$ – €200,000$_{\text{closing stock}}$).
- Cost of sales of Subsidiary includes €150,000 in respect of inter-company items. As far as the group is concerned, these goods are not sold. Therefore, the cost of sales adjustment is €150,000 and the provision for unrealised profit is €50,000.

Consolidated profit and loss account working schedule

	Parent		Subsidiary		Adjustment	Total
	€000		€000		€000	€000
Turnover	2,000		700	incl 200	(200)	2,500
Cost of sales	(1,000)	incl 200	(450)	incl 150	150	(1,300)
Gross profit	1,000		250		(50)	1,200

Solution (c)

- As before, adjustment to turnover is €(200,000) because sales by Subsidiary to Parent are not external revenues.
- Parent's cost of sales includes €160,000 (€200,000$_{\text{purchases}}$ – €40,000$_{\text{closing stock}}$) for inter-company items. The cost to the group of these goods is already included in Subsidiary's cost of sales. The €160,000 must be eliminated to avoid double counting.
- Cost of sales of Subsidiary includes €30,000 in respect of goods which have not yet been sold outside the group. Cost of inter-company sales is analysed as follows:
  - 20% of goods sold to Parent are not sold from group point of view. Therefore €30,000 (20% × €150,000) is not cost of sales from the group perspective.
  - 80% of goods sold to Parent are sold from the group point of view. Therefore, €120,000 (80% × €150,000) is cost of sales from the group perspective.
- Total cost of sales adjustment is €190,000 (€160,000 + €30,000).
- Unrealised profit is €10,000 in total. This is 20% of the total profit (€50,000$_{\text{€200,000 – €150,000}}$) arising on inter-company sales.

Consolidated profit and loss account working schedule

	Parent		Subsidiary		Adjustment	Total
	€000		€000		€000	€000
Turnover	2,000		700	incl 200	(200)	2,500
Cost of sales	(1,000)	incl 160	(450)	incl 150	190	(1,260)
Gross profit	1,000		250		(10)	1,240

Example 10.2 (a) illustrates the most straightforward situation, where all the inter-company goods have been sold outside the group by the year-end. The adjustments to

consolidated turnover and to consolidated cost of sales are identical. This ensures that the group sales figure represents sales revenue to external parties alone. In addition, it ensures that group cost of sales does not double count the cost of goods which are sold internally in the first instance, before being sold outside the group.

Example 10.2 (b) illustrates the situation where none of the goods sold by the subsidiary to the parent has been sold outside the group by the year-end. In this case, the cost of sales adjustment is a different amount to the turnover adjustment. This enables the provision for unrealised profit in stock to be recognised.

Example 10.2 (c) captures the most complex situation of the three illustrated. In this case, there is a combination of inter-company goods sold externally to the group and inter-company goods in stock at the year-end.

Distribution costs and administrative expenses

Group distribution costs and administrative expenses are the sum of parent and subsidiary company amounts, with the following adjustments:

- there may be inter-company items included under these headings which will have to be eliminated
- goodwill amortised in accordance with group accounting policies may be included within one of these headings (or within other operating expenses).

As with the earlier captions, only post-acquisition amounts of subsidiaries acquired during the year are included in the year of acquisition and only amounts up to the date of disposal are included for subsidiaries disposed of during the year.

Investment income

Group income from financial assets is the sum of parent and subsidiary company amounts, with the following adjustments:

- take out dividends received and receivable by the parent from its subsidiaries. This income is already included in group profits because 100% of subsidiaries' profits are included
- adjust for any inter-company interest income. This might arise where one group company holds debenture or other loan capital of another group company.

Dividends payable by a sub-subsidiary require a further adjustment in the consolidated profit and loss account workings. Minority interest must be adjusted for the double counting caused by the minority being allocated with their share of the profits of the subsidiary (including dividend receivable from the sub-subsidiary) and their share of the profits of the sub-subsidiary (from which the dividend was paid). We return to this topic later in the chapter.

Other profit and loss account adjustments

Any other consolidation adjustments should be made against the relevant figure in the profit and loss account. For example:

- unrealised profit or loss on inter-company sales of fixed assets should be made against that profit or loss, which will be recorded under the most relevant profit and loss account caption, depending on the nature of the fixed asset

- adjustment should be made to depreciation arising from:
  - fair value adjustments of fixed assets for the purpose of consolidation; or
  - transfers of fixed assets from one group company to another, at a profit or loss
- depreciation adjustments should be made against the relevant depreciation charge which may be included as part of cost of sales, administrative expenses or distribution costs.

Taxation

Group taxation charge is the sum of the parent and all subsidiary undertakings' tax charges. To the extent that revenue authorities allow group taxation relief, the tax effect is reflected in the tax charge of the individual company availing of the relief. Individual companies are the taxable entities, rather than the group.

Minority interest

Minority interest in the group profit for the year is the sum of the minority share of each individual subsidiary's profit or loss. The following points should be borne in mind:

- identify the minority share of any preference dividend first
- only then is the minority share of the remaining profit after tax accruing to the equity shareholders calculated.

Minority interest in the group profit for the year is the sum of minority interest in preference dividends and in the remaining profits of all subsidiaries, less adjustment for the minority share of provisions for unrealised profit in stock or inter-company dividends recorded by sub-subsidiaries (see Example 10.4).

The minority share of profit for the year does not link into the minority interest account in the workings for the consolidated balance sheet. The minority interest in profit for the year reflects all profit earned in the current year by the minority, whether paid out by the subsidiary in dividends or not. The minority interest account in the balance sheet workings calculates the amount of group net assets financed by the minority at the balance sheet date. This reflects the minority share of share capital and accumulated *retained* earnings of the subsidiary.

Dividends

Dividends provided out of group profits are those payable to parent company shareholders only. However, at this point in the consolidation workings, the *group's share of subsidiary dividends* needs to be removed from the profits in the subsidiary columns and added to the adjustment column. These dividends are already included in the parent's profit, although excluded from group totals by earlier adjustment (see step 4 in Table 10.1 and earlier section on investment income). The tidying up of group share of dividends received and receivable from subsidiaries ensures that the workings correctly indicate the location of all retained earnings of the group (i.e., the amount of profit retained by the subsidiary or in the parent company revenue reserves/profit and loss account). This tidying up exercise is referred to, very graphically, as the *dividend shuffle* in Barker and Ó hÓgartaigh (1998). Examples 10.3 and 10.4 illustrate this *dividend shuffle* in the columnar profit and loss account workings.

Retained profit at the beginning and end of the period

Retained profits of the group at the beginning of the period should comprise all retained earnings of the parent, together with the group share of post-acquisition profits (less losses) of all subsidiaries up to the beginning of the period. This total is reduced by consolidation adjustments, such as provisions for unrealised profit on inter-company items at the beginning of the period and goodwill write-offs.

Under UK and Irish professional accounting regulations, goodwill arising on acquisitions must be eliminated from the balance sheet. Until 1997 such goodwill was more commonly written off directly against reserves, without going through the profit and loss account of any period. However, a minority of companies adopted the alternative treatment allowed under SSAP 22 *Accounting for Goodwill* of capitalisation and amortisation through the profit and loss account. Since 1997 FRS 10 *Goodwill and Intangible Assets* requires capitalisation and amortisation over the useful economic life of the goodwill. To the extent that goodwill was written off directly against revenue reserves or amortised through the profit and loss account, retained earnings of the group at the beginning of the period will be reduced by the aggregate of such write-offs.

Retained profits at the end of the period is arrived at by adding profit retained for the year (from the consolidated profit and loss account) to the group retained profits at the beginning of the period. This total can be arrived at independently, by adding retained earnings of the parent at the end of the year to the group share of post-acquisition profits (less losses) of subsidiaries to the same year-end. As for the retained profits at the beginning of the year, the combined parent and subsidiary profits are reduced by the cumulative consolidation adjustments, such as provisions for unrealised profit on inter-company items at the end of the period and goodwill write-offs.

Simple worked example

Example 10.3 illustrates the technique involved in preparing a consolidated profit and loss account from summary profit and loss accounts of Parent and Subsidiary.

Example 10.3 Consolidated profit and loss account (1)

Example

Parent owns 75% of Subsidiary's ordinary shares and 40% of Subsidiary's preference shares. Subsidiary's revenue reserves at acquisition were €3,400. The following are the summarised profit and loss accounts of Parent and Subsidiary at 31.12.20X1.

Profit and loss accounts		**Parent**	**Subsidiary**
	€	€	€
Sales		100,000	50,000
Operating expenses		(60,000)	(26,000)
Operating profit		40,000	24,000
Investment income			
Ordinary dividends	4,500		
Preference dividends	1,600	6,100	—
Profit before taxation		46,100	24,000
Taxation		(14,000)	(8,400)
Profit after taxation		32,100	15,600
Transfer to reserves		(10,000)	(2,000)
		22,100	13,600
Proposed dividends			
Ordinary		(12,000)	(6,000)
Preference		—	(4,000)
Profit retained for year		10,100	3,600
Retained profit b/f		20,000	8,000
Retained profit c/f		30,100	11,600

Required

Prepare the consolidated profit and loss account workings from the information given.

Solution

W_1 Inter-company dividends receivable and payable

		€
Preference	40% × €4,000	1,600
Ordinary	75% × €6,000	4,500
		6,100

W_2 Minority interest (preference and ordinary)

		€
Preference dividends 60% × €4,000		2,400
Ordinary dividends 25% × €6,000	} or 25% x	1,500
Residual profit 25% × (15,600–10,000)	} (15,600–4,000)*	1,400
		5,300

* After the preference dividend is provided for, the minority equity shareholders are entitled to their share of profit for the year, regardless of whether it is paid/payable as dividends.

W_3 Transfers to reserves

	€
Parent	10,000
Subsidiary 75% × €2,000	1,500
	11,500

W_4 Retained profit brought forward

	€	€
Parent		20,000
Subsidiary	8,000	
Less: Pre-acquisition reserves	(3,400)	
	4,600 × 75%	3,450
		23,450

W_5 Consolidated profit and loss account columnar workings

	Parent	Subsidiary	Adjustment	Total[1]
	€	€	€	€
Sales	100,000	50,000	—	150,000
Expenses	(60,000)	(26,000)	—	(86,000)
Investment income (W_1)	6,100	—	(6,100)	—
Profit before taxation	46,100	24,000	(6,100)	64,000
Taxation	(14,000)	(8,400)	—	(22,400)
Profit after taxation	32,100	15,600	(6,100)	41,600
Minority interest (W_2)	—	(5,300)	—	(5,300)
Attributable to group	32,100	10,300	(6,100)	36,300
Transfer to reserves (W_3)	(10,000)	(1,500)[2]	—	(11,500)
	22,100	8,800	(6,100)	24,800
Dividends: Parent	(12,000)	—	—	(12,000)
Subsidiary (W_1)	—	(6,100)[2]	6,100	—
	10,100	2,700	—	12,800
Profit b/f (W_4)	20,000	3,450[2]	—	23,450
Profit c/f	30,100	6,150	nil	36,250[3]

continued overleaf

Example 10.3 Continued

1 Total column provides the data for the consolidated profit and loss account.
2 Once minority interest in profit after tax for the year is deducted in Subsidiary's column, all subsequent amounts going through that column must be group share only (e.g., group share of Subsidiary's transfers to reserves).
3 The total profit c/f should correspond with the balance in the consolidated revenue reserves account in the consolidated balance sheet workings.

Dividends payable by a sub-subsidiary

Adjustments to the consolidation profit and loss account workings for inter-company dividends have been discussed earlier in this chapter. Where the group structure includes a sub-subsidiary with an indirect minority interest, additional care is required when calculating these adjustments. While inter-company dividends are eliminated in the columnar working schedule for the consolidated profit and loss account, the minority's share of the dividend receivable from the sub-subsidiary must be recognised in the amount for minority interest. Example 10.4 includes dividends received by the parent from the subsidiary and by the subsidiary from the sub-subsidiary. A risk of double counting within minority interest arises when the minority percentages are applied to each subsidiary's profit after tax. Some of the income of the sub-subsidiary is therefore included twice, in its own profit after tax and then when the dividend payable out of that profit is treated as receivable, in the subsidiary's profit after tax. This double counting is avoided by including an adjustment for the minority's share of the dividend received from the sub-subsidiary (see Workings 3 and 5 in the solution to Example 10.4).

Example 10.4 Consolidated profit and loss account (2)

Example

Parent acquired 60% of Subsidiary for €7.5m on 1.11.20X1, when Subsidiary's revenue reserves amounted to €3m (share capital €9m). On 1.11.20X2, Subsidiary acquired 75% of the shares in Sub-subsidiary for €6m, when Sub-subsidiary's revenue reserves amounted to €1m (share capital €6m). Profit and loss accounts for the three companies for the year ended 31.10.20X4 are as follows:

Profit and loss accounts	**Parent €000**	**Subsidiary €000**	**Sub-subsidiary €000**
Sales	30,000	20,000	16,000
Cost of sales	(15,000)	(10,000)	(8,000)
Gross profit	15,000	10,000	8,000
Other operating expenses	(7,500)	(5,000)	(4,000)
Operating profit	7,500	5,000	4,000
Investment income			
Interest receivable	300	—	—
Dividends receivable	810	675	—
Interest payable	(700)	(500)	(400)
Profit before taxation	7,910	5,175	3,600
Taxation	(2,650)	(1,700)	(1,200)
Profit after taxation	5,260	3,475	2,400
Dividends	(1,500)	(1,350)	(900)
Profit retained for year	3,760	2,125	1,500
Retained profit b/f	8,740	4,920	1,300
Retained profit c/f	12,500	7,045	2,800

Notes
1 All investment income is inter-company.
2 Goodwill on acquisition is amortised over ten years.
3 Goodwill amortisation is included in *Other operating expenses*.

Required
Prepare the consolidated profit and loss account from the information given

As the solution to Example 10.4 is quite long, it is divided into four parts as follows:

- Solution 10.4 (1) contains all the workings except for the columnar profit and loss account working.
- Solution 10.4 (2) contains the consolidated profit and loss account columnar working.
- Solution 10.4 (3) contains the consolidated profit and loss account as it would appear in the published accounts.
- Solution 10.4 (4) shows the consolidated balance sheet T account working for revenue reserves/retained earnings. This part of the solution illustrates how the final balance in retained earnings, arrived at from a completely different approach in the consolidated balance sheet workings, agrees with the bottom line total in the detailed consolidated profit and loss account (Solution 10.4 (3)).

Solution 10.4 (1) Consolidated profit and loss account (2) – workings

W_1 Group structure

Parent
↓ 60%
Subsidiary
↓ 75%
Sub-subsidiary

		Subsidiary	Sub-subsidiary	
		%	%	
Group share	Direct	60	—	
	Indirect	—	45	(60% × 75%)
		60	45	
Minority share	Direct	40	25	
	Indirect	—	30	(40% × 75%)
		40	55	

continued overleaf

Solution 10.4 (1) Continued

W_2 Goodwill on acquisition	**Subsidiary €000**	**Sub-subsidiary €000**	**Total €000**
Investment at cost	7,500		
Group share of Subsidiary's cost of investment			
(60% × €6m)		3,600	
Group share of net assets acquired			
60% × €12m	(7,200)		
45% × €7m	—	(3,150)	
Goodwill	300	450	750
Cumulative amortisation to start of year ($^2/_{10}$;$^1/_{10}$)	(60)	(45)	(105)
Amortisation in current year	(30)	(45)	(75)
Balance sheet amount at year end	210	360	570

W_3 Investment income

As all investment income of Parent is inter-company, it is all eliminated in the consolidated profit and loss account columnar workings.

W_4 Minority interest in dividends received

Dividends received by Subsidiary from Sub-subsidiary (900 × 75%)	675
Minority share (40%) already included in Sub-subsidiary's minority interest*	270

* The adjustment to minority interest ensures that the minority's share of Sub-subsidiary's profits are not double counted.

W_5 Retained profit brought forward	**€000**	**€000**	**€000**
Parent			8,740
Subsidiary	4,920		
Less pre-acquisition	(3,000)	1,920	
Group share (60%)			1,152
Sub-subsidiary	1,300		
Less pre-acquisition	(1,000)	300	
Group share (45%)			135
Less: Cumulative goodwill written off at start of year (W_2)			(105)
			9,922

Solution 10.4 (2) Consolidated profit and loss account (2) – columnar workings

W_6 Consolidated profit and loss account columnar workings

	Parent	Subsidiary	Sub-subsidiary	Adjustment	Total
	€000	€000	€000	€000	€000
Sales	30,000	20,000	16,000		66,000
Cost of sales	(15,000)	(10,000)	(8,000)		(33,000)
Gross profit	15,000	10,000	8,000		33,000
Other operating expenses	(7,500)	(5,000)	(4,000)	(75) W2	(16,575)
Operating profit	7,500	5,000	4,000	(75)	16,425
Investment income					
Interest income	300	—	—	(300) W3	—
Dividend income	810	675	—	(1,485) W3	—
Interest payable	(700)	(500)	(400)	300*	(1,300)
Profit before taxation	7,910	5,175	3,600	(1,560)	15,125
Taxation	(2,650)	(1,700)	(1,200)		(5,550)
Profit after taxation	5,260	3,475	2,400	(1,560)	9,575
Minority interest 40%/55%		(1,390)	(1,320)	270 W4	(2,440)
	5,260	2,085	1,080	(1,290)	7,135
Dividends: Parent	(1,500)				(1,500)
Subsidiary €1,350 × 60%		(810)		810	—
Sub-subsidiary €900 x 45%			(405)	405	—
Profit retained for year	3,760	1,275	675	(75)	5,635
Retained profit b/f (W_5)	8,740	1,152	135	(105)	9,922
Retained profit c/f	12,500	2,427	810	(180)	15,557

* As all Parent's investment income is inter-company (Note 1 in Example 10.4), €300,000 of interest expense is inter-company.

The consolidated profit and loss account required by Example 10.4 is taken from the *total* column in Working 6, and is set out in Solution 10.4 (3).

Solution 10.4 (3) Consolidated profit and loss account (2) – published accounts

Consolidated profit and loss account for year ended 31.10.20X4

	€000
Sales	66,000
Cost of sales	(33,000)
Gross profit	33,000
Other operating expenses	(16,575)
Operating profit	16,425
Interest payable	(1,300)
Profit before taxation	15,125
Taxation	(5,550)
Profit after taxation	9,575
Minority interest	(2,440)
Profit attributable to members of the group	7,135
Dividends	(1,500)
Profit retained for year	5,635
Retained earnings b/f	9,922
Retained earnings c/f	15,557

It is useful as a self-check to complete the T account for consolidated reserves in the balance sheet workings at this point. The T account approaches calculation of the total for retained profits from a completely different angle from that used in the detailed profit and loss account columnar workings. It works on year-end totals rather than building up that total from the detailed components of profit and retained earnings brought forward from the previous year. Nonetheless, the balance in the T account at the end of the period should agree with the bottom line on the consolidated profit and loss account for the period. The T account for the balance sheet consolidation workings is set out in Solution 10.4 (4).

Solution 10.4 (4) Consolidated profit and loss account (2) – revenue reserves T account

Consolidated revenue reserves

	€000		**€000**
Cost of control		Parent	12,500
Subsidiary $_{3,000 \times 60\%}$	1,800	Subsidiary	7,045
Sub-subsidiary $_{1,000 \times 45\%}$	450	Sub-subsidiary	2,800
Goodwill written off ($W_{2 - \text{Solution 10.4 (1)}}$)	180		
Minority interest			
Subsidiary $_{(40\% \times 7,045)}$	2,818		
Sub-subsidiary $_{(55\% \times 2,800)}$	1,540		
Consolidated balance sheet	15,557		
	22,345		22,345

Summary

This chapter has illustrated the basic workings for the consolidated profit and loss account using, as a starting point, the detailed profit and loss accounts of the parent and individual subsidiary companies. Adjustments for inter-company transactions were also illustrated in the examples in this chapter. The treatment of associated companies in the profit and loss account is the topic of Chapter 11, which builds on the material in this chapter, using the equity basis of accounting for associates, which has already been explained in Chapter 7 (in the context of the consolidated balance sheet).

Learning outcomes

After studying this chapter you should have learnt:

- how to prepare a detailed consolidated profit and loss account from data on individual group companies
- how to set out your workings for the consolidated profit and loss account in a columnar format
- how to incorporate adjustments for unrealised profit, fair value depreciation and goodwill into the columnar workings
- how to calculate minority interest in subsidiaries' profits for the reporting period
- how to cancel inter-company dividends in the columnar workings.

Multiple choice questions

Solutions to these questions are presented in Appendix 1.

10.1 Alpha and Beta

Alpha has owned 100% of the share capital of **Beta** for many years. On 1 October 20X2, Alpha transferred a machine, purchased in June 20X0 for €100,000, to Beta for €95,000. Both companies charge a full year's depreciation on all machinery owned at the end of each financial year, at a rate of 10% straight line. Neither company charges depreciation in the year of disposal.

The balance sheet of each company at 31 March 20X3 included fixed assets at the following net amounts respectively:

Alpha €1,565,000
Beta €872,000

Consolidation adjustments in respect of the transfer of machinery, required in preparing the consolidated profit and loss account for the year ended 31 March 20X3 will:

(a) increase profits by €14,500
(b) increase profits by €15,500
(c) reduce profits by €14,500
(d) reduce profits by €15,500

10.2 Tom and Jerry

The called-up share capital of **Jerry** consists of the following:

1,000,000 ordinary shares of €1 each
800,000 10% preference shares of €1 each

On 1 April 20X4, **Tom** acquired 80% of the ordinary shares in Jerry. The profit and loss account of Jerry for the year ended 31 December 20X4, disclosed *Profit for the year after tax* of €320,000.

The minority interest in respect of Jerry which was shown on the consolidated profit and loss account of Tom for the year ended 31 December 20X4 was:

(a) €36,000
(b) €48,000
(c) €64,000
(d) €96,000

10.3 Bridle and Horse

Bridle purchased 80% of the share capital of **Horse** on 1 July 20X1. The profit and loss account of Horse for the year ended 31 December 20X1, disclosed the following:

	€
Operating profit after taxation	360,000
Exceptional gain net of taxation (closure of branch on 31 October 20X1)	60,000

The amount disclosed as *Minority interest* in the consolidated profit and loss account of Bridle for the year ended 31 December 20X1 is:

(a) €36,000
(b) €42,000
(c) €48,000
(d) €72,000

10.4 Roy and Paul

Roy owns 80% of the ordinary shares of **Paul** but none of its 100,000 10% €1 preference shares. The profit and loss account of Paul for the year ended 31 July 20X5 shows:

	€	€
Profit after taxation		140,000
Dividends		
Ordinary	40,000	
Preference	10,000	50,000
Retained profit		90,000

In the consolidated profit and loss account for the year ended 31 July 20X5 the figure for minority interest is:

(a) €28,000
(b) €30,000
(c) €34,000
(d) €36,000

10.5 Hal and Sid

Hal acquired 80% of the ordinary share capital and 40% of the preference share capital of **Sid** many years ago. The profit and loss account of Sid for the year ended 31 March 20X0 included the following:

	€	€
Profit after taxation		260,000
Dividends – Preference	10,000	—
Ordinary	80,000	90,000
Profit retained for year		170,000

The minority interest shown in the consolidated profit and loss account of Hal for the year ended 31 March 20X0 was:

(a) €50,000
(b) €52,000
(c) €56,000
(d) €58,000

10.6 Drum, Gold and King

Drum owns	80% of Gold
	90% of King
	50% of Nut
Gold owns	20% of Nut
King owns	70% of Queen

During the year ended 31 October 20X6 each of the companies had a profit after tax of €10,000 and there were no transfers to reserves or dividends.

The minority interest in the consolidated profit and loss account of Drum and its subsidiaries for the year was:

(a) € 9,000
(b) € 9,400
(c) € 9,700
(d) €10,100

10.7 Acorn and Oak

Acorn is a wholly owned subsidiary of **Oak**. Their respective profit and loss accounts for the year ended 31 December 20X2, included the following:

	Cost of sales
	€ million
Oak	3.0
Acorn	2.0

The turnover of Oak included €1.2 million in respect of goods sold to Acorn and the stocks of Acorn included €400,000 of these goods. Oak invoices Acorn at cost plus a standard mark-up of $33^1/_3$%.

The amount disclosed as *Cost of sales* in the consolidated profit and loss account of Oak for the year ended 31 December 20X2, is:

(a) €3.7 million
(b) €3.8 million
(c) €3.9 million
(d) €5.0 million

Data for questions 10.8 and 10.9

Bill acquired 75% of the share capital of **Ben** many years ago. The consolidated accounts at 31 March 20X8, included a provision of €10,000 for unrealised profit on stock which has been carried forward to the 20X9 accounts.

The following information relates to the year ended 31 March 20X9:

	Bill	**Ben**
	€000	**€000**
Sales (including inter-company sales)	2,400	1,500
Cost of sales	1,250	875

During the year Ben sold goods with an invoice value of €200,000 to Bill. Ben fixed its selling price at cost plus $33^1/_3$%. At 31 March 20X9, the stocks of Bill included one-quarter of the purchases during the year from Ben.

10.8 Bill and Ben (1)

The turnover shown in the 20X9 consolidated profit and loss account of the Bill Group was:

(a) €3,325,000
(b) €3,700,000
(c) €3,750,000
(d) €3,900,000

10.9 Bill and Ben (2)

The cost of sales shown in the 20X9 consolidated profit and loss account of the Bill Group was:

(a) €1,925,000
(b) €1,927,500
(c) €2,012,500
(d) €2,127,500

Data for questions 10.10 and 10.11

Alba purchased all the equity shares of **Beba** on 1 January 20X0. The profit and loss accounts of the two companies for the year ended 30 June 20X0 included the following:

	Alba	**Beba**
	€000	**€000**
Turnover	4,650	2,865
Cost of sales	3,260	1,980

The turnover of Alba included sales to Beba during the period 1 January to 30 June 20X0 amounting to €600,000, which represented cost plus a standard mark-up of $33\frac{1}{3}$%. The stocks of Beba during the period 1 January to 30 June 20X0 included goods invoiced by Alba at €90,000.

10.10 Alba and Beba (1)

The turnover disclosed in the consolidated profit and loss account of the Alba Group for the year ended 30 June 20X0 was:

(a) €5,482,500
(b) €5,782,500
(c) €6,082,500
(d) €7,215,000

10.11 Alba and Beba (2)

The cost of sales disclosed in the consolidated profit and loss account of the Alba Group for the year ended 30 June 20X0 was:

(a) €3,680,000
(b) €3,672,500
(c) €4,670,000
(d) €4,617,500

10.12 Knave and Ace

On 1 July 20X5, **Knave** purchased 80% of the share capital of **Ace**. The net profit after tax of Ace for the year ended 31 December 20X5 amounted to €120,000 and Ace proposed a first and final dividend for the year of €40,000. The minority interest in respect of Ace disclosed in the consolidated profit and loss account of Knave for the year ended 31 December 20X5 was:

(a) € 8,000
(b) €12,000
(c) €16,000
(d) €24,000

Self-assessment exercises

Solutions to these self-assessment exercises can be found at:
www.thomsonlearning.co.uk/accountingandfinance/piercebrennan

10.1 Large, Medium and Small

The following profit and loss accounts were prepared for **Large**, **Medium** and **Small** for the year ended 31 December 20X9:

	Large	**Medium**	**Small**
	€000	**€000**	**€000**
Sales	17,000	10,000	1,500
Cost of sales	(12,000)	(6,000)	(1,000)
Gross profit	5,000	4,000	500
Operating expenses	(3,600)	(2,400)	(280)
Investment income	216	—	—
Profit before taxation	1,616	1,600	220
Taxation	(628)	(650)	(70)
Profit after taxation	988	950	150
Dividends	(400)	(240)	(60)
Profit retained for year	588	710	90
Retained profit 1 January 20X9	912	540	310
Retained profit 31 December 20X9	1,500	1,250	400

Notes:

1 Large acquired 90% of the ordinary shares in Medium on 1 January 20X2 when Medium had retained profits of €140,000, and 60% of the ordinary shares in Small on 1 May 20X3 when Small had retained profits of €110,000.

2 Small sold all its output to Large. At 31 December 20X9, the stocks of Large included goods which it had bought from Small for €300,000. Small earned a constant rate of gross profit of $33^1/_3$% on sales throughout 20X9.

3 Dividends paid by Medium include €40,000 in respect of preference shares, all of which are held outside the group.

Required

Prepare the consolidated profit and loss account of Large for the year ended 31 December 20X9.

10.2 Head and Toe

On 1 October 20X4 **Head** acquired 80% of the ordinary share capital of **Toe** by way of share exchange. Head issued five of its own shares for every two shares it acquired in Toe. The market value of Head's shares on 1 October 20X4 was €3 each. The share issue has not yet been recorded in Head's books. The summarised financial statements of both companies are:

Profit and loss accounts year to 31 March 20X5

	Head		**Toe**	
	€000	**€000**	**€000**	**€000**
Turnover		1,200		1,000
Cost of sales		(650)		(660)
Gross profit		550		340
Operating expenses		(120)		(88)
Debenture interest		nil		(12)
Operating profit		430		240
Taxation		(100)		(40)
Profit after tax		330		200
Dividends – Interim	(40)		—	
– Final	(40)	(80)	(60)	(60)
Retained profit for the year		250		140
Retained profit brought forward		160		500
Retained profit carried forward		410		640

Balance sheets as at 31 March 20X5

Fixed assets				
Land and buildings		400		150
Plant and machinery		220		510
Investments		20		10
		640		670
Current assets				
Stock	240		280	
Debtors	170		210	
Bank	20		40	
	430		530	
Creditors: Amounts falling due within one year				
Trade creditors	170		155	
Taxation	50		45	
Dividends	40		60	
	(260)		(260)	
Net current assets		170		270
		810		940
Creditors: Amounts falling due after more than one year				
8% debentures		nil		(150)
Net assets		810		790
Capital and reserves				
Ordinary shares of €1 each		400		150
Profit and loss account		410		640
		810		790

The following information is relevant:

1 At the date of acquisition, the fair values of Toe's assets were equal to their book values with the exception of its land and an item of plant. These had fair values of €125,000 and €50,000 respectively in excess of their book values. The plant had a remaining life of five years. Depreciation is charged to cost of sales.
2 In the post-acquisition period, Head sold goods to Toe at a price of €100,000, a mark-up on cost of 25% to Head. Toe had half of these goods in stock at the year-end.
3 Consolidated goodwill is to be written off as an operating expense over a five-year life. Time apportionment should be used in the year of acquisition.
4 Head's policy is to include only post-acquisition dividends in income. Profits and dividends are deemed to accrue evenly over the year. Head has not accounted for the proposed dividend of Toe.
5 The current accounts of the two companies disagreed due to a cash remittance of €20,000 to Head on 26 March 20X5 not being received until after the year-end. Before adjusting for this, Toe's debtor balance in Head's books was €56,000.

Required

Prepare a consolidated profit and loss account and balance sheet for Head and group for the year to 31 March 20X5.

Examination-style questions

10.1 McTavish and Patel

The following are the trial balances of **McTavish** and its subsidiary **Patel** as at 31 March 20X9:

	McTavish	Patel
	€000	€000
Ordinary share capital (€1 shares)	30,000	15,000
Sales	128,000	36,000
Creditors	5,550	2,960
Profit and loss account – balance at 31 March 20X8	3,600	4,000
	167,150	57,960
	€000	€000
Cost of goods sold	87,000	27,320
Freehold land and buildings (net book value)	12,300	7,500
Plant and machinery (net book value)	5,875	8,100
Motor vehicles (net book value)	—	900
Expenses, including depreciation of fixed assets	23,000	5,440
Trade debtors	6,273	3,750
Balance at bank	8,482	770
Stock at 31 March 20X9	7,320	4,180
Investment: 12 million ordinary €1 shares in Patel at cost	16,600	—
Interim dividend paid	300	—
	167,150	57,960

The following information should be taken into account:

1 McTavish acquired its shares in Patel on 1 April 20X8.
2 Included in the stock of Patel at 31 March 20X9 is an amount of €2,400,000 for goods purchased from McTavish, which had cost the latter 70% of that figure.
3 Sales by McTavish to Patel during the year ended 31 March 20X9 amounted to €8,400,000. Of these, goods with a sales value of €200,000 were dispatched by McTavish on 30 March 20X9 but were not received by Patel until 3 April 20X9. The cost to McTavish of all sales to Patel was 70% of the sales figure.
4 McTavish has charged Patel €100,000 for management services for the year. This charge has not yet been recorded in the books of Patel.
5 The trade debtors figure in the books of McTavish and the trade creditors figure in the books of Patel include *Current account – Patel* and *Current account – McTavish* balances of €550,000 and €250,000 respectively.

6 Both companies proposed a final dividend of 10% in respect of the year ended 31 March 20X9.
7 Estimated taxation on the profits for the year is:

McTavish: €8,000,000
Patel: €1,400,000

Required

Prepare the consolidated profit and loss account for the year ended 31 March 20X9 and the consolidated balance sheet as at that date.
(Ignore taxation)

10.2 Own and group

Own made the following investments over a period of years:

Year	Company	Price paid	No. of shares purchased	% Holding purchased	Balance on profit and loss account
		€			€
20X4	Flag	4,000	3,000	15%	12,000
20X5	Goal	63,000	45,000	75%	24,000
20X6	Penalty	48,750	40,000	80%	10,000

In 20X7 **Goal** purchased the remaining 10,000 shares in **Penalty** for €12,000. Penalty had €15,000 on its profit and loss account at that date. On 1 January 20X9, Goal made a 1 for 2 bonus issue. €30,000 was transferred from the profit and loss account to the share capital account. Each company prepared final accounts for the year ended 31 December 20X9 as follows:

Profit and loss accounts for year ended 31 December 20X9

		Own	Flag	Goal	Penalty
		€	€	€	€
Gross profit		158,000	47,000	36,000	6,000
Dividends received:	Flag	300			
	Goal	1,500			
Dividends receivable:	Flag	600			
	Goal	3,600			
		164,000	47,000	36,000	6,000
Overhead expenses		86,000	25,000	20,000	4,000
Profit before taxation		78,000	22,000	16,000	2,000
Taxation		35,000	7,000	6,000	—
		43,000	15,000	10,000	2,000
Dividends:	Paid	6,000	2,000	2,000	
	Proposed	10,000	4,000	4,800	
		16,000	6,000	6,800	
Retained profit for year		27,000	9,000	3,200	2,000
Balance b/f at 1 January 20X9		55,000	25,000	40,000	14,000
		82,000	34,000	43,200	16,000
Transfer to share capital account				30,000	
Retained profit c/f		82,000	34,000	13,200	16,000

Balance sheets at 31 December 20X9

	Own	Flag	Goal	Penalty
	€	€	€	€
Fixed assets	270,750	35,900	66,500	39,600
Cost of shares purchased	115,750		12,000	
Stock	75,300	20,600	12,700	8,600
Debtors	68,700	12,100	20,400	18,400
Dividends receivable	4,200			
Cash in hand	20,200	13,000	15,200	9,600
	554,900	81,600	126,800	76,200
	€	€	€	€
Ordinary share capital	400,000	20,000	90,000	50,000
Profit and loss account	82,000	34,000	13,200	16,000
	482,000	54,000	103,200	66,000
Trade creditors	27,900	16,600	12,800	10,200
Proposed dividends	10,000	4,000	4,800	
Taxation	35,000	7,000	6,000	
	554,900	81,600	126,800	76,200

Required

Prepare:

(a) A consolidated profit and loss account for Own and its subsidiary companies for the year ended 31 December 20X9.

(b) A consolidated balance sheet as at that date.

10.3 Athens and Group

Athens acquired 70% of the ordinary share capital and 50% of the preference share capital of **Bergen** when that company was incorporated many years ago. On 1 October 20X0, Athens acquired 60% of the ordinary share capital of **Graz** for €699,000. The companies' draft financial statements for the year ended 31 December 20X0 were as follows:

Balance sheets at 31 December 20X0

	Athens	Bergen	Graz
	€000	€000	€000
Tangible fixed assets	1,403	478	280
Investment in subsidiaries	761	—	—
	2,164	478	280
Current assets			
Stock	120	50	360
Debtors	190	120	180
Cash	150	30	90
	460	200	630
Creditors: Amounts falling due within one year	(320)	(92)	(200)
Net current assets	140	108	430
Total assets less current liabilities	2,304	586	710
Creditors: Amounts falling due after one year	(840)	(96)	(140)
	1,464	490	570
Ordinary shares (nominal value €1 each)	600	60	80
5% preference shares (nominal value €1 each)	—	40	—
Share premium account	300	—	120
Profit and loss account	564	390	370
	1,464	490	570

Profit and loss accounts for the year ended 31 December 20X0

	Athens	Bergen	Graz
	€000	€000	€000
Turnover	2,520	852	1,416
Cost of sales	(1,288)	(510)	(852)
Gross profit	1,232	342	564
Distribution costs	(496)	(50)	(84)
Administrative expenses	(260)	(100)	(168)
Operating profit	476	192	312
Interest payable	(56)	(14)	(24)
Dividends received from Graz	36	—	—
Profit before taxation	456	178	288
Tax on profit	(226)	(66)	(108)
Profit after taxation	230	112	180
Dividends paid	(30)	—	(60)
Dividends proposed	—	(42)	—
Retained profit for year	200	70	120

The following information is relevant to the preparation of the group financial statements:

1 At the date of acquisition, the value of the tangible fixed assets of Graz at open market price was €400,000. Book value at that date was €290,000. The group depreciation policy is to provide 20% per annum on the fair value at acquisition, depreciation in the year of acquisition to be time apportioned and classified as a distribution cost. No disposals or acquisitions of fixed assets took place between the date of acquisition and the year end date. All other assets and liabilities of Graz were stated at their fair values at the time of acquisition.

2 Graz paid ordinary dividends on 1 December 20X0. No further dividends were declared for the year ended 31 December 20X0.

3 Goodwill arising on acquisition is to be amortised against the profit and loss account over a six year period on the straight-line basis. A full year's charge is to be included in administrative expenses for the year ending 31 December 20X0.

4 There were no intercompany transactions between Graz and other group companies during the financial year and it is assumed that the profit of Graz accrues evenly over the year. Graz had not issued any shares since the acquisition by Athens.

5 Bergen sold goods to Athens for €250,000 during the current year. Year-end stock of Athens includes stock of €50,000 bought from Bergen. Bergen earns a constant gross profit percentage of 40% on all sales.

Required

Using acquisition accounting principles, prepare the consolidated balance sheet at 31 December 20X0 and a consolidated profit and loss account for the Athens Group for the year ended on that date.

(Notes to the accounts are not required.)

Consolidated profit and loss account: equity accounting

Learning objectives

After studying this chapter you should be able to:

- incorporate the results of an equity accounted entity into the detailed consolidated profit and loss account
- explain the difference between full consolidation and equity accounting in the context of the consolidated profit and loss account
- link the consolidated profit and loss account amounts with the consolidated balance sheet workings for an equity accounted entity
- deal with amortisation of an associate's goodwill in the consolidated profit and loss account workings
- eliminate unrealised profit on intra-group trading with equity accounted entities

Introduction

The rationale for preparing the consolidated profit and loss account is that the profit and loss account of the parent undertaking, which shows dividend income from subsidiaries, does not give shareholders sufficient information about an undertaking which the parent is able to *control*. The consolidated profit and loss account replaces dividend income from subsidiaries with their underlying profits and losses (less the minority interest, if any). This method of consolidation is known as *line-by-line consolidation* or *full consolidation*.

Chapter 7 has already explained *equity accounting* in the context of the consolidated balance sheet where parent companies invest in associates. This chapter deals with equity accounting in the context of the consolidated profit and loss account.

As discussed in Chapter 7, the equity basis of accounting is an intermediate form of accounting between cost-based accounting and full consolidation. It was introduced because of the inadequacy of both methods of accounting where the interest of the investor was significant, but control could not be exercised. Under equity accounting, the consolidated profit and loss account includes the group's share of the investee's profits or losses and taxation for the year. This is to be contrasted with including dividend income alone under the cost basis and including all of the investee's revenues and expenses (less minority interests) under full consolidation.

Definitions of the equity basis and the gross equity basis of accounting (which is required by FRS 9 for most joint ventures) are included in Chapter 7, as is an explanation of the equity basis of accounting as it is applied in the context of the consolidated balance sheet. A review of that chapter is recommended before continuing with the current chapter. This chapter expands on the material dealt with in Chapter 7 and explains how the equity method of accounting is applied in the consolidated profit and loss account.

Comparison between methods

Comparison between full consolidation and equity method of accounting

It is useful at this point to highlight the differences in the consolidated profit and loss account between using full consolidation and the equity basis of accounting for a given investment. Example 11.1 illustrates these differences.

Example 11.1 Comparison between full consolidation and equity method: consolidated profit and loss account

Example

Investor acquired 9m of Investee's 12m €1 shares for €10.75m on 31.12.20X3 when Investee's reserves were €1m. Goodwill on consolidation is amortised over a ten-year period starting in the year ended 31.12.20X4.

The profit and loss accounts for the year ended 31.12.20X9 are:

	Investor	**Investee**
	€000	**€000**
Turnover	9,000	4,500
Operating costs	(4,500)	(2,200)
Operating profit	4,500	2,300
Investment income from Investee	600	—
Profit before taxation	5,100	2,300
Taxation	(1,500)	(800)
Profit after taxation	3,600	1,500
Proposed dividends	(2,000)	(800)
Retained profit for year	1,600	700
Retained profit at 1.1.20X9	10,900	2,300
Retained profit at 31.12.20X9	12,500	3,000

Required

Prepare the consolidated profit and loss account, assuming investment in Investee is to be (i) fully consolidated and (ii) accounted for using the equity method of accounting.

Note: Full consolidation is normally appropriate where a majority of equity shares is owned by investor. The equity method is used in this example for illustrative purposes only.

Solution

Group structure

Investor —— 75% ——► Investee

continued overleaf

Example 11.1 Continued

Consolidated profit and loss accounts for the year ended 31.12.20X9

	(i) Full	**(ii) Equity**
	€000	**€000**
Turnover	13,500	9,000
Operating costs	(6,700)	(4,500)
Operating profit	6,800	4,500
Amortisation of goodwill (W_1)	(100)	(100)
Share of profit of Investee (W_2)	—	1,725
Profit before taxation	6,700	6,125
Taxation (W_3)	(2,300)	(2,100)
Profit after taxation	4,400	4,025
Minority interest (W_4)	(375)	—
Profit attributable to group	4,025	4,025
Proposed dividends	(2,000)	(2,000)
Retained profit for year	2,025	2,025
Retained profit at 1 January (W_5)	11,375	11,375
Retained profit at 31 December	13,400	13,400

W_1 Goodwill	**Full €000**	**Equity €000**
Investment at cost	10,750	10,750
Share of net assets at acquisition date (75% × €13m)	(9,750)	(9,750)
Goodwill on acquisition	1,000	1,000
Amount amortised at beginning of year ($^5/_{10}$ – W_5)	(500)	(500)
Goodwill amortised in current year	(100)	(100)
Closing balance sheet amount for goodwill	400	400

W_2 Share of profits of Investee	**Full €000**	**Equity €000**
Profit before tax: €2.3m × 75%	* —	1,725

* **Note:** Under full consolidation, Investee's profits are included on a line-by-line basis, therefore, *Share of Investee's profit* is an irrelevant concept.

W_3 Taxation charge		**Full €000**	**Equity €000**
Investor		1,500	1,500
Investee:	Full consolidation	800	—
	Equity: €800 × 75%	—	600
		2,300	2,100

W_4 Minority interest	**Full €000**	**Equity €000**
In profit after tax of Investee (25% × €1,500)	375	—

W_5 Consolidated reserves at beginning of year	**Full €000**	**Equity €000**
Investor	10,900	10,900
Share of Investee's post-acquisition reserves (75% × [€2.3m – €1m])	975	975
Goodwill written off (20X4 – 20X8; W_1)	(500)	(500)
	11,375	11,375

The following additional comments on Example 11.1 should help clarify points of detail that might otherwise be confusing:

- equity accounting includes only the *group share* of the profit before taxation and taxation charge of Investee in the profit and loss account. Therefore, there is no minority interest under the equity method
- full consolidation includes 100% of Investee's revenues and expenses on a line-by-line basis (except any amounts related to inter-company transactions with Investor). Therefore, minority interest of 25% of Investee's profit after tax must be shown in the consolidated profit and loss account
- consolidated retained earnings carried forward and brought forward are the same under both methods.

Gross equity method

The gross equity method is the same as the equity method as far as the consolidated profit and loss account is concerned. However, as indicated in Chapter 7, the investor's share of turnover of the joint venture is disclosed on the face of, or in a note to, the consolidated profit and loss account. Under the equity method, the associate's turnover is neither included in group turnover nor disclosed in the notes to the consolidated profit and loss account (except in the case of some substantial associates under FRS 9 where additional disclosures are required, see Chapter 14). Example 11.2 illustrates the disclosure required.

Example 11.2 Gross equity method: disclosure of joint venture turnover

Consolidated profit and loss account (extract)	**€m**
Turnover: Group and share of joint ventures	320
Less: Share of joint ventures' turnover	(120)
Group turnover	200
Cost of sales	(120)
Gross profit	80

Consolidated profit and loss account workings

The technique for preparing consolidated profit and loss accounts using columnar workings was introduced in Chapter 10. This chapter uses the structure detailed in Chapter 10 to incorporate the additional entries required where the group holds investments for which equity accounting is appropriate.

Incorporating associates into columnar workings

Associates are treated differently in the consolidated profit and loss account compared with their treatment in the individual profit and loss account of the investor. However, they are not treated the same as subsidiaries on consolidation. Nonetheless, details and entries concerning associates can be incorporated into the columnar workings described previously in Chapter 10 for subsidiaries. This is done in such a way as to acknowledge their difference from subsidiaries, but at the same time to allow their systematic inclusion in the consolidation.

The step-by-step approach is summarised in Table 11.1. This is a development of the step-by-step approach described for the consolidated profit and loss account with subsidiaries in Table 10.1.

Table 11.1 Technique for including associates in consolidated profit and loss account columnar workings

1. Open a column for each associate in the columnar workings, to the right-hand side of the total column (see solution to Example 11.3)
2. Enter associate's amounts for all captions from *sales* to *profit before taxation* in this column
3. Do not include any amount for the associate in group totals for these captions. The associate column is described as *memorandum only*, i.e., associate amounts are not added into group totals either in whole or in part for any of these captions. These *memorandum* amounts are shaded in the solutions to examples in this chapter to highlight their exclusion from consolidated profit and loss account totals
4. Insert a double underline below the associate's profit before taxation (see solution to Example 11.3)
5. Insert a new row into the columnar workings for *group share* of associate's profit before taxation
6. Include the *group's share* of associate's profit before taxation in the total column and in the associate's column
7. Group profit before taxation is the sum of profit before taxation of parent and subsidiaries (combined) and group's share of associate's profit before taxation
8. Calculate the group taxation charge as described in Chapter 10
9. Insert a new row into the columnar workings for *group share* of associate's taxation
10. Include the *group's share* of associate's taxation in the total column and in the associate's column
11. For remaining captions in the columnar workings, include the group's share in the associate's column and in the group totals or adjustment columns as appropriate, e.g., group share of dividends payable by the associate (associate and adjustment columns) and group's share of retained earnings brought forward (associate and total columns)

Worked example

Example 11.3 illustrates the preparation of a simple consolidated profit and loss account where the group includes a subsidiary and an associate. The example also requires the preparation of a consolidated balance sheet, which allows the comprehensive application of the equity method to be illustrated. The solution to this example is presented in four separate parts. The first two parts (Solution 11.3 (1) and Solution 11.3 (2)) present the consolidated profit and loss account workings. Solution 11.3 (3) presents workings for the consolidated balance sheet. Finally, Solution 11.3 (4) presents the consolidated profit and loss account and balance sheet.

Example 11.3 Equity accounting and the consolidated final accounts

Example

Parent bought 75% of the shares in Subsidiary in 20X3 for €27m when Subsidiary had retained profits of €7m, and 25% of the ordinary shares in Associate in 20X4 for €6m when Associate had retained profits of €2m. Their profit and loss accounts for the year ended 31.12.20X9 and balance sheets as at that date were as follows:

	Parent	**Subsidiary**	**Associate**
Profit and loss accounts	**€000**	**€000**	**€000**
Profit before taxation	20,000	12,000	8,000
Taxation	(8,000)	(4,000)	(2,000)
Profit after taxation	12,000	8,000	6,000
Dividends paid	(4,000)	(2,000)	(2,000)
Profit retained	8,000	6,000	4,000
Retained profit 1 January	17,000	9,000	6,000
Retained profit 31 December	25,000	15,000	10,000

Balance sheets	**Parent €000**	**Subsidiary €000**	**Associate €000**
Fixed assets	80,000	25,000	17,000
Investments	33,000	—	—
Stocks	70,000	26,000	12,000
Debtors	60,000	16,000	9,000
Cash at bank	7,000	4,000	2,000
	250,000	71,000	40,000
Share capital	150,000	25,000	20,000
Profit and loss account	25,000	15,000	10,000
	175,000	40,000	30,000
Creditors	75,000	31,000	10,000
	250,000	71,000	40,000

The creditors of Subsidiary and the debtors of Parent include €6m due by Subsidiary to Parent.
Dividends received by Parent from Subsidiary and Associate have been included in Parent's profit and loss account.
Goodwill is amortised over five years, including a full year's amortisation in the year of acquisition.

Required

Prepare the consolidated profit and loss account and balance sheet of Parent and group.

Solution 11.3 (1) Consolidated profit and loss account – workings

W_1 Group structure

Parent → 75% → Subsidiary
Parent → 25% → Associate

W_2 Goodwill on acquisition	**Subsidiary €000**	**Associate €000**	**Total €000**
Investment at cost	27,000	6,000	
Group share of net assets acquired			
75% × €32m	(24,000)		
25% × €22m		(5,500)	
Goodwill	3,000	500	3,500
Cumulative amortisation to start of year ($^5/_5$;$^5/_5$)	3,000	500	3,500
Balance sheet amount at year-end	—	—	—

W_3 Investment income		**€000**
Dividends received from Subsidiary	75% × €2,000	1,500
Dividends received from Associate	25% × €2,000	500
		2,000

W_4 Retained profit brought forward	**€000**	**€000**	**€000**
Parent			17,000
Subsidiary	9,000		
Less: Pre-acquisition profit	(7,000)	2,000	
Group share (75%)			1,500
Associate	6,000		
Less: Pre-acquisition profit	(2,000)	4,000	
Group share (25%)			1,000
Less: Cumulative goodwill written off (W_2)			(3,500)
			16,000

Solution 11.3 (2) Consolidated profit and loss account columnar workings

W_5 Consolidated profit and loss account columnar workings

	Parent	Subsidiary	Adjustment	Total	Associate*
	€000	**€000**	**€000**	**€000**	**€000**
Operating profit	18,000	12,000	—	30,000	8,000
Investment income (W_3)	2,000	—	(2,000)	—	—
	20,000	12,000	(2,000)	30,000	8,000
Group share of A's profit 25%				2,000	2,000**
Profit before taxation	20,000	12,000	(2,000)	32,000	2,000
Taxation: Group	(8,000)	(4,000)		(12,000)	
Associate 25%	—	—	—	(500)	(500)
Profit after taxation	12,000	8,000	(2,000)	19,500	1,500
Minority interest 25% × 8,000	—	(2,000)	—	(2,000)	
Profit attributable to group	12,000	6,000	(2,000)	17,500	1,500
Dividends: Parent	(4,000)			(4,000)	
Subsidiary €2,000 × 75%		(1,500)	1,500		
Associate €2,000 × 25%			500		(500)
Profit retained for year	8,000	4,500	—	13,500	1,000
Retained profit c/f (W_4)	17,000	1,500	(3,500)	16,000	1,000
	25,000	6,000	(3,500)	29,500	2,000

* The *memorandum* section of Associate's column is shaded and bordered by broken lines in this and subsequent examples in this chapter to highlight that these amounts for Associate are not included in group profit and loss account totals.

** Once group share of Associate's profit before tax is calculated, all amounts in Associate's column are group share only.

Solution 11.3 (3) Consolidated balance sheet – additional workings

W_6 Investment in Associate

	€000
Share of net assets at year-end (25% × €30m)	7,500
Plus: Unamortised goodwill	—
	7,500

Alternative working: **Investment in Associate T account**

	€000		**€000**
Investment at cost	6,000	Goodwill written off	500
Group share of post-acquisition reserves 8,000 × 25%	2,000	Consolidated balance sheet	7,500
			—
	8,000		8,000

W_7 Minority interest in Subsidiary's net assets

	€000
25% × €40m	10,000

The consolidated profit and loss account is now presented in Solution 11.3 (4) based on the amounts in the total column in the columnar workings in Solution 11.3 (2). The consolidated balance sheet is also presented in Solution 11.3 (4), as a check on the consistency of the consolidation exercise. Note that the retained earnings figure included in the balance sheet is the bottom line from the detailed consolidated profit and loss account.

Solution 11.3 (4) Consolidated profit and loss account and balance sheet

Consolidated profit and loss account year ended 31.12.20X2 (W_5)

	€000
Profit before taxation	30,000
Share of profit of Associate	2,000
Profit before taxation	32,000
Tax: Group	(12,000)
Share of taxation of Associate	(500)
Profit after taxation	19,500
Minority interest*	(2,000)
Profit attributable to group	17,500
Dividends	(4,000)
Profit retained	13,500
Retained profit 1 January	16,000
Retained profit 31 December	29,500

Consolidated balance sheet as at 31.12.20X2	**€000**	**€000**
Fixed assets (€80,000$_{Parent}$ + €25,000$_{Subsidiary}$)		105,000
Investment in Associate (W_6)		7,500
		112,500
Current assets		
Stocks (€70,000$_{Parent}$ + €26,000$_{Subsidiary}$)	96,000	
Debtors		
(€60,000$_{Parent}$ + €16,000$_{Subsidiary}$ – €6,000$_{inter\text{-}company}$)	70,000	
Bank (€7,000$_{Parent}$ + €4,000$_{Subsidiary}$)	11,000	
	177,000	
Creditors due in one year		
(€75,000$_{Parent}$ + €31,000$_{Subsidiary}$ – €6,000$_{inter\text{-}company}$)	(100,000)	
Net current assets		77,000
		189,500
Share capital		150,000
Retained earnings (W_5)		29,500
		179,500
Minority interest* (W_7)		10,000
		189,500

* Minority interest in both consolidated profit and loss account and consolidated balance sheet relate to Subsidiary only.

Associates' goodwill amortisation

It was shown in Chapter 7 that goodwill is calculated when an investment is classified as an associate and is accounted for using the equity method. Any goodwill arising on acquisition of associates is accounted for in accordance with the parent's accounting policy. Assuming that policy to be amortisation over the goodwill's useful life, the associate's goodwill is offset against the group's share of the associate's profit in the consolidated profit and loss account. Example 11.4 illustrates this treatment.

Example 11.4 Amortisation of associate's goodwill

Example

The profit and loss accounts of Parent, Subsidiary and Associate for the year ending 31.12.20X4 are as follows:

	Parent	Subsidiary	Associate
	€000	€000	€000
Sales	29,900	15,600	12,480
Cost of sales	(17,940)	(9,360)	(7,488)
Gross profit	11,960	6,240	4,992
Other operating expenses	(2,000)	(1,000)	(800)
Operating profit	9,960	5,240	4,192
Investment income	1,000	—	—
Interest payable	(480)	(240)	(192)
Profit before taxation	10,480	5,000	4,000
Taxation	(6,000)	(3,000)	(2,400)
Profit after taxation	4,480	2,000	1,600
Proposed dividends	(2,000)	(1,000)	(800)
Profit retained for year	2,480	1,000	800
Retained profit 1 January	15,520	2,000	1,600
Retained profit 31 December	18,000	3,000	2,400

Parent acquired 8m of the 10m ordinary shares in Subsidiary on 31.12.20X0 for €9.5m when the profit and loss account of Subsidiary amounted to €1.5m. Parent acquired 2m of the 8m ordinary shares in Associate on 31 Dec 20X2 for €2.5m when Associate had retained profits of €1.2m. Goodwill is amortised over ten years, commencing in the year following acquisition.

Required

Prepare the consolidated profit and loss account of Parent group.

Solution 11.4 (1) Consolidated profit and loss account – workings

W_1 Group structure

Parent

80% → Subsidiary

25% → Associate

W_2 Goodwill amortisation	**Total**	**Annual amortisation**
Goodwill on acquisition of Subsidiary	**€000**	**€000**
Acquisition at cost	9,500	
80% of net assets acquired (€11.5m)	(9,200)	
	300	30*
Goodwill on acquisition of Associate		
Acquisition at cost	2,500	
25% of net assets acquired (€9.2m)	(2,300)	
	200	20**

* Included in 'Other operating expenses'.
** Offset against group's share of Associate's profit before tax.

W_3 Inter-company dividends receivable and payable	**€000**
Subsidiary: 80% × €1m	800
Associate: 25% × €0.8m	200
	1,000

W_4 Retained profit brought forward	**€000**	**€000**
Parent		15,520
Subsidiary	2,000	
Less: Pre-acquisition reserves	1,500	
	500	
Group share (80%)		400
Associate	1,600	
Less: Pre-acquisition reserves	1,200	
	400	
Group share (25%)		100
Less: Goodwill written off at beginning of year		
Subsidiary ($^3/_{10}$ – 20X1 to 20X3)	(90)	
Associate ($^1/_{10}$ – 20X3)	(20)	(110)
		15,910

Solution 11.4 (2) Consolidated profit and loss account – columnar working

W_5 Consolidated profit and loss account columnar workings

	Parent	Subsidiary	Adjustment	Total	Associate
	€000	**€000**	**€000**	**€000**	**€000**
Sales	29,900	15,600	—	45,500	12,480
Cost of sales	(17,940)	(9,360)	—	(27,300)	(7,488)
Gross profit	11,960	6,240	—	18,200	4,992
Other operating expenses	(2,000)	(1,000)	(30)*	(3,030)	(800)
Operating profit	9,960	5,240	(30)	15,170	4,192
Investment income (W_3)	1,000	—	(1,000)		—
Interest payable	(480)	(240)	—	(720)	(192)
Profit before taxation	10,480	5,000	(1,030)	14,450	4,000
Group share of A's profit			(20)*	980	1,000
Group profit before tax	10,480	5,000	(1,050)	15,430	1,000
Taxation: Group	(6,000)	(3,000)		(9,000)	
Group share of A's taxation				(600)	(600)
Profit after taxation	4,480	2,000	(1,050)	5,830	400
Minority interest		(400)		(400)	
	4,480	1,600	(1,050)	5,430	400
Dividends: Parent	(2,000)	—	—	(2,000)	
Subsidiary W3		(800)	800		
Associate W3			200		(200)
Profit retained for year	2,480	800	(50)	3,430	200
Profit b/f (W_4)	15,520	400	(110)*	15,910	100
Profit c/f	18,000	1,200	(160)	19,340	300

* Goodwill amortisation (W_2)

Notes
- The *memorandum* section of Associate's column is shaded and bordered by broken lines to highlight that these amounts for Associate are not included in group profit and loss account totals.
- Once group share of Associate's profit before tax is calculated, all amounts in Associate's column are group share only

Solution 11.4 (3) Published consolidated profit and loss account

Consolidated profit and loss account for year ended 31.12.20X4

	€000
Sales	45,500
Cost of sales	(27,300)
Gross profit	18,200
Other operating expenses	(3,030)
Operating profit	15,170
Interest payable	(720)
Profit before taxation	14,450
Share of profit of Associate	980
Group profit before taxation	15,430
Tax: Group	(9,000)
Share of taxation of Associate	(600)
Profit after taxation	5,830
Minority interest	(400)
Profit attributable to group	5,430
Dividends	(2,000)
Profit retained	3,430
Retained profit 1.1.20X4	15,910
Retained profit 31.12.20X4	19,340

Intra-group trading

Under full consolidation, intra-group profits and losses are eliminated in full in the consolidated financial statements. Where the profit is recorded in a subsidiary that is not wholly owned, the minority is charged with their share of the unrealised profit. The rationale behind these adjustments and the technique involved were explained in Chapter 3.

UK regulation (FRS 9) requires that a similar adjustment should apply for transactions between a group member and an associate or joint venture. Where the associate is accounted for using the equity method, the *group's share* of the unrealised profit or loss should be eliminated. As indicated in Chapter 7, it is necessary to look back to the exposure draft which preceded FRS 9 (ED 50) to find explicit guidance on how this adjustment should be implemented. ED 50 recommended that the adjustment should be taken in the consolidated profit and loss account against either the group profit or against the group's share of associate's profit, according to which of them recorded the profit on the transaction. Example 11.5 illustrates the approach adopted where the *profit is recorded by a full member of the group* (the parent company in this example).

Example 11.5 Unrealised profit from sales to associate

Example

Parent has a number of subsidiaries and also has a 40% investment in the equity share capital of Associate. During the year ended 31.3.20X5, Parent sold goods which cost €800,000, to Associate for €1.2m, reflecting a uniform mark-up on cost of 50%. At 31.3.20X5, the stocks of Associate included €300,000 of goods bought from Parent, but unsold at the year-end. In addition, the stock of Associate at 31.3.20X4 had included €210,000 relating to goods bought from Parent under the same pricing structure.

Required

Explain how the provision for unrealised profit is dealt with in the consolidated profit and loss account for the year ended 31.3.20X5.

Solution

- The adjustment in the consolidated profit and loss account is based on the *increase* in the provision during the year (€30,000 – see working).
- Adjustment for unrealised profit is *group's share* only because the transaction is between a full group member and the associate (€12,000).
- Group sales figure is not adjusted because the corresponding purchase amount is not included in group purchases (group share of Associate's profit before tax is the first amount included in consolidated profit and loss account in respect of Associate's results).
- Adjustment, in the consolidated profit and loss account workings, of €12,000 (see working), is charged against group gross profit.
- Adjustment in consolidated balance sheet is against Investment in Associate and Consolidated revenue reserves because the stock is held by the associate and is therefore not included in group stock.

Working	**Total unrealised profit** €	**Group share (40%)** €
Unrealised profit in Associate's stock		
Year-end (50/150 × €300,000)	100,000	40,000
Beginning of year (50/150 × €210,000)	70,000	28,000
Increase in provision	30,000	12,000

Example 11.6 illustrates the approach where the *profit is made by the associate* from sales to full group members. As in Example 11.5, the adjustment for the increased provision for unrealised profit is limited to the group's share. This is because the transaction is between an associate and full members of the group. Unlike Example 11.5, the adjustment in Example 11.6 is offset against stock in the consolidated balance sheet. This is because the stock incorporating the unrealised profit is included in the consolidated balance sheet, as it is the parent company's stock.

Example 11.6 Unrealised profit from sales by associate

Example

Parent has a number of subsidiaries and also has a 30% investment in the equity share capital of Associate. During the year ended 31.12.20X4, Associate sold goods to full group members (Parent and subsidiaries). At 31.12.20X4, the stocks of the full group members included goods purchased from Associate, which had been marked up by €20,000 (20X3, €15,000). The balance sheet of Associate at year-end included net assets of €800,000 and a profit for the year ended 31.12.20X4 of €80,000.

Required

Explain how the provision for unrealised profit is dealt with in the consolidated profit and loss account for the year ended 31.12.20X4.

Solution

- The adjustment in the consolidated profit and loss account is based on the *increase* in the provision during the year (€5,000 – see working)
- Adjustment for unrealised profit is *group's share* only because the transaction is between the associate and full group members (€1,500).
- Group sales figure is not adjusted because the sale was not included in any full member's sales amount
- Group purchases (cost of sales) figure is not adjusted because the corresponding amount is not included in group sales (group share of Associate's profit before tax is the first amount included in consolidated profit and loss account in respect of Associate's results).
- The adjustment in the consolidated profit and loss account of €1,500 (see working) is charged against group's share of Associate's profit.
- Adjustment in the consolidated balance sheet is against Stock and Consolidated revenue reserves because the stock is held by full group members and is therefore included in group stock.

Working	**Total unrealised profit** €	**Group share (30%)** €
Unrealised profit in group member's stock		
Year-end	20,000	6,000
Beginning of year	15,000	4,500
Increase in provision	5,000	1,500

Consolidated profit and loss account (extract)*	€
Group's share of Associate's profit (30% × €80,000)	24,000
Less: Increase in provision for unrealised profit	(1,500)
	22,500

* Assuming no goodwill amortisation in respect of Associate.

Consolidated balance sheet (extract)**	€
Group's share of Associate's net assets (30% × €800,000)	240,000
Group stock (Parent + subsidiaries – €1,500)	X

** Assuming no unamortised goodwill in respect of Associate.

Majority held subsidiary with associate

Where a subsidiary which is not wholly owned by the parent has an associate, the group's interest in that associate must be included in the consolidated profit and loss account in the same way as the group's interest in other revenues and expenses of the subsidiary would be included. That is, the entire interest of the subsidiary in the profit before tax and tax charge of the associate must be included under the appropriate captions and the minority interest in the subsidiary's share of the associate's profit after tax must be included in the minority interest. Example 11.7 summarises the required treatment.

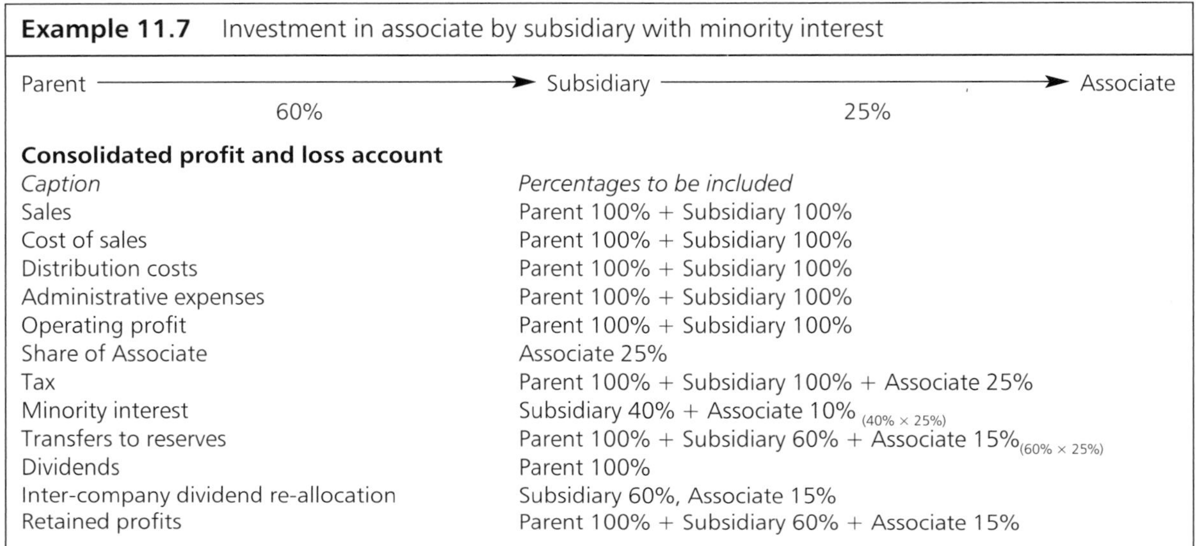

Example 11.7 Investment in associate by subsidiary with minority interest

Parent → (60%) → Subsidiary → (25%) → Associate

Consolidated profit and loss account

Caption	*Percentages to be included*
Sales	Parent 100% + Subsidiary 100%
Cost of sales	Parent 100% + Subsidiary 100%
Distribution costs	Parent 100% + Subsidiary 100%
Administrative expenses	Parent 100% + Subsidiary 100%
Operating profit	Parent 100% + Subsidiary 100%
Share of Associate	Associate 25%
Tax	Parent 100% + Subsidiary 100% + Associate 25%
Minority interest	Subsidiary 40% + Associate 10% (40% × 25%)
Transfers to reserves	Parent 100% + Subsidiary 60% + Associate 15% (60% × 25%)
Dividends	Parent 100%
Inter-company dividend re-allocation	Subsidiary 60%, Associate 15%
Retained profits	Parent 100% + Subsidiary 60% + Associate 15%

Summary

This chapter has explained and illustrated the implications of adopting equity accounting for the detailed entries in the consolidated profit and loss account. In particular, examples were provided of columnar consolidation profit and loss account workings incorporating associated company results. Until the group share of the profits of an associate is brought into the consolidation totals, the amounts of the associate's detailed profit and loss account captions are included in the columnar profit and loss account workings for memorandum purposes only. Once the group's share of the associate's profit is included in the consolidation totals, the associate's amounts under subsequent profit and loss account captions are included in the cross-casting, but only the group's share. This chapter has focused on the techniques involved in applying the equity method of accounting in the consolidated profit and loss account. Regulations governing the use of the equity method are explained and illustrated in Chapter 15.

Learning outcomes

After studying this chapter you should have learnt:

- how to incorporate the results on an equity accounted entity into the detailed consolidated profit and loss account
- the difference between full consolidation and equity accounting in the context of the consolidated profit and loss account

- that amounts included in the consolidated profit and loss account for equity accounted entities link into the consolidated balance sheet T account workings for Investment in associate
- how to deal with amortisation of an associate's goodwill in the consolidated profit and loss account workings
- how to eliminate unrealised profit on intra-group trading with equity accounted entities.

Multiple choice questions

Solutions to these questions are presented in Appendix 1.

11.1 Leebase, Stringer and Temple

Leebase owns 75% of the issued ordinary share capital of **Stringer** and 40% of the issued ordinary share capital of **Temple**.

Turnover for the year ended 30 June 20X7 is as follows:

	€000
Leebase	100
Stringer	120
Temple	360

The figure for turnover, which should be included in the consolidated profit and loss account for the year ended 30 June 20X7, is:

(a) €190,000
(b) €220,000
(c) €334,000
(d) €580,000

11.2 Preserve, Jam, Marmalade and Honey

Preserve owns 75% of **Jam** which owns 60% of **Marmalade**. Preserve also owns 45% of **Honey**.

Profits for the year ended 31 May 20X9 were as follows:

	€000
Preserve	600
Jam	300
Marmalade	240
Honey	540

The figure for profit attributable to the members of Preserve group, which should be included in the consolidated profit and loss account for the year ended 31 May 20X9, is:

(a) €1,176,000
(b) €1,212,000
(c) €1,383,000
(d) €1,680,000

Data for questions 11.3 and 11.4

Hop has a subsidiary undertaking **Skip** and an associated undertaking **Jump**. For the year ended 31 May 20X4 the following balances were extracted from the accounts of the three companies:

	Hop	**Skip**	**Jump**
	€000	**€000**	**€000**
Turnover	840	510	180
Cost of sales	630	375	135

During the year under review, sales by Hop to Skip amounted to €200,000 on which Hop earned a gross profit of 25%. At 31 May 20X4 €80,000 worth of these goods were included in the closing stock of Skip.

11.3 Hop, Skip and Jump (1)

The figure for turnover, which should be included in the consolidated profit and loss account for the year ended 31 May 20X4, is:

€000

(a) 1,150
(b) 1,330
(c) 1,350
(d) 1,530

11.4 Hop, Skip and Jump (2)

The figure for cost of sales, which should appear in the same consolidated profit and loss account, is:

€000

(a) 805
(b) 825
(c) 940
(d) 1,140

11.5 Constable, Turner and Whistler

Constable owns 40% of **Turner** which it treats as an associated undertaking in accordance with FRS 9. Constable also owns 60% of **Whistler**. Constable has held both of these shareholdings for more than one year. Turnover of each company for the year ended 30 June 20X2 was as follows:

	€m
Constable	400
Turner	200
Whistler	100

The figure for turnover, which should be included in the consolidated profit and loss account for the year ended 30 June 20X2, is:

(a) €460m
(b) €500m
(c) €580m
(d) €700m

11.6 Stephen, Alison and Hugo

Stephen, its 90% subsidiary, **Alison**, and its 20% associate, **Hugo**, have made the following transfers to reserves:

	Stephen	**Alison**	**Hugo**
	€000	**€000**	**€000**
Transfers to reserves	450	300	250

The transfer to reserves reported in Stephen's consolidated profit and loss account will be:

(a) €720,000
(b) €750,000
(c) €770,000
(d) €800,000

Self-assessment exercises

Solutions to these self-assessment exercises can be found at:
www.thomsonlearning.co.uk/accountingandfinance/piercebrennan

11.1 Golf, Club, Ball and Tee

Golf is a trading company which has recently sought to diversify its interests by purchasing shares in other companies. It has been its policy to insist on appointing a director to the board of any company, so as to take an active part in the management, where its investment comprises more than 20% of the equity share capital.

The following investments have been made:

1 On 1 January 20X2, 15% of the ordinary share capital of **Club**.
2 On 1 July 20X2, 30% of the ordinary share capital of **Ball**.
3 On 1 November 20X2, 75% of the ordinary share capital of **Tee** and also 50,000 of the 100,000 9% preference shares of €1 each in that company.

The draft profit and loss accounts of the four companies for the year ended 30 June 20X3 show:

	Golf	**Club**	**Ball**	**Tee**
	€	€	€	€
Turnover	2,100,000	3,900,000	1,900,000	1,200,000
Expenses	(1,850,000)	(3,500,000)	(1,690,000)	(1,074,000)
Operating profit	250,000	400,000	210,000	126,000
Dividends receivable	46,500	—	—	—
	296,500	400,000	210,000	126,000
Taxation	(90,000)	(170,000)	(85,000)	(51,000)
	206,500	230,000	125,000	75,000
Less: Proposed dividends				
Preference	—	(6,000)	—	(9,000)
Ordinary	(132,000)	(100,000)	(60,000)	(32,000)
	74,500	124,000	65,000	34,000
Balance brought forward	450,000	306,000	235,000	200,000
Balance carried forward	524,500	430,000	300,000	234,000

The following information is ascertained:

1 Included in the stock of Tee was €24,000 for goods purchased from Golf subsequent to 1 November 20X2. Golf realised its usual 25% gross profit, based on selling price, when it sold these goods.
2 The dividend due from Club has not been incorporated in the draft profit and loss account of Golf.

Required

(a) Prepare the consolidated profit and loss account of Golf for the year ended 30 June 20X3, using only the information given.

(b) Identify how your answer would differ if the inter-company sale (and related stock) had taken place in the opposite direction (i.e., the stock was purchased from Tee and included in the closing stock of Golf at the year-end).

11.2 Kale, Leek, Neep and Sage

Kale, **Leek**, **Neep** and **Sage** have issued share capital in ordinary shares of €500,000, €250,000, €200,000 and €100,000 respectively.

The summarised profit and loss accounts of the companies for the year ended 28 February 20X5 are set out as follows:

	Kale	Leek	Neep	Sage
	€000	€000	€000	€000
Turnover	15,721	5,488	6,900	6,102
Cost of sales	(8,018)	(3,183)	(3,795)	(2,563)
Gross profit	7,703	2,305	3,105	3,539
Distribution costs	(1,964)	(622)	(875)	(1,135)
Administrative expenses	(4,584)	(1,384)	(1,799)	(1,696)
Operating profit	1,155	299	431	708
Dividends from group and associated companies	429	—	—	—
	1,584	299	431	708
Tax on profit on ordinary activities	(504)	(112)	(148)	(257)
Profit for the financial year	1,080	187	283	451
Dividend paid and proposed	(500)	(180)	(150)	(250)
Retained profit for the year	580	7	133	201
Retained profit at 1 March 20X4	3,216	175	197	463
Retained profit at 28 February 20X5	3,796	182	330	664

You obtain the following information:

1 The par values of the ordinary shares are as follows:

Kale	€1
Leek	25 cent
Neep	50 cent
Sage	€1

2 Kale acquired 800,000 shares in Leek on 1 March 20X0 when there was a debit balance of €15,000 on the profit and loss account of Leek.

3 On 1 April 20X4 Kale acquired 90,000 shares in Sage whose profits accrue evenly throughout the year.

4 Kale acquired 160,000 shares in Neep on 1 March 20X4. Neep was incorporated and first commenced to trade on 1 March 20X3.

5 Kale purchases goods for resale from Neep. On 28 February 20X5 Kale held a stock of those goods amounting to €222,435. Neep manufactures only one product and has a standard selling price to all customers.

Required

Prepare the consolidated profit and loss account of Kale and its subsidiaries, incorporating the results of the associated undertaking, for the year ended 28 February 20X5.

Examination-style questions

11.1 Dejay, Carey and Gowran

Dejay has adopted a strategy of growth by acquisition and over the last two years has bought the following:

1 On 1 April 20X1, 2.8m €1 ordinary shares in **Carey** for cash of €4.16m. At the date of acquisition the balance on reserves was €750,000 credit.
2 On 1 April 20X2, 80,000 €1 ordinary shares in **Gowran** for cash of €300,000. This holding gives Dejay significant influence but not control.
3 On 1 April 20X2, €1.4m debentures in Carey for cash of €1.4m.

The summarised balance sheets, as at 31 March 20X3, of the three companies are as follows:

	Dejay	**Carey**	**Gowran**
	€000	**€000**	**€000**
Tangible fixed assets	24,400	6,600	500
Investments	5,860	—	—
Net current assets	2,340	1,500	240
10% debentures	(3,000)	(3,500)	—
	29,600	4,600	740
Issued ordinary €1 shares	10,000	3,500	200
Reserves	19,600	1,100	540
	29,600	4,600	740

The summarised profit and loss accounts, for the year ended 31 March 20X3, of the three companies are as follows:

	Dejay	**Carey**	**Gowran**
	€000	**€000**	**€000**
Turnover	55,000	16,500	7,700
Operating expenses	(49,000)	(15,000)	(7,570)
Operating profit	6,000	1,500	130
Investment income from Carey			
Dividend proposed	400	—	—
Debenture interest	140	—	—
Investment income from Gowran			
Dividend proposed	24	—	—
Interest payable	(300)	(350)	—
Profit before taxation	6,264	1,150	130
Taxation	(2,000)	(520)	(30)
Profit after taxation	4,264	630	100
Dividend proposed	(1,700)	(500)	(60)
Retained profit for year	2,564	130	40
Balance brought forward	17,036	970	500
Balance carried forward	19,600	1,100	540

Additional information:

1 Dejay purchased goods for resale from Gowran during the year ended 31 March 20X3. At the year-end, Dejay held a stock of these goods which had cost Dejay €80,000. Gowran earns a standard 25% margin on sales.
2 It is group policy to amortise goodwill, over five years, on all acquisitions of both subsidiaries and associates.

Required

(a) Prepare a consolidated:
  (i) profit and loss account for the Dejay Group for the year ended 31 March 20X3
  (ii) balance sheet as at 31 March 20X3.

(b) Discuss the implications of trading between a parent and its associated undertaking, for the preparation of consolidated accounts.

11.2 Rush, Slow and Tardy

You are given the following information about **Rush, Slow and Tardy.**

1 Profit and loss accounts for the year ended 30 June 20X9

	Rush	**Slow**	**Tardy**
	€000	**€000**	**€000**
Turnover	13,500	7,200	4,500
Cost of sales	(9,000)	(4,056)	(2,475)
Gross profit	4,500	3,144	2,025
Investment income	45	—	—
Distribution costs	(1,282)	(756)	(528)
Administrative expenses	(1,193)	(948)	(637)
Profit on ordinary activities before taxation	2,070	1,440	860
Taxation	(675)	(480)	(220)
Profit on ordinary activities after taxation	1,395	960	640
Dividends paid	(225)	—	(150)
Dividends proposed	(225)	(450)	(220)
Retained profit for current year	945	510	270
Retained profit at beginning of year	3,600	1,575	855
	4,545	2,085	1,125

2 Rush acquired a 30% interest in the ordinary shares (and voting power) of Tardy on 1 July 20X6. At that date the retained profits of Tardy were €455,000.

3 Rush acquired an 80% interest in the ordinary shares (and voting power) of Slow on 30 September 20X8.

4 The investment income of €45,000 in the accounts of Rush represents a dividend received from Tardy.

5 The stock of Tardy at 1 July 20X8 contained €300,000 of goods which had been purchased from Rush. These items had cost Rush €150,000 to manufacture. Rush had provided for the unrealised profit in the 20X8 group accounts.

6 Profits of Slow accrue evenly over time.

Required

(a) Prepare the consolidated profit and loss account of Rush and group for the year ended 30 June 20X9.

(b) Explain your treatment of unrealised profit in Tardy's opening stock.

11.3 Bergin, Cullen, Doyle and Evans

The draft accounts of four companies for the year ended 31 December 20X4 include the following details:

Balance sheets as at 31 December 20X4 (extracts)

	Bergin	Cullen	Doyle	Evans
	€	€	€	€
Issued share capital (€1 ordinary)	48,000	18,000	30,000	16,000
Share premium	22,000	—	14,000	8,000
Profit and loss account	58,000	20,000	64,000	16,000
	128,000	38,000	108,000	40,000

Profit and loss accounts for year ended 31 December 20X4

	Bergin	Cullen	Doyle	Evans
	€	€	€	€
Turnover	352,000	130,000	218,000	110,000
Cost of sales	(180,000)	(66,000)	(112,000)	(56,000)
Gross profit	172,000	64,000	106,000	54,000
Other net operating expenses	(128,000)	(46,000)	(78,000)	(40,000)
Operating profit	44,000	18,000	28,000	14,000
Other income	6,000	2,000	4,000	2,000
Interest payable	(16,000)	(4,000)	(6,000)	(4,000)
Profit before taxation	34,000	16,000	26,000	12,000
Taxation	(16,000)	(6,000)	(10,000)	(4,000)
Profit after taxation	18,000	10,000	16,000	8,000
Dividends				
Paid 30.6.20X4	(5,000)	(4,000)	(2,000)	(1,000)
Proposed	(5,000)	(5,000)	(3,334)	(1,000)
Retained	8,000	1,000	10,666	6,000

Additional information:

1 Bergin has made the following acquisitions:
   - In 20W7 when Cullen was established, Bergin subscribed at par for 14,400 €1 ordinary shares in Cullen.
   - In 20W8 Bergin acquired 18,000 €1 ordinary shares in Doyle for €74,400. Doyle's shareholders' funds on the date of acquisition amounted to €64,000 (including share premium of €14,000 and profit and loss account balance of €20,000).

2 Cullen acquired 10,000 €1 shares in Evans on 1 July 20X4 for €45,300. Evans' share capital and share premium are unchanged since acquisition.

3 Doyle owns certain licences and rights, which although not recorded, had a fair value on acquisition of €60,000. These licences have a ten-year life of which four years were outstanding at 1 January 20X4.

4 At acquisition Evans held stocks with a book value of €2,000 but which were considered to have a fair value of only €400. Evans did not record the fair value in its own accounts. Between acquisition and the year-end, all of these stocks were sold.

5 Bergin has not recorded dividends receivable. Cullen has credited dividends receivable of €750 to the profit and loss account.

6 Between July and the year-end Evans sold goods to Doyle for €4,000 (making a profit of €1,000) and to Cullen for €8,000 (making a profit of €3,000). These goods were all sold to customers by the year-end.

7 Bergin group adopts the following accounting policies:
   Goodwill: Goodwill is capitalised and amortised over the five years following acquisition on a straight-line basis.
   Intangible assets: The cost of intangible assets is written off on a straight-line basis over the expected useful life of the asset.

Required

(a) Prepare the cost of control account to indicate, separately, the goodwill attributable to the acquisition of (i) Doyle and (ii) Evans.

(b) Prepare the consolidated profit and loss account for the year ended 31 December 20X4. (*Show your columnar workings*.)

(c) Discuss *briefly* your treatment of the fair value at acquisition of stocks in Evans detailed in item 4.

12

Disposal of shares in subsidiaries

Learning objectives

After studying this chapter you should be able to:

- calculate the group profit or loss on disposal of a subsidiary or associate
- distinguish between the profit or loss in the individual accounts of the investing company and that in the consolidated accounts
- explain the impact of amortised goodwill on the calculation of group profit or loss on disposal
- identify the appropriate method of accounting, in the consolidated accounts, for the remaining investment (if any)

Introduction

In earlier chapters, we explained techniques for preparing consolidated balance sheets and consolidated profit and loss accounts under the assumption that (i) the group composition was unchanged during the year or (ii) a subsidiary or associate was acquired during the accounting period. Although we referred to the situation where a subsidiary was disposed of in earlier chapters (particularly in Chapter 10), we have not explained the impact of a disposal on the preparation of consolidated accounts – until now.

In this chapter, we will explain the effect of a disposal on the individual accounts of the investing company, in addition to the effect on the consolidated accounts of the investing group. The chapter commences with a discussion of how to calculate the profit or loss on disposal. Then, the impact of a parent selling its entire holding in a subsidiary is explained before dealing with the more difficult area of selling part of the parent's shareholding in the subsidiary.

In particular, four different situations which can arise in the context of disposal of shares in a subsidiary will be explained and illustrated. These are:

1. Sale of the investor's entire holding, either at
   - the beginning of the period; or
   - during the accounting period.
2. Sale of part of the investor's holding but control is retained, i.e., the investee remains a subsidiary and there is a new or increased minority interest.
3. Sale of part of the investor's holding but significant influence is maintained, i.e., the investee ceases to be a subsidiary and becomes an associate.
4. Sale of part of the investor's holding where only a simple investment remains, i.e., the investee ceases to be a subsidiary and becomes a simple investment.

Calculating the profit or loss on disposal

This section discusses how to calculate the profit or loss on disposal. A distinction is made initially between the profit or loss that is recognised in the individual accounts of the investor and the profit or loss that is recognised in the group accounts. In both cases, the profit or loss is the difference between the proceeds of disposal and the carrying amount of the investment at the date of disposal.

Individual accounts of the parent

In the individual profit and loss account of the investing company, the profit or loss on disposal of shares in a subsidiary is the difference between the proceeds and the carrying amount of the investment, usually its cost.

Until the early 1990s, this profit or loss was likely to be shown in the published accounts as an extraordinary item, where it was material. Under FRS 3 *Reporting Financial Performance*, profits or losses on disposal of fixed assets and on the sale or termination of an operation are required to be disclosed on the face of the profit and loss account as exceptional items (paragraph 20, FRS 3).

Many disposals of subsidiaries qualify as discontinued operations under FRS 3. The FRS indicates in paragraph 20 that profits or losses on the termination of an operation and on disposal of fixed assets should be separately disclosed:

> The following items, including provisions in respect of such items, should be shown separately on the face of the profit and loss account after operating profit and before interest, and included under the appropriate heading of continuing or discontinued operations:
>
> (a) profits or losses on the sale or termination of an operation;
> (b) costs of a fundamental reorganisation or restructuring having a material effect on the nature and focus of the reporting entity's operations; and
> (c) profits or losses on the disposal of fixed assets.

Consolidated accounts

FRS 2 *Accounting for Subsidiary Undertakings* provides guidance in paragraph 46 on how a subsidiary, which ceases to be a subsidiary during the accounting period, should be treated:

> When an undertaking ceases to be a subsidiary undertaking during a period, the consolidated financial statements for that period should include the results of that subsidiary undertaking up to the date that it ceases to be a subsidiary undertaking and any gain or loss arising on that cessation, to the extent that these have not already been provided for in the consolidated financial statements.

The profit or loss on disposal of shares in a subsidiary will be a different amount in the group accounts to that recorded in the parent's accounts. Although the proceeds of disposal are the same in both the individual accounts of the parent and the group accounts, the value at which the subsidiary is carried in the consolidated accounts is different from the value of the investment in the individual accounts of the parent company. Investments in subsidiaries are usually included in the individual accounts of the parent at cost, whereas in the consolidated accounts they are carried at the group share of net assets plus unamortised goodwill. The difference between these two amounts is the group's share of post-acquisition retained profits, net of goodwill amortised.

Example 12.1 summarises the relationship between the carrying amount of the investment in the subsidiary in the parent undertaking's balance sheet and the carrying amount in the group balance sheet, distinguishing between the position at acquisition and the position at a date subsequent to acquisition. As explained in Chapter 2, investment in subsidiary in the parent's balance sheet is replaced by the group's share of the subsidiary's net assets plus goodwill in the consolidated balance sheet. At the date of acquisition, *cost* and *group's share of net assets plus goodwill* are equal in amount. (Example 7.6 demonstrated the equivalence between cost and group share of net assets plus goodwill at acquisition for an associate. The same principle applies in the context of subsidiaries.)

Example 12.1 Group carrying amount of investment in subsidiary

At acquisition

- Carrying amount in Parent's individual balance sheet and in the consolidated balance sheet correspond.

Parent's balance sheet		*Group balance sheet*
Cost	=	Group share of net assets + goodwill

- 100% of Subsidiary's assets
- plus goodwill on acquisition
- 100% of Subsidiary's liabilities
- less minority interest

Post-acquisition

- Carrying amount in Parent's individual balance sheet and in the consolidated balance sheet no longer correspond.

Parent's balance sheet	*Group balance sheet*		
Cost	*Carrying amount at acquisition*	*Annual change in carrying amount*	*Over useful life of goodwill*
	Group share of net assets + goodwill	± group share of post— acquisition profits/losses	– goodwill amortised

During the period subsidiaries remain as members of the group, the group's share of their post-acquisition reserves is credited to consolidated reserves. Goodwill on acquisition is systematically amortised against group profits, thereby reducing the amount of these post-acquisition reserves recorded by the group. The dual aspect of this activity is that group net assets are increasing simultaneously with the net increase in group reserves. (The net increase referred to here is group share of post-acquisition retained earnings of subsidiaries, less aggregate goodwill amortised against profits since acquisition.)

From the date of acquisition to the eventual date of disposal, the carrying amount of subsidiaries in the group balance sheet changes every time a consolidated balance sheet is prepared, while the carrying amount in the parent's balance sheet usually remains at cost. The carrying amount in the group balance sheet increases by the group's share of retained earnings and other post-acquisition surpluses (such as revaluation surpluses), and/or decreases by the group's share of retained losses and goodwill amortised.

FRS 2 (paragraph 47) explains how the profit or loss on disposal should be calculated:

> The gain or loss directly arising for the group on an undertaking ceasing to be its subsidiary undertaking is calculated by comparing the carrying amount of the net assets of that subsidiary undertaking attributable to the group's interest before the cessation with any remaining carrying amount attributable to the group's interest after the cessation together with any proceeds received. The net assets compared should include any related goodwill not previously written off through the profit and loss account.

If we assume initially that the parent disposes of all of its shares in the subsidiary, the comparison referred to in paragraph 47 of FRS 2 can be simplified to:
The gain or loss *equals* proceeds received *minus* net assets attributable to the group's interest before the cessation (including any related goodwill not previously written off through the profit and loss account).

Example 12.2 compares the calculation of (i) profit or loss on disposal of shares in a subsidiary in the parent's accounts with (ii) the profit or loss in the group accounts. In both cases profit (or loss) equals proceeds minus carrying amount. Proceeds do not differ between parent and group. However, carrying amounts differ. Consequently, the difference between the profit as calculated in the individual profit and loss account of the parent and as calculated for group profit and loss account purposes is the difference in carrying amount at the date of disposal.

Example 12.1 has already indicated that the difference in carrying amounts is the group share of post-acquisition retained profits or losses of the subsidiary less any goodwill amortised. Example 12.2 also illustrates this, but in a different way. When a subsidiary is disposed of, the parent no longer has access to these retained profits (net of any consolidation goodwill amortised). Effectively, group profit (or loss) on disposal is the difference between the profit (or loss) in the parent's individual accounts and the group's share of post-acquisition net retained profit of the disposed subsidiary.

Example 12.2 Profit on disposal: Parent and group compared

Profit	= **Proceeds**	minus	**Carrying amount**
Parent accounts	Same amount as group		Cost
Group accounts	Same amount as Parent		Group share of net assets at date of disposal plus unamortised goodwill
Difference	=		Post-acquisition retained profits, less goodwill amortised

Sale of investor's entire holding

Sale of the investor's entire holding was the first of four different situations regarding disposal of shares referred to in the introduction to this chapter. A number of examples are provided in this section to illustrate the treatment of such disposals. In addition, two complicating factors, goodwill and taxation, are illustrated in these otherwise straightforward examples.

Impact of goodwill on profit/loss on disposal

Goodwill can complicate the calculation of group profit or loss on disposal. As indicated in Example 12.2, the carrying amount of investment in subsidiary in the group accounts changes each period by the group's share of the subsidiary's post-acquisition retained earnings (or losses), net of goodwill amortisation. Consequently, the unrealised profit accumulated in group reserves in respect of each subsidiary is reduced to the extent that goodwill on acquisition has been written off against that profit.

Example 12.3 illustrates the effect of different treatments of goodwill on the calculation of profit or loss on disposal. The difference between profit or loss on disposal as recorded in the parent's individual profit and loss account and the group profit or loss on disposal is also reconciled in Example 12.3 using the three different assumptions with respect to the treatment of goodwill on acquisition.

Example 12.3 Disposal of shares in subsidiary: reconciliation of profit in parent with profit in group

Example

Parent purchased all of Subsidiary's 30,000 €1 shares for €42,000, when revenue reserves of Subsidiary were €5,000.

Parent sold its shares in Subsidiary for €50,000 when revenue reserves of Subsidiary were €15,000.

Required

Calculate the profit or loss on disposal:

(a) in the individual accounts of Parent
(b) in the group accounts, assuming *no* goodwill has been written off
(c) in the group accounts, assuming *all* goodwill has been written off against consolidated profits
(d) in the group accounts, assuming €3,000 goodwill has been written off against consolidated profits.

Reconcile the differences between your answer to (a) and your answers to (b), (c) and (d).

Solution

(a) Disposal in individual accounts of Parent	€
Proceeds	50,000
Carrying amount of investment in Parent's accounts (cost)	42,000
Profit on disposal	8,000

(b) Disposal in consolidated accounts: No goodwill written off		€	€
Proceeds			50,000
Less: Carrying amount of investment in group accounts			
Unamortised goodwill			
[€42,000$_{cost}$ – (€30,000$_{share\ capital}$ + €5,000$_{pre\text{-}acquisition\ reserves}$)]		7,000	
+ Parent's share of net assets – represented by	€		
Share capital	30,000		
Revenue reserves at disposal	15,000	45,000	52,000
Loss on disposal			(2,000)

continued overleaf

Solution (b) (*continued*)

Reconciling the difference

			€
Profit in Parent's individual accounts			8,000
Post-acquisition revenue reserves no longer consolidated (€15,000$_{\text{reserves at disposal}}$ – €5,000$_{\text{pre-acquisition reserves}}$)			(10,000)
Group loss			(2,000)

(c) Disposal in consolidated accounts: All goodwill written off

		€	€
Proceeds			50,000
Less: *Carrying amount of investment in group accounts*			
Unamortised goodwill		Zero	
Parent's share of net assets – represented by:	€		
Share capital	30,000		
Revenue reserves at disposal	15,000	45,000	45,000
Profit on disposal			5,000

Reconciling the difference

			€
Profit in Parent's individual accounts			8,000
Post-acquisition revenue reserves no longer consolidated (€15,000 – €5,000$_{\text{pre-acquisition}}$ – €7,000$_{\text{goodwill written off}}$)			(3,000)
Group profit			5,000

(d) Disposal in consolidated accounts: Some goodwill written off

		€	€
Proceeds			50,000
Less: *Carrying amount of investment in group accounts*			
Unamortised goodwill (€7,000$_{\text{goodwill}}$ – €3,000$_{\text{amount written off}}$)		4,000	
+ Parent's share of net assets – represented by	€		
Share capital	30,000		
Revenue reserves – at disposal	15,000	45,000	49,000
Profit on disposal			1,000

Reconciling the difference

			€
Profit in Parent's individual accounts			8,000
Post-acquisition revenue reserves no longer consolidated (€15,000 – €5,000$_{\text{pre-acquisition}}$ – €3,000$_{\text{goodwill written off}}$)			(7,000)
Group profit			1,000

Mid-year disposals

Example 12.4 illustrates the disposal of Parent's entire holding nine months into the current year. The investor started the year with two wholly owned subsidiaries and its consolidated accounts at the end of the previous year included the results and net assets of both subsidiaries, in addition to those of the parent. Nine months into the current year, Parent disposes of its shares in Subsidiary$_1$. This has the following implications:

- consolidated profit for the year includes all profits of Parent and Subsidiary$_2$, and only nine months' profit of Subsidiary$_1$. Because Parent had no stake in Subsidiary$_1$ for the final three months of the year *and* the consolidated profit and loss account reports group results for the 12 months ended 31 March 20X8, profits of Subsidiary$_1$ for the three months after disposal are excluded from the consolidated profit and loss account

- group profit on disposal must include the effect of relinquishing access to retained profits earned in the current year up to the date of disposal, in addition to the post-acquisition retained earnings of Subsidiary_1 up to the beginning of the year
- the consolidated balance sheet at 31 March 20X8 will include assets and liabilities of Parent and Subsidiary_2. The balance sheet reports net assets controlled by the group on the last day of the year. Assets and liabilities of Subsidiary_1 are excluded because the group no longer controls these net assets.

Example 12.4 also illustrates the effect of two different policies for goodwill. Solution 1 assumes that all goodwill has been fully written off against consolidated reserves by the end of March 20X7 and Solution 2 assumes that goodwill was capitalised and not amortised.

Example 12.4 Mid-year disposal of shares in subsidiary: sale of total shareholding

Example

Balance sheets at 31.3.20X7	**Parent**	**Subsidiary_1**	**Subsidiary_2**
	€	€	€
Sundry net assets	6,000	4,000	4,500
Investment in			
Subsidiary_1 100%	4,000	—	—
Subsidiary_2 100%	5,000	—	—
	15,000	4,000	4,500
Share capital	10,000	2,000	3,000
Revenue reserves	5,000	2,000	1,500
	15,000	4,000	4,500

Parent acquired its shares in the two subsidiaries when pre-acquisition revenue reserves were:

Subsidiary_1	€500
Subsidiary_2	€1,000

Parent sells its shares in Subsidiary_1 for €6,500 on 31.12.20X7.

Profit and loss accounts for year ended 31.3.20X8	**Parent**	**Subsidiary_1**	**Subsidiary_2**
	€	€	€
Operating profit	4,000	2,400	1,500
Exceptional item: Profit on disposal ($€6{,}500_{\text{proceeds}} - €4{,}000_{\text{cost}}$)	2,500	—	—
Profit before taxation	6,500	2,400	1,500
Taxation	(2,000)	(800)	(700)
Profit after taxation	4,500	1,600	800
Retained profit b/f	5,000	2,000	1,500
Retained profit c/f	9,500	3,600	2,300

Required

Prepare the consolidated profit and loss account for the year ended 31.3.20X8, assuming:

1. All goodwill has been amortised by 31.3.20X7.
2. Goodwill is not amortised.

continued overleaf

Example 12.4 Continued

Solution 1 Goodwill amortised
Consolidated profit and loss account for year ended 31.3.20X8

	€
Profit [€4,000$_{Parent}$ + (€2,400 x $^9/_{12}$)$_{Subsidiary_1}$ + €1,500$_{Subsidiary_2}$]	7,300
Exceptional item (W_2)	1,300
Profit before taxation	8,600
Taxation [€2,000$_{Parent}$ + (€800 x $^9/_{12}$)$_{Subsidiary_1}$ + €700$_{Subsidiary_2}$]	(3,300)
Profit after taxation	5,300
Retained profit b/f (W_3)	4,500
Retained profit c/f (W_4)	9,800

Workings

W_1 Goodwill on acquisition	**$Subsidiary_1$**	**$Subsidiary_2$**
	€	€
Investment at cost	4,000	5,000
Net assets at acquisition		
Share capital	(2,000)	(3,000)
Reserves	(500)	(1,000)
Goodwill	1,500	1,000
W_2 Group profit on disposal	€	€
Profit in Parent's profit and loss account [€6,500$_{proceeds}$ – €4,000$_{cost}$]		2,500
Less: Post-acquisition retained profit 'sold'		
At 31.3.20X7 (€2,000$_{retained\ profits\ at\ disposal}$ – €500$_{pre\text{-}acquisition}$)	1,500	
Profit for year ($^9/_{12}$ x €1,600)	1,200	
	(2,700)	
Less goodwill amortised (W_1)	1,500	(1,200)
Group profit*		1,300

W_3 Retained profit b/f	€
Parent	5,000
$Subsidiary_1$ (€2,000 – €500$_{pre\text{-}acquisition}$)	1,500
$Subsidiary_2$ (€1,500 – €1,000$_{pre\text{-}acquisition}$)	500
Less: Goodwill written off (W_1) (€1,500$_{Subsidiary_1}$ + €1,000$_{Subsidiary_2}$)	(2,500)
	4,500
W_4 Retained profit c/f	€
Parent	9,500
$Subsidiary_2$ (€2,300 – €1,000$_{pre\text{-}acquisition}$)	1,300
Less: Goodwill written off ($Subsidiary_2$)	(1,000)
	9,800

* **Alternative approach to calculating group profit on disposal**		€	€
Proceeds			6,500
Less: *Carrying amount of investment in group accounts*			
Unamortised goodwill – $Subsidiary_1$		0	
+ Parent's share of net assets – represented by	€		
Share capital	2,000		
Revenue reserves at disposal (2,000 + ($^9/_{12}$ × 1,600))	3,200	5,200	(5,200)
Group profit on disposal			1,300

Solution 2 Goodwill not amortised
Consolidated profit and loss account for year ended 31.3.20X8

	€
Profit [€4,000$_{Parent}$ + (€2,400 x $^9/_{12}$)$_{Subsidiary_1}$ + €1,500$_{Subsidiary_2}$]	7,300
Exceptional item (W_1)	(200)
Profit before taxation	7,100
Taxation [€2,000$_{Parent}$ + (€800 x $^9/_{12}$)$_{Subsidiary_1}$ + €700$_{Subsidiary_2}$]	(3,300)
Profit after taxation	3,800
Retained profit b/f (W_2)	7,000
Retained profit c/f (W_3)	10,800

Workings

W_1 Group loss on disposal

	€	€
Profit in Parent's profit and loss account [€6,500$_{proceeds}$ – €4,000$_{cost}$]		2,500
Less: Post-acquisition retained profit 'sold':	€	
At 31.3.20X7 (€2,000$_{retained\ profit\ at\ disposal}$ – €500$_{pre\text{-}acquisition}$)	1,500	
Profit for year ($^9/_{12}$ x €1,600)	1,200	
	2,700	
Less: Goodwill amortised	—	(2,700)
Group loss*		(200)

W_2 Retained profit b/f

	€
Parent	5,000
$Subsidiary_1$ (€2,000 – €500$_{pre\text{-}acquisition}$)	1,500
$Subsidiary_2$ (€1,500 – €1,000$_{pre\text{-}acquisition}$)	500
	7,000

W_3 Retained profit c/f

	€
Parent	9,500
$Subsidiary_2$ (€2,300 – €1,000$_{pre\text{-}acquisition}$)	1,300
	10,800

* **Alternative approach to calculating group loss on disposal**		€	€
Proceeds			6,500
Less: *Carrying amount of investment in group accounts*			
Unamortised goodwill – $Subsidiary_1$		1,500	
+ Parent's share of net assets – represented by	€		
Share capital	2,000		
Revenue reserves at disposal (2,000 + ($^9/_{12}$ × 1,600))	3,200	5,200	(6,700)
Group loss on disposal			(200)

Working 2 in Solution (1) and Working 1 in Solution (2) refer to *post-acquisition retained profit 'sold'*. This descriptive label requires further explanation. The consolidation procedure predominantly used so far in this book is the acquisition method of consolidation. One of the consequences of using this method is that post-acquisition retained earnings of subsidiaries are accumulated in group reserves. By definition, these reserves are retained by the subsidiary concerned and are not distributed to its shareholders. As long as the parent maintains its investment in the subsidiary, there is the possibility that these reserves will be distributed (either in cash or through the issue of bonus shares). Even without being distributed, accumulated retained earnings add value to the investment because the subsidiary has increased its net worth. The parent, as the majority shareholder, recognises its share of that increased net worth by adding the group's share of post-acquisition retained earnings to group reserves as they arise.

Once the parent sells the shares in its subsidiary, it relinquishes access to these retained earnings. Ideally, the proceeds of disposal will compensate for the earnings foregone. In effect, the group has anticipated earnings by including them in group profits prior to their being realised through dividend income or through proceeds of disposal. When the shares are disposed of, the profit recognised in the group accounts must be reduced to the extent that some of it has been anticipated in previous periods. In Example 12.4, profit/loss on disposal was calculated using two different approaches (W_2 in Solution 1 and W_1 in Solution 2). The approach set out in the workings highlighted the adjustment to the amount included in the parent company profit and loss account for the post-acquisition retained profits of the disposed subsidiary. The alternative approach focused on profit or loss as the difference between proceeds and carrying amount of the disposed asset.

The solutions to Example 12.4 do not include consolidated balance sheets. It would be useful at this point to test your understanding of the material covered in Part 2 of this book by preparing consolidated balance sheets for Example 12.4 under each of the two assumptions regarding goodwill treatment. The critical point to remember when preparing consolidated balance sheets after disposal of a subsidiary is that the consolidated balance sheet only includes the assets and liabilities of subsidiaries remaining at the balance sheet date. This should be contrasted with the position relating to the profit and loss account, where the profit of the subsidiary disposed of during the year is included in the consolidated profit and loss account up to the date of disposal.

Treatment of taxation on disposal profit

Companies are taxable on profits earned. The individual company is the taxable entity, rather than the group. Consequently, tax charged on disposal profit is calculated by reference to the profit earned by the parent company. Detailed discussion of provisions of tax legislation is beyond the scope of this book. Rather, a relatively simplistic approach is adopted in calculating tax charges on gains on disposals of subsidiaries. This allows illustration of the principle that the tax charge recognised by the parent is also the tax charge on disposal profits included in the group profit and loss account. Example 12.5 illustrates the treatment of taxation charged on disposal profits.

Example 12.5 Tax on disposal of shares in subsidiary

Example

Parent purchased all Subsidiary's €100,000 share capital for €180,000 when Subsidiary's revenue reserves were €60,000.

Parent sold all its shares in Subsidiary for €300,000 when Subsidiary's revenue reserves were €140,000.

Assume capital gains tax is 30% and that goodwill has not been written off.

Required

Calculate the profit on disposal, after tax, in both the individual accounts of the parent and in the group accounts. Reconcile the parent's and the group's profit.

Solution

Individual accounts of Parent		€
Profit (€300,000$_{proceeds}$ – €180,000$_{cost}$)		120,000
Taxation at 30%		(36,000)
Profit after taxation		84,000

Consolidated accounts		
Parent's share of Subsidiary's net assets at disposal date	€	€
Share capital	100,000	
Revenue reserves	140,000	240,000
Unamortised goodwill (€180,000$_{cost}$ – €160,000$_{net\ assets\ at\ acquisition}$)		20,000
Carrying amount of investment in group accounts		(260,000)
Proceeds		300,000
Profit		40,000
Taxation (same amount as in Parent's accounts)		(36,000)
Profit after taxation		4,000

Reconciliation of individual company and group profit	€
Profit after taxation in individual accounts of Parent	84,000
Less: Post-acquisition reserves no longer consolidated (€140,000$_{reserves\ at\ date\ of\ disposal}$ – €60,000$_{reserves\ at\ acquisition\ date}$)	(80,000)
Group profit after taxation	4,000

Sale of part of investor's shares in subsidiary

The preceding section dealt with disposals where the parent disposed of its entire holding in a subsidiary, either at the beginning of the period or during the accounting period. In this section, disposal of part of the parent's shareholding is dealt with. Three possible outcomes of the part-disposal are addressed. After the disposal of shares in the investee the investor can:

1 continue to control the subsidiary
2 exercise significant influence over the investee
3 have a simple trade investment remaining.

Part-disposal – control retained

There are two consequences when an investor sells some of its shares in a subsidiary but retains control. Minority interest is either created (where the subsidiary is wholly owned before the disposal) or increased. In addition, profit or loss on disposal is recorded in both the individual accounts of the parent and in the group accounts. The principles already explained in the context of a parent undertaking selling its entire holding of shares in a subsidiary are also applied when only part of the parent's holding is disposed of. In summary, these include:

- profit or loss in the individual accounts of the parent is the difference between proceeds and cost of the shares disposed of.
- profit or loss in the group accounts is:
  - the parent's profit or loss adjusted for
  - the proportion of the subsidiary's retained post-acquisition profits disposed of, net of goodwill amortisation.

In addition, where control is retained, the entire revenues and expenses of the subsidiary are included in the consolidated profit and loss account for the period under review. However, the minority interest is calculated in stages, i.e., the minority's share of pre-disposal profit after taxation of the subsidiary is added to the minority's share of post-disposal profit after tax. The percentage minority share will be different pre- and post-disposal.

Example 12.6 illustrates how disposal of 25% of shares of a wholly owned subsidiary, half-way through the year, is dealt with in the consolidated profit and loss account. The group profit on disposal is based on Parent's profit on disposal in the first instance. However, this must be reduced by the group's share of post-acquisition profits of Subsidiary which are now effectively sold. Working 1 in Example 12.6 details the calculations of disposal profits. Parent's profit is €1,500, while the group profit is €1,075. The difference of €425 is the group's share of Subsidiary's post-acquisition retained profits (25% of €1,700), which were included in consolidated retained profits from earlier periods and to which the group relinquishes access on disposal of 25% of its shares.

Example 12.6 Disposal of shares in subsidiary: sale of part-shareholding, control retained

Example

Parent acquired 100% of Subsidiary when pre-acquisition profits were €1,000.

Balance sheets at 31.12.20X7

	Parent	Subsidiary	Consolidated
	€	€	€
Assets	8,000	6,000	14,000
Investment in Subsidiary (cost)	8,000	—	—
Goodwill	—	—	3,000
	16,000	6,000	17,000
Share capital	10,000	4,000	10,000
Revenue reserves	6,000	2,000	7,000
	16,000	6,000	17,000

On 30.6.20X8 Parent sold 25% of Subsidiary for €3,500. Profit on disposal is not included in the extract from Parent's profit and loss account for the year ended 31.12.20X8 which follows. Goodwill is not amortised.

Extract from profit and loss accounts: year ended 31.12.20X8

	Parent	Subsidiary
	€	€
Operating profit before taxation	4,000	2,500
Taxation	(1,900)	(1,100)
Profit after taxation	2,100	1,400

Ignore taxation on disposal profit

Required

Set out the consolidated profit and loss account columnar workings for the year ended 31.12.20X8.

Solution

Consolidated profit and loss account columnar workings: year ended 31.12.20X8

	Parent	Subsidiary	Adjustment	Total
	€	€	€	€
Operating profit	4,000	2,500		6,500
Exceptional profit (W_1)	1,500		(425)	1,075
Profit before taxation	5,500	2,500	(425)	7,575
Taxation	(1,900)	(1,100)		(3,000)
Profit after taxation	3,600	1,400	(425)	4,575
Minority interest				
(€1,400 x $^6/_{12}$ x 0%)		—		
(€1,400 x $^6/_{12}$ x 25%)		(175)		(175)
	3,600	1,225	(425)	4,400
Profit b/f	6,000	1,000		7,000
Reserves no longer consolidated		(425)	425	
	9,600	1,800	—	11,400

Workings

W_1 Profit on disposal	€	€
Proceeds of disposal		3,500
Investment at cost (25% x €8,000)		(2,000)
Profit in Parent's accounts		1,500
Post-acquisition retained profits 'sold':		
Retained at 1.1.20X8 (€2,000 – €1,000 $_{\text{pre-acquisition}}$)	1,000	
Retained to date of disposal ($^6/_{12}$ x €1,400)	700	
	1,700	
25% 'sold'	425	(425)
Group profit*		1,075

* **Alternative approach to calculating group profit on disposal**		€	€
Proceeds			3,500
Less: *Carrying amount of investment in group accounts*			
Unamortised goodwill – Subsidiary_1		3,000	
+ Parent's share of net assets – represented by	€		
Share capital	4,000		
Revenue reserves at disposal (€2,000 + ($^6/_{12}$ × €1,400))	2,700	6,700	
		9,700	
Group share disposed of: 25%			(2,425)
Group profit on disposal			1,075

One further point worth highlighting in Example 12.6 is the minority interest amount in the columnar consolidated profit and loss account workings. There was no minority interest in Subsidiary before the disposal of Parent's shares. After disposal, Parent only owns 75% of Subsidiary. Therefore, the minority is entitled to their share of profits from 30 June 20X8, i.e., for the last six months of the current year. Therefore, minority interest in the group profit after taxation is 25% of six months' profits of Subsidiary (25% x $^6/_{12}$ x €1,400).

The adjustment to retained earnings brought forward for *reserves no longer consolidated* in Example 12.6 represents the group's share of post-acquisition profits which have been disposed of (and which are subsequently part of minority interest in the consolidated balance sheet). As a result of this adjustment, the proportion of Subsidiary's reserves previously included in group retained earnings (as part of post-acquisition retained earnings of Subsidiary at the beginning of the year), but no longer available to the group, is removed from Subsidiary's column. The adjustment does not affect the total column. Group retained earnings at the end of the year are not adjusted. However, the group share of the post-acquisition retained earnings of Subsidiary associated with the disposed shares has now been realised by Parent and is included in its profit and loss account balance rather than in Subsidiary's.

Part-disposal – significant influence retained

When an investor sells some of its shares but retains significant influence over the former subsidiary, the investment is classified as an associate and is accounted for using the equity method from the date of disposal. This means that the entire revenues and expenses of the subsidiary are included in the consolidated profit and loss account only up to the date of disposal (and the appropriate minority interest is identified). From the date the investment becomes an associate, the group's share of profit before taxation and the group's share of taxation are included in the consolidated profit and loss account. In addition, profit or loss on disposal is recorded in both the individual accounts of the parent and in the group accounts. The principles of accounting for disposals, already explained in the context of a parent undertaking selling its entire holding of shares in a subsidiary (and in the context of selling some of its holding but retaining control), are also applied when there is a loss of control through disposal of the parent's majority holding. In summary, these include:

- Profit or loss in the individual accounts of the parent is the difference between proceeds and cost of the shares disposed of.
- Profit or loss in the group accounts is:
  - parent's profit or loss on disposal adjusted for
  - the proportion of the subsidiary's retained post-acquisition profits disposed of, net of goodwill amortisation.

If the subsidiary was not wholly owned before disposal, there will be a minority interest up to the date of disposal. The minority interest is based on the proportion of profits earned while the investment was classified as a subsidiary. From the time the investment is classified as an associate, the equity basis of accounting requires a one-line consolidation in the consolidated balance sheet and only group share of profit before taxation, and group share of taxation, in the consolidated profit and loss account. Thus, there is no minority interest under the equity method of accounting.

Example 12.7 illustrates how disposal of 75% of shares of a previously wholly owned subsidiary is dealt with in the consolidated profit and loss account.

Example 12.7 Disposal of shares in subsidiary: sale of part-shareholding, associate remains

Example

Parent acquired all the shares in $Subsidiary_1$ and $Subsidiary_2$ when pre-acquisition revenue reserves were:

$Subsidiary_1$ €500
$Subsidiary_2$ €1,000

Balance sheets at 31.12.20X7

	Parent	$Subsidiary_1$	$Subsidiary_2$
	€	€	€
Assets	6,000	4,000	4,500
Investment in			
$Subsidiary_1$	4,000	—	—
$Subsidiary_2$	5,000	—	—
	15,000	4,000	4,500
Share capital	10,000	2,000	3,000
Revenue reserves	5,000	2,000	1,500
	15,000	4,000	4,500

Profit and loss accounts for year ended 31.12.20X8 (extract)

	Parent	$Subsidiary_1$	$Subsidiary_2$
	€	€	€
Operating profit for year	2,000	1,600	800

On 1.1.20X8, Parent sold 75% of its shares in $Subsidiary_1$ for €4,300. Profit on disposal is not included in operating profit. Assume goodwill is not amortised.
Ignore taxation

Required

(i) Prepare the consolidated profit and loss account for the year ended 31.12.20X8.
(ii) Indicate how investment in $Subsidiary_1$ would be dealt with in the consolidated balance sheet at that date.
(iii) Reconcile the balance sheet amount for *Investment in associate*.

Solution

(i) Consolidated profit and loss account for year ended 31.12.20X8

	€
Profit for year (€2,000 + €800)	2,800
Share of profit of associate (25% x €1,600)	400
Group profit before exceptional item	3,200
Exceptional item (W_1)	175
	3,375
Retained profit c/f [€5,000$_{\text{Parent}}$ + €1,500$_{\text{Subsidiary 1}}$ + €500$_{\text{Subsidiary 2}}$]	7,000
	10,375

(ii) Consolidated balance sheet at 31.12.20X8 (extract)

	€
Investment in associate	
Share of net assets [25% x €5,600]	1,400
Unamortised goodwill [25% x (€4,000$_{\text{cost}}$ – €2,500$_{\text{net assets at acquisition}}$)]	375
	1,775

(iii) Reconciliation of balance sheet amount

Cost + post-acquisition retained profit of associate – goodwill amortised	
[€1,000 + (25% x (€1,500$_{\text{to beginning of year}}$ + €1,600$_{\text{current year}}$)) – 0]	1,775

continued overleaf

Example 12.7 Continued

Workings

W_1 Group profit on disposal

	€	€
Profit in Parent's profit and loss account$_{[€4,300 - (75\% \times €4,000)]}$		1,300
Less: Post-acquisition retained profit 'sold'		
[75% x (€2,000$_{\text{retained profit at disposal}}$ – €500$_{\text{at acquisition}}$)]	1,125	
Less: Goodwill amortised	—	(1,125)
Group profit*		175

*** Alternative approach to calculating group profit on disposal**

	€	€	€
Proceeds			4,300
Less: *Carrying amount of investment in group accounts*			
Unamortised goodwill (€4,000$_{\text{cost}}$ – €2,500$_{\text{net assets}}$)		1,500	
+ Parent's share of net assets – represented by	€		
Share capital	2,000		
Revenue reserves at disposal	2,000	4,000	
		5,500	
Group share disposed of: 75%			(4,125)
Group profit on disposal			175

Part-disposal – simple trade investment remains

When an investor sells the majority of its shares in an investee (which was previously categorised as a subsidiary) and retains insufficient shares for the investment to be classified as either a subsidiary or an associate, the remaining investment must be accounted for as a simple investment. This means that the investment is included at cost in the consolidated balance sheet and that dividend income alone is included in the consolidated profit and loss account. The meaning of 'cost' where a simple investment remains after a part disposal of shares in a former associate has been clarified by FRS 9 *Associates and Joint Ventures.* Paragraph 43 of FRS 9 states:

> The initial carrying amount of any interest retained in a former associate or joint venture is a surrogate cost derived from the former carrying amount rather than any consideration paid.

FRS 9 also refers (in paragraph 43) to the equivalence of this treatment to that required for former subsidiaries under paragraph 47 of FRS 2:

> The treatment required for remaining investments in former associates and joint ventures is similar to that applied to any remaining interest in an entity that has ceased to be a subsidiary (paragraph 47 of FRS 2).

Although paragraph 47 of FRS 2 does not specify the amount at which any remaining simple investment should be carried following a part-disposal of shares in a former subsidiary, FRS 9 describes the required treatment clearly in paragraph 42:

> When an entity ceases to be either an associate or joint venture, the initial carrying amount of any interest retained in the entity is based on the percentage retained of the final carrying amount for the former associate or joint venture at the date the entity ceased to qualify as such, including any related goodwill as required by paragraph 40.

Paragraph 40 of FRS 9 requires that profit or loss on disposal of an investment (in an associate or joint venture) should be calculated after taking into account any related goodwill that has not previously been either written off through the profit and loss account or attributed to prior period amortisation or impairment applying the transitional provisions of FRS 10 *Goodwill and Intangible Assets*. Chapter 17 discusses FRS 10 in more detail.

Consequently, the calculation of profit or loss on disposal of a part-interest in a former subsidiary, where a simple investment remains, is exactly the same as the profit or loss on disposal explained earlier in this chapter. This includes:

- profit or loss in the individual accounts of the parent is the difference between proceeds and cost of the shares disposed of
- profit or loss in the group accounts is:
  - parent's profit or loss adjusted for
  - the proportion of the subsidiary's retained post-acquisition profits disposed of, net of goodwill amortisation.

The simple investment will be included in the consolidated balance sheet at its *surrogate* cost. According to FRS 9, this is group share of net assets of the investee plus the group's remaining share of unamortised goodwill at the time of change of status to simple investment. An alternative way of identifying surrogate cost is by taking actual cost plus group share of post-acquisition retained earnings (to the date of disposal of the majority share), minus accumulated amortisation on related goodwill up to the date of disposal. This initial post-disposal carrying amount should be reviewed and written down, if necessary to its recoverable amount.

Example 12.8 illustrates the treatment of a disposal where the remaining investment is categorised as a simple investment. Profit on disposal in the consolidated profit and loss account is based on the group's carrying amount at the date of disposal of the 90% of shares sold. The remaining 10% investment in the former subsidiary is included in the consolidated balance sheet at the surrogate cost. As detailed earlier, the surrogate cost is the actual cost of €500 plus the group's share (10%) of the post-acquisition retained earnings up to the date of disposal (€1,300 – see W_1 in Example 12.8).

Example 12.8 Disposal of shares in subsidiary: sale of part-shareholding, simple investment remains

Example

Details are as for Example 12.7, but instead of disposing of Subsidiary_1, assume Parent sells 90% of Subsidiary_2 for €6,500 on 31.12.20X8.

Required

(i) Prepare the consolidated profit and loss account for the year ended 31.12.20X8.
(ii) Indicate how investment in Subsidiary_2 would be dealt with in the consolidated balance sheet at that date.
(iii) Reconcile the balance sheet amount for Investment in associate.

Solution

(i) Consolidated profit and loss account for year ended 31.12.20X8

	€
Profit for year (€2,000$_{\text{Parent}}$ + €1,600$_{\text{Subsidiary 1}}$ + €800$_{\text{Subsidiary 2}}$)	4,400
Exceptional item (W_2)	830
	5,230
Retained profit b/f [€5,000$_{\text{Parent}}$ + €1,500$_{\text{Subsidiary}_1}$ + €500$_{\text{Subsidiary}_2}$]	7,000
	12,230

continued overleaf

Example 12.8 Continued

(ii) Consolidated balance sheet at 31.12.20X8 (extract)

		€
Simple investment		
Share of net assets [10% x €5,300 $_{€4,500 + €800}$]		530
Unamortised goodwill [10% x (€5,000$_{cost}$ – €4,000$_{net\ assets\ at\ acquisition}$)]		100
		630

(iii) Reconciliation of balance sheet amount

Cost + post-acquisition retained profit to date of reclassification as simple investment [€500 + (10% x €1,300$_{post\text{-}acquisition\ to\ date\ of\ disposal}$)][1]	630

Workings

		€
W$_1$ Post-acquisition profits of Subsidiary$_2$ to date of disposal [€1,500$_{reserves\ at\ 1\ January}$ – €1,000$_{pre\text{-}acquisition}$ + €800$_{earnings\ for\ year}$]		1,300

	€	€
W$_2$ Group profit on disposal		
Profit in Parent's profit and loss account$_{[€6,500 - (90\% \times €5,000)]}$		2,000
Less: Post-acquisition retained profit 'sold'		
90% x €1,300$_{(W1)}$	1,170	
Less: Goodwill amortised	—	(1,170)
Group profit[2]		830

[1] Had the goodwill been fully amortised at the date of disposal, the carrying amount would have been reduced by €100 (10% of goodwill of €1,000).

[2] **Alternative approach to calculating group profit on disposal**

	€	€	€
Proceeds			6,500
Less: *Carrying amount of investment in group accounts*			
Unamortised goodwill (€5,000$_{cost}$ – €4,000$_{net\ assets}$)		1,000	
+ Parent's share of net assets – represented by	€		
Share capital	3,000		
Revenue reserves at disposal (€1,500 + €800)	2,300	5,300	
		6,300	
Group share disposed of: 90%			(5,670)
Group profit on disposal			830

In the full consolidated balance sheet for Example 12.8, Subsidiary$_1$ would be consolidated on a line-by-line basis. Since Subsidiary$_2$ is a simple investment at year-end, its assets and liabilities are no longer included in the consolidated balance sheet. It is now included at its surrogate cost.

Summary

This chapter focused on the treatment of disposals of shares in subsidiaries. In particular, it explained why the profit or loss on disposal of shares in the investing company's own accounts is usually different from the profit or loss on disposal in the group accounts. In addition, it explained the impact of disposals on the consolidated profit and loss account for different disposal dates and for different proportions of shareholdings disposed.

Illustrations were provided to ensure that the multiple choice question, self-assessment exercises and the examination-style questions that follow can now be attempted with a reasonable expectation that the issues involved are understood.

Learning outcomes

After studying this chapter you should have learnt:

- how to calculate the group profit or loss on disposal of shares in a subsidiary or associate
- how to distinguish between the profit or loss in the individual accounts of the investing company and that in the consolidated accounts
- how amortised goodwill impacts on the calculation of group profit or loss on disposal
- how to identify the appropriate method of accounting, in the consolidated accounts, for the remaining investment (if any).

Multiple choice question

The solution to this question is presented in Appendix 1.

12.1 Gutman and Wilmer

Gutman bought 100% of the issued share capital of **Wilmer** for €3 million some years ago. On 30 June 20X9 it sold 80% of the shares for €5 million.

The summarised balance sheet of Wilmer as at 30 June 20X9 is as follows:

	€000
Net assets	6,000
Called up share capital	2,000
Profit and loss account	4,000
	6,000

The book value of Wilmer's net assets on acquisition by Gutman had been €2.9 million and this was considered to equate to fair value. Goodwill on acquisition is fully amortised through the profit and loss account by 1 July 20X8.

Ignoring taxation, the profit on disposal of the shares in Wilmer to be included in Gutman's consolidated profit and loss account for the year ended 30 June 20X9 is:

(a) €100,000
(b) €200,000
(c) €920,000
(d) €2.6 million

Self-assessment exercises

Solutions to these self-assessment exercises can be found at:
www.thomsonlearning.co.uk/accountingandfinance/piercebrennan

12.1 Atley, Bartram and Conway: Disposal of entire holding mid-year

Balance sheets as at 31 December 20X6

	Atley	**Bartram**	**Conway**
	€000	**€000**	**€000**
Fixed assets	1,200	700	510
Shares in subsidiary			
150,000 shares in Bartram	700	—	—
Net current assets/(liabilities)	100	100	(10)
	2,000	800	500

continued overleaf

	Atley €000	Bartram €000	Conway €000
Ordinary shares of €1 each	700	200	100
Reserves	900	600	400
12% debentures	400	—	—
	2,000	800	500

Summarised profit and loss accounts for year ended 31 December 20X6

	Atley	Bartram	Conway
Profit before taxation	500	100	50
Taxation	260	52	26
	240	48	24
Proposed dividend	60	20	—
Retained profit	180	28	24

The following information is relevant:

1. Atley acquired 75% of the issued ordinary share capital of Bartram on 30 September 20X6.
2. On 1 July 20X6, Atley sold its 100% holding in Conway for €3 per share. Atley originally acquired the shares ten years ago at a cost of €1.50 per share when the reserves of Conway were €200,000. Conway's share capital has remained unchanged since that date.
3. In its draft accounts, Atley has credited its profit on disposal of the shares directly to reserves.
4. Profits accrue evenly throughout the year.
5. Atley does not take credit in its own accounts for dividends until they have been received.

Required

(a) Compute the profit on disposal of the investment in Conway to be shown in the individual accounts of Atley (ignore taxation).
(b) Calculate the consolidated reserves for the consolidated balance sheet as at 31 December 20X5.
(c) Prepare the consolidated balance sheet of the group as at 31 December 20X6.
(d) Prepare the consolidated profit and loss account for the year ended 31 December 20X6.
(e) Prepare a reconciliation of the movement in the consolidated reserves of the group for the year to 31 December 20X6.

12.2 Hot, Cross and Bun: Part-disposal – control retained

The following are the summarised accounts of **Hot**, **Cross** and **Bun** for the year ended 30 September 20X6:

Summarised profit and loss accounts

	Hot €000	Cross €000	Bun €000
Operating profit/(loss)	250	(20)	65
Taxation	128	—	25
	122	(20)	40
Proposed dividend	80	—	20
Retained profit/(loss) for the year	42	(20)	20

Summarised balance sheets at 30 September 20X6

	Hot €000	Cross €000	Bun €000
Sundry net assets	430	110	160
70,000 ordinary shares in Cross at cost	84	—	—
90,000 ordinary shares in Bun at cost	180	—	—
	694	110	160
Share capital – ordinary shares of €1 each	400	100	100
Profit on sale of shares in Cross	10	—	—
Retained profits	284	10	60
	694	110	160

You are provided with the following additional information:

1 On 1 October 20X0, Hot purchased 90% of the share capital of Cross at a price of €1.20 per share. On that date the retained profits of Cross were equivalent to 40 cent per share.
2 On 31 March 20X6, Hot disposed of 20,000 shares in Cross at a price of €1.70 per share.
3 On 1 July 20X6, Hot purchased 90,000 shares in Bun for €180,000.
4 Hot does not take credit in its own accounts for dividends until they have been received.
5 The operating profits/(losses) of each company have arisen evenly throughout the year.
6 Cross has not paid any dividends since 1 October 20X0 and Bun has not declared any dividends, except as shown in the accounts, since 1 October 20X5.

Required

Prepare the consolidated profit and loss account for the year ended 30 September 20X6 and the consolidated balance sheet of Hot and its subsidiaries as at 30 September 20X6.

12.3 Leap, Jump and Step: Part-disposal – associate remains

Set out here are the draft accounts of **Leap**, **Jump** and **Step**.

Balance sheets as at 31 March 20X4

	Leap	Jump	Step
	€000	€000	€000
Fixed assets	3,205	1,200	1,760
Investments (note 1)	2,975	—	—
Stocks	1,740	960	1,060
Debtors	910	380	840
Bank balance	950	230	—
Bank overdraft	—	—	(130)
Creditors	(1,850)	(940)	(910)
Proposed dividends	(200)	(100)	(100)
Total net assets	7,730	1,730	2,520
Ordinary shares of €1 each	2,000	800	700
10% preference shares of €1 each	—	300	—
Share premium account	1,500	—	—
Revenue reserves	2,030	630	1,620
	5,530	1,730	2,320
Long-term loan	2,200	—	200
Total capital employed	7,730	1,730	2,520

Profit and loss accounts for year ended 31 March 20X4 (extract)

	Leap	Jump	Step
	€000	€000	€000
Profit for year	523	430	310
Dividends: Preference shares – paid 30.9.20X3	—	(30)	—
Ordinary shares – proposed	(200)	(100)	(100)
– paid 30.9.20X3	—	(100)	—
	323	200	210

Additional information is given as follows:

1 The investments were acquired several years ago and the figure in the balance sheet of Leap is made up as follows:

	Jump	Step	Total
	€000	€000	€000
800,000 ordinary shares at cost	1,880		1,880
560,000 ordinary shares at cost		1,655	1,655
Dividend received		(50)	(50)
200,000 preference shares at cost	190		190
Less: Proceeds of sale of 500,000 ordinary shares on 1.10.20X3	(700)		(700)
	1,370	1,605	2,975

continued overleaf

2 The revenue reserves of Jump and Step at acquisition were €520,000 and €900,000, respectively. There were no changes in share capital since dates of acquisition.
3 The profit and loss account of Leap includes the relevant dividends paid by the subsidiaries for the year ended 31 March 20X4, but none of the dividends proposed.
4 The profits of each of the companies accrue evenly throughout the year.

Required
Prepare the consolidated profit and loss account and consolidated balance sheet of Leap and group, for the year ended 31 March 20X4.

12.4 Knife, Fork and Spoon: Part-disposal – variety of outcomes

The following are the balance sheets of **Knife**, **Fork** and **Spoon** at 31 December 20X8:

	Knife	Fork	Spoon
	€	€	€
Sundry assets	200	800	500
Investments*	800	—	—
	1,000	800	500
Ordinary share capital in shares of €1 each	600	400	200
Revenue reserves	400	400	300
	1,000	800	500

* Knife acquired 300 shares in Fork for €500 when the balance on Fork's profit and loss account was €200, and 160 shares in Spoon for €300 when the balance on Spoon's profit and loss account was €100.

The companies' profit and loss accounts for the year ended 31 December 20X9 were as follows:

	Knife	Fork	Spoon
	€	€	€
Profit before taxation	500	400	300
Taxation	(200)	(100)	(100)
Profit after taxation	300	300	200
Dividends	(100)	—	—
Retained profit for year	200	300	200
Retained profit b/f	400	400	300
Retained profit c/f	600	700	500

Required
Prepare the consolidated profit and loss account of Knife for the year ended 31 December 20X9 and its consolidated balance sheet as at that date under each of the following assumptions:
(a) Knife sold 160 shares in Spoon on 1 January for €700 cash.
(b) Knife sold 40 shares in Spoon on 1 April for €180 cash.
(c) Knife sold 150 shares in Spoon on 1 July for €600 cash.
(d) Knife sold 100 shares in Spoon on 1 October for €500 cash.

Note: Disposal proceeds were all received in cash.

Examination-style questions

12.1 Adam, Bono and Clayton: Disposal of entire holding mid-year

Adam acquired 160,000 shares in **Bono** for €440,000 cash during 20X3. Bono's net assets amounted to €420,000 at the date of acquisition.

During 20X6 Adam formed a wholly owned subsidiary, **Clayton**, by subscribing for 100,000 shares at par.

On 30 September 20X8, Adam sold all of its shares in Bono to **Florist**. The consideration received was €600,000 in cash and 100,000 €1 8% preference shares in **Florist** valued at €1.20 each.

Adam amortises goodwill arising on consolidation over ten years, charging a full year's amortisation in the year of purchase and none in the year of sale.

The summarised accounts for the year ended 31 December 20X8 are as follows:

Balance sheets at 31 December 20X8

	Adam	Bono	Clayton
	€	€	€
Tangible fixed assets	624,768	374,693	184,759
Investments: Shares in subsidiaries	540,000	—	—
Net current assets	254,432	164,487	100,865
	1,419,200	539,180	285,624
Ordinary share capital (€1 shares)	400,000	200,000	100,000
Profit and loss account	1,019,200	339,180	185,624
	1,419,200	539,180	285,624

Profit and loss accounts for year ended 31 December 20X8

	€	€	€
Turnover	2,748,538	1,828,692	631,229
Operating expenses	(2,508,538)	(1,668,692)	(579,229)
Operating profit	240,000	160,000	52,000
Dividends received	20,000	—	—
Profit before taxation	260,000	160,000	52,000
Taxation	(80,000)	(60,000)	(18,000)
Profit after taxation	180,000	100,000	34,000
Dividends			
Interim paid 31 July 20X8	(40,000)	(20,000)	(4,000)
Final proposed	(40,000)	(20,000)	(10,000)
Retained for year	100,000	60,000	20,000

Additional information:

1. The transactions relating to the disposal of the shares in Bono have not been reflected in the summarised accounts of Adam.
2. Tax would be charged at 25% on any gains on disposal of shares.
3. Dividends receivable have not been accrued by Adam.

Required

(a) Calculate the profit or loss on the disposal of the shares held in Bono as it would be included in the individual accounts of Adam and in the consolidated accounts of Adam Group.

(b) Prepare the consolidated balance sheet as at 31 December 20X8 and the consolidated profit and loss account for the year ended on 31 December 20X8 in as much detail as the information given permits.

Note: You may ignore the requirements of FRS 3 to highlight the impact of discontinued activities on the profit and loss account.

12.2 Pen and Nib: Part-disposal – control retained

On 30 December 20X6, **Pen** purchased 120,000 ordinary shares, *cum* dividend, in **Nib**, for €150,000. The balance on the profit and loss account of Nib, after provision for a final dividend of €15,000, was €25,000.

In 20X7, Nib paid the final dividend for 20X6 and Pen credited its portion to the profit and loss account for 20X7.

On 30 June 20X9, Pen purchased an additional 15,000 shares in Nib for €20,000.

On 30 December 20X9, Pen sold 30,000 of the shares which it had purchased in 20X6 for €50,000. It recorded this by debiting the bank account and crediting shares in Nib with €50,000.

During 20X9 Pen sold goods to Nib at invoice prices equal to cost price plus 25%. On 31 December 20X9 Nib still had some of these goods in stock valued at the invoiced price of €15,000.

Summarised final accounts for the year ended 31 December 20X9 were as follows:

	Pen	Nib
Profit and loss accounts	€	€
Profit after taxation	86,000	1,000
Proposed dividend	5,000	—
	81,000	1,000
Balance brought forward 1 January 20X9	62,000	27,000
	143,000	28,000
Balance sheets at 31 December 20X9	€	€
Fixed assets	287,000	126,000
Shares in Nib	120,000	—
Net current assets	136,000	52,000
	543,000	178,000
Ordinary shares of €1 each fully paid	400,000	150,000
Profit and loss account	143,000	28,000
	543,000	178,000

Required

Prepare:

(a) The consolidated profit and loss account for Pen, and its subsidiary, for the year ended 31 December 20X9.

(b) The consolidated balance sheet as at that date.

12.3 Holdings: Mid-year disposal of entire holding or of majority holding – associate remaining

Holdings had acquired a 75% holding of 150,000 €1 ordinary shares in **Subbat** on 1 November 20X0 for €700,000, at which date there was a credit balance on reserves of €200,000 in Subbat and the net assets of the company at fair values totalled €800,000.

Holdings makes up its accounts to 31 October each year and the goodwill arising on consolidation was amortised over five years, commencing the year after acquisition.

Acquisitive offered to purchase some or all of the shares in Subbat from Holdings with effect from 30 June 20X2 on the following terms:

- Offer 1 was to purchase 150,000 shares for €1,350,000.
- Offer 2 was to purchase 100,000 shares for €720,000.

The following information was available for the year ending 31 October 20X2 prior to the acceptance of either offer:

	Holdings €000	Subbat €000
Profit after tax	500	240
Dividends paid prior to 30 June	60	40
Dividends proposed	125	100
Profit retained	315	100
Retained profit brought forward	1,025	400

Holdings accounts for dividends on a cash-received basis. Assume a corporation tax rate of 35%.

Required

(a) Calculate the gain or loss on disposal that will appear both in the accounts of Holdings and of the Holdings group as at 31 October 20X2 on the assumption that Offer 1 was accepted and Acquisitive purchased 150,000 €1 ordinary shares in Subbat on 30 June 20X2.

(b) Prepare the following statements on the assumption that Acquisitive purchased 100,000 €1 ordinary shares in Subbat on 30 June 20X2 (Offer 2):

(i) a profit and loss account starting with the profit after tax figure for the year ended 31 October 20X2, consolidating the results of Holdings and Subbat

(ii) a statement of movement on reserves for the group and for the parent company.

Part Four

Regulatory framework

13

Introduction to European, UK and international accounting regulations

Learning objectives

After studying this chapter you should be able to:

- discuss the sources of regulation underlying the preparation of group accounts
- appreciate the approaches to standard setting under UK GAAP and IAS GAAP
- summarise the accounting standards applicable to the preparation of group accounts
- differentiate between accounting requirements under UK GAAP and IAS GAAP
- apply different formats in presenting group profit and loss accounts and balance sheets

Introduction

Company financial accounting and reporting is governed by the requirements of companies' legislation, pronouncements of professional accountancy bodies and stock exchange regulations. Until about 25 years ago the publication of a company's accounts was viewed largely as a duty imposed by law to compel the directors of companies to account to shareholders for the funds entrusted to their management. The disclosures required by law were minimal and there was considerable discretion available to the directors in deciding on the accounting treatment of many of the major items in the accounts.

For EU countries, legal requirements changed consequent on EU company law directives, issued with the objective of promoting free trade among EU countries. Many of these directives deal with accounting issues in an effort to harmonise accounting treatment across countries. In relation to financial statements generally, the Fourth Directive standardised the format for presentation of profit and loss accounts and balance sheets and imposed substantial disclosure requirements. In relation to group accounts in particular, the Seventh Directive has had a significant impact. This Directive has been incorporated into the legislation of all EU countries. Many professional accounting pronouncements have put flesh on the legal requirements where technical accounting terminology has been used in the legislation or where the legislation provides opportunities for creative interpretations or variations in accounting practices which would be inconsistent with the harmonisation objective of the Directive.

Part 4 of this book discusses the professional accounting requirements in Financial Reporting Standards (FRSs) and in Statements of Standard Accounting Practice (SSAPs) currently applying to UK/Irish groups (referred to as *UK GAAP*), and those in the International Accounting Standards (IASs) of the International Accounting Standards Board (IASB), referred to as *IAS GAAP*.

In June 2000, the European Commission (EC) proposed that all EU-listed companies should be required to comply with IASs by the year 2005 (European Commission (2000). From the perspective of groups currently reporting under UK GAAP, this book highlights the impact on the presentation of group accounts arising from the impending switch to IASs.

This chapter provides an overview of the regulations applying to the preparation of group accounts in Europe. The chapters to follow in this part of the book expand on the detailed regulatory requirements.

Regulatory framework

In an attempt to harmonise accounting practice among EU countries, the EC published a number of documents, notably the Fourth and Seventh Company Law Directives on annual and consolidated accounts which have been adopted by EU countries in their national legislation. These have been successful in improving the comparability of accounts, thus facilitating cross-border business.

However, these Directives are not accepted as a basis for adequate financial reporting in major securities markets outside Europe. Consequently, in 1996, the EC put forward a new strategy to improve the financial reporting framework for European companies. The objectives of the new strategy were to promote:

- easier access for European companies in international capital markets
- improved comparability of consolidated accounts within the single European market.

The Commission's strategy is to associate the EU with the efforts of the International Accounting Standards Committee (IASC), now the International Accounting Standards Board (IASB) and IOSCO (International Organization of Securities Commissions) with a view to EU companies preparing consolidated accounts in conformity with IASs (soon to be International Financial Reporting Standards (IFRSs)) of the IASB. It is beyond the scope of this book to discuss the role and history of the IASB. However, this topic is well covered in the many publications on international accounting (see Bibliography).

In June 2000, the EC issued a policy document proposing that all European companies listed on regulated markets (including banks and other financial institutions) should be required to prepare consolidated accounts in accordance with IASs. In June 2002, the Council of Ministers of the EU approved the Commission's proposal. The Regulation that is now adopted will require the use of IASs and IFRSs by 1 January 2005, after a formal endorsement process. It is intended also that, within two years, the requirement will be extended to all companies preparing a public offer prospectus in accordance with the EU's Listing Particulars Directive.

Unlike Directives, EU Regulations have the force of law without requiring transposition into national legislation. The requirement to use IASs applies to the consolidated accounts of listed companies. However, member states can either require or allow unlisted companies to publish financial statements in accordance with the same set of standards as those for listed companies.

The Regulation also established an endorsement mechanism comprising the Accounting Regulatory Committee (chaired by the Commission) assisted by the European Financial Reporting Advisory Group (EFRAG).

European Directives

As has already been stated, the most important directives from an accounting point of view are the Fourth and Seventh Company Law Directives on annual and consolidated accounts.

The EU Fourth Directive, already enacted into law in EU member states, significantly extended legal financial reporting and disclosure requirements over those previously required. Incorporation of the requirements of the Fourth Directive has had a significant impact on the presentation of the profit and loss account and balance sheet (in particular by prescribing formats) and on the disclosures made therein.

The EU Seventh Directive deals with the preparation of group accounts and the provision of financial information on groups of companies. It was adopted by the EEC in 1983, to be implemented by member states by 1 January 1988, with enforcement from 1990.

The main provisions of the Seventh Directive deal with:

- requirement to prepare group accounts
- exemptions from requirement to prepare group accounts
- exclusion of subsidiaries and how to account for them.

As a result of the Directive, legal definitions of subsidiaries are based on the concept of control rather than ownership, i.e., having the ability to direct the financial and operating policies of other undertakings with a view to gaining economic benefit from their activities.

UK GAAP

Not only are consolidated accounts influenced by the Seventh Directive (through the legislation implementing that Directive in each EU country), but they are also influenced by local accounting standards. These standards are, to all intents and purposes, the same in the UK and the Republic of Ireland and the term *UK GAAP* is used in this book to refer to these regulations. (All professional accounting pronouncements in force at July 2002 are listed in Appendix 2. SSAPs and FRSs relating specifically to group accounts covered in this book are listed in Table 13.1 further on in this chapter.)

The Accounting Standards Board's (ASB) *Foreword to Accounting Standards* explains the authority, scope and application of accounting standards. Accounting standards are authoritative statements of how transactions should be reflected in financial statements. They are applicable to all financial statements whose purpose is to give a true and fair view.

The requirement that accounts give a true and fair view comes from legislation. While emanating from UK legislation, the Fourth Directive spread this requirement throughout the EU. Compliance with standards is generally necessary if financial statements are to give a true and fair view. The authority of the standards derives from the fact that they represent the views of the accounting profession on the appropriate treatment of particular items if accounts are to give a true and fair view. Accounting standards in the UK have explicit legal backing (but do *not* in the Republic of Ireland). In addition, members of six professional accounting bodies (including members of professional accounting bodies in Ireland) are expected to observe accounting standards.

True and fair view override

However, legislation allows directors to depart from legal requirements in order to comply with the true and fair view. The true and fair view overrides the detailed requirements of legislation. FRS 18 *Accounting Policies* provides guidance on the interpretation of statutory disclosure requirements where the true and fair view override provisions of legislation are invoked. Groups departing from explicit requirements of legislation must disclose (i) particulars of any departure, together with (ii) the reasons for any such departure and (iii) its effect.

Specifically, FRS 18 clarifies the legal disclosure requirements as follows:

- *particulars of any departure:*
  - a clear and unambiguous statement that there has been a departure and that the departure is necessary to give a true and fair view
  - the treatment the legislation would normally require and a description of the treatment actually adopted.
- *reasons for it:*
  - a statement explaining why the treatment adopted would not give a true and fair view.
- *its effect:*
  - a description of how the position in the accounts differs as a result of the departure, with quantification except (i) where quantification is already evident in the accounts; and (ii) when the effect cannot be quantified, in which case the directors should explain the circumstances.

These provisions are relevant to group accounts and crop up in subsequent chapters in exhibits which invoke these override provisions to depart from provisions of legislation (see, for example, Exhibits 15.6, 16.2, 17.9, 17.10 and 17.12).

IAS GAAP

IASs influence accounts in two ways. First, domestic standard setters are increasingly attempting to produce standards that comply as much as possible with IASs. Over recent years, there has been considerable cooperation between standard setters across the world. Consequently, with some exceptions, UK GAAP are consistent with IASs (as will be illustrated later in this chapter).

Second, companies that are quoted on stock exchanges outside their own country may adopt IASs to improve their acceptability in other jurisdictions. For example, the London Stock Exchange accepts from its registrants accounts prepared under IAS GAAP. However, the New York Stock Exchange does not yet do so.

Standard setting in the UK and Ireland

The institutional environment of corporate financial reporting began to change in the UK and Ireland in 1970 with the establishment of the Accounting Standards Committee (ASC). This body developed accounting standards which stipulated the appropriate accounting treatment for various transactions and which required disclosure of significant items in company accounts. ASC operated for 20 years. Following criticisms of standards and the standard setting process, it was replaced by the ASB in 1990.

The changes introduced by the expanded disclosure requirements of the Fourth and Seventh Directives have been accompanied by a change in the attitude of the management of many companies to the role of a company's accounts (although the two are not necessarily related). Accounts are now seen as not merely fulfilling a statutory obligation but as having a key role in projecting the corporate image and in conveying useful information to an increasingly financially sophisticated audience.

Accounting standards under UK GAAP

Accounting standards are authoritative statements of accounting practice on how particular transactions/events should be reflected in financial statements. They aim to reduce the variety of practice in the accounting treatment of the matters with which they deal. There are two types of accounting standard: SSAP and FRS.

SSAPs were developed between 1970 and 1990 by ASC, a body representative of the six main professional accounting bodies in Ireland and the UK. In all, 25 standards were issued, of which all but nine (at the time of writing) have since been withdrawn (see Appendix 2 for a list of SSAPs still in force at the time of writing).

Until August 1990, SSAPs were issued by the Councils of each of the six professional accounting bodies, which in turn required their members to comply with them. Criticisms of the standard setting process led to major changes in the system in 1990. To achieve greater independence and objectivity, a new standard setting regime, somewhat independent of the accounting profession, was established to replace the ASC. The revised structure is outlined diagrammatically in Figure 13.1 (only the basic structure is shown – not shown are a number of additional specialist committees that have also been established).

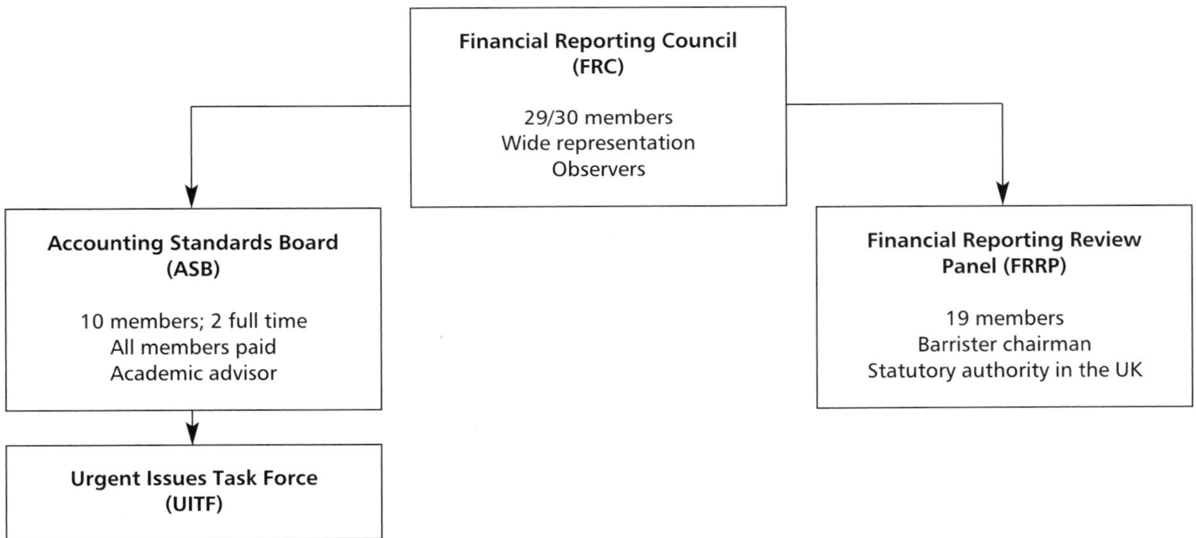

Figure 13.1 Standard-setting structure in the UK

The FRC determines general policy with regard to standard setting. It operates broadly as a board of directors, with responsibility for appointing the members of ASB, the FRRP and the UITF, ensuring they are adequately financed and guiding their activities so that all parties interested in financial reporting have their major concerns dealt with in a timely way. Members of the FRC represent users and preparers of financial statements, the profession, the financial community and the world of business and administration.

The ASB develops and issues FRSs in the UK. In the Republic of Ireland, all FRSs continue to be issued through the Institute of Chartered Accountants in Ireland (ICAI). The ASB is the first independent standard setting body in the UK and Ireland. First chaired by Sir David Tweedie (now Chairman of the IASB), and now chaired by Mary Keegan, formerly a partner with PricewaterhouseCoopers, the ASB adopted the extant SSAPs on its establishment. Since then, the ASB has issued 19 of its own FRSs (by December 2002).

The UITF was established by the ASB to provide a forum for the prompt review of urgent accounting issues that, in the absence of statutory or professional guidance, may be the subject of disparate or unsatisfactory treatment in practice. It assists the ASB by providing interim solutions to urgent accounting problems. This assists in preventing bad practice taking hold. The UITF has issued 35 *Abstracts* (by July 2002). Many of these have subsequently been incorporated into FRSs. (The remaining Abstracts in force at the time of writing are shown in Appendix 2.)

Enforcement of accounting standards under UK GAAP

Implementation of standards has some legal backing in the UK. UK legislation requires large companies to state whether the accounts have been prepared in accordance with applicable accounting standards and to disclose details of material departures.

The system operates differently in the Republic of Ireland. Because of funding requirements and changes in legislation which would be required to implement the new system, the Irish government decided in 1990 not to become directly involved in the activities of the FRC. However, in recognition of the importance of maintaining the correspondence between UK and Irish financial reporting practice, the government requested ICAI to act as the Irish standard setting body and to maintain a link with ASB. There is an ICAI representative and a government observer on FRC. ICAI adopts standards developed by ASB, adjusting them where necessary to reflect Irish legislation.

The position in Ireland will change on establishment of the Irish Auditing and Accounting Supervisory Authority, a new body formed to supervise the regulation of accountancy bodies. One of its recommended functions is to make '*arrangements for examining the validity of material departures from accepted accounting standards and practice by public limited companies*' (Report of the Review Group on Auditing, Government Publications, Dublin, 2000, p.126).

The ASB's *Foreword to Accounting Standards* states that compliance with accounting standards will normally be necessary for accounts to show a true and fair view. In applying accounting standards, it is important to be guided by the spirit and reasoning behind them. The six professional accounting bodies in Ireland and the UK expect their members to observe accounting standards and may enquire into apparent failures to do so or to ensure adequate disclosures of significant departures.

The FRRP examines departures from accounting standards by UK companies and may take court action if necessary. It examines and questions any identified or alleged material departures from accounting standards by large and listed companies and has the power to petition the courts to order the withdrawal of a company's accounts. So far, FRRP has not had to take court action, but it has used its considerable influence to effect changes in accounting practices with which it disagreed. By July 2002, FRRP had issued 74 *Press Notices* explaining action taken against companies and the issues giving rise to FRRP disagreement. These Press Notices provide useful insights of the regulator's view where standards are open to interpretation. FRRP does not have authority in Ireland but exerts moral suasion through its published views and rulings.

The UK system aims to produce more independent accounting standards which reflect a wide constituency of views and which have stronger legal backing than was the case with those developed by ASC. The FRRP provides an authoritative enforcement mechanism, which is seen to take action against wayward or inappropriate accounting practices.

Standard setting internationally

The IASC was established in 1973 through agreement between the professional accountancy bodies in nine countries. It grew to over 140 member organisations from over 100 countries before it was reconstituted as IASB in 2001. Much progress has been made in promoting IASs and in harmonising accounting practice internationally. National rules and accounting pronouncements are generally moving to an international benchmark. In 1998 new laws were introduced in Belgium, France, Germany and Italy to allow large companies to use IASs. In the UK, the ASB indicated in October 2001 that it was unlikely to issue any new standards in the UK, except those required to implement IASs. ASB would instead be monitoring existing standards to facilitate harmonisation with IASs. The potential for IASs to provide a basis for comparable cross-border financial reporting is increasingly discussed.

In February 2000 the US Securities and Exchange Commission (SEC) issued a *Concept Release* exploring the possibility that multinational companies raising new capital in the US could use IASs for such cross-border offerings. In May 2000 IOSCO recommended that multinational enterprises should be able to use IASs in financial statements used for cross-border listings and offerings. In June 2000 the European Commission recommended that Europe's listed companies should all prepare their consolidated financial statements in accordance with IASs by the year 2005. That proposal was adopted by the EU in June 2002.

The objectives of the IASC are:

(a) to develop, in the public interest, a single set of high quality, understandable and enforceable global accounting standards that require high quality, transparent and comparable information in financial statements and other financial reporting to help participants in the world's capital markets and other users make economic decisions;
(b) to promote the use and rigorous application of those standards; and
(c) to bring about convergence of national accounting standards and International Accounting Standards to high quality solutions. (*IASC Constitution*, paragraph 2, 24 May 2000)

The IASC was restructured in 2000 and a new constitution was adopted. The IASC foundation was established to oversee a new professional accounting standard-setting body. Sir David Tweedie was appointed chairman to this new body, the IASB.

By 2001 seven national accounting standard setters have an IASB member resident in their jurisdiction (Australia and New Zealand (combined), Canada, France, Germany, Japan, the United Kingdom and the United States). The IASB Constitution envisages a 'partnership' between IASB and national bodies in these seven jurisdictions to work together to achieve convergence of accounting standards worldwide. The IASB website presents useful country-by-country information about the use of IASB standards by stock exchanges and in developing national accounting standards.

The new structure came into effect on 1 April 2001. Figure 13.2 shows the structure of the IASB. If this figure is compared with the standard setting structure of the ASB (Figure 13.1), some similarities in approach can be identified. For example, both are independent of professional accounting bodies, have independent funding and a full-time staff. The Standing Interpretations Committee (SIC) – which became the International Financial Reporting Interpretations Committee (IFRIC) in December 2001 – acts similarly to the UITF in providing quick guidance on areas where requirements of standards are not clear or are being abused. However, the standard-setting structure under IAS GAAP is more complex than under UK GAAP, allowing for more input from interested parties. This is probably important where standards aim to have global impact.

The IASB will issue International Financial Reporting Standards (IFRSs) in the future rather than IASs. On its establishment in April 2001 it announced that it was adopting all IASs in force at that time. As already stated, previously SIC issued interpretations to assist companies in complying with IASs. The IASB will issue interpretations of the IFRIC in the future rather than of SIC. These interpretations do not have the same status as IASs, but they must be complied with under IAS 1 *Presentation of Financial Statements* which in paragraph 11 states:

> Financial statements should not be described as complying with International Accounting Standards unless they comply with all the requirements of each applicable Standard and each applicable Interpretation of the Standing Interpretations Committee.

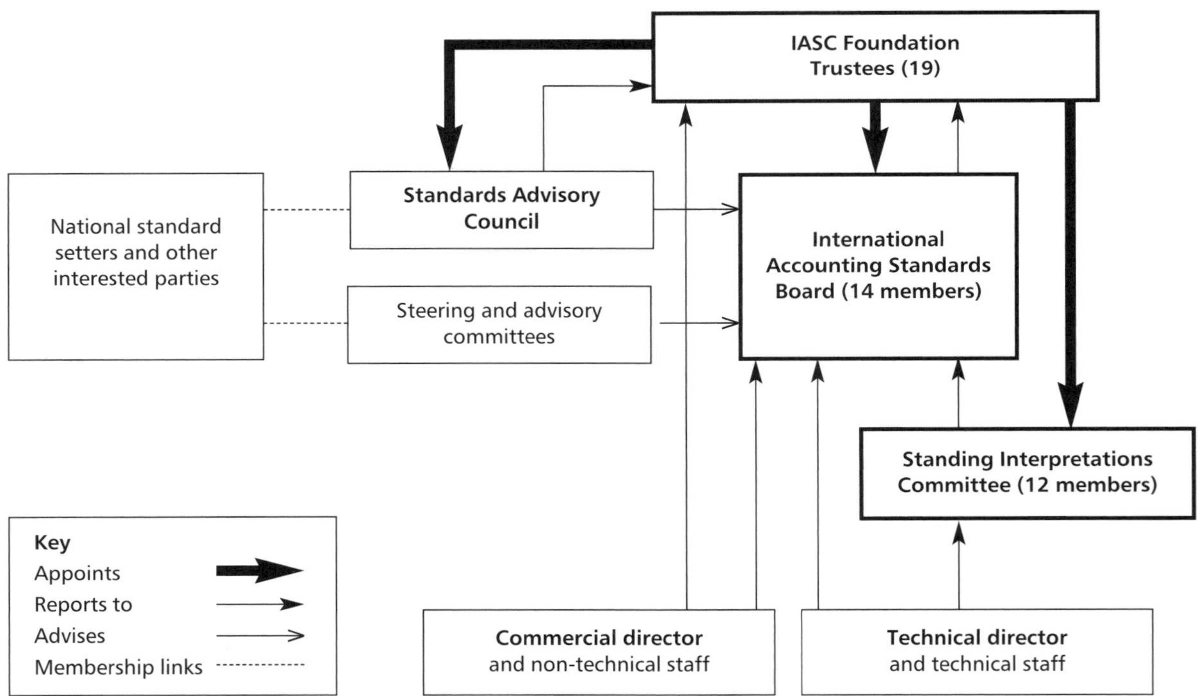

Figure 13.2 Standard-setting structure of the IASB

International accounting standards

As at December 2002 41 IASs have been issued, of which seven have been withdrawn, leaving 34 currently applying. In addition, 33 final Interpretations of SIC have been issued, of which two have been withdrawn. (IASs and SIC Interpretations in force at the time of writing are listed in Appendix 2.)

Enforcement of IASs

IASB currently has no authority to require compliance with its standards. Consequently, compliance with IASs is not mandatory unless the individual entity or country chooses to adopt those standards. Many countries, however, require the financial statements of publicly traded enterprises to be prepared in accordance with IASs, and (where necessary) to give particulars of any material departure from those standards and the reasons for it (for details of which countries see the IASB website, www.iasb.org.uk). In addition, companies and/or securities legislation in many countries requires management and directors of publicly traded companies (and, in many cases, all enterprises) to prepare financial statements in accordance with IASs, that present fairly (or give a true and fair view of) the financial position of the enterprise at the end of the financial year and the results of its operations and cash flows for the year.

UK and international standards relevant to the preparation of group accounts

Table 13.1 provides an overview of the UK standards and IASs applicable in the preparation of group accounts. Ten accounting standards and four UITF Abstracts influence the preparation and presentation of consolidated accounts under UK GAAP. Nine IASs and 11 SIC Interpretations influence the preparation and presentation of consolidated accounts internationally. The table also indicates the chapter in this book where the particular regulation is discussed.

Table 13.1 Regulations under UK GAAP and IAS GAAP relevant to group accounts

UK GAAP	IAS GAAP
Consolidated financial statements (Chapter 14)	
FRS 2 *Accounting for Subsidiary Undertakings*	IAS 27 *Consolidated Financial Statements and Accounting for Investments in Subsidiaries* SIC 12 *Consolidation – Special Purpose Entities*
Associates and joint ventures (Chapter 15)	
FRS 9 *Associates and Joint Ventures*	IAS 28 *Accounting for Investments in Associates* IAS 31 *Financial Reporting of Interests in Joint Ventures* SIC 3 *Elimination of Unrealised Profits and Losses on Transactions with Associates* SIC 13 *Jointly Controlled Entities – Non-monetary Contributions by Venturers* SIC 20 *Equity Accounting Method – Recognition of Losses* SIC 33 *Consolidation and Equity Method – Potential Voting Rights and Allocation of Ownership Interests*
Business combinations (Chapter 16)	
FRS 6 *Acquisitions and Mergers* Abstract 15 *Disclosure of substantial acquisitions*	IAS 22 *Business Combinations* SIC 9 *Business Combinations – Classification either as Acquisitions or Unitings of Interests*
Goodwill (Chapter 17)	
FRS 7 *Fair Values in Acquisition Accounting* FRS 10 *Goodwill and Intangible Assets* FRS 11 *Impairment of Fixed Assets and Goodwill* Abstract 27 *Revision to estimates of the useful life of goodwill and intangible assets* Abstract 31 *Exchange of businesses or other non-monetary assets for an interest in a subsidiary, joint venture or associate*	SIC 22 *Business Combinations – Subsequent Adjustment of Fair Values and Goodwill Initially Reported* SIC 28 *Business Combinations – 'Date of Exchange' and Fair Value of Equity Instruments*
Foreign currencies (Chapter 18)	
SSAP 20 *Foreign currency translation* Abstract 9 *Accounting for operations in hyper-inflationary economies*	IAS 21 *The Effects of Changes in Foreign Exchange Rates* IAS 29 *Financial Reporting in Hyperinflationary Economies* SIC 11 *Foreign Exchange – Capitalisation of Losses resulting from Severe Currency Devaluations* SIC 19 *Reporting Currency – Measurement and Presentation of Financial Statements under IAS 21 and IAS 29* SIC 30 *Reporting Currency – Translation from Measurement Currency to Presentation Currency*
Cash flow statements (Chapter 19)	
FRS 1 *Cash Flow Statements*	IAS 7 *Cash Flow Statements*
Segmental reporting (Chapter 20)	
SSAP 25 *Segmental reporting*	IAS 14 *Segment Reporting*
Quasi-subsidiaries (Chapter 20)	
FRS 5 Reporting the Substance of Transactions	IAS 1 *Presentation of Financial Statements*

Overview of differences between UK GAAP and IAS GAAP

As stated in the introduction to this chapter, one of the objectives of this part of the book is to identify the similarities and differences between UK GAAP and IAS GAAP. An overview of the main similarities and differences in the context of group accounts is therefore provided in this section.

For the most part, UK GAAP regulations are consistent with the requirements of IASs. However, as shown in Table 13.2, Nobes (2000) identifies four major areas where UK GAAP and IAS GAAP are inconsistent.

Table 13.2 Major differences between UK GAAP and IAS GAAP relevant to group accounts

Inconsistency	*FRS/UITF Abstract (number, paragraph)*	*IAS (number, paragraph)*
Greater restriction under UK GAAP on provisions arising from business combinations accounted for as acquisitions	FRS 7,7	IAS 22,31
Goodwill can be treated as having an indefinite life under UK GAAP and in such circumstances is not amortised	FRS 10,19–21	IAS 22,44 and 51
Different criteria used in FRS 6 to determine whether a business combination is a pooling/uniting of interests to which merger accounting rules can be applied	FRS 6,6–12	IAS 22,8
Financial statements of a hyperinflationary subsidiary can be remeasured using a stable currency as a measurement currency in the UK	Abstract 9,6	IAS 21,36

Source: Adapted from Nobes, C. (ed.) 2000. *GAAP 2000 – A Survey of National Accounting Rules in 53 Countries*, PricewaterhouseCoopers, London, pp.59–60 and 108–109

PricewaterhouseCoopers (2000) identifies both similarities and differences between the provisions of IASs and UK GAAP, and the aspects of relevance to group accounts are summarised in Table 13.3.

Table 13.3 Similarities and differences between UK GAAP and IAS GAAP relevant to group accounts

Subject	*UK GAAP*	*IAS GAAP*
Group reporting		
• Definition of subsidiary	Based on voting control	Based on voting control
• Exclusion of subsidiaries from consolidation	Only if severe long-term restrictions or if acquired and held for resale in the near future. Dissimilar activities are not a justification	Only if severe long-term restrictions or if acquired and held for resale in the near future. Dissimilar activities are not a justification
• Definition of associate	Requires evidence of exercise of significant influence	Based on significant influence: presumed if 20% interest or participation in entity's affairs
• Presentation of associate results	Use expanded equity method. Share of operating profit, exceptional items and tax shown separately	Use equity method. Show share of profits and losses
• Disclosures about significant associates	Give detailed information on significant associates' assets, liabilities and results	Minimal
• Equity method or proportional consolidation for joint ventures	Generally use gross equity method. Consolidate own assets/liabilities in limited circumstances such as oil and gas joint arrangements	Both proportional consolidation and equity method permitted. Consolidate own assets/ liabilities in limited circumstances such as oil and gas joint arrangements

continued overleaf

Table 13.3 Continued

Subject	*UK GAAP*	*IAS GAAP*
Business combinations		
• Purchase method – fair values on acquisition	Comparable to IAS. Few acquisition provisions allowed	Fair value assets and liabilities of acquired entity. Some plant closure and restructuring liabilities relating to the acquired entity may be provided in the fair value exercise if specific criteria met
• Purchase method – subsequent adjustments to fair values	Broadly comparable to IAS, except investigation of values must have been ongoing	Fair values can be corrected against goodwill up to the end of the year after acquisition if additional evidence of values becomes available. Record subsequent adjustments in income statement. Reversals of acquisition provisions: always adjust goodwill
• Purchase method – contingent consideration	Reasonable estimate of fair value should be included in cost of acquisition	If the adjustment is probable and the amount can be measured reliably, estimate at acquisition then subsequently correct against goodwill
• Purchase method – minority interests at acquisition	State at share of fair value of net assets	State at share of fair value of net assets or at share of pre-acquisition carrying value of net assets
• Purchase method – disclosure	Broadly comparable to IAS, but must also present table showing book values, fair value adjustments and fair values of acquired assets and liabilities	Disclosures include names and descriptions of combining entities, method of accounting for acquisitions, date of acquisition and impact on results and financial position of acquirer
• Purchase method – goodwill	Comparable to IAS, although indefinite life may be used in certain circumstances	Capitalise and amortise over useful life, normally not longer than 20 years
• Purchase method – negative goodwill	Record as negative asset and recognise in income to match depreciation of non-monetary depreciable assets; any excess over the fair values of such assets is recognised in income over period likely to benefit	Contrary to UK GAAP, if it relates to expected future losses/costs, recognise in income along with these. Otherwise record as negative asset and recognise over useful lives of identifiable, non-monetary assets. Any excess over the fair values of such assets is recognised in income immediately
• Pooling of interests method	Restrictions similar to IAS. Criteria include size of entities and low-level limits of non-share consideration	Severely restricted to 'true mergers of equals'. Rules focus on lack of identification of an acquirer
Foreign currency translation		
• Foreign entities within consolidated financial statements	Use closing rate for balance sheets; either average or closing rate for income statements. Take exchange differences to statement of total recognised gains and losses (STRGL). Not included in gain on disposal of subsidiary	Use closing rate for balance sheets; average rate for income statements. Take exchange differences to equity and include in gain on disposal of subsidiary
• Hyperinflation – foreign entity	Either adopt IAS method or remeasure local currency statements using the reporting currency as the functional currency	Adjust local statements of foreign entity to current price levels prior to translation

Source: Adapted from PricewaterhouseCoopers, 2000. *International Accounting Standards Similarities and Differences IAS, US GAAP and UK GAAP*, PricewaterhouseCoopers, London

The overview of similarities and differences between UK GAAP and IAS GAAP introduced here is developed in the chapters to follow. Most chapters in this section of the book conclude with a table summarising the similarities and differences between UK GAAP and IAS GAAP in the area covered by the chapter.

Format of group financial statements

The formats of company financial statements are prescribed by the EU Fourth Directive. Content is influenced by provisions of company law in each country which, in turn, has been influenced by the provisions of the EU Company Law Directives, particularly the Fourth and Seventh Directives.

The basic format of financial statements is determined primarily by the requirements of the Fourth Directive. Under UK GAAP, FRS 3 *Reporting Financial Performance* imposes additional requirements which have influenced the format and presentation of profit and loss accounts in particular. In addition, FRS 3 requires a further statement, the 'statement of total recognised gains and losses' (STRGL), which the ASB describes as a 'primary' financial statement. There are four primary financial statements according to the ASB: the profit and loss account, the balance sheet, the STRGL and the cash flow statement.

IASs are flexible in the formats and headings to be used in primary financial statements, whereas the Directives are more prescriptive.

A cash flow statement is generally required under UK GAAP and IAS GAAP, but is not referred to in the Directives. Requirements dealing with cash flow statements are discussed further in Chapter 20.

Table 13.4 provides an overview of the regulations governing the format of primary financial statements required under UK GAAP and IAS GAAP.

Table 13.4 Regulations governing the format of primary financial statements under UK GAAP and IAS GAAP

Primary statement	*UK GAAP*	*IAS GAAP*
Profit and loss account	Fourth Directive specifies formats to be followed FRS 3 requires additional disclosures	More flexible on format
Balance sheet	Fourth Directive specifies formats to be followed	More flexible on format
Cash flow statement	Presentation prescribed by FRS 1	Presentation prescribed by IAS 7
STRGL	Primary financial statement required by FRS 3	Not required

Formats of profit and loss account

As summarised in Table 13.5, the Fourth Directive requires companies to follow one of four formats – operational or type-of-expenditure analysis, combined with vertical or horizontal layout – in preparing their profit and loss accounts.

Table 13.5 Profit and loss account formats under the Fourth Directive

Layout:	Vertical	Horizontal
Analysis:		
Operational	①	③
Type-of-expenditure	②	④

The Directive specifies the headings to be used and the order of presentation of items. The headings and items are preceded by either letters (e.g., A, B, C), Roman numerals (e.g., I, II, III) or Arabic numerals (e.g., 1, 2, 3). The exact wording of headings preceded by a letter or Roman numeral must be followed, with no deviation. Items preceded by Arabic numerals can be combined on the face of the profit and loss account or balance sheet. However, for such items combined, the detail must be shown in the notes to the accounts. Each format is illustrated in the Directive. Some items specifically relevant to group accounts were added to the Fourth Directive formats on enactment of the Seventh Directive.

Example 13.1 reproduces the most common formation used – operational analysis, in vertical layout (① in Table 13.5). In particular, there are five items specifically relevant to group accounts which are highlighted in bold in Example 13.1. Two items are shown after operating profit in the individual accounts of the parent company. These are:

- *income from shares in group undertakings*
- *income from participating interests.*

In the consolidated accounts, *Income from shares in group undertakings* will be replaced by the detailed profit and loss account items of the subsidiaries. In relation to associated companies and joint ventures, two items may appear in the consolidated accounts:

- *income from interests in associated undertakings*
- *income from other participating interests.*

In the consolidated profit and loss account, shown after *Profit or loss on ordinary activities after taxation* but before any appropriations, where subsidiaries are not wholly owned, will be:

- *minority interest.*

Example 13.1 Fourth Directive operational analysis and vertical layout for the profit and loss account

	€
Turnover	X
Cost of sales	(X)
Gross profit or loss	X
Distribution costs	(X)
Administrative expenses	(X)
Other operating income	X
Operating profit	X
Income from shares in group undertakings (company)	**X**
Income from participating interests (company)	**X**
Income from interests in associated undertakings (group)	**X**
Income from other participating interests (group)	**X**
Income from other financial assets	X
Other interest receivable and similar income	X
Amounts written off financial assets and investments held as current assets	(X)
Interest payable and similar charges	(X)
Profit before taxation	X
Tax on profit or loss on ordinary activities	(X)
Profit or loss on ordinary activities after taxation	X
Minority interest (group)	**(X)**
Profit or loss for the financial year	X

All profit and loss account items in the required formats are preceded in the Fourth Directive by Arabic numerals (thus the numerals are not reproduced in Examples 13.1 and

13.2). This means that the items do not have to be shown on the face of the profit and loss account and can be relegated to the notes.

The less common type-of-expenditure analysis, in vertical layout (② in Table 13.5), is illustrated in Example 13.2. Again, the five items specifically relevant to group accounts are highlighted in bold.

Example 13.2 Fourth Directive type-of-expenditure analysis and vertical layout for the profit and loss account

	€
Turnover	X
Variation in stocks of finished goods and in work in progress	X/(X)
Own work capitalized	X
Other operating income	X
(a) Raw materials and consumables	(X)
(b) Other external charges	(X)
Staff costs: (a) Wages and salaries	(X)
(b) Social welfare costs	(X)
(c) Other pension costs	(X)
(a) Depreciation and other amounts written off tangible and intangible fixed assets	(X)
(b) Exceptional amounts written off current assets	(X)
Other operating charges	(X)
Income from shares in group undertakings (company)	**X**
Income from participating interests (company)	**X**
Income from interests in associated undertakings (group)	**X**
Income from other participating interests (group)	**X**
Income from other financial assets	X
Other interest receivable and similar income	X
Amounts written off financial assets and investments held as current assets	(X)
Interest payable and similar charges	(X)
Tax on profit or loss on ordinary activities	(X)
Profit or loss on ordinary activities after taxation	X
Minority interest (group)	**(X)**
Profit or loss for the financial year	X

Statutory profit and loss account disclosure requirements

Legislation imposes additional disclosure requirements on companies over and above those arising from requirements of UK GAAP and IAS GAAP. The nature of these additional disclosure requirements varies from country to country. However, in the context of group accounts a number of general points can be made.

The disclosure requirements apply to amounts disclosed in consolidated accounts. Generally speaking the amount to be disclosed from the consolidated profit and loss account will be:

- 100% of the item as it appears in the parent's individual company accounts
- 100% of the item as it appears in the subsidiary's accounts, subject to the inclusion of the post-acquisition element only in the year of acquisition.

These amounts should be adjusted for any consolidating adjustments arising from intercompany transactions, etc.

In the case of directors' remuneration, only the remuneration paid to directors of the holding company is disclosed, whether the remuneration is paid by the parent or the subsidiary or both. Thus, remuneration paid to directors of subsidiary companies who are not directors of the parent company is not disclosed.

Disclosure of holding company's profit and loss account

Legislation in the UK and Ireland permits holding companies to dispense with the need to provide their own individual profit and loss accounts provided the consolidated accounts show how much of the consolidated profit or loss is dealt with in the individual accounts of the holding company. Thus, UK and Irish companies usually include a note to the accounts disclosing the profit after tax which the parent would have shown in its own accounts. The parent column in the profit and loss account columnar workings (discussed in Chapter 10) should provide the amount for disclosure.

Note 11 to Abbey National's individual company balance sheet in Exhibit 13.1 indicates that a separate profit and loss account for the parent company is not presented as that company's results are included in the consolidated profit and loss account. The amount of the parent company's profit or loss is separately disclosed.

Exhibit 13.1 **Parent company profit and loss account**
The Abbey National Group Annual Report 2000

Notes to the Financial Statements (extract)
Note 11 Profit on ordinary activities after tax
The profit after tax of the Company attributable to the shareholders is £864m (£1,446m). As permitted by section 230 of the Companies Act 1985, the Company's profit and loss account has not been presented in these financial statements.

Elan Corporation discloses the same information in Exhibit 13.2, but in a different format. It first analyses the consolidated retained profits between the holding company and subsidiaries and associates. Then the amount of the parent company's own profit dealt with in the consolidated accounts is disclosed separately in a note underneath the analysis.

Formats of balance sheets

The Fourth Directive prescribes two formats for balance sheets: vertical and horizontal. Unlike the profit and loss account (where all items are preceded by Arabic numerals in the Fourth Directive) some balance sheet items are preceded by letters or Roman numerals (i.e., they must be shown separately on the face of the balance sheet), while some balance sheet items are preceded by Arabic numerals (i.e., they can be combined on the face of the balance sheet and disclosed in the notes to the accounts). The Fourth Directive balance sheet formats were amended on enactment of the Seventh Directive to require disclosure of minority interests on the face of the balance sheet (only group accounts).

Exhibit 13.2 **Parent company profit and loss account**
Elan Corporation plc Annual Report 2000

Notes to the Financial Statements (extract)
19 Profit and loss account

	At 31 December 2000 $m	At 31 December 1999 $m
Holding company	2,623.4	2,517.9
Subsidiary and associated undertakings	(1,492.4)	(1,729.0)
Goodwill written-off	(574.3)	(580.8)
	556.7	208.1

Elan Corporation plc has availed of the Companies (Amendment) Act 1986 exemption from the requirement to present its separate non-consolidated profit and loss account. Of the consolidated net profit after tax, profit of $105.5 million (1999: $2,081.7 million) is dealt with in the profit and loss account of the Company.

Example 13.3 illustrates the vertical balance sheet format. Totals are required for two items: *Net current assets (liabilities)* and *Total assets less current liabilities*. Otherwise it is not clear where the two balance sheet totals should be struck and some variations are found in practice.

Example 13.3 Balance sheet vertical format

A Fixed assets
I Intangible assets
1 Development costs
2 Concessions, patents, licences, trademarks and similar rights and assets
3 Goodwill (group)
4 Payments on account
II Tangible assets
1 Land and buildings
2 Plant and machinery
3 Fixtures, fittings, tools and equipment
4 Payments on account and assets in course of construction
III Financial assets
1 Shares in group undertakings (company)
2 Loans to group undertakings (company)
3 Participating interests / other participating interests (company/group)
4 Loans to undertakings in which a participating interest is held (company/group)
5 Investments other than loans
6 Other loans
7 Own shares

B Current assets
I Stocks
1 Raw materials and consumables
2 Work in progress
3 Finished goods and goods for resale
4 Payments on account

continued overleaf

Example 13.3 Continued

II Debtors
- 1 Trade debtors
- **2 Amounts owed by group undertakings (company)**
- **3 Amounts owed by undertakings in which a participating interest is held (company/group)**
- 4 Other debtors
- 5 Called-up share capital not paid
- 6 Prepayments and accrued income

III Investments
- **1 Shares in group undertakings**
- 2 Own shares
- 3 Other investments

IV Cash at bank and in hand

C Creditors: Amounts falling due within one year
- 1 Debenture loans
- 2 Bank loans and overdrafts
- 3 Payments received on account
- 4 Trade creditors
- 5 Bills of exchange payable
- **6 Amounts owed to group undertakings (company)**
- **7 Amounts owed to undertakings in which a participating interest is held (company/group)**
- 8 Other creditors including tax and social welfare
- 9 Accruals and deferred income

D Net current assets (liabilities)

E Total assets less current liabilities

F Creditors: Amounts falling due after more than one year
- 1 Debenture loans
- 2 Bank loans and overdrafts
- 3 Payments received on account
- 4 Trade creditors
- 5 Bills of exchange payable
- **6 Amounts owed to group undertakings (company)**
- **7 Amounts owed to undertakings in which a participating interest is held (company/group)**
- 8 Other creditors including tax and social welfare
- 9 Accruals and deferred income

G Provisions for liabilities and charges
- 1 Pensions and similar obligations
- 2 Taxation, including deferred taxation
- 3 Other provisions

H Capital and reserves

I Called-up share capital

II Share premium account

III Revaluation reserve

IV Other reserves
- 1 The capital redemption reserve fund
- 2 Reserves for own shares
- 3 Reserves provided for by the articles of association
- 4 Other reserves

V Profit and loss account

Minority interest

The Roman and Arabic numerals are also shown in Example 13.3 to indicate whether the item must be shown on the face of the balance sheet or may be disclosed in the notes to the accounts.

Items relevant to group accounts are highlighted in bold. There are 13 items in the balance sheet specifically relevant to group accounts.

1 *Goodwill.*

Goodwill is shown as an intangible fixed asset. Goodwill arising on consolidation appears only in group accounts rather than in individual company balance sheets.

Financial fixed assets contains four items relating to group accounts:

2 *Shares in group undertakings.*
3 *Loans to group undertakings.*
4 *Participating interests / Other participating interests.*
5 *Loans to undertakings in which a participating interest is held.*

Shares in group undertakings and *Loans to group undertakings* will only appear in the individual accounts of the parent. The shares will be replaced by the underlying net assets of the group undertaking on consolidation. The loans will cancel with the corresponding liability in the group undertaking's balance sheet on consolidation.

The individual accounts of the parent may contain three balances in current assets relating to group accounts:

6 *Amounts owed by group undertakings.*
7 *Amounts owed by undertakings in which a participating interest is held.*
8 *Shares in group undertakings.*

Shares in group undertakings would only appear in current assets in rare circumstances and are more likely to be found in financial fixed assets as explained earlier. For the same reasons as explained earlier, the shares and *Amounts owed by group undertakings* will only appear in the individual accounts of the parent undertaking.

9 *Amounts owed to group undertakings.*
10 *Amounts owed to undertakings in which a participating interest is held.*
11 *Amounts owed to group undertakings.*
12 *Amounts owed to undertakings in which a participating interest is held.*

Liabilities of the parent to group undertakings and participating interests may appear in *Creditors: amounts falling due within one year* and/or *Creditors: amounts falling due after more than one year*, depending on repayment dates. Amounts owed by the parent to group undertakings will cancel on consolidation and only appear in the individual accounts of the parent.

13 *Minority interest.*

The Seventh Directive introduced a requirement to disclose minority interests on the face of the (consolidated) balance sheet. As a result of these provisions, the Fourth Directive formats were amended to include minority interests. In Format 1 of the balance sheet, minority interests should be shown either immediately before or immediately after *Capital and reserves* in the vertical balance sheet format. In the horizontal format, minority interests should be shown under the heading '*Liabilities*' immediately after capital and reserves.

The horizontal format balance sheet is similar in detail to the vertical format (details are consequently not shown in Example 13.4). However, it follows a different layout. Assets are totalled independently of liabilities and equity, and a T account horizontal layout is adopted as is illustrated in Example 13.4. This format is rarely seen in practice.

Example 13.4 Balance sheet horizontal format (summarised)

Assets		Liabilities	
A	Fixed assets	A	Capital and reserves
			Minority interest
B	Current assets	B	Provisions for liabilities and charges
		C	Creditors

Summary

This chapter has introduced regulations influencing the preparation of group accounts by companies under UK GAAP and under IAS GAAP. In addition, the influence of EU Directives has been discussed and illustrated.

Chapters to follow will expand on the requirements of these regulations. Chapter 14 considers the regulations applying to group accounts generally, while Chapter 15 considers those applying to associated undertakings and joint ventures. Regulations applying to business combinations using either acquisition or merger accounting are discussed in Chapter 16 and accounting for goodwill follows in Chapter 17. Foreign currency issues are considered in Chapter 18 followed by Chapter 19 dealing with cash flow statements. Finally, Chapter 20 covers quasi-subsidiaries and segmental reporting.

Learning outcomes

After studying this chapter you should have learnt:

- the sources of regulation underlying the preparation of group accounts
- the different approaches to standard setting under UK GAAP and IAS GAAP
- the accounting standards applicable to the preparation of group accounts
- the differences between UK GAAP and IAS GAAP requirements applying to the preparation of group accounts
- how to present group profit and loss accounts and balance sheets in compliance with EU Directives.

Company legislation and professional accounting regulations: parent and subsidiary undertakings

Learning objectives

After studying this chapter you should be able to:

- understand regulations applying to parent and subsidiary undertakings under UK GAAP
- understand regulations applying to parent and subsidiary undertakings under IAS GAAP
- compare and contrast UK GAAP and IAS GAAP regulations applying to parent and subsidiary undertakings

Introduction

This chapter examines the accounting regulations governing consolidated accounts deriving from (i) UK GAAP and (ii) IAS GAAP in the context of requirements to prepare consolidated accounts. Specific topics covered include definitions of group undertakings, grounds for exemption from preparing consolidated accounts, excluding subsidiary undertakings from consolidated accounts, and other related topics concerning parent and subsidiary relationships.

Methods of preparing group accounts are not addressed. Parts 2 and 3 explained the detailed mechanics of preparing group accounts, primarily under the acquisition method of accounting, but also under the equity method (including gross equity method). Chapter 9 introduced merger accounting, and contrasted that method of accounting with the traditional acquisition method of consolidation.

As explained in Chapter 13, presentation of group financial statements is influenced by the requirements of the EU Seventh Directive which has been enacted through legislation in all EU countries. The Seventh Directive aimed to standardise the form and content of consolidated accounts in the EU. The main requirements of the Directive deal with:

- requirements for preparing group accounts
- exemptions from requirements to prepare group accounts
- exclusion of subsidiaries and how to account for excluded subsidiaries.

FRS 2 *Accounting for Subsidiary Undertakings* was issued by the ASB in July 1992 replacing SSAP 14. It provides guidance on the implementation of the Seventh Directive in the UK and Ireland and interprets certain items and phrases in the Directive in the context of the *true and fair view* requirement. FRS 2 is consistent with UK legislation implementing the Directive and wherever possible uses the same definitions and terminology. It is written in terms of UK legislation and more than any other standard is predominantly based on UK legal provisions. Paragraphs 95 to 96 cross-reference FRS 2 to UK legal requirements, paragraph 97 deals with Northern Irish legislation and paragraph 98 does the same in respect of legislation in the Republic of Ireland.

The objective of FRS 2 is to require parent undertakings to provide financial information about activities of groups, showing groups as single economic entities, by preparing consolidated financial statements. FRS 2 emphasises the requirements of legislation that parent undertakings should consolidate all subsidiary undertakings over which the group exercises *dominant influence*, subject only to certain specified exclusions. It reduces the possibility of using quasi-subsidiaries to move assets and liabilities off balance sheet by circumventing the legal definition of subsidiary undertakings. Quasi-subsidiaries are discussed further in Chapter 20.

Two pronouncements of the IASB deal with consolidated financial statements generally: IAS 27 *Consolidated Financial Statements and Accounting for Investments in Subsidiaries* and SIC 12 *Consolidation – Special Purpose Entities*. These are discussed in this chapter. IAS 22 *Business Combinations* is considered in Chapter 16 as it deals with the acquisition and merger methods of accounting.

IAS 27 was issued in 1989 to replace IAS 3 *Consolidated Financial Statements*, issued in 1976. The IAS was reformatted in 1994 and a number of small editorial changes have been made to the standard since then. As both FRS 2 and IAS 27 were prepared to conform with the Seventh Directive, their respective provisions are similar.

This chapter considers these three accounting pronouncements (i.e., FRS 2, IAS 27 and SIC 12) under a number of headings. In this chapter, the scope of the regulations is discussed, as are the definitions determining classification of undertakings as subsidiaries. The composition of group accounts is then considered, followed by exemptions from the requirement to prepare consolidated accounts and grounds for exclusion of subsidiaries from consolidation. Methods of consolidation are only briefly mentioned as these are more thoroughly dealt with elsewhere, especially in Parts 2 and 3 and in Chapters 15 and 16. Regulations concerning coterminous year-ends and uniform accounting policies are described, as are those applying to minority interests. Consolidation adjustments are discussed, as are the effects of changes in group composition. Other disclosures required by the three accounting pronouncements (i.e., FRS 2, IAS 27 and SIC 12) are then listed. The chapter concludes with a comparison of the main differences between UK GAAP and IAS GAAP.

UK GAAP

Scope

FRS 2 extends the legal requirement for limited companies with subsidiaries to prepare group financial statements to all parent undertakings (including partnerships and other unincorporated businesses).

Definitions

FRS 2 definitions are based on UK legislation and derive from the Seventh Directive. These definitions are based on the concept of control rather than ownership. Control is having the ability to direct the financial and operating policies of other undertakings with a view to gaining economic benefit from their activities. The Seventh Directive definition of a subsidiary was summarised in Chapter 1.

The Directive widened the definition of a subsidiary to include situations where an entity controls another, regardless of the strict percentage of shares owned. Thus, companies previously escaping consolidation (very often through artificial ownership structures designed to circumvent legal definitions) must now be brought in. The emphasis of the legal definition of a subsidiary was changed from ownership of a specific proportion of shares to one including various ways in which parents control subsidiaries. The definition centres around the parent rather than, as previously was the case, the subsidiary. FRS 2 definitions are not exactly the same as the Seventh Directive.

Under FRS 2 (paragraph 14), an undertaking is a parent undertaking of another, the subsidiary undertaking, if *any* of the following apply:

- (a) It holds a majority of the voting rights in the undertaking.
- (b) It is a member of the undertaking and has the right to appoint or remove directors holding a majority of the voting rights at meetings of the board on all, or substantially all, matters.
- (c) It has the right to exercise a dominant influence over the undertaking:
  - (i) by virtue of provisions contained in the undertaking's memorandum or articles; or
  - (ii) by virtue of a control contract. The control contract must be in writing and be of a kind authorised by the memorandum or articles of the controlled undertaking. It must also be permitted by the law under which that undertaking is established.
- (d) Is a member of the undertaking and controls alone, pursuant to an agreement with other shareholders or members, a majority of the voting rights in the undertaking.
- (e) It has a participating interest in the undertaking and:
  - (i) it actually exercises a dominant influence over the undertaking; or
  - (ii) it and the undertaking are managed on a unified basis.
- (f) A parent undertaking is also treated as the parent undertaking of the subsidiary undertakings of its subsidiary undertakings.

A number of key phrases in this definition are defined in FRS 2 including *dominant influence*, *control* and *managed on a unified basis*.

Dominant influence is defined (in paragraph 7) as:

> Influence that can be exercised to achieve the operating and financial policies desired by the holder of the influence, notwithstanding the rights or influence of any other party.
>
> (a) … *the right to exercise a dominant influence* means that the holder has a right to give directions with respect to the operating and financial policies of another undertaking with which its directors are obliged to comply, whether or not they are for the benefit of that undertaking.
>
> (b) *The actual exercise of dominant influence* is the exercise of an influence that achieves the result that the operating and financial policies of the undertaking influenced are set in accordance with the wishes of the holder of the influence

> and for the holder's benefit whether or not those wishes are explicit. The actual exercise of dominant influence is identified by its effect in practice rather than by the way in which it is exercised.

It is clear from the definition of dominant influence that an undertaking shall not be regarded as having the right to exercise a dominant influence over another undertaking unless it has a right to give directions with respect to the operating and financial policies of that other undertaking. This definition emphasises the actual exercise of dominant influence, as determined by its effect in practice. Reflecting the importance of the term, *dominant influence* is referred to in Bass's *Basis of consolidation* accounting policy note in Exhibit 14.1.

Exhibit 14.1 **Exercise of dominant influence**
Bass plc Annual Report 2000

Notes to the Financial Statements (extract)
Basis of consolidation
The Group financial statements comprise the financial statements of the parent company and its subsidiary undertakings. The results of those businesses acquired or disposed of during the year are consolidated for the period during which they were under the Group's dominant influence.

Control is defined in FRS 2 (paragraph 6) as:

> The ability of an undertaking to direct the financial and operating policies of another undertaking with a view to gaining economic benefits from its activities.

Managed on a unified basis is relevant to holding a participating interest and is defined in FRS 2 (paragraph 12) as follows:

> Two or more undertakings are managed on a unified basis if the whole of the operations of the undertakings are integrated and they are managed as a single unit. Unified management does not arise solely because one undertaking manages another.

Different parental relationships with group entities are distinguished in Exhibit 14.2. GlaxoSmithKline distinguishes between (i) exercise of dominant influence for subsidiaries, (ii) joint control for joint ventures, (iii) significant influence for associates and

Exhibit 14.2 **Parent's relationship with subsidiaries, associates and joint ventures**
GlaxoSmithKline plc Annual Report 2000

Notes to the Financial Statements (extract)
3 Accounting policies (extract)
Consolidation
Undertakings in which the Group has a material interest are accounted for as subsidiaries where the Group exercises dominant influence, as joint ventures where the Group exercises joint control and as associates where the Group can exercise significant influence. ESOTs are accounted for as subsidiaries on the grounds that the Group has de facto control.

(iv) *de facto* control for ESOTs (employee share ownership trusts). *De facto* control refers to Article 1 (D) of the Seventh Directive (referred to in Chapter 1). *De facto* control arises where, although the parent does not itself hold a majority of voting rights, (i) it has, through the exercise of its voting rights, appointed a majority to the board or (ii) controls alone or with agreement of other shareholders a majority of voting rights. The exercise of significant influence and joint control for associates and joint ventures are discussed further in Chapter 15.

Group accounts

Legislation enacted by the Seventh Directive specifies that group accounts comprise:

- consolidated balance sheet
- consolidated profit and loss account
- notes thereon.

Group accounts must comply with formats set out in the Fourth Directive (discussed in Chapter 13) and are required to give a true and fair view.

Under FRS 2, consolidated financial statements are defined as *the financial statements of a group prepared by consolidation* (paragraph 4). A parent is required to prepare consolidated financial statements for its group unless it uses one of the exemptions listed in the following.

Exemptions from requirements to prepare group financial statements

Under FRS 2, a parent undertaking is exempt from preparing consolidated accounts on size grounds, or because the parent is itself a subsidiary, or because all of its subsidiaries can or must be excluded. In particular:

- the group is small or medium sized *and* all members of the group are private companies
- the parent undertaking is wholly owned and its immediate parent is established under the law of an EU member state (provided the parent undertaking has no securities listed on an EU state stock exchange)
- the parent undertaking is a majority-owned subsidiary and meets all the conditions for exemption set out in the Seventh Directive (i.e., (a) the exempted undertaking and all of its subsidiary undertakings are consolidated in the accounts of a larger body of undertakings, the parent undertaking of which is governed by the law of a member state; (b) the notes to the annual accounts of the exempted undertaking must disclose (i) the name and registered office of the parent undertaking that draws up the consolidated accounts and (ii) the fact that the exemption from the obligation to draw up consolidated accounts has been taken)
- all the parent undertaking's subsidiary undertakings are permitted or required to be excluded from consolidation under the Seventh Directive.

Size exemption

Under the Seventh Directive, parent undertakings need not prepare consolidated financial statements if they fall within specified size criteria for medium sized companies. The group must satisfy two or more of the size criteria in the Fourth Directive to qualify for the size exemption. Table 14.1 sets out these criteria as originally included in the Fourth Directive and currently applying in the UK and in the Republic of Ireland. The exemption is held until the parent undertaking fails to meet the criteria for two consecutive years.

Table 14.1 Size criteria for exemption from preparing group financial statements: medium-sized companies

Group must satisfy two of the following	*Original Fourth Directive**	*UK*	*Republic of Ireland*
Annual turnover less than	8 million EUA	£11.2 million	IR£12 (€15.237) million
Balance sheet total less than	4 million EUA	£5.6 million	IR£6 (€7.618) million
Average number employed not more than	250	250	250

* Member states were allowed to increase the first two size criteria. EUA = European Unit of Account

The size criteria are defined in terms of turnover, balance sheet total and number of employees. Turnover means the amount in the consolidated profit and loss account. Balance sheet total is defined as fixed and current assets. Employee numbers are those of the parent and its subsidiaries combined.

FRS 2 points out that there could be cases where a company is exempt from preparing group financial statements but where, as a result, the individual financial statements do not give a true and fair view of its results and financial position. Sufficient disclosures should be made to enable the parent company's financial statements to give a true and fair view.

Where parent undertaking is a subsidiary

Unlisted parent undertakings, which are themselves subsidiaries of companies incorporated in the EU (i.e., intermediate holding companies), are exempt from preparing consolidated financial statements:

- if the parent is a wholly owned subsidiary and its immediate parent is established under EU law
- where the parent undertaking holds 90% or more of the nominal value of the shares in the subsidiary and the minority shareholders approve the exemption and have not requested the preparation of consolidated accounts. (The Seventh Directive specified 90%, but allowed a derogation for ten years from 1 January 1990. The 90% limit was legislated for in the Republic of Ireland, but the limit in the UK Companies Act 1989 was set at a majority (i.e. more than 50%).)

Under the Seventh Directive, exemption is dependent on compliance with a number of conditions and is not available to listed companies. The conditions for exemption are:

- the exempt intermediate holding company must be included in the consolidated accounts of a company incorporated in an EU member state
- a parent company's consolidated accounts are prepared in compliance with the provisions of the Seventh Directive
- a parent company's consolidated accounts must have the same year-end date as the exempt intermediate holding company or an earlier date during the same financial year
- a parent company's consolidated accounts must be filed with the Registrar of Companies translated into the language of the exempt intermediate holding company.

Example 14.1 illustrates these requirements.

Example 14.1 Exemption for parents that are intermediate holding companies

Example

Four companies form part of a group of companies, as follows:

	Scenario 1	*Scenario 2*	*Scenario 3*
Group structure	*Country of incorporation*	*Country of incorporation*	*Country of incorporation*
A	UK	France	France
↓100%			
B	US	Germany	UK
↓100%			
C	UK	UK	UK
↓100%			
D	UK	UK	UK

Note: All group companies have the same year-end date.

Required

For each of the three scenarios, indicate which of the four companies in the group must prepare consolidated accounts and which would be exempt intermediate holding companies.

Solution

Scenario 1

Company	*Not exempt/Exempt*	*Explanation*
A	Not exempt	Parent undertaking of largest group of companies
B	Not applicable	Not subject to EU regulation
C	Not exempt	Immediate parent is incorporated outside the EU
D	Not applicable	D is not a parent

Scenario 2

Company	*Not exempt/Exempt*	*Explanation*
A	Not exempt	Parent undertaking of largest group of companies
B	Exempt (conditional)	Exempt, provided A prepares consolidated accounts that comply with the Seventh Directive and that a translation of those accounts into German is filed
C	Exempt (conditional)	Exempt, provided A or B prepares consolidated accounts that comply with the Seventh Directive and that a translation of those accounts into English is filed
D	Not applicable	D is not a parent

Scenario 3

Company	*Not exempt/Exempt*	*Explanation*
A	Not exempt	Parent undertaking of largest group of companies
B	Exempt (conditional)	Exempt, provided A prepares consolidated accounts that comply with the Seventh Directive and that a translation of those accounts into English is filed
C	Exempt (conditional)	Exempt, provided A or B prepares consolidated accounts that comply with the Seventh Directive. If only A, then a translation of those accounts into English must be provided
D	Not applicable	D is not a parent

Source: Adapted from Davies, M., Paterson, R. and Wilson, A. 1999. *UK GAAP*, 6th edition, Ernst & Young and Butterworths Tolley, London, p.290

If the exemption applies, the following should be disclosed in the notes to the accounts of the exempted parent:

- statement that the company is exempt from the requirements to prepare group financial statements
- in relation to the parent undertaking in whose consolidated financial statements the exempt company's accounts are included:
  - that parent undertaking's name
  - that parent undertaking's country of incorporation or registration.

For a parent company exempt from preparing group financial statements, the Seventh Directive suggests that the fixed assets, turnover, profit/loss for year, capital and reserves and average numbers employed of subsidiary undertakings of the exempted parent should be disclosed in a note to the ultimate parent company's consolidated accounts.

The following should be disclosed:

- name of that parent undertaking(s)
- country of parent's incorporation (or place of business if unincorporated)
- address from which group financial statements may be obtained (if group financial statements are available publicly).

In addition to the disclosure requirements of the Seventh Directive for parents not required to prepare group accounts, paragraph 22 of FRS 2 requires the parent to state that its financial statements present information about it as an individual undertaking and not about its group. This should include or refer to a note setting out the grounds for exemption from the requirement to prepare consolidated accounts.

Exclusion of subsidiaries

Some subsidiaries may be excluded from group accounts, and accounted for in a manner other than full consolidation.

Under FRS 2, the consolidated financial statements should include the accounts of the parent undertaking and all its subsidiary undertakings except those required to be excluded by the standard. FRS 2 discusses exclusions under the Seventh Directive distinguishing between *required* and *permitted* exclusions, i.e., exclusions may be (i) required or (ii) permitted on five grounds under the Directive as follows:

- dissimilar activities (*must* exclude under Seventh Directive)
- immaterial subsidiaries (*may* exclude under Seventh Directive)
- disproportionate expense or undue delay (*may* exclude under Seventh Directive)
- severe long-term restrictions (*may* exclude under Seventh Directive)
- interest held exclusively with a view to subsequent resale (*may* exclude under Seventh Directive).

As standards only apply to material items, exclusion on the grounds of immateriality is not covered by, and need not be referred to, under FRS 2.

FRS 2 accepts the Seventh Directive's exclusion of subsidiaries on the grounds of dissimilar activities but states (consistent with the Seventh Directive) that it would be exceptional for such circumstances to occur. FRS 2 indicates that the contrast between banking companies and other companies, or between profit and not-for-profit undertakings is not sufficient to justify exclusion. It goes on to say (paragraph 25(c)) that it could not provide an example of dissimilar activities justifying exclusion:

> It is exceptional for such circumstances to arise and it is not possible to identify any particular contrast of activities where the necessary incompatibility with the true and fair view generally occurs.

Implicit in this is the view that presentation of segmental information is a better means of dealing with companies carrying on dissimilar activities rather than excluding such undertakings from consolidation.

FRS 2 is more definitive about exclusions *permitted* under the Seventh Directive:

- under FRS 2, neither disproportionate expense nor undue delay in obtaining necessary information can justify excluding from consolidation a subsidiary that is material in the context of the group
- exclusions on the grounds of severe long-term restrictions are *required* under FRS 2 (rather than *permitted* under the Seventh Directive)
- interests held with an immediate intention to sell within one year (and the interest has not previously been included in consolidated accounts) *must* be excluded from consolidation under FRS 2 (whereas their exclusion is *permitted* under the Seventh Directive).

In relation to exclusions from consolidation, the requirements of the Seventh Directive and FRS 2 are summarised and compared in Table 14.2.

Table 14.2 Exclusions from consolidation under the Seventh Directive and FRS 2

	Seventh Directive	*FRS 2*
Immaterial subsidiaries	May be excluded	Not covered, standards only deal with material items
Severe long-term restrictions	May be excluded	Must be excluded
Disproportionate expense, undue delay	May be excluded	Not a justifiable reason for exclusion
Held with a view to resale	May be excluded	Must be excluded
Dissimilar (incompatible) activities	Must be excluded	Must be excluded – although such a scenario is considered unrealistic

FRS 2 specifies accounting treatment for excluded subsidiaries which varies with the reason for exclusion:

- *incompatible activities*: include the investment in consolidated accounts using the equity method
- *severe long-term restrictions*: include the investment as a fixed asset. The carrying amount should be cost (if restrictions were in place from the date of initial investment) or amount under the equity method of accounting (if restrictions came into effect after acquisition). Book value should be written down for any permanent diminution in value. If the parent undertaking still exercises significant influence, ongoing profits and losses can be accrued, in which case the subsidiary undertaking is equity accounted. Otherwise, no further accrual of the subsidiary's profits or losses is allowed
- *held exclusively with a view to subsequent resale*: include as a current asset, at the lower of cost and net realisable value.

Additional disclosure requirements under FRS 2 for excluded subsidiaries are:

- particulars of balances between excluded subsidiaries and the group
- nature and extent of transactions of excluded subsidiaries with the group
- for subsidiaries excluded and *not* accounted for using the equity method:
  - dividends received/receivable from that subsidiary
  - any write-downs during the period, of investments in that subsidiary, or in amounts due from that subsidiary
- for subsidiaries excluded because of dissimilar activities, disclosure of their separate financial statements (summarised financial information suffices in some cases).

Schroders does not consolidate subsidiaries operating under severe long-term restrictions. Instead these investments are accounted for as investments under current assets (not fixed assets as required by FRS 2). Exhibit 14.3 does not tell us how the investments are valued.

Exhibit 14.3 **Subsidiaries under severe long-term restrictions**
Schroders Annual Report 2000

Notes to the Accounts (extract)
1 Principal accounting policies (extract)
(c) Basis of consolidation (extract)
Private equity investments (venture capital and buy-out funds) which the Group manages and/or in which it is a general partner are not consolidated because there are severe long term restrictions on the rights of the general partners. The Group accounts for general partnership interests as 'Equity shares' within 'Investments held as current assets'.

Coterminous year-ends

Under FRS 2, group undertakings should have the same (or coterminous) financial year-ends. Where any subsidiary's year-end differs, interim accounts to the group year-end should be prepared. If this is not practicable, subsidiary financial statements not more than three months before the group year-end should be used. Any material intervening events should be adjusted for in the consolidated financial statements.

For subsidiaries with different accounting year-ends or accounting periods, FRS 2 requires disclosure of:

- name of subsidiary undertaking
- accounting date or period
- reason for using a different date or accounting period.

As can be seen in Exhibit 14.4, Schroders uses management accounts where subsidiary year-ends are not the same as the group reporting date.

Exhibit 14.4 **Coterminous year-ends**
Schroders Annual Report 2000

Notes to the Accounts (extract)
1 Principal accounting policies (extract)
(c) Basis of consolidation (extract)
The accounts of subsidiary and associated undertakings are coterminous with those of the Company apart from those of certain undertakings which have accounting reference dates other than 31 December for commercial reasons. Management accounts made up to 31 December are used for such undertakings.

In Exhibit 14.5, AstraZeneca uses financial statements prepared one month earlier than the rest of the group to consolidate one subsidiary. Non-coterminous year-ends are permitted under FRS 2 provided the financial statements are no more than three months before the group reporting date. The three required disclosures are present in the note – the name of the subsidiary, the year-end of that subsidiary and the reason (*local conditions and to avoid undue delay*) for not using coterminous financial statements.

Exhibit 14.5 **Different reporting dates**
AstraZeneca plc Annual Report 2000

Notes relating to the Financial Statements (extract)
1 Composition of the Group
The Group financial statements consolidate the financial statements of AstraZeneca PLC and its subsidiaries, of which there were 235 at 31 December 2000. Owing to local conditions and to avoid undue delay in the presentation of the Group financial statements, Salick Health Care prepares its financial statements to 30 November.

Uniform accounting policies

FRS 2 requires uniform group accounting policies to be used in consolidated financial statements, if necessary by adjusting amounts for consolidation. Departures from this principle may be permitted in 'exceptional cases'. Particulars of the different accounting policies used should be disclosed, together with reasons for and effect of the departure, which must be disclosed in the notes to the consolidated accounts.

Schroders discloses how it deals with subsidiaries that do not follow the same accounting policies as the group. Exhibit 14.6 shows that the group adjusts subsidiary and associate accounts to conform with UK accounting policies and the adjusted amounts are then incorporated into the consolidated accounts.

Exhibit 14.6 **Uniform group accounting policies**
Schroders Annual Report 2000

Notes to the Accounts (extract)
1 Principal accounting policies (extract)
(c) Basis of consolidation (extract)
The accounts of certain subsidiary and associated undertakings incorporated outside the United Kingdom are drawn up initially to conform with local regulations and adjusted subsequently on consolidation to conform with United Kingdom company law and accounting standards.

Minority interests

Where subsidiaries are not wholly owned, the consolidated profit and loss account and the consolidated balance sheet includes 100% of all subsidiary revenues, expenses, assets and liabilities under full line-by-line consolidation. Then, in a single line in both the consolidated profit and loss account and the consolidated balance sheet, the interest of minority shareholders is recognised.

FRS 2 requires the aggregate of capital and reserves attributable to minority shareholders to be disclosed in the balance sheet separately from shareholders' funds. When a subsidiary undertaking is acquired, minority interest should be calculated by reference to assets and liabilities recorded at fair value or at adjusted carrying value. Goodwill arising on acquisition should not be attributed to minority interests.

Where a subsidiary has net liabilities, the minority interest would be a debit balance, suggesting the group can recover some of the subsidiary's deficit from the minority shareholders. The figure for minority interest in the profit and loss account and the consolidated balance sheet would be shown accordingly. However, it is possible that the minority shareholders have no binding legal or commercial obligation to contribute in the event that the subsidiary shows a deficiency of net assets. In that event, this debit balance should be charged in the profit and loss account. The corresponding liability in the balance sheet should only be provided for to the extent the group has any commercial or legal obligation to provide finance that may not be recoverable in respect of the accumulated losses attributable to the minority.

Under FRS 2, the profit or loss attributable to the minority should be shown separately in the consolidated profit and loss account after profit after tax.

Safeway provides a note in its financial review, shown in Exhibit 14.7, on how it dealt with the minority interest in a post-tax loss of a fully consolidated activity. This entity is a joint venture accounted for as a subsidiary. Normally joint ventures, where there is joint control, are accounted for using the gross equity method of accounting. It is not clear how 'management control' differs from 'joint control' but this is the basis of accounting for the joint venture as a subsidiary. As the joint venture is loss making, the minority interest in the profit and loss account is a credit entry to remove losses from the consolidated profit and loss account which have not been suffered by the group.

Exhibit 14.7 **Minority interest in losses for year**
Safeway plc Annual Report 2000

Financial review (extract)
Minority Interest
In accordance with applicable accounting standards, our Northern Ireland joint venture is accounted for as a subsidiary since we have management control. However, as we own only 50% of the shares, there is a minority interest credit on our Profit and Loss Account to reflect our partner's, Fitzwilton, share of the post tax loss. This was £7 million compared with nearly £10 million last year.

Consolidation adjustments

As only realised profits of the group can be included in the consolidated accounts, consolidation adjustments may be required when aggregating parent and subsidiary accounts into one set of group accounts. Profits are only realised when the transaction involves a third party outside the group. Thus, intra-group transactions (i.e., transactions between companies in the same group) may need to be adjusted for. These are sometimes referred to as inter-company (between companies) transactions, although the term intra-group is more accurate as the companies must be group companies for the transaction to merit adjustment.

The Seventh Directive clarified the treatment of consolidation adjustments under acquisition accounting by requiring the group share only of consolidating adjustments to be charged against consolidated revenue reserves. Prior to this, adjustments on consolidation could be charged in full against consolidated revenue reserves.

Intra-group profits or losses included in assets in the balance sheet should be eliminated in full under FRS 2 in respect of all subsidiaries (whether consolidated or not). Consistent with the requirements of the Seventh Directive, the amount should be charged against the group and the minority interest in proportion to their holdings in the subsidiary that recorded the profit or loss. Techniques for dealing with such adjustments were explained and illustrated in Parts 2 and 3 of the book.

Exhibit 14.8 shows how GlaxoSmithKline treats intra-group transactions. The note also refers to the deferred tax implications of these adjustments.

Exhibit 14.8 **Adjustments for intra-group transactions**
GlaxoSmithKline Annual Report 2000

Notes to the financial statements (extract)
3 Accounting policies (extract)
Consolidation (extract)
Transactions and balances between subsidiary undertakings are eliminated; no profit is taken on sales between subsidiary undertakings or sales to joint ventures and associated undertakings until the products are sold to customers outside the Group.

Deferred taxation relief on unrealised intra-Group profit is accounted for only to the extent that the related taxation effect is expected to reverse.

Sundry other disclosures

Under the Seventh Directive (which amends the Fourth Directive), where a company is itself a subsidiary undertaking, particulars must be given of:

- parent undertaking of the largest group of undertakings which prepares group accounts of which the company is a member
- parent undertaking of the smallest group of undertakings that prepares consolidated accounts of which the company is a member.

Particulars to be disclosed include:

- name of parent undertaking
- country of incorporation/principal address (if not incorporated) of parent undertaking
- address at which the group accounts are available (if available for public inspection).

Exhibit 14.9 illustrates these requirements.

Exhibit 14.9 **Disclosures concerning parent undertakings**
Powergen Energy Regulatory finance statements 2001

Notes to the summary Regulatory accounts (extract)
14 Parent undertaking and ultimate parent undertaking
The Distribution Business is an operating division of Powergen Energy plc (PGE) which is wholly owned by Powergen (East Midlands) Investments (PEMI). The ultimate parent undertaking and controlling party is Powergen plc.
The smallest Group to consolidate the financial statements of PGE is that of which PEMI is the parent undertaking. The largest group which has published financial statements in which the results of PGE are consolidated is that of which Powergen plc is the parent undertaking. The consolidated accounts in the year ended 31 December 2000 can be obtained from:

Company Secretary
Powergen plc
City Point
1 Ropemaker Street
London EC2Y 9HT

FRS 2 requires some miscellaneous disclosures additional to legal requirements and to those FRS 2 disclosures mentioned already:

- proportion of voting rights held by the group (for principal subsidiaries only)
- indication of the nature of subsidiaries' businesses (for principal subsidiaries only)
- basis of exercise of dominant influence (where relevant to including the undertaking as a subsidiary).

IAS GAAP

Scope

IAS 27 applies to the preparation and presentation of consolidated accounts and to accounting for investments in subsidiaries in the individual accounts of parent undertakings. All subsidiaries must be consolidated, except those which *must* be excluded under the IAS.

Definitions

A number of definitions in IAS 27 (paragraph 6), which are short compared with the equivalent definitions in the Seventh Directive and FRS 2, are as follows:

> A parent is an enterprise that has one or more subsidiaries.
>
> A subsidiary is an enterprise that is controlled by another enterprise (known as the parent).
>
> Control … is the power to govern the financial and operating policies of an enterprise as to obtain benefits from its activities.

Guidance is provided in IAS 27 on what constitutes control. Evidence of control includes the parent:

- owning directly or indirectly more than half the voting power of the enterprise

- having the power over more than half the voting rights by virtue of an agreement with other investors
- having the power to govern the financial and operating policies of the enterprise under a statute or an agreement
- having the power to appoint or remove the majority of the members of the board of directors or equivalent governing body
- having the power to cast the majority of votes at board/governing body meetings.

SIC 33 *Consolidation and Equity Method – Potential Voting Rights and Allocation of Ownership Interests* clarifies that the existence and effect of potential voting rights that are presently (i.e., currently) exercisable or presently convertible (e.g., share warrants, share call options, debt or equity instruments that are convertible into ordinary shares) to give the enterprise voting power (or reduce another party's voting power) over the financial and operating policies of another enterprise (potential voting rights) should be considered, in addition to the other factors described in IAS 27. All facts and circumstances that affect potential voting rights should be examined, except the intention of management and the financial capability to exercise or convert. However, the calculations in the accounts should be determined based solely on present ownership interests.

While the definition and guidelines are similar to those in FRS 2, a number of differences are highlighted in Table 14.3. The differences are highlighted in italics.

Table 14.3 Comparisons of definitions of control under UK GAAP and IAS GAAP

FRS 2	*IAS 27*
Majority of voting rights	More than half the voting rights
Member of, and has right to appoint or remove directors *holding majority of voting rights* on *substantially all matters*	Appoint or remove the majority of the members of the board of directors or equivalent governing body
Right to give directions on operating and financial policies by virtue of *provisions in memorandum or articles of association* or by virtue of *control contract*	Power to govern the financial and operating policies
Is a *member of*, and controls alone pursuant to an agreement with other shareholders/members a majority of the voting rights	Power over more than half the voting rights by virtue of an agreement with other investors
Participating interest in the undertaking and actually exercises a dominant influence or it and the undertaking are managed on a unified basis	No equivalent in the IAS

Source: Adapted from Cairns, D. and Nobes, C. 2000. *The Convergence Handbook: A Comparison between International Accounting Standards and UK Financial Reporting Requirements*, Institute of Chartered Accountants in England and Wales, London

Although IAS 27 requires consolidation of all entities controlled by the reporting entity, it does not provide explicit guidance on the circumstances in which an enterprise should consolidate a special purpose entity (an entity created to accomplish a narrow and well-defined objective). Further guidance on this narrow point is provided in SIC 12 which deals with consolidation of special purpose entities. The consensus of the SIC is that special purpose entities should be consolidated when the substance of the relationship indicates that the special purpose entity is controlled by the reporting entity. UK GAAP has no equivalent guidance to SIC 12, although it has resonance with FRS 5 (discussed in Chapter 20) which requires quasi-subsidiaries to be consolidated in accordance with their commercial substance rather than strict legal form.

Group accounts

Consolidated financial statements are defined in IAS 27 as the 'financial statements of a group prepared as those of a single enterprise'. They include all enterprises controlled by the parent other than those excluded under the requirements of IAS 27.

Exemptions from requirements to prepare group financial statements

IAS 27 does not require parents that are wholly owned (or 'virtually' wholly owned) subsidiaries to prepare consolidated financial statements where they themselves control subsidiaries. The IAS makes it clear that 'virtually' wholly owned means being owned 90% or more. Where the exempt parent is virtually wholly owned, the permission of minority shareholders must be obtained.

This is similar to the provisions of FRS 2 except that under FRS 2 the exemption is only available where (i) the ultimate parent is established in an EU member state and (ii) the enterprise to be exempted is not listed. Also, FRS 2 exempts 'majority' owned (not 'virtually' wholly owned) parent companies from having to prepare consolidated accounts if they meet the exemption criteria under legislation.

Under IAS 27, if a parent does not prepare consolidated accounts for its group, it (the exempted parent) must disclose:

- reasons why consolidated financial statements are not prepared
- bases on which subsidiaries have been accounted for in the exempted parent's financial statements
- name of ultimate parent that publishes consolidated financial statements
- registered office of the ultimate parent that publishes consolidated financial statements.

Exclusion of subsidiaries

IAS 27 requires subsidiaries to be excluded from consolidation when:

- control is intended to be temporary because the subsidiary is held with a view to subsequent disposal in the near future
- the subsidiary operates under severe long-term restrictions which significantly impair its ability to transfer funds to the parent.

The IAS specifically states that subsidiaries with dissimilar activities should be consolidated.

Excluded subsidiaries should be accounted for in accordance with IAS 39 *Financial Instruments, Recognition and Measurement*. IAS 39 classifies investments in excluded subsidiaries as financial assets that are available for sale. This is a default classification category and would include investments under severe long-term restrictions as well as assets held under temporary control. IAS 39 requires that such assets be carried at fair values.

Table 14.4 summarises the differences between UK GAAP and IAS GAAP (i) in subsidiaries that are excluded from consolidation and (ii) in how such excluded subsidiaries are accounted for.

Table 14.4 Excluded subsidiaries – differences between UK GAAP and IAS GAAP

FRS 2		*IAS 27*	
Exclusion In exceptional circumstances, where subsidiary's activities are so different that consolidation would be incompatible with requirement to give true and fair view		**No exclusion** Consolidate subsidiaries with dissimilar activities	
Accounting for excluded subsidiaries		**Accounting for excluded subsidiaries**	
Grounds	*Accounting*	*Grounds*	*Accounting*
Temporary control	Current asset at lower of cost and net realisable value	Temporary control	'Available-for-sale' financial assets should be included in current assets at fair value under IAS 39
Severe long-term restrictions	Use equity method (if exercise of significant influence) or cost (if no significant influence exercised)	Severe long-term restrictions	Classified as 'available-for-sale' financial assets and should be recorded at fair value under IAS 39

Source: Adapted from Cairns, D. and Nobes, C. 2000. *The Convergence Handbook: A Comparison between International Accounting Standards and UK Financial Reporting Requirements*, Institute of Chartered Accountants in England and Wales, London

As shown in Exhibit 14.10, Siemens (which reports under German GAAP) excludes subsidiaries for three reasons that are permitted under IAS 27. These are (i) the subsidiary is *not significant*; (ii) subsidiaries *whose assets Siemens is not permitted to use* and (iii) subsidiaries *acquired exclusively as temporary investments*.

Exhibit 14.10 **Exclusion of subsidiaries**
Siemens Annual Report 2000

Consolidated financial statements – Notes (extract)
Summary of significant accounting policies (extract)
Companies included in consolidation (extract)
The worldwide consolidated financial statements include the accounts of Siemens AG ('the Company') and all subsidiaries which are directly or indirectly controlled (collectively referred to as 'Siemens'). Subsidiaries that are not significant in terms of external sales, earnings and total assets are not included in the consolidated financial statements on the basis of immateriality. In addition, retirement benefit corporations and housing companies whose assets Siemens is not permitted to use because they are assigned for a specific purpose, as well as those companies whose shares were acquired exclusively as temporary financial investments, are not included in the consolidated financial statements.

Exhibit 14.11 shows how Nestlé treats the fixed asset investment in subsidiaries operating under severe long-term restrictions (or as Nestlé put it 'where the political, economic or monetary situation might … carry a greater than normal level of risk'). Such investments are fully written down (to a nominal value of 1 franc).

Exhibit 14.11 **Fixed asset investment under severe long-term restrictions**
Nestlé Annual Report 2001

Annex to the annual accounts of Nestlé S.A.
Accounting policies (extract)
Financial assets (extract)
Participations located in countries where the political, economic or monetary situation might be considered to carry a greater than normal level of risk are carried at a nominal value of one franc.

As shown in Exhibit 14.12, Aegon (which reports under Dutch GAAP) does not consolidate some subsidiaries on the grounds of (i) *insignificance*, (ii) *not intended to be held for long-term ownership* and others on the grounds of (iii) *dissimilar activities*. Separate financial statements in respect of subsidiaries excluded on the ground of dissimilar activities are included in the notes and the investments are '*included in the income statements on a separate line*' (presumably using the equity method of accounting although this is not absolutely clear).

Exhibit 14.12 **Exclusion of dissimilar subsidiaries Aegon Annual Report 2000**

Notes to the Consolidated Financial Statements (extract)
Consolidated principles (extract)
In the consolidated statements of AEGON N.V. all group companies have been included, except for some group companies for which the aggregate financial effect is relatively insignificant and for companies which are not intended to be held for a long-term ownership. Also group companies of which consolidation would not result in a fair view of the group because of dissimiliar activities have not been consolidated. The financial statements of these latter companies have been added separately in the notes. Their results have been included in the income statements on a separate line.

In Exhibit 14.13, Akzo Nobel (which also reports under Dutch GAAP) provides a reconciliation of the fixed financial asset representing the group of subsidiaries not consolidated. They use the equity method of accounting for these excluded subsidiaries. Akzo prepares its accounts in millions of euro.

Exhibit 14.13 **Non-consolidation of subsidiaries Akzo Nobel Annual Report 2000**

Notes to the Consolidated Financial Statements

Financial Non current Assets		Nonconsolidated companies			
	Total	Share in capital	Loans	Deferred tax assets	Other
Situation at December 31, 1999	1,282	465	179	244	394
Acquisitions/deconsolidations/investments	84	7	6	25	46
Disinvestments/repayments	(175)	(25)	(83)		(67)
Equity in earnings	154	154			
Dividends received	(32)	(32)			
Taxes on income	54			54	
Changes in exchange rates	4	2	—	2	—
Situation at December 31, 2000	1,371	571	102	325	373

Some Akzo Nobel companies are general partners in a number of partnerships that are included in the balance sheet under nonconsolidated companies. Akzo Nobel's equity in the capital of these partnerships was EUR 141 million at year-end 2000 (at December 31, 1999: EUR 124 million). Equity in 2000 earnings was EUR 31 million, against EUR 22 million in 1999. At year-end 2000, these partnerships accounted for EUR 4 million of short-term receivables from nonconsolidated companies (at December 31, 1999: EUR 38 million).

These subsidiaries are clearly significant, as Akzo Nobel also has a note providing further details about the earnings shown in the consolidated income statement in respect of non-consolidated subsidiaries.

Danone's note on non-consolidated financial fixed assets (which follows French GAAP) in Exhibit 14.14 is informative in that it distinguishes between non-consolidated subsidiaries, associates and simple investments. The wording suggests that the companies named in the note were not consolidated because they were acquired during the year. The equity method of accounting appears to have been used for these non-consolidated subsidiaries although the wording and positioning of the phrase 'using the equity method of accounting' is awkward so one cannot be absolutely sure of this.

Exhibit 14.14 **Non-consolidated subsidiaries**
Danone Group Annual Report 2000

Consolidated financial statements Notes (extract)

NOTE 7 – Long-term investments in non-consolidated companies

(€ millions) and at net book value at December 31	1999	2000
Acquired previous year-end, and consolidated at the beginning of subsequent year	158	206
Subsidiaries (more than 50% owned)	175	43
Affiliates (20% to 50% owned)	5	2
Other investments (less than 20% owned)	245	320
Net long-term investments	583	571

Net long-term investments in non-consolidated subsidiaries and affiliates are mainly comprised of investments in the companies Paulista (Dairy products in Brazil), Salus (Water in Uruguay) Danone Roumanie (Dairy products in Romania) and Société du Mont Dore (Water in France) which will be included in the consolidation in 2001, and investments in companies that are not consolidated due to their size (including the Japanese Yakult company).

Coterminous year-ends

Under IAS 27, financial statements to be consolidated should normally be drawn up to the same reporting date. Where this is not the case, the difference between reporting dates should be no more than three months. IAS 27 indicates that for consistency, the reporting periods should be the same even where the reporting dates are different. Where there are different reporting dates, adjustments should be made for effects of significant transactions or other events occurring between the different date and the group reporting date.

Exhibit 14.15 **Coterminous year-ends**
Swiss Air Annual Report 2000

Accounting Policies (extract)

4 Balance sheet date

The balance sheet date for the SAirGroup is December 31. The consolidation is based on subsidiary financial statements with year-ends between September 30 and December 31. Those subsidiaries with year-ends which do not fall between these two dates are consolidated using interim financial statements for the period ended December 31.

In Exhibit 14.15 Swiss Air discloses that, for subsidiary year-ends not the same as the group year-end, it uses either (i) financial statements ending within three months of the reporting date or (ii) interim financial statements.

Uniform accounting policies

IAS 27 requires uniform accounting policies to be used. Where group companies use different accounting policies, the IAS indicates that, normally, appropriate adjustments should be made to bring the accounting policies into line. Where this is not practicable, that fact should be disclosed, together with the proportions of items in the consolidated accounts to which different accounting policies have been applied. Bayer illustrates these requirements in Exhibit 14.16

Exhibit 14.16 **Uniform group accounting policies**
Bayer Annual Report 2001

Notes to the Consolidated Financial Statements of the Bayer Group
Accounting policies (extract)
The financial statements of the consolidated companies are prepared according to uniform recognition and valuation principles. Valuation adjustments made for tax reasons are not reflected in the Group statements.

Minority interests

Under IAS 27, minority interests should be presented separately in the consolidated balance sheet, outside shareholders' equity and liabilities. The consolidated income and expenditure account should also show minority interests in income separately.

Where losses applicable to the minority exceed the minority's equity interest in the subsidiary, the excess, and any further losses attributable to the minority, are charged against the minority except where the minority has a binding obligation to make good the losses and is in a position to so do. This requirement differs from FRS 2 which requires all minority interest debit balances to be recorded in consolidated financial statements. In addition, FRS 2 requires a provision to be made where the parent has an obligation to provide finance to subsidiaries and where such finance may not be recoverable.

IAS 27 also refers to minority interests in cumulative preference shares and states that the minority dividend on such shares should be deducted before the parent computes its share of profits from the subsidiary, even where the dividend has not been declared. There is no equivalent requirement in FRS 2, although the practice is normal under UK GAAP.

In Exhibit 14.17, ABN Amro provides a useful description of what the balance sheet amount for minority interests represents. The note provides an analysis of the balance for minority interests which, in effect, distinguishes between non-equity and equity minority interests. In addition, the note provides a reconciliation of the movements on the account during the period. These movements mainly comprise issue and redemption of preference shares, foreign currency translation adjustments and 'other minority interests'. ABN Amro (which follows Dutch GAAP) reports in millions of euro.

In Exhibit 14.18, AXA (which reports under French GAAP) also discloses the movements in minority interests during the year. They are made up of acquisitions (three acquisitions which are separately identified), dividends paid to minority shareholders by subsidiaries, foreign currency translation differences, 'other changes' and, lastly, minority share of income which is the minority interest identified in the consolidated profit and loss account for the year.

Exhibit 14.17 **Balance sheet minority interests**
ABN Amro Annual Report 1999

Notes to the Financial Statements (extract)
17 Minority interests
This item comprises the share of third parties in the equity of subsidiaries and other group companies, as well as preferred stock issued to third parties by subsidiaries in the United States. The right to repayment of this preferred stock is in all cases vested in the issuing institution but repayment is also subject to approval of the supervisory authorities. If this right is not exercised, preference shares without fixed dividend entitlement qualify for a dividend step-up. In terms of dividend and liquidation rights, Trust preference shares are comparable to ABN AMRO Holding N.V. preference shares.

	1999	**1998**	**1997**
Cumulative preference shares	109	94	101
Non-cumulative preference shares			
• Trust preference shares with fixed dividend	2,488	1,070	
• Other shares with fixed dividend	547	471	504
• Other shares with dividend step-up	1,209	1,040	1,113
Other minority interests	592	855	336
Total	4,945	3,530	2,054

	1999	**1998**	**1997**
Opening balance	3,530	2,054	955
Currency translation differences	556	(195)	191
Issue of preference shares	1,180	1,133	1,025
Redemption of preference shares			(234)
Other movements	(321)	538	117
Closing balance	4,945	3,530	2,054

Exhibit 14.18 **Balance sheet minority interest**
AXA plc Annual Report 1999

Notes to the Financial Statements (extract)
9 Minority Interests
Changes in minority shareholders' interests are summarized as follows:

	Years Ended December 31,		
(in euro millions)	**1999**	**1998**	**1997**
Minority interests at January 1,	5,237	7,090	3,132
AXA Royale Belge acquisition	—	(2,325)	—
GRE acquisition	1,025	—	—
Additions from UAP acquisition	—	—	2,913
Dividends paid by consolidated subsidiaries	(507)	(188)	(304)
Impact of foreign currency fluctuations on minority interests	851	(355)	389
Other changes (including Internal Restructurings)	(10)	42	157
Minority interests in income of consolidated subsidiaries	858	974	802
MINORITY INTERESTS AT DECEMBER 31,	**7,454**	**5,237**	**7,090**

Consolidation adjustments

Intra-group balances and intra-group transactions should be eliminated in full under IAS 27, as should any resulting unrealised profits. Unrealised losses resulting from intra-group transactions should also be eliminated except where the cost cannot be recovered. IAS 27 refers to IAS 12 *Income Taxes* in relation to the deferred tax implications arising from timing differences generated from these adjustments.

Sundry other disclosures

In addition to disclosures concerning (i) method of accounting, (ii) exempted parents, (iii) uniform accounting policies and (iv) changes in group composition, IAS 27 requires the following disclosures:

- listing of significant subsidiaries, including:
  - name of significant subsidiaries
  - country of incorporation/residence of significant subsidiaries
  - proportion of ownership interest held
  - proportion of voting power held (if different from proportion of ownership interest).
- where applicable:
  - reasons for not consolidating a subsidiary
  - nature of parent–subsidiary relationship where not more than half of the voting power is held
  - name of enterprise owning more than half of voting power, but not exercising control.

Comparison of UK GAAP and IAS GAAP

There are a number of differences between FRS 2 and IAS 27, the main ones having already been summarised in Tables 14.3 and 14.4. The main differences relate to definitions, methods of accounting and disclosure requirements.

Many of the disclosure requirements under FRS 2 and IAS 27 are the same. Therefore, only the extra disclosure requirements under UK GAAP and IAS GAAP are compared in Table 14.5.

Table 14.5 Extra disclosure requirements under UK GAAP and IAS GAAP

FRS 2	*IAS 27*
■ Excluded subsidiaries: – Balances between subsidiary and rest of group – Nature and extent of transactions between subsidiary and rest of group – Subsidiary not accounted for by the equity method – dividends received and receivable; any write-down of investment in or amounts due from subsidiary ■ Nature of business of principal subsidiaries ■ Different reporting dates – name of subsidiary, accounting date or period, reasons for different date/period ■ Name of undertaking ceasing to be a subsidiary during the period and circumstances if not a disposal ■ Circumstances of undertaking becoming/ceasing to be subsidiary, if not by means of purchase or exchange of shares ■ Nature and extent of significant statutory, contractual or exchange control restrictions on distributions of subsidiary	■ Proportions of items determined using non-uniform accounting policies ■ Nature of relationship, where parent does not own more than half of the voting power ■ Name of enterprise that is not a subsidiary even though more than half the voting power is owned

Source: Adapted from Cairns, D. and Nobes, C. 2000. *The Convergence Handbook: A Comparison between International Accounting Standards and UK Financial Reporting Requirements*, Institute of Chartered Accountants in England and Wales, London

Summary

This chapter has discussed general regulations underlying the preparation of consolidated financial statements. These include requirements to prepare group accounts, definitions of subsidiaries, exemptions from requirements to prepare consolidated accounts and exclusion of subsidiaries from consolidation. Also considered were regulations dealing with subsidiaries with non-uniform accounting policies, non-coterminous year-end dates and for dealing with intra-group transactions. Regulations on minority interests were also addressed.

Later chapters develop some of the issues briefly raised in this chapter. In particular, changes in group composition are discussed further in Chapter 16, as are the two methods of accounting for business combinations, acquisition and merger accounting. Chapter 17 deals with regulations covering one of the consequences of the acquisition method of accounting, i.e., goodwill.

Learning outcomes

After studying this chapter you should have learnt:

- UK GAAP regulations applying to the preparation of group accounts for parents and their subsidiary companies
- IAS GAAP regulations applying to the preparation of group accounts for parents and their subsidiary companies
- how UK GAAP and IAS GAAP regulations applying to parent and subsidiary undertakings compare and contrast.

Multiple choice questions

Solutions to these questions are prepared under UK GAAP and are shown in Appendix 1.

Classification as subsidiary

14.1 Colours

Colours made the following acquisitions during the year ended 31 December 20X7:

Red Acquired 55% of voting equity. Colours changed the composition of the Board of Red since acquisition.

Blue Acquired a 90% holding, of which 35% relates to voting equity. Colours has so far failed to have one of its directors appointed to the Board of Blue.

Orange Acquired 70% of the voting equity.

Purple Acquired 48% of the voting equity. By virtue of a provision in the Memorandum and Articles of Association of Purple, Colours has a right to exercise control over the financial and operating policies of Purple.

Which of these four companies would be treated as subsidiary companies under FRS 2 *Accounting for Subsidiary Undertakings* in the consolidated accounts of Colours for the year ended 31 December 20X7?

	Red	Blue	Orange	Purple
(a)	Subsidiary	Subsidiary		Subsidiary
(b)		Subsidiary	Subsidiary	Subsidiary
(c)	Subsidiary	Subsidiary	Subsidiary	
(d)	Subsidiary		Subsidiary	Subsidiary

14.2 Easy

The issued share capital of **Easy** comprises:

5,000 non-participating, non-voting 10% preference shares
10,000 non-voting A ordinary shares
1,000 voting ordinary shares

of which **Indy** owns:

5,000 preference shares
1,695 'A' ordinary shares
505 voting ordinary shares

In the consolidated accounts of Indy, the investment in Easy should be treated as:

(a) a subsidiary undertaking
(b) an associated undertaking
(c) a trade investment
(d) none of these

Exemptions from requirement to prepare group financial statements

14.3 Cairo

Cairo is 100% owned by Joel. Cairo owns 80% of **Card**, which owns 30% of **Gardenia**. None of these companies has any other long-term investments. Assuming relevant conditions for exemption (not mentioned in this MCQ) are met, which investing companies must prepare consolidated financial statements under FRS 2?

(a) Joel, Cairo and Card
(b) Joel and Card only
(c) Joel and Cairo only
(d) Joel only

EXCLUSION OF SUBSIDIARIES

14.4 Subsidiary must be excluded

FRS 2 *Accounting for Subsidiary Undertakings* states that a subsidiary must be excluded from consolidated accounts if:

(a) Subsidiary operates under severe long-term restrictions which impair control
(b) Inclusion of the subsidiary would involve disproportionate expense
(c) Activities and assets of the subsidiary are insignificant in relation to the group as a whole
(d) Inclusion of the subsidiary would have a harmful effect on the group

14.5 Exclusion of a subsidiary

Under FRS 2, which one of the following *would not* give rise to the exclusion of a subsidiary undertaking from consolidation:

(a) where severe long-term restrictions substantially hinder the rights of the parent undertaking over the assets of the subsidiary undertaking
(b) where the interest in the subsidiary undertaking is held exclusively with a view to subsequent resale
(c) where the information necessary for the preparation of the group accounts cannot be gathered without undue delay
(d) where the subsidiary carries on activities dissimilar to those of the parent, the inclusion of which in the accounts would be incompatible with the obligation to give a true and fair view.

14.6 Pheasant

Pheasant owns 90% of the equity share capital of **Partridge**, a company incorporated and operating in a foreign country. The military government of that country imposed severe long-term restrictions (four years after the acquisition by Pheasant), and the directors of Pheasant are of the opinion that these restrictions significantly impair control, so much so that significant influence cannot be exercised.

In accordance with FRS 2 *Accounting for Subsidiary Undertakings*, which of the following best represents how the requirements of FRS 2 would be applied to accounting for the investment in Partridge in the consolidated accounts of Pheasant?

(a) As a subsidiary, based on the latest available accounts of Partridge.
(b) Using the equity method, as for an associate, based on the latest available accounts of Partridge.
(c) Using the equity method based on the accounts on the date the restrictions came into force.
(d) As a simple investment, shown at cost.

14.7 Ant Pheas

Ant Pheas owns 90% of the equity share capital of **Swallow**, a company incorporated and operating in a foreign country. The military government of that country imposed severe long-term restrictions (four years after the acquisition by Ant Pheas), and the directors of Ant Pheas are of the opinion that these restrictions significantly impair control, so much so that significant influence cannot be exercised.

In accordance with FRS 2 *Accounting for Subsidiary Undertakings*, which of the following best represents how the requirements of FRS 2 would be applied to disclosing the investment in Swallow in the consolidated accounts of Ant Pheas?

(a) A note giving an indication of the nature of the restrictions and the date they came into force.
(b) A note of the balances and nature and extent of transactions between the excluded subsidiary and the rest of the group, of dividends received and of any write down relating to the investment in Swallow.
(c) A note containing summarised financial information for the excluded subsidiary, Swallow.
(d) A note of the balances and nature and extent of transactions between the excluded subsidiary, Swallow, and the rest of the group.

14.8 Control is intended to be temporary

FRS 2 requires a subsidiary to be excluded from consolidation if control is intended to be temporary (i.e., where a subsidiary is held exclusively with a view to resale). In these circumstances, FRS 2 requires that the subsidiary be accounted for:

(a) under the equity method of accounting
(b) as a fixed asset investment at cost less any provision required
(c) as a fixed asset investment at valuation
(d) as a current asset investment at the lower of cost and net realisable value

14.9 Activities are so dissimilar

A subsidiary should be excluded from consolidation because its activities are so dissimilar from those of other companies in the group that its inclusion in consolidated financial statements would be incompatible with the obligation to give a true and fair view. How does FRS 2 require such an investment to be treated in the consolidated financial statements?

(a) Stated in the consolidated balance sheet at cost or valuation, less provisions.
(b) Stated in the consolidated balance sheet at cost or valuation, less provisions, and reconciled in a note to summary separate financial statements.
(c) Stated in the consolidated balance sheet under the equity method of accounting with no further disclosures.
(d) Stated in the consolidated balance sheet under the equity method of accounting with separate financial statements for the excluded subsidiary undertaking (summarised in some cases) also disclosed.

Examination-style questions

14.1 Seventh Directive

(a) FRS 2 *Accounting for Subsidiary Undertakings* reflects the provisions of the Seventh Directive. Under FRS 2 in what circumstances does a parent/subsidiary relationship arise?
(b) (i) Under the Seventh Directive, in what five circumstances may a subsidiary be excluded from the consolidated accounts of a parent company?
(ii) In what additional circumstances to those permitted under the Seventh Directive does FRS 2 require/permit subsidiaries to be excluded from the consolidated accounts of a parent company?

14.2 Jasmin, Kasbah and Fortran

Relevant balance sheets of **Jasmin**, **Kasbah** and **Fortran** as at 31 March 20X4 are as follows:

	Jasmin	Kasbah	Fortran
	€000	€000	€000
Tangible fixed assets	289,400	91,800	7,600
Investments			
Shares in Kasbah (at cost)	97,600		
Shares in Fortran (at cost)	8,000		
	395,000		
Current assets			
Stock	285,600	151,400	2,600
Cash	319,000	500	6,800
	604,600	151,900	9,400
Creditors: Amounts falling due within one year	(289,600)	(238,500)	(2,200)
Net current assets/(liabilities)	315,000	(86,600)	7,200
Total assets less current liabilities	710,000	5,200	14,800
Capital and reserves			
Called-up share capital			
Ordinary €1 shares	60,000	20,000	10,000
10% €1 preference shares	—	4,000	—
Revaluation reserve	40,000	—	1,200
Profit and loss reserve	610,000	(18,800)	3,600
	710,000	5,200	14,800

You have recently been appointed chief accountant of Jasmin and are about to prepare the group balance sheet at 31 March 20X4. The following points are relevant to the preparation of those accounts:

1 Jasmin owns 90% of the ordinary €1 shares and 20% of the 10% €1 preference shares of Kasbah. On 1 April 20X3 Jasmin paid €96 million for the ordinary €1 shares and €1.6 million for the 10% €1 preference shares when Kasbah's reserves were a credit balance of €45 million.

2 Jasmin sells part of its output to Kasbah. The stock of Kasbah on 31 March 20X4 includes €1.2 million of stock purchased from Jasmin at cost plus one-third.

3 The policy of the group is to revalue its tangible fixed assets on a yearly basis. However, the directors of Kasbah have always resisted this policy preferring to show tangible fixed assets at historical cost. The market value of the tangible fixed assets of Kasbah at 31 March 20X4 is €90 million. The directors of Jasmin wish you to follow the requirements of FRS 2 *Accounting for Subsidiary Undertakings* in respect of the consistency of accounting policies for all group companies.

4 The ordinary €1 shares of Fortran are split into 6 million A ordinary €1 shares and 4 million 'B' ordinary €1 shares. Holders of A shares are assigned 1 vote and holders of B ordinary shares are assigned two votes per share. On 1 April 20X3 Jasmin acquired 80% of the A ordinary shares and 10% of the B ordinary shares when the profit and loss reserve of Fortran was €1.6 million and the revaluation reserve was €2 million. The A ordinary shares and B ordinary shares carry equal rights to share in the company's profit and losses.

5 The fair values of Kasbah and Fortran were not materially different from their book values at the time of acquisition of their shares by Jasmin.

6 Goodwill arising on acquisition is amortised over five years.

7 Kasbah has paid its preference dividend for the current year but no other dividends are proposed by the group companies. The preference dividend was paid shortly after the interim results of Kasbah were announced and was deemed to be a legal dividend by the auditors.

8 The directors of Jasmin wish to exclude the financial statements of Kasbah from the group accounts on the grounds that Kasbah's output is not similar to that of Jasmin and that the resultant accounts therefore would be misleading. Jasmin produces synthetic yarn and Kasbah produces garments.

Required

(a) List the conditions for exclusion of subsidiaries from consolidation under FRS 2 for the directors of Jasmin and state whether Kasbah may be excluded on these grounds.

(b) Prepare a consolidated balance sheet for Jasmin Group for the year ending 31 March 20X4. (All calculations should be made to the nearest thousand euro.)

14.3 FSR group

The **FSR group** consists of the holding company **FSR** and two subsidiary companies, **GBH** and **Short**. FSR had acquired 75% of the ordinary shares in GBH and 80% of the ordinary shares in Short on 1 December 20X2. The ordinary shares in Short are held exclusively with a view to subsequent resale; the ordinary shares in GBH are held on a long-term basis. FSR prepares its accounts to 30 November each year.

A trainee accountant, working on the consolidation for the year ended 30 November 20X3, has proposed the following adjustments:

(i) Treatment of profit arising from intra-group sales:
During October 20X3 GBH sold goods costing it €200,000 to FSR for €220,000. All goods were in stock as at 30 November 20X3.

The trainee accountant proposed reducing the stock and consolidated profits by €15,000.

During September 20X3 FSR sold goods costing €60,000 to GBH for €72,000. All goods were in stock as at 30 November 20X3.

The trainee accountant proposed reducing the stock and consolidated profits by €12,000.

(ii) Treatment of goodwill arising on acquisition of GBH:
The 75% shareholding in GBH was acquired on 1 December 20X2 for €3,000,000 when the fair value of the total net assets in GBH was estimated to be €3,000,000.

The trainee accountant proposed to credit the minority interest with €250,000 and record the goodwill at 1 December 20X2 at €1,000,000. In accordance with group policy, this goodwill was to be written off over five years. The charge in the 20X3 accounts was to be €200,000.

(iii) Treatment of profit arising from sale by Short:
Short sold goods costing €100,000 to FSR for €110,000 on 31 August 20X3. All goods were in stock as at 30 November 20X3.

The trainee accountant proposed to reduce the stock and the consolidated profit and loss account by €8,000.

Required

(a) Describe the accounting treatment required in the consolidated accounts of the FSR group as at 30 November 20X3 of the investment in Short to comply with financial reporting standards.

(b) Inform the trainee accountant whether the proposed consolidation adjustments in (i) to (iii) in the list comply with accounting standards. State any additional information which could affect the accounting treatment.

(c) Explain briefly the reasons for the accounting treatment recommended for (i) to (iii) in the list.

15

Company legislation and professional accounting regulations: associated undertakings and joint ventures

Learning objectives

After studying this chapter you should be able to:

- understand regulations applying to associated undertakings under UK GAAP
- understand regulations applying to associated undertakings under IAS GAAP
- describe the accounting treatment applying to joint ventures
- apply UK regulations to accounting for joint arrangements that are not entities (JANEs)
- compare and contrast UK GAAP and IAS GAAP regulations

Introduction

The underlying rationale for using equity accounting for investments classified as associates or joint ventures was explained in Chapters 7 and 11. Techniques for applying the equity method of accounting were also described and illustrated in those chapters. In addition, the detailed mechanics and accounting entries involved were explained and illustrated.

This chapter sets out the regulatory background and requirements applying in accounting for (i) associated undertakings, (ii) joint ventures and (iii) joint arrangements that are not entities (JANEs). Two sources of regulations are discussed: UK GAAP and IAS GAAP. The chapter has four parts: first, we consider the two sources of regulations as they apply to associates. Joint ventures are considered separately from associates in the next part. Joint arrangements that are not entities (JANEs) are then discussed. The chapter concludes by comparing UK and IAS GAAP.

UK GAAP – associates

SSAP 1 *Accounting for Associated Companies* was first issued in 1971. In November 1997, ASB issued FRS 9 *Associates and Joint Ventures* to supersede SSAP 1. FRS 9 provides guidance on defining and accounting for associates and joint ventures. The requirements of FRS 9 retained much of the approach of SSAP 1 on associated companies but introduced new requirements for reporting joint ventures. Many changes were prompted by the need to bring professional accounting regulations into line with legal provisions consequent on legislating for the Seventh Directive in the UK and the Republic of Ireland.

The standard addresses two areas where accounting for associates had sometimes been criticised. First, SSAP 1 had been interpreted as identifying associates according to whether the investor held 20% or more of the voting rights in its investment (even though the standard had a broader test of identification, based on whether the investment was for the long term and the investor was in a position to exercise significant influence). The excessive focus on a 20% threshold allowed companies to choose (or avoid) equity accounting for the investments by minimal adjustments to their stake.

The second criticism of SSAP 1 was that investments accounted for under the equity method might be used to facilitate off balance sheet finance as, under the equity method, the share of assets and liabilities of associates is included as a net amount in the consolidated balance sheet. The problem was created by the strict interpretation of the pre-Seventh Directive definition of subsidiary where the emphasis was on holdings of more than 50% in order to be classified as a subsidiary. At that time, holdings up to and including 50% were classified as associates even where control existed.

Definitions

Some of the definitions relevant to equity accounting have already been introduced in Chapter 7. These introductory definitions are expanded on in this chapter.

The Seventh Directive defined an associate as existing when another undertaking:

> exercises a significant influence over the operating and financial policy of an undertaking not included in the consolidation (an associated undertaking) in which it holds a participating interest … that participating interest shall be shown in the consolidated balance sheet as a separate item with an appropriate heading. An undertaking shall be presumed to exercise a significant influence over another undertaking where it has 20% or more of the shareholders' or members' voting rights in that undertaking.

The definition of associate in FRS 9 (paragraph 4) is similar to the definition in the Seventh Directive:

> An entity (other than a subsidiary) in which another entity (the investor) has a participating interest and over whose operating and financial policies the investor exercises a significant influence.

This definition leads, in turn, to two further key definitions (paragraph 4). The first is the definition of participating interest, which is:

> An interest held in shares of another entity on a long-term basis for the purpose of securing a contribution to the investor's activities by the exercise of control or influence arising from or related to that interest. The investor's interest, must, therefore, be a beneficial one and the benefits expected to arise must be linked to the exercise of its significant influence over the investee's operating and financial policies. An interest in the shares of another entity includes an interest convertible into an interest in shares or an option to acquire shares.
>
> Companies legislation provides that a holding of 20 per cent or more of the shares of an entity is to be presumed to be a participating interest unless the

> contrary is shown. The presumption is rebutted if the interest is either not long-term or not beneficial.

The second key element of the definition relates to the exercise of significant influence. FRS 9 gives guidance on what constitutes significant influence. It involves participation in the financial and operating policy decisions of the company (including dividend policy) but without control of these policies. Exercise of significant influence is defined in paragraph 4 as follows:

> The investor is actively involved and is influential in the direction of its investee through its participation in policy decisions covering aspects of policy relevant to the investor, including decisions on strategic issues such as:
> (a) the expansion or contraction of the business, participation in other entities or changes in products, markets and activities of its investee; and
> (b) determining the balance between dividend and reinvestment.

The guidance given in FRS 9 on what constitutes significant influence specifies two conditions to help in assessing whether investors can exercise influence over the operating and financial policies of investees. These are:

- investor is actively involved and is influential through participation in policy decisions including decisions on strategic issues
- investor is involved in determining the balance between dividends and reinvestment.

Three types of strategic issue are identified (i) expansion/contraction of the business, (ii) participation in other entities and (iii) changes in products, markets and activities.

Tomkins' definition of associates in Exhibit 15.1 refers to the investment being (i) substantial, (ii) long term and involves (iii) minority equity interest and (iv) participation in commercial and financial policy decisions.

Exhibit 15.1 **Definition of associates**
Tomkins plc Annual Report 2000

Principal accounting policies (extract)
Investments (extract)
An associated undertaking ('associate') is an investment in which the group has a substantial long-term minority equity interest and in which it participates in commercial and financial policy decisions.

The investor's percentage ownership of shares in the associated undertaking is clearly given a subordinate role to the relationship in substance between investor and investee. The relationship between investor and investee is determined by arrangements such as the number of directors the investor can nominate to the board and by considering the relative dispositions of other shareholders' holdings in the investee. This is more restrictive than the Seventh Directive where investors holding 20% or more of the equity of undertakings are presumed to exercise significant influence.

In relation to the definition of significant influence, FRS 9 (paragraph 4) goes on to state:

> Companies legislation provides that an entity holding 20 per cent or more of the voting rights in another entity should be presumed to exercise a significant influence over that other entity unless the contrary is shown. For the purpose of applying the

presumption, the shares held by the parent and its subsidiaries in that entity should be aggregated. The presumption is rebutted if the investor does not fulfil the criteria for the exercise of significant influence set out above.

Smith & Nephew uses a different wording in its definition of associates in Exhibit 15.2. Only the upper limit percentage (of 50%) is specified in the policy note, but not a lower limit. The exercise of significant influence over commercial and financial policy decisions is identified as a key determinant.

Exhibit 15.2 **Alternative definition of associates**
Smith & Nephew Annual Report 2000

Associated undertakings are those companies in which the group has a beneficial interest of 50% or less in the equity capital and where the group exercises significant influence over commercial and financial policy decisions.

Examples of the calculation of aggregate holdings in determining the percentage holding relevant in assessing whether significant influence is exercised were given in Chapter 7.

To summarise, the key element identifying an associate as distinct from a subsidiary relationship or a simple investment is the ability to exercise significant influence in the absence of control. Many examples exist of investments in the 20% to 50% range which are not equity accounted. Exhibit 15.3 is one such example. RMC Group discloses in Exhibit 15.3 that it does not account for a 22.17% investment as an associate because it cannot exercise significant influence.

Exhibit 15.3 **Absence of significant influence**
RMC Group p.l.c. Annual Report 2000

d Other investments (extract)
At 31st December 2000, RMC Group p.l.c. held 22.17% of the issued Ordinary share capital of Alexander Russell PLC, a company registered and principally operating in Scotland and listed in the United Kingdom. The latest date to which accounts have been published is 31st December 1999. These disclosed a profit for the year of £4.2 million, and capital and reserves of £36.7 million. The company is not regarded as an associate undertaking as RMC Group p.l.c. is not in a position to exercise significant influence in management.

Investments of less than 20% are sometimes accounted for using the equity method because of the investor's ability to exercise significant influence. Exhibit 15.4 illustrates this situation. In Exhibit 15.4 (note (d)), Rio Tinto discloses two investments (Freeport-McMoRan Copper & Gold Inc and Lihir Gold Limited) which are accounted for as associates even though the shareholdings are not within the 20 to 50% range specified by FRS 9. Only 16.26% of the shares of Lihir Gold Limited are owned by the group but note (d) states that nonetheless significant influence is exercised. Only 16.61% of Freeport-McMoRan Copper & Gold Inc is owned by the group, although it holds 36.59% of a particular class of shares (which may be voting shares, through which significant influence is exercised).

Exhibit 15.4 **Equity method of accounting for holdings less than 20%**
Rio Tinto plc Annual Report 2000

30 PRINCIPAL ASSOCIATES
At 31 December 2000

Name and country of incorporation/operation	Principal activities	Number of shares held by the Group	Class of shares held	Proportion of class held %	Group interest %
Papua New Guinea					
Lihir Gold Limited (note d)	Gold mining	185,758,126	Ordinary Kina 0.1	16.26	16.26
Portugal					
Sociedade Mineira de Neves-Corvo S.A.	Copper and tin mining	7,178,500	Esc 1000	49	49
South Africa					
Tisland (Pty) Limited	Rutile and zircon mining	7,353,675	R1	49	50
United States of America					
Cortez	Gold mining		(b)		40.0
Freeport-McMoRan Copper & Gold Inc (note d)	Copper and gold mining in Indonesia	23,931,100	Class 'A' Common US$0.10	36.59	16.61
Argentina					
Minera Alumbrera Limited	Copper and gold mining	92,901,000 1,000,000	Common Preference	50	25

(a) The Group comprises a large number of companies and it is not practical to include all of them in this list. The list, therefore, only includes those companies that have a more significant impact on the profit or assets of the Group.
(b) Those joint ventures, associates and joint arrangements marked (b) are unincorporated entities.
(c) All entities operate mainly in the countries in which they are incorporated.
(d) The Group equity accounts for its interests in Freeport-McMoRan Copper & Gold Inc and Lihir Gold Limited because it exercises significant influence over their activities.

Equity method of accounting

Associated companies should be accounted for using the equity method of accounting. This method of accounting was not defined in SSAP 1, but this omission was initially rectified in paragraph 8 of FRS 2 *Accounting for Subsidiary Undertakings* as follows:

> A method of accounting for an investment that brings into the consolidated profit and loss account the investor's share of the investment undertaking's results and that records the investment in the consolidated balance sheet at the investor's share of the investment undertaking's net assets including any goodwill arising to the extent that it has not previously been written off.

As set out in Chapter 7, the description of the equity method of accounting in FRS 9 is different from that in FRS 2. FRS 9's definition spells out explicitly the technique involved in applying the equity method. The difference in the definition does not affect the application of equity accounting in practice. FRS 9's definition is just more descriptive of the approach. It describes the equity method (paragraph 4) as follows:

> A method of accounting that brings an investment into its investor's financial statements initially at its cost, identifying any goodwill arising. The carrying amount of the investment is adjusted in each period by the investor's share of the results of its investee, less any amortisation or write-off for goodwill, the investor's share of any relevant gains or losses, and any other changes in the investee's net assets including distributions to its owners, for example by dividend. The investor's share of its investee's results is recognised in its profit and loss account. The investor's cash flow statement includes the cash flows between the investor and its investee, for example relating to dividends and loans.

Dixons' accounting policy note explains the equity method in Exhibit 15.5.

Exhibit 15.5 **Accounting policy for equity method of accounting**
Dixons Group plc Annual Report 1999/2000

Accounting Policies (extract)
2.6 Investments (extract)
Shares in associated undertakings are accounted for using the equity method. The consolidated profit and loss account includes the Group's share of the pre-tax results and attributable taxation of the associated undertaking. In the consolidated balance sheet, the investment is shown as the Group's share of the net assets of the associated undertakings. Goodwill arising on the acquisition of an associate is capitalised as part of the carrying amount in the consolidated balance sheet, and amortised over its estimated useful life.

3i Group does not account for its associates using the equity method of accounting as required by UK legislation. The true and fair view override provision of legislation is invoked. This provision has already been discussed in Chapter 13. The statement in Exhibit 15.6 that 'The treatment adopted is in accordance with Financial Reporting Standard 9 – Associates and Joint Ventures' is somewhat contradictory. The justification for the treatment adopted is vague in Exhibit 15.6 because the company is less than clear about whether significant influence is exercised or not. In effect, these investments are accounted for as simple investments as only dividends received and interest income is included in the profit and loss account in relation to these investments.

Exhibit 15.6 **Associates – significant influence not exercised**
3i Group plc Annual Report 2001

Accounting policies (extract)
B Joint ventures and associated undertakings (extract)
The Directors consider that, in general, the Group's equity share investments do not come within the Companies Act definition of associated undertakings, since 3i does not usually exercise significant influence over the operating and financial policies of investees. However, it is possible that, in a small number of equity share investments, 3i does in fact exert significant influence on occasions, and that the Companies Act provides that these be treated as associated undertakings and accounted for using the equity method of accounting. The Directors believe that the equity accounting for Investments would not give a true and fair view of the income from the investment activities of the Group, since this is better measured by the inclusion of dividends and interest income. It is impracticable to quantify the effect of this departure on the revenue profit for the year and there would be no effect on net assets. The treatment adopted is in accordance with Financial Reporting Standard 9 – Associates and Joint Ventures.

Paragraphs 31 to 37 of FRS 9 spell out the application of the equity method. Similar principles to those applied in consolidating subsidiaries should be followed, including:

- use of fair values on acquisition and in calculating goodwill on acquisition
- any goodwill on the associate's own balance sheet should not be included as an asset in computing the goodwill arising on acquisition of the associate
- inter-company profits and losses should be eliminated (investor's share only, offset against relevant profit or loss in the consolidated profit and loss account)
- same accounting policies as those of the investor should be applied. The associate's results may need to be adjusted
- results of the entity should be included to the same year-end as the investor or, where not practicable, not more than three months before the investor's year-end
- share of associate to be taken into account is that of the parent and subsidiaries only, excluding holdings of the group's other associates and joint ventures
- results and net assets to be taken into account under the equity method are those recorded in the associate's own group accounts (i.e., including the associate's share of the results and net assets of its associates and joint ventures).

Granada Media does not comply with the requirements of FRS 9 in the way it accounted for an investment in an associated undertaking. The extract in Exhibit 15.7 states that, on acquisition, assets and liabilities of the investee *should* be recorded at fair values and that goodwill on the acquisition *should* be recognised. The directors state that the acquisition was in effect a reorganisation and use this explanation to justify applying merger accounting principles in accounting for the acquisition. They state that they cannot quantify the effect of the departure from FRS 9.

Exhibit 15.7 **Disposal of associated company**
Granada Media plc Annual Report 2000

Accounting policies (extract)

2 Basis of Consolidation (extract)

The Group accounts comprise a consolidation of the accounts of the Company and all of its subsidiaries and includes the Group's share of the results and net assets of its associates and gross equity of joint ventures. The accounts of principal subsidiaries, associates and joint ventures are made up to 30 September.

During the year an investment held by Granada Group PLC in 50% of the ordinary share capital of ONdigital was transferred to the Company in return for the issue of ordinary shares in the Company. At the time of the transfer the Company was a wholly owned subsidiary of Granada Group PLC. In the accounts of the Company, the investment of ONdigital has been recorded at the book value of the investment in the accounts of the transferor, in accordance with section 132 Companies Act 1985. In the consolidated accounts of the Company, FRS 9 Associates and Joint Ventures requires that, when an entity acquires a joint venture, fair values should be attributed to the investee's underlying assets and liabilities and goodwill recognised. However, the directors consider that the transaction is in substance a group reorganisation, since it took place while the Company was wholly owned by the transferror and that the treatment required by FRS 9 would fail to give a true and fair view. Accordingly the directors have applied the principles of merger accounting to the transfer so as to include the results, assets and liabilities of ONdigital, a joint venture, as if the investment had always been held by the Company. It is not possible to quantify the effect of this departure.

Paragraphs 26 to 30 of FRS 9 detail how entities accounted for under the equity method should be dealt with in the published accounts:

- interests in associates should be included as part of fixed asset investments in the parent's balance sheet
- share of net assets of associates should be included in fixed asset investments in the consolidated balance sheet, together with goodwill on acquisition of associates not written off and this should be separately disclosed
- share of associate's operating profit should be shown immediately after group operating profit in the consolidated profit and loss account (and *after* the investor's share of the results of any joint ventures)
- amortisation or write-off of goodwill arising on acquisition of associates should appear immediately after the share of associate's operating profit
- group share of associate's exceptional items should be separately disclosed
- group share of associate's interest should be shown separately
- group share of associate's relevant amounts at or below profit before taxation should be included in group amounts, with separate disclosure of the amounts relating to associates, e.g., taxation
- investor's share of turnover should be separately disclosed where helpful as an indication of the size of associates
- the group share of associated company recognised gains and losses should be included in the statement of total recognised gains and losses and should be disclosed separately if material.

The balance sheet formats of the Fourth Directive require the following headings and disclosures for associated companies:

- participating interests
- loans to undertakings with which the company is linked by virtue of participating interests
- debtors – amounts owed by undertakings with which the company is linked by virtue of participating interests
- creditors – amounts owed to undertakings with which the company is linked by virtue of participating interests.

(*Note*: Interests in associated companies and participating interests are, for practical purposes, the same.)

The Fourth Directive requires disclosure of *Income from participating interests* on the face of the profit and loss account after operating profit before taxation.

Barclays plc discloses in Exhibit 15.8 that it changed its presentation of results of joint ventures and associated undertakings in 2000. The former treatment of including results of joint ventures and associates in *Other operating income* is not as recommended in the Fourth Directive. It is not clear why the former treatment was adopted – it is possible that income from joint ventures and associates was not material and therefore did not require separate disclosure.

Exhibit 15.8 **Results of associates in the profit and loss account Barclays plc Annual Report 2000**

Additional Information (extract)
Changes in accounting presentation (extract)
The Group's share of the results of Joint Ventures and Associated Undertakings are shown separately below operating profit having previously been included in Other operating income. For the purposes of Business Group analysis the share of the results is still included in Operating profit.

Example 15.1 spells out the issues to be considered in deciding what should be disclosed in the profit and loss account to comply with FRS 9, in respect of an entity accounted for under the equity method.

Example 15.1 Disclosure of equity accounted results

Example
FRS 9 requires most associates and joint venture entities to be equity accounted, with specified separate disclosures, in consolidated financial statements.

Required
Identify which elements of the disclosures required in the profit and loss account have to be shown on the face of the account and which can be relegated to the notes.

Solution
It is not clear from FRS 9 which elements of the required disclosures have to be shown on the face of the profit and loss account and which can be shown in the notes. The only help on this issue is given in example 1 in Appendix IV to FRS 9, which notes that subdivisions for which the statutory prescribed heading is '*Income from interests in associated undertakings*' may be shown in a note rather than on the face of the profit and loss account. This seems to imply that the disclosures specified can be relegated to the notes and yet the example in FRS 9 (that directly follows the note) shows each of the required disclosures, with the exception of taxation, on the face of the profit and loss account (albeit the example does not include any super-exceptional items (i.e., exceptional items requiring disclosure on the face of the profit and loss account under FRS 3 *Reporting Financial Performance*)).

In addition, all these disclosures show the share of joint ventures' and associates' results separately on the face of the profit and loss account, which for many groups would be impracticable because of printing space constraints.

To further compound the issue, the Fourth and Seventh Directives require that '*Income from interests in associated undertakings*' in the specified formats for the profit and loss account should be treated as if it is preceded by an Arabic numeral, which means that the item can be relegated to the notes.

We therefore suggest the following practical solution:

- the share of joint ventures' turnover should be shown separately from that of the group on the face of the profit and loss account, in order to comply with the legal requirement to show the group turnover. It is also possible, however, to show a total figure for turnover including joint ventures, as long as joint ventures' turnover and the group's turnover excluding that of its joint ventures, is clearly shown
- where the share of associates' turnover is disclosed voluntarily, it should be shown on the face of the profit and loss account. It may be combined with that of joint ventures, but must be separately analysed in the notes. It is also possible to give a total for the group's turnover including both joint ventures and associates, as long as the group's turnover, excluding that of its associates and joint ventures, is clearly shown

continued overleaf

Example 15.1 Continued

- share of operating results of joint ventures and associates should be shown on the face of the profit and loss account immediately after group operating result, but may be combined in a single-line item *'Share of joint ventures' and associates' operating profit'*, as long as they are shown separately in the notes, with the share of joint ventures' operating results shown first
- amortisation of goodwill arising on the acquisition of joint ventures or associates should be included within *'Share of joint ventures' and associates' operating profit'*. There should be separate disclosure of this item in the notes.
- share of each super-exceptional item of joint ventures and associates should be shown separately on the face of the profit and loss account below the group's super-exceptional items, if any. For each super-exceptional item, the investor's share of joint ventures' and associates' figures may be combined in a single-line item suitably styled on the face of the profit and loss account, but should be shown separately in the notes, with the joint ventures' share shown first
- share of interest and format line items below the level of profit before tax should be included within the amounts shown on the face of the profit and loss account for the group. The share should then be separately disclosed in the notes, with the share of joint ventures' items shown first
- in addition, the share of associates' and joint ventures' results has to be analysed between continuing activities (including acquisitions) and discontinued activities, as required by FRS 3, *Reporting Financial Performance*.

Furthermore, it should be noted that the definition of the gross equity method for joint ventures requires the investor's share of the gross assets and liabilities underlying the net amount to be shown on the face of the balance sheet.

Source: Adapted from Holgate, P. and McCann, H. 1998. 'Accounting solutions – disclosure of equity accounted results', *Accountancy*, June, p.94

Where the associate itself prepares consolidated accounts, the amounts to be included in the investor's accounts should be based on the associate's consolidated amounts. This is illustrated in Example 15.2 which highlights how the minority interest in the associate's consolidated accounts is treated.

Example 15.2 Treatment of minority interest in associate's consolidated accounts

Example

A company's associate has a subsidiary, which is partly owned by outside shareholders. The investing group, when equity accounting in accordance with FRS 9, bases its share of the associate's results and net assets on the associate's consolidated accounts.

Required

Indicate where the group should include its share of the minority interest shown in the associate's consolidated accounts.

Solution

In the investing group's profit and loss account, paragraph 27 of FRS 9 states that for items below the level of profit before tax the group's figures should include the investor's share of the relevant amounts for associates. Minority interests appear below profit before tax, and so the investing group's profit and loss account should include in its minority interest, the group's share of the associate's minority interest. The amount related to the associate should be disclosed separately.

In the balance sheet, the group shows its share of the associate's net assets as a one-line asset. This amount is calculated after deducting the minority interest in the associate's consolidated balance sheet. The group's share of the minority interest does not have to be disclosed separately.

Source: Adapted from Holgate, P. and Nailor, H. 2000. 'Accounting solutions – associate with minority interest', *Accountancy*, September, p.111

Sundry issues under FRS 9

This section covers a number of issues dealt with under FRS 9 such as non-coterminous year-ends, uniform group accounting policies and consolidating adjustments.

Non-coterminous year-ends

FRS 9 states that the financial statements of the holding company and associate should be coterminous. If financial statements are not coterminous, the associate's financial statements should end not more than three months before the group's year-end date. However, where this would result in release of price-sensitive information, a period of not more than six months before the investor's year-end is permitted. Material changes after the associate's year-end and before the investor's year-end should be taken into account. Example 15.3 discusses an interesting problem which arises on acquisition of listed associates with a year-end two months after the group's reporting date.

Example 15.3 Acquisition of associate with different year-end date

Example

On 1.10.20X0 a group acquired an interest in an associate. The group's year-end is 31 December and the associate's is 28 February. The associate is a listed company and it publishes interim accounts for the six months to 31 August.

Required

What accounts for the associate should the group include in its December 20X0 financial statements?

Solution

Under the normal principles of equity accounting, the group's share of the associate's net assets is determined at the date of acquisition and the balance of the purchase consideration is goodwill. The group's share of the associate's results is recognised in the group's profit and loss account from the date of acquisition. FRS 9 requires that, where practicable, the associate's figures that go into the group's financial statements should be based on financial statements prepared to the same date. This is not possible where an associate with a different year-end is listed on a recognised stock exchange and the inclusion of financial information up to the group's year-end would release price-sensitive information relating to the associate. In those circumstances, paragraph 31(d), FRS 9, allows the use of financial statements prepared for a period that ends not more than six months before the group's year-end.

In the situation described, the associate has been acquired after the date of its latest published financial statements, which are the interim accounts to 31.8.20X0. If paragraph 31(d) is invoked, a practical solution for the December 20X0 financial statements, which avoids using unpublished financial information relating to the associate, is to include in the group's balance sheet provisional figures for the group's share of the net assets and goodwill, based on the interim accounts to 31.8.20X0. No post-acquisition results would be included in the group's profit and loss account for the year to 31.12.20X0. The notes should disclose that the figures for the associate are based on its financial statements to 31.8.20X0.

If this approach were followed, the group's financial statements for the year to 31.12.20X1 would include figures for the associate based on its published financial statements relating to the year to 31.8.20X1. Therefore the group's share of the associate's post-acquisition results would be derived from the associate's year to 31.8.20X1, adjusted to eliminate the results for September 20X0, which pre-date the acquisition, leaving the 11 months to 31.8.20X1 to be included. The adjustment for the pre-acquisition results should also be reflected as an adjustment to the provisional amounts of goodwill and net assets previously recorded. The associate's management accounts may be used to determine the adjustment.

Source: Adapted from Holgate, P. and Nailor, H. 2000. 'Accounting solutions – acquisition of associate', *Accountancy*, November, p.112

In Exhibit 15.9, Cadbury Schweppes provides a real-life example of the treatment explained in Example 15.3. Its year-end is 31 December 2000. The share of profits of its non-coterminous associate, Camelot, is for a period ending not more than three months before the investor's year-end (i.e., 30 September 1999).

Exhibit 15.9 **Non-coterminous year-ends**
Cadbury Schweppes plc Annual Report and Form 20-F 2000

Principal Accounting Policies (extract)
(p) Associated undertakings
All companies where the Group exercises significant influence, normally by board representation and/or ownership of 20% of the voting rights on a long-term basis, are treated as associated undertakings. The value of associated undertakings reflects the Group's share of net assets of the companies concerned. The Group's share of the profit before tax of associated undertakings is included in the Group Profit and Loss Account. All associated undertakings have financial years which are coterminous with the Group's, with the exception of Camelot Group plc ('Camelot') whose financial year ends in March. The Group's share of the profits of Camelot is based on its most recent, published, unaudited financial statements to 30 September.

Group accounting policies

The same accounting policies as those of the investor should be followed by the associate. Because the investor cannot control the associate, it is conceivable that the associate's accounting policies may differ from those used by the investor. Consequently, the associate's results may need to be adjusted in arriving at the amounts to be included in the investor's financial statements under the equity method.

Inter-company transactions and balances

Transactions, balances and cash flows with associates and joint ventures are not eliminated under FRS 9. However, the group share of any inter-company profits and losses carried in the value of assets in the consolidated balance sheet should be eliminated.

Balance sheet

Under FRS 9, the individual balance sheet of the investing company should include investment in associate at cost less any amounts written off. Where there has been a permanent impairment in value of the investment, it should be written down and the amount written off should be disclosed separately.

The consolidated balance sheet should present the investment as:

- investing group's share of net assets, if possible at fair value (excluding goodwill in the associate's own accounts)
- premium/discount on acquisition of the associate to the extent it is unamortised.

Example 15.4 discusses how goodwill on investments in joint ventures and associates should be treated in the consolidated accounts. Although the example primarily relates to a joint venture investment (considered later in this chapter), the points made in the example are also relevant to associates.

Example 15.4 Joint venture and goodwill

Example

A parent company acquired a subsidiary for a consideration that included goodwill of €20 million. The subsidiary itself has an investment in a joint venture entity. It is estimated that €8 million of the €20 million goodwill arising on the acquisition is attributable to the joint venture.

Required

(i) Discuss whether it is acceptable to apportion the total goodwill in this way and to show the goodwill of €8 million relating to the joint venture in fixed asset investments and the remaining €12 million as capitalised goodwill under intangible assets, in the parent company's consolidated balance sheet.

(ii) What difference would there be if the subsidiary had an investment in an associate rather than a joint venture investment?

Solution

(i) Treatment of goodwill relating to the joint venture

It is appropriate to apportion the total goodwill between the subsidiary undertaking and the joint venture, based on their fair values at the date of the acquisition, where the joint venture was acquired as part of an overall acquisition. Although allocation of goodwill is not specifically dealt with in FRS 7 *Fair Values in Acquisition Accounting*, it would appear to be required by FRS 11 *Impairment of Fixed Assets and Goodwill.*

This is because, under FRS 11, capitalised goodwill should be allocated to income-generating units along with other assets and liabilities for the purpose of impairment reviews.

Paragraph 34 of FRS 11 also requires goodwill on an acquisition comprising two dissimilar businesses to be reviewed separately for impairment so that any impairment loss arising, say, in the subsidiary undertaking does not fall to be offset against an increase in value of the joint venture.

(ii) If subsidiary's investment were an associate

If the acquired subsidiary had an investment in an associate rather than a joint venture, the goodwill arising on the subsidiary's acquisition of the associate would have been included in the subsidiary's financial statements as part of the carrying amount relating to the associate under the equity method and disclosed separately, in accordance with paragraph 29 of FRS 9 *Associates and Joint Ventures.*

Paragraph 21 of FRS 9 requires that, under the gross equity method, the joint venture should receive the same treatment as set out for associates, except that in the consolidated balance sheet the parent company's share of the gross assets and liabilities underlying the net equity amount for the joint venture should be shown in 'amplification of that net amount'.

It follows, therefore, that it is appropriate to include the goodwill of €8 million arising on the joint venture's acquisition as part of the gross asset disclosure on the face of the balance sheet and to show it as a separate item either there or in the notes. Alternatively, the €8 million could be included in the net amount by disclosing it as a separate item on the face of the balance sheet, after the subtotal comprising the share of gross assets less the share of gross liabilities.

Source: Adapted from Holgate, P. and Ghosh, J. 1999. 'Accounting solutions – joint venture and goodwill', *Accountancy*, April, p.84

Total goodwill on acquisition of equity accounted investments, less any amortisation or write-down, should be included in the balance sheet as part of the carrying amount of the investment, with separate disclosure of unamortised goodwill. Any profit or loss on disposal of an equity accounted investment should take into account the remaining goodwill element of the investment. Example 12.3 illustrated the impact of goodwill on calculating profit or loss on disposal in the context of subsidiaries. The example is equally valid in the context of associates.

Impairment of goodwill attributable to associates or joint ventures should be recognised. The amount written off should be separately disclosed in the accounting period.

To review the treatment of associates in consolidated balance sheets (already addressed in Chapter 7), Example 15.5 summarises the approach taken under the equity method of accounting. As explained in Chapter 7, the presentation required under FRS 9 focuses on group share of net assets plus unamortised goodwill. The technique for including associates in the workings for the consolidated balance sheet combines cost and group share of post-acquisition profits (less goodwill amortised). The total under each approach is the same, as is illustrated in Example 15.5.

Example 15.5 Goodwill on acquisition of associates

Example

Parent acquired a 25% investment in Associate for €750 on 1.1.20X7. The balance on Associate's retained profits was €1,860 and share capital consisted of 500 €1 ordinary shares at the date of acquisition. At 31.12.20X8 Associate's retained profits were €2,960. Parent's policy is to write off goodwill over four years.

Required

Show the investment in Associate in the consolidated balance sheet at 31.12.20X8.

Solution

Goodwill on acquisition	€	€
Cost of investment		750
Net assets of Associate at acquisition:		
Share capital	500	
Retained profits	1,860	
	2,360	
Group share – 25%		590
Goodwill		160
Written off 20X7 and 20X8		(80)
Unamortised goodwill at 31.12.20X8		80

Investment in Associate in consolidated balance sheet at 31.12.20X8

As presented in published accounts	€
Share of net assets	
([500$_{\text{share capital}}$ + 2,960$_{\text{retained profit at 31.12.20X8}}$] @ 25%$_{\text{group share}}$)	865
Unamortised goodwill	80
	945
As calculated	
Cost of investment	750
Share of post-acquisition profits	
([2,960$_{\text{retained profit at 31.12.20X8}}$-1,860$_{\text{pre-acquisition}}$] @ 25%$_{\text{group share}}$)	275
Goodwill written off	(80)
	945

Earlier versions of accounting standards on associates and joint ventures (e.g., SSAP 1) required the amount/balance on investment in associates to be presented in a different way to the current standard. Previously, investment in associates was presented as:

- cost plus
- post-acquisition profits; minus
- goodwill written off

This continues to be the way the figures are calculated (as this accords with how the investment is recorded under the double entry system – see Chapter 7). Some companies still use the terminology of the old standard. RMC Group presents the investment in both ways in Exhibit 15.10.

Exhibit 15.10 **Presentation of investment in associate**
RMC Group p.l.c. Annual Report 2000

	2000 £m	1999 £m
c) Associated undertakings (extract)		
Shares at cost	55.7	24.2
Share of post-acquisition net retained earnings and reserves	10.0	4.3
	65.7	28.5
Loans	11.3	2.9
At 31st December	77.0	31.4
Represented by:		
Net tangible assets	64.9	29.5
Goodwill	12.1	1.9
	77.0	31.4

Net liabilities in associates

Share of net liabilities (rather than net assets) of associated undertakings should be included in the carrying amount for associates, except where there is evidence (e.g., public statement) that the investor has irreversibly withdrawn from its investment in the investee and takes no further responsibility for the associate. Example 15.6 provides a discussion of the issues to be considered in deciding how to account for group's share of net liabilities of an associate.

Example 15.6 Interest in associate's net liabilities

Example
A company has an interest of 25% in an associated undertaking. The associate has made losses, which have resulted in net liabilities in its balance sheet. A provision has been made against the investment's carrying value in the investor's books.

Required
Explain how the associate should be treated in the investor's consolidated financial statements under FRS 9.

Solution
Paragraph 44 of FRS 9 *Associates and Joint Ventures* says that the investor should continue to record changes in the carrying amount for each associate and joint venture, even if application of the equity method (or gross equity method) results in an increase in net liabilities. The only exception to equity accounting for such deficits is where there is enough evidence that an event has irrevocably changed the relationship between the investor and its investee, marking its irreversible withdrawal from its associate or joint venture.

This means that a group will not be able to exclude its share of an associate's losses on the grounds that there is no intention to support the undertaking. Mere intention alone will not be adequate and the standard is looking for a demonstrable commitment to the withdrawal, including a public statement to that effect.

continued overleaf

Example 15.6 Continued

Therefore, where a group intends to dispose of its investment, the associate's results should continue to be equity accounted until there is a binding contract for sale. An irreversible withdrawal will also arise where the direction of the associate's operating and financial policies has become the responsibility of its creditors (including bankers) or a liquidator.

Where the interest in a joint venture or an associate is in net liabilities, paragraph 45 of FRS 9 says that the amount recorded should be shown as a provision or a liability. The most appropriate line item in the balance sheet formats within which to show the group's share of the joint venture's or associate's deficit is 'other provisions'.

Where a group has a number of investments, then it may have an investment in a joint venture or an associate that has a deficit, as well as the more normal situation of joint ventures and associates with net assets. In this situation, it is necessary to decide how to show the deficit in the consolidated financial statements. It would not be appropriate to net the positive interest in some joint ventures or associates against the negative interest in others to show a net asset or net provision. Consequently, the group's interest in the other joint ventures' or associates' net assets should be shown separately from the provision made for the group's share of net liabilities of its joint ventures or associates that are in deficit.

Source: Adapted from Holgate, P. and McCann, H. 1998. 'Accounting solutions – interest in associate's net liabilities', *Accountancy*, June, p.94

Consolidated accounts not prepared

Where the investing company does not prepare consolidated accounts, the information required by FRS 9 in respect of associates should be shown by preparing separate financial statements, or by showing the relevant amounts as additional information to the investing company's own profit and loss account/balance sheet.

Acquisitions and disposals

Acquisitions and disposals of investments in associates and joint ventures should be accounted for similarly to acquisitions and disposals of subsidiaries under paragraphs 50 to 52 of FRS 2:

- for an interest acquired in stages, the investment is to be calculated by reference to the net assets at the date it became an associate
- for increases in interests in associates, the investment is to be calculated by reference to the fair value of net assets at the date of increase
- profit and loss on disposal should be calculated by reference to the difference between the carrying amount of the investment before and after disposal.

Where the investment ceases to meet the definition of an associate, it should be carried at an amount reflecting the investor's share at the date of cessation of the relationship, together with related goodwill. The carrying amount is referred to as its *surrogate* cost in FRS 9. (Example 12.7 illustrated this treatment.)

Identification of carrying amount at date of disposal was explained in Chapter 12, as was the complication caused by goodwill in that calculation. Further explanation of the impact of goodwill written off against reserves in calculating profit or loss on disposal of subsidiaries is included in Chapter 17. The discussion in Example 15.7 reinforces the explanations provided in Chapter 12 and to come in Chapter 17.

Example 15.7 Accounting for disposal of associates

Example

A parent company has an investment of 40% in an associated company that was acquired some years ago at a cost of €24 million. In the opening consolidated balance sheet, the investment is carried at the group's share of net assets of €16 million, after writing off to reserves €10 million goodwill arising on acquisition. During 20X9, the company disposed of 50% of its investment in the associate for €18 million and no longer has board representation. Consequently, the remaining interest of 20% represents a trade investment. The company's share of the associate's net assets at the date of disposal amounted to €20 million.

Required

How should this transaction be reflected in the parent's individual and consolidated financial statements for the year ended 31.12.20X9?

Solution

The parent, in its own financial statements, would report a gain of €6 million (disposal proceeds of €18 million less cost of disposal of 50% of €24 million) and show the remaining 20% interest at a carrying value of €12 million (half of original investment of €24 million still held).

In the consolidated financial statements, the gain on disposal is €3 million, which is calculated as proceeds of €18 million less share of net assets at the date of disposal of €10 million (50% of €20 million), less attributable goodwill previously written off to reserves of €5 million (50% of €10 million).

However, the key issue is whether the carrying value of the 20% investment retained should be shown in the consolidated balance sheet on the basis of the share of net assets at the date of disposal of €10 million, leaving €5 million (50% of €10 million) goodwill attributable to the interest retained in reserves or whether the €5 million goodwill should be added to the share of net assets in the consolidated balance sheet to report a carrying value of €15 million.

Paragraph 42 of FRS 9 states that the carrying amount of any interest retained in the entity that ceases to qualify as an associate or a joint venture should include any related goodwill. The question, therefore, is whether the paragraph 42 requirement applies to goodwill that has previously been written off to reserves. We believe it does. Paragraph 42 makes a reference to paragraph 40 that deals with the calculation of the profit or loss on disposal of an interest in an associate or joint venture. Paragraph 40 refers to the inclusion in the profit and loss on disposal of the relevant proportion of goodwill that has not previously been either written off through the profit and loss account or attributed to prior period amortisation or impairment on applying the transitional arrangements of FRS 10 *Goodwill and Intangible Assets*.

Although paragraph 40 deals with the proportion of goodwill disposed of and not to the proportion retained, the specific reference in paragraph 42 to the inclusion of any related goodwill as required by paragraph 40 leads us to conclude that the carrying value of the investment retained should be recorded at €15 million inclusive of the attributable goodwill retained. Failure to do this could distort the reported gain or loss on eventual disposal.

The difference of €3 million between the carrying value of €15 million shown in the parent's consolidated balance sheet and the cost of €12 million shown in the parent's individual balance sheet is simply the profit retained in respect of the 20% interest while the investment was an associate (50% of: share of net assets at date of disposal of €20 million *less* share of net assets on acquisition of €14 million (cost of €24 million *less* goodwill of €10 million)).

It is also necessary to ensure that the carrying value of the investment in the group is not impaired. But as long as this is not the case, it would be possible to revalue the investment to €15 million in the parent's balance sheet and credit the difference of €3 million to the revaluation reserve, thus making the carrying values in the parent's and the group's balance sheets identical.

Source: Adapted from Holgate, P. and Ghosh, J. 1999. 'Accounting solutions – associate becomes trade investment', *Accountancy*, December, p.82

Disclosures

From the perspective of users of accounts, a disadvantage of the equity method of accounting is that the investor's share of net assets and net profit of associated undertakings are included as one-line adjustments in the consolidated accounts. Compared with the line-by-line approach taken in full consolidation, this provides readers of accounts with considerably less information. The disclosure requirements of FRS 9 attempt to compensate for this deficiency of the equity method of accounting, particularly in the case of substantial associates.

FRS 9 requires the following particulars to be disclosed.

For each principal associate

Nine items must be disclosed for all associate investments as follows:

1 name
2 proportion of the issued shares of each class held
3 details of any special rights attaching to the shares held
4 accounting period or date if different from those of the investing group
5 indication of the nature of the business
6 notes relating to the financial statements of associates material to understanding the effect of the investment (in particular indicating the share of contingent liabilities and capital commitments)
7 extent of significant statutory, contractual or exchange control restrictions
8 amounts reported under FRS 8 *Related Party Disclosures* as owing and owed between an investor and its associates and joint ventures should be analysed into amounts relating to loans and amounts relating to trading balances
9 explanation why the facts rebut the presumptions attaching to a greater than or less than 20% shareholding and the exercise of significant influence.

Thresholds for substantial associates

Additional disclosures are required where certain thresholds are exceeded. Assessment of whether the threshold is exceeded is based on *any one* of the four following amounts:

1 gross assets
2 gross liabilities
3 turnover
4 operating results (based on a three-year average).

For equity accounted entities, where the investor's share of any one of gross assets, gross liabilities, turnover or operating results exceeds 15% of the investor's equivalent amounts, additional disclosures should be made of the investor's share in each of the following five items:

1 turnover
2 fixed assets
3 current assets
4 liabilities due within one year
5 liabilities due after more than one year.

Where the investor's share of gross assets, gross liabilities, turnover or operating results exceeds 25% of the investor's equivalent amounts, condensed balance sheet and profit and loss account information should be included. The investor's share of eight items must be disclosed in the condensed accounts as follows:

1 turnover
2 profit before taxation
3 taxation
4 profit after taxation
5 fixed assets
6 current assets
7 liabilities due within one year
8 liabilities due after more than one year.

Example 15.8 illustrates how the thresholds are calculated for determining whether extra disclosures are required under FRS 9.

Example 15.8 Determining disclosure thresholds for associates

Example
On 1.10.20X0 a group acquired an interest in an associate. The group's year-end is 31 December and the associate's is 28 February. The associate is a listed company and it publishes interim accounts for the six months to 31 August.

Required
What figures for the associate should the group use to determine whether the 15% or 25% thresholds that trigger additional disclosures under FRS 9 *Associates and Joint Ventures* have been reached?

Solution
Special disclosures relating to associate's results, assets and liabilities are required by paragraph 58, FRS 9, where those items have a significant impact on the investing group. These arise where the group's share in its associates in aggregate exceeds 15% of certain thresholds. If the group's share in any of its individual associates exceeds 25% of those thresholds, additional disclosures have to be given for that associate. The thresholds compare the group's share of associate's gross assets, gross liabilities, turnover or operating results (on a three-year average) with the corresponding amounts for the group. For the newly acquired associate, the asset and liability tests would be based on the associate's assets and liabilities at 31.8.20X0. The turnover and operating profit tests would be based on the associate's results for the year to 31.8.20X0.

As explained in Example 15.3, however, the group's profit and loss account for the year to 31.12.20X0 would not include any post-acquisition results relating to the newly acquired associate. Hence the group's share of associate's turnover and other profit and loss account items that must be disclosed under paragraph 58, if any of the thresholds are exceeded, would include nil in respect of this associate for the year ended 31.12.20X0.

Source: Adapted from Holgate, P. and Nailor, H. 2000. 'Accounting solutions – acquisition of associate', *Accountancy*, November, p.112

Exhibit 15.11 shows the additional disclosures made by Cadbury Schweppes in respect of associates that (i) exceeded the 15% threshold and (ii) exceeded the 25% threshold. The first part of the note discloses five items in respect of 'associated undertakings' which suggests these associated undertakings exceeded the 15% threshold. The note goes on to disclose additional information in respect of one associated undertaking, Camelot. The eight additional disclosures required where the 25% threshold is exceeded are disclosed, so presumably Camelot exceeds the 25% threshold.

Exhibit 15.11 **Additional disclosures in respect of substantial associates under UK GAAP Cadbury Schweppes Annual Report 2000**

Notes to the Financial Statements (extract)
12 Investments (extract)
(c) Additional associated undertaking disclosures
The Group's share in its associated undertakings' selected profit and loss and balance sheets items is as follows:

	2000	1999
	£m	£m
Turnover	**1,930**	1,750
Fixed assets	**123**	157
Current assets	**241**	210
Liabilities due within one year	**(208)**	(159)
Liabilities due after one year	**(298)**	(220)

The Group's share in selected profit and loss and balance sheet items for its associated undertaking Camelot is as follows:

	2000	1999
	£m	£m
Turnover	**1,382**	1,348
Profit before tax	**16**	18
Tax	**(5)**	(4)
Profit after tax	**11**	14
Fixed assets	**7**	12
Current assets	**123**	112
Liabilities less than one year	**(91)**	(86)
Liabilities greater than one year	**—**	(12)

Operating profit from associates can be split into the following geographic regions:

	2000	1999	1998
	£m	£m	£m
North American Beverages	**31**	—	5
Central	**14**	16	17
Africa, India and Middle East	**13**	14	12
Other	**7**	5	4
Total	**65**	35	38

During the year the Group purchased packaging materials from, and paid bottling fees to, L'Européenne D'Embouteillage SNC totalling £3m and £49m respectively. The year-end net payable by Group companies was £4m. The Group sold beverages concentrate totalling £231m to DPSUBG and the amount owing by DPSUBG at the year-end was £26m. All transactions are on an arms' length basis.

Goodwill included in the carrying value of associates is £301m.

Pearson's note on associates is shown in Exhibit 15.12. During the year, the group combined its television interests with another company and retained a 22% interest in this business. The note is extensive and only two parts of it are reproduced:

- a reconciliation of movements on the investment in associates in the consolidated balance sheet. These comprise exchange adjustments, reclassification from associates to joint ventures, additions, disposals, group share of losses during the period, goodwill adjustment on disposals and goodwill amortised

- additional disclosures in relation to group interests in associates.

Exhibit 15.12 **Additional disclosures in respect of substantial associates under UK GAAP Pearson Annual Report 2000**

Notes to the Accounts

15. Associates (extract)

All figures in £ millions	**equity**	**share of loans**	**reserves**	**total**	**goodwill**	**total net assets**
Summary of movements						
At 31 December 1999	98	67	43	208	26	234
Exchange differences	2	—	2	4	15	19
Transfer to joint ventures	(8)	—	2	(6)	—	(6)
Additions	18	13	—	31	58	89
Combination of television interests:						
– Television assets contributed	(4)	(64)	51	(17)	(48)	(65)
– Share of combined television interests	183	—	—	183	633	816
Combination of Asset Valuation interests						
– DBC	5	—	—	5	117	122
Disposals	(104)	(12)	(45)	(161)	—	(161)
Retained loss for the year	—	—	(14)	(14)	—	(14)
Goodwill written back on disposal	41	—	—	41	—	41
Goodwill amortisation	—	—	—	—	(51)	(51)
At 31 December	231	4	39	274	750	1,024

The aggregate of the Group's share in its associates, excluding the Group's interest in the RTL Group, and Lazard in 1999, is shown below.

All figures in £ millions	**2000**	**1999**
Sales	384	299
Fixed assets	42	72
Current assets	132	165
Liabilities due within one year	(73)	(105)
Liabilities due after one year or more	(32)	(73)
Net assets	69	59

The disclosure requirements applying to joint ventures (considered later in this chapter) are the same as for associates.

Presentation

FRS 9 provides an example of the normal presentation of information relating to associates in company accounts. This example is reproduced in Example 15.10 later in this chapter (because the example also includes joint ventures which are dealt with at that stage).

IAS GAAP – associates

This section of the chapter discusses the regulations applying to associates. One IAS and three SICs deal with accounting issues relating to associates:

- IAS 28 *Accounting for Investments in Associates*
- SIC 3 *Elimination of Unrealised Profits and Losses on Transactions with Associates*
- SIC 20 *Equity Accounting Method – Recognition of Losses*
- SIC 33 *Consolidation and Equity Method – Potential Voting Rights and Allocation of Ownership Interests*.

IAS 28 was issued in 1989 to supersede IAS 3 *Consolidated Financial Statements* and was revised in 1998 and 2000. SIC 3 was issued in 1997, SIC 20 in 2000 and SIC 33 in 2001.

Definitions

IAS 28 considers that an associate is an entity over which the investor is in a position to exercise significant influence and defines the term (in paragraph 3) as follows:

> An associate is an enterprise in which the investor has significant influence and which is neither a subsidiary nor a joint venture of the investor.

If the investor owns (either directly or indirectly through subsidiaries) 20% or more of the voting capital of the investee, the exercise of significant influence is presumed (and *vice versa*), unless it can be clearly demonstrated to the contrary. SIC 33 *Consolidation and Equity Method – Potential Voting Rights and Allocation of Ownership Interests* clarifies that the existence and effect of potential voting rights that are presently (i.e., currently) exercisable or presently convertible (e.g., share warrants, share call options, debt or equity instruments that are convertible into ordinary shares) to give the enterprise voting power (or reduce another party's voting power) over the financial and operating policies of another enterprise (potential voting rights) should be considered, in addition to the other factors described in IAS 28. All facts and circumstances that affect potential voting rights should be examined, except the intention of management and the financial capability to exercise or convert. However, the calculations in the accounts should be determined based solely on present ownership interests.

The IAS defines significant influence (in paragraph 3) as follows:

> Significant influence is the power to participate in the financial and operating policy decisions of the investee but is not control over those policies.

Paragraph 5 of the IAS provides further guidance by stating that indications of the exercise of significant influence include representation on the board of directors, participation in policy making, material transactions between the investor and investee, interchange of management personnel and provision of essential technical information.

Allianz Group, which adopts IAS GAAP, discloses a definition of associated undertakings in Exhibit 15.13 which is at variance with IAS 28. Investments are treated as associated undertakings even where significant influence is not exercised, provided the shareholding is more than 20%.

Exhibit 15.13 **Definition of associates**
Allianz Group Annual Report 2000

Investments in affiliated enterprises, joint ventures and associated enterprises (extract)
Associated enterprises are all those enterprises, other than affiliated enterprises, in which the Group has an interest of between 20 percent and 50 percent, regardless of whether significant control is exercised or not.

Banco Santander Central Hispano discloses in Exhibit 15.14 that it accounts for investments in listed companies of 3% or more as if they were associated undertakings.

Exhibit 15.14 **Listed companies of 3% or more accounted for as associates**
Banco Santander Central Hispano Annual Report 1999

Accounting Policies (extract)
Consolidation principles (extract)
The holdings in companies controlled by the Bank and not consolidable because their business activity is not directly related to that of the Bank (Note 11) and the holdings in other companies ('associated companies' – Note 10) with which the Group has a lasting relationship and which are intended to contribute to the Group's business activities, in which the Group's ownership interests are equal to or exceed 20% (3% if listed), are carried at the fraction of the investees' net worth corresponding to such holdings, net of the dividends collected from them and other net worth eliminations (equity method).

The criteria for identification of associates are more restrictive under FRS 9 than IAS 28. For example, FRS 9 requires that the investor be *actively* involved and influential in the investee through participation in policy decisions. Under FRS 9, an agreement (formal or informal) is required to provide the basis for the exercise of significant influence. Consequently, some entities that would be accounted for as associates under IAS 28 would not be so treated under FRS 9.

Equity method of accounting

IAS 28 also requires the equity method of accounting to be applied to associates, except where the associate has been acquired with a view to disposal in the near future. The consolidated profit and loss account should include the 'share of results' of associates but the IAS is not as explicit as FRS 9 in indicating what amounts should be disclosed in the consolidated profit and loss account.

Similar to FRS 9, the investor's balance sheet should include the share of net assets of the associate, including any unamortised goodwill arising on acquisition of the associate.

Investments which are *prima facie* associates should be accounted for using the cost-based approach (i.e., investment at cost in the balance sheet, dividends received and receivable in the profit and loss account) in any of the following circumstances:

- cessation of the exercise of significant influence (even where investment is retained)
- associate operates under severe long-term restrictions that impair its ability to transfer funds
- investment is acquired with a view to disposal in the near future.

The carrying amount of the investment after any of the above events should be the cost thereafter (i.e. after the event).

Where the investment has previously been recorded under the equity method, the carrying value of the investment at the date of change of status should be regarded as cost.

SIC 20 *Equity Accounting Method – Recognition of Losses* clarifies computation of the carrying amount of the investment in an associate. This amount should include ordinary and preferred shares that provide unlimited rights of participation in earnings or losses and a residual equity interest in the associate. If the investor's share of losses of an associate exceeds the carrying amount of the investment, recognition of further losses should be discontinued, unless the investor has incurred obligations to satisfy liabilities of the associate that the investor has guaranteed or otherwise committed, whether the liability is funded or not. Financial interests in an associate which are not included in the carrying amount of the investment are accounted for in accordance with other applicable IASs, for example IAS 39 *Financial Instruments: Recognition and Measurement*. Additionally, continuing losses of an associate should be considered objective evidence that financial interests in that associate may be impaired. Impairment of the carrying amount of the investment in an associate is determined based on the carrying amount after adjustment for equity method losses.

Sundry issues under IAS 28

This section covers a number of issues, dealt with under IAS 28, such as non-coterminous year-ends, uniform group accounting policies, consolidating adjustments and net liabilities in associates.

Non-coterminous year-ends

The most recent financial statements of the associate should be used in applying the equity method of accounting. Where the reporting dates of the investor and investee are different, the investor should use interim financial information of the associate if available. When this is impractical, the investor may use financial statements drawn up to a different reporting date. The length of reporting period and any difference between reporting dates should be consistent from period to period. Significant events or transactions between the date of the associate's financial statements and the investor's year-end should be adjusted for.

Group accounting policies

IAS 28 states that uniform accounting policies for like transactions and events should be adopted. Where the associate uses accounting policies other than those adopted by the investor appropriate adjustments should be made to the associate's financial statements when those are used in applying the equity method.

In Exhibit 15.15, Siemens (which reports under German GAAP) provides an interesting policy on how it deals with adjustments arising for associated companies prepared using

Exhibit 15.15 **Uniform group accounting policies**
Siemens Annual Report 2000

Consolidated financial statements – Notes (extract)
Summary of significant accounting policies (extract)
Principles of consolidation (extract)
Valuations in the annual statements of associated companies accounted for under the equity method that deviate from these uniform principles have not been adjusted on the basis of immateriality.

different accounting policies to the group accounting policies. There is no adjustment to make the policies uniform, justified on the grounds of immateriality.

Accounting adjustments

IAS 28 does not give explicit guidance on elimination of unrealised profits and losses arising from inter-company transactions between associates and other group companies. SIC 3 *Elimination of Unrealised Profits and Losses on Transactions with Associates* clarifies the position and requires such unrealised profits to be eliminated to the extent of the investor's interest in the associate. SIC 3 goes on to state that unrealised losses should not be eliminated where the transaction provides evidence of the impairment of the asset transferred. Agfa-Gevaert provides a good example of this treatment in Exhibit 15.16.

Exhibit 15.16 **Adjustments for intra-group transactions**
Agfa-Gevaert N.V. Annual Report 2000

Notes to the Consolidated Financial Statements (extract)
1 Significant accounting policies (extract)
Transactions eliminated on consolidation
All intra-group balances and transactions, including unrealised gains arising on intra-group transactions, are eliminated in preparing the consolidated financial statements. Unrealised gains arising from transactions with associated entities are eliminated to the extent of the Group's interest in the enterprise. Unrealised gains resulting from transactions with associates are eliminated against the investments in the associate. Unrealised losses are eliminated in the same way as unrealised gains except that they are only eliminated to the extent that there is no evidence of impairment.

Net liabilities in associates

Under IAS 28, where there is a deficiency of net assets in the associate (i.e., net liabilities) and the investor's share in the associate's equity becomes negative, the equity method of accounting should be discontinued and the investment should be recorded at a nil valuation. However, where the investor has made guarantees or commitments in respect of the associate, such losses should be provided for in the accounts.

Acquisitions and disposals

Under IAS 28, after acquisition, the investor should include its share of profits of the investee in the consolidated profit and loss account. Where the conditions for recognising the investee as an associate cease because the investor can no longer exercise significant influence (possibly as a result of disposal of shares) or because of severe long-term restrictions, the equity method should be discontinued and the investment should be carried at its book value at the date of ceasing to apply the equity method.

Disclosures

The following disclosures in respect of associates are required under IAS 28:

- listing of associates
- description of significant associates
- proportion of ownership interest in significant associates

- proportion of voting power held (if different from ownership interest)
- methods used to account for associates.

Table 15.1 summarises the differences in disclosure requirements under FRS 9 and IAS 28. It is clear from the table that the disclosure requirements under UK GAAP are considerably greater than under IAS GAAP. IAS GAAP requires the method of accounting for associates to be disclosed – this is not a specific requirement under FRS 9 although under FRS 18 *Accounting Policies* accounting policies for material items should be disclosed. All other IAS disclosure requirements are also required under UK GAAP, and UK GAAP requires considerably more disclosures in relation to substantial associates exceeding specified thresholds.

Table 15.1 Comparison of disclosures concerning associates (and joint ventures) required under UK GAAP and IAS GAAP

UK GAAP		*IAS GAAP*
Name		Listing of associates
Proportion of the issued shares of each class held		Proportion of ownership interest in significant associates
Details of any special rights attaching to the shares held		Proportion of voting power held (if different from ownership interest)
Accounting period or date if different from those of the investing group		
Indication of the nature of the business		Description of significant associates
Notes relating to the financial statements of associates material to understanding the effect of the investment, in particular indicating the share of contingent liabilities and capital commitments		
Extent of significant statutory, contractual or exchange control restrictions		
Amounts reported under FRS 8 *Related Party Disclosures* as owing and owed between an investor and its associates and joint ventures should be analysed into amounts relating to loans and amounts relating to trading balances		
Explanation why the facts rebut the presumptions attaching to a greater than or less than 20% shareholding and the exercise of significant influence		Methods used to account for associates
Additional disclosures		
Exceed thresholds by 15%	*Exceed thresholds by 25%*	
Turnover	Turnover	
Fixed assets	Profit before taxation	
Current assets	Taxation	
Liabilities due within one year	Profit after taxation	
Liabilities due after more than one year	Fixed assets	
	Current assets	
	Liabilities due within one year	
	Liabilities due after more than one year	

Joint ventures

Both UK GAAP and IAS GAAP have explicit regulations dealing with joint ventures.

UK GAAP – joint ventures

Joint ventures are also covered in FRS 9. The gross equity method of accounting is required for joint ventures and this is now explained.

Definition

FRS 9 defines a joint venture (in paragraph 4) as:

> An entity in which the reporting entity holds an interest on a long-term basis and is jointly controlled by the reporting entity and one or more other venturers under a contractual arrangement

The key term in this definition is 'jointly controlled' which is defined (also in paragraph 4) as follows:

> A reporting entity jointly controls a venture with one or more other entities if none of the entities alone can control that entity but all together can do so and decisions on financial and operating policy essential to the activities, economic performance and financial position of that venture require each venturer's consent.

No percentage interest is required in the case of an investment in a joint venture or consortium provided joint control can be exercised. Joint control is more than the exercise of significant influence relevant to associates. It implies the ability to exert control at high levels of strategic decision making. A joint venture must be a separate entity carrying on its own business, otherwise it would be classified as a joint arrangement which is subject to different provisions in FRS 9.

An example of a joint venture is provided by Debenhams in Exhibit 15.17. The venture is owned jointly (50: 50) with Freemans. An explanation is provided of the way in which the two investors exercise joint control.

Exhibit 15.17 **Joint venture investment**
Debenhams plc Annual Report 2000

11 Investments in Joint Venture – Group (extract)
The Group owns the whole of the 'A' ordinary shares in Debenhams Direct Limited, giving a 50 per cent economic interest through an entitlement to 50 per cent of the profits and net assets of the company. The Otto Versand GmbH subsidiary Freemans owns the remainder of the share capital. Both parties have equal voting rights and equal entitlement to board representation. Accordingly, Debenhams Direct Limited has been accounted for as a joint venture in the consolidated financial statements.

Debenhams Direct Limited is registered in England and Wales and operates in the United Kingdom. The accounting and reporting date of Debenhams Direct Limited is 26 February. However, adjustments have been made in these financial statements to reflect the results of the joint venture for the financial year ended 26 August 2000.

Lloyds TSB jointly owns a company with two other investors and only owns 24.5% of the joint venture as shown in Exhibit 15.18. This example highlights that it is joint control rather than percentage holdings that is critical in establishing joint venture status for FRS 9 purposes.

Exhibit 15.18 **Joint venture**
Lloyds TSB Group Annual Report 2000

24 Joint venture

During 2000 the Group was party to the creation of a new payments processing company, Intelligent Processing Solutions Limited ('IPSL'), in conjunction with Unisys and Barclays Bank. This new company began operating in December 2000 and now handles all of the Group's UK cheque processing activities, for which fees are charged by IPSL to the Group. The staff previously employed by the Group in its UK cheque processing activities have been transferred to the employment of IPSL.

The Group's investment in IPSL, which comprised 24.5 per cent of the issued ordinary share capital of the company, is being accounted for as a joint venture. The carrying value of the investment at 31 December 2000 was £4 million, which has been included within other assets on the balance sheet.

In the year ended 31 December 2000 £4 million of fees payable to IPSL have been included in the Group's administrative expenses. The Group has also prepaid £7 million of fees in respect of 2001 and this amount is included in prepayments and accrued income; in addition at 31 December 2000 IPSL owed £2 million to the Group, which is included in other assets.

Accounting for joint ventures

Under FRS 9, joint ventures should be accounted for using the gross equity method. As already indicated in Chapter 7, this is defined in FRS 9 (paragraph 4) as:

> A form of equity method under which the investor's share of the aggregate gross assets and liabilities underlying the net amount included for the investment is shown on the face of the balance sheet and, in the profit and loss account, the investor's share of the investee's turnover is noted.

(This method of accounting has already been explained in Chapter 7. Example 7.1 compared full line-by-line consolidation with the equity method of accounting. Example 7.2 briefly showed the differences between the equity method and the gross equity method of accounting.)

Examples 7.1 and 7.2 are reworked in Example 15.9 to highlight the differences between the equity method and gross equity method of accounting. In the consolidated profit and loss account, the only difference in the two methods is the presentation of turnover. Under the equity method, group turnover is that of the investor and its subsidiaries. Under the gross equity method, the consolidated profit and loss account starts with gross turnover including the investor's share of turnover of the joint venture. Then the investor's share of turnover of the joint venture is deducted, leaving group turnover (the starting point in the consolidated profit and loss account under the equity method).

Example 15.9 Equity and gross equity methods compared

Example

On 31.12.20X3 Investor acquired 3 million shares (25%) of Investee when Investee's reserves were €1 million. Goodwill on acquisition is to be amortised over ten years commencing with a full year's charge in 20X4.

The summarised balance sheets of Investor and Investee at 31.12.20X9 and profit and loss accounts for the year ending on the same date are as follows:

Summarised balance sheets	*Investor group excluding Investee*		*Investee*
	€000	**€000**	**€000**
Tangible fixed assets	14,500		10,000
Investment in Investee	3,583		—
Current assets		8,800	
Liabilities		(3,800)	
Net assets	6,850		5,000
	24,933		15,000
Share capital (€1 shares)	20,000		12,000
Reserves	4,933		3,000
	24,933		15,000
Summarised profit and loss accounts			
Turnover	9,000		4,500
Operating costs	(4,500)		(2,250)
Operating profit	4,500		2,250
Investment income (from Investee)	200		—
Profit before taxation	4,700		2,250
Taxation	(1,500)		(750)
Profit after taxation	3,200		1,500
Proposed dividends	(2,000)		(800)
Retained profit for year	1,200		700
Retained profit c/f	3,733		2,300
Retained profit b/f	4,933		3,000

Required

Prepare the consolidated accounts of the investor under (i) the equity method and (ii) the gross equity method of accounting.

Solution

Consolidated balance sheet	*(i) Equity method*		*(ii) Gross equity method*
	€000	**€000**	**€000**
Tangible fixed assets	14,500		14,500
Investment in Investee ($[15{,}000_{\text{net assets}}$ @ 25%] + $133_{\text{unamortised goodwill W1}}$)	3,883		
Share of Investee's gross assets ([10,000 + 8,800] @ 25%)		4,700	
Unamortised goodwill (see W_1)		133	
Share of Investee's gross liabilities (3,800 @ 25%)		(950)	3,883
Net assets	6,850		6,850
	25,233		25,233

continued overleaf

Example 15.9 Continued

Solution (*continued*)

Consolidated balance sheet	*(i) Equity method*	*(ii) Gross equity method*
	€000	**€000**
Share capital (€1 shares)	20,000	20,000
Reserves		
(4,933 + [(3,000 – 1,000) @ 25%] – [200$_{\text{goodwill written-off W1}}$])	5,233	5,233
	25,233	25,233
Consolidated profit and loss account		
Turnover (9,000 + [€4,500$_{\text{joint venture}}$ @ 25%])		10,125
Less: Share of Investee's turnover		(1,125)
Group turnover	9,000	9,000
Operating costs	(4,500)	(4,500)
Operating profit	4,500	4,500
Amortisation of goodwill (1/10 × 333)	(33)	(33)
Share of profits of Investee (2,250 @ 25%)	563	563
Profit before taxation	5,030	5,030
Taxation [1,500 + (750 @ 25%)]	(1,688)	(1,688)
Profit after taxation	3,342	3,342
Proposed dividends	(2,000)	(2,000)
Retained profit for year	1,342	1,342
Retained profit b/f		
(3,733 + [(2,300–1,000) @ 25%] – [333 × 5/10$_{\text{goodwill amortised}}$])	3,891	3,891
Retained profit c/f	5,233	5,233

(W1) Goodwill

Cost of investment	3,583
Share of net assets acquired	
[25% × (12,000$_{\text{share capital}}$ + 1,000$_{\text{reserves}}$)]	(3,250)
Goodwill	333
Amortised (20X4 to 20X9 – 6$_{\text{years}}$ ➡ 6/10ths)	(200)
Consolidated balance sheet	133

In the balance sheet, the only difference between the two methods is in the *presentation* of the investment in investee. Under the gross equity method, the presentation expands the information given by the traditional equity method without changing its nature. Under the equity method, group share of the investee's net assets is shown as a single amount. Unamortised goodwill on acquisition of the investee is included in the asset total. Under the gross equity method, the investor's share of gross assets of the investee is disclosed separately. Unamortised goodwill is added to this. The investor's share of the gross liabilities of the investee is then deducted leaving the same net carrying amount as shown under the equity method for investment in investee in the consolidated balance sheet.

The gross equity method is only prescribed for joint ventures under FRS 9. The gross assets and gross liabilities of the joint venture are memorandum figures only and are not assets or liabilities of the group. It is the share of the joint venture's *net* assets that forms part of the group's balance sheet.

FRS 9 provides an example of the normal presentation of information relating to associates and joint ventures in company accounts, reproduced in Example 15.10. Under the gross equity method, in the consolidated profit and loss account, the group's share of turnover of the joint venture is shown deducted from total turnover. The operating profit and interest payable relating to joint ventures is also shown separately. Note that share of operating profit from joint ventures is shown before the group share of profit from associates. In the consolidated balance sheet, the investment in joint ventures is analysed between share of gross assets and share of gross liabilities.

Example 15.10 FRS 9 presentation of information about associates and joint ventures

Consolidated profit and loss account

The format is illustrative only. The amounts shown for 'Associates' and 'Joint ventures' are subdivisions of the item for which the statutory prescribed heading is 'Income from interests in associated undertakings'. The subdivisions may be shown in a note rather than on the face of the profit and loss account.

	£m	£m
Turnover: group and share of joint ventures	320	
Less: share of joint ventures' turnover	(120)	
Group turnover		200
Cost of sales		(120)
Gross profit		80
Administrative expenses		(40)
Group operating profit		40
Share of operating profit in: Joint ventures	30	
Associates	24	54
		94
Interest receivable (group)		6
Interest payable: Group	(26)	
Joint ventures	(10)	
Associates	(12)	(48)
Profit on ordinary activities before tax		52
Tax on profit on ordinary activities*		(12)
Profit on ordinary activities after tax		40
Minority interests		(6)
Profit on ordinary activities after taxation and minority interest		34
Equity dividends		(10)
Retained profit for group and its share of associates and joint ventures		24
*Tax relates to the following: Parent and subsidiaries	(5)	
Joint ventures	(5)	
Associates	(2)	

Consolidated balance sheet	£m	£m	£m
Fixed assets			
Tangible assets		480	
Investments			
Investments in joint ventures:			
Share of gross assets	130		
Share of gross liabilities	(80)	50	
Investments in associates		20	
			550

continued overleaf

Example 15.10 Continued

	£m	£m
Current assets		
Stock	15	
Debtors	75	
Cash at bank and in hand	10	
	100	
Creditors (due within one year)	(50)	
Net current assets		50
Total assets less current liabilities		600
Creditors (due after more than one year)		(250)
Provisions for liabilities and charges		(10)
Equity minority interest		(40)
		300
Capital and reserves		
Called up share capital		50
Share premium account		150
Profit and loss account		100
Shareholders' funds (all equity)		300

Notes

In the example, there is no individual associate or joint venture that accounts for more than 25% of any of the following for the investor group (excluding any amount for associates and joint ventures):

- gross assets
- gross liabilities
- turnover
- operating results (on a three-year average)

Additional disclosures for joint ventures (which in aggregate exceed the 15% threshold)

	£m	£m
Share of assets		
Share of fixed assets	100	
Share of current assets	30	
		130
Share of liabilities		
Liabilities due within one year or less	(10)	
Liabilities due after more than one year	(70)	
		(80)
Share of net assets		50

Additional disclosures for associates (which in aggregate exceed the 15% threshold)

	£m	£m
Share of turnover of associates		90
Share of assets		
Share of fixed assets	4	
Share of current assets	28	
		32
Share of liabilities		
Liabilities due within one year or less	(3)	
Liabilities due after more than one year	(9)	
		(12)
Share of net assets		20

Source: Example 1, Appendix IV, FRS 9 *Associates and Joint Ventures*

Profit and loss account and the gross equity method

Example 15.11 discusses the approach to calculating the amounts to be shown in the consolidated profit and loss account concerning turnover of joint ventures.

Example 15.11 Accounting adjustment under the equity method of accounting

Example

A group has a 50% interest in a joint venture entity. The group sells goods to the joint venture, which in turn sells on to third parties at a margin. During the financial year ended 31.12.20X8, the group made sales of €10 million to the joint venture, which cost €6 million to produce. The joint venture sold the goods to third parties at €12 million and none was held in stock at the year-end.

Assume these group sales to the joint venture are its only sales during the year and that sales of goods bought from the investor are the only sales made by the joint venture.

Required

Indicate how this information should be reflected in the consolidated profit and loss account of the group for the year ended 31.12.20X8.

Solution

FRS 9 *Associates and Joint Ventures* requires the investor's share of its joint venture's turnover to be shown in the consolidated profit and loss account – but not as part of group turnover (FRS 9, paragraph 21). This is because the turnover required to be disclosed under legislation is that of the group excluding its joint venture (that is, €10 million).

However, it would clearly be misleading to show a total group turnover including share of the joint venture's turnover of €16 million (€10 million + 50% of €12 million) and then deduct the group's share of the joint venture's turnover of €6 million to arrive at group turnover of €10 million (i.e., without adjusting for intra-group sales).

It is necessary to eliminate €5 million from group turnover, being 50% of €10 million sales made by the group to the joint venture. The €5 million should be set off both against the total turnover of €16 million and the group's share of the joint venture's turnover of €6 million. In other words, the elimination of €5 million is effectively made against the share of the joint venture's turnover of €6 million to reflect the group's share of the incremental sales made by the joint venture to third parties. This would result in the following presentation:

Consolidated profit and loss account extract	**€m**	
Turnover including share of joint venture	11	$(€10_{million} + (50\% \times €12_{million}) - €5_{million})$
Less: Share of joint venture turnover	(1)	
Group turnover	10	
Cost of sales	(6)	
Group operating profit	4	
Share of operating profit of joint venture	1	
Operating profit including share of joint venture	5	

Depending on how material the group's share of its joint venture turnover is, it may be necessary to indicate that the reported share of joint venture turnover is stated after eliminating turnover between the group and the joint venture of €5 million.

Source: Adapted from Holgate, P. and Ghosh, J. 1999. 'Accounting solutions – joint venture and group accounts', *Accountancy*, February, p. 83

Minority interest in joint ventures

Example 15.12 clarifies the treatment of joint ventures in which there is a subsidiary with a minority interest.

Example 15.12 Minority interest in joint venture

Example

A company's joint venture investment has a subsidiary, which is partly owned by outside shareholders. The investing group, when equity accounting in accordance with FRS 9, bases its share of the joint venture's results and net assets on the joint venture's consolidated accounts.

Required

Where should the group include its share of the minority interest shown in the joint venture's consolidated accounts?

Solution

The group's joint venture investment should be included in the consolidated accounts using the gross equity method. In the group's profit and loss account, the treatment of the group's share of the joint venture's minority interest is the same as for an associate described in Example 15.2.

In the group's balance sheet, the group's share of the joint venture's gross assets and gross liabilities should be shown separately under the heading *Investment in joint ventures*. Since the joint venture's minority interest is not an asset or a liability, the most appropriate presentation is to show the group's share of the minority interest as a separate item deducted from its share of gross assets and liabilities.

Source: Adapted from Holgate, P. and Nailor, H. 2000. 'Accounting solutions – associate with minority interest', *Accountancy*, September, p.111

Disclosures

The disclosures applying to joint ventures are identical to those applying to associates, described earlier.

IAS GAAP – joint ventures

Separate regulations apply to joint ventures in the form of IAS 31 *Financial Reporting of Interests in Joint Ventures* which was issued in 1990, reformatted in 1994 and revised in 1998 and 2000. SIC 13 *Jointly Controlled Entities – Non-Monetary Contributions by Venturers* was issued in 1998.

The criteria in FRS 9 for identification of joint ventures are potentially more restrictive than those for jointly controlled entities under IAS 31. Joint ventures are defined under IAS 31 (paragraph 2) as follows:

> A joint venture is a contractual arrangement whereby two or more parties undertake an economic activity which is subject to joint control.

IAS 31 identifies three types of joint venture: (i) jointly controlled operations, (ii) jointly controlled assets and (iii) jointly controlled entities. The benchmark treatment for accounting for joint ventures under IAS 31 is proportionate consolidation, although the IAS allows the use of the equity method for reporting interests in jointly controlled *entities* (i.e., type (iii)).

Under the Seventh Directive member states may require or permit proportional consolidation for joint ventures. Proportional consolidation involves including the investor's share of the individual assets and liabilities, profits and losses and cash flows on a line-by-line basis.

The proportionate method of consolidation is defined in IAS 31 (paragraph 2) as follows:

> Proportionate consolidation is a method of accounting and reporting whereby a venturer's share of each of the assets, liabilities, income and expenses of a jointly controlled entity is combined on a line-by-line basis with similar items in the venturer's financial statements or reported as separate line items in the venturer's financial statements.

Proportionate consolidation is a cross between full consolidation (as used for subsidiaries) and the equity method of accounting (as used for associates). Under proportionate consolidation, the *group share* of assets, liabilities, profits and losses of the joint venture is included in each line of the consolidated financial statements. The logic of proportionate consolidation where a joint venture is unincorporated is that the investor legally shares in the individual assets and liabilities rather than owns shares therein.

Example 15.13 illustrates the method.

Example 15.13 Proportionate consolidation

Example

Parent invested in 40% of Joint Venture (an unincorporated entity) at commencement of Joint Venture's activities in 20X6. The consolidated accounts of Parent and the individual accounts of Joint Venture for 20X8 are as follows:

Balance sheets	*Consolidated balance sheet of Parent*	*Joint Venture*
	€000	**€000**
Net assets	45	10
Investment in Joint Venture (at cost)	1	—
	46	10
Share capital	30	—
Capital account[1]	—	10
Profit and loss account	16	—
	46	10
Profit and loss accounts		
Profit before taxation	25	10
Taxation	(10)	(5)
Profit after taxation	15	5
Retained profit	1	—
Capital b/f[1]	—	5
Retained profit/capital c/f	16	10

It is assumed that profits of the unincorporated entity are taxable as shown.

Required

Prepare the consolidated balance sheet after including the joint venture using proportionate consolidation.

Solution

Balance sheet after proportionate consolidation	**€000**
Net assets [45 + 40% (10)]	49
Investment in Joint Venture (at cost)	—
	49
Share capital/capital account	30
Profit and loss account [(16 + 40% (7.5)][2]	19
	49

continued overleaf

Example 15.13 Continued

Profit and loss account after proportionate consolidation	**€000**
Profit before taxation [(25 + 40% (10)]	29
Taxation [(10 + 40% (5)]	(12)
Profit after taxation	17
Retained profit/capital b/f [1 + 40% (2.5)][1]	2
Retained profit/capital c/f	19

[1] Unincorporated entities do not have retained reserves – all undistributed profits are included in the capital account
[2] The 40 % investment in Joint Venture cost €1 million. Therefore, the capital of Joint Venture at commencement must have been €1 million × 100/40 = €2.5 million. Post-acquisition profits are therefore €10 million–2.5 million=7.5 million.

Example 15.14 compares four methods of accounting described in this book using simple data:

- full consolidation
- equity method of accounting
- proportional consolidation
- gross equity method of accounting.

Example 15.14 Acquisition/equity/proportional consolidation/gross equity methods

Example
Investor acquired 50% of Investee for €185 when Investee's revenue reserves were €150. The balance sheets were as follows:

		Investor		Investee
		€		€
Fixed assets		820		420
Investment in Investee		185		—
Current assets			260	
Creditors: Amounts falling due within one year			(120)	
Net current assets		625		140
		1,630		560
Share capital		700		200
Reserves		930		360
		1,630		560

Required
Prepare group balance sheets using:
(a) full consolidation under (i) the acquisition method
(b) non-consolidation techniques under (ii) the equity method, (iii) the gross equity method and (iv) proportional consolidation to account for the investment in Investee (assume no amortisation of goodwill).

Solution

	Acquisition method	Equity method		Gross equity method	Proportional consolidation
Fixed assets – group	1,240	820		820	1,030
Investment in Investee	—	290		—	—
(560 @ 50%+10_{goodwill}); or					
(185_{cost} + $105_{\text{post-acquisition profits}}$)					
Share of gross assets					
([$420_{\text{fixed assets}}$ + $260_{\text{current assets}}$] @ 50%)			340		
Share of gross liabilities (120 @ 50%)			(60)	280	
Goodwill (185 – $175_{200+150@50\%}$)	10	—		10	10
Net current assets – group	765	625		625	695
	2,015	1,735		1,735	1,735
Share capital	700	700		700	700
Reserves (930 + $105_{360-150\ @\ 50\%}$)	1,035	1,035		1,035	1,035
	1,735	1,735		1,735	1,735
Minority interest	280	—		—	—
	2,015	1,735		1,735	1,735

All these methods have been explained in this and earlier chapters, but this single example brings the four methods together to allow them to be compared. In the consolidated balance sheet in all four cases, the share capital and the reserves are the same. Share capital is that of the investor only. Reserves are the investor's, together with the group share of post-acquisition reserves of the investee.

This comparison of the treatment in the consolidated balance sheet can be summarised as follows:

- under the full consolidation, line-by-line, acquisition method:
  - fixed assets and net current assets are investor's and investee's combined on a line-by-line basis
  - goodwill is the difference between the cost of the investment and the fair value of the net assets acquired
  - minority interest is the minority share of the net assets of investee
- under the equity, single-line method:
  - fixed assets and net current assets are those of the investor only
  - investment in investee is included as a single-line item which is the group share of the net assets of the investee plus any related goodwill on the investment not amortised
  - goodwill is included as part of investment in investee and is not shown separately
  - there is no minority interest
- under the gross equity method:
  - fixed assets and net current assets are those of the investor and the group's share of the investee's gross assets and gross liabilities which are separately disclosed
  - goodwill is the difference between the cost of the investment and the net assets acquired
  - there is no minority interest
- under proportional consolidation:
  - fixed assets and net current assets are those of the investor plus the group's share of the investee's on a line-by-line basis

- goodwill is the difference between the cost of the investment and the net assets acquired
- there is no minority interest.

FRS 9 does not permit the use of proportionate consolidation for joint ventures and instead requires the use of the gross equity method. The ASB rejected proportional consolidation for joint ventures on the following grounds (paragraph 13, Appendix III to FRS 9):

> The Board rejects proportional consolidation for joint ventures because it believes that it can be misleading to represent each venturer's joint control of a joint venture – which allows it to direct the operating and financial policies of the joint venture only with the consent of the other venturers – as being in substance equivalent to its having sole control of its share of each of that entity's assets, liabilities and cash flows. The key features of control are that the controlling party has the ability to direct or deploy what it controls without consultation and ability to take the benefit from what it directs or deploys without question of entitlement.

IAS 31 *prefers* – whereas FRS 9 *prohibits* – the use of the line-by-line proportionate consolidation method for joint venture entities.

DaimlerChrysler, which reports under US GAAP, accounts for a material joint venture using proportional consolidation. Under US GAAP, the equity method should be used for accounting for joint ventures. The auditors of DaimlerChrysler refer to this treatment in their audit report in Exhibit 15.19 and justify the use of proportional consolidation on the basis that this is the recommended treatment under the Seventh Directive and under IASs.

Exhibit 15.19 **Auditors' comments on accounting for joint ventures DaimlerChrysler Annual Report 2000**

Independent Auditor's Report (Extract)
In 1998, DaimlerChrysler accounted for a material joint venture in accordance with the proportionate method of consolidation as is permitted under the Seventh Directive of the European Community and the Standards of the International Accounting Standards Committee. In our opinion, United States generally accepted accounting principles required that such joint venture be accounted for using the equity method of accounting. The United States Securities and Exchange Commission stated that it would not object to DaimlerChrysler's use of the proportionate method of consolidation as supplemented by the disclosures in Note 3.

IAS 31 requires venturers who contribute or sell assets to a joint venture to recognise the portion of gain or loss on the transfer of the asset in accordance with the substance of the transaction. SIC 13 *Jointly Controlled Entities – Non-Monetary Contributions by Venturers* deals with the special case where an investor makes a non-monetary contribution to a jointly controlled entity in return for an equity interest in that entity. In such circumstances, the investor is permitted to recognise the share of gain or loss on the transaction except when:

- significant risks and rewards of ownership of the contributed non-monetary assets have not been transferred
- gain or loss on the non-monetary contribution cannot be measured reliably
- non-monetary assets contributed are similar to those contributed by other investors.

IAS 31 requires a venturer to separately disclose the following in relation to joint ventures:

- aggregate contingent liabilities
- aggregate commitments
- listing and description of interests in significant joint ventures, and the proportion of ownership interest held in jointly controlled entities.

Joint arrangements that are not entities (JANEs)

A variation of proportional consolidation is required under FRS 9 for joint arrangements that are not entities. These are defined in FRS 9 (paragraph 4) as follows:

> A contractual arrangement under which the participants engage in joint activities that do not create an entity because it would not be carrying on a trade or business of its own. A contractual arrangement where all significant matters of operating and financial policy are predetermined does not create an entity because the policies are those of its participants, not of a separate entity.

Paragraphs 8 and 9 of FRS 9 provide guidance on this definition. In particular, indications of a joint arrangement are offered, including:

- participants derive their benefit from products or services taken in kind rather than by receiving a share in the financial results of trading
- each participant's share of the output or result of the joint activity is determined by its supply of key inputs to the process producing that output or result.

The standard provides examples of such arrangements – a joint marketing (e.g., mutually beneficial advertising campaign), distribution network or a shared production facility.

Investors should account for such joint arrangements directly for the investor's share of the assets, liabilities and cash flows relating to the joint arrangements. The share should be measured by reference to the terms of the joint arrangement. This approach is therefore very similar to proportional consolidation.

Comparison of UK GAAP and IAS GAAP

There are a number of differences between FRS 9 and IASs 28 and 31. The main differences are summarised in Table 15.2. These relate to definitions, methods of accounting and disclosure requirements. Disclosure requirements under FRS 9 are more extensive than under IASs. These differences were summarised earlier in Table 15.1.

Table 15.2 Main differences in accounting for associates and joint ventures between UK GAAP and IAS GAAP

	UK GAAP	*IAS GAAP*
Associates		
Definition	Demonstration of ability to exercise significant influence more restrictive	Exercise of significant influence
Method of accounting	Equity method	Equity method
Profit and loss account	Disclose investor's share of operating profit, exceptional items and interest on face of profit and loss account	No explicit guidance on presentation in profit and loss account
Balance sheet	Disclose goodwill element separately	Single amount to be disclosed with no analysis of underlying components
Disclosures	More detailed disclosures required	Limited disclosures required
Joint ventures		
Method of accounting	Gross equity method	Proportionate consolidation benchmark treatment, equity method permitted
Profit and loss account	Separate disclosure of gross (inclusive of joint venture) turnover, with deduction of joint venture turnover to present group turnover	No separate identification of amounts relating to joint ventures
Balance sheet	Gross assets and gross liabilities of joint venture to be separately disclosed	No separate identification of amounts relating to joint ventures
Net liabilities	Include investor's share of net liabilities unless it can be demonstrated that investor has withdrawn from the relationship	Cease to apply equity method of accounting unless investor has obligations to make payments

Sources: Cairns, D. and Nobes, C. 2000. *The Convergence Handbook: A Comparison between International Accounting Standards and UK Financial Reporting Requirements*. Institute of Chartered Accountants in England and Wales, London
Connor, L., Dekker, P., Davies, M., Robinson, P. and Wilson, A. 2001. *IAS/UK GAAP Comparison* Ernst & Young, London.
PricewaterhouseCoopers. 2000. *International Accounting Standards Similarities and Differences. IAS, US GAAP and UK GAAP.* PricewaterhouseCoopers, London

Summary

This chapter has primarily dealt with the regulations applying to accounting for associates and the use of the equity method of accounting under UK GAAP and under IAS GAAP. Joint ventures were also considered under these two sources of regulation. The special treatment of JANEs under FRS 9 was also briefly discussed. The chapter concluded by comparing regulations under UK GAAP and under IAS GAAP. Three different methods of accounting have been considered in the chapter: the equity method of accounting, a variation thereon for joint ventures in the form of the gross equity method and the proportionate method of consolidation.

Learning outcomes

After studying this chapter you should have learnt:

- to record associated undertakings in group accounts following UK GAAP regulations
- to record associated undertakings in group accounts following IAS GAAP regulations
- to account for joint ventures in group accounts
- to apply UK regulations to accounting for joint arrangements that are not entities (JANEs)
- the differences between UK GAAP and IAS GAAP regulations applying to accounting for associated undertakings and joint ventures.

Multiple choice questions

Solutions to these questions are prepared under UK GAAP and are shown in Appendix 1.

15.1 Polka

Polka has acquired several investments in other companies, with stakes ranging from 1% to 100%. On consolidation, the equity method of accounting for investments is normally appropriate where:

(a) the majority of the consideration was a share for share exchange
(b) not less than 90% of the fair value of the total consideration given is in the form of equity share capital
(c) the group stake is less than 20% of the ordinary share capital
(d) the group stake is between 20% and 50% of the ordinary share capital

15.2 Prolific

Equity shareholdings of **Prolific**

Name of company	Equity held	Other shareholders
Ready	30%	No other shareholder holds more than 15%
Steady	25%	Progress owns 70% of the equity share capital, has two directors on the board and refuses to answer any correspondence from Prolific
Go	18%	Stop owns 36% and Start owns 46%. The company was set up as a joint venture. All three companies have a director on Go's board

Which investments qualify as associated undertakings of Prolific under FRS 9?

(a) Ready only
(b) Ready and Steady only
(c) Ready and Go only
(d) All three

15.3 Jenkins

Jenkins has the following shareholdings:

Gypsy — 20% of ordinary share capital held, no board representation. The remaining 80% of Gypsy's share capital is held by Craggs, a company unconnected with Jenkins

Jean — 50% of ordinary share capital held. The remaining 50% of Jean's ordinary share capital is held by Brent, which is at loggerheads with Jenkins over the control of Jean. Each shareholder is in a continuous struggle to buy the other's shareholding and each has appointed one of Jean's three directors to exercise influence over the company. The third director is neutral

Isobel — 100% of ordinary share capital held, full control of board.

What is the status of each investment?

	Associated undertaking (FRS 9 definition)	Subsidiary undertaking (FRS 2 definition)	Neither
(a)	Gypsy & Jean	Isobel	—
(b)	Jean	Isobel	Gypsy
(c)	Gypsy	Jean & Isobel	—
(d)	—	Isobel	Jean & Gypsy

15.4 Music

Music holds the following long-term investments:

25% of the ordinary shares in Violin. The remaining shares are owned by a large number of small shareholders, the largest of which owns 4%.

25% of the ordinary shares in Trumpet. 60% of the ordinary shares in Trumpet are held by Concert and the remainder by a large number of small shareholders, the largest of which owns 3%.

25% of the ordinary shares and 80% of the 7% preference shares in Cello. The remaining shares are held by a large number of small shareholders, the largest of which owns 6% of the ordinary shares in Cello.

The following companies are associated undertakings of Music:

(a) Violin and Cello
(b) Violin and Trumpet
(c) Violin
(d) Trumpet and Cello

15.5 Mona

Mona has the following long-term shareholdings:

- 25% of Templer's ordinary share capital
- 30% of Quiggin's preference share capital
- 87% of Erridge's A ordinary shares (non-voting)
- 45% of Erridge's B ordinary shares (voting)

Which of these shareholdings should be accounted for under the equity accounting method to comply with FRS 9?

(a) Templer only
(b) Templer and Quiggin only
(c) Templer and Erridge only
(d) Quiggin and Erridge only

Examination-style questions

15.1 The equity method

The equity method of valuing certain forms of investment made by one company in another has been in common use since the early 1970s.

Required

(a) Define concisely the term 'equity method' and outline the accounting procedures by which it is applied.
(b) Describe the present position regarding the use of the method, as referred to in FRSs 2 and 9.
(c) Assess the validity of the equity method as an alternative to other modes of accounting for the relevant investments.

15.2 Deb

The financial accountant has supplied you with the draft financial statements of **Deb** for the year ended 30 June 20X1, which include the following:

Trade investments €4,910,000 purchased on 1 April 20X0

Part of these investments are held in the books at cost – €2,720,000:

- Of these, €1,420,000 are equity investments in listed companies intended to be held on a short-term basis (market value at the balance sheet date – €1,750,000).
- In addition, there are equity investments in unlisted companies which cost €1,300,000. The directors of Deb are satisfied that the unlisted securities are worthwhile investments in the long term.

The balance of the trade investments figure refers to an equity investment in a private company Sob. Deb holds 25% of the equity of Sob. The cost of this investment was €3,810,000 which exactly matched the fair value of the tangible assets acquired. Sob's most recent financial statements are made up to 31 March 20X1 and these indicate losses (after tax relief of €2,300,000) for the year of €2,280,000. No dividends have been received. Because of these poor results, the directors have written down the investment.

Required

You are required, as financial director, to:

(a) Show how the listed and unlisted investments should be accounted for in the group accounts of Deb, setting out appropriate entries to the financial statements and appropriate disclosures required to comply with good accounting practice.

(b) Set out any additional information which you would require in respect of the above items, prior to finalising the financial statements.

15.3 Scirocco

The following information relates to an investment in an associated undertaking, **Scirocco**.

	€000
At acquisition	
Ordinary share capital (10 cent each)	420
Reserves (including revaluation surpluses reflecting the fair value of net assets at acquisition)	2,290
At 31.12.20X9	
Ordinary share capital (10 cent each)	480
Reserves (including share premium)	3,120

The investing company, Golf, originally acquired 30% of the share capital of Scirocco at a cost of €1,252,000. At a later date, Scirocco had a 1 for 7 rights issue at 110 cent per share and Golf took up its full entitlement to the rights.

Required

(a) Define 'associated undertaking' under FRS 9.

(b) Discuss the application of the definition in (a), where an investing group or company holds:
  (i) 20% or more of the equity voting rights of another company; and
  (ii) less than 20% of the equity voting rights of another company.

(c) On the basis of the information given, prepare the note to the consolidated balance sheet of Golf at 31.12.20X9 in respect of *Investment in Scirocco*, to provide the disclosures required under FRS 9.

15.4 Octopus and Uncertain

FRS 2 (and the Seventh Directive that preceded it) changed the definitions relating to the composition of a group for the purpose of presenting the group accounts of a commercial organisation.

Consider the following data relating to the year ended 31 August 20X5 of **Octopus and Uncertain**.

Balance sheet	**Octopus**		**Uncertain**	
	€000	**€000**	**€000**	**€000**
Fixed assets				
Tangible (net book value)	6,500			4,000
Investment in Uncertain at cost	2,000			
		8,500		
Current assets	3,500		3,000	
Current liabilities	(4,550)		(2,500)	
Net current (liabilities) / assets		(1,050)		500
		7,450		4,500
Debentures		(2,000)		(1,500)
		5,450		3,000

continued overleaf

Balance sheet (*continued*)	**Octopus**	**Uncertain**
	€000	**€000**
Capital and reserves		
Ordinary shares	2,000	1,000
Reserves	3,450	2,000
	5,450	3,000

Profit and loss account	**Octopus**	**Uncertain**
	€000	**€000**
Trading profit before tax	1,100	500
Dividend from Uncertain	100	—
Taxation	(600)	(200)
Profit after tax	600	300
Dividends paid	(300)	(200)
Retained	300	100

Octopus acquired 50% of the ordinary share capital of Uncertain on 1 September 20X4 for €2,000,000 when its reserves were €1,900,000 and sold this holding on 3 September 20X5 for €2,050,000.

Required

(a) Prepare the group profit and loss account and balance sheet on three bases:
- (i) when Uncertain is treated as a subsidiary
- (ii) when Uncertain is treated as an associated undertaking
- (iii) when Uncertain is treated as an investment.

(b) Comment on the validity of these three alternative bases.

You may ignore the requirement of FRS 10 to amortise purchased goodwill.

15.5 Intra-associated Dealing

The following is an extract from paragraph 31(b) and (c) of Financial Reporting Standard 9 *Associates and Joint Ventures*:

> Where profits and losses resulting from transactions between the investor and its associate or joint venture are included in the carrying amount of assets in either entity, the part relating to the investor's share should be eliminated.
>
> In arriving at the amounts to be included by the equity method, the same accounting policies as those of the investor should be applied.

Required

(a) An investing company, **Intra-associated Dealing**, holds 30% of the equity capital of an associate which purchases stocks at full commercial terms from the investing company. You are required to illustrate and explain the adjusting entries you would make in consolidated workings so as to allow for an unrealised profit content in the stocks so purchased and carried by the associated company.

(b) State your understanding of the term 'accounting policies' as used in the context of the extract from FRS 9 quoted in this question.

15.6 Archer

Archer owns a number of subsidiaries, and prepares its consolidated financial statements to 31 December each year. During 20X8 Archer purchased interests in Bow and Arrow. Draft profit and loss accounts for the year ended 31 December 20X8 and balance sheets as at that date for the Archer Group (excluding Bow and Arrow) and for Bow and Arrow are as follows:

Profit and loss account for the year ended 31 December 20X8

	Archer Group	**Bow**	**Arrow**
	€ million	**€ million**	**€ million**
Turnover	3,000	200	1,800
Cost of sales	(1,800)	(125)	(900)
Gross profit	1,200	75	900
Operating expenses	(500)	(25)	(260)
Operating profit	700	50	640
Interest payable	(20)	(5)	(10)
Profit before tax	680	45	630
Tax	(200)	(10)	(190)
Profit after tax	480	35	440
Dividends	(180)	–	(40)
Retained profit for year	300	35	400

Balance sheet as at 31 December 20X8

	Archer Group	**Bow**	**Arrow**
	€ million	**€ million**	**€ million**
Fixed assets			
Tangible assets	2,200	40	2,100
Investment in Bow	200	—	—
Investment in Arrow	800	—	—
	3,200	40	2,100
Current assets			
Stocks	400	125	250
Debtors	300	–	240
Bank and cash	80	200	110
	780	325	600
Creditors: Amounts due within one year	(480)	(30)	(300)
Net current assets	300	295	300
	3,500	335	2,400
Share capital and reserves			
€1 ordinary shares (equity)	1,200	100	600
Revaluation reserve	600	–	300
Profit and loss account	1,700	235	1,500
	3,500	335	2,400

Notes

1 The directors of Archer have decided to reinstate goodwill, written off to reserves in previous years, as an asset in the balance sheet.

Goodwill previously written off to reserves amounts to €120 million and relates to the purchase of a 100% interest in Quiver in January 20X6. The directors have taken the view that the estimated useful economic life of the goodwill at the date of acquisition was ten years.

No adjustment has been made to the financial statements in respect of this.

2 On 1 January 20X8 Archer purchased 100% of the ordinary share capital of Bow. The details are as follows:

	€ million
Cost of investment	200
Fair value of net assets acquired	
Fixed assets	50
Stock	250

Fixed assets are to be depreciated over five years.

During 20X8, 50% of the stock was sold outside the group on normal trading terms, with the remaining stock expected to be sold in 20X9. The acquisition of Bow has not yet been incorporated into the financial statements of the Archer Group.

3 On 1 January 20X8 Archer purchased 30% of Arrow. Archer contributes to the activities of Arrow and is actively involved in Arrow's financial and operating policy decisions. The balance sheet of Arrow at 1 January 20X8 showed the following:

	€ million
Share capital	600
Revaluation reserve	300
Profit and loss account	1,100
	2,000

Goodwill is to be capitalised and amortised over five years. The acquisition of Arrow has not yet been incorporated into the financial statements of the Archer Group.

Required

(a) Explain, in the context of FRS 9 *Associates and Joint Ventures*, the difference between an associate and a joint venture.

(b) Prepare the consolidated profit and loss account for the year ended 31 December 20X8 and the balance sheet as at that date for the Archer Group.

15.7 Textures

Textures was incorporated in 20W5. Its financial year-end is 30 November 20X6. It manufactures in the Republic of Ireland and exports more than 60% of its output. It has a number of foreign subsidiary companies.

It has developed a number of arrangements to support its export sales. These include two agreements with (1) Pills, (2) Eduaids and Mr Bracos. Information on these agreements is as follows:

1 Agreement with Pills

An agreement was made in 20X2 with Pills, a pharmaceutical company, jointly to fund on a 50:50 basis an entity, Textures & Pills Joint Venture, to operate a marketing office in Asia which would advertise each of the company's products but not trade in the products. Both Textures and Pills have guaranteed to meet liabilities if the other party fails to meet its share of the costs and risks.

Accounts prepared for Textures & Pills Joint Venture for the year ended 30 November 20X6 showed the following:

	€000
Fixed assets	
Premises	300
Current assets	
Bank and cash	30
	330
Capital	
As at 1 December 20X5	
Textures	211
Pills	211
	422
Less: Expenses	(92)
As at 30 November 20X6	330

2 Agreement with Eduaids and Mr Bracos

Textures entered into an agreement on 1 December 20X1 with Eduaids, a company that manufactured educational equipment, and Mr Bracos, a South American lawyer, to set up under their three-way joint control an unincorporated import undertaking in South America to trade as Eurohelp. Textures had an effective 30% interest in Eurohelp. The balance sheet of Textures as at 30 November 20X6 showed an investment at cost in Eurohelp of €750,000.

The balance sheet of Eurohelp for the year ended 30 November 20X6 showed:

	€000
Fixed assets	7,500
Net current assets	1,100
	8,600
Capital account	
As at 30 November 20X5	6,750
Retained profit for the year	1,850
	8,600

Textures has used proportional consolidation to account for its interest in Eurohelp since entering into the agreement.

Required

(a) (i) Explain the advantages of using expanded equity accounting to account for associates in consolidated accounts

(ii) Discuss the advantages and disadvantages of using proportional consolidation to account for joint ventures.

(b) (i) Explain how the joint activity of Textures & Pills Joint Venture would be dealt with in the accounts of Textures as at 30 November 20X6

(ii) Calculate the retained profit of Eurohelp as at 1 December 20X5 that would be included in the consolidated retained profit brought forward in the accounts of Textures at 30 November 20X6.

15.8 Baden

FRS 9 *Associates and Joint Ventures* deals not only with the accounting treatment of associated companies and joint venture operations but covers certain types of joint business arrangements not carried on through a separate entity. FRS 9, inter alia, restricts the circumstances in which equity accounting can be applied and provides detailed rules for accounting for joint ventures.

The following financial statements relate to **Baden**, a public limited company.

Profit and loss account for year ended 31 December 20X8

	€m	**€m**
Turnover		212
Cost of sales		(170)
Gross profit		42
Distribution costs	17	
Administrative expenses	8	
		(25)
		17
Other operating income		12
Operating profit		29
Exceptional item		(10)
Interest payable		(4)
Profit on ordinary activities before tax		15
Taxation on profit on ordinary activities		(3)
		12
Ordinary dividend – paid		(4)
Retained profit for year		8

continued overleaf

Balance sheet at 31 December 20X8

	€m	€m
Fixed assets – tangible	30	
goodwill	7	37
Current assets	31	
Creditors: Amounts falling due within one year	(12)	
Net current assets		19
Total assets less current liabilities		56
Creditors: Amounts falling due after more than one year		(10)
		46
Capital and reserves		
Called-up share capital		
Ordinary shares of €1		10
Share premium		4
Profit and loss account		32
		46

1 Cable, a public limited company, acquired 30% of the ordinary share capital of Baden at a cost of €14 million on 1 January 20X7. The share capital of Baden has not changed since acquisition when the profit and loss reserve of Baden was €9 million.
2 At 1 January 20X7 the following fair values were attributed to the net assets of Baden but not incorporated in its accounting records.

	€m
Tangible fixed assets (carrying value €20m)	30
Goodwill (estimate)	10
Current assets	31
Creditors: Amount falling due within one year	20
Creditors: Amount falling due after more than one year	8

3 Guy, an associated company of Cable, also holds a 25% interest in the ordinary share capital of Baden. This was acquired on 1 January 20X8.
4 During the year to 31 December 20X8, Baden sold goods to Cable to the value of €35 million. The inventory of Cable at 31 December 20X8 included goods purchased from Baden on which the company made a profit of €10 million.
5 The policy of all companies in the Cable Group is to amortise goodwill over four years and to depreciate tangible fixed assets at 20% per annum on the straight-line basis.
6 Baden does not represent a material part of the group and is significantly less than the 15% additional disclosure threshold required under FRS 9 *Associates and Joint Ventures*.

Required

(a) Explain the criteria which distinguish an associate from an ordinary fixed asset investment.
(b) Explain the principal difference between a joint venture and a 'joint arrangement' and the impact that this classification has on the accounting for such relationships.
(c) Show how the investment in Baden would be stated in the consolidated balance sheet and profit and loss account of the Cable Group under FRS 9 *Associates and Joint Ventures*, for the year ended 31 December 20X8 on the assumption that Baden is an associate.
(d) Show how the treatment of Baden would change if Baden was classified as an investment in a joint venture.

15.9 Rusher

Rusher decided to expand its operations and entered into a joint venture agreement with the government of a developing country to form a new company, **Belaruse**, to manufacture plastic containers. The share capital of Belaruse is owned equally by Rusher and the government of the country and amounts to €3 million. The board of directors of the joint venture company is made up of equal numbers of government officials and directors of Rusher. In alternate years a chairman is appointed from Rusher and the chairman has the casting vote in any dispute.

The financial and business policies of Belaruse have to conform with the goals and objectives of the five-year operating plan determined by the government. Belaruse is an incorporated company. Profits are distributed to Rusher according to the legislation applying to overseas joint ventures. The first profit and loss account of Belaruse is set out as follows and has been drawn up in accordance with the accounting regulations of the overseas country and has been translated into euro (€).

Belaruse profit and loss account year ended 30 November 20X5

	€000
Sales	1,000
Expenses (cost of sales)	(600)
Profit from sales	400
Profit from other activities	50
Total profit	450
Allocation to reserve fund	(18)
Pre-tax profit	432
Profits tax (30%)	(129)
Net profit	303
Allocations to economic stimulation and social welfare reserve	(53)
Profit for distribution to joint venture partners	250
Share of profits of foreign partner (Rusher) to be repatriated	125
Tax on profits for repatriation (12%)	(15)
Net repatriated profit	110

(*Note*: There is no exchange difference as the value of the local currency has been fixed in relation to the euro since the inception of the joint venture.)

The auditors of Rusher are a large firm of international accountants with offices in the overseas country. The government of the country has agreed that the auditors may have access to the accounting records of Belaruse. Other details of the joint agreement are as follows:

(a) Before any profits are shared, there must be a transfer to the reserve fund and an allocation to a fund to provide for the economic stimulation of the country and the social welfare of the people. These funds can never be distributed to Rusher.

(b) The developing country will prepare all the documents for the registration of the company.

(c) Rusher will provide the know-how, selling and marketing and expertise training for personnel.

(d) In the event of the termination of the agreement, the developing country will receive repayment of capital in preference to Rusher and Rusher can never receive more than its original investment plus repatriated profit not yet paid in the event of a liquidation.

The accountant of Rusher is having some difficulty in deciding how to treat the joint venture in the financial statements of the company. It is proposed to treat Belaruse as a 'quasi-subsidiary' and consolidate it into the financial statements of Rusher Group. The auditors do not agree with this treatment and wish the company to use the equity method for inclusion of Belaruse in the group accounts.

Required

(a) Discuss the possible reasons behind the auditor's recommendation to use the equity method as opposed to acquisition accounting for the inclusion of Belaruse in the group accounts.

(b) Explain the main criticisms of the equity method of accounting and how these criticisms might be overcome.

(c) Calculate the amounts which would be included in the group financial statements of Rusher for Belaruse if the accountant used:

(i) the equity method of accounting

(ii) acquisition accounting.

(The principles involved in the calculations should be explained.)

15.10 Espur

Details of investments held by **Espur** at 31 December 20X2.

1 Investment in Heclo

This company's shareholders' funds at 31 December 20X2 consisted of:

	€000
7% preference shares at €1 per share	500
Ordinary shares of €1 per share	3,000
Reserves	760

On 1 April 20X1, Espur had acquired a 40% holding of the ordinary share capital at a (gross) cost of €1,670,000 under an arrangement by which Espur controls the composition of the board of directors of Heclo.

Of the dividends which Espur received from Heclo in 20X1, €16,000 were from pre-acquisition profits of €540,000. At 31 December 20X1, reserves were €600,000. The proposed 20X1 final ordinary dividend of 7 cent per share was paid in May 20X2.

Heclo paid an interim dividend of 3 cent per share on 1 August 20X2 and at 31 December 20X2 proposed a final dividend of 10 cent per share.

2 Investment in Terand

At 31 December 20X2 this company's shareholders' funds consisted of:

	€000
Ordinary shares of €1 per share	800
Reserves	126

On 31 December 20X1, Espur had acquired a long-term interest of 30% in the ordinary share capital at a cost of €290,000 under an arrangement by which Espur actually exercises a significant influence over the operating and financial policies of Terand. At that date, Terand's reserves were €76,000.

Terand proposed a dividend of 3 cent per share on 31 December 20X2. For the year ended 31 December 20X2, Terand's profit and loss account disclosed a profit before tax figure of €98,000 and a taxation charge of €24,000.

3 Investment in Unive

At 31 December 20X2, this company's shareholders' fund consisted of:

	€000
7% preference shares of €1 per share	200
Ordinary share capital of €1 per share	500
Reserves	460

On 30 June 20X1, Espur had acquired a 60% holding of the 7% preference share capital and a participating interest of 25% in the ordinary share capital at a (gross) cost of €145,700 and €170,600 respectively. At that date Unive's reserves were €310,500.

Unive paid the 20X1 preference dividend in January 20X2, the proposed 20X1 final ordinary dividend of 6 cent per share in April 20X2 and an ordinary interim dividend of 2 cent per share on 31 July 20X2. At 31 December 20X2, Unive proposed a year's dividend on the preference shares and a final dividend of 8 cent per share on the ordinary shares.

Espur's participating interest in Unive conferred neither a dominant nor a significant influence over the operating and financial policies of that company.

4 Investment in Ledec

At 31 December 20X2 this company's shareholders' funds consisted of:

	€000
8% preference shares of €1 per share	1,000
Ordinary shares of €1 per share	6,000
Reserves	976

In addition to which there was loan capital of:

	€000
6% debentures	2,800

On 31 March 20X1, when the reserves of Ledec were €565,000, Espur acquired a 5% holding of the ordinary share capital at a cost of €327,000. The reserves had risen to €592,000 by 1 August 20X1 when Espur acquired a 25% holding of the 6% debentures at a cost of €639,000 *cum int*. Interest on these debentures is paid half-yearly on 30 June and 31 December.

Ledec proposed an ordinary dividend of 5 cent per share at 31 December 20X1 which was paid in April 20X2 together with the second half-year's preference dividend.

The first half-year's preference dividend for 20X2 was paid in August 20X2 and at 31 December 20X2 Ledec proposed the second half year's preference dividend together with a dividend of 8 cent per share on the ordinary shares.

Required

(a) From an accounting treatment point of view, identify the status of each of the four investments.

(b) Prepare detailed extracts from the profit and loss account for the year ended 31 December 20X2 and the balance sheet at that date, as far as the information is available, incorporating the financial effects of the four investments, separately for:
   (i) Espur (the parent undertaking);
   (ii) Espur group (consolidated accounts).

Note: It is the policy of Espur to ignore dividend income until actually received and to write off goodwill on consolidation over a period of five years. You should ignore the taxation aspects of the transactions.

16

Acquisition and merger accounting

Learning objectives

After reading this chapter you should be able to:

- discuss the regulations under UK GAAP and IAS GAAP applying to the acquisition method of accounting
- explain the regulations under UK GAAP and IAS GAAP applying to the merger method of accounting
- understand how to account for demergers
- explain reverse acquisitions
- compare and contrast UK GAAP and IAS GAAP regulations applying to the acquisition and merger methods

Introduction

Chapter 9 introduced the basic techniques for preparing consolidated accounts using the merger method of accounting, rather than the more traditional acquisition method. As explained in that chapter, legal and professional accounting regulations restrict the use of merger accounting. In addition, in some countries the legality of the merger method is uncertain. As a result, the merger method is used infrequently in practice.

This chapter considers first the regulations governing acquisition accounting. It then reviews the regulations governing merger accounting. The remainder of the chapter explains the specialised concepts of demergers and reverse acquisitions that come within professional regulations governing mergers and acquisitions. Lastly, the disclosure requirements of accounting standards relating to acquisitions and mergers are summarised.

Acquisition accounting – regulations

Acquisition accounting techniques have been comprehensively explained and illustrated in Parts 2 and 3 of this book and should by now be familiar to readers. To recap, under acquisition accounting:

- assets and liabilities of the subsidiary acquired are included on a line-by-line basis in the consolidated financial statements at fair value at the date of acquisition
- goodwill on acquisition is the difference between the fair value of the consideration paid and the fair value of the net assets acquired
- minority interests in the net assets at fair value are shown as a one-line item in the balance sheet, outside shareholders' funds

- pre-acquisition profits of the subsidiary acquired are not distributable
- group's share of post-acquisition profits (net of adjustments and goodwill amortisation and write-offs) are included in group reserves
- results of the subsidiary acquired are included from the date of acquisition
- results of subsidiaries disposed of are included only to the date of disposal.

The accounting policy of Prudential in Exhibit 16.1 clearly explains the approach taken in acquisition accounting.

Exhibit 16.1 **Acquisition accounting policy Prudential plc Annual Report 2000**

Notes on the Financial Statements (extract)
Basis of Presentation (extract)
The consolidated financial statements of the Group include the assets, liabilities and results of the Company and subsidiary undertakings in which Prudential has a controlling interest. The results of subsidiaries are included in the financial statements from the date acquired to the effective date of disposal. All intercompany transactions are eliminated on consolidation except for investment management fees charged by M&G to long-term business funds.

The regulations dealing with acquisition accounting are considered in this section. Relevant regulations are to be found in FRS 2 *Accounting for Subsidiary Undertakings*, FRS 6 *Acquisitions and Mergers* and FRS 7 *Fair Values in Acquisition Accounting* under UK GAAP. Relevant regulations under IAS GAAP are to be found in IAS 22 *Business Combinations*, with clarification of IAS 22 contained in SIC 28 *Business Combinations – 'Date of Exchange' and Fair Value of Equity Instruments*.

Only the parts of the relevant accounting standards dealing specifically with acquisition accounting and merger accounting are covered in this chapter. Fair values and goodwill are discussed in Chapter 17.

Changes in group composition have already been considered in Chapter 14 and material covered in that chapter is not repeated here. Consequences of changes in composition of groups are also examined. A change in the composition of a group can be categorised as either an increase or a reduction in an interest in a subsidiary or as the addition or removal of a subsidiary. A group may reduce its interest in subsidiaries either by selling some or all of its shares. In addition, where the subsidiary issues new shares to another shareholder, the percentage owned by the group is effectively reduced.

Regulations clarifying the date of acquisition/disposal, and the treatment of piecemeal acquisitions are discussed as are the disclosure requirements relating to activities acquired and disposed (that are accounted for using the acquisition method).

UK GAAP

Changes in group composition

Three standards deal with changes in group composition: FRS 2, FRS 6 and FRS 7.

FRS 2 sets out the conditions under which consolidated accounts should be prepared, and provides guidance on the manner of preparation of these accounts. The acquisition method of accounting is not defined in the standard, but it is clear from the description of how to account for acquisitions and disposals of subsidiaries that the standard is based on the acquisition method. The standard deals with definitions, exemptions from preparing consolidated accounts and exclusions of subsidiaries therefrom. In addition, guidance is given on consolidating adjustments, on the accounting treatment for changes in composition of a group and for changes in stake. FRS 2 clarifies issues relevant to acquisition accounting such as identification of the effective date of acquisition and calculation of pre-acquisition profits.

FRS 6 was issued in September 1994. Its objectives are to ensure that:

- merger accounting is only used for those business combinations that are not acquisitions. Under FRS 6, merger accounting is restricted to very rare cases where the business combination cannot be properly viewed as a takeover of one company by another
- acquisition accounting is used for all other business combinations
- financial statements provide sufficient information for users concerning the effect of combinations.

Under FRS 6, acquisition accounting should be used for all business combinations with two exceptions. These are:

1 Acquisitions:
   - not prohibited by legislation from using merger accounting
   - meeting all the criteria for merger accounting in FRS 6 and falling within the definition of a merger.
2 Group reconstructions and combinations affected by using a new parent company may be treated as mergers. In practice, group restructuring accounts for a majority of cases where merger accounting is used (*Company Reporting*, 104, February 1999, p.4).

Under UK GAAP, there are slightly different approaches to dealing with reductions in interests depending on whether the investment ceases to be classified as a subsidiary or whether the interest in a continuing subsidiary is being reduced.

For an undertaking ceasing to be a subsidiary, the acquisition method of accounting usually applied in preparing consolidated accounts requires:

- inclusion of that subsidiary's profits up to date of cessation
- gain or loss on cessation to be calculated by comparing the carrying amount of the net assets in the subsidiary (before the cessation, minus any carrying amount after the cessation) with the proceeds. The net assets compared should include any related goodwill not previously written off or amortised. Profit or loss is the difference between the group share of net assets (including goodwill not written off through the profit and loss account) after reduction and group share before reduction compared with proceeds.

Where only part of an interest is sold, but an interest in subsidiary is retained, the gain or loss is calculated by comparing the sale proceeds with the consolidated net asset value attributable to the shares sold at the date of disposal (including any related goodwill not written off or amortised). The mechanics of such calculations are explained in Chapter 12.

Effective date of acquisition and disposal

The effective date of acquisition or disposal under FRS 2 is the date on which control passes. FRS 2 states that this date is a matter of fact and cannot be backdated or otherwise altered. Control is defined (in paragraph 6) as:

> The ability of an undertaking to direct the financial and operating policies of another undertaking with a view to gaining economic benefits from its activities.

Indications of the date on which control passes (i.e., of the effective date of acquisition) are set out in FRS 2, as follows:

- date the acquiring party commences directing the operating and financial policies of the acquired undertakings
- date from which there are changes in the flow of economic benefits
- date on which consideration passes (but this is not conclusive evidence of the date of acquisition).

Situations are also given in the standard indicating dates on which control is transferred including:

- control as a result of public offer – the date the offer becomes unconditional (i.e., after a specified number of acceptances of the offer)
- private treaties – the date an unconditional offer is accepted
- control as a result of issue or cancellation of shares – date of issue/cancellation.

The date for accounting for an undertaking ceasing to be a subsidiary undertaking is the date on which its former parent undertaking relinquishes control.

Piecemeal acquisitions

The Seventh Directive clarified the treatment of piecemeal acquisitions (already discussed in Chapter 5). Pre-acquisition profits are calculated by reference to the fair value of assets and liabilities at the date control is obtained, even where the investment was purchased in stages. Prior to the Seventh Directive, pre-acquisition profits could be calculated based on revenue reserves at each stage of acquisition. In the case of acquisitions in two or more stages, the Seventh Directive requires goodwill to be calculated on the date the undertaking became a subsidiary.

FRS 2, consistent with the Seventh Directive, requires assets and liabilities of subsidiaries acquired in stages to be included at fair value on the date the undertaking becomes a subsidiary, rather than the date of earlier purchases. This is a practical approach to acquisition accounting and does not require retrospective assessment of fair values. However, as indicated in Chapter 5, where the equity method of accounting was adopted prior to control being achieved, fair values at the date of achieving associate status are used for the relevant proportion of shares.

Under FRS 2, any increase in interest in a subsidiary should be accounted for by reference to the fair value of the subsidiary at the date of increase (except where the differences between fair values and book values at that date are immaterial). Thus, assets and liabilities at the date of increase in stake should be revalued and goodwill on the increased stake calculated accordingly. There is no need to recalculate goodwill previously arising.

Cable & Wireless acquired a subsidiary in stages. Previously its investment was recorded as an associate, but after the acquisition, control was obtained and the investment was then classified as a subsidiary. Exhibit 16.2 clearly shows that the step-by-step method was applied in recording this piecemeal (two-stage) acquisition (see Chapter 5 for an explanation of the step-by-step approach). Cable & Wireless acknowledges that this approach does not comply with the requirements of the Seventh Directive and the company invokes the true and fair view override provisions of legislation to justify the departure (see Chapter 13 for a discussion of the true and fair override provisions). As is required by legislation and by FRS 18 *Accounting Policies*, the note discloses the effect of the departure on amounts recorded in the consolidated financial statements.

Exhibit 16.2 **Piecemeal acquisition**
Cable & Wireless Annual Report 2000

Notes to the Accounts (extract)
32 Acquisitions (extract)
The following major acquisitions were made by the Group in the year:
On 15 June 1999 the Group acquired a further 80% of Cable & Wireless IDC (formerly International Digital Communications) Inc. for cash consideration of Yen 55.2bn (£288m). This increased the Group's holding in IDC to 97.7%.

Prior to becoming a subsidiary undertaking, Cable & Wireless IDC was accounted for as an associated undertaking. In accordance with FRS 2 – *Accounting for Subsidiary Undertakings* – and in order to give a true and fair view, purchased goodwill has been calculated as the sum of the goodwill arising on each purchase of shares in Cable & Wireless IDC, being the difference at the date of each purchase between the fair value of the consideration given and the fair value of the identifiable assets and liabilities attributable to the interest purchased. This represents a departure from the statutory method, under which goodwill is calculated as the difference between cost and fair value on the date that Cable & Wireless IDC became a subsidiary undertaking. The statutory method would not give a true and fair view because it would result in the Group's share of Cable & Wireless IDC retained reserves, during the period that is was an associated undertaking, being recharacterised as goodwill. The effect of this departure is to increase retained profits and purchased goodwill by £6m.

Exhibit 16.3 shows that IWP International increased its stake in a subsidiary and thereby eliminated the minority interest shown in the consolidated accounts in respect of that investment. Unusually, the minority shareholders were bought out and the investment was acquired, at no cost. This was because the subsidiary had a net deficit situation and the group took over all liabilities. As a result, most of the credit balance relating to the minority interest was released to the profit and loss account (shown as an exceptional profit) and the remaining credit balance is being carried as negative goodwill which is being amortised.

Exhibit 16.3 **Minority interest in net liabilities acquired**
IWP International plc Annual Report 2000

Notes to the Financial Statements (extract)
21 Minority Interest
The minority interest with a book value at 1 April 1999 of €4,478,000 was acquired during the year for €nil. In accordance with FRS 10, an amount of €3,092,000 has been released to the profit and loss account during the year. The balance of €1,386,000 is being carried in the balance sheet at 31 March 2000 as negative goodwill and will be released over the estimated useful lives of the non-monetary assets to which it relates.

Disclosure requirements

Many disclosure requirements of FRS 6 come from legal requirements. FRS 6 also includes disclosure requirements relating to fair value and goodwill, which are summarised in Chapter 17. Under FRS 6, the date of the business combination must be disclosed for both acquisitions and mergers. Additional disclosures are required by FRS 6 specifically relating to acquisition accounting and they repeat some of the requirements of FRS 3 *Reporting Financial Performance* relevant to changes in composition of groups.

- in the period of acquisition, post-acquisition results of acquired entities should be shown as part of continuing operations in the profit and loss account, unless they have also been discontinued in the period
- where it is not practicable to determine the post-acquisition results of an operation to the end of the period of acquisition, an indication should be given of the contribution of the acquired entity to the turnover and operating profit of the continuing operations. If this cannot be done, that fact should be stated and reasons provided
- any exceptional profit or loss in periods following acquisition that is determined using the fair values recognised on acquisition should be disclosed
- costs incurred in reorganising, restructuring and integrating the acquisition included in the profit and loss account after the acquisition should be disclosed
- cash paid on acquisition, net of cash balances taken over, should be disclosed in the cash flow statement.

FRS 6 also requires disclosure of amounts not included in consolidated accounts including:

- profit after tax and minority interests should be disclosed for material acquisitions for the current year up to the date of acquisition and for the previous financial year
- for substantial acquisitions, turnover, operating profit, exceptional items requiring disclosure under FRS 3, profit before taxation and taxation should be disclosed for the current year up to the date of acquisition and for the previous financial year.

UITF Abstract 15 *Disclosure of substantial acquisitions* clarifies the scope of FRS 6 disclosure requirements in relation to substantial acquisitions. Where specified ratios (e.g., net assets of acquired entity/net assets of acquiring entity, operating profits of acquired entity/operating profits of acquiring entity, fair value of consideration issued/net assets of acquiring entity) exceed 15%, the acquisition should be treated as substantial.

Where an acquisition or disposal has a material impact on a major business segment, FRS 3 requires that this should be disclosed and explained. In Exhibit 16.4, Cadbury Schweppes includes a note on its disposals and comprehensively describes how the gain on disposal was calculated and what effect the disposal had on some of the results of the group.

Exhibit 16.4 **Disposal of subsidiaries**
Cadbury Schweppes Annual Report and Form 20-F 2000

Notes to the Financial Statements (extract)
Nature of Operations and Accounting Policies (extract)
(4) Preparation of Financial Statements (extract)
Profit on sale of subsidiaries and investments (extract)
The most significant disposals during the year were Amalgamated Beverage Industries Ltd ('ABI'), the Group's South African associated undertaking, and beverage brands in Zambia. The overall profit on disposals was £27m.

The most significant disposal during 1999 was the disposal of beverages brands in 160 markets. An analysis of the profit on disposal is set out below:

	£m
Proceeds less costs and tangible assets	467
Goodwill previously written off to reserves	(51)
Brands disposed	(66)
Profit on disposal before taxation	350

The operating results of the beverages operations disposed of during 1999 have been treated as discontinued operations. The net cash inflow included in the Group Cash Flow in relation to the disposed beverages brands in 1999 was £23m.

IAS GAAP

Acquisition accounting is considered in IAS 22 *Business Combinations*. Aspects of IAS 22 dealing with fair values in acquisition accounting and with the accounting treatment of goodwill are considered in Chapter 17.

IAS 22 was issued in September 1983 and revised in 1993 and 1998. Its objectives are to prescribe an accounting treatment for business combinations. The standard covers the acquisition method of accounting ('*virtually all*' cases) and the '*rare situation*' of '*uniting of interests*' when an acquirer cannot be identified (i.e., merger accounting).

Changes in group composition

Acquisitions should be accounted for using the purchase method of accounting. An acquisition is defined in IAS 22 as:

> A business combination in which one of the enterprises, the acquirer, obtains control over the net assets and operations of another enterprise, the acquiree, in exchange for the transfer of assets, incurrence of a liability or issue of equity.

Identification of an acquirer is key to accounting for a combination as an acquisition and guidance is given on indications that an acquirer exists. Further guidance on this is given in SIC 9 *Business Combinations – Classification either as Acquisitions or Unitings of Interests*.

The IAS described the acquisition (or the purchase) method of accounting in detail (many of the aspects described in IAS 22 have already been covered in Parts 2 and 3 of this book).

Changes in composition of the Akzo Nobel group arose partly because of a reorganisation which is described in Exhibit 16.5. All these changes (including acquisitions and disposals) are explained in the exhibit.

Exhibit 16.5 **Changes in composition of group**
Akzo Nobel plc Annual Report 2000

Notes to the Consolidated Financial Statements (extract)
Changes in Consolidated Interests
After the acquisition of Courtaulds plc in 1998, the fibers operations of Akzo Nobel and Courtaulds were combined into a separate organization, named Acordis. At December 31, 1999, Acordis was sold for EUR 640 million to a newly established company. Akzo Nobel acquired a 21% interest in this company and extended a subordinated loan of EUR 138 million. In 1999, the Company recognized an extraordinary loss after taxes of EUR 515 million for the separation and divestment of Acordis.

Early in November 1999, the Company acquired Hoechst Roussel Vet, the veterinary business of Hoechst AG. The total consideration was EUR 546 million, leading to goodwill of EUR 300 million in 1999. In 2000, additional goodwill of EUR 16 million was recognized as a charge to shareholders' equity.
At year-end 2000, Chefaro, Akzo Nobel's Over-The-Counter activity, was divested for EUR 140 million. The gain on this divestment was EUR 90 million.

During 1999 and 2000 Akzo Nobel acquired and deconsolidated various other businesses, none of which were significant to the consolidated financial statements.

As shown by Exhibit 16.6, the Siemens group appears to comprise over 700 subsidiaries – one can only imagine the complexities in practice of having to prepare consolidated workings (such as those described in simple terms in this book) for a group of that size. Siemens provides an interesting estimate of the effect on consolidated sales (2%) of not consolidating immaterial subsidiaries.

Exhibit 16.6 **Changes in composition of group**
Siemens Annual Report 2000

Consolidated financial statements – Notes (extract)
Summary of significant accounting policies (extract)
Companies included in consolidation (extract)
In addition to Siemens AG, the consolidated financial statements at September 30, 2000 include the accounts of 167 (1999: 177) subsidiaries in Germany and 551 (1999: 565) subsidiaries in foreign countries. Companies that are either inactive or have a low business volume are not included in the consolidated financial statements because their effect was not significant. Full consolidation of these companies would have increased consolidated sales by approximately 2%.

Compared to September 30, 1999, a total of 22 domestic subsidiaries and 92 foreign subsidiaries have been consolidated for the first time, while 32 domestic companies and 106 foreign companies are no longer included in the consolidated financial statements. Sixteen of these companies were merged with and into Siemens AG or other consolidated companies.

Bayer applies the acquisition method to account for business combinations, citing IAS 22 as its reference point. It calls this method 'capital consolidation' but, the different terminology notwithstanding, it is clear from Exhibit 16.7 that the method is the same as the method more usually known as the acquisition method or purchase method.

Exhibit 16.7 **Capital consolidation Bayer Annual Report 2001**

Consolidation methods (extract)
Capital consolidation is performed according to IAS 22 (Business Combinations) by offsetting investments in subsidiaries against the underlying equities at the dates of acquisition. The identifiable assets and liabilities of subsidiaries and joint ventures are included at their fair values in proportion to Bayer's interest. Remaining differences are recognized as goodwill.

Where the statements of individual consolidated companies reflect write-downs or write-backs of investments in other consolidated companies, these are reversed for the Group statements.

Intragroup sales, profits, losses, income, expenses, receivables and payables are eliminated.

Deferred taxes are recognized for temporary differences related to consolidation entries.

Joint ventures are included by proportionate consolidation according to the same principles.

Under IAS 27, the gain or loss on disposal of the interest in a subsidiary is calculated as the difference between the proceeds and the carrying amount of the subsidiary's net assets at the date of disposal. The resulting profit or loss on disposal should be recorded in the consolidated income and expenditure account.

Effective date of acquisition and disposal

As already explained, the results and net assets of the acquired subsidiary should be included in the consolidated accounts from the date of acquisition. The date of acquisition is the date on which control is effectively transferred to the acquirer (paragraph 20):

> In substance, the date of acquisition is the date from when the acquirer has the power to govern the financial and operating policies of an enterprise so as to obtain benefits from its activities. Control is not deemed to have been transferred to the acquirer until all conditions necessary to protect the interests of the parties involved have been satisfied. However, this does not necessitate a transaction being closed or finalised at law before control effectively passes to the acquirer. In assessing whether control has effectively been transferred, the substance of the acquisition needs to be considered.

SIC 28 *Business Combinations – 'Date of Exchange' and Fair Value of Equity Instruments* addresses when the 'date of exchange' occurs where shares are issued as purchase consideration in an acquisition.

Piecemeal acquisitions

SIC 28 confirmed that when an acquisition is achieved in one exchange transaction (i.e., not in stages), the 'date of exchange' is the date of acquisition; that is, the date when the acquirer obtains control over the net assets and operations of the acquiree. When an acquisition is achieved in stages (e.g., successive share purchases), the fair value of the equity instruments issued as purchase consideration at each stage should be determined at the date that each individual investment is recognised in the financial statements of the acquirer.

In relation to successive purchases, IAS 22 requires the step-by-step approach to be applied in computing pre-acquisition profits and goodwill (see Chapter 5 for a discussion of the mechanics of this method). The value of the net assets acquired should be ascertained at the date of each exchange transaction (even if these occur before the date on which control is obtained). As a result of this requirement, adjustments relating to previously held interests should be accounted for as revaluations. However, where the investment is accounted for as an associated undertaking (prior to obtaining control), the computation of pre-acquisition profits and goodwill should be from the date when the equity method of accounting is applied.

IAS 22 and FRS 6 differ on their requirements concerning successive purchases. FRS 6 requires fair values of net assets acquired, pre-acquisition profits and goodwill to be calculated from the date the undertaking becomes a subsidiary rather than from the date of earlier purchases as in IAS 22. But, as discussed earlier in this chapter (and also in Chapter 5), FRS 2 acknowledges the conundrum with prior associate status. Where the equity method of accounting was adopted prior to control being achieved, fair values at the date of achieving associate status are used for the relevant proportion of shares.

Disclosure requirements

IAS 22 specifies disclosures that should be made for all business combinations and specifically in respect of acquisitions and for mergers. Disclosure requirements relating to mergers are dealt with later in this chapter. All disclosure requirements also apply to business combinations taking place after the balance sheet date. If this is impracticable, that fact should be disclosed.

Disclosure requirements in IAS 22 relating to fair value and goodwill are summarised in Chapter 17. The disclosure requirements applying (i) to all business combinations and (ii) to acquisitions are as follows.

For all business combinations:

- name and description of combining entities
- method of accounting for the combinations
- effective date of combination for accounting purposes
- operating results of combinations that are to be disposed of.

For acquisitions only:

- percentage voting shares acquired
- cost of acquisition
- description of purchase consideration paid or contingently payable
- nature and amount of restructuring provisions and other plant closure expenses consequent on acquisition, and recognised at the date of acquisition.

IAS 27 requires disclosure of the effect of acquisitions and disposals of subsidiaries on:

- financial position at the reporting date
- results for the reporting period
- corresponding amounts for the previous accounting period.

Regulations applying to merger accounting

Under UK GAAP FRS 6 (paragraph 2) defines a merger as:

> A business combination that results in the creation of a new reporting entity formed from the combining parties, in which the shareholders of the combining entities come together in a partnership for the mutual sharing of the risks and benefits of the combined entity and in which no party to the combination in

> substance obtains control over any other, or is otherwise seen to be dominant, whether by virtue of the proportion of its shareholders' rights in the combined entity, the influence of its directors or otherwise.

IAS GAAP uses the term 'uniting of interests' rather than merger. The term is defined in IAS 22 (paragraph 8) as follows:

> A uniting of interests is a business combination in which the shareholders of the combining enterprises combine control over the whole, or effectively the whole, of their net assets and operations to achieve a continuing mutual sharing in the risks and benefits attaching to the combined entity such that neither party can be identified as acquirer.

The related terms to highlight in these two definitions are:

- '*combining entities come together in a partnership for the mutual sharing of the risks and benefits*' (FRS 6), '*continuing mutual sharing in the risks and benefits*' (IAS 22)
- '*no party ... seen to be dominant*' (FRS 6), '*neither party can be identified as acquirer*' (IAS 22).

UK GAAP and IAS GAAP permit merger accounting in limited circumstances. The spirit of the regulations is that it should only be used in rare or exceptional cases. Of the 100 or more European annual reports consulted in the preparation of this book, only six cases were found where merger accounting methods were applied and most of these are reproduced later in this chapter.

UK GAAP

Criteria for merger accounting

The definition of merger accounting in FRS 6 has already been reproduced earlier in this chapter. For a business combination to qualify for merger accounting, it must meet the requirements of legislation and thereafter comply with five criteria specified in the FRS. The requirements of legislation derive from the Seventh Directive which sets out conditions to be met when accounting for a combination as a merger. Thus, on an exceptional basis, merger accounting is considered acceptable under the Directive.

Pre-FRS 6 conditions for merger accounting in the UK met with considerable abuse. Transactions in the UK (which, in substance, were acquisitions) were manipulated so that merger accounting provisions could be availed of. Consequently, those provisions did not promote consistency of accounting practice and more definitive regulations were required to narrow the conditions for merger accounting.

Under FRS 6, there are five criteria which must be satisfied for merger accounting to apply:

1. No party to the combination is portrayed as either acquirer or acquired.
2. All parties to the combination participate in establishing the management structure for the combined entity.
3. The relative sizes are not so disparate that one party dominates.
4. Consideration received comprises primarily equity shares, and any non-equity consideration or shares carrying reduced voting rights, represent an immaterial proportion of the fair value of consideration.

5 No equity shareholders retain any material interest in the future performance of only a part of the combined entity.

Where the five criteria for merger accounting under FRS 6 are satisfied the combination *must* be accounted for as a merger. These criteria are more restrictive than the conditions in the Seventh Directive. The Directive specifies three conditions that must be met for a business combination to be accounted for as a merger:

1 At least 90% of the nominal value of the relevant shares (i.e., shares carrying unrestricted rights to participate in distributions and assets on liquidation) in the undertaking acquired is held by the group.
2 The 90% holding was obtained primarily by an issue of shares by the parent or its subsidiaries.
3 The fair value of any non-share consideration does not exceed 10% of the *nominal* value of the shares issued as part consideration.

Even if these criteria are satisfied, the Seventh Directive does not compel companies to adopt merger accounting. The decision rests with the business in question, once it qualifies under the criteria.

Table 16.1 summarises the conditions for merger accounting under the Seventh Directive and FRS 6.

Table 16.1 Conditions for merger accounting under the Seventh Directive and FRS 6

Seventh Directive	*FRS 6*
At least 90% of the nominal value of the shares in the undertaking acquired is held by the group	No party to the combination is portrayed either as acquirer or acquired
The 90% holding was obtained primarily by an issue of shares by the parent or its subsidiaries	All parties to the combination participate in establishing the management structure for the combined entity
The fair value of any non-equity consideration does not exceed 10% of the nominal value of the shares issued as part consideration	The relative sizes are not so disparate that one party dominates
	Consideration received primarily comprises equity shares, and any non-equity consideration or shares carrying reduced voting rights, represent an immaterial proportion of the fair value of consideration
	No equity shareholders retain any material interest in the future performance of only a part of the combined entity

Size criterion

There is a rebuttable presumption in FRS 6 that one party will dominate the combined entity if it is more than 50% larger than each of the other parties to the combination, judged by reference to ownership interests – i.e., by considering the proportion of equity of the combined entity attributable to the shareholders of each of the combining parties.

This criterion is illustrated in Example 16.1 and shows that the focus is voting shares when deciding whether the size criterion is met. Under assumption (i), the disparity in ownership and voting between Parent and Subsidiary shareholders is 25%, i.e., Parent shareholders are 25% larger as a group than Subsidiary shareholders. However, under assumption (ii) the disparity in sizes is much greater with Parent shareholders 67% larger as a group compared with Subsidiary shareholders.

Example 16.1 Size criterion under FRS 6

Example

Parent and Subsidiary combine by means of a share exchange. Their balance sheets before the combination are as follows:

	Parent	Subsidiary
	€000	€000
Net assets	17,500	3,500
Share capital	12,500	3,000
Reserves	5,000	500
	17,500	3,500

Required

In the context of the relative sizes, indicate whether merger accounting would be appropriate, assuming Parent issues

(i) 10 million

(ii) 7.5 million

€1 ordinary voting shares in exchange for all of Subsidiary's shares.

Solution

	Assumption (i)		*Assumption (ii)*	
	Voting shares	%	Voting shares	%
	000		000	
Parent	12,500	56	12,500	62.5
Subsidiary	10,000	44	7,500	37.5
	22,500	100	20,000	100.0
Disparity in size	12,500/10,000 = 1.25		12,500/7,500 = 1.67	

A proportional split up to a maximum of 60:40 between parent and subsidiary shareholders is acceptable to meet the size criterion for merger accounting (i.e., the parent shareholder group holds no more than 50% more shares than the former shareholders of the subsidiary).

However, a proportional split of 61:39 may not be acceptable. The original shareholders in the parent now hold over 56% more shares in the combined entity than the former shareholders of the subsidiary. (Parent shareholders are 56% larger, exceeding the limit (which is rebuttable) set down in FRS 6 of 50%.)

Non-equity consideration

The consideration received should primarily comprise equity shares, with any non-equity element making up an immaterial element of the total consideration. Under UK and Irish law (and under the Seventh Directive), the fair value of the non-equity consideration cannot exceed 10% of the *nominal value* of the equity shares exchanged as part of the combination. FRS 6 provides guidance on what constitutes consideration. Any acquisition of shares by one combining party in the other party within two years before the combination should be taken into account in determining whether the non-equity consideration is an immaterial proportion.

Reconstructions

Under FRS 6, group reconstructions *may* be accounted for using merger accounting, even though the FR5 6 merger criteria may not be met, provided:

- merger accounting is not prohibited by legislation
- ultimate shareholders remain the same and their respective rights remain unchanged
- minority interests are not altered by the transaction.

The definition of a group reconstruction includes the transfer of shares in a subsidiary from one group company to another, and the addition of a new parent company to a group. Where the transaction does not alter the relative rights of the ultimate shareholders, acquisition accounting (involving restatement of assets and liabilities to fair values and recognition of goodwill) is unlikely to be appropriate.

Examples of two group reconstructions, where the existing group is rearranged, but otherwise the relative rights of shareholders are not altered, are shown in Example 16.2. Rearrangements such as those shown in this example may be done for tax purposes or for other commercial reasons. In case 1, before the reconstruction, Parent owned shares in Subsidiary$_2$ directly. These shares are transferred from Parent to its wholly owned subsidiary, Subsidiary$_1$. After the reconstruction, Parent owns shares in Subsidiary$_2$ indirectly through its holdings in Subsidiary$_1$. Before the reconstruction, the group comprised a parent company and two subsidiaries. After reconstruction, the group comprises a directly owned subsidiary and an indirectly owned subsidiary.

In case 2, shares in Parent$_1$ are transferred to a new holding company, Parent$_2$ in exchange for shares in that company, i.e., former shareholders of Parent$_1$, now own shares in Parent$_2$. They own shares in the two subsidiaries indirectly through Parent$_1$. Case 2 involves the addition of a new parent company to the group. These reorganisations qualify for merger accounting because they are implemented through share exchanges and relative shareholdings remain unchanged.

Example 16.2 Group reconstructions

Example

Case 1

Subsidiary$_1$ is wholly owned and Subsidiary$_2$ is 75% owned by Parent. Parent transfers its shares in Subsidiary$_2$ to Subsidiary$_1$.

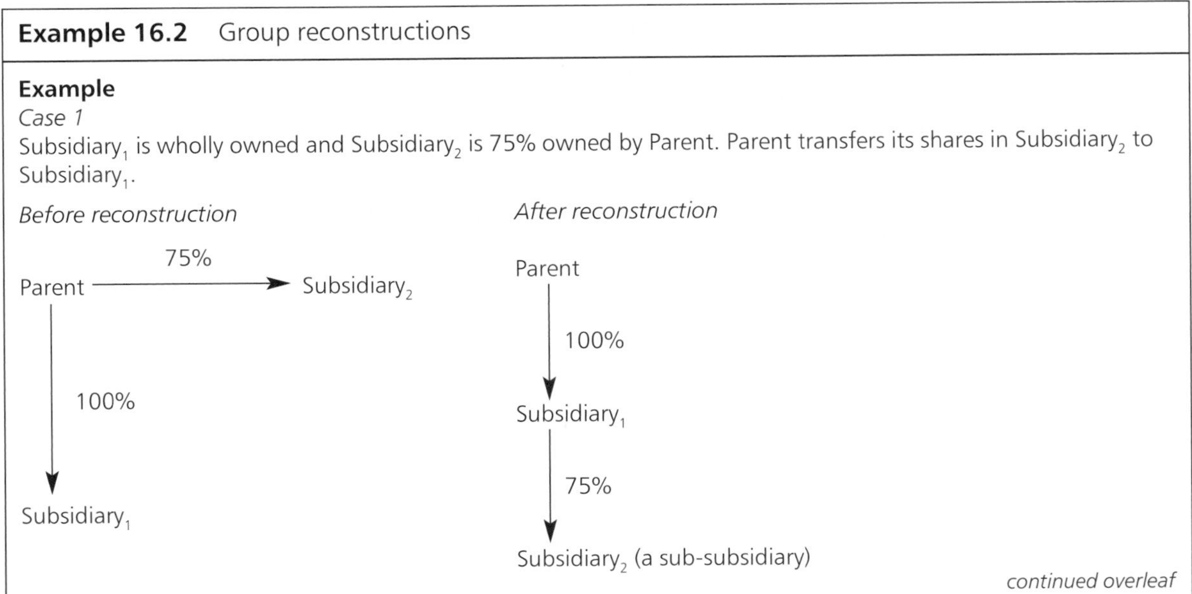

continued overleaf

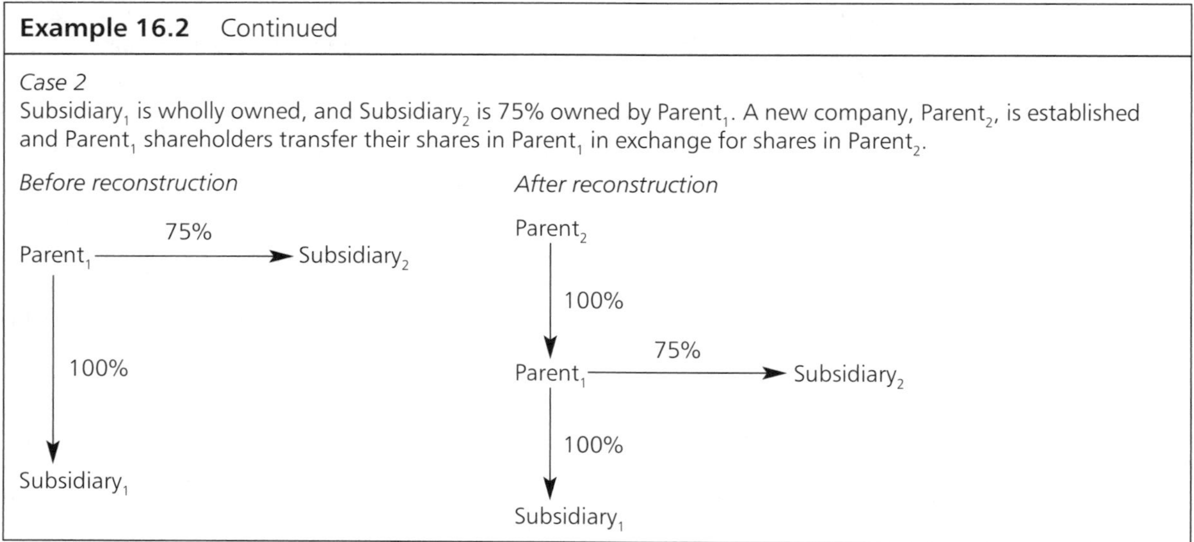

Disclosure requirements

As stated in relation to the disclosure requirements relating to acquisition accounting, the date of the combination should be disclosed for both acquisitions and mergers. Disclosure requirements of FRS 6 specifically relating to merger accounting are as follows:

- analysis of principal components of the profit and loss account and of total recognised gains and losses into:
  - post-merger period
  - period up to the date of merger for each party to the merger
  - previous period for each party to the merger.

  The analysis should show as a minimum, turnover, operating profit and exceptional items, (split between continuing operations, discontinued operations and acquisitions), profit before taxation, taxation and minority interests
- composition and fair value of consideration given
- aggregate book value of net assets of each party at the date of the merger
- nature and amount of significant accounting adjustments to net assets to achieve consistency of accounting policies and explanation of any other adjustments to net assets made as a consequence of the merger
- adjustments to reserves resulting from the merger.

Examples of merger accounting under UK GAAP

As shown in Exhibit 16.8, the merger of GrandMet and Guinness in 1998 was accounted for using the merger method.

Exhibit 16.8 **Merger Accounting under UK GAAP**
Diageo Annual Report 1998

Notes to the Accounts (extract)
(1) Basis of preparation (extract)
i Merger accounting
The financial statements have been prepared under merger accounting principles in relation to the merger of GrandMet and Guinness. Under merger accounting, the results and cash flows of GrandMet and Guinness are combined from the beginning of the financial period in which the merger occurred. Profit and loss account and balance sheet comparatives are restated on the combined basis and adjustments are made to achieve consistency of accounting policies.

The combination of Glaxo Wellcome and SmithKline Beecham provides another example of merger accounting. In the extract shown in Exhibit 16.9, the use of merger accounting is justified on the basis of the 'intentions' of the merging parties and on their 'sizes'. The second paragraph describes the mechanics of merger accounting.

Exhibit 16.9 **Accounting for merger**
GlaxoSmithKline plc Annual Report 2000

Notes to the financial statements (extract)
6 Merger of Glaxo Wellcome and SmithKline Beecham (extract)
Accounting for the merger
Reflecting the intentions, and the respective sizes of the merging parties, the combination of Glaxo Wellcome plc and SmithKline Beecham plc has been treated as a merger at 27th December 2000 under UK GAAP.

Under merger accounting, the shares issued by GlaxoSmithKline plc to acquire Glaxo Wellcome and SmithKline Beecham are accounted for at par and no share premium arises; the shares acquired by GlaxoSmithKline in Glaxo Wellcome and SmithKline Beecham are similarly accounted for at the nominal value of the shares issued. In the consolidated accounts of GlaxoSmithKline, the results and net assets of Glaxo Wellcome and SmithKline Beecham are combined, at their book amounts, subject to the alignment adjustments discussed below.

Each of GlaxoSmithKline plc, Glaxo Wellcome plc and SmithKline Beecham plc has an accounting reference date of 31st December. In view of the proximity of the merger date to the financial year-end date, and the relative insignificance of any business activity between 27th December 2000 and 31st December 2000, the accounting date of the merger has for practical purposes been taken as 31st December 2000. The whole of the profit for the financial year 2000 of each of Glaxo Wellcome plc and SmithKline Beecham plc is deemed to relate to the period prior to the merger date.

In Exhibit 16.10, also dealing with the merger of Glaxo Wellcome and SmithKline Beecham, adjustments required to bring the two sets of accounts and accounting policies into line are described. Commendable detail is provided in disclosure of these adjustments.

Exhibit 16.10 **Merger adjustments**
GlaxoSmithKline plc Annual Report 2000

Notes to the financial statements (extract)
6 Merger of Glaxo Wellcome and SmithKline Beecham (extract)
Accounting alignment
Certain adjustments have been made, and reflected in the results of GlaxoSmithKline, to align the accounting policies and classifications previously adopted by Glaxo Wellcome and SmithKline Beecham, as follows:

Accounting policy:
(A) Interest on finance for major construction projects, previously capitalised by SmithKline Beecham, is now expensed.
(B) Deferred tax relief on unfunded post-retirement benefits, previously recognised by SmithKline Beecham only on post-retirement healthcare is now recognised additionally on unfunded pension costs.

Accounting presentation:
(C) Standard sales discounts in the USA, previously classified by SmithKline Beecham to selling, general and administrative expenditure, are now reclassified as a deduction from sales.
(D) Royalty and similar recurring income, and significant one-off items of operating income/expense, previously classified by SmithKline Beecham to selling, general and administrative expenditure, are now classified to other operating income/expense.

Balance sheet reclassification:
(E) Certain items have been reclassified for consistency.

Investment reclassification:
(F) Certain equity investments held by SmithKline Beecham have been reclassified in 2000 from fixed assets to current assets and written down to current market value, to reflect the fact that GlaxoSmithKline now considers these investments to be available for sale.

Consolidation adjustment:
(G) Royalties paid by Glaxo Wellcome to SmithKline Beecham have been eliminated on consolidation.

Segment reclassification:
Glaxo Wellcome's over-the-counter products are being managed in GlaxoSmithKline by Consumer Healthcare. The sales and profits of these products have been classified to the Consumer Healthcare sector.
The adjustments have been made for all years presented, with the exception of the investment reclassification, which has been made from the date of the merger. Only the accounting policy adjustments and the investment reclassification affect the book value of net assets. The adjustments are identified by the relevant letter in the following tables of balance sheet and profit and loss account. [Table not reproduced]

The note goes on to show how the two separate balance sheets are brought together under merger accounting. A separate column identifies the adjustments made. (This material is not reproduced here.)

Rio Tinto also used merger accounting. Exhibit 16.11 includes considerable justification (considerably more than GlaxoSmithKline in Exhibit 16.9) as to why merger accounting is appropriate in the context of the business combination. The example is interesting in that it refers to the use of merger accounting not complying with legal provisions in the UK. The merger in this case was effected through 'contractual arrangements' and there was 'no change in the ownership of any existing shares'. Legislation anticipates that a merger will be effected through share exchange. The exhibit describes why the treatment adopted does not comply with legal requirements in the UK and justifies the departure from the provisions of legislation by invoking the true and fair view override provisions of legislation.

Exhibit 16.11 **Merger accounting under UK GAAP**
Rio Tinto Annual Report 2000

Notes to the Consolidated Financial Statements (extract)
These are the financial statements of the Rio Tinto Group (the Group), formed through the merger of economic interests (merger) of Rio Tinto plc and Rio Tinto Limited, and presented by both Rio Tinto plc and Rio Tinto Limited as their consolidated accounts in accordance with both United Kingdom and Australian legislation and regulations.

On 21 December 1995, Rio Tinto plc and Rio Tinto Limited, which are listed respectively on Stock Exchanges in the United Kingdom and Australia, entered into a dual listed companies (DLC) merger. This was effected by contractual arrangements between the companies and amendments to their memoranda and articles of association.

As a result, Rio Tinto plc and Rio Tinto Limited and their respective groups operate together as a single economic enterprise, with neither assuming a dominant role. In particular, the arrangements:

- confer upon the shareholders of Rio Tinto plc and Rio Tinto Limited a common economic interest in both groups;
- provide for common boards of directors and a unified management structure;
- provide for equalised dividends and capital distributions; and
- provide for the shareholders of Rio Tinto plc and Rio Tinto Limited to take key decisions, including the election of directors, through an electoral procedure in which the public shareholders of the two companies effectively vote on a joint basis.

The merger involved no change in the legal ownership of any assets of Rio Tinto plc or Rio Tinto Limited, nor any changes in the ownership of any existing shares or securities of Rio Tinto plc or Rio Tinto Limited, nor the issue of any shares, securities or payment by way of consideration, save for the issue by each Company of one special voting share to a trustee company which provides the joint electoral procedure for public shareholders.

The financial statements have been drawn up in accordance with United Kingdom accounting standards. The merger of economic interests is accounted for as a merger under United Kingdom Financial Reporting Standard (FRS) 6.

In order to present a true and fair view of the Rio Tinto Group, in accordance with FRS 6, the principles of merger accounting have been adopted. This represents a departure from the provision of the Companies Act 1985 which sets out the conditions for merger accounting based on the assumption that a merger is effected through the issue of equity shares.

The main consequence of adopting merger rather than acquisition accounting is that the balance sheet of the merged group includes the assets and liabilities of Rio Tinto Limited at their carrying values prior to the merger, subject to adjustments to achieve uniformity of accounting policies, rather than at their fair values at the date of the merger. In the particular circumstances of the merger, the effect of applying acquisition accounting cannot reasonably be quantified.

In order that the financial statements should present a true and fair view, it is necessary to differ from the presentational requirements of the United Kingdom Companies Act 1985 by including amounts attributable to both Rio Tinto plc and Rio Tinto Limited public shareholders in the capital and reserves shown in the balance sheet and in the profit for the financial year. The Companies Act 1985 would require presentation of the capital and reserves and profit for the year attributable to Rio Tinto Limited public shareholders (set out in note 21) as a minority interest in the financial statements of the Rio Tinto Group. This presentation would not give a true and fair view of the effect of the Sharing Agreement under which the position of all public shareholders is as nearly as possible the same as if they held shares in a single company.

IAS GAAP

'Uniting of interests' is the term used in IASs to refer to a merger.

Criteria for merger accounting

The definition in IAS 22 for a uniting of interests was reproduced earlier in this chapter. Key terms in this definition are 'continuing mutual sharing in the risks and benefits' and 'neither party can be identified as acquirer'. The standard indicates that failure to identify an acquirer would occur in 'exceptional circumstances'.

The IAS indicates that mutual sharing of risks and benefits is achieved only where:

1 The substantial majority, if not all, of the voting common shares of the combining enterprises are exchanged or pooled.
2 The fair value of one enterprise is not significantly different from that of the other enterprise.
3 The shareholders of each enterprise maintain substantially the same voting rights and interest in the combined entity, relative to each other, after the combination as before.

SIC 9 *Business Combinations – Classifications as either Acquisitions or Unitings of Interests* clarifies that all three criteria must be present for the combination to be accounted for as a uniting of interests and even then, it is only classified as a uniting of interests when an acquirer cannot be identified.

IAS 22 requires a uniting of interests to be accounted for using the 'pooling of interests' method of accounting (referred to under UK GAAP as the merger method).

IAS 22 describes the pooling of interests method of accounting. Assets and liabilities of the combining entities should be included, together with comparative amounts, as if the enterprises had been combined from the beginning of the previous period. The difference between the share capital issued and any additional consideration, and any share capital acquired, should be adjusted against equity. Merger expenses should be recorded in the period in which they are incurred.

Table 16.3 (shown towards the end of this chapter) summarises the conditions required to justify the use of merger accounting, comparing UK and IAS GAAP. Where conditions are met, the combination must be accounted for using the merger method under the relevant regulation. Both regulations are more prescriptive than the Seventh Directive.

If the conditions exist or are met, the combination must be accounted for as a merger under both UK GAAP and IAS GAAP. This is expected to be 'rare' under FRS 6, or to occur in 'exceptional circumstances' under IAS 22. This is in contrast to the Seventh Directive, which provides companies satisfying the relevant criteria with the *option* of using merger accounting. As already indicated, the conditions under FRS 6 are more extensive than those under IAS 22.

Reconstructions

IAS 22, unlike FRS 6, does not address the issue of reconstructions.

Disclosure requirements

IAS 22 disclosure requirements for business combinations accounted for as acquisitions were discussed earlier in this chapter. Disclosures in respect of mergers include:

- description and number of shares issued
- percentage of each entity's voting shares exchanged to effect uniting of interests

- amounts of assets and liabilities contributed by each enterprise
- sales revenue, other operating revenues, extraordinary items and net profit or loss of each enterprise prior to the date of the combination included in consolidated financial statements.

DaimlerChrysler which reports under US GAAP, used merger accounting in 1998 to account for the coming together of Daimler-Benz and Chrysler Corporation. As shown in Exhibit 16.12, the 2000 annual report continues to refer to the combination as having been accounted for as a merger and to alert readers to the consequences of having used that method of accounting.

Exhibit 16.12 **Merger accounting**
DaimlerChrysler Annual Report 2000

Notes to Consolidated Financial Statements (extract)
All amounts herein are shown in millions of euros
Certain prior year balances have been reclassified to conform with the Group's current year presentation. DaimlerChrysler was formed through the merger of Daimler-Benz Aktiengesellschaft ('Daimler-Benz') and Chrysler Corporation ('Chrysler') in November 1998 ('Merger').

The Merger was accounted for as a pooling of interests and accordingly, the historical results of Daimler-Benz and Chrysler for 1998 have been restated as if the companies had been combined for all periods presented. In connection with the Merger, €685 of merger costs (€401 after tax) were incurred and charged to expense in 1998. These costs consisted primarily of fees for investment bankers, attorneys, accountants, financial printing, accelerated management compensation and other related charges.

Demergers

A demerger refers to splitting a group of companies into two or more separate groups and can be done through transferring the shareholding in a subsidiary from the parent company to the individual shareholders of the parent. In this way, shareholders of the parent own the subsidiary directly, rather than indirectly through their shareholding in the parent. This is called a distribution *in specie* (also called a dividend in kind). A distribution *in specie* is a dividend paid in a form other than cash.

Demergers can be part of a group restructuring. In fact, FRS 6 states that group reconstructions may include 'arrangements such as … the splitting off of one or more subsidiary undertakings as in some demergers'. To be consistent with merger accounting principles, shareholders should end up with the same relative rights in the demerged entities as they had in the combined group.

The demerger can be effected in a number of ways but two common approaches are shown in Example 16.3. In alternative 1, Parent has effectively transferred its shareholding in Subsidiary to its own shareholders and this is referred to as a distribution *in specie*. Alternative 2 shows how the same effect can be achieved by establishing a second subsidiary (owned by the shareholders of the parent) to which the parent's shareholding in the subsidiary to be demerged can be transferred. Shares in the newly formed parent are issued to shareholders of the old parent. Shares in the demerged subsidiary are transferred to the newly formed parent.

Example 16.3 Demerger illustrated

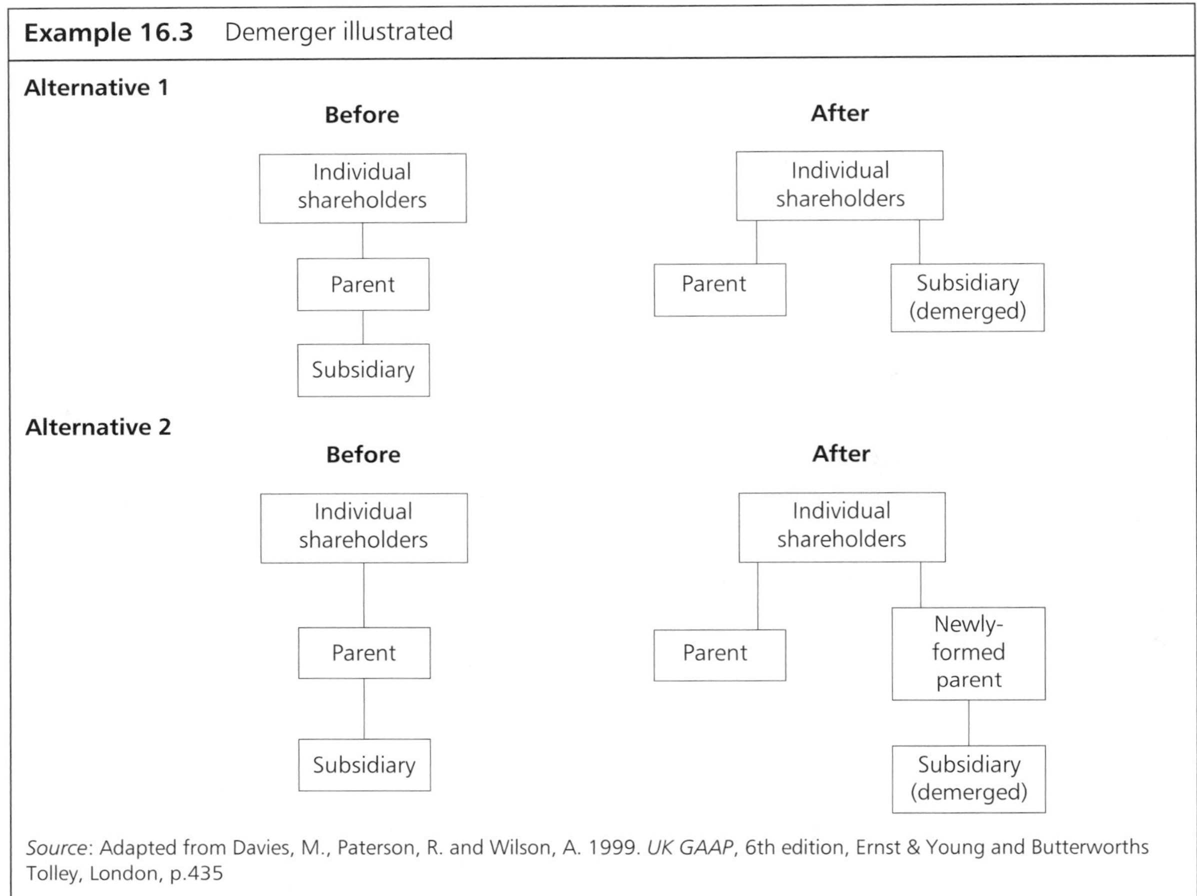

Source: Adapted from Davies, M., Paterson, R. and Wilson, A. 1999. *UK GAAP*, 6th edition, Ernst & Young and Butterworths Tolley, London, p.435

Under both alternatives, the parent no longer holds shares in the demerged subsidiary. The subsidiary is therefore no longer consolidated. Instead the demerged subsidiary's shares are owned by shareholders of the parent, either (i) directly or (ii) indirectly through the establishment of a new parent owned by the 'old' parent's shareholders. Under alternative 1, Subsidiary is demerged from Parent and (assuming no other group companies) there is no longer a group. Under alternative 2, Subsidiary is demerged from 'old' Parent and 'old' Parent (assuming no other group companies) no longer constitutes a group. Instead a new group is formed by the newly formed parent.

The demerger of a subsidiary is structured as a distribution in kind, i.e., the subsidiary's shares are distributed to the parent undertaking's shareholders. Because the owners of the demerged subsidiary are effectively the same owners of the company as when it was owned by 'old' Parent, it is logical that demergers are accounted for in a way that is consistent with merger accounting principles. Merger accounting is appropriate for group restructurings under FRS 6. For example, the transfer is recorded without fair value adjustments, and shares issued are recorded at nominal value. Book value is normally used to value the dividend when the subsidiary is demerged. The amount of the dividend shown in the consolidated profit and loss account is equal to the carrying value of the subsidiary's net assets attributable to the group's interest. Thus, the demerger reduces the shareholders' stake in Parent group and this reduction is effected through the dividend *in specie*. The shareholders obtain either a direct interest or a new indirect interest in the subsidiary in return for the reduction of their interest in the parent. An alternative to the distribution *in specie* is that the parent disposes of its shares in the subsidiary for equity consideration. Under normal acquisition accounting principles, book value of assets disposed of would be compared with the fair value of the shares received as consideration for the disposal. This would usually involve a share premium and the difference would be recorded as a profit or loss on disposal. As shown in Chapter 12, the amount of the profit or loss on disposal will differ in the individual accounts of the parent from that in the consolidated accounts.

Example 16.4 illustrates accounting for the demerger where alternative 2 in Example 16.3 is the format of the demerger. The demerger is a disposal of Subsidiary to the individual shareholders of Parent_1. This is achieved by establishing a new holding company, Parent_2. Parent_2 issues shares to Parent_1's shareholders in exchange for the shares in Subsidiary held by Parent_1. There is no profit or loss on disposal as the disposal is recorded at book value. Thus, in the balance sheets in Example 16.4, the wholly-owned subsidiary has a book value of €800m (group) and €500m (parent company). This is the value at which the demerger is recorded and there is no profit or loss on disposal. The corresponding entry is the dividend *in specie* appropriated out of the profit and loss account. By way of contrast, the entries under acquisition accounting (assuming Parent_1 disposes of shares in Subsidiary for equity in Parent_2) are also shown in part (b) of the solution.

Example 16.4 Accounting for demergers

Example

Parent_1 has a 100% investment in Subsidiary. Parent_1 acquired the entire share capital at Subsidiary's date of incorporation. The balance sheets of (i) Parent_1 and (ii) Subsidiary and (iii) the group balance sheet at 31.12.20X5 are as follows:

	(i)	(ii)	(iii)
	Parent_1 €m	Subsidiary €m	Parent_1 Group €m
Investment in Subsidiary	500		
Other net assets	1,200	800	2,000
	1,700	800	2,000
Share capital (€1 ordinary)	1,000	500	1,000
Profit and loss account	700	300	1,000
	1,700	800	2,000

Subsidiary is to be demerged from the group. Parent_2 is to issue 500 million €1 ordinary shares to shareholders of Parent_1 in exchange for shares held by Parent_1 in Subsidiary.

Required

(a) Show how the demerger would be reflected in the balance sheets of (i) Parent_1, (ii) Parent_2 and (iii) the Parent_1 group.

(b) Show how the disposal (and acquisition by Parent_2) would be recorded under acquisition accounting principles, assuming the shares in Parent_2 were valued at €2 each and that Parent_1 received these shares as consideration for the shares disposed of.

continued overleaf

Example 16.4 Continued

Solution **(a) Demerger**	€	**(i)** **Parent$_1$** **€m**	**(ii)** **Parent$_2$** **€m**	**€m**	**(iii)** **Parent$_1$** **Group** **€m**
Investment in Subsidiary			500		
Other net assets		1,200			1,200
		1,200	500		1,200
Share capital (€1 ordinary)		1,000	500		1,000
Profit and loss account	700			1,000	
Distribution *in specie*	(500)	200		(800)	200
		1,200	500		1,200
(b) Disposal by Parent$_1$ and acquisition by Parent$_2$					
Investment in Subsidiary			1,000		
Shares in Parent$_2$		1,000			1,000
Other net assets		2,200			1,200
		2,200	1,000		2,200
Share capital (€1 ordinary)		1,000	500		1,000
Share premium			500		
Profit and loss account	700			1,000	
Profit on disposal ($1{,}000_{\text{500 shares} \times €2} - 500_{\text{investment at cost}}$)	500	1,200			
Profit on disposal ($1{,}000_{\text{500 shares} \times €2} - [500_{\text{investment at cost}}$ $+ 300_{\text{post-acquisition retained profits}}]$)				200	1200
		2,200	1,000		2,200

Source: Adapted from Davies, M., Paterson, R. and Wilson, A. 1999. *UK GAAP*, 6th edition, Ernst & Young and Butterworths Tolley, London, pp.436–7

While demergers are not common, they occur with sufficient frequency to justify including this topic in a specialist book on group accounts.

UK GAAP

Eircom disposed of its mobile communications business to Vodafone using a demerger to effect the transaction. Rather than disposing of the business segment itself, it first demerged that segment by transferring the business to its shareholders, who then disposed of the business to Vodafone. This is explained in Exhibit 16.13.

Exhibit 16.13 **Demerger used to dispose of business segment Eircom plc Proposed Merger Prospectus 2000**

Summary Overview (extract)

The two-part process

The Demerger and separate Vodafone Offer enable *eircom* shareholders to receive Vodafone Shares directly as consideration for the disposal of Eircell in a tax efficient manner for the majority of shareholders. This will take place as follows:

(1) Demerger
The Eircell business will be demerged from *eircom* to a new company called Eircell 2000 plc. *eircom* shareholders at the Demerger Record Time will be allotted one share in Eircell 2000 for each share they hold in *eircom*. The Demerger, which is the subject matter of this Circular, requires approval by the holders of a majority of *eircom* Shares who vote either by proxy or attend and vote at the EGM; and

(2) Vodafone Offer
Vodafone will offer to acquire all of the Eircell 2000 Shares in exchange for Vodafone Shares. Under the terms of the Vodafone Offer, Eircell 2000 shareholders will receive 0.9478 Vodafone Shares for every two Eircell 2000 Shares they hold. The Vodafone Offer is formally set out in the Offer Document issued separately by UBS Warburg on behalf of Vodafone.

Definitions (extract)
'Demerger'

The reconstruction of the Group whereby, pursuant to the First Asset Distribution Agreement, Eircell Limited will distribute business, assets and liabilities of Eircell Limited and its subsidiaries (as more particularly described in the First Asset Distribution Agreement) to *eircom*, following which, pursuant to the Second Asset Distribution Agreement, *eircom* will distribute the business, assets and liabilities of Eircell Limited and its subsidiaries (as more particularly described in the Second Asset Distribution Agreement) to *eircom*'s shareholders by way of the transfer of such business, assets and liabilities to Eircell 2000 in consideration for Eircell 2000 issuing ordinary shares to *eircom*'s shareholders at the Demerger Record Time on the basis of one share in Eircell 2000 for each share in *eircom* held by such shareholders as noted on *eircom*'s register of members at the Demerger Record Time.

IAS GAAP

Zeneca Agrochemicals provides an example of a demerger under IAS GAAP in Exhibit 16.14. The transaction has been accounted for as a '*dividend in specie*'. A note to the preliminary announcement of results states that the demerger by dividend *in specie* was effected by distributing shares in Syngenta to shareholders on the basis of one Syngenta share for every 40.237651 AstraZeneca shares held.

Exhibit 16.14 **Demerger under IAS GAAP**
AstraZeneca Annual Report and Form 20F 2000

Notes to the Consolidated Financial Statements
27 Zeneca Agrochemicals demerger
On 13 November 2000 Zeneca Agrochemicals was demerged from the AstraZeneca Group and merged with the agribusiness of Novartis to form Syngenta AG. The Zeneca Agrochemicals results for the period to 13 November have been reported as discontinued in the AstraZeneca accounts for the year ended 31 December 2000 and prior years. The demerger of Zeneca Agrochemicals was accounted for as a dividend *in specie*. The impact of the demerger is set out below.

	$m
Fixed assets	1,491
Current assets	2,130
Creditors due within one year	(1,306)
Creditors due after more than one year and provisions	(246)
Book value of Zeneca Agrochemicals net assets disposed	2,069
Minority interest share of net assets	(10)
Goodwill previously charged to reserves written back	813
	2,872

continued overleaf

Exhibit 16.14 Continued

Repayment of debt by Zeneca Agrochemicals	
Net payment of debt per Cash Flow Statement	(909)
Net financial liabilities demerged	(294)
	(1,203)
Dividend *in specie*	1,669

Prior to its demerger, the Agrochemicals business contributed \$173m to operating cash flows before exceptional items, and absorbed \$78m in respect of exceptional items and \$149m in respect of capital expenditure.

Reverse acquisitions

Paragraph 12 of IAS 22 refers to occasions where, in a share exchange transaction, voting control passes to the acquiree. Such a situation is described as a reverse acquisition. This leads to the unusual situation that the company issuing shares is deemed to have been acquired by the other enterprise which is deemed to be the acquirer. IAS 22 requires the purchase (i.e., acquisition) method of consolidation to be applied in such situations.

Appendix 2 of FRS 6 states that the requirements of FRS 6 are consistent with those of IAS 22 except for the provision in paragraph 12 of IAS 22 relating to reverse acquisitions. This is because reverse acquisitions are incompatible with legal requirements in the UK and Republic of Ireland. However, although there is no equivalent to reverse acquisitions in UK GAAP, the UITF has issued an information sheet (No. 17) on the topic (in which the UITF refers to '*reverse takeovers*'). The UITF concludes that it is acceptable to invoke the true and fair override provisions of legislation to apply reverse acquisition accounting.

Example 16.5 is a simple example of a reverse acquisition. It shows how, although one company (Subsidiary) is a wholly owned subsidiary, the reverse of normal applies whereby the wholly owned subsidiary ends up preparing the group accounts. This is because, as a result of the share exchange, the new shareholders of Parent (i.e., the shareholders of Subsidiary) outnumber the old shareholders by two to one, and therefore, they effectively control the Parent group.

Example 16.5 Reverse acquisition

Example
The share capital of Parent is 100 ordinary €1 shares. Parent issued 200 new shares in exchange for all the ordinary shares in Subsidiary.

Required
(i) Show the group structure after the new issue of shares by Parent and (ii) explain the transaction as a reverse acquisition.

Solution

(i) Group structure after the new issue of shares

Before reverse acquisition	€	*Comment*
Net assets	100	
Original share capital of Parent	100	Parent is owned 100% by its shareholders
After reverse acquisition		
Investment in Subsidiary	200	Parent is the holding company of Subsidiary.
Other net assets	100	
	300	
Original share capital of Parent	100	At the same time Parent is now only 33% owned by its original shareholders. Subsidiary now owns 67% of Parent and in that context is itself a parent undertaking.
New shares issued	200	
	300	

(ii) Reverse acquisition

Although Parent 100% owns Subsidiary, there has been a change in control of Parent. Shareholders of Subsidiary now own 67% of the shares in Parent. In reverse acquisition, Subsidiary would prepare consolidated accounts.

Redbus Interhouse (which follows UK GAAP and reports under UK legislation) accounted for its combination (between Redbus Interhouse and Horace Small Apparel) as a reverse acquisition, citing the provisions of IAS 22 to support this accounting treatment. Exhibit 16.15 explains that under UK legislation, the company issuing the shares, Horace Small Apparel plc (i.e., the legal parent), is required to prepare consolidated accounts. The true and fair override provisions of legislation are invoked to allow the other enterprise Redbus Interhouse plc to prepare consolidated accounts, as that company's shareholders have acquired control of the parent (Horace Small Apparel plc) as a result of the share-for-share exchange. The company explains the effect of using reverse acquisition accounting by comparing reserves under reverse acquisition accounting with those which would have arisen had acquisition accounting been followed.

Exhibit 16.15 **Reverse acquisition**
Redbus Interhouse plc Annual Report 2000

Notes on the Financial Statements (extract)
Basis of consolidation
On 5th April, 2000 the Company, then named Horace Small Apparel plc, became the legal parent company of Redbus Interhouse Limited in a share-for-share transaction. Due to the relative values of the companies, the former Redbus Interhouse Limited shareholders became the majority shareholders with 69% of the enlarged share capital. Further, the Company's continuing operations and executive management were those of Redbus Interhouse Limited. Accordingly, the substance of the combination was that Redbus Interhouse Limited acquired Horace Small Apparel plc in a reverse acquisition. As part of the business combination Horace Small Apparel plc changed its name to Redbus Interhouse plc and changed its year-end to 31st December.

Under the requirements of the Companies Act 1985 it would normally be necessary for the Company's consolidated accounts to follow the legal form of the business combination. In that case the pre-combination results would be those of Horace Small Apparel plc and its subsidiary undertakings, which would exclude Redbus Interhouse Limited. Redbus Interhouse Limited would then be brought into the Group from 5th April,

continued overleaf

Exhibit 16.15 Continued

2000. However, this would portray the combination as an acquisition of Redbus Interhouse Limited by Horace Small plc and would, in the opinion of the directors, fail to give a true and fair view of the substance of the business combination. Accordingly, the directors have adopted reverse acquisition accounting as the basis of consolidation in order to give a true and fair view.

In invoking the true and fair override the directors note that reverse acquisition accounting is endorsed under International Accounting Standard 22 and that the Urgent Issues Task Force of the UK's Accounting Standards Board considered the subject and concluded that there are instances where it is right and proper to invoke the true and fair override in such a way.

As a consequence of applying reverse acquisition accounting, the results for the year ended 31st December, 2000 comprise the results of Redbus Interhouse Limited for its year ended 31st December, 2000 plus those of Horace Small Apparel plc from 5th April, 2000, the date of reverse acquisition, to 31st December, 2000. The comparative figures are those of Redbus Interhouse Limited for the 17 months ended 31st December, 1999. As set out in note 23, goodwill amounting to £47,231,000 arose on the difference between the fair value of Horace Small Apparel plc's share capital and the fair value of its net assets at the reverse acquisition date. The goodwill has been written off in the year ended 31st December, 2000 because Horace Small Apparel plc had no continuing business and therefore the goodwill has no intrinsic value.

The effect on the consolidated financial statements of adopting reverse acquisition accounting, rather than following the legal form, are widespread. However, the following table indicates the principal effect on the composition of the reserves.

	Reverse acquisition accounting (as disclosed) £000	Normal acquisition accounting £000	Impact of reverse acquisition accounting £000
Called-up share capital	1,508	1,508	—
Capital redemption reserve	46	46	—
Share premium account	102,147	102,147	—
Merger reserve	—	111,433	(111,433)
Other reserves	14,306	—	14,306
Profit and loss account	(5,652)	8,809	(14,461)
	112,355	223,943	111,588

Comparison of UK GAAP and IAS GAAP

FRS 6 and IAS 22 are broadly similar. Table 16.2 summarises, from an overall perspective, the main differences between the two sets of regulations. The most significant difference relates to the accounting treatment of reverse acquisitions. Also, the conditions under which merger accounting may be used are more detailed and prescriptive in FRS 6.

Table 16.2 Main differences in group accounting methods between UK GAAP and IAS GAAP

	UK GAAP	*IAS GAAP*
Scope		Transactions between entities under common control are not covered in IAS 22
Criteria for merger	Five criteria, in addition to legal requirements arising from the Seventh Directive	Three criteria – no specifications concerning percentages of shares exchanged or the amount of non-equity consideration
Piecemeal acquisitions/ successive purchases	Computations from the date control is acquired	Step-by-step approach
Reconstructions	Group reconstructions may be accounted for as mergers	Reconstructions not mentioned
Reverse acquisition accounting	Not permitted by legislation, but requirement to give true and fair view can be invoked to apply this method of accounting	Enterprises issuing shares treated as acquirees; enterprise whose existing shareholders receive shares are treated as the acquirer

Sources: Cairns, D. and Nobes, C. 2000. *The Convergence Handbook: A Comparison between International Accounting Standards and UK Financial Reporting Requirements*, Institute of Chartered Accountants in England and Wales, London
Connor, L., Dekker, P., Davies, M., Robinson, P. and Wilson, A. 2001. *IAS /UK GAAP. Comparison,* Ernst & Young, London
PricewaterhouseCoopers. 2000. *International Accounting Standards Similarities and Differences IAS, US GAAP and UK GAAP.* PricewaterhouseCoopers, London

Table 16.3 compares differences in the conditions for merger accounting under UK GAAP and IAS GAAP.

Table 16.3 Comparison of conditions requiring merger accounting under UK GAAP and under IAS GAAP

UK GAAP	*IAS GAAP*
Conditions in legislation (Seventh Directive) At least 90% of the nominal value of the shares in the undertaking acquired is held by the group	*IAS 22* The shareholders of each enterprise maintain substantially the same voting rights and interest in the combined entity, relative to each other, after the combination as before
The 90% holding was obtained primarily by an issue of shares by the parent or its subsidiaries	The substantial majority, if not all, of the voting common shares of the combining enterprises are exchanged or pooled
The fair value of any non-equity consideration does not exceed 10% of the nominal value of the shares issued as part consideration	
Conditions of FRS 6 No party to the combination is portrayed either as acquirer or acquired	
All parties to the combination participate in establishing the management structure for the combined entity	
The relative sizes are not so disparate that one party dominates	The fair value of one enterprise is not significantly different from that of the other enterprise
Consideration received primarily comprises equity shares and any non-equity consideration, or shares carrying reduced voting rights, represent an immaterial proportion of the fair value of consideration	
No equity shareholders retain any material interest in the future performance of only a part of the combined entity	

Differences in disclosure requirements between the two standards are compared in Table 16.4, which summarises the disclosure requirements of FRS 6 and of IAS 22.

Table 16.4 Comparison of disclosures concerning business combinations required under UK GAAP and IAS GAAP

FRS 6	*IAS 22*
For both acquisitions and mergers	*For all business combinations*
Names of the combining entities	Names and descriptions of combining entities
Whether the combination has been accounted for as an acquisition or a merger	Method of accounting for the combination
Date of the combination	Effective date of combination for accounting purposes
	Operating results of combinations that are to be disposed of
For acquisitions only	*For acquisitions only*
Post-acquisition profits should be shown separately in the profit and loss account as a component of continuing operations (in accordance with FRS 3)	Percentage voting shares acquired
Costs incurred in reorganising, restructuring and integrating the acquisition included in the profit and loss account after the acquisition	Cost of acquisition
Cash paid on acquisition, net of cash balances taken over, should be disclosed in the cash flow statement	Description of purchase consideration paid or contingently payable
	Nature and amount of restructuring provisions and other plant closure expenses consequent on acquisition, and recognised at the date of acquisition
For mergers only	*For mergers only*
Analysis of principal components of the profit and loss account and of total recognised gains and losses into: (1) post-merger period; (2) period up to date of merger for each party to the merger; (3) previous period for each party to the merger. The analysis should show as a minimum turnover, operating profit and exceptional items (split between continuing operations, discontinued operations and acquisitions), profit before taxation, taxation and minority interests	Description and number of shares issued
Composition and fair value of consideration given	Percentage of each entity's voting shares exchanged to effect uniting of interests
Aggregate book value of net assets of each party at the date of the merger	Amounts of assets and liabilities contributed by each enterprise
Nature and amount of significant accounting adjustments to net assets to achieve consistency of accounting policies and explanation of any other adjustments to net assets made as a consequence of the merger	Sales revenue, other operating revenues, extraordinary items and net profit or loss of each enterprise prior to the date of the combination included in consolidated financial statements
Adjustments to reserves resulting from the merger	

Note: Disclosure requirements relating to goodwill and fair values are not included in this table, as they are dealt with in Chapter 17.

Summary

Although regulators expect merger accounting to be applied in 'rare' or 'exceptional' cases, in practice it is found sufficiently often to require students and practitioners to be familiar with this method of accounting. The chapter first discussed the acquisition method of accounting, followed by a consideration of the rationale behind, techniques involved in, and regulations relating to merger accounting. Two sources of regulations were considered: UK GAAP and IAS GAAP. References were also made to the Seventh Directive as this influenced the UK and IAS GAAP regulations. The more specialist topics of demergers and reverse acquisitions were discussed and the chapter concluded by comparing UK and IAS GAAP regulations. The requirements of UK GAAP and IAS GAAP are fairly consistent, with minor exceptions as described in this chapter.

Learning outcomes

After studying this chapter you should have learnt:

- to differentiate between the regulations applying to the acquisition method of accounting under UK GAAP and IAS GAAP
- to differentiate between the regulations applying to the merger method of accounting under UK GAAP and IAS GAAP
- how to account for demergers
- what is meant by reverse acquisitions.

Multiple choice questions

Solutions to these questions are prepared under UK GAAP and are shown in Appendix 1.

CONDITIONS FOR MERGER ACCOUNTING – CASH ELEMENT

16.1 Macrae

If **Macrae** acquires 95% of Urquhart's equity for consideration of 10% equity and 90% cash, does this business combination qualify as a merger under (i) Seventh Directive and (ii) FRS 6 *Acquisitions and Mergers*?

	Seventh Directive	**FRS 6 Acquisitions and Mergers**
(a)	Yes	Yes
(b)	Yes	No
(c)	No	Yes
(d)	No	No

16.2 EU Seventh Directive

Provided that other criteria are also satisfied, the **EU Seventh Directive** states that the merger method of consolidation may be used when the cash element of the consideration for the subsidiary's shares does not exceed:

(a) 10% of the nominal value of the shares issued
(b) 10% of the fair value of the shares issued
(c) 10% of the fair value of the total consideration
(d) 10% of the nominal value of the shares acquired

16.3 Jump, Hop and Skip

Jump was formed to acquire the whole of the equity share capital of both **Hop** and **Skip**. The shareholders in Hop were given three shares in Jump for every two in Hop and those in Skip received four shares in Jump for every three in Skip. Shares in Jump are valued at 250 cent each. In addition, all shareholders received €40 of 10% debenture stock at par for each 100 shares sold to Jump. Hop has 300,000 €1 ordinary shares and Skip has 150,000 €1 ordinary shares.

Considering the criterion of the Seventh Directive that the cash value of any non-share consideration should not exceed 10% of the nominal value of the shares issued as part consideration, is Jump eligible to use merger accounting for either Hop or Skip?

(a) Hop only
(b) Skip only
(c) Both Hop and Skip
(d) Neither Hop nor Skip

CONDITIONS FOR MERGER ACCOUNTING – PROPORTION OF EQUITY ACQUIRED

16.4 Mason and Lockwood

Mason's issued share capital consists of 700,000 non-voting restricted A shares and 7,000 voting equity B shares. **Lockwood**'s issued share capital consists of 1,000,000 €1 ordinary shares. Lockwood acquires 644,908 A shares and 6,231 B shares of Mason's issued share capital, issuing €600,000 equity voting shares (market value €986,055) of its own as consideration.

Does this business combination qualify as a merger under (i) Seventh Directive and (ii) FRS 6 *Acquisitions and Mergers*?

	Seventh Directive	FRS 6
(a)	No	No
(b)	Yes	No
(c)	No	Yes
(d)	Yes	Yes

MERGER ACCOUNTING TECHNIQUE

16.5 Alleyn and Fox

Alleyn merged with **Fox** on 31 July 20X9. Both companies' accounting periods ended on 30 September 20X9. Consolidated profit under the merger method for the year can be analysed as follows:

	Alleyn	Fox	Group
	€000	€000	€000
Pre-merger	25	12	37
Post-merger	35	28	63
	60	40	100

Under FRS 6, which of these figures must be shown separately in a note to the consolidated accounts?

(a) €25,000, €35,000, €12,000 and €28,000
(b) €25,000, €12,000 and €63,000
(c) €37,000 and €63,000
(d) €60,000 and €40,000

16.6 Arm and Leg

The balance sheets of **Arm** and **Leg** at 30 April 20X0, disclosed the following

	Arm	Leg
	€	€
Ordinary shares of €1 each	80,000	70,000
Share premium	8,000	3,500
Undistributed profits	12,650	15,000
	100,650	88,500

On 1 May 20X0, Arm acquired 66,500 shares in Leg in exchange for 83,125 of its own shares. At close of business on 30 April 20X0, the respective market values of the shares of the two companies were as follows:

Arm	€2.00
Leg	€2.50

Using the merger accounting method, the consolidated undistributed profits of Arm on 1 May 20X0 on completion of the share exchange were:

(a) €10,275
(b) €12,650
(c) €26,900
(d) €27,650

16.7 Cart and Horse

Cart and **Horse** were parties to a business combination on 1 January 20X6. On that date the shareholders of Horse received shares in Cart and it has been agreed that the criteria for merger accounting set out in FRS 6 *Acquisitions and Mergers* have been satisfied. On 1 January 20X6, the fixed assets of Horse had a net book value of €300,000, and were estimated to have used up 50% of their useful life. In their condition on 1 January 20X6, these fixed assets had a realisable value of €265,000, and Cart could have purchased identical new fixed assets for €450,000.

Using the merger method of accounting for the combination, what value should be attributed to the fixed assets of Horse for the purposes of calculating any difference arising on consolidation?

(a) €225,000
(b) €265,000
(c) €300,000
(d) €450,000

16.8 Matisse and Goldfish

Matisse acquired 95% of the shares of **Goldfish** on 1 May 20X9. Both companies have a 31 December year-end.

How many months' profit of Goldfish will be included in Matisse's consolidated profit and loss account for the year ended 31 December 20X9 under each of the acquisition and merger methods?

	Acquisition method	**Merger method**
(a)	Eight months	Eight months
(b)	Eight months	Twelve months
(c)	Twelve months	Eight months
(d)	Twelve months	Twelve months

16.9 Orange and Peach

On 1 July 20X2, **Orange** acquired 95% of the share capital of **Peach** by means of a share exchange. The respective profit and loss accounts for the year ended 31 December 20X2, disclosed *Profit attributable to the group for the year* as follows:

	€000
Orange	400
Peach	360

Using the merger method of accounting, the consolidated profit and loss account for the year ended 31 December 20X2, will disclose *Profit for the year* as:

(a) €571,000
(b) €580,000
(c) €742,000
(d) €760,000

16.10 Beef and Gravy

Beef acquired 100% of the equity of **Gravy** on 31 December 20X8. Both companies' accounting periods ended on 30 November 20X9. Beef made €132,000 profit for the year and Gravy made €90,000 profit. Under the acquisition and merger methods, what is Beef's consolidated profit for the year?

	Acquisition	**Merger**
(a)	€214,500	€214,500
(b)	€214,500	€222,000
(c)	€222,000	€214,500
(d)	€222,000	€222,000

Self-assessment exercises

Solutions to these self-assessment exercises can be found at:
www.thomsonlearning.co.uk/accountingandfinance/piercebrennan

16.1 Cormorant and Albatross

Cormorant has a share capital of 3 million ordinary shares of €1 each. It acquired 15% of the ordinary share capital of **Albatross** within the past two years, having purchased the shares for €287,000 cash.

It has now bid for, and acquired, the remainder of the 5 million ordinary shares on the basis of three of its own ordinary shares at 140 cent per share (nominal value €1) plus 30 cent in cash for every five shares of Albatross.

Required

In the circumstances given, indicate whether:
(i) the conditions for merger accounting under the Seventh Directive, and (ii) the additional conditions (i.e., additional to the Seventh Directive) for merger accounting under FRS 6 *Acquisitions and Mergers* are complied with.

16.2 Bogart and Bacall

Bogart has a share capital of 1.3 million ordinary shares of €1 each. Bogart made an offer to acquire all two million equity shares of **Bacall** and succeeded in buying 1,910,000 shares. A share exchange was arranged so that Bacall shareholders who accepted the offer received one €1 ordinary share in Bogart for every two shares held in Bacall. The market value of Bogart's shares was then €2.80 (nominal value €1). Bogart had no previous investment in Bacall.

Required

Discuss whether Bogart would be eligible to use merger accounting under FRS 6 assuming it also gave shareholders in Bacall:

(a) 20 cent per equity share acquired

(b) one convertible 6% preference share, nominal value €1 but worth €1.20, for every 6 equity shares acquired?

Examination-style questions

16.1 Sturdy, Technic and Compos

Sturdy is a company engaged in the manufacture of printed circuit boards. On 1 October 20X0 it had acquired shares in **Technic** and **Compos**.

The balance sheet as at 30 September 20X2 of each of the companies is set out as follows:

	Sturdy €000	Technic €000	Compos €000
Fixed assets			
Tangible fixed assets	19,380	1,040	2,890
Investment property	1,500	—	—
Investments			
Ordinary shares in Compos (note 1)	1,200	—	—
Ordinary shares in Technic (note 2)	4,000	—	—
	26,080	1,040	2,890
Current assets			
Stock	13,920	928	228
Debtors	10,498	812	938
Investments	—	580	—
Preference shares in Technic (note 3)	200	—	—
Cash	—	116	—
	24,618	2,436	1,166
Current liabilities			
Creditors	9,773	1,688	1,172
Proposed dividends	609	53	—
Overdraft	3,596	—	104
	(13,978)	(1,741)	(1,276)
Net current assets / (liabilities)	10,640	695	(110)
Non-current liabilities			
8% loan stock	(9,280)	—	(178)
Deferred tax	—	—	(1,334)
	(9,280)	—	(1,512)
Net assets (note 5)	27,440	1,735	1,268
Shareholders' funds (note 4)			
Ordinary shares of €1 each	12,000	250	40
5% preference shares	—	350	—
Share premium	3,000	—	—
Investment property revaluation reserve	500	—	—
Revaluation reserve	2,000	—	—
Other reserves	9,940	1,135	1,228
	27,440	1,735	1,268

Notes:

1 On 1 October 20X0 the company acquired 20% of the ordinary shares in Compos from F. McRae for a cash consideration of €1,200,000. At that date the fixed assets had a book value of €4m and a fair value of €6m. The net assets had a fair value of €3.2m.

Compos is a family-owned company that purchases circuit boards from Sturdy to use in the manufacture of control equipment. It is managed by its principal shareholder F. McRae who had acquired 90% of the ordinary shares in the company in 20W7. The company has returned to profitability under his management.

On 1 October 20X0 Sturdy negotiated a contract with Compos for the sale of circuit boards for a three-year period.

2 Technic was a family-owned company that operated in the same industry as Sturdy and Compos, manufacturing printed circuit boards. Sturdy planned to acquire the company in order to gain the services of Technic's design team.

On 1 October 20X0 the company acquired 100% of the ordinary shares in Technic. The consideration for these shares was €4 million. The consideration was satisfied by the issue of five Sturdy ordinary shares and €3.50 loan stock issued at par for each ordinary share in Technic. The premium on the issue of the shares was taken to the credit of the share premium account. On the date of the share exchange the net assets of Technic had a fair value of €3m.

3 On 1 October 20X0 the company acquired 100% of the preference shares in Technic. The consideration for these preference shares was €175,000 based on a market earnings yield of 10%. The market earnings yield at 30 September 20X1 was 8.75% and at 30 September 20X2 was 12.5%. It was expected to remain at 12.5% for the next year.

The investment was initially classified as a fixed asset investment and Sturdy revalued the investment to €200,000 on 30 September 20X1. The classification was reviewed on 30 September 20X2 and, on the basis that it had not been intended to retain the preference shares, the investment was reclassified from fixed to current assets. It was expected that the preference shares would be sold during the next three years.

4 The share capital of Technic and Compos has remained unaltered since 20X0.

5 The fair value of the net assets of Technic as at 30 September 20X2 for consolidation purposes was €3,800,000.

Summarised results for each company are set out for the years ended 30 September 20X1 and 20X2 as follows:

	Sturdy		**Technic**		**Compos**	
	20X1	**20X2**	**20X1**	**20X2**	**20X1**	**20X2**
	€000	**€000**	**€000**	**€000**	**€000**	**€000**
Turnover	34,900	34,900	6,696	9,280	2,622	4,319
Profit after tax	966	1,204	360	429	321	624
Dividends	650	600	66	63	—	—

Required

In the context of preparing accounts for the year ended 30 September 20X2, advise the directors of Sturdy on:

(a) the difference between acquisition accounting and merger accounting

(b) whether the investment in Technic satisfies the qualifying conditions for merger accounting under FRS 6

(c) the changes that would be made to the parent company balance sheet of Sturdy as at 30 September 20X2 if the company used merger accounting.

16.2 Hurley and Sliothar (2)

Using the information provided in examination-style question 9.1 (in Chapter 9), you are now required to complete the consolidated profit and loss account for Hurley and group using both merger and acquisition accounting principles.

Required

Prepare the consolidated profit and loss account for the year ended 31 December 20X2 on the basis that:

(i) Merger accounting is applied.
(ii) Acquisition accounting is applied.

17

Goodwill

Learning objectives

After studying this chapter you should be able to:

- define goodwill and fair value
- measure goodwill using book values of net assets acquired and adjustments where fair values of net assets differ from book values
- explain the implications of the fair value principle for measuring purchase consideration
- apply the requirements of FRS 7, FRS 10 and IAS 22 in the context of goodwill
- illustrate the application of the UK and IAS regulations by reference to published accounts data
- outline the main differences between UK GAAP and IAS GAAP regulations for measuring, accounting for and reporting goodwill

Introduction

Accounting for goodwill and intangible assets has been the subject of considerable debate in the UK and elsewhere. The debate has settled for the moment in the UK with the publication in 1997 of FRS 10 *Goodwill and Intangible Assets*. The objectives of FRS 10 (paragraph 1) are to ensure that:

(a) capitalised goodwill and intangible assets are charged in the profit and loss account in the periods in which they are depleted; and
(b) sufficient information is disclosed in the financial statements to enable users to determine the impact of goodwill and intangible assets on the financial position and performance of the reporting entity.

Objective (a) is based on the fundamental principle of matching income with related expenditure. Objective (b) is driven by the desire of regulators to make accounts more useful, particularly in assessing the stewardship of the entity's management and to assist in making economic decisions.

Intangible assets are defined in FRS 10 (paragraph 2) as:

> Non-financial fixed assets that do not have physical substance but are identifiable and are controlled by the entity through custody or legal rights.

Goodwill is an example of such an asset. In Chapter 1, goodwill was described as the difference between the amount paid for an acquisition and the value of the net assets acquired. In Part 2 of this book, a technique for calculating goodwill (in the cost of control account in the consolidated balance sheet workings) was presented. The effect on this calculation, of differences between *book* value of net assets acquired and their *fair* value, was referred to. In most cases in Part 2, the simplifying assumption was made that fair value of net assets was equal to their book value. In the small number of cases where that assumption was relaxed, the mechanics of fair value adjustments in the consolidation workings were explained and illustrated. In Part 3 of the book, goodwill on consolidation was often amortised against group profits in the consolidated profit and loss account. Alternatively, for simplicity, it was left as a permanent asset in the balance sheet and, therefore, only affected consolidated profits when the investment to which the goodwill related was disposed of.

A more holistic discussion of goodwill in the context of the regulatory framework of financial reporting is provided in this chapter. Two major aspects of goodwill are dealt with:

- how to measure goodwill
- how to account for the asset once it has been quantified.

First of all, the issues involved in measuring goodwill are considered, the fair value principle is explained and professional regulations dealing with fair value are discussed. In particular, the requirements of FRS 7 *Fair Values in Acquisition Accounting*, UITF Abstract 31 *Exchanges of businesses or other non-monetary assets for an interest in a subsidiary, joint venture or associate* and IAS 22 *Business Combinations* are outlined and illustrated. The focus is initially on UK GAAP, and IAS GAAP is subsequently dealt with.

After *measurement* of goodwill, we go on to consider regulations governing how to *account* for goodwill. In particular, FRS 10 *Goodwill and Intangible Assets*, FRS 11 *Impairment of Fixed Assets and Goodwill*, IAS 22 *Business Combinations* and UITF Abstract 27 *Revision to estimates of the useful economic life of goodwill and intangible assets* are discussed and illustrated. Once again, we focus first on UK GAAP, then go on to deal with IAS GAAP.

Disclosures required under the various regulations are summarised and illustrated, including disclosures relating to fair value and to accounting for goodwill. Unusually, the disclosures required in relation to fair values are not contained in FRS 7. Rather, they are in FRS 6 *Acquisitions and Mergers*. Therefore, although FRS 6 has already been dealt with in Chapter 16, the disclosure requirements of that standard relevant to fair values are covered in this chapter. Disclosures under IAS GAAP are dealt with towards the end of the chapter.

Measuring goodwill

Two types of goodwill are discussed in the accounting literature: purchased goodwill and internally generated (or non-purchased) goodwill. The valuation of internally generated goodwill is a highly subjective exercise. Consequently, goodwill is only recorded in the financial statements when it arises through the purchase of a business. This is one of the anomalies in accounting for goodwill. If purchased goodwill is capitalised as an asset, such accounting treatment is inconsistent with the accounting treatment of internally generated goodwill, which is never capitalised or recognised separately in financial statements.

Purchased goodwill is defined in FRS 10 (paragraph 2) as:

> The difference between the cost of an acquired entity and the aggregate of the fair values of that entity's identifiable assets and liabilities.

Nokia, in Exhibit 17.1, illustrates the potential significance of goodwill in accounts. Note 6 to its accounts discloses substantial amounts of goodwill arising on acquisitions during the current year. The note discloses fair value of net assets for three acquisitions in the current year of €37 million (€43m, €(4m) and €(2m), respectively). These fair values are significantly different from the consideration paid of €1,051 million (€492m, €223m and €336m, respectively), resulting in goodwill of €1,014m for the three acquisitions. The amount of goodwill recognised is clearly dependent on the consideration paid and the fair values attributable to the net assets acquired.

Exhibit 17.1 **Significance of goodwill**
Nokia Financial Statements 2000

Notes to the Consolidated Financial Statements (extract)
6 Acquisitions (extract)
In October 2000, Nokia increased its ownership of the Brazilian handset manufacturing joint venture NG Industrial (NGI) from 51% to 100% by acquiring all the shares of NGI held by Gradiente Telecom S.A. for EUR 492 million in cash. The fair value of net assets acquired was EUR 43 million giving rise to a goodwill of EUR 449 million.

In August 2000, Nokia acquired DiscoveryCom, a company which provides solutions that enable communications service providers to rapidly install and maintain Broadband Digital Subscriber Line (DSL) services for fast Internet access. The acquisition price was EUR 223 million, which was paid in Nokia stock and Nokia stock options. The fair value of net assets acquired was EUR –4 million giving rise to a goodwill of EUR 227 million.

In March 2000, Nokia acquired Network Alchemy, a provider of IP Clustering solutions for EUR 336 million, which was paid in Nokia stock and Nokia stock options. The fair value of net assets acquired was EUR –2 million giving rise to a goodwill of EUR 338 million.

The fair value principle

Under legal and professional requirements, acquisition accounting requires that the purchase consideration and net assets acquired be recorded at fair value. In the context of acquisition accounting, the valuation of assets and liabilities acquired at fair value is essentially an application of the principle of historic cost. From a group perspective, the net assets of the subsidiary (or associate) at the date of acquisition become net assets of the group at the date of acquisition rather than when acquired by the individual subsidiary. Therefore, the historic cost principle applied at the date of acquisition requires an estimate of what it would cost an arm's length purchaser to acquire the individual assets and liabilities of the subsidiary or associate at the date of acquisition. For the remainder of this chapter, we will refer to subsidiaries only, although the principles of goodwill accounting apply equally well to associates and joint ventures.

In practice, the individual accounts of the acquired subsidiary do not include net assets at their fair value at the date of acquisition. The carrying value of the newly acquired subsidiary's net assets will usually be at cost (i.e., historic cost to the subsidiary), which reflects the conditions prevailing at the date the asset or liability was purchased by the individual subsidiary. Differences between fair value at the date of acquisition and carrying value in the financial statements of the individual subsidiary are most likely to be greatest in the case of fixed assets. However, they can also arise in certain circumstances for current assets and for liabilities. The consolidation adjustments to record fair values affect balance sheet values (including goodwill and minority interest), and also amounts in the post-acquisition consolidated profit and loss account when these assets are consumed or sold. Examples 17.1 and 17.2 illustrate the effect of fair value adjustments in relation to stock (17.1) and fixed assets (17.2) on calculations of goodwill and on post-acquisition profits.

Example 17.1 considers the situation where the fair value of stock at acquisition is €2 million higher than its book value. The effect of recognising the fair value at acquisition is to create goodwill that is €2 million less than it would have been had the goodwill been based on book values. Post-acquisition profits in the year following acquisition are also reduced when the consolidated cost of goods sold is increased by €2 million to reflect fair values at acquisition.

Example 17.1 Fair value of stock different at acquisition

Example

Parent acquires 100% of Subsidiary for €50m cash. At the date of acquisition Subsidiary's balance sheet showed net assets of €40m, including stocks which had cost Subsidiary €9m. The fair value of the stock to the group is estimated to be €11m. Fair value of all other assets and liabilities of Subsidiary were considered to be equal to their book values. The stock was subsequently sold by Subsidiary for €13m.

Required

Outline the effect on (i) goodwill and (ii) post-acquisition profit of applying the fair value principle.

Solution

(i) Goodwill

- Stock of Subsidiary is brought into the consolidated balance sheet at the date of acquisition at its fair value to the group, €11m.
- Goodwill is €8m at the date of acquisition [€50m –(€40m + €11m – €9m)].

(ii) Post-acquisition profit

- Assuming goodwill is amortised, post-acquisition profits of the group will be charged with a portion of €8m each year, the portion depending on the goodwill's useful life.
- Consolidated profit and loss account for the period after acquisition will include profit on sale of stock of €2m (€13m – €11m), whereas Subsidiary's individual profit and loss account will include a profit of €4m (€13m – €9m).

Example 17.2 considers the situation where the fair value of a tangible fixed asset at acquisition is €2 million higher than its book value. In addition, there is a 20% minority in Example 17.2, whereas Subsidiary was wholly owned in Example 17.1. Goodwill is the difference between the cost of the investment and the group's share of the fair value of net assets acquired. The group's share (of the fair value of net assets acquired) includes 80% of the €2 million fair value surplus when calculating goodwill. The minority is also credited with their share of the revaluation surplus.

The effect of the fair value adjustment on post-acquisition profits is not as immediate in Example 17.2 as it was in Example 17.1. Unlike the treatment of stock in Example 17.1, the cost of the asset consumed in Example 17.2 is not charged against the consolidated profit and loss account in its entirety in the year immediately following acquisition. The group's share of the revaluation surplus is charged against consolidated profits over the asset's remaining useful life of five years. The minority is also charged with their share of the additional depreciation for each of the five years. (Fair value adjustments in the context of revaluing tangible fixed assets were explained in Chapter 3.)

Example 17.2 Fair value of fixed asset different at acquisition

Example

Details are as for Example 17.1, except assume that:

- Parent acquires 80% of the shares in Subsidiary for €38m.
- The asset with the fair value difference is a fixed asset subject to depreciation.
- The remaining useful life of the fixed asset is five years and it has no residual value at the end of that period.

Required

Outline the effect on (i) goodwill, (ii) post-acquisition profits and (iii) minority interest of applying the fair value principle.

Solution

(i) Goodwill

- Fixed asset of Subsidiary is brought into the consolidated balance sheet at the date of acquisition at its fair value to the group, €11m.
- Goodwill is €4.4m (€38m – (80% × [€40m + €11m – €9m]) at the date of acquisition.
- Minority interest at the date of acquisition is €8.4m (20% × €42m).

(ii) Post-acquisition profits

- Assuming goodwill is amortised, post-acquisition profits of the group will be charged with a portion of €4.4m each year, the portion depending on the goodwill's useful life.
- A consolidation adjustment for depreciation of €0.4m [(€11m ÷ 5) – (€9m ÷ 5)] is required in the consolidated profit and loss account.

(iii) Minority interest

- Minority interests will be charged with 20% of the consolidation depreciation adjustment.

Professional regulations on fair value

Professional regulations governing fair value calculations were relatively minor until 1994, when FRS 7 was introduced to control the many abuses of the fair value principle evidenced in the 1980s in the UK. Much of the detail in FRS 7 was prompted by experience of creative accounting practices associated with widespread merger and acquisition activity in the UK in the 1980s.

Pre-FRS 7

In the past, there was no specific guidance under UK GAAP on how to arrive at fair values of either purchase consideration or net assets. Although FRS 10's predecessor, SSAP 22 *Accounting for Goodwill* (which was published in 1984) also used the term *fair value* in its definition of goodwill, little practical guidance was given on how it should be interpreted. Much of the controversy which surrounded the implementation of SSAP 22 in the 1980s and 1990s was caused by the magnitude of goodwill amounts recognised. This was considered at the time to be due to loose regulations. At the end of the 1990s and since then, large amounts of goodwill are again very evident, as was highlighted for Nokia in Exhibit 17.1. Large goodwill amounts nowadays are more likely to be caused by the value of intellectual capital (much of which is not included on the balance sheet) whereas in the 1980s, valuation of brands and similar intangibles in addition to generous acquisition provisions contributed to substantial goodwill amounts. Creative compliance with SSAP 22 commonly involved recognising at acquisition large, and often unnecessary, provisions for future costs or future losses. Such provisions reduced the total fair value of net assets acquired, thereby increasing goodwill. However, as the preferred accounting treatment for goodwill under SSAP 22 was immediate write-off against reserves, increasing goodwill at acquisition did not affect post-acquisition earnings per share (EPS). Moreover, these provisions could actually improve post-acquisition EPS by shielding the post-acquisition profit and loss account from restructuring costs (which were charged against the provision) or by directly increasing post-acquisition profits when unnecessary provisions, created at acquisition, were subsequently released back to consolidated profit and loss account.

Much of the debate which preceded publication of FRS 10 focused on the merits and demerits of various approaches to accounting for goodwill, e.g., the relative strengths of the two alternatives available under SSAP 22, i.e., immediate write-off against reserves or capitalisation and amortisation through the profit and loss account. However, it became clear during this debate that the scale of the problem was exaggerated by the unscrupulous creation of pre-acquisition provisions with the express objective of boosting post-acquisition performance. Such provisions were not prohibited by regulations at that time. Example 17.3 illustrates the impact of such pre-acquisition provisions on goodwill calculations and subsequent group profits.

Example 17.3 Effect of pre-acquisition provisions on goodwill when goodwill is written off directly against reserves

Example

Parent purchases 100% of shares in Subsidiary for €100m, when net assets in the balance sheet of Subsidiary are €80m. The fair value of the net assets at the date of acquisition also amounts to €80m. Parent initiates a reorganisation of the activities of Subsidiary following acquisition and estimates the cost of the reorganisation to be €5m.

Required

In the context of a goodwill policy of immediate write-off against reserves, explain the effect of providing for the reorganisation costs at acquisition (rather than charging these costs against profits when incurred) and discuss the advantages of making such provisions at the date of acquisition.

Solution

- Goodwill after provision for reorganisation costs amounts to €25m. It would have been €20m had the provision not been made.
- When reorganisation costs are actually incurred (after the acquisition), they can bypass the consolidated profit and loss account by being charged against the provision, thereby protecting post-acquisition profits from the charge of €5m.
- There is no periodic charge against consolidated profits when goodwill is written off directly against reserves.

Current UK regulations

FRS 7 *Fair Values in Acquisition Accounting* was issued in 1994. It provides guidance on quantifying the amounts for goodwill recognised in financial statements. The standard regulates the measurement of goodwill in three ways by focusing on:

- fair values of assets and liabilities included in the goodwill calculation
- controlling (mainly by prohibiting) provisions being made at the time of acquisition
- fair value of the purchase consideration, including deferred and contingent consideration.

Fair value was first defined in FRS 7 (paragraph 2) as:

> The amount at which an asset or liability could be exchanged in an arm's length transaction between informed and willing parties, other than in a forced or liquidation sale.

FRS 7 tackled a significant component of the problem of accounting for goodwill in advance of the ASB replacing the discredited SSAP 22 by FRS 10. The objective of FRS 7 was to reform acquisition accounting practices. In particular (paragraph 1), its objectives are:

> To ensure that when a business entity is acquired by another, all the assets and liabilities that existed in the acquired entity at the date of acquisition are recorded at fair values reflecting their condition at that date; and that all changes to the acquired assets and liabilities, and the resulting gains and losses, that arise after control of the acquired entity has passed to the acquirer are reported as part of the post-acquisition financial performance of the acquiring group.

The ASB was particularly worried about the practice of creating provisions at the time of an acquisition in respect of anticipated future losses or post-acquisition expenditure. The effect of this was to avoid charging such items against future profits. Under FRS 7, provision for future losses in acquired businesses and for reorganisation costs following an acquisition should not be accounted for as liabilities of the acquired businesses. Instead, both should be treated as post-acquisition items in the consolidated profit and loss account of the acquirer.

Determining the fair value of purchase consideration

FRS 7 requires purchase consideration to be recorded at fair value when calculating goodwill. The FRS provides guidance on measuring fair value of the purchase consideration, thereby quantifying the cost of acquisition. Under FRS 7 the cost of acquisition includes:

- cash and other monetary consideration
- expenses of acquisition
- fair value of other purchase consideration given by the acquirer.

Normally, quantifying the cash consideration is straightforward. However, if cash settlement is to be deferred, fair value can be calculated by discounting cash payments back to present value using a discount rate equivalent to the interest rate which the acquirer could obtain on similar borrowing.

Professional fees and similar costs can be included in the cost of acquisition. Internal costs (e.g., cost of directors' time) and expenses that cannot be directly attributable to the acquisition cannot be included.

Other purchase consideration (such as capital instruments) should be valued at market price on the date of acquisition or, where there is no reliable market, fair value should be estimated by other means (e.g., value of similar quoted securities).

UITF Abstract 31, *Exchanges of businesses or other non-monetary assets for an interest in a subsidiary, joint venture or associate*, was issued in October 2001. The aim of the Abstract is to clarify the fair value principles involved in measuring consideration when a business is transferred by the investor in exchange for shares acquired in a new subsidiary.

Abstract 31 addresses the issue of valuing non-monetary consideration paid when the equity interest acquired qualifies as a subsidiary, associate or joint venture of the investing company, particularly in the context of transferring ownership rights in a business as some or all of the consideration paid. Prior to the Abstract being issued, there was ambiguity relating to whether transactions should be reported at book value or fair value. Abstract 31 requires that such transactions be analysed in terms of net changes in ownership interests. It requires the following accounting treatment:

- the part of the business exchanged that is owned by the parent directly before and indirectly after the transaction remains at book value
- the parent's share of net assets acquired through its new interest in the subsidiary should be accounted for at fair value
- goodwill should be recognised in respect of the parent's new interest in the subsidiary
- a gain or loss should be recognised in respect of the part of the business that is no longer directly or indirectly owned by the parent.

Example 17.4 illustrates the issues involved and the accounting treatment required by Abstract 31.

Example 17.4 Exchange of business for equity interest in another

Example

Parent and Subsidiary$_2$ are initially unconnected companies. Parent transfers all of its shares in a wholly owned subsidiary, Subsidiary$_1$ to Subsidiary$_2$. In exchange, Subsidiary$_2$ issues equity shares to Parent giving Parent a 50% interest in Subsidiary$_2$.

Immediately before the transaction, the net assets of Subsidiary$_1$ amounted to €300 and they had a fair value of €500. At the same date, the net assets of Subsidiary$_2$ (excluding the shares in Subsidiary$_1$) had a book value of €400 and a fair value of €700. For the purpose of the exchange transaction, both businesses were valued at €1,200.

After the transaction, the enlarged Subsidiary$_2$ group could be:

- a subsidiary of Parent
- a joint venture interest of Parent; or
- an associate of Parent

depending on the rights attaching to the shares acquired by Parent in Subsidiary$_2$.

Assuming Subsidiary$_2$ becomes a subsidiary of Parent, Subsidiary$_1$ becomes a sub-subsidiary of Parent.

Required

(i) Show the group structure before and after the exchange transaction.

(ii) Discuss whether, under UITF Abstract 31, net assets in Subsidiary$_1$ should be accounted for at fair value at the date of the exchange transaction or at their previous book values in the consolidated accounts of Parent.

Solution

(i) Group structure: Before

Group structure: After

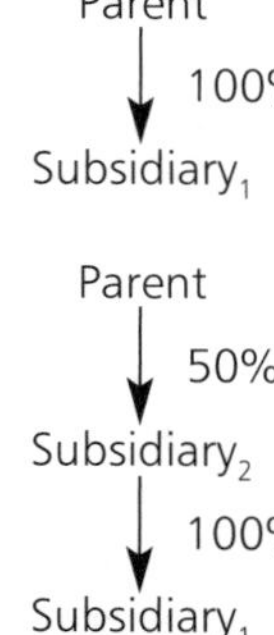

(ii) Net assets of $Subsidiary_1$ after exchange

- Any part of $Subsidiary_1$ that is owned by Parent throughout the transaction (directly before and indirectly after the exchange) remains at book value in the consolidated accounts of Parent. Therefore, 50% of the net assets of $Subsidiary_1$ (50% × €300 = €150) remain at book value.
- Only 50% of the net assets of $Subsidiary_1$ are considered disposed of by Parent.
- As it may be difficult to value the consideration given for shares in $Subsidiary_2$, the best estimate of its value may be given by valuing what is acquired, i.e., €600 (50% × €1,200).
- Net assets acquired through Parent's investment in $Subsidiary_2$ are included in Parent's consolidated balance sheet at fair value at the date of acquisition (€$700_{\text{Fair value of net assets of Subsidiary}_2}$ less minority interest of €$350_{50\%}$).
- Goodwill of €250 arises (€$600_{\text{Fair value of consideration for 50\% of Subsidiary}_1}$ – (50% × €$700_{\text{Fair value of net assets of Subsidiary}_2}$)).
- The gain on disposal of 50% of $Subsidiary_1$ is €450. This is the difference between the proceeds of €600 (50% × €1,200) and the carrying amount of the net assets no longer owned of €150 (50% × €300).

Source: Adapted from the proposed Abstract on *Exchanges of businesses or other non-monetary assets for equity in a subsidiary, associate or joint-venture*, Information Sheet 47, UITF, May 2001

Where the amount of purchase consideration is contingent on one or more future events (e.g., performance of the acquired entity), the cost of acquisition should include a reasonable estimate of the fair value amounts expected to be payable. Elan Corporation plc, in Exhibit 17.2, discloses contingent consideration within creditors.

Exhibit 17.2 **Disclosure of contingent consideration**
Elan Corporation plc Annual Report 2000

Notes relating to the Financial Statements (extract)
17 Creditors (extract)
Included in creditors is an amount relating to future contingent cash payments which Elan may be liable to make relating to the acquisition of the Naprelan and Verelan products. At 31 December 2000, the balance outstanding was $18.0 million, all of which has been included in amounts falling due within one year.

Exhibit 17.3, Incepta Group plc, a UK listed public relations company, discloses contingent purchase consideration and the fact that this has been reclassified from creditors to provisions.

Exhibit 17.3 **Deferred and contingent consideration**
Incepta Group plc Annual Report 2001

Provisions
In a note to the accounts, Incepta discloses that its acquisitions typically involve an earn-out arrangement whereby the consideration payable includes a deferred element that is subject to the future financial performance of the acquired entity. Incepta discloses further that in order to better reflect the nature of the liability, deferred consideration for acquisitions is now carried in provisions where in the past these amounts were included in creditors. The maximum deferred cash and loan note consideration payable under all earn-out arrangements amounts to £71.5 million. Provision has been made for only £33.4 million of this amount as the directors are of the opinion that the remaining £38.1 million represents a contingent liability, as the likelihood of payment is considered remote. A further deferred acquisition consideration amounting to £67.3 million is payable in shares and this amount is carried in the balance sheet as shares to be issued.

Source: *Company Reporting*, July 2001, p.13

Example 17.5 explains the impact on goodwill of deferred consideration which is contingent on uncertain future events.

Example 17.5 Deferred contingent consideration

Example

A purchaser of an acquired entity is required to pay additional consideration. The value of the additional consideration depends on the acquired entity's future performance. The additional consideration may give rise to more goodwill.

Required

Discuss how this future goodwill should be accounted for under FRS 7 and FRS 10.

Solution

FRS 7 deals specifically with the treatment of deferred consideration where the amount payable is uncertain because it is contingent on the outcome of future events. FRS 7 requires a reasonable estimate of the fair value of amounts expected to be payable in the future to be included in the cost of acquisition when the fair value exercise is undertaken. This amount will have to be adjusted, if necessary, when the final amount payable is determined or when revised estimates are made. Such adjustments should continue to be made to the cost of the acquisition and, therefore, to goodwill, until the consideration is finally determined.

It follows that any additional goodwill should be accounted for in the same way as the previous goodwill was accounted for. Therefore, if the goodwill on the acquisition was capitalised under FRS 10, any additional goodwill should be accounted for as an adjustment to the value of the existing goodwill carried on the balance sheet. On the other hand, if the acquisition pre-dated FRS 10 and the previous goodwill remains eliminated against reserves, any additional goodwill will be treated as an adjustment to the goodwill eliminated against reserves.

Source: Adapted from Holgate, P. and Ghosh, J. 1998. 'Accounting solutions – deferred consideration', *Accountancy*, March, p.90

Subsequent events can also cause the amount of consideration recorded for an acquisition to be revised (even where the contingency was not formally recognised as part of the original transaction). Example 17.6 teases out the issues where vendors were awarded additional consideration following legal action.

Example 17.6 Subsequent adjustment to consideration

Example

Ten years ago a company made an acquisition. Some time afterwards the vendors commenced legal action over the amount of the purchase consideration, claiming additional amounts in relation to the acquired business's performance. The court required the company to pay additional amounts to the vendors.

The goodwill originally recorded on the acquisition was written off to reserves. The company adopted FRS 10 early, but did not reinstate the goodwill previously written off directly to reserves (see section on transitional arrangements later in this chapter).

Required

(i) Discuss whether the additional payment now required by the court can be treated as goodwill or must it be expensed because the time limit for fair value adjustments has expired.

(ii) If the additional payment can be treated as goodwill, discuss whether it must be capitalised under FRS 10 or if it can be written off to reserves.

Solution

(i) Adjustment to payment

The time limit for fair value adjustments (paragraph 25, FRS 7) applies only to the amounts determined for the assets and liabilities acquired. There is no time limit on the recognition of goodwill in relation to contingent consideration (paragraph 27, FRS 7). That is, goodwill continues to be adjusted until the final amount in known.

(ii) Treatment of additional goodwill

The transitional provision in paragraph 69, FRS 10 means that the goodwill remaining eliminated against reserves should comprise, at most, 'all goodwill previously eliminated'. It is possible to interpret this as requiring any goodwill arising after the adoption of FRS 10 to be recognised as an asset and not eliminated against reserves, even when it arises in relation to contingent consideration.

However, as the previous estimate is being revised, it seems logical that the additional goodwill should be treated in the same way as the goodwill that was accounted for when the acquisition was made. In this case, therefore, the adjustment to the original goodwill should be eliminated against reserves.

Source: Adapted from Holgate, P. and Calderwood, K. 1998. 'Accounting solutions – goodwill', *Accountancy International*, November, p.86

Determining the fair values of identifiable assets and liabilities acquired

FRS 7 requires identifiable assets and liabilities to be recorded at fair value when calculating goodwill. Identifiable assets and liabilities are defined in both FRS 7 and FRS 10 (paragraph 2 in both), as follows:

> The assets and liabilities of an entity that are capable of being disposed of or settled separately, without disposing of a business of the entity.

To counter abuses evident under SSAP 22, FRS 7 provides that identifiable net assets to be initially brought into the consolidated balance sheet should be those of the acquired entity that existed at the date of acquisition. However, the assets and liabilities that are brought into account need not necessarily have been previously recognised in the financial statements of the acquired entity. For example, pension surpluses and deficiencies may be recorded which have not previously been shown in the financial statements of the subsidiary acquired.

As already explained, net assets should be identified and valued using the acquirer's accounting policies and should not be increased or decreased by changes resulting from the acquirer's intentions for future actions regarding the acquired entity. Liabilities of the acquired entity should not include provisions for future operating losses of the acquired entity or for reorganisation and integration costs expected to be incurred as a result of the acquisition. Such losses and costs are part of the post-acquisition financial performance of the acquiring group.

The recognition and measurement of acquired assets and liabilities should be completed by the date on which the first post-acquisition financial statements of the acquirer are approved. If this is not possible, provisional valuations should be made. These should then be amended, if necessary, in the next financial statements, with a corresponding adjustment to goodwill. Exhibit 17.4 illustrates amendment to goodwill arising from revisions to fair value estimates.

Exhibit 17.4 **Adjustments to provisional fair value estimates Cable & Wireless Annual Report 2000**

Notes on the Financial Statements (extract)

14 Intangible fixed assets (extract)

Included in additions is a net increase of £49m in the goodwill which arose on the acquisition of the US internet business in September 1998 to reflect finalisation of the fair values of the separable net assets acquired and the consideration given. The principal changes to the provisional fair values established in 1999 relate to (i) consideration received on the sale of the Dial-up business recorded on acquisition as an asset held for re-sale, (ii) the outcome of negotiations on the amount of deferred consideration due, and (iii) amounts received from the vendor in full and final settlement of a claim by the Company in respect of various matters associated with the acquisition.

FRS 7 sets out guidelines for establishing fair values of specific assets and liabilities. These guidelines are summarised in Table 17.1.

Table 17.1 FRS 7 and fair values of specific assets and liabilities

Asset/liability	*Fair value*
Tangible fixed assets	Market value (if similar assets traded on open market) or
	Depreciated replacement cost
Intangible assets	Replacement cost – normally estimated market value
Stocks and work in progress	Lower of replacement cost and net realisable value (allows for subsequent realisation of trading profit)
Commodity stocks	Current market price
Quoted investments	Market price
Monetary assets and liabilities	Market price or
	Current price to acquire similar asset/liability or discounting future cash flows to present value
Contingent assets and liabilities	Recognise where reasonably expected to crystallise. Value where capable of calculation – use reasonable estimates of the expected outcome
Businesses held exclusively with a view to subsequent resale	Estimated sale proceeds. If not sold within a year, consolidate at fair values at date of acquisition
Pensions	Recognise fair value of deficiency or surplus in a funded pension (if expected to be realised)
Deferred taxation	Calculate deferred tax liabilities by considering group as a whole. Recognise benefit of any tax losses attributable to acquired entity

IAS GAAP

IAS 22 *Business Combinations* was first published in 1983 and was last revised in 1998. In broad terms, IAS 22 takes a similar approach to FRS 7 in regulating fair value measurements. However, there are a number of differences between FRS 7 and IAS 22. The following is a summary:

- FRS 7 requires that a reasonable estimate of the fair value of the future expected payments in respect of contingent purchase consideration should be included in the cost of acquisition. IAS 22 requires that the cost of acquisition should be adjusted only when the contingency is resolved and the additional payment is both probable and capable of reliable measurement

- IAS 22 requires a reorganisation or restructuring provision that was not a liability of the investee to be recognised as an acquired liability, provided certain conditions are met. IAS 22 deals with the reversal of such provisions and the consequences of the expenditure not being incurred. FRS 7 requires that any such provision should be recognised as a post-acquisition expense
- in an acquisition, IAS 22 requires that minority interest be measured by reference to the pre-acquisition carrying amounts of the net assets in the accounts of the acquired company. This treatment is not allowed under UK GAAP, which requires that both group and minority interests be measured using fair values
- there are differences in detail between FRS 7 and IAS 22 when determining the fair value of particular assets and liabilities acquired. For example, FRS 7 requires that a separate business of the investee which is sold within a year of acquisition should, in certain circumstances, be measured at an amount based on its subsequent sale proceeds. IAS 22 does not deal with this issue.

Accounting for goodwill

Three main approaches to accounting for goodwill have already been discussed and illustrated in Part 2 of this book. They are:

1. immediate write-off against reserves
2. capitalisation as an asset and amortisation over the goodwill's useful economic life
3. capitalisation without amortisation.

Only the second treatment affects periodic reported income and, therefore, EPS. As indicated earlier, SSAP 22 allowed a choice between the first two options. The vast majority of companies chose immediate write-off against reserves in preference to taking annual amortisation charges against profits. Under UK and IAS GAAP, a choice is no longer allowed when accounting for goodwill. Both FRS 10 and IAS 22 require goodwill to be capitalised and amortised over its useful life. However, because transitional arrangements under FRS 10 allowed companies to continue to write off goodwill against reserves for acquisitions occurring before FRS 10 came into effect, immediate write-off against reserves is explained later in this chapter.

Companies do not have to amortise goodwill under FRS 10 where they can justify that the goodwill has an indefinite useful life. Consequently, the third option just listed (capitalisation without amortisation) is found in practice in a minority of cases under UK GAAP. IAS 22 does not allow companies to assume an indefinite useful life for goodwill and so examples of the third approach listed are not found under IAS GAAP.

Diageo, in Exhibit 17.5, indicates in its accounting policy for *Brands, goodwill and other intangible assets* that it wrote off goodwill against reserves prior to 1 July 1998 and that goodwill thus written off has not been reinstated. Since 1 July 1998 it adopts a policy of capitalisation. Some of the capitalised goodwill is amortised and some of it is not. Thus, Diageo adopts all three policies for goodwill in respect of acquisitions remaining as subsidiaries and associates at the year-end. The exhibit refers to impairment reviews which are discussed later in this chapter.

Exhibit 17.5 **Accounting policy for goodwill Diageo Annual Report 2000**

Accounting Policies (extract)
Brands, goodwill and other intangible assets (extract)
When the cost of an acquisition exceeds the fair values attributable to the group's share of the net assets acquired, the difference is treated as purchased goodwill. Goodwill arising from 1 July 1998 is capitalised; prior to that date it was eliminated against reserves, and this goodwill has not been reinstated.

Where capitalised goodwill and intangible assets are regarded as having limited useful economic lives, their cost is amortised on a straight-line basis over those lives – up to 20 years. Where goodwill and intangible assets are regarded as having indefinite useful economic lives, they are not amortised. Impairment reviews are carried out to ensure that goodwill and intangible assets are not carried at above their recoverable amounts. Any amortisation or impairment write downs are charged to the profit and loss account.

Immediate write-off

Immediate write-off of goodwill against reserves was very common in the UK prior to the publication of FRS 10. The reasoning behind immediate write-off of goodwill and SSAP 22's preference for this method was:

- consistency with treatment of non-purchased goodwill
- write-off should not go through profit and loss account because goodwill is written off for accounting reasons and not because of any diminution in value of the asset
- the write-off is unrelated to the results for the year.

However, there were inconsistencies in the application of the immediate write-off policy under SSAP 22. The standard did not specify the reserve to be used. Many companies applying SSAP 22's preferred treatment did not have adequate reserves for the write-off of very large amounts of goodwill. Some innovative interpretations of the standard's requirements developed from this. These included a variety of methods for writing off goodwill against reserves. Table 17.2 lists some interpretations found in practice under SSAP 22. Each of these is discussed in the following paragraphs.

Table 17.2 Methods of writing goodwill off against reserves

Accounting policy	*In practice*
Immediate write off against reserves	Against revenue reserves Against share premium account Negative reserve 'Dangling debit'

Against revenue reserves

The most straightforward interpretation of the SSAP 22 requirement was that goodwill would be subtracted from retained earnings (revenue reserves or the total on profit and loss account reserve). Diageo, in Exhibit 17.6, indicates in note 23 to the accounts that goodwill written off immediately on acquisition against reserves under the old regulation was written off against the profit and loss account reserve.

Exhibit 17.6 **Goodwill written off against reserves on acquisition Diageo Annual Report 2000**

Notes to the Consolidated Accounts (extract)
23 Reserves attributable to equity shareholders (extract)

	Profit and loss account £ million
At 30 June 1999	(1,343)
Retained earnings	263
Exchange adjustments	27
Tax charge on exchange in reserves	(7)
Premiums on share issues, less expenses	(6)
Repurchase of own shares	(54)
Goodwill on disposals of businesses	446
Transfers	23
At 30 June 2000	(651)

Aggregate goodwill written off against the profit and loss account, net of disposals, is £4,094 million (1999 – £4,498 million) including £156 million (1999 – £162 million) in respect of associates. The exchange adjustments include losses of £119 million in respect of foreign currency net borrowings (1999 – £208 million).

Against share premium account

However, where retained earnings were insufficient, or where companies wished to protect them from significant reductions, some of the other approaches in Table 17.2 were used. Occasionally, application was made to the courts to have the share premium reclassified to enable goodwill to be written off against the resulting non-distributable reserve.

Under UK and Irish legislation, share premium may only be used to issue bonus shares and for writing off certain share and debenture redemption premiums and issue expenses. Goodwill may not be written off against share premium. However, application can be made to the courts to have the share premium account reclassified as a non-distributable reserve. Although there is a valid argument that this practice is not within the spirit of the law, the approach was used in practice. Exhibit 17.7 illustrates how that policy continues to be relevant in respect of goodwill arising before FRS 10 came into effect. The significance of the €43 million goodwill write-off (in effect against share premium) in Barlo's case can be gauged by reference to retained earnings, which amount to just under €60 million.

Exhibit 17.7 **Use of share premium to write off goodwill Barlo plc Annual Report 2000**

Notes forming part of the Financial Statements (extract)
24 Other Reserves (extract)
In accordance with High Court Orders, goodwill amounting to €42,848,000 has previously been written off against capital reserves created by transfers from the share premium account.

Negative reserve

Some companies created a negative reserve in respect of goodwill written off. In effect, the goodwill write-off did not reduce any individual reserve. The negative goodwill reserve reduced total reserves. At first glance, Glanbia plc in Exhibit 17.8 illustrates the use of a negative reserve. However, closer examination reveals that its previously written off goodwill is separately disclosed as a negative constituent of revenue reserves rather than as a separate reserve within shareholders' funds. This latter treatment is expressly prohibited by FRS 10. However, the presentation in Exhibit 17.8 is reminiscent of the use of negative reserves under SSAP 22.

Exhibit 17.8 **Negative reserve for goodwill write-off**
Glanbia plc Annual Report 2000

Notes to the Financial Statements (extract)
27 Revenue reserves

	At 1 January 2000 IR£000	Currency translation difference IR£000	Goodwill on disposal IR£000	Profit retained/ (loss absorbed) for year IR£000	At 30 December 2000 IR£000
Company	12,260	—	—	(491)	11,769
Subsidiaries	17,944	—	2,916	37,098	57,958
Joint venture and associates	2,344	—	—	348	2,692
Total profit and loss reserves	32,548	—	2,916	36,955	72,419
Currency translation reserve	(24,575)	(3,145)	—	—	(27,720)
Goodwill reserve	(99,626)	(388)	(540)	—	(100,554)
Total revenue reserves	(91,653)	(3,533)	2,376	36,955	(55,855)

'Dangling debit'

Under the 'dangling debit' approach, accumulated goodwill is recorded in a goodwill account. Balances on profit and loss account and other reserves are recorded separately. In the published balance sheet, share capital and adjusted reserves are subtotalled. Goodwill is then subtracted from this subtotal.

Capitalisation of goodwill

Following substantial debate over a long period, FRS 10 finally prohibited immediate write-off of goodwill against reserves when it was issued in 1997. The standard requires capitalisation of purchased goodwill and amortisation over its useful economic life, unless that life is considered to be indefinite. However, FRS 10 did not *require* a prior year adjustment in respect of goodwill which had been previously written off against reserves under SSAP 22. As a result, companies which had previously written goodwill off against reserves were not required to record large charges against retained profits arising from prior year adjustments.

The Diageo policy for goodwill in Exhibit 17.5 illustrates the adoption of a policy which complies with FRS 10, in addition to continuing the previous SSAP 22 policy for acquisitions completed before FRS 10 came into effect (accounting periods ending on or after 23 December 1998).

Kingfisher in Exhibit 17.9 provides a comprehensive description of its goodwill policy. FRS 10 has been applied in accounting periods since (and including) the year ended on 31 January 1999. Goodwill for prior accounting periods was eliminated directly against reserves. The policy then goes on to explain that such goodwill will be charged in the profit and loss account in the period in which the business to which it relates is disposed of. In addition, goodwill arising on an acquisition during the year is considered to have an indefinite life and is therefore not amortised. The true and fair override is invoked to justify this departure from the UK Companies Act requirement. The group also refers to undertaking an annual impairment test on the carrying amount of goodwill, as required by FRS 10. Impairment reviews are discussed later in this section.

Exhibit 17.9 **Comprehensive goodwill accounting policy Kingfisher plc Annual Report 2001**

Notes to the Accounts (extract)

1 Accounting policies (extract)

Goodwill and intangible assets

Intangible assets, which comprise goodwill arising on acquisitions and acquired licences and copyrights, are stated at cost less amortisation.

Goodwill arising on all acquisitions prior to 31 January 1998 remains eliminated against reserves. This goodwill will be charged in the profit and loss account on subsequent disposal of the business to which it relates. Purchased goodwill arising on acquisitions after 31 January 1998 is treated as an asset on the balance sheet. Where goodwill is regarded as having a limited estimated useful economic life it is amortised on a systematic basis over its life. Where goodwill is regarded as having an indefinite life it is not amortised. The estimated useful economic life is regarded as indefinite where goodwill is capable of continued measurement and the durability of the acquired business can be demonstrated. Where goodwill is not amortised an annual impairment review is performed and any impairment will be charged to the profit and loss account.

In estimating the useful economic life of goodwill arising, account has been taken of the nature of the business acquired, the stability of the industry, the extent of continuing barriers to market entry and expected future impact of competition. With the exception of BUT S.A. all acquisitions since 31 January 1998 are considered by the directors to have an estimated useful economic life of 20 years.

Goodwill arising on the acquisition of shares in BUT S.A. is £135.4 million. The directors consider that BUT S.A. has a proven ability to maintain its market leadership over a long period and will adapt successfully to any foreseeable technological or customer-led changes and that barriers to entry into its market place exist, such that the business will prove to be durable. BUT S.A.'s record since 1972, when it commenced trading, has been one of consistent growth in both turnover and operating profits. Accordingly, the goodwill is not amortised and, in order to give a true and fair view, the financial statements depart from the requirement of amortising goodwill over a finite period, as required by the Companies Act. Instead an annual impairment test is undertaken and any impairment that is identified will be charged to the profit and loss account. It is not possible to quantify the effect of the departure from the Companies Act, because no finite life for goodwill can be identified.

Goodwill arising on purchase of pharmacy businesses is amortised over a useful economic life of 20 years. Acquired licences and copyrights are amortised over the period of the underlying legal agreement, which do not exceed 20 years.

Various aspects of capitalising goodwill are addressed in FRS 10. They are discussed in the following paragraphs under the headings:

- initial recognition
- amortisation
- determining useful economic life
- review of useful economic life
- impairment reviews
- negative goodwill
- revaluation of goodwill
- transitional arrangements.

Initial recognition

Internally generated goodwill should not be capitalised. Positive purchased goodwill should be capitalised and classified as an asset on the balance sheet. If the value of an intangible asset purchased as part of a business acquisition cannot be measured reliably, it should be subsumed within the amount of the purchase price of goodwill.

In Example 17.7, the treatment of goodwill on an acquired subsidiary's balance sheet is discussed.

Example 17.7 Goodwill on subsidiary's balance sheet

Example

$Parent_1$ group had capitalised purchased goodwill in respect of previous acquisitions. $Parent_1$ group was subsequently acquired by $Parent_2$ group.

Required

How should the goodwill in $Parent_1$ group's balance sheet be dealt with in $Parent_2$ group's balance sheet?

Solution

$Parent_2$ group is required to recognise the $Parent_1$ group's identifiable assets and liabilities that existed at the date of acquisition. FRS 7 defines identifiable assets and liabilities as those that are capable of being disposed of or settled separately, without disposing of one of $Parent_1$ group's businesses. Goodwill is not an identifiable asset, because it cannot be sold separately from a business. Therefore, any purchased goodwill recognised as an asset in $Parent_1$ group's balance sheet in respect of its previous acquisitions should be disregarded in the fair value exercise. Such goodwill is in effect subsumed within the calculation of goodwill arising on the new acquisition. The elimination of previously recognised purchased goodwill in the fair value exercise should be shown in the fair value table* as an adjustment to the book values of $Parent_1$ group's assets and liabilities.

[* Fair value table is explained later in this chapter.]

Source: Adapted from Holgate, P. and Nailor, H. 1997. 'Accounting solutions – goodwill', *Accountancy International*, May, p.67

Amortisation

Where purchased goodwill is considered to have a limited useful economic life, it should be amortised on a systematic basis over that life. Residual value may not be assigned to goodwill. Straight-line amortisation should be used unless another method can be shown to be more appropriate.

The precise caption in the profit and loss account under which goodwill amortisation should be included is not specified in FRS 10 or in the prescribed layouts for the profit and loss account under the Seventh Directive. Example 17.8 discusses whether presentation after *Operating profit* in the profit and loss account is an appropriate place for disclosing the goodwill amortisation charge.

Example 17.8 Locating goodwill amortisation in profit and loss account

Example

Following the requirements of FRS 10, goodwill arising on a current year acquisition will be capitalised in the balance sheet and amortised over its useful economic life.

Required

Discuss whether the amortisation charge should be shown after *Operating profit* in the profit and loss account.

Solution

Where goodwill and intangible assets are regarded as having limited useful economic lives, paragraph 15 of FRS 10 requires that they should be amortised on a systematic basis over those lives.

The note on legal requirements in Appendix 1 of FRS 10 says that the profit and loss account formats in the Companies Act 1985 prescribe the headings under which *depreciation and other amounts written off tangible and intangible fixed assets* are to be included. Under Format 1 (see Example 13.1), such amounts are to be included in cost of sales, distribution costs and administrative expenses. Under Format 2 (see Example 13.2), such amounts are shown as a separate heading.

Operating profit is not shown in the Companies Act 1985 formats. However, paragraph 39 of FRS 3 *Reporting Financial Performance* states that *Operating profit* is normally profit before income from shares in group undertakings. The format headings to which amortisation of goodwill and intangible assets should be allocated appear before the line item *Income from shares in group undertakings*. Therefore, the amortisation of goodwill should be charged in arriving at (i.e., before) *Operating profit*.

Source: Adapted from Holgate, P. and McCann, H. 1998. 'Accounting solutions – goodwill amortisation', *Accountancy International*, April, p.76

In certain circumstances, purchased goodwill is considered *not* to have a limited useful economic life. Where this is the case, it should not be amortised. This is a departure from specific requirements of companies' legislation. Where this policy is applied, the true and fair override is invoked (for further discussion of the true and fair override provisions see Chapter 13).

Both Kingfisher plc in Exhibit 17.9 and Incepta Group plc in Exhibit 17.10 disclose the use of the true and fair override in their goodwill accounting policies. As in Exhibit 17.9, Incepta in Exhibit 17.10 refers to undertaking annual impairment reviews (in the absence of goodwill amortisation) to assess the appropriateness of the goodwill's carrying amount. Impairment reviews are discussed later in this section.

Exhibit 17.10 **True and fair override for goodwill not amortised**
Incepta Group plc Annual Report 2000

Notes to the financial statements (extract)
1 Accounting policies (extract)
(8) Goodwill and intangible assets (extract)
Goodwill arising on acquisitions of businesses, associated undertakings or subsidiary undertakings is calculated as the excess of the fair value of the consideration given and costs of acquisition over the fair value of the separable net assets acquired. Goodwill arising on acquisitions up to and including 28 February 1998 was written off against reserves immediately on acquisition. In accordance with FRS 10 *Goodwill and Intangible Assets*, goodwill arising on acquisitions on or after 1 March 1998 is capitalised as an intangible fixed asset and amortised over its estimated useful economic life. Goodwill previously written off directly to reserves has not been reinstated on the balance sheet, but written off directly against the profit and loss reserve in accordance with the transitional provisions of FRS 10.

The directors are of the opinion that the intangible assets of the Group have an indefinite economic life given the durability of the Group's brand names, their ability to sustain long-term profitability, their proven ability to maintain market leadership and the Group's commitment to develop and enhance their value across its network of offices worldwide. In accordance with FRS 10 and FRS 11, *Impairment of Fixed Assets and Goodwill*, the carrying values of intangible assets are reviewed annually for impairment on the basis stipulated in FRS 11 and adjusted to the recoverable amount if required. The individual circumstances of each acquisition are assessed to determine the appropriate treatment of any related goodwill.

The financial statements depart from the requirement of companies' legislation to amortise goodwill over a finite period in order to give a true and fair view, for the reasons outlined above. If the goodwill arising on all acquisitions made since 1 March 1998 had been amortised over a period of 20 years, operating profit for the year ended 29 February 2000 would have decreased by £1.6 million (1999 – £0.5 million).

Cadbury Schweppes in Exhibit 17.11 discloses that it does not amortise goodwill arising on its associate.

Exhibit 17.11 **Goodwill on associate not amortised**
Cadbury Schweppes Annual Report and Form 20-F 2000

Accounting Policies (extract)
o Intangibles and goodwill (extract)
The Group has concluded that goodwill arising on its associate, Dr Pepper/Seven Up Bottling Group ('DPSUBG'), should not be amortised as it has an indefinite useful economic life. This investment is considered to have indefinite durability that can be demonstrated, and the value of the investment can be readily measured.

DPSUBG operates in a longstanding and profitable market sector; the US soft drinks bottling industry has over 100 years of history. The sector has high market entry barriers due to the nature of licence agreements with soft drinks concentrate owners (including the Group's subsidiary Dr Pepper/Seven Up, Inc ('DPSU') and the capital required to operate as a bottler and distributor. As an associate, the company is managed separately from the Group and can be valued on a discounted cash flow basis.

The Group has not amortised this goodwill, a departure from the Companies Act 1985 paragraph 21 of Schedule 4, for the over-riding purpose of giving a true and fair view of the Group's results, for the reasons outlined above. If the goodwill arising on DPSUBG and ABI had been amortised over a period of 20 years, operating profit and investment in associates would have decreased by £15m in 2000 (1999: £10m; 1998: £5m).

Determining useful economic life

Although there are many examples of companies justifying an indefinite useful life for goodwill on specific acquisitions, a finite useful life is more typical for the vast majority of goodwill on acquisition.

FRS 10 (paragraph 2) defines useful economic life as follows:

> The useful economic life of purchased goodwill is the period over which the value of the underlying business acquired is expected to exceed the values of its identifiable net assets.

Under FRS 10, there is a rebuttable presumption that useful economic life is 20 years or less. However, useful economic life can be shown to be greater than 20 years or indefinite. A useful life of greater than 20 years can be adopted only if:

- the durability of the acquired business can be demonstrated and justifies estimating useful life at more than 20 years
- goodwill is capable of continued measurement.

These requirements are illustrated in Exhibits 17.5, 17.9, 17.10 and 17.11. Kingfisher in Exhibit 17.9 justifies not amortising goodwill arising on its acquisition of shares in BUT S.A. The directors consider that the track record of the subsidiary combined with entry barriers operating in the industry demonstrate the durability of the business. Similarly, Cadbury Schweppes in Exhibit 17.11 justifies not amortising goodwill arising on an associate, referring to the longstanding profitable history of the associate, combined with industry barriers to entry.

Review of useful economic life

Useful economic lives should be reviewed at the end of each reporting period and revised if necessary. UITF Abstract 27 *Revision to estimates of the useful economic life of goodwill and intangible assets* reiterates the requirement of FRS 10 that if the useful economic life is revised (either extended or shortened), the carrying value should be amortised over the remaining useful economic life. If revision increases useful life to more than 20 years from the acquisition date, the additional requirements of FRS 10 with respect to such goodwill come into effect (i.e., demonstrate durability and capability of continued measurement; and annual impairment review is required).

Abstract 27 also clarifies the treatment of a change from an indefinite to a finite useful life. The Abstract acknowledges that an entity may initially rebut the presumption that useful economic life of goodwill is 20 years or less because there is evidence that its goodwill has an indefinite life. In a subsequent year, the entity may decide that it is no longer able to rebut the presumption. Amortisation over a period of up to 20 years from the date of acquisition would then be necessary. Such a change is not to be treated as a change of accounting policy. Rather, it is a change in the way in which useful life is estimated. Consequently, the carrying amount at the date of the change in estimate should be amortised over the goodwill's revised remaining useful life.

WPP Group plc in Exhibit 17.12 discloses that the directors have reassessed their opinion that all goodwill and intangible assets have an infinite life. Certain goodwill is now amortised over a period up to a maximum of 20 years, where in the past no goodwill was amortised. The true and fair override is invoked for the goodwill which continues not to be amortised. The revision of asset life leads to amortisation being charged on gross goodwill of £131 million, with a charge for the year of £6.6 million (i.e., £131m ÷ 20 years).

Exhibit 17.12 **Change from infinite to finite useful life of goodwill**
WPP Group plc Annual Report 2000

Accounting policies (extract)
3 Goodwill and intangible fixed assets (extract)
The directors have reassessed their opinion that all the goodwill and intangible assets of the Group have an infinite life. For certain acquisitions, where the directors consider it more appropriate, goodwill is now amortised over its useful life up to a 20 year period, from the date of acquisition. The remaining goodwill and intangible assets of the Group are considered to have an infinite economic life because of the institutional nature of the corporate brand names, their proven ability to maintain market leadership and profitable operations over long periods of time and WPP's commitment to develop and enhance their value. The carrying value of these intangible assets will continue to be reviewed annually for impairment and adjusted to the recoverable amount if required.

The financial statements depart from the specific requirement of companies legislation to amortise goodwill over a finite period in order to give a true and fair view. The directors consider this to be necessary for the reasons given above. Because of the infinite life of these intangible assets, it is not possible to quantify its impact.

Notes to the consolidated balance sheet (extract)
13 Intangible fixed assets (extract)

Goodwill	**£m**
1 January 1999	158.0
Additions	252.3
31 December 1999	410.3
Additions	3,102.1
Amortisation	(6.6)
Impairment	(8.5)
31 December 2000	**3,497.3**

Gross goodwill of £131.0 million is subject to amortisation.

Impairment reviews

Impairment is a reduction in recoverable amount below carrying value. Under FRS 10, goodwill amortised over a useful life of 20 years or less should be reviewed for impairment:

- at the end of the first full financial year following acquisition
- in other periods, if events or changes in circumstances indicate carrying value may not be recoverable.

Goodwill amortised over a useful life of greater than 20 years should be reviewed for impairment at the end of each reporting period. If goodwill on acquisition is found to be impaired, the carrying amount of the investment in the parent's accounts should also be reviewed for impairment.

In July 1998 FRS 11 *Impairment of Fixed Assets and Goodwill* was issued to increase consistency in the treatment of fixed assets and goodwill whose values have fallen below the amounts at which they are recorded in the balance sheet. The FRS sets out the method to be used for measuring the extent of any impairment. Impaired assets must be written down, irrespective of whether the impairment is viewed as permanent or temporary. The objective of the standard is to ensure that fixed assets are recorded at no more than their recoverable amount. Recoverable amount is the higher of net realisable value and value in use. Value in use is measured by forecasting future cash flows that will be generated by using the asset and discounting these cash flows to their present value.

Much of the detail in FRS 11 is concerned with the methods to be applied in measuring value in use. The methods incorporate constraints to make forecasts of future cash flows as reliable as possible. For example, restrictions are placed on long-term growth assumptions to discourage unwarranted optimism. There is also a requirement to monitor forecasts in subsequent years and to recalculate recoverable amount if inaccurate forecasting has caused a past impairment to be overlooked.

Impairment of assets should be recognised when it occurs. Examples of indications of impairment are provided in the standard, e.g., operating losses, significant decline in market value, significant adverse change in market of operation (e.g., entrance of major competitor or change in the regulatory environment). Under FRS 11, in the absence of an obvious impairment of specific assets within the subsidiary, the impairment should be allocated in the following order:

- first, to any goodwill capitalised in the balance sheet
- thereafter, to any capitalised intangible assets
- finally, to the tangible assets on a pro rata or more appropriate basis.

The reversal of past impairment losses should be recognised when the recoverable amount of the asset has increased because of a change in economic conditions or in the expected use of the asset.

The adoption of a policy of impairment review for goodwill with indefinite useful economic lives was illustrated earlier in the chapter, in Exhibits 17.9, 17.10 and 17.12. Incepta Group in Exhibit 17.10 undertakes impairment reviews for all intangible assets not amortised. The group explains how the carrying values of intangibles are reviewed annually for impairment and these values are adjusted to recoverable amount, for any impairment identified.

The question of where impairment of goodwill should be charged in the published consolidated profit and loss account, when the goodwill relates to an overseas associate/equity accounted entity, is addressed in Example 17.9.

Example 17.9 Impaired overseas associate

Example

A group has an overseas associate, which it considers is impaired such that the share of net assets and the goodwill should be provided against. The associate has not provided for the impairment of the net assets in its own financial statements, so the impairment is being reflected in the investor's group accounts.

Required

Should the impairment (of goodwill and net assets) be shown (i) in the *share of associate's operating profit* line or (ii) as *amounts written off financial assets and investments held as current assets* (i.e., the heading in the consolidated profit and loss account after *interest receivable)?*

Solution

Paragraph 27, FRS 9 requires amortisation or write-down of goodwill arising on investments in associates to be shown at the same point as the share of associates' operating results, i.e., immediately after the group operating result. Accordingly, any further impairment of the associate's net assets (over and above that charged by the associate itself) should also be included in the *share of associates' operating profit* in the investing group's profit and loss account.

The impairment of goodwill should be disclosed separately from the share of associate's results in the notes to the financial statements. Goodwill arising on the investor's acquisition of its associates, less any amortisation or write-down, should be included in the carrying amount for the associates and should be disclosed separately.

Source: Adapted from Holgate, P., King, H., and Gaull M. 2002. 'Accounting solutions – impaired overseas associate', *Accountancy*, February, p.87

Negative goodwill

Where negative goodwill results from the comparison of cost and fair value of identifiable assets and liabilities, fair values of acquired assets should be tested for impairment and fair values of liabilities should be tested for completeness. Where negative goodwill persists, it should be shown on the face of the balance sheet as a separate part of *Goodwill*. Negative goodwill, up to the fair values of non-monetary assets acquired (e.g., tangible fixed assets, stock), should be recognised in the profit and loss account in the periods in which non-monetary assets are recovered (through depreciation or sale). Negative goodwill in excess of the fair value of non-monetary assets acquired should be recognised in the profit and loss account in the periods expected to benefit from such assets.

Example 17.10 illustrates how amortisation of negative goodwill through the consolidated profit and loss account is determined by matching that goodwill with the costs of consuming the non-monetary assets acquired.

Example 17.10 Amortisation of negative goodwill

Example

Parent acquires 100% of Subsidiary on 31.12.20X0 for €100,000 when Subsidiary's net assets comprised fixed assets €175,000, stock €25,000 and net monetary assets €50,000. Parent's year-end is 31 December.

The stock was sold during 20X1 and the fixed assets were depreciated over seven years from the date of acquisition.

Required

Show how the negative goodwill is treated in the consolidated profit and loss account.

Solution	**€000**	**€000**
Cost of investment		100
Fair value of net assets acquired		
Fixed assets	175	
Stock	25	
Net monetary assets	50	(250)
Negative goodwill		(150)

Amortisation in the 20X1 consolidated profit and loss account

Non-monetary assets recognised through the profit and loss account in 20X1

	€000
Stock	25
Depreciation (€175,000 ÷ 7 years)	25
	50
Total non-monetary assets at acquisition (175,000 + 25,000)	200
Proportion recognised in 20X1	1/4

This means that a credit of €37,500 (€150,000 × ¼) for negative goodwill will go to the profit and loss account in 20X1. The remaining €112,500 will be carried in the balance sheet as a deduction from positive goodwill as part of intangible fixed assets.

Over the following six years (the remaining useful life of the non-monetary assets originally purchased), the negative goodwill will be released into the consolidated profit and loss account (€18,750 a year).

Source: Adapted from Saksida, M. 1998. 'Another new standard: How should we recognise, amortise and disclose goodwill and intangibles?', *Accountancy*, May, pp.80–81

Example 17.11 discusses how negative goodwill should be treated in the context of acquiring a property investment company whose property assets are not normally depreciated.

Example 17.11 Negative goodwill where non-monetary assets are not depreciated

Example

A company is intending to acquire a property investment company whose shares have traditionally traded at a discount to its asset values. As a result of the acquisition, it is likely that negative goodwill will arise when the assets are fair valued.

Required

Given that investment properties are unlikely to be depreciated, how should the negative goodwill be treated under FRS 10?

Solution

Before recognising any negative goodwill, it is important to ensure that all assets are valued properly at fair value (testing for any impairment) and that all liabilities are checked carefully to ensure that none has been omitted or understated. If negative goodwill then arises, it should be carried as a negative asset and shown separately on the face of the balance sheet, next to any positive goodwill. In the normal situation, the negative goodwill will be amortised (i.e., credited to the consolidated profit and loss account) as the non-monetary assets are recovered through depreciation or sale.

If some investment properties are held on leases and if these are being depreciated over the period of the lease, being less than 20 years, then the negative goodwill should be amortised over that period. In that situation, the total negative goodwill should be apportioned between investment properties that are being depreciated and those that are not, the apportionment being done pro rata on the basis of their fair values.

Where investment properties are not being depreciated, it would not be correct to recognise the negative goodwill attributable to them as an immediate gain, reflecting the fact that the acquirer has made a bargain purchase. To do so would mean recognising gains on non-monetary assets before they are realised.

The correct treatment would be to carry the negative goodwill attributable to them without amortisation and release it to the consolidated profit and loss account if and when the properties are sold. This treatment is based on the fact that the benefit of the bargain purchase is not realised until the properties are sold.

Source: Adapted from Holgate, P. and Ghosh, J. 1999. 'Accounting solutions – negative goodwill', *Accountancy International*, January, p.76

IWP International in Exhibit 17.13 recognises negative goodwill. The group discloses negative goodwill separately from positive goodwill in its intangible fixed assets note, although not on the face of the balance sheet. In its accounting policy note, it discloses that negative goodwill is 'amortised to the profit and loss account over the estimated useful lives of the non-monetary assets to which it relates'.

Exhibit 17.13 **Negative goodwill**
IWP International Annual Report 2000

1 Accounting policies (extract)
Goodwill and intangible assets (extract)
Negative goodwill is offset against positive goodwill and amortised to the profit and loss account over the estimated useful lives of the non-monetary assets to which it relates.

10 Intangible fixed assets (extract)

	Goodwill
	€000
At 1 April 1999	61,079
On acquisition of subsidiaries	—
Additions	11,749
Negative goodwill	(1,386)
Amortisation	(3,776)
At 31 March 2000	67,666

An amount of negative goodwill in the sum of €4,478,000 was crystallised during the year on the acquisition of minority interest (see note 21).

21 Minority interest
The minority interest with a book value at 1 April 1999 of €4,478,000 was acquired during the year for €nil. In accordance with FRS 10, an amount of €3,092,000 has been released to the profit and loss account during the year. The balance of €1,386,000 is being carried in the balance sheet at 31 March 2000 as negative goodwill and will be released over the estimated useful lives of the non-monetary assets to which it relates.

Under FRS 10, purchased goodwill arising on a single transaction should not be divided into positive and negative components. However, Example 17.12 discusses an interesting situation where both positive and negative goodwill arose in a piecemeal acquisition. Positive goodwill arose on the initial purchase of a majority stake in the subsidiary. Negative goodwill resulted from the later transaction when the group bought out the minority shareholder. The group believed the negative goodwill arose from a bargain purchase because the vendor needed to divest quickly.

Example 17.12 Positive and negative goodwill

Example
A company has bought out a minority shareholder in a subsidiary. The acquisition of the original stake in the subsidiary gave rise to a goodwill asset in the acquirer's consolidated financial statements. The consideration paid for the purchase of the minority interest was lower than the fair value of the assets and liabilities attributed to the minority. The company believes the purchase price was a bargain because the vendor needed to divest quickly from that business.

Required
Should the negative goodwill arising from this latest purchase be shown separately on the balance sheet or should it be deducted from the unamortised balance of the positive goodwill that was previously capitalised?

Solution

Accounting for negative goodwill is something of an accounting conundrum at the best of times. If the purchase price for the minority interest had been a fair price, applying the rules in FRS 10 would limit or eliminate any apparent negative goodwill. Paragraph 48 requires an impairment review of the acquired subsidiary's assets when negative goodwill appears to arise. In those circumstances, the original goodwill's carrying value would probably have been impaired and it is unlikely that both positive and negative goodwill would have remained after writing down assets' carrying values to their recoverable amounts.

The situation is unusual because the purchase price for the minority interest was a bargain. If there is no impairment to recognise, negative goodwill should normally be shown as a separate (negative) item on the asset side of the balance sheet, immediately below positive goodwill. Negative goodwill should normally be credited in the profit and loss account in the periods in which the acquired non-monetary assets are depreciated or sold. Paragraph 51 of FRS 10 prohibits both positive and negative goodwill being recognised in respect of a single acquisition transaction. In this case, however, the positive and negative goodwill amounts have arisen from separate transactions, i.e., the original purchase of a majority interest and the subsequent purchase of the minority.

Accordingly, although some may believe it would be sensible to account for a single net amount of goodwill attributable to the subsidiary (since the amounts relate to an increased stake in an existing subsidiary where no new assets are acquired), strictly speaking, FRS 10 requires a separate negative goodwill balance to be recognised.

Source: Adapted from Holgate, P. and Nailor, H. 2000. 'Accounting solutions – positive and negative goodwill', *Accountancy*, December, p.94

Revaluation of goodwill

While impairment of goodwill must be recognised in the period it occurs and reversal of past impairment losses should be recognised when such reversal is demonstrated to have taken place, FRS 10 does not permit goodwill to be revalued upwards under any circumstances. Moreover, legislation following EU Directives prohibits such revaluation.

Transitional arrangements

Reinstatement of goodwill written off against reserves under SSAP 22, which under FRS 10 would not be fully amortised by the balance sheet date, is preferred but not required. There is very little evidence of companies reinstating previously written off goodwill since FRS 10 came into effect (*Company Reporting*, September 1999, 111, p.7). Where goodwill is reinstated under FRS 10, somewhat selective treatment is permitted by the standard (paragraph 69). Reinstatement can be of all goodwill:

- previously eliminated
- arising after 23 December 1989
- arising since the effective date of FRS 7 (accounting periods ending after 23 December 1994).

Reinstatement of goodwill previously written off on the introduction of FRS 10 is illustrated in Exhibit 17.14. Emap was one of the few companies that chose to capitalise goodwill retrospectively. Its *Prior year adjustment* to effect the change was disclosed in note 24 to the accounts. In prior years, £309 million of goodwill had been written off directly to reserves. Emap reinstated this goodwill. Had the capitalisation policy always applied, £130 million accumulated amortisation would have been charged against profits in previous years. Consequently, the net amount reinstated in the balance sheet is £179 million (£309 million – £130 million). As a result of the prior year adjustment, the company's profits from 1999 onwards will be charged with £179 million through goodwill amortisation. These charges would not have gone through the consolidated profit and loss account (unless the businesses to which the goodwill relates were sold) had there been no change of accounting policy and had goodwill been left in reserves.

Exhibit 17.14 **Retrospective capitalisation of goodwill Emap plc Annual Report 1999**

Notes to the accounts (extract)
24 Reserves

	Share premium account £m	Profit and loss account £m	Goodwill reserve £m
At 1 April 1998 as originally reported	200.3	358.8	(308.8)
Prior year adjustment – implementation of FRS 10	—	(130.2)	308.8
At 1 April 1998 as restated	200.3	228.6	—
Exchange movement	—	13.4	—
Rights issue	357.4	—	—
Costs associated with rights issue	(8.1)	—	—
Premium on other shares issues, including QUEST	22.0	(13.3)	—
Retained profit for the year	—	34.3	—
At 31 March 1999	**571.6**	**263.0**	—

As discussed earlier, any goodwill remaining eliminated under FRS 10's transitional provisions may not be shown either in a separate goodwill write-off reserve or as a separate element of reserves on the face of the balance sheet. It must be offset against the profit and loss account or other appropriate reserve. The amount of eliminated goodwill (both positive and negative) must be disclosed in notes and must be put through the profit and loss account on disposal or closure.

Diageo discloses aggregate goodwill written off against the profit and loss account, net of disposals, of £4,094 million (including £156 million in respect of associates) in note 23 to the accounts which was reproduced in Exhibit 17.6.

Example 17.13 discusses the implications, at the time of disposal, of goodwill previously written off against reserves, when the proceeds of disposal of the related investment is an equity stake in an unrelated company.

Example 17.13 Pre-FRS 10 goodwill

Example
A company has sold one of its subsidiaries in exchange for a 10% stake in an unrelated listed company, giving rise to a gain on disposal.

Required
Should the pre-FRS 10 goodwill that was written off directly to reserves be written back to profit and loss account now that the subsidiary has been sold?

Solution
The transitional rules of FRS 10 state that, in the year of disposal, the amount included in the profit and loss account in respect of the profit or loss on disposal should include attributable goodwill, to the extent that it has not previously been charged in the profit and loss account. In this case, the goodwill in question was taken

directly to reserves on acquisition and hence it would appear that it should now be charged to the profit and loss account as part of the gain or loss on disposal.

This is fine if the gain on disposal of the subsidiary is a realised gain (for example, if the company intends to hold its 10% stake in the listed company as a current asset). In this case, the net gain on disposal, after charging the goodwill that was taken directly to reserves, should be recognised in the profit and loss account as an exceptional profit on disposal.

However, if the company intends to hold its investment in the listed company for the long-term, as a fixed asset investment, then any gain on the sale of the subsidiary would be unrealised. Unrealised gains on disposal should be recognised in the statement of total recognised gains and losses (STRGL), rather than the profit and loss account. Therefore, under these circumstances the goodwill should be written back to the STRGL as part of the net unrealised gain on disposal.

Source: Adapted from Holgate, P., King, H., and Gaull, M. 2001. 'Accounting solutions – pre-FRS 10 goodwill', *Accountancy*, August, p.100

In Exhibit 17.8, Glanbia illustrated how goodwill previously written off against reserves can be shown as a negative constituent of revenue reserves, while not being shown as a separate negative reserve (which would conflict with the requirements of FRS 10). Example 17.14 discusses the legitimacy of this presentation and the possible implications for distributable profits.

Example 17.14 Goodwill reserve

Example

Under FRS 10, it is no longer permitted to show a separate negative reserve in respect of goodwill previously written off to reserves.

Required

Discuss whether it is possible, under FRS 10, to show a split of the reserve to which the goodwill is written off and whether there are any implications for distributable profits.

Solution

Reserve against which goodwill is written off

Paragraph 71 of FRS 10 requires that goodwill that remains written off to reserves when the standard is adopted should not be shown as a debit balance on a separate goodwill write-off reserve, but should be offset against the profit and loss account or another appropriate reserve. Groups that have previously carried such debit reserves will have to transfer them to another reserve. This would be accomplished as a prior period adjustment.

The FRS also prohibits companies from showing separately on the face of the balance sheet the amount by which a reserve has been reduced by goodwill write-offs, thus precluding, for example, showing separate totals for the profit and loss account reserve before and after goodwill written off. However, the cumulative goodwill eliminated against reserves must still be disclosed in the notes. There is nothing to prevent a company from analysing, in the notes, the balance of the reserve to which goodwill has been written off between goodwill and other amounts.

Effect on distributable profits

Where, under the old rules, a group wrote off goodwill arising on consolidation immediately to reserves, the write-off did not affect the distributable profits of the group, as these are determined on an individual company basis. Consequently, the transfer of pre-FRS 10 goodwill to the group profit and loss account reserve has no effect on distributable profits.

Where goodwill arises in a company as opposed to a group, then it does affect that company's realised and distributable profits. This is considered in Appendix V to FRS 10, which states that realised reserves should not be reduced immediately where goodwill is written off as a matter of accounting policy and there is no actual

continued overleaf

Example 17.14 Continued

diminution in value. A transfer should be made to realised reserves over the goodwill's useful economic life on a systematic basis in the same way as if the company had amortised goodwill.

Where goodwill debit reserves have to be transferred to a company's profit and loss reserve on adoption of FRS 10, then we consider that the elimination of goodwill does not become a realised loss as this is primarily a matter of presentation. Therefore, FRS 10's prohibition of a separate goodwill write-off reserve should make no difference to the basis on which a company had previously been allocating such goodwill from unrealised to realised reserves, i.e., over its estimated useful economic life.

Source: Adapted from Holgate, P. and McCann, H. 1998. 'Accounting solutions – goodwill reserve', *Accountancy International*, April, p.76

The treatment of goodwill (which was previously written off against reserves) on disposal requires some further explanation. In Example 12.3, the effect of a number of accounting treatments for goodwill on group disposal profit or loss was illustrated. Where goodwill had been fully written off, it did not form part of the carrying amount of the subsidiary disposed of. In general terms, profit was calculated as the difference between proceeds of disposal and the group's share of net assets of the subsidiary at the date of disposal plus any *unamortised* goodwill. Goodwill that has been written off directly against reserves under SSAP 22 is deemed to be unamortised goodwill as far as the consolidated profit and loss account is concerned. Although that goodwill was eliminated from the consolidated balance sheet, it has not been charged against profits *through* the profit and loss account. The FRS 10 requirement that goodwill eliminated directly against reserves must be put through the profit and loss account on disposal or closure aims to ensure that the goodwill cost is matched with revenues from the acquisition at least once in its period of ownership by the investing group.

Incepta explains in Exhibit 17.15 the treatment of goodwill previously written off against reserves and the treatment of the unamortised goodwill remaining in respect of a disposed subsidiary, when calculating profit or loss on disposal.

Exhibit 17.15 **Treatment of goodwill on disposal**
Incepta Group plc Annual Report 2000

Notes to the financial statements (extract)
1 Accounting policies (extract)
(8) Goodwill and intangible assets (extract)
On the subsequent disposal or termination of a previously acquired business, the profit or loss on disposal or termination is calculated after charging the amount of any related goodwill taken directly to reserves on acquisition and the net book value of any related goodwill capitalised in the balance sheet.

Goodwill that was capitalised and amortised under SSAP 22 is now subject to FRS 10's recognition, amortisation and impairment rules. Prior period adjustments are not allowed with respect to amortisation and impairment adjustments. They are changes of estimate arising within the context of applying an amortisation policy.

IAS GAAP

Under IAS 22, goodwill must be amortised over its useful life, with a rebuttable presumption that life will not exceed 20 years. The straight-line method is preferred unless another method better reflects the pattern of consumption of benefits. If the life is taken to exceed 20 years, goodwill should be amortised over the longer life and must be tested for impairment at least annually. In addition, the company must disclose why the 20-year life presumption is rebutted and the factors that played a significant role in determining the useful life. Unlike FRS 10, it is not possible under IAS 22 to avoid amortisation altogether by presuming an indefinite life.

Similarly to FRS 10, negative goodwill is the excess of the investor's interest in the fair values of the investee's net assets over the cost of the acquisition. Negative goodwill must be presented in the balance sheet as a deduction from positive goodwill. The previous treatment of allocating the negative goodwill to reduce the fair values of identifiable assets acquired (which was the benchmark treatment before the 1998 revision of IAS 22) is no longer permitted. Negative goodwill should be recognised in income as follows:

- to the extent that it relates to expectations of future losses and expenses that are identified in the investor's plan for the acquisition and can be measured reliably, it should be recognised as income when the identified future losses and expenses occur
- negative goodwill not exceeding the fair values of the non-monetary assets acquired, however, should be recognised as income over the remaining weighted average useful life of the depreciable/amortisable non-monetary assets acquired. Negative goodwill in excess of the fair values of the non-monetary assets acquired should be recognised as income immediately.

The first treatment, permitted by IAS 22 for releasing negative goodwill to profit and loss account, is not permitted under FRS 10. Although the second treatment is similar to that required by FRS 10, it is more restrictive. The credit to income is mirrored by depreciation and amortisation charges only, otherwise negative goodwill must be released to income immediately under IAS 22. FRS 10 requires negative goodwill to be recognised in the profit and loss account in the periods in which non-monetary assets are recovered through depreciation *or sale*. Moreover, FRS 10 does not refer to immediate release to profit and loss account in any circumstances. Rather it refers, somewhat vaguely, to recognising negative goodwill in the profit and loss account in the periods expected to benefit.

Disclosure requirements

Substantial disclosures are required under both UK and IAS GAAP in relation to goodwill. UK GAAP disclosure requirements are outlined and illustrated in the early parts of this section. Disclosures concerning the fair value of consideration paid are addressed below. Disclosures concerning the fair value of net assets acquired, the detailed disclosure requirements for goodwill under UK GAAP and an outline of IAS GAAP disclosure requirements follow.

Fair value of consideration paid

FRS 7 contains no disclosure requirements as all disclosures concerning fair values were included in FRS 6 *Acquisitions and Mergers*. In relation to purchase consideration, FRS 6 requires disclosure of:

- composition and fair value of consideration given, including details of deferred or contingent consideration

- where there is contingent consideration, the range of possible outcomes and the principal factors that affect the outcome
- where the fair value of the consideration can only be determined on a provisional basis at the end of the accounting period, this should be stated and reasons given. Subsequent material adjustments causing adjustment to goodwill should be disclosed and explained
- cash paid on acquisition, net of cash balances taken over, should be disclosed in a note to the cash flow statement.

Exhibits 17.2 and 17.3 illustrated disclosures relating to contingent and deferred consideration.

Fair value of net assets acquired

FRS 6 requires extensive disclosures relating to fair values and provisions, in addition to those required for purchase consideration already outlined. In relation to fair values of assets and liabilities, FRS 6 requires disclosure of a table ('fair value table') showing:

- book values in the acquired company's books of each major category of assets and liabilities acquired
- fair values of those assets and liabilities at the date of acquisition
- differences between fair values and book values should be analysed between:
  - revaluations
  - adjustments to achieve consistency of accounting policies
  - other significant adjustments (including reasons)
- purchased (positive or negative) goodwill arising on acquisition.

Diageo in Exhibit 17.16 discloses a relatively simple fair value table relating to acquisitions, in note 27 to the accounts.

Exhibit 17.16 **Simple fair value table**
Diageo Annual Report 2000

Notes to the Consolidated Accounts (extract)
27 Purchase of subsidiaries (extract)

	Balance sheet at acquisition £ million	**Fair value adjustments £ million**	**Fair value balance sheets £ million**
Fixed assets	34	—	34
Working capital	13	(2)	11
Net assets acquired	47	(2)	45
Goodwill arising on acquisition			106
Purchase consideration paid			151

Elan in Exhibit 17.17 provides a comprehensive illustration of the fair value table. In detailed commentary following the fair value table, Elan provided additional details on the three specified acquisitions and on the 'other' category. The commentary included explanations of the fair value adjustments, a sample of which (relating to the Dura acquisition) is included in Exhibit 17.17.

Exhibit 17.17 **Fair value table**
Elan Corporation plc Annual Report and Form 20-F 2000

Notes relating to Financial Statements (extract)
22 Acquisitions (extract)
Details of the acquisition of subsidiary undertakings are given below:

2000	Net book values $m	Fair value adjustments $m	Net assets acquired $m	Cost of acquisition $m	Goodwill capitalised $m
Dura	417.3	8.8	426.1	1,590.7	1,164.6
Liposome	97.4	263.1	360.5	731.8	371.3
Neuralab	(9.7)	—	(9.7)	76.4	86.1
Other	(6.0)	—	(6.0)	107.8	113.8
	499.0	271.9	770.9	2,506.7	1,735.8

Details of the book value of net assets acquired are as follows:

	Dura $m	Liposome $m	Neuralab $m	Other $m	Total $m
Intangible assets other than goodwill	421.7	—	1.6	1.9	425.2
Tangible assets	83.0	18.7	—	7.9	109.6
Investments	—	—	—	2.0	2.0
Stocks	24.2	5.9	—	4.7	34.8
Debtors	104.9	8.9	—	10.9	124.7
Liquid resources	170.5	43.7	—	—	214.2
Creditors	(190.5)	(24.9)	(11.9)	(49.1)	(276.4)
Long-term debt	(288.0)	—	—	(9.3)	(297.3)
Cash	91.5	45.1	0.6	25.0	162.2
Net assets/(liabilities) acquired	417.3	97.4	(9.7)	(6.0)	499.0

Dura (extract)
The purchase of Dura has been accounted for as an acquisition under Irish GAAP. The fair value adjustment relates to patents and current products of Dura valued at the date of acquisition, which are separable from the business, of $29.9 million, offset by a deferred tax adjustment of $18.4 million and the write-off of financing costs of $2.7 million. Patents and licences arising on acquisition will be amortised over twenty years. Goodwill arising on acquisition of $1,164.6 million will be amortised over a period of twenty years.

FRS 7 provides that in attributing fair values to assets and liabilities acquired, the basic principle is that fair value should reflect the circumstances at the time of acquisition and should reflect neither the acquirer's intentions nor events subsequent to acquisition. Under FRS 6 paragraph 26, provisions for reorganisation and restructuring costs that are included in the liabilities of the acquired entity and any related asset write-downs made in the 12 months up to the date of acquisition should be shown separately in the fair value table.

For consideration paid, where the fair values of the identifiable assets and liabilities can be determined only on a provisional basis at the end of the accounting period in which the acquisition took place, this should be stated and the reason given. Any material subsequent adjustment to the provisional fair values, with corresponding adjustments to goodwill, should be disclosed and explained.

FRS 6 also requires disclosure of movements on provisions relating to acquisitions. These should be analysed between (i) the amounts used for the specific purpose for which they were created and (ii) amounts released unused or applied for another purpose.

The profit and loss account for periods following the acquisition should disclose costs that have been incurred in reorganising, restructuring or integrating the acquisition. The costs required to be disclosed are those that would not have been incurred had the acquisition not taken place. In addition, they must relate to a project identified and controlled by management as part of an integration programme set up at the time of acquisition or as a direct consequence of an immediate post-acquisition review.

Goodwill

Under FRS 10, the following disclosures are required in relation to goodwill:

- description of the methods used to value intangible assets
- disclose separately for positive and negative goodwill:
  - cost at beginning of financial period and at balance sheet date
  - cumulative amount of provisions for amortisation or impairment at the beginning of the financial period and at the balance sheet date
  - reconciliation of movements during the period, disclosing separately additions, disposals, amortisation, impairment losses, reversals of past impairment losses and amount of negative goodwill written back in the financial period
  - net carrying amount at balance sheet date
- disclose profit or loss on each material disposal of a previously acquired business or business segment
- disclose (i) methods and (ii) periods of amortisation and (iii) reasons for choosing those periods
- where amortisation period is shortened or extended following a review of remaining useful economic life of goodwill (i) the reason and (ii) the effect, if material, should be disclosed in the year of change
- where there has been a change in amortisation method used, the reason and the effect, if material, should be disclosed in the year of change
- where goodwill is amortised over a period of greater than 20 years from the date of acquisition, or is not amortised, the grounds for rebutting the 20-year presumption should be given
- where goodwill is not amortised, a statement of departure from specific requirements of companies' legislation to amortise goodwill must be included in financial statements
- the period over which negative goodwill is being written back to profit and loss account must be disclosed
- where negative goodwill exceeds the fair values of non-monetary assets, (i) the amount and (ii) the source of the 'excess' negative goodwill and (iii) the period(s) in which it is being written back should be explained.

FRS 11 requires disclosure of impairment losses charged in the profit and loss account and in the STRGL.

Diageo provides a good illustration of many of these disclosures. Methods adopted in accounting for goodwill and amortisation periods are disclosed in the accounting policy note 'brands, goodwill and other intangible assets' (Exhibit 17.5). In Exhibit 17.18, goodwill charged during the year is disclosed in note 4 to the accounts, while note 12 discloses movements on goodwill and accumulated amortisation during the year. Note 28 discloses details of subsidiaries sold, including loss on disposal and unamortised goodwill written off on disposal.

Exhibit 17.18 **Goodwill disclosures**
Diageo Annual Report 2000

Notes to the Consolidated Accounts (extracts)

4 Operating costs (extract)

Goodwill and exceptional operating costs Operating costs in the year include goodwill amortisation of £17 million (1999 – £4 million) and exceptional operating costs of £181 million (1999 – £382 million) as follows: other external charges £125 million; staff costs £64 million; depreciation and amortisation of fixed assets £9 million; and other operating income £17 million (1999 – £164 million; £138 million; £80 million; and £nil, respectively).

12 Fixed assets – intangible assets (extract)	**Goodwill £ million**
Cost	
At 30 June 1999	297
Exchange adjustments	13
Additions	106
Disposals	—
At 30 June 2000	416
Amortisation	
At 30 June 1999	4
Provided during the year	17
At 30 June 2000	21
Net book value	
At 30 June 2000	395
At 30 June 1999	293

28 Sale of subsidiaries and businesses (extract)

	2000 £ million	**1999 £ million**
Brands	149	60
Other fixed assets	222	36
Working capital and provisions	(1)	102
Cash	71	—
Minority interest	(10)	—
Goodwill	446	141
Loss on sale	(168)	(9)
Sale consideration	709	330
Cash	(71)	—
Sale consideration received	638	330

IAS GAAP

IAS 22 requires the following disclosures relating to combinations accounted for as acquisitions:

- accounting treatment of goodwill and negative goodwill, including the period of amortisation

- justification if the period of amortisation exceeds 20 years
- where the straight-line basis of amortisation is not used, the basis of amortisation used (with justification for not using the straight-line basis)
- the line items in the profit and loss account in which amortisation of goodwill is included
- reconciliation of goodwill and negative goodwill and related accumulated amortisation at the beginning and end of the period, showing (i) opening balances, (ii) additions, (iii) amortisation charged, (iv) other adjustments, (v) write-offs and (vi) closing balances
- statements where fair values can be determined only on a provisional basis
- any subsequent adjustments to provisional fair values
- to the extent that negative goodwill is carried forward to offset future losses and expenses, a description, the amount and the expected timing of those losses and expenses.

In Exhibit 17.1, Nokia (which reports under IAS GAAP) discloses consideration, fair values of net assets acquired and goodwill arising on each acquisition in note 6 to the accounts. It does not, however, provide this information in a table, neither does it analyse the components of net assets acquired or disclose fair value adjustments by component, as would be required under UK GAAP.

In Exhibit 17.19, Nokia (in note 10 to the accounts) discloses movement on goodwill. Movements on accumulated amortisation (described as 'depreciation' in Nokia's accounts) are not disclosed, although this is required under IAS 22.

Exhibit 17.19 **Goodwill disclosures – IAS GAAP**
Nokia Annual Report 2000

Notes to the Consolidated Financial Statements (extract)

10 Intangible assets (extract)

	2000	**1999**
	EURm	**EURm**
Goodwill		
Acquisitions cost Jan. 1	554	347
Additions	1016	210
Disposals	—	–3
Accumulated depreciation Dec. 31	–458	–318
Net carrying amount Dec. 31	1112	236

Overview of differences between UK GAAP and IAS GAAP

While both FRS 10 and IAS 22 define goodwill and negative goodwill as a residual (i.e., the difference between the fair value of consideration paid and the fair value of net assets acquired), the amounts attributed to goodwill and negative goodwill are likely to differ under the two regulations. This is primarily because of differences in the recognition and measurement of acquired assets and liabilities. In addition, differences in the timing of the recognition of contingent consideration, in amortisation of goodwill and negative goodwill and in the determination of the useful life of goodwill could potentially be significant in individual cases.

Table 17.3 summarises UK GAAP and IAS GAAP regulations concerning goodwill.

Table 17.3 Comparison of requirements relating to measurement, disclosures and accounting for goodwill under UK GAAP and IAS GAAP

UK GAAP	*IAS GAAP*
Measurement	*Measurement*
Fair values at acquisition to reflect conditions at date of acquisition	Fair values to be determined at date of exchange transaction which could be different from date of acquisition
Fair values of identifiable acquired assets and liabilities to be determined at date of acquisition	
Value those inventories that acquiree trades on a market in which it acts as both a buyer and seller at current market prices	
Fair values of other inventories to be lower of replacement cost and net realisable value	Other inventories to be included at selling price less costs to completion, costs of disposal and reasonable profit margin
Include reasonable estimate of fair value of future expected payments in respect of contingent purchase consideration	Such estimates not included in initial cost. Cost adjusted when contingency resolved and additional payment is both probable and capable of reliable measurement
Identifiable net assets should be revalued to fair value at date of increases in stake	Revaluation prohibited on any subsequent increase in stake
Provisions for reorganisation or restructuring should be recognised as post-acquisition	Recognise such provisions at acquisition provided conditions met
Value separate business of acquiree, sold within 12 months, using subsequent sale proceeds	
Disclosures	*Disclosures*
Range of possible outcomes and principal factors affecting estimates of contingent consideration	
Fair value table required	
Separate disclosure of provisions for reorganisation and restructuring costs included in liabilities of acquiree and related write-downs	
Any exceptional profit or loss arising from use of fair values recognised in the acquisition	
Costs incurred in reorganising, restructuring and integrating the acquisition	
Disclose reasons for choice of useful life – all cases	Disclosure of reasons for choice of useful life only required where useful life exceeds 20 years
	Disclose income statement line item within which goodwill amortisation is charged/credited
	Negative goodwill recognised as income when related losses anticipated at acquisition are recognised
Accounting treatment	*Accounting treatment*
Goodwill should not be amortised if its useful life is indefinite, provided durability can be demonstrated and it is capable of continuing measurement and impairment review	Useful life of goodwill is always finite
Negative goodwill is recognised as income when acquired non-monetary assets are consumed or in the periods expected to benefit	Negative goodwill is recognised as income when related future losses and expenses are recognised or on a systematic basis over life of acquired non-monetary assets or immediately if any remains
Impairment review required for goodwill after first full year	First year review not required
Goodwill that is amortised over a period exceeding 20 years (or is not amortised) is subject to an annual impairment review	Goodwill that is amortised over a period exceeding 20 years is subject to an annual impairment review
Review of fair values required when negative goodwill arises	Caution expressed relating to fair values if negative goodwill arises

Summary

This chapter has described the regulations governing the measurement of goodwill and its accounting treatment, including disclosure. In addition, some of the ongoing effects of accounting methods allowed under previous regulations which are now prohibited in the UK (but continue for old acquisitions under transitional arrangements) were discussed and illustrated. Many examples of company disclosures were provided to illustrate the requirements under both UK GAAP and IAS GAAP and examples discussing requirements in particular practical contexts were included.

Learning outcomes

After studying this chapter you should have learnt:

- how to define goodwill and fair value
- how to measure goodwill using book values of net assets acquired and adjustments where fair values of net assets differ from book values
- the implications of the fair value principle for measuring purchase consideration
- how to apply the requirements of FRS 7, FRS 10 and IAS 22 in the context of goodwill
- how to illustrate the application of the UK and IAS regulations by reference to published accounts data
- the main differences between UK GAAP and IAS GAAP regulations for measuring, accounting for and reporting goodwill.

Multiple choice questions

Solutions to these questions are prepared under UK GAAP and are presented in Appendix 1.

17.1 Road and Street

Road purchased 70% of the shares in **Street** on 1 January 20X4. At that date the fixed assets of Street had a net book value of €400,000 and were estimated to have exhausted 50% of their useful life. In their condition at 1 January 20X4 these fixed assets had a realisable value of €350,000 and Road could have purchased identical new fixed assets for €600,000.

The value attributed to the fixed assets of Street under FRS 7 for the purpose of calculating goodwill on acquisition is:

(a) €280,000
(b) €350,000
(c) €400,000
(d) €600,000

17.2 FRS 10

Which of the following is allowed under **FRS 10** *Goodwill and Intangible Assets?*:

(a) The revaluation of goodwill from €10,000 to €15,000 during the period of amortisation
(b) A revision of the estimated useful economic life of goodwill from 5 years to 8 years during the period of amortisation
(c) An accounting policy which permits an excess of the aggregate of the fair values of the separable net assets acquired over the fair value of the consideration given to be credited directly to reserves or amortised through the profit and loss account
(d) An accounting policy which permits purchased goodwill to be written off on acquisition against reserves or to be amortised through the profit and loss on ordinary activities

17.3 Rook

Rook purchased the net assets of a business. The consideration for the purchase was the issue of 100,000 €1 ordinary shares with a fair value of €1.10 each. On the date of purchase the books of the acquired businesses showed the following assets:

	Book value	Fair value
	€	€
Goodwill	2,500	
Separable net assets		
Patents	7,000	10,000
Plant	60,000	69,000
Net current assets	15,000	

Under the provisions of FRS 10, the goodwill arising on this purchase is:

(a) € 3,500
(b) € 6,000
(c) €13,500
(d) €16,000

Self-assessment exercises

Solutions to these self-assessment exercises can be found at:
www.thomsonlearning.co.uk/accountingandfinance/piercebrennan

17.1 Charlton and Venables

Charlton purchased 75% of the share capital of **Venables** on 1 April 20X4. The purchase consideration was €3,500,000 payable in cash immediately and a further sum of €750,000 due on 1 April 20X5. In addition, in order to encourage the original owners to maintain their interest in the company and to retain the goodwill acquired, a further sum of €1,000,000 will be payable on 1 January 20X8 if the profit before taxation of Venables for the three years ending 30 June 20X7 exceeds €1,500,000.

The draft balance sheets of both companies have just been prepared to 30 June 20X4 and are as follows:

	Charlton	Venables
	€000	€000
Fixed assets	5,250	1,600
Investment in Venables	3,500	—
Stock	2,150	800
Debtors	1,500	600
Cash	200	500
Creditors	(1,800)	(1,000)
	10,800	2,500
Share capital (€1 ordinary shares)	3,000	500
Revenues	7,800	2,000
	10,800	2,500

The following information is available:

1 The draft profit and loss account indicates that the pre-tax profits for the year ended 30 June 20X4 are €400,000 and are expected to grow by approximately 10% per annum.
2 The draft accounts indicate that the net assets of Venables had increased by €180,000 during the post-acquisition period.
3 The directors of Charlton were aware that there was a need to substantially reorganise the business of Venables and they have assessed these costs at €450,000. These have yet to be reflected in the financial statements of Charlton.

4 The group amortises goodwill over a period of five years from the date of acquisition, with goodwill calculated on a pro rata basis in the year of acquisition.
5 Charlton has already paid an interim dividend of €420,000 on 1 January 20X4 based on directors' expectations of profits for the year ended 30 June 20X4 and are proposing to offer a share scrip issue of €600,000 for the final proposed dividend. The market value of the shares is currently €2 each. No entry has been made to reflect this scrip dividend in the company's books.

   Venables has paid an interim dividend of €160,000 on 1 January 20X4 based on directors' expectations for the year to 30 June 20X4. Venables is now proposing to pay a final dividend of €400,000. No entry has been made in either company's books to reflect the proposed dividend.

Required

(a) Prepare journal entries to record the transactions in note 5.

(b) Prepare the consolidated balance sheet of Charlton and its subsidiary as at 30 June 20X4 in accordance with standard accounting practice.

17.2 Palma International and Pizza

Palma International is an important participant in the world's food, electronics and leisure industries. An entrepreneurial management recognises the importance to marketing strategy of brand names and has been prepared to pay a high price to acquire **Pizza**, a company with a well-known brand in the food industry.

However, funding constraints obliged Palma to phase its acquisition over four years as follows:

Date of acquisition		Number of shares millions	Cost €m
30.9.20X0	purchased *cum* div.	50	150
1.4.20X1	purchased *ex* div.	75	300
1.4.20X2	purchased *ex* div.	150	550
1.4.20X3	purchased *ex* div.	100	400

The following are the summarised financial statements of the two companies:

Pizza: Summarised balance sheets as at 31 March

	20X1 €m	20X2 €m	20X3 €m	20X4 €m
Goodwill	500	400	300	200
Other net assets	513	645	800	977
	1,013	1,045	1,100	1,177
Ordinary €1 shares	500	500	500	500
Reserves	513	545	600	677
	1,013	1,045	1,100	1,177

Pizza: Summarised profit and loss accounts for year ended 31 March

	20X1 €m	20X2 €m	20X3 €m	20X4 €m
Profit after tax	38	65	110	132
Dividends: Interim	(10)	(15)	(25)	(25)
Final	(7)	(18)	(30)	(30)
Retained profit for year	21	32	55	77

Palma International: Draft summarised balance sheets as at 31 March

	20X1	20X2	20X3	20X4
	€m	€m	€m	€m
Investment in Pizza	150	450	1,000	1,400
Other net assets	4,240	4,190	4,000	3,800
	4,390	4,640	5,000	5,200
Ordinary €1 shares	1,000	1,000	1,000	1,000
Reserves	3,390	3,640	4,000	4,200
	4,390	4,640	5,000	5,200

Palma International: Draft summarised profit and loss accounts for year ended 31 March

	20X1	20X2	20X3	20X4
	€m	€m	€m	€m
Profit after tax	104	330	520	400
Dividends: Interim	(30)	(40)	(80)	(100)
Final	(30)	(40)	(80)	(100)
Retained profit for year	44	250	360	200

The following information is also available:

1. Palma credited the income account in the general ledger with the dividend received from Pizza on 15 October 20X0.
2. During the year ended 31 March 20X3 Pizza made sales to Palma (all of which are still in stock at year-end) of €100m with a mark-up of 20% on the transfer price.
3. It is group policy to recognise goodwill as an asset and carry it in the balance sheet. Goodwill is written off to the profit and loss account on a straight-line basis over a life of ten years.
4. The assets in the financial statements are shown at fair values.
5. A holding of more than 20% would give Palma significant influence over Pizza.

Required

(a) Prepare the summarised consolidated balance sheet for Palma International and its subsidiaries for each of the four years 20X1, 20X2, 20X3 and 20X4, including the investment in Pizza in accordance with accounting treatments prescribed in any relevant regulations. Include the relevant note to the accounts for those statements in which goodwill would be shown.

(b) Draft a reply to a director's request that, since purchased goodwill is capitalised even though volatile and unidentifiable, then to be consistent, internally generated goodwill should be similarly treated and carried in the balance sheet. He argues that this would have the double advantage of increasing the group's net worth which, in turn, would facilitate raising funding for further acquisitions.

(Work to the nearest €m.)

Examination-style questions

17.1 Fair value

Fair value as a concept to underpin external financial reporting has long been a controversial topic.

Required

(a) Explain what fair value accounting means.
(b) Explain how the fair value concept is applied in the context of FRS 7.
(c) List three other areas of potential application of fair value accounting in the context of UK and International Accounting Standards.

17.2 Territory and Yukon

FRS 10 *Goodwill and Intangible Assets* regulates the accounting treatment of goodwill in the UK and Ireland. Accounting for goodwill was a contentious issue for several years. FRS 10 attempts to eliminate the problems associated with its predecessor, SSAP 22 *Accounting for goodwill*.

Required

(a) Describe the requirements of FRS 10 regarding the initial recognition and measurement of goodwill and intangible assets.
(b) Explain the approach set out in FRS 10 for the amortisation of positive goodwill and intangible assets.
(c) **Territory** acquired 80% of the ordinary share capital of **Yukon** on 31 May 20X6. The balance sheet of Yukon at 31 May 20X6 was:

Fixed assets	**€000**
Intangible assets	6,020
Tangible assets	38,300
	44,320
Current assets	
Stocks	21,600
Debtors	23,200
Cash	8,800
	53,600
Creditors: Amounts falling due within one year	(24,000)
Net current assets	29,600
Total assets less current liabilities	73,920
Creditors: Amounts falling due after more than one year	
Provision for liabilities and charges	(12,100)
Accruals and deferred income	(886)
Deferred government grants	(2,700)
	58,234
Capital and reserves	
Called-up share capital in ordinary shares of €1	10,000
Share premium account	5,570
Profit and loss account	42,664
	58,234

Additional information relating to the balance sheet:

1 The intangible assets of Yukon were brand names currently utilised by the company. The directors felt that they were worth €7million but there was no readily ascertainable market value at the balance sheet date or any information to verify the directors' estimated value.
2 The provisional market value of the land and buildings was €20 million at 31 May 20X6. This valuation had again been determined by the directors. A valuer's report received on 31 November

20X6 stated the market value of land and buildings to be €23 million as at 31 May 20X6. The depreciated replacement cost of the remainder of the tangible fixed assets was €18 million.

3 The replacement cost of stock was estimated at €25 million and its net realisable value was deemed to be €20 million. *Debtors* and *Creditors: Amounts falling due within one year* are stated at the amounts expected to be received and paid.

4 *Creditors: Amounts falling due after more than one year* was a long-term loan. The initial loan on 1 June 20X5 was €11 million at an interest rate of 10% per annum. The total amount of the interest is to be paid at the end of the loan period on 31 May 20X9. The current bank lending rate is 7% per annum.

5 The provision for liabilities and charges relates to costs of reorganisation of Yukon. This provision had been set up by the directors of Yukon prior to the offer by Territory and the reorganisation would have taken place even had Territory not purchased the shares of Yukon. Additionally, Territory wishes to set up a provision for future losses of €10 million which it feels will be incurred by the group.

6 The purchase consideration was 25 million €1 ordinary shares of Territory at an agreed price of €2 per share (the market price of the shares at the date of acquisition was €2.25), plus €1 per Yukon ordinary share.

7 Goodwill is to be dealt with in accordance with FRS 10. The estimated useful economic life is deemed to be ten years. The directors of Yukon informed Territory that as at 31 May 20X7 the brand names were worthless as the products to which they related had recently been withdrawn from sale because they were deemed to be a health hazard.

8 A full year's amortisation is charged in the year of purchase.

Required

Calculate the charge for goodwill in the group financial statements for accounting periods ending on 31 May 20X6 and 31 May 20X7.

17.3 Heywood and Fast Trak

On 1 July 20X9 **Heywood** was finally successful in acquiring the entire share capital of **Fast Trak**. The terms of the bid by Heywood had been improved several times as rival bidders also made offers for Fast Trak. The terms of the initial bid by Heywood were:

- 20 million €1 ordinary shares in Heywood. Each share had a stock market price of €3.50 immediately prior to the bid
- a cash element of €15 million.

The final bid that was eventually accepted on 1 July 20X9 by Fast Trak's shareholders had improved the cash offer to €25 million and included a redeemable loan note of a further €25 million that will be redeemed on 30 June 20Y3. It carried no interest but market rates for this type of loan note were 13% per annum. There was no increase in the number of shares offered but at the date of acceptance the price of Heywood's shares on the stock market had risen to €4.00 each.

The present value of €1 receivable in a future period where interest rates are 13% can be taken as:

at end of year three	€0.70
at end of year four	€0.60

The fair value of Fast Trak's net assets, other than its intangible assets, was assessed by Heywood to be €64 million. This value had not changed significantly throughout the bidding process. The details of Fast Trak's intangible assets acquired were:

1 The brand name of 'Kleenwash' a dishwashing liquid: A company called 'Brands-R-Us' was commissioned to value the brand. Their report, based on a 'multiple of product turnover', attached a figure of €12 million to the brand.

2 A government licence to extract a radioactive ore from a mine for the next ten years: The licence is difficult to value as there was no fee payable for it. However, as Fast Trak is the only company that can mine the ore, the directors of Heywood have estimated the licence to be worth €9 million. The mine itself has been included as part of Fast Trak's property.

3 A fishing quota of 10,000 tonnes per annum in European waters: A specialist company called Quotasales actively trades in these and other EU quotas. The price per tonne of fishing quotas at

the date of acquisition was €1,600. The quota is for an indefinite period of time, but in order to preserve fish stocks the EU has the right to vary the weight of fish that may be caught under a quota. The weights of quotas are reviewed annually.

4 The remainder of the intangible assets is attributable to the goodwill of Fast Trak.

Required

(a) Discuss the initial recognition criteria, and subsequent accounting treatment for goodwill and intangible assets contained in FRS 10 *Goodwill and Intangible Assets*.

(b) Prepare an extract of the intangible fixed assets of Fast Trak that would be separately recognised in the consolidated financial statements of Heywood on 1 July 20X9. Your answer should include an explanation justifying your treatment of each item.

17.4 Louth and Meath

Louth, whose financial year-end is 30 June 20X5, acquired 90% of **Meath** on 31 March 20X5. Summary balance sheets as at 30 June 20X5 for both Louth and Meath were as follows:

	Louth	**Meath**
	€000	**€000**
Tangible fixed assets	11,825	3,440
Investment in Meath	6,200	—
Net current assets	9,475	275
Long-term liabilities	(2,200)	—
	25,300	3,715
Share capital		
Ordinary shares of €1 each, fully paid up	5,500	1,100
Share premium	2,750	—
Revaluation reserve	7,150	—
Profit and loss account	9,900	2,615
	25,300	3,715

In addition the following information has been provided:

1 The book values of the tangible fixed assets of Meath as at 31 March 20X5 were recorded at €3,000,000 but they were valued by professional valuers at €4,500,000. In addition the net current assets as at 30 June 20X5 were valued at €800,000 but Louth has estimated that further obsolete stock and bad debts still needed to be provided for at 31 March 20X5, amounting to €50,000 and €30,000 respectively.

2 In the three months to 30 June 20X5, Meath made profits of €160,000 and these are reflected within current assets.

3 Louth paid €6,200,000 for its shares in Meath on 31 March 20X5. However, the final price will depend on the profitability of Meath for the three years ended 30 June 20X8. Provided the company achieves a total of €1,900,000 target profits, a further cheque for €1,500,000 will be payable to the vendors. The company believes that there is an 80% probability that the target profits will be met.

4 Over the years, Meath has been able to build up valuable brands. Professional valuers have indicated that these should have been valued at €600,000 on 31 March 20X5. In addition Louth has itself built up its own brands which are worth €1,100,000 at the year-end.

5 The directors of Louth have estimated that in order to develop the business of Meath on a proper footing, redundancies are inevitable and these have been estimated at €600,000 at the time of acquisition.

6 The acquisition expenses amounted to €50,000 for professional fees and it is estimated that the directors' own time on the acquisition amounted to €40,000.

7 Meath has always valued its stocks on the FIFO (first-in first-out) basis in its financial statements. However, on 31 March 20X5, had the company adopted the weighted average basis, a downward stock adjustment of €110,000 would have been necessary.

8 The group amortises goodwill over a five-year period.

9 The directors of Louth require an immediate investment of €850,000 in new plant and machinery in Meath in order to make that company profitable.

Required

(a) Prepare the consolidated balance sheet of Louth and its subsidiary as at 30 June 20X5.

(b) Prepare the 'fair value table' that should be disclosed in the Group financial statements under FRS 6 *Acquisitions and Mergers*.

(c) Prepare a memorandum to the managing director outlining which method of business combination would be required under FRS 6 and explaining how each of the matters raised in this question should be treated in the business combination.

Part Five

Other aspects of consolidation

18

Foreign subsidiaries

Learning objectives

After studying this chapter you should be able to:

- explain how foreign currency transactions are accounted for in the individual accounts under UK GAAP and IAS GAAP
- translate foreign currency financial statements using the closing rate method
- translate foreign currency financial statements using the temporal method
- outline the disclosure requirements applying to foreign currency transactions under UK GAAP and IAS GAAP
- account for subsidiaries operating in hyperinflationary economies under UK GAAP and IAS GAAP
- differentiate between the regulations applying to foreign subsidiaries under UK GAAP and IAS GAAP

Introduction

Most European public companies engage in international trading activities. Such international business is normally transacted in currencies other than the local reporting currency. The move towards a single European market has added to the scale and breadth of international business activity. However, the introduction of a single European currency, the euro, heralds a reduction in the volume of foreign currency transactions and a consequent reduction in the accounting problems arising from conducting business through foreign currencies. That said, this aspect of accounting is still important as many companies have operations outside the eurozone, such as in the UK and the US.

The treatment of transactions denominated in foreign currencies can have a significant impact on a company's reported results and financial position. A definitive standard on foreign currency took a considerable length of time to develop in the UK, which reflected the complexity of the topic, the diversity of treatments being used and the perceived impact of the various proposals on those accounts where changes would be required.

Accounting standards on accounting for foreign currency transactions and translations, and further guidance thereon, have been issued under both UK GAAP and IAS GAAP.

UK GAAP

This section starts with an overview of the regulations applying to foreign currency transactions and foreign currency translation under UK GAAP. The treatment of foreign currency transactions in individual accounts is then discussed, followed by the treatment of foreign subsidiaries and associates in consolidated financial statements. The two methods of translation, closing rate/net investment method and the temporal method are then explained and the section concludes by setting out the disclosure requirements in relation to foreign currency under UK GAAP.

Regulations

SSAP 20 *Foreign Currency Translation* was issued in 1983. It distinguishes between accounting practice required in individual company accounts and that required in consolidated financial statements.

Further guidance on accounting for foreign currency transactions and translations is provided in UITF Abstract 9 *Accounting for operations in hyper-inflationary economies*, which was issued in 1993, and in UITF Abstract 19 *Tax on gains and losses on foreign currency borrowings that hedge an investment in a foreign enterprise*, issued in 1998.

Individual company accounts

Although not immediately germane to a book on group accounts, a discussion of the accounting treatment of foreign currency transactions in the accounts of individual companies is considered to be a necessary precursor to a consideration of foreign currency translations in the context of group accounts. Before considering the issues involved in translating foreign subsidiary and associated undertaking financial statements for consolidation, it is necessary to understand how these investments, and related debt financing, have been dealt with in the accounts of investors.

The aspect most relevant to the preparation of group accounts is translation of the financial statements of foreign entities classified as subsidiaries or associates into the currency of the reporting entity (i.e., the parent undertaking), to be included in the consolidated financial statements. This issue is returned to later in this chapter.

Assets, liabilities, revenues and expenses from transactions denominated in foreign currencies should be translated at the rate of exchange ruling on the date of the transaction (or at an average rate, if it is a reasonable approximation of the actual rate). If the transaction is to be settled at a contracted rate or is covered by a forward rate, then the contract or forward rate (respectively) should be used instead of the actual rate.

If the transaction is unsettled at the year-end, the question of retranslation arises. Normally, non-monetary assets (e.g., fixed assets, stock) should not be retranslated when foreign exchange rates change prior to settlement. However, monetary assets and liabilities should be retranslated at the balance sheet date using the rate of exchange ruling on that date. Table 18.1 lists assets and liabilities that would be classified as either non-monetary or monetary.

Table 18.1 Non-monetary and monetary assets and liabilities

Non-monetary assets	*Monetary assets and liabilities*
Buildings, plant and machinery	Cash and bank balances
Investments	Loans
Stock (inventories)	Amounts receivable
	Amounts payable

Treatment of exchange differences

If the foreign exchange rate when the transaction is settled differs from that used when the transaction was originally recorded, or when monetary items were retranslated at the balance sheet date, a gain or loss arises. Exchange differences which have arisen on settled transactions during the period, and those arising on unsettled retranslated items at the balance sheet date, should be included in the profit or loss of the period. Their categorisation as normal or exceptional, and their inclusion in continuing or discontinued activities is determined in accordance with the criteria of FRS 3. Where gains arise on unsettled long-term items, SSAP 20 recommends a cautious approach to their recognition.

SSAP 20 suggests that unrealised gains on long-term monetary items may require special consideration, but that normally they should be included in the results of the period. Equally, where there are doubts as to the marketability or convertibility of the currency in question, it may be necessary to restrict the amount of gains (or the amount by which exchange gains exceed past losses on the same item) recognised in the profit and loss account. It may be necessary instead to record them in reserves.

Where a foreign currency transaction is covered by a foreign currency forward contract, the settlement rate of exchange will be known on the date of the transaction. In such cases, the transaction is initially recorded at the forward contract rate. As a result, no settlement exchange gain or loss will subsequently arise.

Table 18.2 summarises the requirements of SSAP 20 in relation to recognition of foreign exchange differences on transactions.

Table 18.2 Accounting for exchange differences in individual company accounts

Difference arising on:	*Accounting treatment*
Settled transactions	→ Profit and loss account for year
Unsettled short term	→ Profit and loss account for year
Unsettled long term: Losses	→ Profit and loss account for year
Unsettled long term: Gains	→ Profit and loss account for year, *but* ◆ amount of gain ◆ amount by which gain exceeds past losses *may require to be restricted where doubts exist with respect to convertibility or marketability of currency*

Where a forward contract exists, it avoids foreign currency exposure risk. Use contract rate to record transaction initially, no subsequent exchange gain or loss

An example of a foreign currency accounting policy also specifying the role of forward contracts under UK GAAP is provided by Rolls-Royce in Exhibit 18.1.

Exhibit 18.1 **Accounting policy incorporating forward contracts Rolls-Royce plc Annual Report 2000**

1 Accounting Policies (extract)

Foreign currencies (extract)

Assets and liabilities denominated in foreign currencies are translated into sterling at the rate ruling at the year end or, where applicable, at the estimated sterling equivalent, taking account of future foreign exchange and similar contracts … Other exchange differences, including those arising from currency conversions in the usual course of trading, are taken into account in determining profit on ordinary activities before taxation.

Examples of the accounting treatment of foreign currency transactions are shown in Examples 18.1 and 18.2. Example 18.1 shows the foreign currency transaction initially recorded at the rate ruling on the date of the transaction. When the debtor settles and pays the sum due, the cash received is translated at the foreign exchange rate on the date of receipt. The rate changed and the euro amount received is lower than the euro amount at which the asset (debtor) was originally recorded. As a result, a loss on exchange has to be recorded to reduce the debtor to the sum actually received. Because the transaction was denominated in Swiss francs, it is settled when the required amount of Swiss francs is received. The risk of changes in the exchange rate is borne by the selling entity and, consequently, the loss is recorded in that entity's accounts.

Example 18.1 Recording foreign currency transactions (1)

Example
A eurozone company sells to a Swiss company in May 20X0
Invoice amount: CHF (Swiss francs) 750,000
Cash received August 20X0

Rates of exchange

May 20X0	CHF 1.6521	= €1
August 20X0	CHF 1.8075	= €1

Required
Show how these transactions are recorded.

Solution

Workings	€	€
Sales (750,000 ÷ 1.6521)	453,968	
Cash received (750,000 ÷ 1.8075)	414,938	
Loss on exchange	39,030	
Double entries		
(i) Initial recording		
Dr Debtors	453,968	
Cr Sales		453,968
Recording sale in May 20X0		
(ii) At settlement date		
Dr Bank	414,938	
Dr Loss on exchange	39,030	
Cr Debtors		453,968
Recording payment in August 20X0		

In Example 18.2, the foreign currency monetary item recorded for the new machine is included in creditors. The creditors are recorded at the rate on the date of purchase. However, by the time the company comes to settle the creditors outstanding, the rate has adversely changed. The euro amount required to settle the foreign currency sum due is greater than that recorded initially. As a result, a loss on exchange has to be recorded.

This example differs from Example 18.1 in that the transaction straddles the year-end. As a result, the loss on exchange is recorded in two stages: (i) between the date of the initial transaction and the year-end and (ii) between the year-end date and the settlement date. Example 18.2 shows that the total loss is €22,222, of which:

- €10,526 $_{\text{loss from date of transaction to year-end date}}$ is recorded at the year-end date
- €11,696 $_{\text{loss from year-end date to settlement date}}$ is recorded at the settlement date.

Example 18.2 Recording foreign currency transactions (2)

Example

A eurozone company with a financial year ending on 31 March purchases fixed assets from Barcland costing 400,000 barcs (B) in November 20X0 when the exchange rate was €1 = B2. The supplier was paid in April 20X1.

Rates of exchange

31.3.20X1	€1 = B1.90
April 20X1	€1 = B1.80

Required

Show how this transaction would be recorded (i) at the date of the transaction, (ii) at the balance sheet date and (iii) at the settlement date.

Solution

Workings	€	€
Fixed assets (400,000 ÷ 2)	200,000	
Creditors retranslation (400,000 ÷ 1.90)	210,526	210,526
Loss on exchange at year-end	10,526	
Cash paid (400,000 ÷ 1.80)		222,222
Loss on exchange (222,222 – 210,526)		11,696

Double entries	€	€
(i) Initial recording		
Dr Fixed assets	200,000	
Cr Creditors		200,000
Recording purchase of fixed assets in November 20X0		
(ii) At balance sheet date		
Dr Exchange loss	10,526	
Cr Creditors		10,526
Recording creditors in March 20X1 at the exchange rate ruling at the balance sheet date		
(iii) At settlement date		
Dr Creditors	210,526	
Dr Exchange loss	11,696	
Cr Bank		222,222
Recording settlement of creditor in April 20X1		

Foreign currency borrowings

There is one exception to the rule that all exchange differences arising in the individual company accounts should be included in the profit or loss for the year and that non-monetary items should not be retranslated. The exception arises where a company uses foreign currency borrowings to finance or provide a hedge against a foreign equity investment (a non-monetary asset). SSAP 20 permits an offset procedure. In this situation, the foreign equity investment *may* be denominated in foreign currency (rather than fixed at the amount at which it was originally translated). It is retranslated at each balance sheet date. Any differences arising should be transferred directly to reserves. Availing of the offset procedure is optional but, once adopted, the policy must be applied consistently.

Where the offset procedure is not invoked, all differences on borrowings are included in the profit or loss for the year. Where the offset procedure is invoked, foreign currency differences on the retranslation of the borrowings can be offset in reserves against, and up to a maximum of, translation differences relating to foreign equity investments in that period.

The purpose of the offset exception is to reflect the effects of hedging (as a defence against exchange rate uncertainty) in the accounts. This would not be possible if borrowings alone were retranslated at each balance sheet date.

Under FRS 3, direct transfers to reserves should be disclosed in the STRGL. UITF Abstract 19 *Tax on gains and losses on foreign currency borrowings that hedge an investment in a foreign enterprise* requires any related tax charges and credits taken to the STRGL to be disclosed separately.

Borrowings used in the offset procedure should not exceed the total cash expected to be generated by the investments over their period of ownership by the reporting entity. UITF 19 clarifies that the amount of cash that the investment is expected to generate should be the after-tax amount of dividends and receipts from disposal.

It is not necessary to match the foreign currencies. The offset procedure can be used when the borrowing and investment are in different currencies and different amounts.

To summarise, for foreign equity investment financed by foreign borrowing:

- foreign borrowing requires retranslation at each balance sheet date until repayment
- differences on retranslation normally go to the profit and loss account
- equity investment, a non-monetary asset, usually remains at the original translated amount
- special circumstances of hedge provided by foreign borrowings against exchange risk attaching to foreign investment are recognised in SSAP 20
- an offset procedure is allowed where foreign equity investment is financed by foreign borrowing
- equity investment is denominated in foreign currency as are borrowings
- both are retranslated at each year-end
- differences on investment retranslation offset against differences on borrowings restatement in reserves. A number of conditions attach to the offset provisions.
  - offset is only allowed to the extent of exchange differences on retranslation of the investment. Any excess of difference on retranslation of borrowings (over difference on retranslating investment) is dealt with in the profit and loss account for the year
  - foreign borrowings used in offset should not exceed cash expected to be generated from the equity investment over the lifetime of the investor's holding
  - policy should be applied consistently.

The offset provisions in individual company accounts are illustrated in Examples 18.3 and 18.4 (and in Example 18.13 later in this chapter). Up to eight steps are involved in arriving at a solution in each case, as follows:

1. Translate investments at exchange rate on date of acquisition.
2. Translate borrowings at rate on date of transaction.
3. Denominate carrying amount of investment in foreign currency and retranslate at closing rate.
4. Calculate difference on investment.
5. Transfer difference on investment directly to reserves.
6. Calculate exchange gain/loss on borrowings.

7 Check limit on offset permitted in reserves.
8 Charge/credit surplus difference on borrowings in profit and loss account.

The solutions in Examples 18.3 and 18.4 are annotated by numbers, representing the eight steps just referred to.

In Example 18.3 foreign currency borrowings were used to finance a foreign currency investment. Both the borrowings and investment are initially recorded at the foreign exchange rate on the date of the transactions. At the year-end date, both balances are retranslated at the closing rate of exchange. The loss incurred on retranslation of the foreign currency borrowings is less than the gain recorded on retranslation of the equity investment. Consequently, all the loss can be offset against the gain and the net gain remaining is dealt with in reserves as permitted under SSAP 20.

Example 18.3 SSAP 20 offset provisions individual company (1)

Example
A eurozone company borrows 100,000 barcs (B) on 30.6.20X1 when the exchange rate was €1 = B2. The borrowings were used on the same day to partly finance an equity investment of B150,000.

Required
Show how these transactions would be recorded (i) at the date of the transaction and (ii) at 31.12.20X1, the balance sheet date, when the rate of exchange was €1 = B1.75.

Solution
(i) Initial recording on 30.6.20X1

	B	Rate	€
① Investment	150,000	2	75,000
② Borrowings	100,000	2	50,000

(ii) At the balance sheet date 31.12.20X1

	B	Rate	€	*Exchange gain/(loss)*	
Investment	③ 150,000	1.75	85,714	④ 10,714	⑤ To reserves
Borrowings	100,000	1.75	57,143	⑥ (7,143)	

⑦ Exchange loss on borrowings is covered by exchange gain on translating the foreign currency investment. The end result of the offset procedure is a net gain in reserves of €3,571:
$(10{,}714_{\text{gain on translation of investment}} - 7{,}143_{\text{loss on translation of borrowings}})$
⑧ There is no surplus difference to be charged/credited in the profit and loss account

Example 18.4 differs from Example 18.3 in that the loss on retranslating the borrowings exceeds the gain on retranslation of the foreign equity investment. The loss can only be offset in reserves to the extent that there is a gain on retranslation of the investment. The excess loss must be accounted for in the profit and loss account.

Example 18.4 SSAP 20 offset provisions individual company (2)

Example

■ Long-term loan raised on 31.3.20X1	B1,000,000
■ Invest in Barc subsidiary 31.3.20X1	B800,000
■ Invest in Sarc subsidiary 31.3.20X1	S220,000

Rates of exchange

31.3.20X1	€1 = S4.4 = B4
31.12.20X1	€1 = S4.8 = B3.8

Required

Show how these transactions would be recorded (i) at the date of the transaction and (ii) at 31.12.20X1, the balance sheet date.

Solution

(i) Initial recording

		Rate	€
① Investment in Barc subsidiary	B800,000	4.0	200,000
① Investment in Sarc subsidiary	S220,000	4.4	50,000
② Barc loan	B1,000,000	4.0	250,000

(ii) Year-end restatement

		Rate	€	Difference
Investment in Barc subsidiary	③ B800,000	3.8	210,526	④ 10,526
Investment in Sarc subsidiary	③ S220,000	4.8	45,833	④ (4,167)
			⑤ To reserves	6,359
Barc loan	1,000,000	3.8	263,158	⑥ (13,158)

Treatment of retranslation differences	Profit and loss account €	Reserves €
Gain on investments – transfer to reserves		⑤ 6,359
Loss on loan	⑥ 13,158	
Loss offset in reserves	⑦ (6,359)	(6,359)
To profit and loss account	⑧ 6,799	

The issues involved in adopting the offset rules are discussed in Example 18.5.

Example 18.5 Hedged equity investment

Example

A company registered in the UK purchased an equity investment in a French company. The investment amounted to €40 million and was funded by a loan of US$8 million. Between the time the investment was made and the year-end, the company has made an exchange loss of £300,000 on the dollar loan. The company generally carries its investments at cost using historical exchange rates. However, if the company were to translate the historical cost of its French equity investment at closing rate it would make a gain of £200,000 on the translation.

Required

Discuss the company's options.

Solution

Normal rules

The company may show its investment in the French company at historical sterling cost. However, it must retranslate the dollar borrowing at closing rate. Unless the company adopts the hedged equity investment treatment the exchange loss of £300,000 must be charged to the profit and loss account.

Offset procedure for foreign currency borrowings

Alternatively, it may consider the hedged equity investment treatment. Where a company has used foreign currency borrowings to finance, or to provide a hedge against, its foreign equity investments and where, also, the conditions set out below apply, a company may denominate its equity investments in the appropriate foreign currency. This means that the investment will be regarded as a currency investment and the company will need to translate the carrying amount at the closing rate for each year. Where a company treats hedged equity investment in this way, it should take to reserves any exchange differences that arise when the investments are retranslated. It should also take the exchange differences on the related foreign currency borrowings to reserves.

Conditions

The conditions for offset, which must all apply, are:

- in any accounting period exchange differences on the borrowings can only be offset to the extent of exchange differences on the related investment
- the borrowings must not exceed in aggregate the total amount of cash that the investments are expected to be able to generate from profits or otherwise
- the treatment should be applied consistently (SSAP 20 para 57).

If all these conditions were complied with, the company should translate the French investment at closing rather than historical rate and offset the £200,000 gain against £200,000 of the loss on the loan charging the remaining £100,000 loss to the profit and loss account.

Source: Adapted from Patient, M., Faris, J. and Holgate, P. 1991. 'Accounting solutions – hedged equity investment', *Accountancy*, September, p.67

Example 18.6 clarifies what is meant by the term 'foreign equity investments'.

Example 18.6 Hedged foreign investment and offset rules in individual holding company accounts

Example

A holding company's investment in a foreign subsidiary comprises ordinary shares and loan notes. It has a matching foreign currency loan to hedge its investment.

Required

State whether the holding company is allowed to take the exchange differences on the loan to reserves by using the offset procedures in SSAP 20 *Foreign Currency Translation*.

Solution

Where foreign currency borrowings are used to finance, or to provide a hedge against, a foreign equity investment, SSAP 20 allows the investment to be recorded in the appropriate foreign currency and retranslated into the reporting currency each year. Provided that certain conditions are met, the exchange differences on both the investment and the related currency loan may be offset as movements on reserves and would not enter the holding company's profit and loss account for the year.

Although SSAP 20's reference to foreign equity investments could be narrowly interpreted as meaning equity shares, paragraph 28 clearly indicates that it is the economic substance of the hedging arrangement that should

continued overleaf

Example 18.6 Continued

be driving the accounting treatment. It is reasonable, therefore, to extend the matching treatment to cover the long-term investment in loan notes. Consequently, as the whole of the investment is hedged by a matching borrowing, the exchange differences on both may be set off as reserve movements, assuming the conditions for offset are met.

Source: Adapted from Holgate, P. and Nailor, H. 1995. 'Accounting solutions – hedged foreign investment', *Accountancy*, February, p.95

The consequences of disposing of a hedged foreign equity investment are discussed in Example 18.7.

Example 18.7 Disposal of hedged overseas subsidiary

Example

A company has an investment in an overseas subsidiary financed by foreign currency borrowing. It has treated the borrowing as hedging the investment and consequently, under SSAP 20, has offset the currency movements on the two in reserves. During the current year it sold the investment but kept the borrowing. At the balance sheet date, the borrowing is showing a profit on translation, which the company proposes to take to the profit and loss account as it no longer hedges anything.

Required

Indicate whether you consider this treatment to be correct.

Solution

This is only correct up to a point. In fact, the borrowing was a hedge of the investment from the beginning of the financial year up to the date of sale and any currency movement should be taken through reserves to that point. At that date it changed its nature and became a borrowing that was not a hedge and any movement from that date through to the balance sheet date should be taken to profit and loss account. Even if that were to show a loss while a hedge, and a profit while not a hedge, that would still be the proper treatment.

Source: Adapted from Patient, M., Faris, J. and Holgate, P. 1993. 'Accounting solutions – overseas subsidiary', *Accountancy*, October, p.94

Consolidated financial statements

Two issues arise from the need to translate foreign currency denominated accounts for inclusion in consolidated accounts:

- what exchange rate(s) should be used to convert a balanced set of accounts denominated in a different currency to that used in the parent company accounts?
- how should the differences arising be accounted for?

Usually the accounts to be translated are those of subsidiary, associated and joint venture undertakings. However, branch accounts denominated in foreign currency may also need to be translated for inclusion in overall entity accounts.

Under SSAP 20 there are two methods of translating the accounts of foreign enterprises, prior to consolidation:

- closing rate/net investment method
- temporal method.

The method chosen depends on the relationship between the investing company and the investee. The closing rate/net investment method is the more commonly used method in practice. This is because investments are normally in the net worth of foreign enterprises as opposed to direct investment in individual assets and liabilities. The foreign enterprise is normally partly financed by local borrowings. Its day-to-day operations are independent of the reporting currency of the investing company. The investing company may receive dividends, but the net investment remains until the investment is disposed of. In these circumstances, the closing rate/net investment method should be used.

The temporal method, on the other hand, is used where the foreign subsidiary is a direct extension of (and thereby directly dependent on) the investing company.

Closing rate/net investment method

The closing rate/net investment method of translating the financial statements of foreign enterprises involves using the closing rate to translate the majority of foreign currency balance sheet amounts for subsidiaries and associates prior to consolidation. It also involves using the closing rate or average rate to translate profit and loss account items (with some exceptions). Because share capital, pre-acquisition reserves and dividends, at a minimum, are translated using a rate other than the closing rate, and because the closing rate differs from year to year, translation differences arise.

This section first considers translation of foreign entity financial statements, including the treatment required for resulting exchange differences. Application of the offset pro-cedures for differences on foreign exchange borrowings used to finance foreign currency equity investments in the context of group accounts is then explained and illustrated. The treatment of this topic in group accounts is compared with that in the individual accounts discussed earlier.

Translation of financial statements of foreign enterprises

Under the closing rate/net investment method, balance sheet items (except for share capital and reserves at acquisition) are translated using the rate ruling at the balance sheet date (closing rate). Profit and loss account items (except for dividends) are translated using either the closing rate or the average rate for the period. Differences arising on the retranslation of the opening net investment in the subsidiary, branch or associated undertaking are transferred directly to reserves, as are differences arising when the profit and loss account is translated using the average rate rather than the closing rate. These reserve movements are reported in the STRGL.

Table 18.3 summarises the rates to be used under the closing rate/net investment method.

Table 18.3 Exchange rates used under the closing rate method for translating foreign financial statements

Item	*Rate*
Balance sheet	
Assets (non-monetary, monetary, short-term, long-term)	Closing rate
Liabilities (non-monetary, monetary, short-term, long-term)	Closing rate
Share capital	Rate on date of acquisition of subsidiary
Pre-acquisition reserves	Rate on date of acquisition of subsidiary
Post-acquisition reserves	Balancing figure
Profit and loss account	
Turnover, purchases, other expenses	Closing rate or average rate
Proposed dividend	Closing rate
Dividends paid	Rate ruling when related dividend received by parent

The closing rate/net investment method is illustrated in Example 18.8. Up to seven steps are involved in arriving at a solution, as follows:

① On acquisition translate net investment in subsidiary at exchange rate on date of acquisition.
② Calculate goodwill on acquisition.
③ Translate year-end net assets on subsidiary at closing rate.
④ Share capital of subsidiary is always translated at exchange rate on date of acquisition.
⑤ Pre-acquisition reserves of subsidiary are always translated at exchange rate on date of acquisition.
⑥ Post-acquisition reserves are the balancing figure (Difference between translated net assets at year-end and at acquisition).
⑦ Prepare consolidated balance sheet, adding the translated amounts for the subsidiary (steps ③ and ⑥) to the respective balances for the parent.

Example 18.8 is a simple worked example of the application of the closing rate. It shows how the investment is recorded on acquisition and subsequent translation of the financial statements of the subsidiary for incorporation into the group accounts. The solution in Example 18.8 is annotated by numbers, representing the seven steps just referred to.

Example 18.8 Closing rate/net investment method

Example

A eurozone company acquired 100% of the share capital of a small Australian company at the beginning of the current year, when the revenue reserves of that company were A$30,000. The rate of exchange at the beginning of the period (i.e., on the date of acquisition) was €1 = A$2. The average rate for the year was €1 = A$1.80 and the year-end rate was €1= A$1.75. The group uses the average rate to translate profit and loss account items.

Balance sheets of Parent and Subsidiary are as follows:

	Parent at year-end	Subsidiary at acquisition	Subsidiary at year-end
	€	A$	A$
Fixed assets	120,000	40,000	45,000
Investment in Subsidiary	60,000		
Net current assets	98,000	40,000	50,000
	278,000	80,000	95,000
Financed by			
Ordinary share capital	100,000	50,000	50,000
Reserves	178,000	30,000	45,000
	278,000	80,000	95,000

Required

(i) Translate the net assets of Subsidiary at acquisition and calculate goodwill; (ii) Translate the balance sheet of Subsidiary at the year-end; and (iii) Prepare the consolidated balance sheet at the year-end (assume goodwill is not amortised).

Solution

(i) ① *Translated net assets of Subsidiary at acquisition*

The net investment is translated as follows at the date of acquisition:

	A$	Rate	€
Ordinary share capital	50,000	2.0	25,000
Reserves	30,000	2.0	15,000
	80,000		40,000

② Goodwill = $€60,000_{\text{Cost}} - €40,000_{\text{Net assets of Subsidiary at acquisition}}$ = €20,000

(ii) *Translated balance sheet of Subsidiary at year-end*
The closing net investment in A$ and € is as follows:

	A$	Rate	€
Fixed assets	45,000	1.75	25,714
Net current assets	50,000	1.75	28,571
	95,000		54,285
Ordinary share capital	50,000	2.00	25,000
Reserves at acquisition	30,000	2.00	15,000
Post-acquisition reserves	15,000	Balancing	14,285
	95,000	1.75	54,285

(iii) *Consolidated balance sheet*

	€
Fixed assets (120,000$_{\text{Parent}}$ + 25,714$_{\text{Subsidiary}}$)	145,714
Goodwill [(i) ②]	20,000
Net current assets (98,000$_{\text{Parent}}$ + 28,571$_{\text{Subsidiary}}$)	126,571
	292,285
Ordinary share capital (Parent only)	100,000
Reserves (178,000$_{\text{Parent}}$ + 14,285$_{\text{Post-acquisition of Subsidiary (ii)}}$)	192,285
	292,285

In Example 18.8, post-acquisition reserves are a balancing amount. This balancing figure can be explained, as shown in Example 18.9. Movements on the subsidiary's post-acquisition reserves for the year are made up of:

- The subsidiary's profit for the year, translated at the average rate of exchange.
- The exchange difference arising on translating opening net assets at the year-end rate rather than the opening rate of exchange.
- The exchange difference arising on translating retained profit for the year at the year-end rate, rather than the average rate of exchange.

Example 18.9 Statement of movements on subsidiary's post-acquisition profits

Example
Assume the same data as in Example 18.8.

Required
Using the data in Example 18.8, provide a statement of movements on Subsidiary's post-acquisition translated reserves.

Solution
Post-acquisition reserves of Subsidiary can be analysed as follows:

	A$	Rate	€	€
Profit retained for year at average rate	15,000	1.80		8,333
Difference on retranslation of opening net assets	80,000	1.75	45,714	
	80,000	2.00	40,000	5,714
Difference on retranslating retained profit for year	15,000	1.75	8,571	
	15,000	1.80	8,333	238
				14,285

Example 18.10 is the same as Example 18.8, except that there is a minority interest. It shows that minority interest is the relevant percentage of the subsidiary's year-end net assets as translated using the year-end rate of exchange.

Example 18.10 Closing rate/net investment method with minority interest

Example

Assume the same data as in Example 18.8, except that the eurozone company only acquired 80% of the share capital of the Australian company for €60,000.

Required

Prepare the consolidated balance sheet.

Solution

Consolidated balance sheet

	€
Fixed assets (120,000$_{\text{Parent}}$ + 25,714$_{\text{Subsidiary}}$)	145,714
Goodwill [60,000$_{\text{cost of investment}}$ – ([25,000$_{\text{share capital}}$ + 15,000$_{\text{pre-acquisition reserves}}$] × 80%)]	28,000
Net current assets	126,571
	300,285
Ordinary share capital	100,000
Consolidated reserves (178,000$_{\text{Parent}}$ + [14,285$_{\text{post-acquisition reserves of Subsidiary}}$ × 80%])	189,428
	289,428
Minority interest (54,285$_{\text{year-end net assets}}$ × 20%)	10,857
	300,285

Example 18.11 provides a further illustration of the closing rate/net investment method.

Example 18.11 Translation of subsidiary accounts – closing rate/net investment method

Example

Parent purchased the entire share capital of Subsidiary in Barcland on 1.1 20X0, on which date the reserves of Subsidiary amounted to 90,000 barcs (B). The summarised balance sheets of Subsidiary on 31.12.20X4 and 20X3, are as follows:

Balance sheets as at 31 December	**20X4**	**20X3**
	B000	**B000**
Fixed assets – at cost	600	600
– accumulated depreciation	(270)	(150)
	330	450
Net current assets	510	210
	840	660
Loan repayable in year 20X9	(180)	(180)
	660	480
Share capital	300	300
Reserves	360	180
	660	480

You are provided with the following additional information:

(1) The net profit of Subsidiary for the year ended 31.12.20X4 amounted to B180,000.

(2) The accounting policy of Parent is to use the closing rate/net investment method, including the closing rate for the profit and loss account.

(3) Exchange rates between the barc (B) and the euro were as follows:

1.1.20X0	B1.25 = €1
31.12.20X3	B1.28 = €1
31.12.20X4	B1.30 = €1

Required

(i) Translate the balance sheet of subsidiary at the year-end (31.12.20X4).

(ii) Show movements on Subsidiary's translated fixed assets.

All calculations should be rounded to the nearest €1.

Solution

(i) *Translated balance sheet using closing rate method*

Balance sheet as at 31.12.20X4	B	Rate	€
Fixed assets – at cost	600,000	1.3	461,538
– accumulated depreciation	(270,000)	1.3	(207,692)
	330,000		253,846
Net current assets	510,000	1.3	392,308
	840,000		646,154
Long-term liability	(180,000)	1.3	(138,462)
	660,000		507,692

Capital and reserves	B	Rate	€
Ordinary share capital	300,000	1.25	240,000
Reserves at acquisition	90,000	1.25	72,000
Reserves – see Example 18.12	270,000	Balancing	195,692
	660,000	1.3	507,692

(ii) *Fixed assets*	B	Rate	€
Cost – at 1.1. 20X4	600,000	1.28	468,750
Exchange difference		Balancing amount	(7,212)
Cost – at 31.12. 20X4	600,000	1.30	461,538
Depreciation – at 1.1.20X4	150,000	1.28	117,188
Exchange difference		Balancing amount	(1,804)
Charge for year	120,000	1.30	92,308
Depreciation – at 31.12. 20X4	270,000	1.30	207,692
Net book value at 31.12. 20X4			253,846

As already explained in relation to Example 18.8, movements on post-acquisition reserves in the current year are made up of ① the subsidiary's profit for the year, ② exchange differences arising on translating opening net assets at the year-end rather than at the opening rate of exchange and ③ exchange differences arising on translating retained profit for the year at the year-end rather than the average rate of exchange (where average rate has been used to translate the profit for the year). Example 18.12 extends the solution in Example 18.11 by analysing the make-up of the subsidiary's post-acquisition reserves. Example 18.12 initially identifies the translated opening post-acquisition reserves of Subsidiary (€63,000) before showing movements for the year in categories ① and ②. As the closing rate is used to translate profit for the year, there is no amount in category ③.

Example 18.12 Statement of movements on subsidiary's post-acquisition reserves

Example

Assume the same data as in Example 18.11.

Required

Prepare a statement of movements on Subsidiary's post-acquisition translated reserves, based on the data in Example 18.11.

Solution

Subsidiary's post-acquisition reserves

Opening post-acquisition reserves at 1.1.20X4	B	Rate	€	€
– Net assets at 1.1.20X4	480,000	1.28	375,000	
– Less: Net assets at acquisition	390,000	1.25	312,000	
Post acquisition reserves at 1.1.20X4	90,000			63,000
① Retained profit for year 20X4	180,000	1.30		138,461
② Difference on retranslation in 20X4 of net assets at 1.1.20X4				
– Opening net assets, translated at opening rate	480,000	1.28	375,000	
– Opening net assets, translated at closing rate	480,000	1.30	369,231	
				(5,769)
(only post-acquisition reserves are included in group reserves on consolidation)				195,692

The accounting treatment for translating overseas subsidiaries is described by Smiths Industries in Exhibit 18.2.

Exhibit 18.2 **Accounting policy for closing rate/net investment method Smiths Industries plc Annual Report 2000**

Accounting policies (extract)

Foreign currencies

The profit and loss accounts of overseas subsidiaries are translated into sterling at average rates of exchange for the year.

Exchange adjustments arising from re-translation of opening net assets in overseas subsidiaries and their results for the year at closing rates, and the translation of foreign currency borrowings to match overseas investments, are taken to the statement of total recognised gains and losses. All other exchange gains and losses are taken to the profit and loss account.

Foreign currency borrowings used to finance foreign equity investments

Similar to individual companies, foreign borrowings used to finance foreign equity investments may be offset in reserves against differences on retranslating the net investment in group accounts. This offset is restricted to situations where the relationship between the entities justifies the use of the closing rate/net investment method (rather than the temporal method which is discussed later). Note that using the offset procedure is optional, but it must be applied consistently. Paragraph 57 of SSAP 20 states (emphasis added):

> Where foreign currency borrowings have been used to finance, or provide a hedge against, group equity investments in foreign enterprises, exchange gains or losses on the borrowings, *which would otherwise have been taken to the profit and loss account, may be offset as reserve movements* against exchange differences arising on the retranslation of the net investments.

The conditions attaching to the use of these offset provisions in group accounts are as follows:

- the relationship justifies the use of the closing rate/net investment method
- the limit of offset is the exchange differences on retranslation of the net investment
- foreign borrowings used in offset should not exceed the cash expected to be generated from the equity investments
- offset rules should be applied consistently.

Comparison of individual and group accounts offset procedure

Amounts offset in reserves in group accounts will not normally be the same as amounts offset in individual company accounts for the following reasons:

- in individual company accounts, offset relates to all equity investments regardless of the relationship between the investor and the investee. In group accounts, subsidiaries translated using the temporal method are excluded
- in individual company accounts, the maximum amount of offset is determined by the exchange difference arising on the carrying value of the investment. This carrying amount is usually cost. In group accounts, the maximum is the difference on retranslation of the opening net investment. This is cost, plus or minus any changes in post-acquisition reserves
- in individual company accounts, differences on loans raised by the company itself can only be offset in reserves. In group accounts, differences on loans raised by any group company can be offset in reserves (subject to criteria).

Each of these is subject to the restriction that borrowings dealt with this way should not exceed the total cash expected from the investments.

Comprehensive example of offset rules in individual and group accounts

Example 18.13 is a comprehensive example of the foreign currency borrowing offset rules which, inter alia, compares the offset treatment in individual accounts of the parent with that in the group accounts. The first part of the solution deals with the entries in the individual accounts of the parent, while the second part covers the treatment in the group accounts.

Example 18.13 Comprehensive example – foreign currency borrowings offset rules

Example

On 1.7.20X0 Parent acquired 80% of the issued ordinary shares of Subsidiary, a Barcland company, for B4,800,000, when its retained earnings were B720,000. At that date, Parent raised a loan of B6,300,000 and used part of the loan to acquire the shares in Subsidiary. The barc (B) has strengthened over the past four years and the rates of exchange have been as follows:

1.7.20X0	B8.00=€1
30.6.20X3	B7.00=€1
30.6.20X4	B6.00=€1
Average for year ended 30.6.20X4	B6.00=€1

continued overleaf

Example 18.13 Continued

The draft balance sheets of Parent and Subsidiary are as follows:

	Parent		Subsidiary	
Draft balance sheet as at 30.6.20X4	**€000**	**€000**	**€000**	**B000**
Tangible fixed assets		3,087		5,418
Investment in Subsidiary		600		—
Net current assets		7,983		4,788
Total assets less current liabilities		11,670		10,206
Loan of B6,300,000 restated at 30.6.20X3		(900)		—
		10,770		10,206
Capital and reserves				
Called-up share capital		5,100		4,800
Share premium account		330		—
Retained earnings b/f	3,150		3,138	
Retained earnings for 20X4	2,190		2,268	
Retained earnings c/f		5,340		5,406
		10,770		10,206

(i) Parent avails of the offset rules of SSAP 20 when dealing with foreign equity investments and related borrowings. The entire barc loan is potentially repayable by the realisation of the investment.
(ii) The loan balance in the balance sheet reflects exchange rates at 30.6.20X3.
(iii) Goodwill is amortised over eight years.
(iv) The subsidiary accounts are translated using the closing rate/net investment method.

Required

Individual accounts of Parent

(a) Show how the investment in Subsidiary and the loan of B6,300,000 would be treated in the individual accounts of Parent at 30.6.20X4.
(b) Indicate the revised amounts for (i) investment in Subsidiary, (ii) loan and (iii) retained earnings to be included in Parent's draft individual company balance sheet.

Group accounts

(c) Translate the opening net assets of Subsidiary at the year-end of 30.6.20X4.
(d) Prepare a statement of movements on Subsidiary's post-acquisition translated reserves for the year 20X3/X4.
(e) Indicate the extent to which the difference on retranslation of the borrowings (of B6,300,000) can be offset against reserves in the group accounts for the year ended 30.6.20X4.
(f) Prepare the consolidated balance sheet of Parent and group as at 30.6.20X4.

Solution

(a) Treatment in individual accounts of Parent

	B	Rate	€
(i) Initial recording at date of acquisition			
Investment in Subsidiary	4,800,000	8	600,000
Borrowings	6,300,000	8	787,500
(ii) At balance sheet date 30.6.20X3			
Investment in Subsidiary	4,800,000	7	685,714
Borrowings	6,300,000	7	900,000
(iii) At balance sheet date 30.6.20X4			
Investment in Subsidiary	4,800,000	6	800,000
Borrowings	6,300,000	6	1,050,000

(iv) Gain on exchange (translation of investment) in 20X3/X4

Investment (800,000$_{(iii)}$ – 685,714$_{(ii)}$) (Credit to reserves)	114,286

(v) Loss on exchange (translation of borrowings) in 20X3/X4

Borrowings (1,050,000$_{(iii)}$ – 900,000$_{(ii)}$)	150,000

(vi) Application of offset rules

Debit loss on translation of borrowings directly to reserves (offset against difference on investment$_{(iv)}$)	114,286
Charge remainder (not offset) in profit and loss account for year	35,714
	150,000

Exchange differences on borrowings can only be offset in reserves to the extent that they are covered by exchange differences on translation of the investment. The balance not covered is dealt with in the profit and loss account.

(b) Revised amounts to be included in Parent's balance sheet as at 30.6.20X4

		€
(i)	Investment at cost (4,800 ÷ 6)	800,000
(ii)	Loan (6,300 ÷ 6)	1,050,000
(iii)	Retained earnings (5,340,000$_{\text{per question}}$ +114,286$_{\text{exchange gain}}$ −150,000$_{\text{exchange loss}}$)	5,304,286

(c) Translation of opening net assets of Subsidiary	**B000**	**Rate**	**€000**
Ordinary share capital	4,800	8	600
Pre-acquisition profits	720	8	90
Post-acquisition profits at 30.6.20X3 (5,406 – 720$_{\text{pre-acquisition}}$ – 2,268$_{\text{profit for year}}$)	2,418	Balancing	444
Net assets at 30.6.20X3	7,938	7	1,134
Profit retained for year	2,268	6	378
Difference on exchange for 20X3/X4		Balancing	189
Net assets at 30.6.20X4	10,206	6	1,701

(d) Movement on Subsidiary's post-acquisition reserves in 20X3/X4

	B000	**Rate**	**€000**	**€000**
Opening post-acquisition reserves at 30.6.20X3 (see solution (c)) (5,406 – 720$_{\text{pre-acquisition}}$ – 2,268$_{\text{profit for year}}$)	2,418			444
Profit retained for year ended 30.6.20X4	2,268	6		378
				822
Difference on retranslation of opening net investment				
– Net assets at 30.6.20X3 translated at opening rate	7,938	7	1,134	
– Net assets at 30.6.20X3 translated at closing rate	7,938	6	1,323	
Gain on retranslation of opening net assets of Subsidiary				189
Closing post-acquisition reserves of Subsidiary at 30.6.20X4				1,011

(e) Extent of offset in group accounts

Gain on retranslation of opening net assets of Subsidiary (see solution (d))	189			
Group share of difference on translation of net assets (189 @ 80%$_{\text{group share}}$)				151.2
Difference on retranslation of borrowings				
– Borrowings translated at opening rate	6,300	7	900	
– Borrowings translated at closing rate	6,300	6	1,050	
Loss on retranslation of borrowings of Parent to finance investment in Subsidiary				150.0

Because the group share of exchange gains on retranslation of net assets (€151,200) exceeds the exchange losses on retranslation of borrowings (€150,000), the entire difference on borrowings can be offset against the difference arising on retranslation of net assets, in reserves.

continued overleaf

Example 18.13 Continued

(f) Consolidated balance sheet at 30 June 20X4

(W_1) Goodwill	**€000**
Investment at cost (B4,800,000 ÷ 8)	600
Group share of net assets at acquisition ([$4{,}800_{\text{share capital}}$ + $720_{\text{pre-acquisition profit}}$] ÷ 8 @ $80\%_{\text{group share}}$)	(552)
Goodwill	48
Less: Amortisation 20X1–20X4	(24)
Written down amount at 30.6.20X4	24

(W_2) Retained earnings	**€000**	**€000**
Parent		5,340.0
Subsidiary		
– Closing post-acquisition reserves of Subsidiary at 30.6.20X4 (from (d))	1,011.0	
– Minority share (1,011@ 20%)	(202.2)	
– Group share of post-acquisition reserves	808.8	
– Loss on translation of borrowings offset in reserves (from (e))	(150.0)	
– Goodwill amortisation (W_1)	(24.0)	634.8
		5,974.8

(W_3) Minority interest	**€000**
Net assets of Subsidiary at 30.6.20X4 (from (c))	1,701
Minority interest 20%	340.2

Consolidated balance sheet	**€000**
Tangible fixed assets ($3{,}087_{\text{Parent}}$ + [$B5{,}418_{\text{Subsidiary}}$ ÷ 6 = 903])	3,990.0
Goodwill (W_1)	24.0
Net current assets ($7{,}983_{\text{Parent}}$ + [$B4{,}788_{\text{Subsidiary}}$ ÷ 6 = 798])	8,781.0
Total assets less current liabilities	12,795.0
Loan due after more than one year (B6,300 ÷ 6)	(1,050.0)
	11,745.0
Called-up share capital (Parent only)	5,100.0
Share premium account	330.0
Retained earnings (W_2)	5,974.8
	11,404.8
Minority interest (W_3)	340.2
	11,745.0

In the individual accounts of Parent, investment in Subsidiary is retranslated using year-end rates, as is the loan of B6,300,000 taken out to finance the investment in Subsidiary. In the individual accounts of Parent, exchange losses on the borrowings (€150,000) are offset directly in reserves to the extent of the opposite difference arising on the investment (i.e., €114,286). The remaining balance of difference on the borrowings not offset (€35,714) is taken to the profit and loss account for the year.

As shown in part (c) of the solution to Example 18.13, in the group accounts, the opening net assets of Subsidiary which were translated at the rate of exchange on 1 July 20X3 in the previous year's group accounts, are retranslated using year-end exchange rates at 30 June 20X4. Subsidiary's net assets on acquisition are always translated at the rate of exchange on the date of acquisition. Thus, any translation exchange gains or losses are dealt with in post-acquisition retained reserves, which are therefore a balancing amount.

As previously explained, this balancing amount for post-acquisition reserves is made up of the subsidiary's profit for the year, exchange differences arising on translating opening net assets at the year-end rather than the opening rate of exchange and exchange differences arising on translating retained profit for the year at the year-end rather than the average rate of exchange (where average rate has been used to translate the profit for the year). This is illustrated in part (d) of the solution to Example 18.13.

The group share of the gain on retranslation of Subsidiary's net assets (€189,000 @ 80% = €151,200) is available for offset against any losses arising retranslating the borrowings used to finance the investment in Subsidiary (€150,000). As the group share of the gain on exchange exceeds the loss on translation of the borrowings, full offset can be availed of.

Example 18.14 explains the reasoning behind the allocation of the minority's share of translation gains and losses.

Example 18.14 Minority interest in exchange differences arising on translation of foreign subsidiary

Example

A company has a 51% holding in a foreign subsidiary undertaking, which it consolidates. When the consolidated financial statements are being prepared, exchange differences arise on the retranslation of the subsidiary's opening net assets and on translating the profit for the year.

Required

Explain whether these exchange differences should be taken to reserves or whether they should be allocated to the minority interest in the balance sheet.

Solution

FRS 2 *Accounting for Subsidiary Undertakings* states in paragraph 80 that 'the effect of the existence of minority interests on the returns to investors in the parent undertaking is best reflected by presenting the net identifiable assets attributable to minority interests on the same basis as those attributable to group interests'.

In accordance with SSAP 20 *Foreign Currency Translation*, under the closing rate/net investment method, the foreign subsidiary's assets and liabilities should be translated at the year-end rate. Since this is the basis for including the subsidiary in the accounts as a whole, it follows from the requirements of paragraph 80 of FRS 2 and from the definition of minority interest in FRS 2 that the minority's share of those assets and liabilities should also be included at the year-end rate. Accordingly, the minority's share of the exchange difference should be allocated to them in the balance sheet and only the amount of the exchange difference attributable to the group should be shown in the statement of total recognised gains and losses.

Source: Adapted from Holgate, P. and Horgan, O. 1997. 'Accounting solutions – exchange differences', *Accountancy*, December, p.72

Temporal method

Although the closing rate/net investment method is more commonly used in practice, there are circumstances where the temporal method is more appropriate. The criterion most relevant in deciding whether to use this method is the degree to which the affairs of a foreign enterprise are linked to those of the investor.

The temporal method of translation is permitted where the trade of the foreign enterprise is more dependent on the investing company's currency than on its own currency. SSAP 20 gives an example where the foreign enterprise acts as a selling agency receiving stocks of goods from the investing company and remitting the proceeds back to the company. The effect of using the temporal method is the same as adopting the individual company approach (i.e., non-monetary assets are translated at historic rates, monetary assets and liabilities are translated at closing rates). It is as if the investor had a direct investment in the investee's individual assets and liabilities. In particular:

- Non-monetary assets and related expenses (depreciation and cost of sales) should be translated at the historic rate, i.e., the rate of exchange ruling when the assets were acquired (or were revalued, if relevant).
- Monetary assets and liabilities should be translated using the closing rate.
- All exchange gains and losses should be included in the profit and loss account for the year as part of profit or loss on ordinary activities.

Under the temporal method there is greater variety in the rates used than under the closing rate/net investment method (see Table 18.3). These rates are summarised in Table 18.4.

Table 18.4 Exchange rates used under the temporal method for translating foreign financial statements

Item	*Rate*
Balance sheet	
Non-monetary assets included at historic cost	Rate at date of purchase
Non-monetary assets that have been revalued	Rate when revalued
Non-monetary assets expressed at current values (e.g., stock at net realisable value)	Closing rate
Monetary assets and liabilities	Closing rate
Share capital and pre-acquisition reserves	Rate on date of acquisition of subsidiary
Post-acquisition reserves	Balancing figure
Profit and loss account	
Depreciation	Rate used for related assets
Opening and closing stock	Rate ruling at date of purchase
Turnover, purchases, other expenses	Average rate
Proposed dividend	Closing rate
Dividend paid	Actual rate when dividend received by the parent

Example 18.15 illustrates application of the temporal method.

Example 18.15 Illustration of the temporal method

Example

On 1.4.20X6 Parent purchased 75% of the share capital of Subsidiary, a company operating in Barcland. At that date the reserves of Subsidiary were B1,200,000. At 31.3.20X8 the financial statements of the two companies were:

Profit and loss accounts for the year ended 31.3.20X8	**Parent**	**Subsidiary**
	€000	**B000**
Turnover	12,000	3,600
Opening stock	600	330
Purchases	8,400	2,610
	9,000	2,940
Closing stock	(900)	(840)
Cost of sales	8,100	2,100
Gross profit	3,900	1,500
Distribution costs	(1,200)	(300)
Administrative expenses	(600)	(360)
Depreciation	(360)	(240)
Dividend receivable from Subsidiary	135	—
Profit before taxation	1,875	600
Taxation	(600)	(180)
Profit after taxation	1,275	420
Dividends proposed	(600)	(360)
Retained profit for year	675	60

Balance sheets as at 31.3.20X8	**Parent**	**Subsidiary**
Fixed assets	**€000**	**B000**
Tangible assets	2,400	2,160
Investment in Subsidiary at cost	900	—
	3,300	2,160
Current assets		
Stock	900	840
Other net current assets	1,200	300
	2,100	1,140
Total assets less current liabilities	5,400	3,300
Long-term loan	—	(240)
	5,400	3,060
Share capital	3,000	1,500
Revenue reserves	2,400	1,560
	5,400	3,060

Note 1 Tangible fixed assets

Tangible fixed assets of Subsidiary has not changed since acquisition, other than for depreciation charged.

Note 2 Goodwill

Goodwill is to be amortised over five years, commencing the year after acquisition.

Note 3 Exchange rates	**B to €1**
1.4.20X6	3.2
28.2.20X7 (date of purchase of opening stock)	2.6
31.3.20X7	2.5
Average for year to 31.3.20X8	2.3
28.2.20X8 (date of purchase of closing stock)	2.1
31.3.20X8	2.0

Required

Using the temporal method, translate (i) the closing balance sheet, (ii) the opening balance sheet and (iii) the profit and loss account of Subsidiary for the year ended 31.3.20X8. (iv) Calculate the exchange differences on translation of the financial statements of Subsidiary. Prepare (v) the consolidated profit and loss account and (vi) the consolidated balance sheet.

continued overleaf

Example 18.15 Continued

Solution

(i) Translate the closing balance sheet of Subsidiary at 31.3.20X8

	B000	Rate	€000
Tangible fixed assets	2,160	3.2	675
Stock	840	2.1	400
Other net current assets	300	2.0	150
	1,140		550
Total assets less current liabilities	3,300		1,225
Long-term loan	(240)	2.0	(120)
Net total assets	3,060		1,105
Share capital	1,500	3.2	469
Reserves: Pre-acquisition	1,200	3.2	375
Post-acquisition ($1{,}560_{\text{closing balance}} - 1{,}200_{\text{pre-acquisition}}$)	360	Balancing	261
	3,060		1,105

(ii) Translate the opening balance sheet of Subsidiary at 31.3.20X7

	B000	Rate	€000
Tangible fixed assets (B$2{,}160_{\text{closing fixed assets}} + 240_{\text{depreciation charge for year}}$)	2,400	3.2	750
Stock	330	2.6	127
Other net monetary assets (balancing figure in B000)	270*	2.5	108
Net total assets (B3,060 – B$60_{\text{retained profit}}$)	3,000*		985
Share capital	1,500	3.2	469
Reserves: Pre-acquisition	1,200	3.2	375
Post-acquisition ($1{,}560_{\text{closing balance}} - 60_{\text{profit for year}} - 1{,}200_{\text{pre-acquisition}}$)	300	Balancing	141
	3,000		985

* In constructing the opening balance sheet the total opening net assets of B3 million are calculated by subtracting the retained profit for the year (B60,000) from the closing total of share capital and reserves (B3,060,000). 'Other net monetary assets' are inserted as the balancing figure of B270,000.

(iii) Translate Subsidiary's profit and loss account

Profit and loss account for year ending 31.3.20X8	B000	Rate	€000
Turnover	3,600	2.3	1,565
Opening stock	330	2.6	127
Purchases	2,610	2.3	1,135
	2,940		1,262
Closing stock	(840)	2.1	(400)
Cost of sales	2,100		862
Gross profit	1,500		703
Distribution costs	(300)	2.3	(130)
Administrative expenses	(360)	2.3	(157)
Depreciation	(240)	3.2	(75)
Profit before taxation	600		341
Taxation	(180)	2.3	(78)
Profit after taxation	420		263
Dividend proposed	(360)	2.0	(180)
Retained profit for year	60		83

(iv) Calculation of exchange difference

	€000
€ amount of closing post acquisition reserves (per closing balance sheet)	261
€ amount of opening post acquisition reserves (per opening balance sheet)	141
Increase	120
Retained profit for year (per profit and loss account)	83
Difference on exchange (gain)	37

(v) Consolidated profit and loss account for the year ended 31.3.20X8

	€000	€000
Turnover ($12{,}000_{\text{Parent}} + 1{,}565_{\text{(iii)}}$)		13,565
Opening stock ($600_{\text{Parent}} + 127_{\text{(iii)}}$)	727	
Purchases ($8{,}400_{\text{Parent}} + 1{,}135_{\text{(iii)}}$)	9,535	
	10,262	
Less: Closing stock ($900_{\text{Parent}} + 400_{\text{(iii)}}$)	1,300	8,962
Gross profit		4,603
Distribution costs ($1{,}200_{\text{Parent}} + 130_{\text{(iii)}}$)	(1,330)	
Administrative expenses ($600_{\text{Parent}} + 157_{\text{(iii)}}$)	(757)	
Depreciation ($360_{\text{Parent}} + 75_{\text{(iii)}}$)	(435)	
Gain on exchange (iv)	37	
Goodwill amortised (W_1)	(54)	2,539
Profit before taxation		2,064
Taxation ($600_{\text{Parent}} + 78_{\text{(iii)}}$)		(678)
		1,386
Minority interest 25% @ ($263_{\text{profit after taxation (iii)}} + 37_{\text{exchange gain (iv)}}$)		(75)
		1,311
Dividends		(600)
Retained profit for year		711

(W_1) Goodwill amortised

$900_{\text{cost}} - 75\%@([1{,}500_{\text{share capital}} + 1{,}200_{\text{pre-acquisition reserves}}] \div 3.2_{\text{exchange rate on 1/4/X6}}) = 267_{\text{goodwill}} \times 1/5 = 54$

(vi) Consolidated balance sheet as at 31.3.20X8

		€000
Fixed assets		
Intangible assets – goodwill ($267_{W1} - 54_{W1}$)	213	
Tangible assets ($2{,}400_{\text{Parent}} + 675_{\text{(i)}}$)	3,075	
		3,288
Current assets		
Stock ($900_{\text{Parent}} + 400_{\text{(i)}}$)	1,300	
Other net current assets ($1{,}200_{\text{Parent}} + 150_{\text{(i)}}$)	1,350	
		2,650
		5,938
Long-term loan $_{\text{(i)}}$		(120)
		5,818
Share capital (Parent only)	3,000	
Revenue reserves (W_2)	2,542	
		5,542
Minority interest ($1{,}105_{\text{Subsidiary net assets at year-end (i)}} \times 25\%_{\text{minority share}}$)		276
		5,818

(W_2) Consolidated reserves	€000	€000
Reserves at 31.3.20X7		
Parent ($2{,}400_{\text{closing reserves}} - 675_{\text{retained profit for year}}$)	1,725	
Subsidiary (post-acquisition) $141_{\text{(ii)}} \times 75\%$	106	1,831
Retained group profit for year per group profit and loss account (iv)		711
Reserves at 31.3.20X8		2,542

Disclosure requirements

The disclosure requirements of SSAP 20 are minimal. SSAP 20 requires the following items to be disclosed:

- methods used (i) in translating the financial statements of foreign enterprises and (ii) in the treatment of exchange differences
- net amount of exchange gains and losses on foreign currency borrowings less deposits, identifying separately:
  - amount offset in reserves
  - net amount credited/charged to the profit and loss account
- net movement on reserves arising from exchange differences.

IAS GAAP

The discussion of IAS GAAP mirrors that under UK GAAP and contains the same section headings.

Regulations

The IASC addressed foreign currency issues in IAS 21 *Accounting for the Effects of Changes in Foreign Exchange Rates* which was issued in 1983. This standard was subsequently revised in 1993 and retitled *The Effects of Changes in Foreign Exchange Rates*. IAS 29 *Financial Reporting in Hyperinflationary Economies* was issued in 1989 and was reformatted (i.e., the format was revised without substantive changes to the original text) in 1994. Further guidance was subsequently provided by IASC in SIC 11 *Foreign Exchange – Capitalisation of Losses Resulting from Severe Currency Devaluations*, in SIC 19 *Reporting Currency – Measurement and Presentation of Financial Statements under IAS 21 and IAS 29* and in SIC 30 *Reporting Currency – Translation from Measurement Currency to Presentation Currency*.

Individual company accounts

Under IAS 21, foreign currency assets, liabilities, revenues and expenses should initially be recognised by translation at the rate of exchange ruling on the date of the transaction (referred to as the spot rate in IAS 21) or at an approximation thereof such as an average rate for a week or month.

As for UK GAAP, monetary assets and liabilities should be retranslated at the balance sheet date using the rate of exchange ruling on that date. Non-monetary assets and liabilities should not be retranslated. However, non-monetary items recorded at fair value should be translated at the rate of exchange on the valuation date.

Treatment of exchange differences

Exchange differences should be recognised as income or expenses in the period in which they arise, except for exchange differences on investments in foreign entities (which are dealt with later).

An example of an accounting policy following IAS GAAP is provided by Agfa-Gevaert in Exhibit 18.3. Unlike the Rolls-Royce exhibit shown earlier (Exhibit 18.1), no reference is made to forward contracts as use of such rates is not permitted under IAS GAAP.

Exhibit 18.3 **Accounting policy not incorporating forward contracts Agfa-Gevaert Annual Report 2000**

Significant accounting policies (extract)
(d) Foreign currency (extract)
Foreign currency transactions
In the individual Group companies, transactions in foreign currencies are translated at the exchange rate at the date of the transaction. Foreign currency monetary assets and liabilities are translated at the exchange rate ruling at the balance sheet date. Resulting foreign exchange differences arising on translation are recognized in the income statement for the year. Non-monetary assets and liabilities denominated in foreign currency, which are stated at historical cost, are translated at the foreign exchange rate ruling at the date of the transaction.

Net investment in foreign entity

IAS 21 requires exchange differences on monetary items that are in effect part of net investments in foreign entities, to be classified as part of the equity (i.e., shown in the statement of changes in equity) in the reporting entity's financial statements until disposal of the net investment. Paragraph 18 of IAS 21 clarifies the requirement by pointing out that monetary items may include long-term receivables or loans but do not include trade receivables or payables.

Exchange differences on foreign currency borrowings used as a hedge against exchange movements on net investments in foreign entities should also be classified as equity until the disposal of the net investment, when the gain or loss on exchange should be recognised as income or expenses in the same period as the gain or loss on disposal of the net investment.

Only the portion of the gain or loss on the hedging instrument that is determined to be an effective hedge should be recognised through the statement of changes in equity. The ineffective portion should be reported immediately in the income statement if the hedging instrument is a derivative. Where the hedging instrument is not a derivative (which, the standard indicates, would arise in limited circumstances) the ineffective portion of the gain or loss may be accounted for through equity.

Under IAS GAAP the conditions for using hedge accounting in paragraph 142 of IAS 39 *Financial Instruments: Recognition and Measurement* must be met. These conditions require, inter alia, that formal documentation exists to confirm the hedge relationship. SSAP 20 is less prescriptive in this respect.

Swiss Air in Exhibit 18.4 provides an example of the foreign currency offset provisions under IAS GAAP. The manner in which the policy is expressed is more restrictive than required. Swiss Air's policy suggests that the currency of the foreign borrowings and the foreign subsidiary must be the same although this is not a condition of IAS 21.

Exhibit 18.4 **Accounting policy for foreign currency borrowings offset provisions under IAS GAAP**

Swiss Air Annual Report 2000

Significant Accounting Policies (extract)
6 Foreign currency translation (extract)
In cases in which an investment in a company outside Switzerland has been effected by a non-current loan (with the character of shareholders' equity) in the same foreign currency, any profit or loss arising from the translation of the loan amount is taken to shareholders' equity and not recorded in the profit and loss account until the interest is sold.

Severe devaluation of currency

Normally exchange differences should be accounted for immediately in the income statement. This is the 'benchmark treatment' in IAS 21. However, paragraph 21 of IAS 21 and SIC 11 allow certain exchange differences arising on severe devaluation to be added to the cost of the related asset.

Consolidated financial statements

IAS 21 distinguishes between 'foreign operations that are integral to the operations of the reporting entity' and those that are 'foreign entities'. The closing rate/net investment method applies to 'foreign entities' and the temporal method applies to other foreign operations.

The closing rate/net investment method is explained and illustrated in the next section and the temporal method is explained in the section that follows.

Closing rate/net investment method

The influence of IAS GAAP on translation of the financial statements of foreign enterprises is first considered in this section and the treatment of exchange differences on foreign currency borrowings used to hedge equity investments in foreign entities is then addressed.

Translation of financial statements of foreign enterprises

The closing rate method is recommended for translation of the financial statements of 'foreign entities' (i.e., those that are not part of the integral operations of the reporting entity). All assets and liabilities of such foreign operations should be translated at the closing rate. Revenues and expenses should be translated at the exchange rates at the date of the transactions (except for hyperinflationary economies – see later). Resulting gains and losses should be classified as part of shareholders' equity until the foreign operation is disposed of.

IAS 21 specifies that exchange differences 'classified as equity' (i.e., dealt with directly in reserves) should be classified separately within reserves. This differs from UK GAAP requirements. SSAP 20 does not specify the category of reserves to which exchange differences arising from translating foreign subsidiaries should be taken.

Agfa-Gevaert uses this approach as shown in Exhibit 18.5 (as does Bayer in Exhibit 18.7).

Exhibit 18.5 **Closing rate method for non-integral subsidiaries Agfa-Gevaert Annual Report 2000**

Significant accounting policies (extract)
(d) Foreign currency (extract)
Financial statements of foreign operations
The Group's foreign operations are not considered an integral part of the Company's operations. Accordingly, the assets and liabilities of foreign operations, including goodwill and fair value adjustments arising on consolidation, are translated at the foreign exchange rate ruling at the balance sheet date, while revenue and expenses of foreign operations, are translated at the average foreign exchange rate for the year. Resulting foreign exchange differences are recognized directly in equity.

Balance sheet items must be translated at the closing rate, but IAS 21 differs from UK GAAP in specifying that the average rate should be used to translate income statement items. Thus, Agfa-Gevaert (Exhibit 18.5) and Bayer (Exhibit 18.7) use the average rate to translate revenues and expenses. A related difference therefore arises because the effect of all revenue and expense items on assets and liabilities is translated at closing rate in the balance sheet. This difference should be classified as equity (i.e., dealt with in reserves) until disposal of the subsidiary.

When a foreign subsidiary is disposed of, IAS 21 requires the cumulative amount of exchange differences relating to that foreign subsidiary which have been deferred to be recognised in the profit and loss account in the same accounting period as the related gain or loss on disposal is accounted for. There is no equivalent requirement under UK GAAP in SSAP 20. FRS 3 allows gains or losses to be excluded from the profit and loss account if required to be taken directly to reserves under another standard. This applies, for example, in relation to translation differences under SSAP 20. Such gains and losses should be shown in the STRGL, not in the profit and loss account (as is required under IAS GAAP).

Foreign currency borrowings used to finance foreign equity investments

IAS 21 requirements on this topic have been dealt with earlier in relation to the individual accounts of parent undertakings. Exchange differences on (i) monetary items that are in substance part of an entity's net investment in a foreign entity and (ii) foreign currency liabilities accounted for as a hedge of an entity's net investment in a foreign entity should be classified as equity until disposal of the net investment in the foreign entity. Nokia illustrates these requirements in a group accounts context in Exhibit 18.6.

Exhibit 18.6 **Foreign currency borrowings offset provisions under IAS GAAP Nokia Annual Report 2000**

Accounting principles (extract)
Foreign Group companies
The Group's policy is to hedge a portion of foreign subsidiaries' shareholders' equity to reduce the effects of exchange rate fluctuations on the Group's net investments in foreign Group companies. Exchange gains and losses resulting from the hedging transactions are offset against the translation differences arising from consolidation and recorded in shareholders' equity.

Temporal method

For foreign operations integral to the operations of the reporting entity, the financial statements of such operations should be translated as if the transactions were those of the reporting entity and the procedures described for individual accounts should be applied in these situations.

In Exhibit 18.7, Bayer uses both the closing rate and temporal methods of translation, depending on classification of foreign operations as integral or not to the operations of the reporting entity.

Exhibit 18.7 **Closing rate and temporal methods**
Bayer Annual Report 2001

Foreign currency translation (extract)
The majority of foreign consolidated companies are to be regarded as foreign entities since they are financially, economically and organizationally autonomous. Their functional currencies according to IAS 21 (*The Effects of Changes in Foreign Exchange Rates*) are thus the respective local currencies. The assets and liabilities of these companies are therefore translated at closing rates, income and expense items at average rates for the year.

Where the operations of a foreign company are integral to those of Bayer AG, the functional currency is the euro.

Property, plant and equipment, intangible assets, investments in affiliated companies and other securities included in investments are translated at the historical exchange rate on the day of addition, along with any relevant amortization, depreciation and write-downs. All other balance sheet items are translated at closing rates. Income and expense items (except amortization, depreciation and write-downs) are translated at average rates for the year.

Disclosure requirements

The disclosure requirements for foreign currency transactions and translations under IAS 21 are more extensive than those under SSAP 20. They include disclosure of:

- amount of exchange differences included in the net profit or loss for the period
- reconciliation of net exchange differences included in equity at the beginning and end of the period
- amount of exchange differences arising during the period included in the carrying value on an asset (in the context of severe currency devaluation)
- reason, where reporting currency is different from the country of domicile of the enterprise
- reason, where there has been a change in reporting currency
- where there has been a change in classification of a significant foreign operation (integral part or not of reporting entity's operations) nature of change, reason for change and impact of change on equity and results
- method of translation for goodwill and fair value adjustments on acquisition of a foreign entity.

The differences in disclosure requirements under UK GAAP and IAS GAAP are summarised in Table 18.5.

Table 18.5 Comparison of disclosure requirements under UK GAAP and IAS GAAP

SSAP 20	*IAS 21*
Methods used in translating the financial statements of foreign enterprises and the treatment of exchange differences	
Net amount of exchange gains and losses on foreign currency borrowings less deposits credited/charged to the profit and loss account	Amount of exchange differences included in the net profit or loss for the period
Net amount of exchange gains and losses on foreign currency borrowings less deposits offset in reserves	Reconciliation of net exchange differences included in equity at the beginning and end of the period
Net movement on reserves arising from exchange differences	Amount of exchange differences included in the carrying value of an asset (in context of severe currency devaluation)
	Reason, where reporting currency is different from the country of domicile of the enterprise
	Reason, where there has been a change in reporting currency
	Where there has been a change in classification of a significant foreign operation (integral part or not of reporting entity's operations) nature of change, reason for change and impact of change on equity and results
	Method of translation for goodwill and fair value adjustments on acquisition of a foreign entity

Source: Adapted from Cairns, D. and Nobes, C. 2000. *The Convergence Handbook: A Comparison between International Accounting Standards and UK Financial Reporting Requirements*, Institute of Chartered Accountants in England and Wales, London

Hyperinflationary economies

Problems arise when subsidiaries operate in hyperinflationary economies. Incorporating the results of these subsidiaries in the consolidated accounts could materially distort group results. This is because the investment in foreign currency might be worth very little in terms of the reporting currency. In times of very high inflation, the local currency is likely to weaken considerably against the reporting currency. This can have two consequences:

- foreign currency carrying amounts of assets and liabilities, and foreign exchange gains, are likely to be considerably higher than in previous years, thereby resulting in large reported profits by the foreign subsidiary. Results of the foreign subsidiary are at inflated amounts which could be considered to reflect unrealistically high profitability
- the exchange rate in the hyperinflationary economy will depreciate against the reporting currency. If the closing rate/net investment method is used, resulting exchange losses will bypass the consolidated profit and loss account, as under the closing rate method such losses are taken directly to reserves.

Guidance has been issued under both UK GAAP and IAS GAAP on how to translate the financial statements of companies operating in hyperinflationary environments. In the case of UK GAAP the guidance is in the form of a UITF Abstract rather than as an accounting standard. The recommendations attempt to avoid distortion of the true and fair view caused by high rates of inflation.

UK GAAP

UITF Abstract 9 *Accounting for operations in hyper-inflationary economies* was issued in 1993 and requires adjustments where (i) the cumulative inflation rate over three years approaches or exceeds 100% and (ii) the foreign operations in such economies are material.

Abstract 9 allows two methods of adjustment. These are:

- adjust local currency financial statements to reflect current price levels before the financial statements are translated for inclusion in the group accounts. As part of this process, any gain or loss on net monetary assets/liabilities should be recognised in the profit and loss account
- use as the functional currency a relatively stable currency for the foreign operations in hyperinflationary economies. Transactions should first be remeasured in the stable currency by applying the temporal method.

Allowing a choice acknowledges the possibility that, in practice, a reliable local price-level index may not be available. The effect of using a stable currency remeasurement procedure is that the movement between the local currency and the stable currency is used as a proxy for the inflation index.

Adjusting the local currency financial statements to reflect current prices (before translating the financial statements into the reporting currency) will result in taking any gain or loss on the net monetary position through the profit and loss account.

Example 18.16 uses a simple case to compare the effect of no adjustment for hyperinflation, on the one hand, and the two methods of dealing with hyperinflation, on the other. The remeasurement method involves a two-stage process. First, the amount in the local currency is translated into the stable currency. Then, the stable currency is translated into the reporting currency.

Example 18.16 Hyperinflationary economies: current price level and stable currency remeasurement methods compared

Example

On 1.1.20X1 Parent established Subsidiary in Barcland (currency barcs (B)) and acquired all the shares at par for B100,000 cash. The cash was used to acquire land. There were no other transactions for year.

The relevant stable currency is the sarc (S). You are given the following information:

	Exchange rate	Stable currency exchange rate	Consumer price index
1.1.20X1	B1=€1	S1.00=€0.60	100
31.12.20X1	B200=€1	S1.58=€1.00	23,000

Required

Consolidated accounts are to be prepared on 31.12.20X1. Show how the net assets of Subsidiary (i.e., land of B100,000) would be recorded in the consolidated balance sheet assuming (i) no adjustment for hyperinflation, adjustment for hyperinflation using (ii) the current price level method and (iii) the stable currency remeasurement method.

Solution

Net assets of Subsidiary (land)	**1.1.20X1**	**31.12.20X1**
	€	**€**
(i) No adjustment	100,000	500
(ii) Current price level adjustment	100,000	
(100,000 × (23,000/100) ÷ 200)		115,000
(iii) Stable currency remeasurement	100,000	
(100,000 ÷ 0.60 = $166,667; $166,667 ÷ 1.58)		105,485

Source: Adapted from Davies, M., Paterson, R. and Wilson, A. 1999. *UK GAAP*, 6th edition, Ernst & Young and Butterworths Tolley, London, pp.587, 589

There is a substantial difference in the amounts in the year-end consolidated financial statements in the case of no adjustment compared with adjusted amounts. The two methods of adjustment give results which, while different, are not materially so in this case.

As shown in Exhibit 18.8, GlaxoSmithKline uses the current price level method to adjust financial statements of group entities operating overseas in hyperinflationary economies.

Exhibit 18.8 **Hyperinflationary economies: current price level method GlaxoSmithKline Annual Report 2000**

3 Accounting policies (extract)
Consolidation (extract)
In translating into sterling assets, liabilities, results and cash flows of overseas subsidiary, joint venture and associated undertakings reported in currencies of hyperinflationary economies, adjustments are made to reflect current price levels. Any loss on net monetary assets is charged to the consolidated profit and loss account.

Although not UK GAAP, Ericsson in Exhibit 18.9 uses the stable currency method by converting the local currency into the 'functional' (i.e., more stable) currency. This treatment is justified as being consistent with US GAAP even though Ericsson prepares its financial statements 'in accordance with accounting principles generally accepted in Sweden'.

Exhibit 18.9 **Hyperinflationary economies: remeasurement in stable currency Ericsson Annual Report 2000**

Accounting principles (extract)
c Translation of foreign currency financial statements (extract)
Financial statements of companies operating for example in countries with highly inflationary economies, whose functional currency is considered to be another currency than local currency, are translated in two steps. In the first step, remeasurement is made into the functional currency. Gains and losses resulting from this remeasurement are included in the consolidated Income Statement. In the second step, from the functional currency to Swedish kronor, balance sheet items are translated at year-end exchange rates, and income statement items at the average rates of exchange during the year. The resulting translation adjustments are reported directly against stockholder's equity. In our opinion, the remeasurement method, which is in accordance with U.S. GAAP FAS 52, gives a more fair view of these financial statements, since companies concerned operate in de facto US dollar-, Euro- or Deutschmark-based economies.

Exhibit 18.9 clearly explains the approach involved. As already indicated, two steps are required. First, amounts in financial statements are remeasured to take account of inflation. Any gains and losses arising in this step are recorded in the profit and loss account. Second, the remeasured amounts are translated into the reporting currency of the parent and any foreign exchange gains or losses are accounted for in reserves against shareholders' equity.

DaimlerChrysler (which reports under US GAAP) explains the temporal method, and the impact of hyperinflation on translation, in more detail in Exhibit 18.10.

Exhibit 18.10 **Hyperinflationary economies: example of temporal method DaimlerChrysler Annual Report 2000**

Foreign Currency Translation (extract)

The assets and liabilities of foreign subsidiaries operating in highly inflationary economies are translated into euro on the basis of period-end rates for monetary assets and liabilities and at historical rates for non-monetary items, with resulting translation gains and losses being recognized in income. Further, in such economies, depreciation and gains and losses from the disposal of non-monetary assets are determined using historical rates. The exchange rates of the significant currencies of non-euro countries used in preparation of the consolidated financial statements were as follows (amounts for the year 1998 have been restated from Deutsche Marks into euro using the Official Fixed Conversion Rate of €1=DM 1.95583):

		Exchange rate at December 31,		Annual average exchange rate		
		2000	1999	2000	1999	1998
Currency:		€1=	€1=	€1=	€1=	€1=
Brazil	BRL	1.84	1.80	1.69	1.93	1.29
Great Britain	GBP	0.62	0.62	0.61	0.66	0.67
Japan	JPY	106.92	102.73	99.47	121.25	144.96
USA	USD	0.93	1.00	0.92	1.07	1.11

IAS GAAP

IAS 29 *Financial Reporting in Hyperinflationary Economies* sets out the procedure for dealing with foreign currency financial statements of companies operating in highly inflationary environments. Only one of the two methods permitted under UK GAAP is allowed – the local financial statements should be adjusted to reflect current price levels by applying a general price index.

Such financial statements should be stated in terms of the measuring unit current at the balance sheet date. The following procedure should be applied in restating the financial statements:

- amounts in the balance sheet not expressed in the measuring unit current at the balance sheet date should be restated by applying a general price index. Balance sheet amounts stated at current cost need not be restated
- monetary amounts need not be restated as these are stated at current cost
- items in the income statement should be restated by applying the change in general price index from the dates of the transactions to the balance sheet date
- the gain or loss on the net monetary position should be calculated using the change in general price index to the weighted average net monetary position for the period
- this gain or loss should be separately disclosed in income.

Thus, under IAS GAAP, only the general price index method may be used, whereas under UK GAAP there is a choice of methods: (i) the current price level method (as it is called under UK GAAP) and (ii) remeasurement using a stable currency.

SIC 30 *Reporting Currency – Translation from Measurement Currency to Presentation Currency* addresses how an enterprise translates items from a measurement to a presentation currency. This interpretation note is considered excessively detailed to be covered here.

Comparison of UK GAAP and IAS GAAP

The main differences between UK GAAP, on the one hand, and IAS GAAP, on the other, are summarised in Table 18.6.

Table 18.6 Main differences in foreign currency requirements between UK GAAP and IAS GAAP

	UK GAAP	*IAS GAAP*
Individual company accounts		
Foreign currency monetary assets and liabilities	At year-end, translated at balance sheet rate or at forward contract rate	At year-end, translated at balance sheet rate
Severe devaluation of currencies	Gain or loss to be recognised immediately in profit and loss account	Gain or loss may be capitalised as part of the cost of the related asset, subject to some restrictions
Consolidated financial statements		
Translation differences taken to reserves	Category of reserve not specified	Reserve arising from foreign currency translation differences must be separately classified in equity
Disposal of foreign subsidiary	FRS 3 and SSAP 20 require exchange differences to be dealt with in the STRGL	Cumulative amount of deferred exchange differences is recognised in income
Disclosures	Minimal	More extensive
Hyperinflationary economies		
Accounting treatment	Choice allowed: remeasure using stable functional currency or IAS method	Restate to current purchasing power and translate

Sources: Cairns, D. and Nobes, C. 2000. *The Convergence Handbook: A Comparison between International Accounting Standards and UK Financial Reporting Requirements*, Institute of Chartered Accountants in England and Wales, London
Connor, L., Dekker, P., Davies, M., Robinson, P. and Wilson, A. 2001. *IAS/UK GAAP Comparison*, Ernst & Young, London
PricewaterhouseCoopers. 2000. *International Accounting Standards Similarities and Differences IAS, US GAAP and UK GAAP*, PricewaterhouseCoopers, London

One difference in individual company accounts is that SSAP 20 allows the use of a forward contract rate, where applicable, for translating monetary assets and liabilities at the balance sheet date. This is not allowed by IAS 21. Under IAS 21, the liability should be measured initially at the exchange rate on the date of the transaction and subsequently at the closing rate.

Translation differences classified as equity must be disclosed separately under IAS 21 and amounts at the beginning and end of the period should be reconciled.

On disposal of a foreign entity under IAS 21, the appropriate amount of the cumulative translation differences in reserves must be transferred to the profit and loss account and included in the gain or loss on disposal. Such translation differences are reported in the STRGL under UK GAAP, in the period in which they arise.

Goodwill on foreign acquisitions is not specifically covered by SSAP 20. Under UK GAAP, goodwill and fair value adjustments on acquisition of foreign entities are normally translated at the historic rate. Under IAS GAAP, goodwill and fair value adjustments may be treated as either:

- assets and liabilities of the foreign enterprise which are translated at closing rate
- or assets and liabilities of the reporting entity, reported at their historical costs expressed in the reporting currency, i.e., no exchange differences are recorded on these items after acquisition.

UITF 9 allows a choice of treatment in translating foreign entities in hyperinflationary economies (the current purchasing power method and the stable currency remeasurement method) whereas IAS allows only current purchasing power method.

Summary

Foreign currency is an important issue in the context of group accounts. Many companies operate in foreign countries through the vehicle of subsidiary companies. The accounts of these foreign subsidiaries must be translated before they can be incorporated into the parent undertaking's group financial statements. The chapter has reviewed the regulations governing this issue, first having as background considered translation of foreign currency transactions in the individual accounts of entities. Two methods of translation and incorporation of foreign subsidiaries into group accounts were considered and illustrated with examples: the closing rate/net investment method and the temporal method. Disclosure requirements under UK GAAP and IAS GAAP were summarised and the chapter concluded by dealing with the more specialised topic of translating the financial statements of foreign entities operating in hyperinflationary economies.

Learning outcomes

After studying this chapter you should have learnt:

- how to account for foreign currency transactions in individual company accounts, under UK GAAP and IAS GAAP
- how to use the closing rate method to translate foreign currency financial statements
- how to use the temporal method to translate foreign currency financial statements
- the disclosure requirements applying to foreign currency transactions under UK GAAP and IAS GAAP
- how to account for companies operating in hyperinflationary economies under UK GAAP and IAS GAAP
- the differences between the regulations applying to foreign subsidiaries under UK GAAP and IAS GAAP.

Multiple choice questions

Solutions to these questions are prepared under UK GAAP and are presented in Appendix 1.

CLOSING RATE/NET INVESTMENT METHOD

18.1 Olive and Oil

On 1 January 20X1, **Olive** purchased the entire share capital of **Oil**, a company incorporated in Caribaland.

The fixed asset note to the balance sheet of Oil at 31 December 20X5, included the following:
Fixed assets at cost at 1 January 20X5 $200,000
Exchange rates between the Caribaland dollar ($) and the euro (€) were as follows:

1 January 20X1	$2.50 = €1
31 December 20X4	$2.56 = €1
31 December 20X5	$2.60 = €1
Average rate for 20X5	$2.57 = €1

Olive uses the closing rate/net investment method of translation.

The amount included in the consolidated fixed asset note of Olive at 31 December 20X5, in respect of Oil under the caption 'fixed assets at cost at 1 January 20X5' is:

(a) €76,923
(b) €77,821
(c) €78,125
(d) €80,000

18.2 Diver and Shultz

Diver acquired 80% of the ordinary shares of **Shultz** on 1 January 20X1 when the issued capital of Shultz was CHF(Swiss francs)720,000 and the reserves CHF288,000. In its day-to-day operations the Swiss company is not dependent on the reporting currency of the parent undertaking. At 31 December 20X4 the capital and reserves of the companies were:

	Diver	**Shultz**
	€	**CHF**
Ordinary shares	1,000,000	720,000
Reserves	540,000	1,005,000
Net assets	1,540,000	1,725,000

Rates of exchange are as follows:

1 January 20X1	€1 = CHF2.40
31 December 20X4	€1 = CHF2.30

In the consolidated balance sheet as at 31 December 20X4 consolidated reserves (to the nearest €000) would amount to:

(a) €870,000
(b) €789,000
(c) €804,000
(d) €779,000

18.3 Pete and Schmidt

Pete acquired 75% of the ordinary shares of **Schmidt** (a company incorporated in Barcland) on 1 October 20X1 when the reserves of Schmidt were Barc120,000. At 30 April 20X3 the following balances were extracted from the financial statements of the individual companies:

	Pete	**Schmidt**
	€	**Barc**
Ordinary shares	1,000,000	500,000
Reserves	570,000	280,000

Relevant exchange rates were:

1 October 20X1	€1 = B2.50
30 April 20X3	€1 = B2.40

In the consolidated balance sheet as at 30 April 20X3 the reserves were (use the closing rate method for translating Schmidt):

(a) €610,000
(b) €627,750
(c) €785,000
(d) €790,000

18.4 Harold and Magath

Harold has an 80% subsidiary **Magath** incorporated in Sarcland, where the currency is the Sarc (S). The following information has been extracted from the accounts of Magath.

	S000
Net assets at 31 December 20X0	80,960
Profit for the financial year	4,730
Dividends paid	(1,500)
Retained profit	3,230

It is the accounting policy of Harold to translate the accounts of Magath according to the closing rate method, using the average rate of exchange in the profit and loss account.
The exchange rate has varied as follows:

	S = €1
31 December 20X0	3.45
31 December 20X1	3.80
Average for 20X1	3.70

What is the exchange loss to the nearest thousand euro which would be included in the consolidated accounts of Harold for the year ended 31 December 20X1?

(a) €1,660,000
(b) €1,678,000
(c) €1,748,000
(d) €2,098,000

FOREIGN CURRENCY OFFSET PROVISIONS

18.5 Jack and Cantona

Jack used foreign currency borrowings to finance a foreign equity investment in **Cantona**. At 31 March 20X3 the exchange gain arising on the equity investment was €10,500 while the exchange loss arising on the borrowings amounted to €8,000. Assuming Jack has taken advantage of the offset provisions of SSAP 20, the financial statements of the company for the year ended 31 March 20X3 should:

(a) Take the gain on the equity investment directly to reserves and include the loss on the borrowings to the profit and loss account
(b) Include both exchange differences in the profit and loss account

(c) Offset the exchange loss on the borrowings as a reserve movement against the exchange gain on the equity investment

(d) Include the exchange gain on the equity investment in the profit and loss account and show the exchange loss on the borrowings as a movement on reserves

18.6 Wren and Bald Eagle

Wren, a company operating in the eurozone, has a subsidiary company in the United States called **Bald Eagle.** It was acquired some years ago and the acquisition was financed by means of a UK £ loan. Bald Eagle Inc generally finances its operations through local borrowings and operates on a relatively autonomous basis, subject to control of long-term policy from the eurozone.

Since the last balance sheet date, the values of both the UK pound and the US dollar have strengthened against the euro. Bald Eagle is an extremely profitable company and its market value is believed to be considerably in excess of the price originally paid for it.

Under the provisions of SSAP 20 *Foreign Currency Translation* when accounting for the loan and the investment in the *separate books* of Wren:

(a) The investment in Bald Eagle *must* be translated (at the historic rate of exchange), and the loss on the loan charged to profit and loss account.

(b) The investment in Bald Eagle *may* be translated (at the closing rate of exchange) with the resulting exchange gain taken to reserves and the loss on the loan charged to reserves.

(c) The investment in Bald Eagle *must* be translated (at the closing rate of exchange) with the resulting exchange gain taken to reserves and the loss on the loan offset in reserves up to the amount of the gain.

(d) The investment in Bald Eagle *may* be translated (at the closing rate of exchange) with the resulting exchange gain taken to reserves and the loss on the loan offset in reserves up to the amount of the gain.

TEMPORAL METHOD

18.7 Clark

Clark has an overseas subsidiary. Certain items in the subsidiary's balance sheet as on 31 December 20X1, translated into euro on two bases, are as follows:

	Using exchange rate on 31 December 20X1	**Using exchange rate at date of purchase of relevant asset**
	€	€
Short-term investments, at cost	10,000	12,000
Stocks, at average cost	15,000	14,000
Plant and machinery, at net book value	52,000	62,000
	77,000	88,000

What is the aggregate euro amount to be included in Clark's consolidated balance sheet in respect of these items assuming (i) the closing rate/net investment method and (ii) the temporal method is used?

	Closing rate/net investment method	**Temporal method**
(a)	€76,000	€86,000
(b)	€77,000	€88,000
(c)	€77,000	€86,000
(d)	€76,000	€88,000

Self-assessment exercises

Solutions to these self-assessment exercises can be found at:
www.thomsonlearning.co.uk/accountingandfinance/piercebrennan

18.1 Cole and Palm

Cole purchased the entire share capital of **Palm** in Bananarama on 1 January 20W7, on which date the reserves of Palm amounted to 30,000 Bananarama dollars ($). The share capital of Palm has remained unchanged since its incorporation in 20W2.

The summarised balance sheets of Palm on 31 December 20X1 and 20X0 are as follows:

Balance sheets as at 31 December	**20X1**	**20X0**
	$000	**$000**
Fixed assets		
At cost	200	200
Accumulated depreciation	(90)	(50)
	110	150
Net current assets	170	70
	280	220
Loan repayable in year 20Y0	(60)	(60)
	220	160
Share capital	100	100
Reserves	120	60
	220	160

Additional information:

1 Palm does not hold any stocks.
2 The net profit of Palm for the year ended 31 December 20X1 amounted to $60,000 after charging depreciation of $40,000.
3 The accounting policy of Cole is to:
   - translate all items, including the profit and loss account, using the closing rate method
   - comply with SSAP 20 *Foreign Currency Translation.*
4 Exchange rates between the Bananarama dollar ($) and the euro were as follows:
   1 January 20W7 $1.25 = €1
   31 December 20X0 $1.28 = €1
   31 December 20X1 $1.30 = €1

Required

(a) Show the amounts which should be included in respect of Palm in the consolidated financial statements of Cole for the year ended 31 December 20X1. Your solution should comprise the following:
   (i) the translated balance sheet amounts as at 31 December 20X1
   (ii) the statement of movements on reserves
   (iii) the fixed asset note.

(b) Draft a suitable accounting policy note to be included in the consolidated financial statements of Cole in respect of the translation of the results of foreign subsidiaries.

(All calculations should be rounded to the nearest €1.)

18.2 Athgoe

Athgoe acquired 21 million ordinary shares of one Norwegian kroner each in Bergen on 1 August 20W2 when the reserves of Bergen were Kr15m and the exchange rate was Kr10 to €1. Goodwill was amortised over five years following acquisition.

The profit and loss accounts of Athgoe and Bergen for the year ended 31 July 20X0 were as follows:

	Athgoe	**Bergen**
	€000	**Kr000**
Turnover	92,253	945,040
Cost of sales	60,274	630,000
Gross profit	31,979	315,040
Distribution costs	12,900	75,520
Administrative expenses	14,697	25,200
Other expenses	1,913	21,040
	2,469	193,280
Dividends from subsidiary	3,150	—
	5,619	193,280
Tax	1,939	75,680
Profit on ordinary activities after tax	3,680	117,600
Dividends paid (31 January 20X0)	1,830	42,000
Retained profit for the year	1,850	75,600

The balance sheets of Athgoe and Bergen as at 31 July 20X0 were as follows:

	Athgoe	**Bergen**
	€000	**Kr000**
Fixed assets		
Tangible assets	17,658	385,000
Investment in Bergen	3,050	—
	20,708	385,000
Current assets		
Stock	22,454	36,750
Debtors	6,153	17,500
Cash	1,562	94,500
	30,169	148,750
Total assets	50,877	533,750
Current liabilities		
Trade creditors	(22,457)	(43,750)
Creditors: Amounts falling due after more than one year		
Loan	(12,310)	(86,800)
	16,110	403,200
Capital and reserves		
Share capital in €1 ordinary shares	6,000	—
Share capital in Kr1 ordinary shares	—	35,000
Profit and loss account	10,110	368,200
	16,110	403,200

Exchange rates have been as follows:

	Kroner to €1
31 July 20W9	9.5
Average for 20W9/20X0	8
31 July 20X0	7

In determining the appropriate method of currency translation, it is established that the trade of Bergen is independent of the economic environment of the investing company's currency. Consequently the closing rate/net investment method is used, including using the average rate to translate the profit and loss account of the subsidiary.

continued overleaf

Required

(a) Prepare the consolidated profit and loss account for the year ended 31 July 20X0 and the consolidated balance sheet as at that date, using the closing rate method of translation.

(b) Analyse the movement on consolidated reserves indicating separately:
  - (i) consolidated reserves at 1 August 20W9
  - (ii) group retained earnings for the year ended 31 July 20X0
  - (iii) difference on exchange arising in the year.

(c) Explain how the difference referred to in b (iii) arose. Your explanation should include quantification of components.

18.3 Glenmore and Plenborg

On 1 July 20X5 **Glenmore** acquired 80% of the issued ordinary shares of **Plenborg**, a Danish company, for DK1,600,000. At that date the company raised a loan of DK2,100,000 and used part of the loan to acquire the shares in Plenborg.

The kroner has strengthened over the past four years and the rates of exchange have been as follows:

	DK to €1
1 July 20X5	8.00
30 June 20X6	7.70
30 June 20X7	7.60
30 June 20X8	7.00
30 June 20X9 and average for year ended 30 June 20X9	6.00

The draft profit and loss accounts and balance sheets of Glenmore and Plenborg are set out as follows:

Draft profit and loss accounts for the year ended 30 June 20X9

	Glenmore €000	Plenborg DK000
Operating profit	2,058	2,130
Income from shares in subsidiary	80	—
Profit on ordinary activities before tax	2,138	2,130
Tax on profit on ordinary activities	(708)	(774)
Profit for the financial year	1,430	1,356
Dividends		
Paid	(300)	—
Proposed	(400)	(600)
Profit retained, transferred to reserves	730	756

Draft balance sheets as at 30 June 20X9

	Glenmore €000	Plenborg DK000
Fixed assets		
Tangible assets		
At cost	—	2,268
At valuation	1,470.00	—
Less: Depreciation	(441.00)	(462)
	1,029.00	1,806
Investment in subsidiary	228.57	—
Net current assets	2,632.43	1,806
Total assets less current liabilities	3,890.00	3,612
Creditors: Amounts falling due after more than one year		
Loan	—	(210)
Loan of DK2,100,000 restated at 30 June 20X8	(300.00)	—
	3,590.00	3,402

	Glenmore €000	Plenborg DK000
Capital and reserves		
Called-up share capital	1,700.00	1,600
Share premium account	40.00	—
Revaluation reserve	70.00	—
Retained earnings	1,780.00	1,802
	3,590.00	3,402

Notes
1 The balance on Plenborg's retained earnings at the date of acquisition was DK240,000.
2 Glenmore avails of the offset rules of SSAP 20 when dealing with foreign equity investments and related borrowings. The entire DK loan is potentially repayable by the realisation of the investment.
The balances in the balance sheet reflect exchange rates at 30 June 20X8.
3 Goodwill is amortised over eight years.
4 The subsidiary accounts are translated using the closing rate method.

Required

(a) Explain, with appropriate supporting computations, the treatment of the investment in Plenborg and the loan of DK2,100,000 in the accounts of Glenmore at 30 June 20X9.

(b) Indicate the revised amounts (for investment in subsidiary, loan and retained earnings) to be included in the draft balance sheet of Glenmore.
(Parts (a) and (b) of this question refer to the individual accounts of the parent company.)

(c) (i) Explain the offset rules of SSAP 20 applicable to group companies when equity investments are financed by foreign borrowings.
(ii) Calculate the difference on retranslation, at 30 June 20X9, of the opening net assets of Plenborg.
(iii) Indicate the extent to which the difference on retranslation of the borrowings of DK2,100,000 can be offset against reserves in the group accounts for the year ended 30 June 20X9.

(d) Calculate the following items for inclusion in the consolidated balance sheet as at 30 June 20X9:
(i) goodwill
(ii) minority interest.

(e) Prepare the consolidated balance sheet as at 30 June 20X9 assuming:
(i) full consolidation
(ii) equity accounting for the investment in Plenborg.

18.4 Carpro

Carpro, a Republic of Ireland company which operates in euro, entered into various transactions involving different foreign currencies which affect the accounts for the year ended 30 June 20X3:

1 Carpro bought a computer-controlled item of automated plant at a cost of 800,000 Oboks (OK) on 1 July 20X2. This acquisition was financed (partly) by a three-year loan, obtained on that date, of 720,000 OK at an interest rate of 15% per annum on the outstanding balance.
The loan is repayable in OKs in three equal instalments, together with the annual interest, on 30 June 20X3, 20X4 and 20X5.
The balance of the purchase consideration was paid in OKs at date of acquisition.
Carpro depreciates plant at the rate of 12½% per annum on cost.

Exchange rates were:	**OK = €1**
1 July 20X2	8
30 June 20X3	10
Average for the year to 30 June 20X3	9

Under the terms of the loan contract, repayments of the principal element of the loans, but not payments of interest, are at a fixed rate of 8 OK = €1.

continued overleaf

2 Carpro bought raw materials on credit from Ingcrow, an overseas supplier whose local currency is Parqs (PQ). Transactions were as follows:

		Parqs	**Exchange rate PQ = €1**
Purchases			
20X2	25 August	10,700	25
	2 September	15,432	24
	9 November	17,094	22
20X3	11 March	14,638	26
	4 April	22,059	27
Payments for these purchases:			
20X2	11 November	9,988	22
	3 December	12,117	21
20X3	27 February	18,000	25
	4 March	16,900	25
	25 May	13,048	28
Balance	30 June	to be derived	24
Payment of balance			
	1 September	to be derived	26

3 Carpro acquired a fixed asset investment in the equity share capital of Herma, an overseas company whose local currency is Arlodds (AD) at a cost of 7,200,000 AD on 1 January 20X3.

At the same time Carpro obtained a hedging loan (in a different currency) of 9,600,000 Skrams (SK), repayable in full in SKs on 31 July 20X9. Interest on this loan is payable, at 8% per annum, half yearly on the outstanding balance on 30 June and 31 December in each year.

Herma, the investee company, declared a dividend on equity shares, of which 36,000 AD was attributable to Carpro's shareholding. At 30 June 20X3, Carpro brought the dividend into account as dividends receivable. The dividend was actually remitted to Carpro in ADs on 7 October 20X3.

Exchange rates were:		**Equity investment AD = €1**	**Hedging loan SK = €1**
20X3	1 January	18	24
	30 June	20	30
	7 October	18	31

4 Carpro obtained a five-year loan of 6,000,000 Parqs (PQ) on 1 January 20X3, repayable in full in PQs on 1 January 20X8. Interest at 15% is payable annually in PQs, starting on 1 January 20X4.

Exchange rates were:		**PQ = €1**
20X3	1 January	20
	30 June	24
	Average for year to 30 June 20X3	23

Required

(a) Write a suitable note 'Foreign currency translation' for inclusion in the accounting policies section of the final accounts of Carpro for the year ended 30 June 20X3.

(b) For each of the four sets of transactions detailed, translate the foreign currency items into euro and show each of these figures, together with any resultant exchange translation differences, against their appropriate revenue, expense, asset or liability item in the final accounts of Carpro for the year ended 30 June 20X3.

Translation and disclosure must comply with the requirements of SSAP 20 *Foreign Currency Translation*.

(All calculations should be correct to the nearest €1.)

(c) Write brief notes for each of the four sets of transactions explaining:

(i) the reasons for your choice of rate used in translating the various items

(ii) the accounting treatment you have applied to the items in (i) and to any resultant exchange translation differences in the final accounts for the year ended 30 June 20X3.

Examination-style questions

18.1 Rowlock, Overseas and Europe

Rowlock was formed in 20V5 to manufacture executive toys. The directors decided to expand their exports and on 1 January 20W9 Rowlock acquired investments in an American company, **Overseas**, and a Swedish company, **Europe**. Overseas is to act as a selling agent for the company's products.

The investments consisted of 800,000 shares of US$10 each in Overseas, when its reserves were US$25m, and of 2,250,000 shares of SEK20 each in Europe, when its reserves were SEK230m.

The directors have instructed their accountant to prepare draft consolidated accounts as at 31 December 20X3 on the basis that Overseas is a subsidiary undertaking due to the fact that they exercise a dominant influence; and that Europe is a participating interest but not an associated undertaking.

The balance sheets as at 31 December 20X3 were as follows:

	Rowlock €m	**Overseas US$m**	**Europe SEKm**
Fixed assets			
Tangible assets	669	458	4,231
Investment in Overseas	12	—	—
Investment in Europe	10	—	—
Current assets			
Stocks	675	44	404
Cash	46	113	1,038
Current liabilities			
Creditors	(490)	(31)	(288)
Creditors falling due after more than one year			
Loan	(370)	(103)	(954)
	552	481	4,431
Capital and reserves			
Share capital	185	20	180
Profit and loss account	367	461	4,251
	552	481	4,431

The profit and loss accounts for the year ended 31 December 20X3 are as follows:

	Rowlock €m	**Overseas US$m**	**Europe SEKm**
Turnover	2,784	1,150	10,615
Cost of sales	(1,822)	(775)	(7,154)
Gross profit	962	375	3,461
Distribution costs	(392)	(90)	(831)
Administrative expenses	(370)	(30)	(278)
Depreciation	(35)	(24)	(230)
Dividend from Overseas	12	—	—
Dividend from Europe	11	—	—
Profit before tax	188	231	2,122
Tax	(93)	(90)	(831)
Profit after tax	95	141	1,291
Dividends paid 31.7.X3	(37)	(51)	(440)
Retained profit	58	90	851

Further information:

1 The fixed assets in both Overseas and Europe were acquired on 1 January 20W5. They are stated at cost less depreciation and there have been no acquisitions or disposals during the year.

2 Stocks:

	31 December 20X2		31 December 20X3	
	Stock	**Exchange rate at purchase date**	**Stock**	**Exchange rate at purchase date**
Overseas US$m	57	2.0	44	1.6
Europe SEKm	523	11.5	404	8.5

3 Exchange rates have been as follows:

	US$ = €1	**SEK= €1**
1 January 20W5	2.4	12.0
1 January 20W9	2.0	12.5
31 December 20X2	1.8	11.0
Average for 20X3	1.7	10.0
31 July 20X3	1.7	10.0
31 December 20X3	1.5	8.0

4 Rowlock's accounting policy is to write off goodwill immediately on acquisition.
5 The foreign exchange translation of the foreign subsidiary is to be on the basis that the functional currency of the American operation is euro.

Required

(a) Prepare a draft consolidated profit and loss account for the Rowlock group for the year ended 31 December 20X3 and a draft consolidated balance sheet as at that date.

(b) (i) Calculate the effect on the consolidated profit and loss account for the year ended 31 December 20X3 if the investment in Europe is classified as an associated interest.

(ii) Calculate the carrying value of the investment in the consolidated balance sheet as at 31 December 20X3.
(Assume closing rate is used to translate accounts of Europe.)

18.2 Erasmus and Heinrich

On 1 October 20X5 **Erasmus** acquired 80% of the issued ordinary shares of **Heinrich** for CHF(Swiss francs)800,000. At that date the company raised a loan of CHF1,000,000 and used part of the loan to acquire the shares in Heinrich.

The Swiss franc has strengthened over the past four years and the rates of exchange have been as follows:

	CHF to €1
1 October 20X5	4.00
30 September 20X6	3.85
30 September 20X7	3.80
30 September 20X8	3.50
30 September 20X9	3.00
Average for year ended 30 September 20X9	3.25

The draft profit and loss accounts and balance sheets of Erasmus and Heinrich are as follows:

Profit and loss accounts for the year ended 30 September 20X9

	Erasmus	**Heinrich**
	€	**CHF000**
Operating profit	1,029,000	1,065
Income from shares in subsidiary	73,600	—
Profit on ordinary activities before tax	1,102,600	1,065
Tax on profit on ordinary activities	(352,800)	(385)
Profit for the financial year	749,800	680
Dividends		
Paid	(150,000)	(299)
Proposed	(200,000)	—
Profit retained, transferred to reserves	399,800	381

Balance sheets as at 30 September 20X9

	Erasmus €	Heinrich CHF000
Fixed assets		
Tangible assets at cost	—	1,150
Tangible assets at valuation	735,000	—
Less: Depreciation	(220,500)	(230)
	514,500	920
Investments		
Shares in subsidiary restated at 30.9.20X8	228,570	—
Net current assets	1,194,490	902
Total assets less current liabilities	1,937,560	1,822
Creditors: Amounts falling due after more than one year		
Loan	—	(105)
Loan of CHF1,000,000 restated at 30.9.20X8	(285,710)	—
	1,651,850	1,717
Capital and reserves		
Called-up share capital	850,000	850
Share premium account	20,000	—
Revaluation reserve	35,000	—
Profit and loss account	746,850	867
	1,651,850	1,717

Notes:

1. The profit and loss account balance of Heinrich on 1 October 20X5 was CHF286,000.
2. The subsidiary accounts are translated using the closing rate method with the average rate used for the profit and loss account for the year.

Required

(a) Explain, with appropriate supporting computations, the treatment of the investment in Heinrich and the loan of CHF1,000,000 in the draft balance sheet of Erasmus at 30 September 20X9.

(b) (i) Explain the offset rules applicable to group companies when equity investments are financed by foreign borrowings.

(ii) Calculate the credit or charge to the consolidated profit and loss account for the year ended 30 September 20X9 arising from the translation of the CHF1,000,000 loan.

(c) Prepare the consolidated profit and loss account for the year ended 30 September 20X9 and the consolidated balance sheet at that date.

18.3 Newton, Darwin and Hoyle

(a) **Newton**, to whom you are financial adviser, is preparing its financial statements for the year ended 31 March 20X2. It has two wholly owned subsidiaries:

- A Polish company, **Darwin**, which it acquired a number of years ago at a cost of 500 million zloty. Newton incorporates the financial statements of Darwin in its consolidated financial statements using the closing rate method. During 20W9, Newton borrowed 1,000 million zloty (repayable in 20X9) to provide a hedge against the investment, which was then considered to be worth in excess of 1,500 million zloty. The net assets of Darwin at 31 March 20X1 were 1,200 million zloty.
- A Swiss company, **Hoyle**, which it set up on 1 June 20X1 at a cost of Swiss fr 25 million. Newton is to incorporate Hoyle in its consolidated financial statements using the temporal method. The exchange loss for the period is €52,000. Newton partially financed the acquisition of the shares by borrowing Swiss fr 20 million repayable in 20X7.

In addition, Newton has a 15% investment in a Japanese company, **Gamow**, which it acquired in 20W0 at a cost of Yen 220 million, financed by means of a Yen loan of the same amount. At 31 March 20X2 none of the loan had been repaid.

The relevant exchange rates were:

	€1 = zloty	€1 = Swiss fr	€1 = yen
31 March 20X1	1,000	—	230
1 June 20X1	—	3.7	—
31 March 20X2	950	4.0	290
Average – period to 31 March 20X2	960	3.8	260

(2) The directors of Newton have asked your advice in respect of the following.

For sound commercial reasons Darwin is to change its year-end to 31 January with effect from 31 January 20X3. The consolidated financial statements will hence forward include results for Darwin drawn up for the period to 31 January. The directors wonder which 'closing exchange rate' to use for the purposes of the 31 March 20X3 financial statements for the Newton group – that at 31 January 20X3 or that at 31 March 20X3.

Required

(a) For the year ended 31 March 20X2 calculate, in accordance with standard accounting practice, the exchange differences in respect of the investments/borrowings in (1) and explain the treatment thereof in both the company and the consolidated financial statements for Newton.

(b) Prepare a memorandum advising the directors of Newton on the accounting considerations to be taken into account in connection with Darwin's change of year end; advise the directors of any appropriate accounting treatments for the purposes of the consolidated financial statements.

(Ignore taxation.)

18.4 Hall

At 31 December 20X3, the consolidated balance sheet of **Hall** and its two foreign subsidiary companies included the following assets, capital and reserves:

	Site A €	Site B €	Site C Barcs	Site D Larcs
Freehold land				
Original cost	100,000	300,000	500,000	300,000
Valuation	150,000	360,000	700,000	—

	€
Share capital – Ordinary shares of 25 cent each – Authorised	10,000,000
– Issued and fully paid	4,000,000
Share premium account	1,565,000
Revaluation reserve	131,052
Profit and loss account	3,460,000

It is group policy to incorporate in the group accounts independent valuations of freehold property. During the year ended 31 December 20X4, the following matters arose:

1. Site A was sold for €160,000. The proceeds of sale were credited to a suspense account pending advice on the correct treatment of this transaction.
2. Site D was revalued by independent professional valuers at Larcs 450,000.
3. On 1 March 20X4, a bonus issue of one share for four was made. The directors decided to maintain reserves in the most flexible form.
4. On 1 April, a rights issue of one share for five at 60 cent each was made and fully taken up.
5. On 1 August, a public issue of 4 million shares at 75 cent each was fully subscribed.

6 On 1 September 20X4 90% of the issued share capital of **Lynx** was obtained in exchange for 1,700,000 25 cent ordinary shares in Hall valued at 70 cent each.

The net assets of Lynx at 1 September 20X4 had the following values:

	Net book value	**Fair value**
	€	**€**
Tangible fixed assets	800,000	910,000
Current assets	1,200,000	1,150,000
Creditors	(860,000)	(860,000)

7 Consolidated retained profit for the year, subject to any adjustment required in respect of **1**, amounted to €300,000.

The following are the relevant exchange rates:

31 December 20X3	Barcs 9.5 = €1	Larcs 2.8 = €1
31 December 20X4	Barcs 9.3 = €1	Larcs 2.7 = €1

It is group policy to use the closing rate at the balance sheet date for the translation of all transactions in the accounts of overseas subsidiaries.

Required

(a) Draft the following notes to the consolidated balance sheet of Hall as at 31 December 20X4:
  (i) share capital
  (ii) reserves.

(b) Explain briefly your treatment of the disposal of Site A.
(Calculations to the nearest €1.)

18.5 Unicum

On 1 January 20X0, **Unicum**, the European parent company of a diversified group, purchased 40% of the shares in **Colbo.** Colbo is incorporated and operating in Monty, a country whose currency is the Montian shilling (MSh). The reserves of Colbo amounted to MSh 3m on 1 January 20X0.

The draft consolidated balance sheet of Unicum (incorporating the investment in Colbo at cost) and the audited balance sheet of Colbo at 31 December 20X1 are as follows:

	Unicum Consolidated balance sheet		**Colbo Individual company**	
	€000	**€000**	**MSh000**	**MSh000**
Tangible fixed assets		72,658		24,450
Investment in Colbo at cost		1,420		—
Current assets				
Stocks	27,704		1,800	
Debtors	8,653		2,400	
Cash in hand and at bank	13,642		600	
	49,999		4,800	
Creditors: Amounts falling due within one year	(28,707)		(3,600)	
Net current assets		21,292		1,200
Creditors: Amounts falling due after one year		(24,710)		—
		70,660		25,650
Capital and reserves				
Called-up share capital		6,000		15,000
Reserves		41,620		10,650
Shareholders' funds		47,620		25,650
Minority interest		23,040		—
		70,660		25,650

continued overleaf

The consolidated profit and loss account of the Unicum group and the individual profit and loss account of Colbo for the year ended 31 December 20X1 include the following:

	Unicum Consolidated profit and loss account €000	**Colbo Individual company profit and loss account MSh000**
Profit before tax	26,629	7,110
Taxation charge	(11,399)	(2,310)
Profit after tax	15,230	4,800
Minority interest	(5,880)	—
Profit attributable to group	9,350	4,800
Dividends	(1,830)	—
Profit retained for year	7,520	4,800

Additional information:

1 Goodwill on acquisition is amortised over five years. Goodwill on acquisition of all group entities except Colbo was fully amortised by the beginning of the current year.

2 No dividends were paid or proposed by Colbo in 20X1.

3 The following were the exchange rates at the relevant dates:

1 January 20X0	MSh 10 = €1
31 December 20X0	MSh 6 = €1
31 December 20X1	MSh 5 = €1
Average for year ended 31 December 20X1	MSh 5.5 = €1

4 Unicum uses the closing rate method to translate the financial statements of foreign subsidiaries and associates, translating profits at the average rate of exchange for the year.

Required

(a) Assuming the equity basis of accounting is adopted in the consolidated accounts for the investment in Colbo, calculate the consolidated reserves of Unicum and group at 1 January 20X1.

(b) Assuming the equity basis of accounting is adopted in the consolidated accounts for the investment in Colbo, calculate the consolidated reserves of Unicum and group at 31 December 20X1.

Your answer to (b) should include a reconciliation of the movement on consolidated reserves for the year 20X1, highlighting in particular, movements associated with profit for the year and those caused by retranslating opening net investment in Colbo at the year-end.

(c) Prepare the consolidated balance sheet of Unicum group as at 31 December 20X1:

(i) assuming the equity basis of accounting is appropriate for the investment in Colbo because Unicum *exercises significant influence* over the activities of Colbo

(ii) assuming that full consolidation is appropriate because Unicum *controls* the activities of Colbo.

(d) *Briefly* discuss the significance of the three different ways of including investment in Colbo (cost, equity and full consolidation) in the consolidated balance sheet of Unicum and group.

19

Consolidated cash flow statements

Learning objectives

After studying this chapter you should be able to:

- appreciate the regulations applying to the preparation of cash flow statements
- prepare cash flow statements
- prepare the disclosures required to support cash flow statements
- identify captions that are unique to group cash flow statements
- compare and contrast UK GAAP and IAS GAAP regulations applying to cash flow statements

Introduction

Many users of accounts consider cash flow reporting to be more useful than traditional accruals-based reporting of company performance and financial position. The profit and loss account highlights profit generated but does not explain why the amount of cash available to an organisation has increased or decreased during the accounting period. The balance sheet sets out the financial position at the end of the year with comparative figures. Activities contributing and absorbing cash are not highlighted in the traditional statements despite the importance of cash generation for the successful continuation and growth of a business. Cash flow statements, by way of contrast, explain where businesses generated cash from, and how they used cash during a period.

This chapter describes the regulations applicable to the presentation of cash flow statements, with particular emphasis on the techniques involved in preparing consolidated cash flow statements. There are four additional issues to deal with in group cash flow statements not appearing in cash flow statements of unconsolidated entities:

- dividends paid by associated undertakings
- acquisition of subsidiaries during the year
- disposal of subsidiaries during the year
- dividends paid to minorities.

UK GAAP

There are no legal requirements for publication of cash flow statements but such statements in one form or another have been required under UK GAAP since 1975.

Regulatory framework

Initially, under SSAP 10, a statement of source and application of funds was required in the UK but this was replaced with a requirement for a cash flow statement in 1991 when FRS 1 *Cash Flow Statements* was issued. Unlike the statement of source and application of funds which showed movements in funds (however defined) between balance sheets prepared at two different dates, a cash flow statement reports actual inflows and outflows of cash during a period, classified according to specified business activities. Transactions are only included if they result in a change in cash or bank balances.

FRS 1 *Cash Flow Statements* recommends the reporting of *cash* flows and provides a standard format to be followed. The objective of the FRS is to require businesses to report on a standard basis their cash generation and absorption for a period. FRS 1 *Cash Flow Statements* was revised in 1996.

A consolidated cash flow statement should be prepared as if the group were a single enterprise. Inter-company cash flows should be eliminated in preparing cash flow statements. For subsidiaries acquired or disposed of during the period, cash flows to be included should be for the same period as profits and losses are included in the consolidated profit and loss account.

FRS 1 provides examples of both an individual and a group cash flow statement in Appendix 1 to the FRS.

Scope

FRS 1 applies to all financial statements intended to give a true and fair view, with the following exceptions:

- subsidiary undertakings where 90% or more of the voting rights are controlled within the group, provided the consolidated financial statements which include the exempt subsidiary are publicly available
- mutual life assurance companies
- pension funds
- certain investment funds
- small private companies as defined in legislation
- unincorporated entities equivalent in size to small companies.

Definitions

Cash is defined in FRS 1 (paragraph 2) as:

> Cash in hand and deposits repayable on demand with any qualifying financial institution, less overdrafts from any qualifying financial institution repayable on demand. … Cash includes cash in hand and deposits denominated in foreign currencies.

The standard requires movements in 'liquid resources' to be disclosed. They are defined in paragraph 2 as:

> Current asset investments held as readily disposable stores of value. A readily disposable investment is one that:

a) is disposable by the reporting entity without curtailing or disrupting its business;

and is either:

b) (i) readily convertible into known amounts of cash at or close to its carrying amount, or
   (ii) traded in an active market.

Presentation of cash flow statements

FRS 1 is quite prescriptive concerning the format and layout of the cash flow statement. It lays down a format for the statement and specifies certain disclosures to be made in the notes to the statement. Comparative amounts are required.

Inflows and outflows of cash are grouped together within headings indicating the type of activity giving rise to them. The standard prescribes nine headings within which cash flows are to be reported. Cash flow statements should list cash inflows and outflows under the following headings (and in that order and showing the total for each heading, a total of cash inflow or outflow before use or source of liquid resources and before financing):

1 cash flows from operating activities
2 dividends received from associated undertakings (introduced by FRS 9)
3 returns on investments and servicing of finance
4 taxation
5 capital expenditure and financial investment
6 acquisitions and disposals
7 equity dividends paid

Subtotal: Cash flow before flows from management of liquid resources and financing

8 management of liquid resources
9 financing activities.

Where the prescribed headings do not suit a specialised business, an alternative suitable presentation may be devised. Where an entity has cash flows not covered by a prescribed heading, the most appropriate heading should be used. A relatively common example is receipts of government capital grants. FRS 1 does not refer to grants. Practice varies between including them in *Capital expenditure and financial investment* or *Financing activities*. The former heading is increasingly being used in practice because these grants are received to support the purchase of tangible fixed assets. Cash flows relating to tangible fixed assets are included under *Capital expenditure and financial investment*.

By creating separate headings for dividends, interest and tax, ASB avoided the need to allocate these on an arbitrary basis to operating, investing and financing activities. Although equity dividends paid are included in a separate category, dividends paid to minority shareholders are included under *Returns on investments and servicing of finance*. Dividends received, other than those from associates, are also included under this heading.

The overall total of the cash flow statement comprises the net movement in cash (net of bank overdrafts) for the period which, when added to the cash balance brought forward, gives the cash balance at the end of the period.

Two reconciliations are required:

- operating profit must be reconciled with cash flows from operating activities
- total net cash flow (increase/decrease) is reconciled with movements in net debt.

Redbus (Exhibit 19.5) follows the format prescribed in FRS 1 in its consolidated cash flow statements and discloses seven of the nine items in the list.

Cash flows from operating activities

Cash flows from operating activities are generally the cash effects of transactions relating to trading activities. Two methods of computing cash flows from operating activities are allowed: the direct method (showing relevant constituent cash flows) and the indirect method (adjustment to the operating result). Both methods should yield the same overall cash flows. These are now discussed further.

Direct method

Under the direct method, cash flows from operations are presented on the face of the cash flow statement, analysed as follows:

- cash receipts from sales
- cash payments to suppliers
- cash payments to and on behalf of employees
- VAT paid or received
- other cash payments.

Marks and Spencer in Exhibit 19.1 reports operating cash flows using the direct method.

Indirect method

The more common presentation of operating cash flows is the indirect approach where cash flows from operations are presented as a single item on the cash flow statement. This amount is reconciled to operating profit (from the profit and loss account) in a note. This reconciliation is the indirect method of calculating operating cash flows and is a required disclosure under FRS 1 even where the direct method is adopted. Redbus (Exhibit 19.5) uses the indirect method.

Under the indirect method, cash flows are calculated using the accruals-based profit figure as the starting point. Profit has to be adjusted for:

- non-operating items
- non-cash items.

As the first category of cash flow reported is cash flows from operating activities, it makes sense that the profit figure used in the indirect approach should exclude all non-operating items. Therefore, profit before investment income and/or finance charges must be isolated. The closer one can get to pure operating profit as the starting point the better. For example, profits or losses on disposal are not operating items as far as FRS 1 is concerned.

Profit calculations, by definition, include non-cash adjustments to ensure completeness of revenues and expenses. For example, turnover includes sales on credit not yet paid for. Cost of sales includes purchases on credit not yet paid for. In addition, depreciation and goodwill amortisation are included in arriving at profit. To the extent that non-cash items increase or reduce revenues and expenses for the period (relative to the cash received or paid), profit is increased or reduced. Consequently, operating profit is a crude starting point for operating cash flow and must be adjusted to identify the real cash flows.

Fleshing out these adjustments a little more, under the indirect method, operating profit reflects cash flow from operations after the following adjustments:

- for non-cash items included in profit calculation:
  - depreciation
  - goodwill amortisation
  - profits/losses on disposal (included in operating profit in the profit and loss account).
- for non-cash increases in profit caused by:
  - increasing trade debtors
  - reducing trade creditors
  - increasing stocks.
- for non-cash reductions in profit caused by:
  - reducing trade debtors
  - increasing trade creditors
  - reducing stocks.

Table 19.1 compares the two approaches to calculating operating cash flows.

Table 19.1 Comparison of direct and indirect method of calculating cash flows from operations

Direct method	*Indirect method*	
Cash from customers	Operating profit	
Cash to suppliers	*Adjust for:*	Depreciation
Cash to and on behalf of employees		Profit or loss on disposal
VAT paid or received		Other non-cash items
Other cash payments		Working capital changes

Example 19.1 uses a very simple situation to illustrate the approach to calculating operating cash flows under the two methods.

Example 19.1 Computing cash flows using the direct and indirect methods

Example

Assume the credit sales are the only transactions during the year (i.e., there are no purchases or expenses)

1.1.20X1 Debtors €10,000

20X1 Credit sales €100,000

31.12.20X1 Debtors €15,000

Required

Calculate operating cash flows using the direct and indirect methods of computation.

continued overleaf

Example 19.1 Continued

Solution
Profit for the year is €100,000.

Direct approach

Debtors control account

	€		€
Balance b/f	10,000	Bank* (balancing amount)	95,000
Sales	100,000	Balance c/f	15,000
	110,000		110,000

* Operating cash flows: Cash receipts from customers €95,000

Indirect approach

	€
Operating profit	100,000
Increase in Debtors ($15{,}000_{\text{closing balance}} - 10{,}000_{\text{opening balance}}$)	(5,000)
Operating cash flows	95,000

Debtors and creditors

Debtor balances in the balance sheet can include receivables other than trade debtors. Under the indirect approach to calculating operating cash flows, it is only changes in trade debtors that affect operating profit and its related cash flows. Under FRS 1, reporting entities have to separate movements in balance sheet amounts from debtors and creditors that relate to operating activities from those that have to be reported under other standard headings such as investing activities or returns on investment and servicing of finance. Table 19.2 shows the standard headings in the cash flow statement under which components of debtor and creditor balances in the balance sheet are dealt with.

Table 19.2 Analysis of debtors and creditors under cash flow headings

Debtors and prepayments in the balance sheet	
	Cash flow statement caption
Trade debtors	Cash flow from operating activities
Dividend receivable	Returns on investments and servicing of finance
Corporation tax refund due	Taxation
Proceeds of disposal due	Capital expenditure
Creditors and accruals in the balance sheet	
	Cash flow statement caption
Trade creditors	Cash flow from operating activities
Proposed dividends	Returns on investments and servicing of finance (Preference dividends and dividends paid to minority shareholders) Equity dividends paid (Proposed ordinary dividend of parent)
Interest accruals	Returns on investments and servicing of finance
Corporation tax	Taxation
Fixed asset accruals	Capital expenditure
Finance lease obligations	Financing and/or Returns on investments and servicing of finance

To identify changes in trade debtors and creditors, balance sheet debtor and creditor amounts have to be analysed to separate operating from non-operating amounts. The cash flows relating to non-operating items have to be reported under other captions in the standard such as *Returns on investments and servicing of finance* or *Capital expenditure and financial investment*'.

Example 19.2 illustrates the analysis required in a simple case to identify movements in *trade* debtors.

Example 19.2 Separation of non-operating amounts from debtors

Example

You are provided with the following information about debtors:

	Beginning of year	End of year
Balance sheet amounts	**€000**	**€000**
Debtors	1,010	1,525
Dividend receivable included in debtors	10	25

Required

Analyse total debtors and show the amount to be included as an adjustment for debtors in the reconciliation of operating profit to operating cash flows required by FRS 1.

Solution

Debtors would have to be analysed as follows:

	Trade debtors	Investment income receivable	Total
	€000	**€000**	**€000**
Opening balance	1,000	10	1,010
Closing balance	1,500	25	1,525
Increase in trade debtors	500		

Amount to be shown in the reconciliation is €500,000

Marks and Spencer calculates cash flows from operating activities using both the direct and the indirect methods in Exhibit 19.1 (overleaf). The direct method is shown on the face of the cash flow statement and, as required by FRS 1, the reconciliation of operating profit and cash flows from operating activities (the indirect method) is shown in a note to the cash flow statement. Both approaches produce the same result for cash inflow from operating activities, i.e., £641.5 million in 2000 (£472.3 million in 1999).

Associates and joint ventures

Cash flows from investments that are accounted for using the equity method should be included in the group cash flow statement only to the extent of the actual cash flows between the group and the entity concerned. FRS 9 *Associates and Joint Ventures* amended FRS 1 (revised) to require that such cash flow should be included and reported under a separate heading *Dividends received from joint ventures and associates*. This item did not feature in the example cash flow statement contained in FRS 1 as FRS 9 was issued after FRS 1 was revised.

Exhibit 19.1 **Direct and indirect methods of computing cash flows from operating activities**
Marks and Spencer plc Annual Report 2000

	2000		1999	
Cash flow statement (extract)	£m	£m	£m	£m
Operating activities				
Received from customers	7,989.9		7,884.1	
Payments to suppliers	(5,357.1)		(5,464.2)	
Payments to and on behalf of employees	(1,138.3)		(1,153.9)	
Other payments	(803.8)		(793.1)	
Cash inflow from operating activities before exceptional items		690.7		472.9
Exceptional operating cash outflow		(49.2)		(0.6)
Cash inflow from operating activities		641.5		472.3

27 Reconciliation of operating profit to net cash inflow from operating activities

	2000	1999
	£m	£m
Operating profit	471.0	512.0
Exceptional operating charges	72.0	88.5
Operating profit before exceptional charges	543.0	600.5
Depreciation (excluding £64.0m impairment provision last year)	261.6	236.4
Decrease/(increase) in stocks	40.3	(7.6)
Increase in customer advances	(206.2)	(363.0)
Decrease/(increase) in other debtors	0.9	(8.0)
Increase in creditors	51.1	14.6
Net cash inflow before exceptional items	690.7	472.9
Exceptional operating cash outflow	(49.2)	(0.6)
Net cash inflow from operating activities	641.5	472.3

Example 19.3 provides a simple example of the approach required to calculate the dividend received from associated undertakings. Two methods are used to carry out the calculations:

- a reconciliation approach
- a T account approach.

Cash received from entities accounted for using the equity method is the difference between:

- the opening and closing 'Investment in associates' asset in the balance sheet (having taken into consideration the share of profits (after tax) of associates reported in the profit and loss account)
- and any adjustments for revaluation surpluses and deficits reported in the STRGL.

Example 19.3 Dividend received from associates

Example

Investment in associate appears in the opening and closing consolidated balance sheets at €1,500 and €1,350 respectively, and in the consolidated profit and loss account at €735 share of profit and €350 share of taxation.

Required

Calculate the dividend received from associates to be reported in the cash flow statement using (i) a reconciliation approach and (ii) a T account approach

Solution

(i) Reconciliation approach	€	€
Opening balance		1,500
Add: Share of profit	735	
Less: Share of tax	(325)	410
Expected closing balance		1,910
Actual closing balance		(1,350)
Cash inflow		560

(ii) T account approach

Associate

	€		€
Balance b/d	1,500	Share of tax (consolidated P/L)	325
Opening dividends receivable	Nil	Dividends received (balancing)	560
Share of pre-tax profits (consolidated P/L)	735	Balance c/d	1,350
		Closing dividend receivable	Nil
	2,235		2,235

These requirements are illustrated in Exhibit 19.2 in respect of Rentokil's disclosures of its dividends received from associates.

Exhibit 19.2 **Disclosures in cash flow statements in respect of associates Rentokil Initial plc Annual Report 2000**

Consolidated Cash Flow Statement (extract)
For the year ended 31st December

		2000	**1999**
		£m	**£m**
Operating activities	Net cash inflow from operating activities	577.5	683.8
Associates' dividends	Dividends received from associates	1.5	1.0
Returns on investments and servicing of finance	Interest received	24.5	29.9
	Interest paid	(59.1)	(40.6)
	Interest element of finance lease payments	(2.7)	(3.6)
	Dividends paid to minority interests	(0.8)	(0.8)
	Net cash outflow from returns on investments and servicing of finance	(38.1)	(15.1)

Returns on investments and servicing of finance

Within this heading are cash receipts resulting from the ownership of investments, and payments to providers of finance, to non-equity shareholders (e.g., preference shareholders) and to minority interests. Cash payments of interest to lenders and other creditors are also included, regardless of whether they have been expensed in the profit and loss account or capitalised in the balance sheet. This includes the interest element of finance lease payments.

Example 19.4 illustrates that the amount to be shown for return on investment is the cash sum received, which is not necessarily the amount of revenue for that item shown in the profit and loss account. In the example, although the dividend income in the period shown in the profit and loss account is €100, only €85 cash was received and the debtor for dividend receivable increased at the year-end over the opening balance.

Example 19.4 Calculation of cash received from dividends

Example

You are provided with the following information about dividends:

	Opening	**Closing**
Balance sheet amounts	€	€
Dividend receivable included in debtors	10	25

The credit in the profit and loss account for dividend income is €100

Required

Calculate the cash received from dividends to be included in Returns on investment and servicing of finance in the cash flow statement

Solution

Dividend income account

	€		€
Balance b/d	10	Cash received (balancing)	85
Profit and loss account	100	Balance c/d	25
	110		110

Non-equity dividends (e.g., preference dividends) paid to parent company shareholders and dividends paid to minority shareholders in subsidiaries are separately disclosed. Similar to Example 19.4 in relation to dividends received, it is the amount *paid* to minority shareholders that must be shown. Dividends paid to minorities must be shown separately under the heading *Returns on investments and servicing of finance*. In Exhibit 19.2, Rentokil discloses *Dividends paid to minority interests* as outflows under the caption *Returns on investments and servicing of finance*.

Dividends paid to minority interests can be difficult to calculate. Example 19.5 illustrates how it might be calculated using a reconciliation approach and a T account approach.

Example 19.5 Minority interest

Example
Minority interest appears in the opening and closing consolidated balance sheets at €1,000 and €1,115 respectively and in the consolidated profit and loss account at €350. An additional minority interest of €75 arose during the year from the acquisition of a subsidiary.

Required
Calculate the minority interest cash flows to be reported in the cash flow statement using (i) a reconciliation approach and (ii) a T account approach.

Solution

(i) Reconciliation approach	€
Opening balance	1,000
Add: Profit for year	350
Add: Arising from acquisition	75
	1,425
Less: Closing balance	(1,115)
Cash outflow	310

(ii) T account approach

Minority interest

	€		€
Dividend paid to minority (balancing)	310	Balance b/d	1,000
Minority dividend c/d	Nil	Minority dividends b/d	nil
Minority interest c/d	1,115	Minority interest in consolidated profit and loss account	350
		Minority interest acquired during year	75
	1,425		1,425

Taxation

Taxation paid must be shown in the cash flow statement under a separate heading *Taxation*. Cash receipts from and payments to the taxation authorities in respect of revenue and capital profits are included under this heading. Taxation cash flows arising where the entity merely acts as a collecting agency (e.g., VAT and PAYE) are not included in this heading, but are included in operating cash flows or other appropriate heading.

The amount to be shown for taxation is the amount paid, not the amount charged in the profit and loss account. Example 19.6 illustrates this. The amount charged in the profit and loss account is €3,999 but the T account for taxation shows that €4,955 was actually paid in the period.

Example 19.6 Computing taxation cash flows

Example

Taxation liabilities for corporation tax in the opening and closing balance sheets are €9,198 and €8,728, respectively. The taxation amounts in the profit and loss account are as follows:

	€
Corporation tax	4,230
Deferred tax	(456)
(Over)/under provisions of previous year	225
	3,999

Required

Calculate the taxation cash flows to be reported in the cash flow statement.

Solution

Corporation taxation account

	€		€
Tax paid (balancing amount)	4,925	Balance b/d	9,198
		Profit and loss account	225
Balance c/d	8,728	Profit and loss account	4,230
	13,653		13,653

Capital expenditure and financial investment

Whereas the heading *Investing activities* is used under IAS GAAP (and was previously used under FRS 1 before it was revised in 1996), FRS 1 now requires two headings to capture all investing activities: *Capital expenditure and financial investment* and *Acquisitions and disposals*. Acquisitions and disposals are considered further on in this chapter.

Cash flows included under the heading *Capital expenditure and financial investment* are generally those related to the acquisition and disposal of assets held as fixed assets (other than purchase and sale of trades or businesses which fall into the separate category *Acquisitions and disposals*). However, fixed assets acquired under finance leases are not included in this category. Although lease payments are cash outflows, these payments comprise a finance cost which is part of *servicing of finance* and a capital element which is a *financing* cash outflow.

Examples of cash inflows and outflows from capital expenditure and financial investment include:

- payments for purchase of tangible fixed assets
- receipts from sale of tangible fixed assets
- payments for purchase of certain investments (e.g., *not* included here are investments in subsidiaries, associates and joint ventures or investments included in management of liquid resources)
- receipts from sale of investments (limited to types of investments as noted earlier)
- receipts/payments for customs tax and VAT in respect of investing activities.

As with working capital movements, a detailed analysis of movements on fixed assets is required to identify cash flows. Cash spent on fixed assets acquired must be identified, as distinct from additions to fixed assets which are reported in the fixed asset note to the balance sheet. This requires analysing additions to fixed assets to exclude capital accruals, finance leases capitalised and interest capitalised. Moreover, additions acquired through a new subsidiary must also be excluded. Assets no longer owned following disposal of a subsidiary should also be accounted for in the analysis. The cash expenditure during the year to purchase fixed assets can be identified as follows:

- additions to fixed assets (the starting point)
- adjusted for non-cash items or for items which belong to other headings such as:
  - capital accruals
  - finance leases capitalised
  - interest capitalised
  - total fixed assets acquired/disposed of during the year through acquisition/disposal of subsidiary.

Acquisitions and disposals

Cash flows relating to the acquisition or disposal of any trade or business or of an investment in an entity that, as a result of the transaction, becomes or ceases to be a subsidiary, associate or joint venture must be included in the cash flow statement under a separate heading *Acquisitions and disposals*. Example 19.7 reproduces an extract from Example 2 in Appendix 1 to FRS 1 illustrating the disclosures that might be expected under this heading. The acquisition of a subsidiary has to be shown as a single figure (representing the cash flow (i.e. the cash consideration, not the total purchase consideration)). Details of the assets and liabilities acquired and of the consideration given for them must be shown by way of note.

Example 19.7 Acquisitions and disposals in cash flow statements

Example 2 Appendix 1 FRS 1

Notes to the cash flow statement (extract)

Acquisitions and disposals	**£000**	**£000**
Purchase of subsidiary undertaking	(12,705)	
Net overdrafts acquired with subsidiary	(5,516)	
Sale of business	4,208	
Purchase of interest in a joint venture	(3,811)	
Net cash outflow for acquisitions and disposals		(17,824)

As mentioned earlier, all assets and liabilities acquired or disposed of in the transaction need to be adjusted for in computing amounts for the cash flow statement. To avoid double counting arising from acquisitions and disposals of subsidiaries, net assets acquired/disposed must be taken into account when reconciling opening and closing balance sheet amounts to identify cash flows. For example, tangible fixed assets obtained through acquisition of a subsidiary are non-cash increases in fixed assets. Similarly, tangible fixed assets released through disposal of a subsidiary are non-cash reductions in net book value of tangible fixed assets.

As can be seen from Example 19.7, net cash flows from acquisition and disposal of subsidiaries and associates have to be shown as a single figure. A similar note to that provided for acquisitions should show assets and liabilities sold through a disposal of subsidiary, including minority interest and proceeds received, analysed between cash and other elements of the consideration.

Equity dividends paid

Dividends paid to equity shareholders of the parent must be shown separately in the cash flow statement. The rationale for showing this under its own heading (separately identified from *Returns on investments and servicing of finance*) is that equity dividends are discretionary by nature, whereas other finance costs (interest, etc.) are mandatory. Dividends paid are calculated by reconciling opening and closing proposed dividend balances with dividends appropriated from profits.

Management of liquid resources

This section of cash flow statements deals with receipts and payment in respect of current asset investments considered to be liquid or readily marketable. *Liquid resources* were defined earlier as investments disposable by an entity without curtailing or disrupting the business, which are readily convertible to cash amounts equal or close to their book value. The purpose of this section of the cash flow statement is to reflect the way in which entities manage their cash and similar assets and to distinguish cash flow from this activity from other investment decisions. Cash flows relating to short-term deposits and similar investments (i.e., treasury management activities) should be reported under this heading. Examples of cash inflows and outflows relating to management of liquid resources are provided in FRS 1 as follows:

Inflows:

- withdrawals from short-term deposits not qualifying as cash under FRS 1
- inflows from disposal of investments (gilts, loan stock, equities and derivatives) held as liquid resources.

Outflows:

- payments into short-term deposits not qualifying as cash under FRS 1
- outflows to acquire other investments (gilts, loan stock, equities and derivatives) held as liquid resources.

FRS 1 requires liquid resources to be identified by each reporting entity in accordance with a disclosed policy. An example of assets included in liquid resources is provided by Colt Telecom in Exhibit 19.3.

Exhibit 19.3 **Liquid resources**
COLT Telecom Group plc Annual Report 2000

1 Basis of Presentation and Principal Accounting Policies (**extract**)
Liquid resources
Liquid resources include surplus cash invested in marketable government securities or placed on short-term deposit.

Financing activities

Financing cash flows comprise receipts from, or cash payments to, external providers of finance. Examples include:

- proceeds from issuing shares
- proceeds from issuing debentures, loans, etc.
- repayments of amounts borrowed
- finance lease capital repayments
- payments to redeem shares
- payments of commission and expenses of share issues
- receipts from collecting repayments on or from selling loans
- disbursements for loans made and payments to acquire debt instruments.

Redbus (Exhibit 19.5) discloses two financing activities, *Receipt from issue of shares* and *Capital element of finance lease and hire purchase contract payments*.

Disclosures

The main disclosure requirements of FRS 1 are:

- operating profit must be reconciled with net cash flow from operating activities (this reconciliation is the indirect method of calculating cash flows from operating activities)
- opening and closing amounts for net debt must be reconciled with movement in cash for the period
- opening and closing amounts for net debt must be analysed
- the net debt reconciliation must be analysed between cash flow movements, exchange rate differences, and other movements.

If not presented adjoining the cash flow statement, the following must be shown as notes:

- reconciliation of operating profit to net cash flow from operating activities
- reconciliation of net debt to movement in cash flow.

Reconciliation of operating profit

Reconciliation of operating profit has already been considered in this chapter. The reconciliation is the indirect approach to calculating operating cash flows. However, the reconciliation is required regardless of whether the direct or indirect method of computing cash flows from operating activities is used. This reconciliation reflects the importance of profit and cash flow as primary performance indicators. Such a reconciliation is shown by Marks and Spencer's cash flow statement reproduced in Exhibit 19.1.

Reconciliation of net debt

Entities must explain how their net debt position has changed in the reporting period. Net debt is the borrowings of an entity less cash and liquid resources. Where cash and liquid resources exceed borrowings, the term *net funds* is used. The reconciliation of movements in cash to movements in net debt links the cash flow statement with the change in net debt as reflected in the opening and closing balance sheets. Moreover, movements in net debt should be capable of being traced to the cash flow statement. The objective of this reconciliation is to provide information which assists in assessing the liquidity, solvency and financial adaptability of the entity.

The reconciliation should include a schedule of changes in net debt (analysing opening and closing net debt components), showing separately changes resulting from cash flows, acquisition/disposal of subsidiaries, non-cash changes and the recognition of changes in market value and exchange rate movements. These requirements are illustrated in Example 2 in Appendix 1 of FRS 1 and are reproduced in Example 19.8.

Example 19.8 Net debt disclosure requirements of FRS 1

Example 2 Appendix 1 FRS 1
Reconciliation of net cash flow to movement in net debt

	£000	£000
Decrease in cash in the period	**(6,752)**	
Cash inflow from increase in debt and lease financing	(2,347)	
Cash inflow from decrease in liquid resources	(700)	
Change in net debt resulting from cash flows		(9,799)
Loans and finance leases acquired with subsidiary		(3,817)
New finance leases		(2,845)
Translation difference		643
Movement in net debt in the period		**(15,818)**
Net debt at 1.1.96		**(15,215)**
Net debt at 31.12.96		**(31,033)**

Note 3 – Analysis of net debt

	At 1 Jan. 1996	Cash flow	Acquisition (excl. cash and overdrafts)	Other non-cash changes	Exchange movement	At 31 Dec. 1996
	£000	£000	£000	£000	£000	£000
Cash in hand, at bank	235	(1,250)			1,392	377
Overdrafts	(2,528)	(5,502)			(1,422)	(9,452)
		(6,752)				
Debt due after 1 yr	(9,640)	(2,533)	(1,749)	2,560	(792)	(12,154)
Debt due within 1 yr	(352)	(1,156)	(837)	(2,560)	1,465	(3,440)
Finance leases	(4,170)	1,342	(1,231)	(2,845)		(6,904)
		(2,347)				
Current asset investments	1,240	(700)				540
TOTAL	(15,215)	(9,799)	(3,817)	(2,845)	643	(31,033)

Example 19.9 illustrates disclosure requirements relating to net debt in a simple example.

Example 19.9 Reconciliation and analysis of net debt

Example

The summarised balance sheet of Parent Group is as follows:

	20X2	20X1
	€000	€000
Fixed assets	6,120	5,832
Current assets		
Stocks	2,160	2,040
Short-term investments (net liquid resources)	561	132
Debtors	2,040	1,620
Cash at bank	72	399
	4,833	4,191
Creditors: Amounts falling due within one year		
Trade creditors	3,900	2,919
Corporation taxation	543	450
Dividends	240	210
Accrued interest	120	90
	(4,803)	(3,669)
Net current assets	30	522
Total assets less current liabilities	6,150	6,354
Creditors: Amounts falling due after more than one year		
Bank borrowings	(558)	(642)
Provisions for liabilities and charges	(90)	(45)
Minority interests – equity	(990)	(1,710)
	4,512	3,957
Capital and reserves		
Called up share capital	1,320	1,320
Share premium	402	453
Profit and loss account	2,790	2,184
	4,512	3,957

Additional information

1. There was a decrease in cash for the period of €327,000.
2. The debt relates to a foreign subsidiary's borrowings which are not repayable until 20X9, on which there was a profit on translation during the year of €84,000.

Required

(i) Calculate the net debt of Parent Group and prepare (ii) the movement in net debt and (iii) the analysis of net debt as required by FRS 1.

Solution

(i) Calculation of net debt	20X2	20X1
	€000	€000
Borrowings	(558)	(642)
Cash	72	399
Liquid resources	561	132
Net funds / net (debt)	75	(111)

continued overleaf

Example 19.9 Continued

(ii) Note: Reconciliation of net cash flow to movement in net debt

	€000
Decrease in cash for the period	(327)
Cash outflow from the increase in liquid resources	429
Change in net debt resulting from cash flows	102
Translation difference	84
Movement in net debt in the period	186
Opening net debt	(111)
Closing net funds	75

(iii) Analysis of net debt	**Opening**	**Cash flow**	**Exchange difference**	**Closing**
	€000	**€000**	**€000**	**€000**
Cash at bank	399	(327)		72
Liquid resources	132	429		561
Debt due after more than one year	(642)	—	84	(558)
Total	(111)	102	84	75

Exhibit 19.4 shows the net debt reconciliation for Marks and Spencer. The starting amount in the reconciliation is the net cash inflow or outflow as reported in the cash flow statement. This amount is adjusted for (i) movements in liquid resources, (ii) movements in debt financing and (iii) exchange movements.

Exhibit 19.4 **Reconciliation of net cash flow to movement in net debt**
Marks and Spencer plc Annual Report 2000

	2000	**1999**
Reconciliation of net cash flow to movement in net debt	**£m**	**£m**
Increase/(decrease) in cash	**7.2**	(198.7)
Cash outflow/(inflow) from increase/(decrease) in liquid resources	**162.5**	(180.6)
Cash inflow from increase in debt financing	**(250.9)**	(482.8)
Exchange movements	**11.4**	(0.2)
Movement in net debt	**(69.8)**	(862.3)
Net debt at 1 April	**(1,181.6)**	(319.3)
Net debt at 31 March	**(1,251.4)**	(1,181.6)

Redbus, in Exhibit 19.5, includes both an analysis and reconciliation of net debt as required by FRS 1. Cash flow and non-cash changes account for the changes in opening and closing net debt balances (note 19c). The movement in net funds for the period (87,724) is reconciled with the increase in cash in the period of 86,854. Non-cash movements (new finance leases and translation differences) and cash flows which reduced borrowings explain this difference.

Exhibit 19.5 **Cash flow statement under UK GAAP**
Redbus Interhouse plc Annual Report 2000

Group Cash Flow Statement	**Year ended 31st December, 2000**	**Restated 17 months ended 31st December, 1999**
	£000	**£000**
Net cash (outflow)/inflow from operating activities	(8,732)	577
Returns on investments and servicing of finance	1,725	22
Taxation	(13)	—
Capital expenditure and financial investment	(16,315)	(5,916)
Acquisitions and disposals	9,029	—
Cash outflow before financing	(14,306)	(5,317)
Financing	101,160	3,735
Increase/(decrease) in cash in the period	86,854	(1,582)

The accompanying notes are an integral part of these accounts.

19 Notes to the Group cash flow statement

a) Reconciliation of operating loss to operating cash flows	**£000**	**£000**
Operating loss	(54,021)	(2,015)
Goodwill write-off	47,231	—
Depreciation	2,079	386
Exceptional item	(855)	—
Share option compensation charge	997	553
Increase in debtors	(9,507)	(1,179)
Increase in creditors and provisions	5,344	2,832
Net cash (outflow)/inflow from operating activities	(8,732)	577

b) Analysis of cash flows	**£000**	**£000**
Returns on investments and servicing of finance		
Interest received and similar income	1,853	51
Interest paid and similar charges	(128)	(29)
Net cash inflow	1,725	22
Taxation		
UK corporation tax paid	(13)	—
Net cash outflow	(13)	—
Capital expenditure and financial investment		
Purchase of tangible fixed assets	(16,315)	(5,916)
Net cash outflow	(16,315)	(5,916)
Acquisition and disposals		
Cash at bank and in hand acquired in reverse acquisition	9,099	—
Purchase of associate	(70)	—
Net cash inflow	9,029	—
Financing		
Receipt from issue of shares	101,511	4,000
Capital element of finance lease and hire purchase contract payments	(351)	(265)
Net cash inflow	101,160	3,735

continued overleaf

Exhibit 19.5 **Continued**

c) Analysis and reconciliation of net (debt)/funds

	At 1st January 2000 £000	Cash flow £000	Non-cash changes 2000 £000	At 31st December, 2000 £000
Cash at bank and in hand	16	85,256	872	86,144
Bank overdrafts	(1,598)	1,598	—	—
Obligations under finance leases and hire purchase contracts	(572)	351	(353)	(574)
	(2,154)	87,205	519	85,570

	Year ended 31st December 2000 £000	Restated 17 months ended 31st December, 1999 £000
Increase/(decrease) in cash in the period	86,854	(1,582)
Cash outflow from decrease in debt and lease financing	351	265
Change in net funds resulting from cash flows	87,205	(1,317)
New finance leases and hire purchase contracts	(353)	(837)
Translation difference	872	—
Movement in net funds/(debt) in the period	87,724	(2,154)
Net debt at the beginning of the period	(2,154)	—
Net funds/(debt) at the end of the period	85,570	(2,154)
Net funds/(debt) analysed as follows:		
Cash at bank and at hand	86,144	16
Bank overdrafts	—	(1,598)
Obligations under finance leases and hire purchase contracts	(574)	(572)
	85,570	(2,154)

Sundry other disclosures

A number of additional disclosures are required by FRS 1. These include:

- explanation and further information on exceptional cash flows
- analysis of acquisitions and disposals of subsidiaries showing the assets and liabilities that have been acquired or disposed of and the extent to which consideration is payable or receivable in cash
- details of material non-cash transactions (i.e., those transactions not resulting in cash movements). This might include, for example, acquisition of assets under finance leases, disposal of assets for paper consideration (shares or debenture stock).

FRS 1 requires material non-cash transactions to be disclosed if their non-disclosure would impair understanding of the underlying transactions. Examples include acquiring a subsidiary using equity consideration, capitalised finance leases and retranslation differences on foreign currency-hedged equity investments.

Redbus (Exhibit 19.5) shows non-cash transactions as a separate column in its analysis of and disclosure of movements on net debt/net funds. This separate disclosure of non-cash items is explicitly required by FRS 1. There are two non-cash transactions: (i) *new finance leases and hire purchase contracts* £353,000 and (ii) *translation difference* £872,000.

Exceptional items

Exceptional items in the profit and loss account can be relevant for a number of FRS 1 classifications, e.g., operating activities, taxation, capital expenditure and financial investment, acquisitions and disposals, etc. Cash flows relating to exceptional items are included under the appropriate heading in the cash flow statement. A note to the cash flow statement should indicate how such items affect the cash flows.

Marks and Spencer in Exhibit 19.1 contains an exceptional item under operating activities. As required, the exceptional item is described in a note to the cash flow statement. It represents redundancy and restructuring costs paid.

Redbus (Exhibit 19.5) also reported an exceptional operating item. It included the exceptional item in its reconciliation of operating loss to operating cash flow. This was necessary because the exceptional item related to a reduction in provisions for environmental remediation costs. Thus, the increase in operating profit caused by the reduction in the provision was not matched by an inflow of cash.

Comprehensive example of cash flow statement

Redbus's cash flow in Exhibit 19.5 provides a comprehensive example of a cash flow statement prepared under UK GAAP.

IAS GAAP

Cash flow statements in one form or another have been required under IAS GAAP since 1977.

Regulatory framework

IAS 7 *Statement of Changes in Financial Position* was issued in 1977 and was revised and renamed *Cash Flow Statements* in 1992.

Scope

IAS 7 requires all enterprises, including all financial institutions (unlike FRS 1), to present cash flow statements for each period for which financial statements are presented. Under IAS GAAP, there are no exemptions such as those in FRS 1 from the requirement to prepare cash flow statements.

Definitions

Cash flows are defined as inflows and outflows of cash and cash equivalents (which are no longer mentioned in FRS 1). Cash comprises *cash on hand and demand deposits*. Cash equivalents according to paragraph 6 of IAS 7 represent:

> short-term, highly liquid investments that are readily convertible to known amounts of cash, and which are subject to an insignificant risk of changes in value.

This definition is quite similar to the one included in the 1991 version of FRS 1. When FRS 1 was revised in 1996, all references to 'cash equivalents' were removed because it had proved difficult in practice to interpret and apply consistently. Thus, this definition is one of the most significant differences between IAS 7 and FRS 1. Cash equivalents under IAS 7 are more likely to include financial instruments used in treasury management that are now, under FRS 1, reported separately as management of liquid resources.

Presentation of cash flow statements

Both FRS 1 and IAS 7 are quite prescriptive concerning the format and layout of the cash flow statement. Under IAS 7, cash inflows and outflows should be classified under three headings:

1 operating activities
2 investing activities
3 financing activities.

As we saw earlier, FRS 1 requires analysis under nine headings. These differing requirements are summarised in Table 19.3. Although not the subject of a separate heading under IAS 7, some of the items provided with a separate heading under FRS 1 must be separately disclosed under IAS 7. These include cash flows from interest and dividends paid and received, taxation cash flows and cash flows from acquisitions and disposals of subsidiaries.

Table 19.3 Comparison of cash flow statement headings required under UK GAAP and IAS GAAP

FRS 1	*IAS 7*
1 Cash flows from operating activities	**1** Operating activities
2 Dividends received from associated undertakings	
3 Returns on investments and servicing of finance	
4 Taxation	
5 Capital expenditure and financial investment	**2** Investing activities
6 Acquisitions and disposals	
7 Equity dividends paid	
8 Management of liquid resources	
9 Financing activities	**3** Financing activities

IAS 7 provides guidance on how to classify cash flows into the three categories.

Comprehensive example of cash flow statement

Nestlé provides a cash flow statement based on IAS GAAP in Exhibit 19.6. It classifies its cash flows under the three headings discussed earlier: *operating*, *investing* and *financing* activities.

Exhibit 19.6 **Cash flow statement under IAS GAAP Nestlé Annual Report 2001**

In millions of CHF		2001		2000
Operating activities				
Net profit of consolidated companies	6,338		5,580	
Depreciation of property, plant and equipment	2,581		2,737	
Impairment of property, plant and equipment	222		223	
Amortisation of goodwill	494		414	
Depreciation of intangible assets	150		179	
Impairment of goodwill	184		230	
Increase/(decrease) in provisions and deferred taxes	(92)		(4)	
Decrease/(increase) in working capital	(870)		(368)	
Other movements	(393)		(140)	
Operating cash flow		8,614		8,851
Investing activities				
Capital expenditure	(3,611)		(3,305)	
Expenditure on intangible assets	(288)		(188)	
Sale of property, plant and equipment	263		355	
Acquisitions	(18,766)		(2,846)	
Disposals	484		780	
Income from associates	133		107	
Other movements	143		39	
Cash flow from investing activities		(21,642)		(5,058)
Financing activities				
Dividend for the previous year	(2,127)		(1,657)	
Purchase of treasury shares	(1,133)		(765)	
Sale of treasury shares and options	880		1,837	
Premium on warrants issued	209		81	
Movements with minority interests	(172)		(221)	
Bonds issued	3,338		1,016	
Bonds repaid	(380)		(1,143)	
Increase/(decrease) in other medium/long-term financial liabilities	(71)		(155)	
Increase/(decrease) in short-term financial liabilities	16,754		921	
Decrease/(increase) in marketable securities and other liquid assets	(2,330)		(2,788)	
Decrease/(increase) in short-term investments	216		1,452	
Cash flow from financing activities		15,184		(1,422)
Translation differences on flows		60		(175)
Increase/(decrease) in cash and cash equivalents		2,216		2,196
Cash and cash equivalents at beginning of year	5,451		3,322	
Effects of exchange rate changes on opening balance	(29)		(67)	
Cash and cash equivalents retranslated at beginning of year		5,422		3,255
Fair-value adjustment on cash and cash equivalents		(21)		—
Cash and cash equivalents at end of year		7,617		5,451

IAS 7 does not make explicit reference to how minority interests should be treated. Nestlé (Exhibit 19.6) discloses *Movements with minority interests* under the heading *Financing* and these movements are cash outflows.

Cash flows from operating activities

Like FRS 1, IAS 7 permits the use of either the direct or indirect method of presenting cash flows from operating activities, but indicates a preference for the direct method.

The heading *Returns on investments and servicing of finance* is not required under IAS 7. Interest and dividends received or paid may be classified under any of the three prescribed headings as (i) operating cash flows, (ii) financing (dividends and interest paid) or (iii) investing (dividends and interest received) activities. Nestlé (Exhibit 19.6) includes dividends paid under the heading *Financing activities*.

There is no separate heading for taxation under IAS 7. Instead, taxation cash flows are required to be treated as part of operating activities. Taxes are not separately identified in Nestlé's cash flow statement (Exhibit 19.6).

Investing activities

Under IAS 7, investing activities include cash flows arising from the acquisition and disposal of long-term assets and other investments not included in cash equivalents. Cash flows from the acquisition and disposal of subsidiaries or business units must be presented separately as investing cash flows.

Mövenpick illustrates these requirements in Exhibit 19.7. All amounts are stated in millions of Swiss francs (CHF).

Exhibit 19.7 **Disclosure of acquisitions in cash flow statements under IAS GAAP Mövenpick Annual Report 2000**

Notes to the Consolidated Financial Statements (extract)
23 Cash flow statement
Acquisitions of subsidiaries

(in CHF million)	**2000**
Fixed assets	–53.7
Inventory	–9.5
Cash and marketable securities	–5.2
Other assets	–7.2
Long-term liabilities	23.1
Provisions	1.3
Short-term liabilities	15.9
Fair value of net assets	**–35.3**
Add back cash and marketable securities	5.2
Fair value, net of cash acquired	**–30.1**
Fair value, net of minority interests	–20.1
Goodwill	–11.0
Cash outflow	**–31.1**

The requirements concerning the treatment of associates in cash flow statements are similar under UK GAAP and IAS GAAP (i.e., cash flows between the group and the associate must be included in the cash flow statement). However, as has already been seen, under UK GAAP there is a separate heading in the cash flow statement for dividends received from associated undertakings. Similar to FRS 1, for simple investments accounted for using the cost method or for investments accounted for using the equity method of accounting, IAS 7 restricts the cash flows to be reported in the cash flow statement to those flows between the two enterprises. Advances and new investments should be classified as investing activities, while dividends received can be shown as either operating or investing. In contrast to this is return of capital which must be shown as an investing activity. Nestlé (Exhibit 19.6) discloses *Income from associates* under investing activities.

Financing activities

Financing activities under IAS 7 comprise those activities that *result in changes in the size and composition of the equity capital and borrowings of the enterprise*. Examples provided in IAS 7 are similar (but not as extensive) to those in FRS 1 and include:

- proceeds from issuing shares
- payments to acquire or redeem shares
- proceeds from issuing debentures, loans, etc.
- repayments of amounts borrowed
- finance lease capital repayments.

Disclosures

Additional disclosures supporting the cash flow statement are required under IAS 7 in respect of acquisitions or disposals of subsidiaries, including:

- total purchase consideration or disposal proceeds
- portion of purchase price or disposal proceeds discharged by cash/cash equivalents
- amount of cash/cash equivalents in the acquired/disposed subsidiary
- amount of assets and liabilities other than cash/cash equivalents in the acquired/disposed subsidiary.

In addition, the following must be disclosed:

- non-cash investing and financing transactions
- analysis of components of cash/cash equivalents and a reconciliation of these amounts with amounts in the balance sheet
- significant cash/cash equivalents held by the entity not available to the group, together with management commentary.

These disclosure requirements are similar to those required under FRS 1. Thus, while there are some differences in the detail of disclosure requirements under UK GAAP and IAS GAAP, they are not significant.

Exceptional items

Exceptional items are not mentioned in IAS 7. However, extraordinary items which are still permitted under IASs (but are virtually extinct under UK GAAP) should be classified under one of the three headings in IAS 7 as appropriate, and should be separately disclosed.

Comparison of UK GAAP and IAS GAAP

The main differences between FRS 1 and IAS 7 relate to the formats followed and to the definition of cash. There are also some differences in scope and in the headings under which cash flows are reported. The main differences are summarised in Table 19.4.

Table 19.4 Main differences in requirements applying to cash flow statements between UK GAAP and IAS GAAP

	UK GAAP	*IAS GAAP*
Scope	Exemptions permitted	No exemptions
Format	*Nine headings*: Operating activities Dividends from associates Returns on investments and servicing of finance Taxation Capital expenditure and financial investment Acquisitions and disposals Equity dividends paid Management of liquid resources Financing activities	*Three headings:* Operating activities Investing activities Financing activities
Taxation	Separate heading	Included under *Operating activities*
Cash	Cash includes overdrafts, cash equivalents no longer recognised	Cash includes overdrafts and cash equivalents
Liquid resources	Some cash equivalents under IAS GAAP are defined as liquid resources under UK GAAP, other cash equivalents come under *Financial investment* or *financing*.	
Interest and dividends paid/received	Included under *Returns on investments and servicing of finance* or under *Equity dividends paid*	Can be included under any of the three headings and classified as either (i) operating or (ii) financing or (iii) investing activities

Sources: Cairns, D. and Nobes, C. 2000. The Convergence Handbook: A Comparison between International Accounting Standards and UK Financial Reporting Requirements, Institute of Chartered Accountants in England and Wales, London
Connor, L., Dekker, P., Davies, M., Robinson, P. and Wilson, A. 2001. *IAS/UK GAAP Comparison*, Ernst & Young, London
PricewaterhouseCoopers. 2000. *International Accounting Standards Similarities and Differences IAS, US GAAP, and UK GAAP.* PricewaterhouseCoopers, London

Summary

This chapter has discussed the preparation and presentation of consolidated cash flow statements. Almost all companies are required to prepare cash flow statements. These primary financial statements follow a prescribed layout and content. Consolidated cash flow statements contain a number of captions unique to group accounts.

Learning outcomes

After studying this chapter you should have learnt:

- the regulations applying to the preparation of cash flow statements
- how to prepare cash flow statements
- the disclosures required to support cash flow statements
- to identify captions that are unique to group cash flow statements
- the differences between UK GAAP and IAS GAAP regulations applying to cash flow statements.

Multiple choice questions

Solutions to these questions are prepared under UK GAAP and are presented in Appendix 1.

19.1 Wood

The financial statements of **Wood** for the year ended 31 December 20X3, included the following items:

(i) dividends received
(ii) government grants received in respect of wages
(iii) profit on sale of fixed asset investments
(iv) bonus issue

Which of these four items should be included in the cash flow statement of Wood for the year ended 31 December 20X3, as part of *net cash inflow from operating activities?*

(a) Items (i), (ii), (iii) and (iv)
(b) Items (i), (ii) and (iii)
(c) Items (i) and (ii)
(d) Item (ii) only

19.2 Sceptre

The balance sheet of **Sceptre** at 31 December 20X4, disclosed that the following changes had occurred during the year to that date:

(i) The value of freehold property had increased by €200,000 as a result of a revaluation during the year.
(ii) Provision for warranties had decreased by €100,000.

Which of these would be disclosed in the note to the cash flow statement, *reconciliation of operating profit to net cash inflow from operating activities?*

(a) Both (i) and (ii)
(b) Neither (i) or (ii)
(c) (i) only
(d) (ii) only

19.3 Gough

During the year ended 31 December 20X3 **Gough** made a bonus issue of one ordinary share for every four shares held. In the cash flow statement of Gough for the year ended 31 December 20X3, the bonus issue will be disclosed under the heading:

(a) Financing
(b) Investing activities
(c) Returns on investments and servicing of finance
(d) None of these

19.4 Newtown

The financial statements of **Newtown** for the year ended 31 December 20X6 included the following items:

(i) Interest received
(ii) Bonus issue of ordinary shares
(iii) Receipts from sale of tangible fixed assets
(iv) Interest paid

Which of these four items should be included, as returns on investment and servicing of finance, in the cash flow statement (prepared in accordance with FRS 1 *Cash Flow Statements*) of Newtown for the year ended 31 December 20X6?

(a) (i) and (ii)
(b) (i), (ii) and (iii)
(c) (iii) only
(d) (i) and (iv)

19.5 Dividends paid to minority

Consolidated profit and loss account for year ended 31 March		**20X4**		**20X3**
		€		**€**
Operating profit		464,000		392,000
Share of profit of associated undertaking		82,000		65,000
Profit before tax		546,000		457,000
Taxation – Group	270,000		178,000	
Taxation – Associated undertaking	30,000	300,000	26,000	204,000
Profit after tax		246,000		253,000
Minority interest		112,000		94,000
Profit for the financial year		134,000		159,000

Consolidated balance sheet as at 31 March (extract)	20X4	20X3
Financial fixed asset: Investment in associate undertaking	120,000	96,000
Minority interest (credit balances)	284,000	265,000

In the cash flow statement of the group for the year ended 31 March 20X4, **dividends paid to minority** interest would appear as:

(a) € 80,000
(b) € 93,000
(c) € 94,000
(d) €112,000

19.6 Geoffrey

Extracts from the financial statements of **Geoffrey** show the following balances for minority interests:

Minority interests	**20X9**	**20X8**
	€000	**€000**
Balance sheet	250	220
Profit and loss account	20	30

- In 20X9, a 75% subsidiary revalued a property, resulting in a revaluation surplus of €100,000.
- A 60% overseas subsidiary is accounted for under the closing rate method.
- Exchange losses shown as a movement on consolidated reserves for the year ended 31 December 20X9 were €9,000.

What will be shown as *dividends to minority interests* in the Geoffrey Group cash flow statement?

(a) € 9,000
(b) €10,000
(c) €11,400
(d) €30,000

19.7 Tom and Harry

During the year ended 31 December 20X3 **Tom** acquired 80% of the ordinary shares of **Harry**. Details of the acquisition were:

	€
Fixed assets	300,000
Stocks	80,000
Debtors	100,000
Cash	20,000
Creditors	(50,000)
	450,000
Minority interest	(90,000)
Goodwill	20,000
	380,000
Settled by	
Shares issued	200,000
Cash paid	180,000
	380,000

In the cash flow statement of the group for the year ended 31 December 20X3 the acquisition of Harry would be shown under *acquisitions and disposals* as:

(a) Purchase of goodwill € 20,000
(b) Purchase of subsidiary undertaking (net of cash acquired) €160,000
(c) Purchase of subsidiary undertaking €380,000
(d) Purchase of net assets of subsidiary undertaking €450,000

19.8 Clare, Jim and Tim

Clare acquired a subsidiary, **Jim**, on 1 April 20X9. Clare also has a longstanding subsidiary, **Tim**. Their stocks at various dates are as follows:

	31.12.X9	**1.4.X9**	**31.12.X8**
	€000	**€000**	**€000**
Clare	2,000	1,900	1,800
Jim	360	350	340
Tim	500	480	460

Clare prepares group accounts under the acquisition method.

What is the adjustment to operating profit for change in group stock in calculating cash flow from operating activities for the year to be shown in the group cash flow statement for the year ended 31 December 20X9?

(a) €240,000
(b) €250,000
(c) €600,000
(d) €200,000

19.9 Elwin and Dunn

Elwin and **Dunn** merged on 1 August 20X9. Their first consolidated accounts were prepared under the merger method to 30 September 20X9. Liz was incorporated to act as the holding company; Elwin and Dunn are 100% subsidiaries.

Cash balances at	**30.9.X8**	**1.8.X9**	**30.9.X9**
	€000	**€000**	**€000**
Elwin	250	290	420
Dunn	240	310	380

continued overleaf

What is the increase in cash to be shown in Liz's consolidated cash flow statement for the year ended 30 September 20X9?

(a) €200,000
(b) €310,000
(c) €600,000
(d) €800,000

19.10 Dividends received from associated undertaking

Consolidated profit and loss account for year ended 31 March		**20X4**		**20X3**
		€		**€**
Operating profit		464,000		392,000
Share of profit of associated undertaking		82,000		65,000
Profit before tax		546,000		457,000
Tax – Group	270,000		178,000	
– Associated undertaking	30,000	300,000	26,000	204,000
Profit after tax		246,000		253,000
Minority interest		112,000		94,000
Profit for the financial year		134,000		159,000
Consolidated balance sheet as at 31 March (extracts)				
Investment in associate undertaking		120,000		96,000
Minority interest		284,000		265,000

In the cash flow statement of the group for the year ended 31 March 20X4, **dividends received from associated undertaking** would be:

(a) €28,000
(b) €40,000
(c) €52,000
(d) €82,000

Self-assessment exercises

Solutions to these self-assessment exercises can be found at:
www.thomsonlearning.co.uk/accountingandfinance/piercebrennan

19.1 Plath

The following are the financial statements with an extract from the notes of **Plath**.

Profit and loss account for the year ended 31 March 20X2

	€million
Turnover	1,162
Cost of sales	(866)
Gross profit	296
Distribution costs	(47)
Administrative expenses	(110)
Operating profit	139
Interest received	79
Interest paid	(55)
Profit before taxation	163
Taxation	(24)
Profit for the financial year	139
Dividends	(49)
Retained profit for the financial year	90

Balance sheet as at 31 March	**20X2 €million**	**20X1 €million**
Fixed assets		
Intangible assets	277	234
Tangible assets	1,023	600
Investments	69	68
	1,369	902
Current assets		
Stocks	246	128
Debtors	460	353
Investments	—	20
Cash at bank and in hand	250	124
	956	625
Creditors: Amounts falling due within one year		
Bank loans and overdrafts	388	185
Trade creditors	244	311
Taxation	42	25
Proposed dividend	49	22
	(723)	(543)
Net current assets	233	82
Total assets less current liabilities	1,602	984
Creditors: Amounts falling due after more than one year	(756)	(555)
Provisions for liabilities and charges		
Deferred taxation	(3)	(2)
	843	427
Capital and reserves		
Called up share capital	29	24
Share premium	447	377
Revaluation reserve	251	—
Profit and loss account	116	26
	843	427

Notes:

1. Debentures were issued at a premium of 5%. The premium was credited to the profit and loss account.
2. The operating profit is after charging depreciation on the tangible fixed assets of €22 million and amortisation on the intangible fixed assets of €7 million.
3. The sale of the short-term investments realised €25 million.
4. During the year ended 31 March 20X2, plant and machinery, costing €1,464 million, written down to €244 million at 31 March 20X1, were sold for €250 million.
5. During the year ended 31 March 20X2 25 million 20 cent shares were issued at a premium of €2.80.

Required

(a) Prepare the cash flow statement of Plath for the year ended 31 March 20X2 in compliance with FRS 1.

Include the following notes to the cash flow statement:

1. reconciliation of operating profit to net cash inflow from operating activities
2. analysis of cash flows netted in the cash flow statement
3. reconciliation of net cash flow to movement in net debt
4. analysis of changes in net debt.

(b) Explain the treatment of the depreciation charge and of the dividends paid.

(c) Comment on the usefulness of the statement prepared for part (a).

19.2 AZ Group

You are given the following information for the **AZ Group**:

Group profit and loss account for the year ended 30 June 20X2	**€m**	**€m**
Net profit before taxation		382
Share of associated undertakings' profit		183
Goodwill amortised		(5)
		560
Interest		(50)
		510
Taxation (of which €49m attributable to associated undertakings)		(137)
		373
Proposed dividend		(58)
Retained profit for year		315
Profits retained: In parent and subsidiaries	301	
In associated undertakings	14	315

Group balance sheet at 30 June	**20X2 €m**	**20X2 €m**	**20X1 €m**	**20X1 €m**
Fixed assets				
Intangible fixed assets		25		—
Tangible fixed assets		3,334		2,579
Investments: associated undertakings		1,536		1,522
		4,895		4,101
Current assets				
Stocks	1,214		972	
Debtors	1,861		1,705	
Cash	29		54	
	3,104		2,731	
Creditors: Amounts falling due within one year				
Creditors	(1,340)		(1,082)	
Bank overdrafts	(647)		(240)	
Taxation	(165)		(140)	
Proposed dividend	(58)		(44)	
	(2,210)		(1,506)	
Net current assets		894		1,225
		5,789		5,326
Creditors: Amounts falling due after more than one year				
Loan		(419)		(457)
Provisions for liabilities and charges				
Deferred taxation		(77)		(126)
		5,293		4,743
Capital and reserves				
Called-up share capital		3,427		3,343
Reserves		1,866		1,400
		5,293		4,743

1 During the year, in relation to its operating activities, the AZ Group received €1,520m from its customers and made the following cash payments:

	€m
To suppliers	430
To and on behalf of employees	326
Other	237

2 During the year the AZ Group acquired 100% of the ordinary share capital of TR. This purchase was financed by €525m in cash and 84m ordinary shares of €1 each with a market value of €235m. The following figures related to TR at the date of acquisition:

	€m
Tangible fixed assets	486
Stock	214
Debtors	130
Bank and cash balances	4
Creditors	(104)
	730
Share capital	280
Reserves	450
	730

3 There were no disposals of fixed assets during the year. Depreciation of fixed assets for the year amounted to €55m.

4 Interest of €40m was paid during the year.

Required

Prepare the cash flow statement, using the direct method to calculate cash flows from operating activities, for the AZ Group for the year ended 30 June 20X2, including the notes to the cash flow statement required by FRS 1.

(All workings should be shown.)

19.3 Hugh Group

You are required to prepare the consolidated cash flow statement of **Hugh Group** based on the information provided.

Consolidated profit and loss account for the year ended 31 December 20X2

	€000	€000
Operating profit		19,157
Share of associated company's profit		61
Interest receivable		458
Interest payable		(2,497)
Interest on finance leases		(373)
Profit before tax		16,806
Tax – Group	5,414	
Tax – Associate	18	(5,432)
Profit for the financial year		11,374
Proposed dividend		(3,219)
Retained profit		8,155
Profit and loss account at 31 December 20X1		20,201
Profit and loss account at 31 December 20X2		28,356

continued overleaf

Consolidated balance sheets at 31 December	**20X2**	**20X1**
	€000	**€000**
Fixed assets (note 1)		
Intangible assets	16,702	—
Tangible assets	27,739	13,791
Investments (in associated company)	457	429
	44,898	14,220
Current assets		
Stocks	41,639	19,992
Debtors (note 2)	38,838	22,798
Cash at bank and in hand	1,041	1,279
	81,518	44,069
Creditors: Amounts falling due within one year (note 3)	68,719	23,893
Net current assets	12,799	20,176
Total assets less current liabilities	57,697	34,396
Creditors: Amounts falling due after more than one year (note 5)	9,439	3,861
	48,258	30,535
Capital and reserves		
Share capital and share premium	19,902	10,334
Profit and loss account	28,356	20,201
	48,258	30,535

Notes:

1 *Fixed assets*: Disposals at net book value amounted to €1,474,000 on which a profit on disposal of €50,000 was made. Depreciation amounted to €3,158,000.

2 *Debtors*:

	20X2	**20X1**
	€000	**€000**
Trade debtors	38,667	21,057
Interest receivable	50	100
Sale of plant and machinery	121	1,641
	38,838	22,798

3 *Creditors: Amounts falling due within one year*:

Bank overdrafts	9,065	1,201
Bank loans (six months)	2,708	1,549
Trade creditors	43,555	13,304
Corporation tax	5,414	2,887
Finance leases	4,454	2,179
Proposed dividend	3,219	2,606
Purchase of fixed assets	94	65
Accrued interest	210	102
	68,719	23,893

A translation loss of €102,000 arose during the year on a bank overdraft denominated in dollars.

4 *Changes in financing*:

	Bank loans		**Finance lease**	
	Short-term	**Long-term**	**Current**	**Non-current**
	€000	**€000**	**€000**	**€000**
Balance at 31/12/X1	1,549	2,100	2,179	1,761
Cash inflows	2,006	2,533	—	—
Cash outflows	(847)	—	(703)	(639)
Subsidiary acquired	—	2,000	1,107	710
Inception of finance lease contracts	—	—	—	2,845
Reclassification of finance leases approaching maturity	—	—	1,871	(1,871)
Balance at 31/12/X2	2,708	6,633	4,454	2,806

5 *Creditors: Amounts falling due after more than one year:*

	20X2	20X1
	€000	€000
Long-term loans	6,633	2,100
Finance leases	2,806	1,761
	9,439	3,861

6 *Acquisition of subsidiary on 31 December 20X2:*

Net assets acquired	€000
Tangible fixed assets	12,194
Stocks	9,384
Debtors	13,856
Cash at bank and in hand	1,439
Trade creditors	(20,579)
Bank overdrafts	(6,955)
Long-term loans	(2,000)
Finance leases, current	(1,107)
Finance leases, non-current	(710)
	5,522
Goodwill	16,702
	22,224
Satisfied by	
Shares	9,519
Cash	12,705
	22,224

(*Source:* Davis, David, Blackwood, Michael and Whitehall, Clark. FRS 1 'Cash flow statements', *Accountants Digest* 287, Institute of Chartered Accountants in England and Wales, Summer 1992, adapted)

19.4 Barolo Group

The following draft financial statements relate to the **Barolo Group**:

Group profit and loss account for the year ended 31 December 20X9

	€000	€000
Operating profit		2,635
Share of profit of associated undertaking		475
Loss on disposal of tangible fixed assets	(35)	
Loss on disposal of subsidiary (note 1)	(125)	(160)
Interest receivable	135	
Interest payable	(95)	40
Profit on ordinary activities before taxation		2,990
Tax on profit on ordinary activities (note 2)		(1,030)
Profit on ordinary activities after taxation		1,960
Minority interests		(375)
Profit attributable to members of the parent company		1,585
Dividends – ordinary dividend		(575)
Retained profit for the year		1,010

Group statement of total recognised gains and losses for the year ended 31 December 20X9

	€000
Profit attributable to members of the parent company	1,585
Deficit on revaluation of land and buildings	(150)
Surplus on revaluation of land and buildings in associate	75
Total recognised gains and losses relating to the year	1,510

Group balance sheet as at 31 December	**20X9 €000**	**20X8 €000**
Fixed assets		
Intangible assets	400	720
Tangible assets (note 3)	7,075	9,000
Investments (notes 1 and 4)	2,975	—
	10,450	9,720
Current assets		
Stocks	3,600	3,400
Short-term investments (note 5)	935	220
Debtors (note 6)	3,300	2,700
Cash at bank and in hand	120	665
	7,955	6,985
Creditors: Amounts falling due within one year (note 7)	(8,005)	(6,115)
Net current (liabilities)/assets	(50)	870
Total assets less current liabilities	10,400	10,590
Creditors: Amounts falling due after more than one year		
Bank loan	(1,070)	(1,070)
Provision for liabilities and charges – Deferred tax	(150)	(75)
Minority interests	(1,650)	(2,850)
	7,530	6,595
Capital and reserves		
Called-up share capital	2,200	2,200
Share premium account	505	505
Revaluation reserve	175	250
Profit and loss account	4,650	3,640
Total shareholders' funds	7,530	6,595

The following information is relevant:

1 The group disposed of a subsidiary, **Samic**, on 1 September 20X9. Barolo held an 80% interest in the subsidiary at the date of disposal.

Samic prepared an interim balance sheet at the date of disposal as follows:

	€000	**€000**
Tangible fixed assets		1,550
Current assets		
Stocks	300	
Debtors	250	
Cash at bank and in hand	650	
	1,200	
Creditors: Amounts falling due within one year (including corporation tax – €125,000)	(650)	
Net current assets		550
		2,100
Called-up share capital		500
Profit and loss account		1,600
		2,100

The consolidated carrying values of all the assets and liabilities at that date are as given. The unamortised goodwill in the group accounts relating to the acquisition of Samic was €320,000 at 1 January 20X8. The group's policy is to amortise goodwill arising on acquisition but not in the year of sale of a subsidiary. The loss on disposal of subsidiary in the group accounts comprises:

	€000
Sale proceeds	1,875
Net assets sold (80% × €2.1m)	(1,680)
Goodwill	(320)
Loss on disposal	125

The consideration for the sale of Samic was 1 million ordinary shares of €1 in **Merlot**, the acquiring company, at a value of €1.5 million, and €375,000 in cash. Merlot has an issued ordinary share capital of 7.5 million ordinary shares.

2 The taxation charge in the profit and loss account is made up as follows:

	€000
Corporation tax	855
Tax attributable to associate	100
Transfer to deferred tax	75
	1,030

3 The movement on group tangible fixed assets during the year was as follows:

Cost or valuation	**€000**
At 1 January 20X9	10,500
Additions	1,900
Revaluation	(150)
Disposals and transfers	(3,400)
At 31 December 20X9	8,850
Accumulated depreciation	
At 1 January 20X9	1,500
Provided during year	750
Disposals and transfers	(475)
At 31 December 20X9	1,775
Net book value at 31 December 20X9	7,075
Net book value at 1 January 20X9	9,000

4 During the year, Barolo had transferred some of its tangible assets to a newly created company, **Grappa**, in part consideration for its 40% share of that company. The total investment at the date of transfer in the associate by Barolo was €1.125 million at carrying value, comprising €500,000 in tangible fixed assets and €625,000 in cash. The group has used equity accounting for the investment in Grappa. The land and buildings transferred have been revalued at the year end.

The investments included under fixed assets comprised the associate Grappa, €1.475 million, and the shares in Merlot, €1.5 million (see note 1).

5 The short-term investments comprised the following items:

	20X9	**20X8**
	€000	**€000**
Government securities (repayable 1 May 20Y0)	255	115
Cash on seven-day deposit	505	105
Investments in corporate bonds (maturing 30 September 20Y0)	175	—
	935	220

6 Interest receivable included in debtors was €25,000 at 31 December 20X9 (€20,000 at 31 December 20X8).

7 Creditors: amounts falling due within one year comprise the following items:

	20X9	**20X8**
	€000	**€000**
Trade creditors	6,500	4,865
Corporation tax	905	750
Dividends	400	350
Accrued interest	200	150
	8,005	6,115

Required

Prepare a cash flow statement for the Barolo Group for the year ended 31 December 20X9 in accordance with the requirements of FRS 1 (Revised 1996) *Cash Flow Statements*. Your answer should include the following:

(i) reconciliation of operating profit to operating cash flows
(ii) an analysis of cash flows for any headings netted in the cash flow statement
(iii) a reconciliation of net cash flow to movement in net debt.
(Analysis of movement in net debt is not required to answer part (iii).)

Examination-style questions

19.1 Cooped

Cooped is a listed company incorporated in 20X0. The consolidated profit and loss account for the year ended 30 June 20X8, and the 20X8 and 20X7 consolidated balance sheets of the Cooped Group are presented as follows.

Consolidated profit and loss account for the year ended 30 June 20X8

	€000	€000
Operating profit		9,579
Goodwill amortisation		(1,670)
Share of associated company's profit		31
Interest receivable		229
Interest payable		(1,248)
Interest on finance leases		(188)
Profit before tax		6,733
Tax – Group	2,707	
– Associate	10	(2,717)
Profit for the financial year		4,016
Proposed dividend		(1,609)
Retained profit		2,407
Profit and loss account at 30 June 20X7		10,100
Profit and loss account at 30 June 20X8		12,507

Consolidated balance sheet at 30 June

	20X8	20X7
Fixed assets	€000	€000
Intangible asset – Goodwill	6,680	—
Tangible assets (note 1)	13,870	6,896
Investment in associated company	228	214
	20,778	7,110
Current assets		
Stocks	20,819	9,996
Debtors (note 2)	19,419	11,399
Cash at bank and in hand	521	639
	40,759	22,034
Creditors: Amounts falling due within 1 year (note 3)	34,360	11,946
Net current assets	6,399	10,088
Total assets less current liabilities	27,177	17,198
Creditors: Amounts falling due after more than one year (note 5)	4,719	1,930
	22,458	15,268
Capital and reserves		
Share capital and share premium	9,951	5,168
Profit and loss account	12,507	10,100
	22,458	15,268

The following additional information is provided:

1 *Fixed assets*: Disposals during the year amounted to €737,000 (net book value) and a profit on disposal of €25,000 was made. Depreciation charged for the year amounted to €1,579,000.

2 *Debtors*

	20X8	20X7
	€000	€000
Trade debtors	19,334	10,528
Interest receivable	25	50
Sale of plant and machinery	60	821
	19,419	11,399

3 *Creditors: Amounts falling due within one year*:

	20X8	20X7
	€000	€000
Bank overdrafts	4,533	601
Bank loans (six months)	1,354	774
Trade creditors	21,778	6,652
Corporation tax	2,707	1,443
Finance leases	2,227	1,090
Proposed dividend	1,609	1,303
Purchase of fixed assets	47	32
Accrued interest	105	51
	34,360	11,946

A translation loss of €51,000 arose during the year on a bank overdraft denominated in sterling.

4 *Movements in selected liabilities over the year*:

	Short-term bank loans	Long-term loans	Finance leases Current	Finance leases Non-current
	€000	€000	€000	€000
Balance at 30/6/20X7	774	1,050	1,090	880
Cash inflows	1,003	1,266	—	—
Cash outflows	(423)	—	(351)	(320)
Subsidiary acquired	—	1,000	554	355
Inception of finance leases	—	—	—	1,422
Reclassification of finance leases approaching maturity	—	—	934	(934)
Balance at 30/6/20X8	1,354	3,316	2,227	1,403

5 *Creditors: Amounts falling due after more than one year*

	20X8	20X7
	€000	€000
Long-term loans	3,316	1,050
Finance leases	1,403	880
	4,719	1,930

6 *Acquisition of subsidiary*:

A subsidiary was acquired during the year, the details of which are as follows:

Net assets acquired	€000
Tangible fixed assets	6,097
Stocks	4,692
Debtors	6,928
Cash at bank and in hand	720
Trade creditors	(10,289)
Bank overdrafts	(3,477)
Long-term loans	(1,000)
Finance leases, current	(554)
Finance leases, non-current	(355)
	2,762
Goodwill	8,350
	11,112
Satisfied by	
Shares	4,760
Cash	6,352
	11,112

Required

(a) Prepare a consolidated cash flow statement for the Cooped Group for the year ended 30 June 20X8.

(b) Present supporting notes for:
  (i) reconciliation of operating profit to net cash flow from operating activities
  (ii) reconciliation of net cash flow to movement in net cash/(debt)
  (iii) analysis of changes in net cash/(debt) over the year.

19.2 Carver

Carver is a listed company incorporated in 20V8 to produce models carved from wood. In 20W5 it acquired a 100% interest in a wood importing company, **Olio**; in 20W9 it acquired a 40% interest in a competitor, **Multi-products**; and on 1 October 20X3 it acquired a 75% interest in **Good Display**. It is planning to make a number of additional acquisitions during the next three years.

The draft consolidated accounts for the Carver Group are as follows:

Consolidated profit and loss account for the year ended 30 September 20X4

	€000	€000
Operating profit		1,485
Amortisation of goodwill		(25)
Share of profits of associated undertakings		495
Income from fixed asset investment		155
Interest payable		(150)
Profit on ordinary activities before taxation		1,960
Tax on profit on ordinary activities		
Corporation tax	391	
Deferred taxation	104	
Tax attributable to income of associated undertakings	145	(640)
Profit on ordinary activities after taxation		1,320
Minority interests		(100)
Profit for the financial year		1,220
Dividends paid and proposed		(400)
Retained profit for the year		820

Consolidated balance sheet as at 30 September

	20X4		20X3	
	€000	**€000**	**€000**	**€000**
Fixed assets				
Intangible fixed assets		75		—
Tangible fixed assets				
Buildings at net book value		2,075		2,200
Machinery: Cost	3,000		1,400	
Aggregate depreciation	(1,200)		(1,100)	
Net book value		1,800		300
		3,950		2,500
Investments in associated undertaking		1,100		1,000
Fixed asset investments		410		410
Current assets				
Stocks	1,975		1,000	
Trade debtors	1,850		1,275	
Cash	4,515		1,820	
	8,340		4,095	
Creditors: Amounts falling due within one year				
Trade creditors	500		280	
Obligations under finance leases	240		200	
Corporation tax	375		217	
Dividends	300		200	
Accrued interest	40		30	
	1,455		927	
Net current assets		6,885		3,168
Total assets less current liabilities		12,345		7,078
Creditors: Amounts falling due after more than one year				
Obligations under finance leases	710		170	
Loans	1,460	2,170	500	670
Provision for liabilities				
Deferred taxation		117		13
Capital and reserves				
Called-up share capital in 25 cent shares	3,940		2,000	
Share premium account	2,883		2,095	
Profit and loss account	3,120		2,300	
Total shareholders' equity		9,943		6,395
Minority interest		115		—
		12,345		7,078

1 There were no acquisitions or disposals of buildings during the year. Machinery costing €500,000 was sold for €500,000, resulting in a profit of €100,000. New machinery was acquired in 20X4 including additions of €850,000 acquired under finance leases.

continued overleaf

2 Information relating to the acquisition of Good Display:

	€000
Machinery	165
Stocks	32
Trade debtors	28
Cash	112
Less:	
Trade creditors	(68)
Corporation tax	(17)
	252
Less: Minority interest	(63)
	189
Goodwill	100
	289
800,000 shares issued as part consideration	275
Balance of consideration paid in cash	14
	289

Goodwill is amortised over four years, including a full year's charge in the year of acquisition.

3 Loans were issued at a discount in 20X4 and the carrying amount of the loans at 30 September 20X4 included €40,000 representing the finance cost attributable to the discount and allocated in respect of the current reporting period.

Required

(a) Prepare the consolidated cash flow statement for the Carver Group for the year ended 30 September 20X4 with supporting notes for:
 (i) reconciliation of operating profit to net cash flow from operating activities
 (ii) analysis of cash flows for amounts shown net in the cash flow statement
 (iii) reconciliation of net cash flow to movement in net cash / (debt)
 (iv) analysis of changes in net cash / (debt).

(b) Explain and illustrate any adjustments that you consider the company should make to the cash flow statement in (a) to take account of the following information:
 (i) Carver had constructed a laser cutter which is included in the machinery cost figure at €73,000. The costs comprise:

	€000
Materials	50
Labour	12
Overheads	6
Interest capitalised	5
	73

 (ii) The cash figures comprised the following:

	30.9.X4 €000	30.9.X3 €000
Cash in hand	15	10
Bank overdrafts	(65)	(770)
Bank	1,890	1,080
10% treasury stock 20X3	—	1,500
Bank deposits	1,125	—
Gas 3% 20X0–20X5	1,550	—
	4,515	1,820

- The 10% treasury stock 20X3 was acquired on 1 September 20X3 and redeemed on 31 October 20X3.
- The bank deposits were made on 1 January 20X4 for a 12-month term.
- The Gas 3% was acquired on 1 June 20X4 and the company proposes to realise this investment on 30 November 20X4.

19.3 Den Batts Group

The following draft financial statements relate to the **Den Batts Group**.

Summarised group profit and loss account for the year ended 31 December 20X1

	€000
Operating profit	5,260
Profit on disposal of tangible fixed assets	20
Loss on disposal of subsidiary (note 1)	(250)
Share of profit of associated undertaking	950
Profit on ordinary activities before taxation	5,980
Tax on profit on ordinary activities (including €200,000 attributable to associate)	(2,060)
Profit on ordinary activities after taxation	3,920
Minority interests	(750)
Profit attributable to members of the parent company	3,170
Dividends paid	(1,150)
Profit retained for year	2,020

Group statement of total recognised gains and losses for the year ended 31 December 20X1

	€000
Profit attributable to members of the parent company	3,170
Deficit on revaluation of land and buildings	(300)
Surplus on revaluation of land and buildings in associate	150
Total recognised gains and losses relating to the year	3,020

Summarised group balance sheet as at 31 December	**20X1 €000**	**20X0 €000**
Fixed assets		
Tangible assets (note 2)	14,210	17,680
Investments (notes 1 and 3)	5,950	—
	20,160	17,680
Current assets		
Stocks	7,200	6,800
Trade debtors	6,600	5,400
Cash at bank and in hand	240	1,330
	14,040	13,530
Less: Creditors amounts falling due within one year		
Trade creditors	(13,400)	(10,030)
Bank overdraft	(2,440)	(2,290)
Net current (liabilities)/assets	(1,800)	1,210
Total assets less current liabilities	18,360	18,890
Capital and reserves		
Called-up share capital	5,410	5,410
Revaluation reserve	350	500
Profit and loss account	9,300	7,280
Total shareholders' funds	15,060	13,190
Minority interests	3,300	5,700
	18,360	18,890

continued overleaf

The following information is also relevant:

1 The group disposed of a subsidiary, **Steam**, on 1 September 20X1. Den Batts held an 80% interest in the subsidiary at the date of disposal.

Steam prepared an interim balance sheet at the date of disposal as follows:

	€000	€000
Tangible fixed assets		3,100
Stocks	600	
Trade debtors	500	
Cash at bank and in hand	1,300	
Trade creditors	(1,300)	1,100
		4,200
Called-up share capital		1,000
Profit and loss account		3,200
		4,200

The consolidated carrying values of all the assets and liabilities at that date are as given. Goodwill was fully amortised by the date of disposal. The loss on disposal of subsidiary in the group accounts comprises:

	€000
Sale proceeds	3,110
Net assets sold (80% × €4.2 million)	(3,360)
Loss on disposal	250

The consideration for the sale of Steam was 2 million ordinary shares of €1 in **Power**, the acquiring company, at a value of €3 million, and €110,000 in cash. Power has an issued ordinary share capital of 15 million ordinary shares.

2 The movements on group tangible fixed assets during the year were as follows:

	Cost or valuation €000	Accumulated depreciation €000	Net book value €000
At 1 January 20X1	21,000	3,320	17,680
Additions/ provided during year	4,180	1,500	
Revaluation	(300)	—	
Disposals and transfers	(6,800)	(950)	
At 31 December 20X1	18,080	3,870	14,210

3 During the year, Den Batts acquired a 40% share of **Energy**. The cost of this investment was €2.25 million, comprising €1 million in tangible fixed assets transferred and €1.25 million in cash. The group has used equity accounting for the investment in Energy. The land and buildings transferred have been revalued at the year-end.

The investments included under fixed assets comprised the associate Energy, €2.95 million, and the shares in Power, €3 million (see note 1).

Required

(a) Prepare the cash flow statement of Den Batts and group for the year ended 31 December 20X1, in as much detail as the information given permits.

(Notes to the cash flow statement, as required by FRS 1, are not required to answer part (a).)

(b) Explain how the disposal of a subsidiary affects the calculation of cash flows. Use the cash flow statement prepared in answer to (a) to illustrate your answer.

20

Other topical issues

Learning objectives

After studying this chapter you should be able to:

- understand the principle of substance over form and its effect on group accounts
- understand what is meant by the term quasi-subsidiary
- describe how quasi-subsidiaries should be accounted for under UK GAAP
- prepare segmental reports in the format required by regulations
- compare and contrast UK GAAP and IAS GAAP regulations applying to segmental reports

Introduction

This chapter deals with two unrelated issues that are relevant to group accounts: (i) off balance sheet financing and quasi-subsidiaries and (ii) segmental reporting. UK GAAP and IAS regulations are outlined and some examples from company accounts are provided by way of illustration.

Off balance sheet finance and quasi-subsidiaries

> Business practice is continually evolving and new forms of transactions are sometimes developed whose true intention or commercial effect is not immediately obvious.
>
> (ED 49 *Reflecting the substance of transactions in assets and liabilities*, ASC, 1990)

Traditional accounting practice developed over a long period of relatively uncomplicated commercial dealings. However, over the last few decades business transactions have become more complex. Accounting has struggled to keep pace with innovative practices, some of which were prompted by genuine commercial considerations, while others arose from explicit efforts to circumvent potentially unfavourable accounting treatments and disclosures. Off balance sheet financing was the term initially used to describe the many schemes devised in the 1980s, whereby entities were provided with finance that was not reflected in their balance sheets. These schemes usually involved a literal interpretation of legislation and a consequent misrepresentation of the spirit of the regulations. Consequently, the commercial substance of transactions was often disguised. One such scheme was to establish entities which did not meet the strict legal definition of a subsidiary. Therefore, they did not have to be consolidated despite being controlled by the parent. Borrowings could be channelled through those entities and, because they were not consolidated, the liabilities were kept off the group balance sheet. Such entities came to be called quasi-subsidiaries (or hidden subsidiaries, non-subsidiary subsidiaries, controlled non-subsidiaries).

UK GAAP

Quasi-subsidiaries are dealt with in FRS 5 *Reporting the Substance of Transactions*. An overview of FRS 5 is provided in this section by way of background, before considering the regulations dealing specifically with quasi-subsidiaries. The standard was issued in April 1994 after a lengthy process which spanned nine years of proposals. FRS 5 broke new ground by prescribing accounting practice in general terms with the aim that the standard would have continued and lasting relevance. The general approach adopted by FRS 5 involves analysing the effects of transactions on assets and liabilities to establish if new assets (and related liabilities) have been acquired and if previously recognised assets and liabilities should continue to be included in the reporting entity's accounts.

Although FRS 5 applies to all transactions, the accounting treatment and disclosure of the vast majority of items are unaffected by the standard. It is particularly relevant to transactions whose substance is not readily apparent and whose true commercial effect may not be fully indicated by their legal form. FRS 5 sets out general principles covering:

- determination of the substance of a transaction
- whether any resulting assets and liabilities should be included in the balance sheet
- reporting these transactions in the profit and loss account
- disclosures necessary
- whether any special 'vehicle' companies incorporated into a transaction should be consolidated.

Underlying the general principles are agreed definitions for assets and liabilities in FRS 5 (paragraphs 2 and 4, respectively), which are as follows:

> [Assets are] rights or other access to future economic benefits controlled by an entity as a result of past transactions or events.
>
> [Liabilities are] an entity's obligations to transfer economic benefits as a result of past transactions or events.

Determining the substance of a transaction

A key step in determining the substance of a transaction is to identify whether the transaction has given rise to new assets or liabilities or whether it has increased or decreased existing assets or liabilities. Central to this judgement are the FRS 5 definitions of assets and liabilities.

Accounting for financing normally follows logically from the treatment of the related asset. To determine the appropriate treatment of the liability, it is often easier to examine what has happened to the asset. Future benefits inherent in assets are never certain. There is always a risk that benefits will differ from those expected. The allocation of risk between parties is important in determining which party has an asset. Assets and liabilities should be recognised in the balance sheet where there is *both* sufficient evidence that an asset or liability exists *and* that the asset or liability can be reliably measured. Recognition is defined in FRS 5 (paragraph 6) as:

> The process of incorporating an item into the primary financial statements under the appropriate heading. It involves depiction of the item in words and by a monetary amount and inclusion of that amount in the statement totals.

Quasi-subsidiaries

Quasi-subsidiaries arise where reporting entities do not have to consolidate the accounts of investees because, under existing legislation, the investee does not qualify as a subsidiary. However, the relationship between the entities is such that the investing company controls the investee giving rise to benefits that are, in substance, no different from those arising where investees are subsidiaries.

In the past, companies could transact part of their business through corporate vehicles over which they had effective control. However, the investment was structured in such a way that these entities did not qualify as subsidiaries. For example, a family-controlled business could transact business through an entity controlled by one member of the family and keep that business out of the accounts of the main family business.

Off balance sheet financing arises in this context by channelling borrowings into a company that is effectively controlled by the parent but is technically not a subsidiary. This is illustrated in Example 20.1.

Example 20.1 Off balance sheet financing through a quasi-subsidiary

Example

The issued share capital of B plc consists of 50,000 ordinary shares of €1 each and 50,000 'A' preference shares of €1 each. All shares carry one vote each. 'A' preference shares carry an entitlement to dividend based on current interest rates. Parent owns the ordinary shares, while Friendly Bank plc holds the 'A' preference shares. All shareholders are entitled to nominate the same number of directors, but Parent nominees have greater voting power at board of directors' meetings.

Required

Comment on how this arrangement could facilitate off balance sheet financing.

Solution

Parent controls B plc as it has majority voting power at board of directors' meetings. Because it only owns 50% of B plc's equity and does not control the composition of the board of directors, prior to the Seventh Directive B plc was not a legal subsidiary and therefore was not consolidated into Parent's group accounts. Consequently any borrowings channelled through B plc would not adversely affect Parent's consolidated gearing ratio.

The EU Seventh Directive widened the definition of a subsidiary and thereby reduced the scope for quasi-subsidiary types of off balance sheet financing.

A parent undertaking is required to prepare consolidated financial statements that deal with the state of affairs of all its subsidiaries based on the position at the year-end. As we saw in Chapter 14, the definition of a subsidiary is comprehensive. The objective of the legislation is that undertakings under control of the reporting entity should be consolidated as subsidiaries. Arrangements that fall outside the definitions of the Seventh Directive and of accounting standards do not confer parent–subsidiary status. It is in such circumstances that the concept of 'quasi-subsidiaries' may become relevant.

To reinforce the pre-eminence of control over ownership, entities over which control is exercised in fact, whether by right or not (*de facto* control), must be consolidated under FRS 5. FRS 5 invokes the 'true and fair view' override provisions to require consolidation where commercial substance indicates control, despite the relationship between the investor and its investee not qualifying (strictly speaking) as a subsidiary under the definitions in regulations. In complex situations, it may be difficult to ascertain who is exercising control or to identify where the entity is acting in accordance with another's wishes. In these cases it is necessary to consider the position of each party, and what has motivated them, so that the overall commercial substance of the arrangement can be determined.

FRS 5 (paragraph 7) defines a quasi-subsidiary as:

> a company … that, though not fulfilling the definition of a subsidiary, is directly or indirectly controlled by the reporting entity and gives rise to benefits for that entity that are in substance no different from those that would arise were the vehicle a subsidiary.

Consistent with the definition of assets, the exposure to risk is taken as primary evidence of access to benefits.

Where a quasi-subsidiary has been identified, FRS 5 requires that it be consolidated in exactly the same way as if it were a legal subsidiary. This may give rise to particular problems. For example, where the reporting entity has no equity in the quasi-subsidiary (as may often be the case) then the minority interest would be 100%! Nonetheless, the profits, losses, assets and liabilities of the quasi-subsidiary will be consolidated, allowing more realistic financial ratios to be calculated.

Because quasi-subsidiaries do not satisfy the strict definition of a subsidiary, FRS 5 requires the consolidated accounts to disclose the fact that they have been included, together with a summary of their own financial statements.

A hypothetical example of a quasi-subsidiary is shown in Example 20.2. The client in the example needs cash, which is provided by the bank in return for a substantial fee. The commercial substance of the transaction described is that the client borrows a substantial sum of cash which, is secured in effect, on the assets comprising the aeroplane fleet. The objective in structuring the transaction in the way described is to avoid having to show the borrowings from the bank as a liability in the consolidated accounts of the client. FRS 5 frustrates this objective by requiring the quasi-subsidiary to be consolidated. The balance sheet of the quasi-subsidiary will contain the aeroplane fleet in assets and will show the liability to the parent bank (in respect of the borrowings) in liabilities.

Example 20.2 Accounting for quasi-subsidiaries under FRS 5

Example

A major bank established a subsidiary for the purpose of facilitating a financing arrangement (sale and leaseback) for one of its financially distressed major clients. The bank's subsidiary purchased a fleet of aeroplanes from the client in return for a substantial cash payment. The client undertook to continue total management of the aircraft in return for a fee. This fee, together with any profits or losses on sale of the aircraft, was the sole source of income for the bank's subsidiary.

Required

Comment on how you would account for this transaction in the accounts of the bank and of the client.

Solution

Under FRS 5, the bank's subsidiary will be regarded as a quasi-subsidiary of the client and not a subsidiary of the bank, even though the bank has legal ownership. The client will therefore be required to consolidate the quasi-subsidiary and to disclose additional information about the quasi-subsidiary as required under FRS 5.

In practice, examples of quasi-subsidiaries are likely to be relatively rare. They could arise where the reporting entity directs the operating and financial policies of another entity with a view to obtaining benefits from that other entity and yet has no equity investment in that other entity. British Airways refers to the acquisition of a quasi-subsidiary in its 1999/2000 annual report as shown in Exhibit 20.1 and makes the disclosures required by FRS 5, i.e., details of the quasi-subsidiary and a summary of the quasi-subsidiary's financial statements are included.

Exhibit 20.1 **Quasi-subsidiary**
British Airways Annual Report 1999/2000

1 Accounting Policies (extract)
Basis of consolidation (extract)
Where an entity, though not fulfilling the legal definition of a subsidiary or subsidiary undertaking, gives rise to benefits for the group that are, in substance, no different than those that would arise were that entity a subsidiary or subsidiary undertaking, that entity is classified as a quasi-subsidiary. In determining whether the group has the ability to enjoy the benefits arising from such entities' net assets, regard is given as to which party is exposed to the risks inherent in the benefits and which party, in practice, carries substantially all the risks and rewards of ownership.

21 Acquisitions of interest in subsidiary undertakings and quasi-subsidiary (extract)
During the year, British Airways acquired the majority of risks and rewards in the activities of the London Eye Company Ltd and has accordingly accounted for it as a quasi-subsidiary from July 1999.

22 Quasi-subsidiary
Summarised financial information of the London Eye Company Limited, prepared in accordance with British Airways' accounting policies, is set out below.

	Total £million
Profit and Loss Account	
Turnover	2
Operating loss, loss before taxation and loss for the period	(2)
Balance Sheet	
Fixed assets	75
Current assets	5
Creditors: Amounts falling due within one year	(10)
Net current liabilities	(5)
Total assets less current liabilities	70
Creditors: Amounts falling due after more than one year	(74)
Capital and reserve deficit	(4)
Cash Flow Statement	
Cash outflow from operating activities	(3)
Capital expenditure and financial investment	(49)
Net cash outflow before management of liquid resources and financing	(52)
Financing	49
Decrease in cash	(3)

There are no recognised gains or losses other than the loss for the period.

IAS GAAP

The IASC has also addressed the general principle of substance over form, although it did not refer specifically to quasi-subsidiaries. *Framework for the Preparation and Presentation of Financial Statements* was issued in April 1989 and sets out the concepts that underlie the preparation and presentation of financial statements. Four principal qualitative characteristics of information are identified in this document, one of which is reliability. According to paragraph 31, information is reliable when it is:

> free from material error and bias and can be depended upon by users to represent faithfully that which it either purports to represent or could reasonably be expected to represent.

Paragraph 35 of the Framework requires transactions and events to be accounted for in accordance with their substance and economic reality, not merely with their legal form. The Framework document defines the consideration of substance over form by stipulating that:

> If information is to represent faithfully the transactions and other events that it purports to represent, it is necessary that they are accounted for and presented in accordance with their substance and economic reality and not merely their legal form.

Paragraph 36 of the Framework indicates that financial statements are not neutral if, by the selection or presentation of information, they influence the decision making or judgement of users in order to achieve a predetermined result or outcome.

Paragraph 20 of IAS 1 identifies a number of considerations to be taken into account by management when selecting accounting policies. Substance over form is one such consideration in the selection of accounting policies. Preparers should ensure that they choose and apply accounting policies that reflect the substance and economic reality of events and transactions.

Comparison of UK GAAP and IAS GAAP

Accounting for the substance of transactions is dealt with in more detail in FRS 5 than in the IASs. More guidance on the application of the principle is provided in FRS 5. In addition, IASs do not mention quasi-subsidiaries specifically.

Segmental reporting for groups

Many companies have multiple products and operate in many geographic markets, often through subsidiary undertakings. For diversified businesses, users need greater detail about the results and resources of the entity than is provided in the profit and loss account and balance sheet. Different segments of the operations of diversified companies may be subject to significantly different rates of profitability, degrees of risk and opportunities for growth. The desirability of including disaggregated financial information concerning distinct segments is well accepted. Both UK GAAP and IAS GAAP have explicit standards dealing with disclosure of segmental information. After a discussion of each one in turn, the two sets of regulations are then compared.

UK GAAP

Enactment of the EU Fourth Directive in 1981 in the UK (and in 1986 in the Republic of Ireland) introduced a legal requirement to analyse turnover by type of business activity and geographically. SSAP 25 *Segmental Reporting* added to legal requirements by requiring segmental analysis of profitability and net assets in addition to turnover. The primary aim of the standard is to provide a better understanding of performance by showing the impact that significant components of the business have on the group as a whole.

SSAP 25 provides guidance on how reportable segments should be determined and it specifies the segmental information to be disclosed.

Scope

The statutory provisions (derived from the Fourth Directive) contained in the standard apply to all companies. The non-statutory provisions apply to:

- plcs
- holding companies that have a plc as a subsidiary
- banking and insurance companies or groups
- private companies that exceed by a multiple of ten the size criteria for medium-sized companies, i.e. exceed any two of:
  - turnover of more than £112 million for UK companies (IR£120 (€152.37) million in the Republic of Ireland)
  - total assets of more than £56 million for UK companies (IR£60 (€76.18) million in the Republic of Ireland)
  - average number of employees more than 2,500 (in both the UK and the Republic of Ireland).

Definitions

A separate class of business is defined by SSAP 25 as a distinguishable component of an entity that provides a separate product or service or a separate group of related products or services. A geographical segment is defined as a geographical area comprising an individual country or group of countries in which an entity operates or to which it supplies products or services. In identifying separate segments the directors should consider the nature of products and services, the nature of production processes, markets for sales, distribution channels for sales, the organisational pattern of activities of the business and any separate legislation relating to parts of the business. Reportable segments should be those that are significant to the business as a whole. Each segment is significant if:

- segment turnover is greater than 10% of total turnover
- segment profit/loss is greater than 10% of total profit or loss
- segment net assets are more than 10% of total net assets.

Disclosures

SSAP 25 requires a total of eight disclosures (marked ① to ⑧ in the following). For each class of business and geographical segment, the company or group must segmentally analyse three items:

- turnover, analysed between:
  - sales to external customers ①
  - sales between segments ②

  - sales analysed by origin ③
  - sales analysed by destination (except where this is not materially different from sales by origin) ④
- results before taxation and minority interests ⑤. This will normally be before interest except where interest income/expense is central to the business
- net assets ⑥, which are not defined in SSAP 25 but will normally be non-interest bearing operating assets less non-interest-bearing liabilities.

In relation to the preparation of group accounting and previous item ② above, inter-segment sales are likely to be eliminated on consolidation. However, as illustrated in Example 20.3, gross sales are disclosed in the segmental analysis, with a separate deduction shown for inter-segment sales.

Associated undertakings

If associated undertakings account for 20% or more of an entity's total result, or account for 20% or more of its total assets, they are considered significant by the standard. The following should be segmentally disclosed in respect of *significant* associates:

- share of results before tax and minority interests ⑦
- share of net assets⑧, including goodwill to the extent not written off, stated after attributing (where possible) fair values to the net assets at the date of acquisition.

(Note, however, that segmental analysis of the turnover of associated undertakings is not required.)

Presentation

The Appendix to SSAP 25 (which does not form part of the standard) provides an example of the form of presentation of segmental information. This Appendix is reproduced in Example 20.3. The first section of the Appendix analyses turnover, profit before tax and net assets by class of business. There are three classes of business in the example. Inter-segment sales are separately identified in the analysis of turnover. Common costs and interest are not analysed segmentally in the analysis of profit, presumably because they cannot be allocated to individual business segments. Similarly, in the segmental analysis of assets, certain assets are 'unallocated'. Note that, as required by SSAP 25, the group's share of associated undertakings' profit and net assets are also segmentally analysed. Associated company turnover is not included in group turnover and is therefore not analysed segmentally.

Geographical analysis requirements are similar to analysis by class of business. In the second section of the Appendix, turnover is analysed geographically both by destination and by origin. Profit before tax and net assets are also analysed by geographic segment.

The eight items required to be disclosed under SSAP 25 are marked ① to ⑧ to highlight implementation of the disclosure requirements in Example 20.3 (these numbered annotations have been added by the authors, and do not appear in the SSAP).

SSAP 25 restates the legal provision that where, in the opinion of the directors, the disclosure of any of the information required by the accounting standard would be seriously prejudicial to the interests of the reporting entity, that information need not be disclosed. The fact of non-disclosure must be stated.

Example 20.3 SSAP 25 Appendix: Illustrative segmental report by class of business

Classes of business	**Industry A**		**Industry B**		**Other industries**		**Group**	
	1990	**1989**	**1990**	**1989**	**1990**	**1989**	**1990**	**1989**
	£000	**£000**	**£000**	**£000**	**£000**	**£000**	**£000**	**£000**
Turnover								
Total sales	33,000	30,000	42,000	38,000	26,000	23,000	101,000	91,000
Inter-segment sales ②	(4,000)	—	—	—	(12,000)	(14,000)	(16,000)	(14,000)
Sales to third parties ①	29,000	30,000	42,000	38,000	14,000	9,000	85,000	77,000
Profit before taxation								
Segment profit ⑤	3,000	2,500	4,500	4,000	1,800	1,500	9,300	8,000
Common costs							300	300
Operating profit							9,000	7,700
Net interest							(400)	(500)
							8,600	7,200
Group share of the profits before taxation of associated undertakings ⑦	1,000	1,000	1,400	1,200	—	—	2,400	2,200
Group profit before taxation							11,000	9,400
Net assets								
Segment net assets ⑥	17,600	15,000	24,000	25,000	19,400	19,000	61,000	59,000
Unallocated assets							3,000	3,000
							64,000	62,000
Group share of the net assets of associated undertakings ⑧	10,200	8,000	8,800	9,000	—	—	19,000	17,000
Total net assets							83,000	79,000

Geographical segments	**United Kingdom**		**North America**		**Far East**		**Other**		**Group**	
	1990	**1989**	**1990**	**1989**	**1990**	**1989**	**1990**	**1989**	**1990**	**1989**
Turnover	**£000**	**£000**	**£000**	**£000**	**£000**	**£000**	**£000**	**£000**	**£000**	**£000**
Turnover by destination ④ – sales to third parties	34,000	31,000	16,000	14,500	25,000	23,000	10,000	8,500	85,000	77,000
Turnover by origin ③										
Total sales	38,000	34,000	29,000	27,500	23,000	23,000	12,000	10,500	102,500	95,000
Inter-segment sales	—	—	(8,000)	(9,000)	(9,000)	(9,000)	—	—	(17,000)	(18,000)
Sales to third parties ①	38,000	34,000	21,000	18,500	14,000	14,000	12,000	10,500	85,000	77,000
Profit before taxation										
Segment profit ⑤	4,000	2,900	2,500	2,300	1,800	1,900	1,000	900	9,300	8,000
Common costs									300	300
Operating profit									9,000	7,700
Net interest									(400)	(500)
									8,600	7,200
Group share of the profit before taxation of associated undertakings ⑦	950	1,000	1,450	1,200	—	—	—	—	2,400	2,200
Group profit before taxation									11,000	9,400

continued overleaf

Example 20.3 Continued

	United Kingdom		North America		Far East		Other		Group	
	1990	1989	1990	1989	1990	1989	1990	1989	1990	1989
Net assets	£000	£000	£000	£000	£000	£000	£000	£000	£000	£000
Segment net assets ⑥	16,000	15,000	25,000	26,000	16,000	15,000	4,000	3,000	61,000	59,000
Unallocated assets									3,000	3,000
									64,000	62,000
Group share of the net assets of associated undertakings ⑧	8,500	7,000	10,500	10,000	—	—	—	—	19,000	17,000
Total net assets									83,000	79,000

Waterford Wedgwood illustrates the basic requirements for segmental reporting in Exhibit 20.2. The items disclosed are numbered ① to ⑥ to pinpoint application of the disclosure requirements of SSAP 25 discussed earlier. There are three classes of business and the three

Exhibit 20.2 **Segmental reporting under UK GAAP Waterford Wedgwood Annual Report 2000**

Notes to the financial statements (extract)
1 Segment information (extract)
(a) Classes of business

	Turnover	Operating profit ⑤	2000 Net assets ⑥
	€Mils	€Mils	€Mils
Crystal	435.7	65.8	211.3
Ceramics	481.4	17.6	285.7
All-Clad/Other Products	167.3	21.0	133.2
Group net borrowings	—	—	(332.8)
	1,084.4	104.4	297.4
Minority interests	—	—	(3.7)
	1,084.4	104.4	293.7

(b) Geographical segment by country of operation

	Turnover by destination ④	Turnover by country of operation ③	Operating profit/(loss) ⑤	2000 Net assets ⑥
	€Mils	€Mils	€Mils	€Mils
Europe	402.3	727.8	83.2	467.3
North America	533.9	522.1	22.6	133.7
Asia Pacific	106.6	84.0	(2.3)	21.2
Rest of world	41.6	27.8	0.9	8.0
	1,084.4	1,361.7	104.4	630.2
Inter-segment sales	—	② (277.3)	—	—
Group net borrowings	—	—	—	(332.8)
	1,084.4	① 1,084.4	104.4	297.4
Minority interests	—	—	—	(3.7)
	1,084.4	1,084.4	104.4	293.7

All inter-segment sales originate from Europe.

items (turnover, profit and net assets) are analysed under these three classes of business. Four geographical segments are identified in the exhibit. As required under SSAP 25, turnover is analysed by both destination (where the goods are sold to) and origin (where the goods are manufactured). Also as required by SSAP 25, inter-segment sales are separately identified.

Two balance sheet items, group net borrowings and minority interests, are not analysed by class of business or geographically (presumably because they cannot be allocated to a single segment). Disclosures are not provided for associated undertakings, presumably because they are not significant.

Goodwill

An interesting question is raised in Example 20.4 relating to the effect of goodwill amortisation on segmental analysis of results.

Example 20.4 Segmental analysis and goodwill

Example

A parent company provides segmental analysis of consolidated results in accordance with SSAP 25. Following implementation of FRS 10, it amortises goodwill through the consolidated profit and loss account.

Required

Can the parent provide the segmental analysis of operating profit before goodwill and then deduct goodwill as a single figure, in the same way as it deducts one figure for interest?

Solution

Goodwill amortisation is a charge against operating profit. SSAP 25 requires segmental analysis of results before accounting for taxation and minority interests. As segmental analysis of results is normally given at the operating profit level, the company's intended presentation does not satisfy SSAP 25.

The company could, however, show a segmental analysis of profit before goodwill amortisation, then a segmental analysis of goodwill amortisation and finally the analysis of operating profit (after goodwill amortisation).

Source: Adapted from Holgate, P. and Ghosh, J. 1999. 'Accounting solutions – segments and goodwill', *Accountancy*, March, p.98

Impact of FRS 3

FRS 3 *Reporting Financial Performance* does not require segmental information to be given for the separate categories of continuing and discontinued activities. However, the standard states in paragraph 53 that if an acquisition or discontinuance has a material impact on a major business segment, this should be explained in the notes to provide a thorough understanding of the results and financial position of the company.

CRH provides very comprehensive disclosure of the impact of acquisitions on geographic segments in Exhibit 20.3.

Exhibit 20.3 Acquisitions and segmental reporting CRH plc Annual Report 2000

Notes on Financial Statements (extract)
1 Segmental information (extract)
Impact of 2000 acquisitions on segmental reporting

The principal acquisitions during 2000 were:

Republic of Ireland Ballintra Concrete and the William Cox joint venture (part of the rooflights operations of Yule Catto & Co plc).

Britain and Northern Ireland Springvale Insulation and Cox Building Products UK (part of the rooflights operations of Yule Catto & Co plc).

Mainland Europe The Jura Group in Switzerland, the German and Dutch rooflights operations of Yule Catto & Co plc, Zwaana, Monoliet and Dijkbouw in the Netherlands, Omnidal, Van Welkenhuyaen, Schelfhout and the buyout of Remacle in Belgium, Codimat and the buyout of Matériaux Service in France, Termo Organika, Drogomex, Polbet and Prefabet Kozienice in Poland, six asphalt businesses and the buyout of Karjalan Murske in Finland.

The Americas The Shelly Company and its add-on businesses Northern Ohio Paving, Waco Stone & Paving, Bluestone Paving and Van Wey Sand & Gravel in Ohio and West Virginia, Hoffer's Inc, Thorn-Orwick and Gollin Supply also in the Mid-West, Strescon and Sabatini in the Mid-Atlantic region, The Dolomite Group and Domine Builders Supply in New York, New Jersey Concrete Pipe, American Stone Mix in Maryland, Chase Precast in Massachusetts, CCI Manufacturing in Texas, England Construction, Owen Excavation, Telluride Gravel and WR White in the Mountain region, Acme Materials and Construction, Larry's/Reeves and Jensen Paving in the North West, and the New Basis utility vault business in California.

The impact of these acquisitions is summarised below:

	Turnover €m	**Trading profit €m**	**Net assets at 31st December 2000 €m**
Republic of Ireland	5.6	0.5	8.8
Britain & Northern Ireland	18.6	(1.1)	22.8
Jura Group (acquired on 30th November, 2000)	26.7	(0.1)	380.2
Mainland Europe – other	173.8	12.5	228.4
Total Mainland Europe	200.5	12.4	608.6
The Shelly Company (acquired on 24th February, 2000)	333.8	38.3	415.1
The Americas – other	480.4	50.1	607.4
Total The Americas	814.2	88.4	1,022.5
Total acquisitions including share of joint ventures	1,038.9	100.2	1,662.7

Analysis by class of business €955.9 million of the turnover and €98.8 million of the trading profit relating to 2000 acquisitions is classified under the building materials segment.

In Exhibit 20.4, Whitbread separately identifies acquired businesses awaiting disposal and excludes these from the segmental analysis. Whitbread's disclosure is commendable in the large number (seven) of business segments identified. Inter-segment sales are disclosed separately. The segmental analysis is accompanied by an interesting note on the effect of changes in transfer prices between divisions on the segmental analysis. The share of turnover of joint ventures is not analysed segmentally and is disclosed separately as a single figure, although the note to the segmental analysis provides further details concerning the joint venture. Amounts relating to central services, which presumably could not be allocated to individual business segments, are also separately identified. However, the exceptional item is separately analysed by business segment.

Nearly all the activities of this company take place in a single geographical location and consequently there are only two geographical segments – (i) UK and (ii) rest of the world. The note points out that sales by country of origin and by destination country are not materially different and are, therefore, not separately disclosed, neither are inter-segment geographical sales as these are not material.

Exhibit 20.4 **Disposals and segmental reporting**
Whitbread PLC Annual Report 1999/2000

Segmental analysis of turnover, profit and net assets (extract)	**Turnover**	**1999/2000 Operating profit**	**Net assets**
By business segment	**£m**	**£m**	**£m**
Beer	1,116.0	46.5	298.9
Pub Partnerships	146.9	64.3	385.9
Inns	859.4	173.5	1,297.1
Restaurants	733.8	56.8	674.1
Hotels	287.5	53.7	1,184.0
Sports, health and fitness	103.6	23.0	405.1
Other drinks	656.7	14.4	131.6
Acquired business awaiting disposal (see note below)	10.8	1.3	129.6
Segmental turnover, operating profit and net assets	3,914.7	433.5	4,506.3
Inter-segment turnover	(244.4)		
Share of joint ventures' turnover	(787.5)		
Central services	68.6	(18.0)	(237.7)
Allocation to Whitbread Share Ownership Scheme		(4.4)	
Exceptional items		(78.5)	
	2,951.4	332.6	4,268.6
By geographical segment			
United Kingdom	2,880.5	327.6	4,249.5
Rest of the world	70.9	5.0	19.1
	2,951.4	332.6	4,268.6

The acquired business awaiting disposal relates to the pubs business acquired with Swallow Group plc.

Inter-divisional pricing for the supply of beer and related services has been rebased to reflect current conditions in the market. The impact of this in the current period is to reduce the profit of the Beer segment by £10.6m and to increase the profits of Pub Partnerships, Inns and Restaurants by £4.4m, £5.6m and £0.6m, respectively.

continued overleaf

Exhibit 20.4 Continued

The exceptional costs are detailed in note 4. The analysis is as follows:

	1999/2000 £m
Beer	—
Pub Partnerships, Inns and Restaurants	10.3
Restaurants	7.2
Hotels	15.0
Other drinks	34.2
Central services	11.8
	78.5

Restaurants' segmental turnover includes the group's share of joint venture turnover amounting to £130.4m (1998/9 – £121.0m) and Other drinks turnover is derived wholly from the group's share of a joint venture (1998/9 – £335.6m). Inter-segment turnover is from Beer to the other segments. Central services turnover comprises, primarily, food distribution services provided to a joint venture. The geographical analysis of turnover and profit is by source. The analysis of turnover by destination is not materially different. Sales between geographical segments are not material. The result and net assets of the majority of Travel Inns are included in the divisions that operate them, not in the Hotels. Net assets included above are total net assets excluding net debt.

In the profit and loss account, turnover of the group and share of joint ventures includes sales from the group to joint ventures amounting to £220.2m (1998/9 – £137.6m) and sales to the group from joint ventures amounting to £24.0m (1998/9 – £11.4m).

IAS GAAP

IAS 14 *Segment Reporting* was substantially revised in 1997 to change the scope of the original standard and to impose additional disclosure requirements.

Scope

IAS 14 is narrower in scope than SSAP 25 and only applies to enterprises whose equity or debt is publicly traded. However, there is no equivalent provision under IAS GAAP similar to the UK GAAP concession that segmental reports need not be provided where, in the opinion of the directors, this would be seriously prejudicial to the business.

Definitions

IAS 14 provides considerable detail defining a class of business or geographical segment. One of the two should be chosen as the primary segment and the other is the secondary segment (to which reduced disclosure applies).

Disclosures

IAS 14 requires disclosure of nine items (only eight are required under SSAP 25) in respect of the primary segmental analysis:

1 segment revenue
2 segment result, which is segment revenues less segment expenses, before minority interest
3 total segment operating assets

4. total segment operating liabilities
5. total cost incurred to acquire segment assets to be used during more than one accounting period (i.e., capital expenditure)
6. segment depreciation and amortisation
7. other significant non-cash expenses of the segment
8. share of net profit/loss from enterprises accounted for under the equity method
9. aggregate investments in any of these enterprises accounted for under the equity method.

Table 20.1 later in this chapter compares the requirements of SSAP 25 and IAS 14, including the disclosure requirements. This comparison of SSAP 25 and IAS 14 shows that both standards require disclosure of ① segment turnover/revenue, ② segment profit/result and ③ segmental analysis of share of net results of associated undertakings/enterprises accounted for under the equity method.

Only UK GAAP requires disclosure of ④ segment turnover by origin, ⑤ segment turnover by destination, ⑥ inter-segment turnover, ⑦ segment net assets and ⑧ segmental analysis of net assets of associated undertakings.

Only IAS GAAP requires disclosure of ④ segment operating assets, ⑤ segment operating liabilities, ⑥ segment capital expenditure, ⑦ segment depreciation and amortisation, ⑧ significant segment non-cash expenses and ⑨ segmental analysis of aggregate investments accounted for using the equity method.

If the primary segment is analysed by class of business then only three items (1, 3 and 5) of the list of requirements under IAS 14 need to be disclosed for the secondary geographical segment. Such disclosures are only required where the item to be disclosed represents 10% or more of the total.

As was the case where class of business was the primary focus, only three items of the secondary basis of analysis require disclosure when the primary segment analysis is geographic analysis (and only for the business segments whose revenue or assets are more than 10% of the total). As before, items 1, 3 and 5 would be disclosed by class of business, in addition to the nine required geographic disclosures.

Presentation

IAS 14 illustrates the disclosures required in Appendix B (which does not form part of the standard). This illustration is reproduced in Example 20.5. The primary segmental analysis is by class of business (of which there are four). Sales, segment assets and capital expenditure are analysed into five geographical segments. The nine items required to be disclosed under IAS 14 are marked ① to ⑨ highlight implementation of the disclosure requirements in the example (these numbered annotations have been added by the authors and do not appear in the original example in the IAS).

Example 20.5 IAS 14: illustrative segmental report [Primary analysis by business segment]

	Paper Products		Office Products		Publishing		Other Operations		Eliminations		Consolidated	
	20X2	20X1	20X2	20X1	20X2	20X1	20X2	20X1	20X2	20X1	20X2	20X1
Revenue												
External sales	55	50	20	17	19	16	7	7				
Inter-segment sales	15	10	10	14	2	4	2	2	(29)	(30)		
Total revenue ①	70	60	30	31	21	20	9	9	(29)	(30)	101	90
Result												
Segment result ②	20	17	9	7	2	1	0	0	(1)	(1)	30	24
Unallocated corporate expenses											(7)	(9)
Operating profit											23	15
Interest expense											(4)	(4)
Interest income											2	3
Share of net profits of associates ⑧	6	5					2	2			8	7
Income taxes											(7)	(4)
Profit from ordinary activities											22	17
Extraordinary loss: Uninsured earthquake damage to factory		(3)									—	(3)
Net profit											22	14
Other information												
Segment assets ③	54	50	34	30	10	10	10	9			108	99
Investment in equity method associates ⑨	20	16					12	10			32	26
Unallocated corporate assets											35	30
Consolidated total assets											175	155
Segment liabilities ④	25	15	8	11	8	8	1	1			42	35
Unallocated corporate liabilities											40	55
Consolidated total liabilities											82	90
Capital expenditure ⑤	12	10	3	5	5		4	3				
Depreciation ⑥	9	7	9	7	5	3	3	4				
Non-cash expenses other than depreciation ⑦	8	2	7	3	2	2	2	1				

Secondary analysis by geographic segment

	Sales Revenue by Geographical Market ①	
	20X2	20X1
United Kingdom	19	22
Other European Union countries	30	31
Canada and the United States	28	21
Mexico and South America	6	2
Southeast Asia (principally Japan and Taiwan)	18	14
	101	90

	Carrying Amount of Segment Assets ③		Additions to Property Plant, Equipment, and Intangible Assets ⑤	
	20X2	20X1	20X2	20X1
United Kingdom	72	78	8	5
Other European Union countries	47	37	5	4
Canada and the United States	34	20	4	3
Indonesia	22	20	7	6
	175	155	24	18

The Bank of Cyprus provides a comprehensive example of segmental reporting under IAS GAAP in Exhibit 20.5. There are three classes of business (including a hotel business segment which is unusual for a bank) and three geographical segments. Class of business is the primary segmental analysis, although disclosures in the secondary geographical segmental analysis are not significantly fewer than in the class of business analysis. Of the nine disclosures required under IAS 14, eight are provided by Bank of Cyprus. Other significant non-cash expenses of the segment are not separately disclosed, possibly because they are not material.

Exhibit 20.5 **Segmental reporting under IAS GAAP**
Bank of Cyprus Group Annual Report 1999

Notes to the Financial Statements (extract)
2 Segmental analysis (extract)
The Group has three principal areas of activity: commercial banking and financial services, life and general insurance business and property and hotel business. The Group's banking and financial services are provided in three geographical markets, Cyprus, Greece and the United Kingdom/Ireland. The other activities of the Group are carried on only in Cyprus. The primary reporting format is for the areas of activity.

Areas of Activity 1999	Banking and financial services C£000	Insurance business C£000	Property and hotel business C£000	Total C£000
Turnover	438,678	93,673	6,957	539,308
Profit before tax	80,077	12,001	1,583	93,661
Associated company		6,484		6,484
Profit and loss account				100,145
Assets	4,877,106	330,156	34,434	5,241,696
Associated company		11,885		11,885
Inter-segment assets				(12,714)
Total assets				5,240,867
Liabilities	4,568,248	298,970	14,353	4,881,571
Inter-segment liabilities				(6,864)
Total liabilities				4,874,707
Additions of property and equipment	23,521	1,419	56	24,996
Life assurance business				(1,229)
Total capital expenditure				23,767
Depreciation	10,544	311	222	11,077
Life assurance business				(150)
Total depreciation				10,927
Profit from sale of long-term investments in equity shares	16,073	1,160		17,233
Insurance business				(1,160)
Profit from sale of long-term investments				16,073

continued overleaf

Geographical areas 1999	**Cyprus C£000**	**Greece C£000**	**United Kingdom/ Ireland C£000**	**Total C£000**
Turnover	432,886	77,660	42,039	**552,585**
Inter-segment turnover, mainly interest	(8,329)	(3,695)	(1,253)	**(13,277)**
Turnover with external customers	424,557	73,965	40,786	**539,308**
Profit before tax	72,531	14,680	6,450	**93,661**
Associated company	6,484			**6,484**
Profit and loss account				**100,145**
Assets	4,085,552	870,323	659,598	**5,615,473**
Associated company	11,885			**11,885**
Inter-segment assets				**(386,491)**
Total assets				**5,240,867**
Additions of property and equipment	11,457	11,511	2,028	**24,996**
Life assurance business				**(1,229)**
Total capital expenditure				**23,767**

The analyses by geographical segment are generally based on the location of the office recording the transaction.

Even though the activities of some of the Group companies are interdependent, the analyses by area of activity and geographical area are presented without adjustments for the cost of the net investment, the allocation of the benefit of earnings on the Group capital and for Group head office expenses, as such adjustments would necessarily be subjective.

Comparison of UK GAAP and IAS GAAP

The requirements of SSAP 25 and of IAS 14, while different, contain no incompatibilities. The main differences are summarised in Table 20.1.

Table 20.1 Main differences in segmental reporting requirements between UK GAAP and IAS GAAP

	UK GAAP	*IAS GAAP*
Definition of reportable segment	Less prescriptive and detailed	More prescriptive and detailed
Other definitions	Less detailed	More detailed
Scope	Plcs, banking and insurance companies and large companies	Entities with publicly traded securities
Disclosure	Turnover (third parties, inter-segment, origin, destination), profit, net assets	Turnover, profit, total assets, total liabilities, capital expenditure, depreciation and other significant non-cash expenses
	Share of (i) results and (ii) net assets of significant associates i.e., if total result or net assets exceed 20%	(i) Share of results of investments accounted for using the equity method, together with (ii) investments in those entities
	No primary/secondary distinction	Different disclosures required of primary and secondary segments
Exemption from disclosure	Permitted	Not permitted

Sources: Cairns, D. and Nobes, C. 2000. *The Convergence Handbook: A Comparison between International Accounting Standards and UK Financial Reporting Requirements*, Institute of Chartered Accountants in England and Wales, London
Connor, L., Dekker, P., Davies, M., Robinson, P. and Wilson, A. 2001. *IAS/UK GAAP Comparison*. Ernst & Young, London
PricewaterhouseCoopers. 2000. *International Accounting Standards Similarities and Differences IAS, US GAAP and UK GAAP* PricewaterhouseCoopers, London

Summary

This chapter outlined the regulations governing two distinct topics: quasi-subsidiaries and segmental reporting. UK GAAP and IAS GAAP in these two areas, while different, are not significantly so. In practice, given the impact of FRS 5, quasi-subsidiaries are not common. However, almost all companies, particularly those operating through subsidiaries conducting a variety of businesses and in varied geographical locations, are required to disclose segmentally analysed financial information.

Learning outcomes

After studying this chapter you should have learnt:

- how the principle of substance over form affects group accounts
- what is meant by the term quasi-subsidiary
- how to account for quasi-subsidiaries under UK GAAP
- how to present segmental reports in the format required by regulations
- the differences between UK GAAP and IAS GAAP regulations applying to segmental reports.

Multiple choice questions

Solutions to these questions are prepared under UK GAAP and are presented in Appendix 1.

20.1 Quasi-subsidiary

FRS 5 *Reporting the Substance of Transactions* defines a **quasi-subsidiary** as which of the following?

(a) A company that meets the definition of a subsidiary, but is not directly or indirectly controlled by the reporting entity and gives rise to benefits for that entity that are in substance no different from those that would arise were the vehicle a subsidiary.

(b) A company that does not fulfil the definition of a subsidiary, but is not directly or indirectly controlled by the reporting entity and gives rise to benefits for that entity that are in substance no different from those that would arise were the vehicle a subsidiary.

(c) A company that does not meet the definition of a subsidiary but is directly or indirectly controlled by the reporting entity and gives rise to benefits for that entity that are in substance no different from those that would arise were the vehicle a subsidiary.

(d) A company that meets the definition of a subsidiary, but is not directly or indirectly controlled by the reporting entity and does not give rise to benefits for that entity that are in substance no different from those that would arise were the vehicle a subsidiary.

20.2 How quasi-subsidiaries are to be accounted for

Which of the following statements best describes the requirements of FRS 5 *Reporting the Substance of Transactions* on how quasi-subsidiaries are to be accounted for?

(a) consolidate quasi-subsidiaries in exactly the same way as if they were legal subsidiaries

(b) do not consolidate quasi-subsidiaries but disclose their summary financial statements in a note to the consolidated accounts

(c) consolidate quasi-subsidiaries in exactly the same way as if they were legal subsidiaries and disclose the fact that they have been included

(d) consolidate quasi-subsidiaries in exactly the same way as if they were legal subsidiaries and disclose the fact that they have been included, together with a summary of their own financial statements

20.3 Disclose which of the following

SSAP 25 *Segmental Reporting* requires a public company to disclose which of the following information for each business segment?

(a) turnover only
(b) turnover and profit or loss (before tax and minority interest)
(c) turnover, profit or loss (before tax and minority interest) and net assets
(d) profit or loss (before tax and minority interest) and net assets

20.4 Disclosure requirements of SSAP 25

Which of the following correctly sets out the disclosure requirements of SSAP 25 *Segmental Reporting*?

(a) Turnover (third parties, inter-segment, origin, destination)
Profit
Net assets
(b) Turnover (inter-segment, origin, destination)
Profit
Net assets
(c) Turnover (third parties, inter-segment, destination)
Profit
Net assets
(d) Turnover (third parties, inter-segment, origin)
Profit
Net assets

20.5 Disclosure requirements of IAS 14

Which of the following correctly sets out the **disclosure requirements of IAS 14** *Segmental Reporting*?

(a) Turnover
Profit
Total assets
Total liabilities
Capital expenditure
Depreciation
Other significant non-cash expenses
(b) Turnover
Profit
Capital expenditure
Depreciation
Other significant non-cash expenses
(c) Turnover
Profit
Total assets
Total liabilities
Capital expenditure
Depreciation
(d) Turnover
Profit
Total assets
Total liabilities
Depreciation
Other significant non-cash expenses

Examination-style questions

20.1 Quasi-subsidiaries

Required

Explain the measures taken by the accounting profession in (a) FRS 2 *Accounting for Subsidiary Undertakings* and (b) FRS 5 *Reporting the Substance of Transactions* to ensure that consolidated accounts provide the holding company shareholders with information that is relevant, understandable, reliable and comparable in situations where **quasi subsidiaries** have been set up.

20.2 Timber Products

Required

(a) (i) Explain the objective of FRS 5 *Reporting the Substance of Transactions*.

(ii) Explain the criteria for ceasing to recognise an asset and give an illustration of the application of each of those criteria.

(b) Explain the appropriate accounting treatment for the following transaction and the entries that would appear in the consolidated profit and loss account for the year ended 31 October 20X5 of Timber Products and in the consolidated balance sheet as at that date for the following transaction.

On 1 December 20X4 **Timber Products** sold a factory that it owned in Scotland to Inter a wholly owned subsidiary of Offshore Banking for €10m. The factory had a book value of €8.5m. Inter was financed by a loan of €10m from Offshore Banking. Timber Products was paid a fee by Inter to continue to operate the factory, such fee representing the balance of profit remaining after Inter paid its parent company loan interest set at a level that represented current interest rates. If there were an operating loss, Timber Products would be charged a fee that would cover the operating losses and interest payable.

For the year ended 31 October 20X5 the fee paid to Timber Products amounted to €3m and the loan interest paid by Inter amounted to €1.5m.

20.3 Textures

Textures was incorporated in 20W5 to manufacture artificial limbs. Its financial year-end is 30 November 20X6. It manufactures in the Republic of Ireland and exports more than 60% of its output. It has a number of foreign subsidiary companies.

Textures has developed a number of arrangements to support its export sales. It entered into an agreement on 1 December 20X3 with **Computer Control** to jointly control **Afrohelp**, a company in which each of the investing companies held a 50% interest. Afrohelp assembled mechanical products from Textures and automated them with control equipment from Computer Control.

The joint venture has been equity accounted by each investor company. One of the newly appointed non-executive directors has questioned whether the investment in Afrohelp should be treated as a quasi-subsidiary and consolidated.

On 1 November 20X6 Textures sold stock costing €110,000 to Afrohelp for €162,000. This stock was unsold at 30 November 20X6.

Required

Assuming that you are the finance director of Textures:

(i) Advise the non-executive director of the conditions that would need to be satisfied to avoid Afrohelp being treated as a quasi-subsidiary as at 30 November 20X6.

(ii) Contrast the treatment of the unrealised gain on the sale of stock to Afrohelp on treating Afrohelp as an associate compared to as a quasi-subsidiary.

20.4 Zodiac

At 30 September 20X3, the **Zodiac** group consisted of Zodiac and three subsidiaries, all of which are based in the United Kingdom, and are engaged in the production and distribution of various types of metal container. During the current year ending 30 September 20X4, Zodiac has expanded its operations by making the following acquisitions:

1 December 20X3	Purchased 90% of the share capital of **Aries**, a company operating in the chemicals industry, which is incorporated and based in Germany.
1 March 20X4	Acquired the entire share capital of **Taurus**, an electronics company incorporated and based in Malaysia.
1 June 20X4	Purchased 80% of the equity of **Pisces**, an American company providing security services throughout the US.

The directors of Zodiac have been informed that in future the group will be required to disclose segmental information. They do not understand why this is necessary or what the implications are for the published financial statements of the group.

Required

(a) Explain the purpose of disclosing segmental information in financial statements.
(b) Describe the criteria to be used for selecting the reportable segments of Zodiac.
(c) State the information which should be included in the financial statements of each segment.
(d) Indicate any significant problems which may be encountered by the Zodiac group in complying with the requirements of SSAP 25 *Segmental Reporting*.

20.5 Diverse

Diverse is a pharmaceutical company based in Ireland. It has two subsidiaries, one based in France, **Mardi**, and one in Germany, **Samstag**. Mardi is involved in the manufacture of tennis balls, while Samstag is also involved in the pharmaceutical business.

The following information is available for the group for the year ended 31 December 20X6:

	Group Total €000	**Diverse €000**	**Mardi €000**	**Samstag €000**
Third-party turnover	22,000	12,000	4,000	6,000
Net profit before taxation	9,000	4,000	1,500	3,500
Net assets at 31 December 20X6	100,000	60,000	15,000	25,000

Required

(a) Explain briefly the purpose of disclosing segmental information in financial statements.
(b) Prepare the note to the published consolidated financial statements of Diverse for the year ended 31 December 20X6 which would comply with SSAP 25 *Segmental Reporting*.

Appendix 1

Solutions to multiple choice questions

Question	Ans	Workings/explanation
1.1 Red	(d)	Green would be accounted for as an associated company, not a subsidiary
1.2 Sam	(b)	*W_1: Group structure*

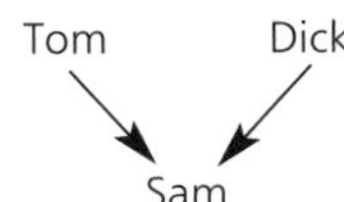

W_2: Determining subsidiary relationship → Exercise of (voting) control

		%	
Tom		54	→ Subsidiary
$\dfrac{1{,}500_{shares} \times 10_{votes}}{(2{,}000 \times 10_{votes}) + (8{,}000 \times 1_{vote})}$	$= \dfrac{15{,}000}{28{,}000}$		
Dick		21	
$\dfrac{(6{,}000_{shares} \times 1_{vote})}{(2{,}000 \times 10_{votes}) + (8{,}000 \times 1_{vote})}$	$= \dfrac{6{,}000}{28{,}000}$		

1.3 Reddie, Ret and Asy (d)

W_1: Determining subsidiary relationship → Exercise of (voting) control

Ret

$$\frac{9{,}000 \times 8_{votes}}{(10{,}000 \times 8_{votes}) + 50{,}000} = \frac{72{,}000}{130{,}000} = 55\% \rightarrow \text{Subsidiary}$$

Asy

$$\frac{45{,}000 \times 1_{vote}}{(10{,}000 \times 8_{votes}) + 50{,}000} = \frac{45{,}000}{130{,}000} = 35\%$$

1.4 Alice, Betty and Carol (d)

W_1: Group structure

Alice
↓ 90%
Betty
↓ 70%
Carol

Carol → Dawn 30%; Carol → Eve 60%; Eve → Dawn 30%

Question 1.4 (continued) **Ans** **Workings/explanation**

W_2: Determining subsidiary relationship → Exercise of control

There is a distinction between the proportion over which the parent exercises control and the effective rate of ownership. To determine whether a subsidiary relationship exists calculate the proportion over which the parent exercises control which is the aggregate of the holdings of the parent and the *whole* of each subsidiary's holding (without deduction for any minority) in a potential subsidiary is taken into account. However, the effective rate used to determine the group share and the minority interest to include in the consolidated accounts allows for minority interests in the shareholdings (see Chapter 6)

	%	
Betty	90	→Subsidiary
Carol	70	→Subsidiary
Dawn	30%+30% 60	→Subsidiary
Eve	60	→Subsidiary

W_3: *Effective ownership in respect of each company (not required for solution)*

	Group %	Minority %	Total %
Betty – Direct	90	10	100
Carol – Direct		30	
Carol – Indirect	90% × 70% 63	10% × 70% 7	
	63	37	100
Dawn – Direct		40.00	
Dawn – Indirect	90%x70%x30% 18.90	10%x70%x30% 2.10	
	90%x70%x60%x30% 11.34	10%x70%x60%x30% 1.26	
		30%x30% 9.00	
		30%x60%x30% 5.40	
		40%x30% 12.00	
	30.24	69.76	100

1.5 Jack, Packie and Kevin (c) *W_1: Group structure*

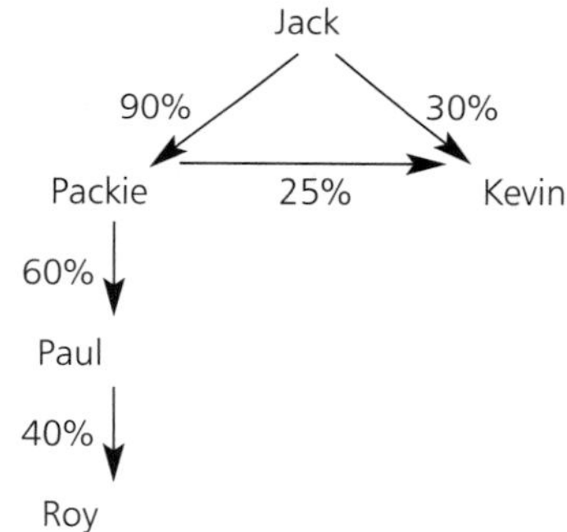

W_2: Determining subsidiary relationship → Exercise of control (see explanation in solution to MCQ 1.4)

	%	
Packie	90	→Subsidiary
Kevin	30% + 25% 55	→Subsidiary
Paul	60	→Subsidiary
Roy	40	

1.5 (*continued*) (c) W_3: *Effective ownership in respect of each company (not required for solution)*

		Group %		**Minority** %	**Total** %
Packie – Direct		90		10	100
Kevin – Direct		30.0		45.0	
Kevin – Indirect	90% × 25%	22.5	10% × 25%	2.5	
		52.5		47.5	100
Paul – Direct				40	
Paul – Indirect	90% × 60%	54	10% × 60%	6	
		54		46	100
Roy – Direct				60.0	
Roy – Indirect	90%x60%x40%	21.6	10%x60%x40%	2.4	
			40%x40%	16.0	
		21.6		78.4	100

1.6 Anna, Bella and Emma (d) W_1: Group structure

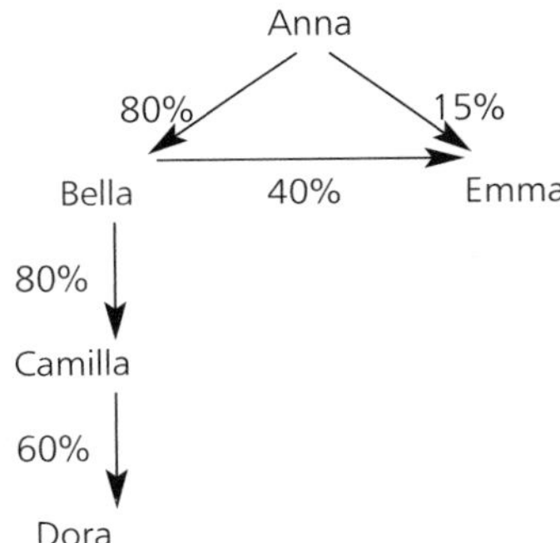

W_2: *Determining subsidiary relationship* → *Exercise of control* (see explanation in solution to MCQ 1.4)

		%	
Bella		80	→Subsidiary
Emma	15% + 40%	55	→Subsidiary
Camilla		80	→Subsidiary
Dora		60	→Subsidiary

Effective interest		**Group** %		**Minority** %	**Total** %
Bella – Direct		80		20	100
Emma – Direct		15		45	
Emma – Indirect	80% × 40%	32	20% × 40%	8	
		47		53	100
Camilla – Direct				20	
Camilla – Indirect	80% × 80%	64	20% × 80%	16	
		64		36	100
Dora – Direct				40.0	
Dora – Indirect	80%x80%x60%	38.4	20%x80%x60%	9.6	
			20%x60%	12.0	
		38.4		61.6	100

Question	Ans	Workings/explanation
1.7 Ash, Beech and Cedar	(d)	*W_1: Group structure*

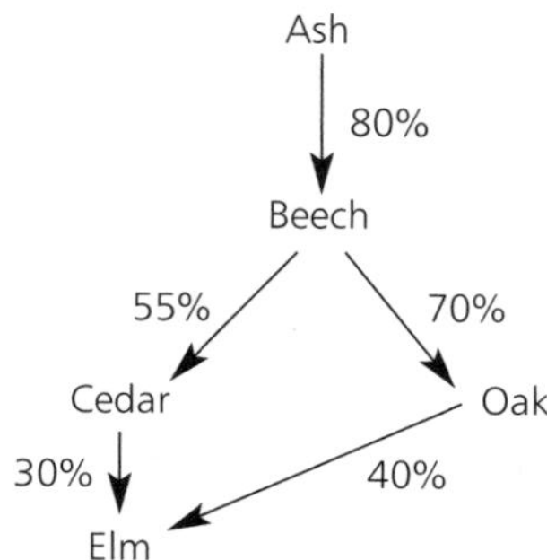

W_2: Determining subsidiary relationship → Exercise of control (see explanation in solution to MCQ 1.4)

	%	
Beech	80	→Subsidiary
Cedar	55	→Subsidiary
Oak	70	→Subsidiary
Elm	30%+40% 70	→Subsidiary

Effective interest	**Group** %	**Minority** %	**Total** %
Beech – Direct	80	20	100
Cedar – Direct		45	
Cedar – Indirect	80% × 55% 44	20% × 55% 11	
	44	56	100
Oak – Direct		30	
Oak – Indirect	80% × 70% 56	20% × 70% 14	
	56	44	100
Elm – Direct		30.0	
Elm – Indirect	80%x55%x30% 13.2	20%x55%x30% 3.3	
	80%x70%x40% 22.4	45%x30% 13.5	
		20%x70%x40% 5.6	
		30%x40% 12.0	
	35.6	64.4	100

Question	Ans	Workings/explanation
1.8 Alan, Brian and Colin	(c)	*W_1: Group structure*

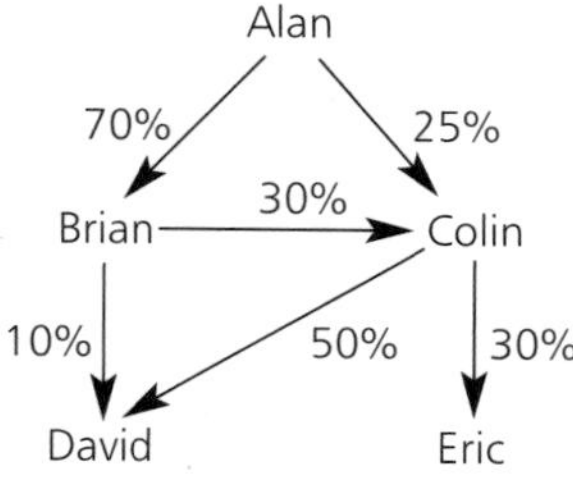

W_2: Determining subsidiary relationship → Exercise of control (see explanation in solution to MCQ 1.4)

	%	
Brian	70	→Subsidiary
Colin	30% + 25% 55	→Subsidiary
David	10% + 50% 60	→Subsidiary
Eric	30	

1.8 (*continued*)

W_3: Effective ownership in respect of each subsidiary (not required for solution)

		Group %		Minority %	Total %
Brian – Direct		70		30	100
Colin – Direct		25		45	
Colin – Indirect	70% × 30%	21	30% × 30%	9	
		46		54	100
David – Direct		—		40.0	
David – Indirect	70% × 10%	7.0	30% × 10%	3.0	
	25% × 50%	12.5	30% × 10%	22.5	
	70% × 30% × 50%	10.5	30% × 30% × 50%	4.5	
		30		70	100

1.9 Orchard, Plum and Damson (b)

W_1: Group structure

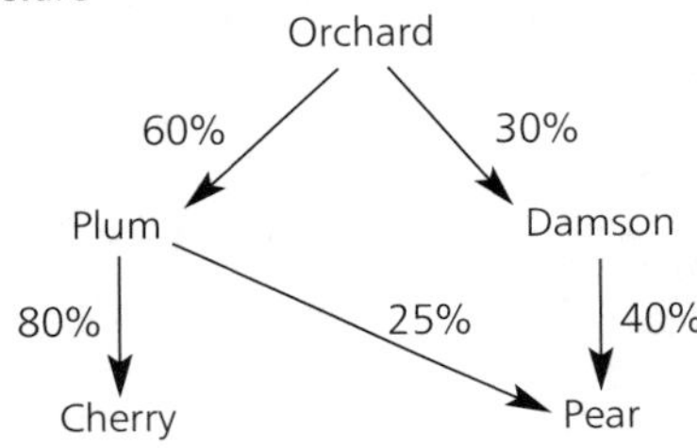

W_2: Determining subsidiary relationship → Exercise of control (see explanation in solution to MCQ 1.4)

	%	
Plum	60	→Subsidiary
Damson	30	
Cherry	80	→Subsidiary
Pear	25	

W_3: *Effective ownership in respect of each subsidiaries (not required for solution)*

		Group %		Minority %	Total %
Plum – Direct		60		40	100
Cherry – Direct		—		20	
Cherry – Indirect	60% × 80%	48	40% × 80%	32	
		48		52	100

1.10 Ovett (b)

1.11 Garden (a)

Question	Ans	Workings/explanation
2.1 Parent and Baby	(b)	Cost €100,000 – €77,000 (€110,000$_{\text{net assets}}$ @ 70%$_{\text{group share}}$)=€23,000

2.2 Rugby and Soccer (b)

Cost of control account

	€000		€000
Cost	100	Ordinary share capital (100,000 @ 60%$_{\text{group share}}$)	60
		Preference share capital (40,000 @ 50%$_{\text{group share}}$)	20
		Retained profit (10,000 @ 60%$_{\text{group share}}$)	6
		Balance c/d	14
	100		100

2.3 Heather and Pearl (a) (c)

Shares issued 100 @ €5
Premium on issue = €4$_{\text{premium per share}}$ × 100$_{\text{shares}}$ = 400$_{\text{share premium}}$
Heather reserves: €400$_{\text{share premium}}$ +400$_{\text{profit and loss account}}$ = €800
Heather Group reserves: €400$_{\text{share premium}}$ +400$_{\text{profit and loss account}}$ = €800

2.4 Heather and Pearl (b) (b)

Consolidated net assets: €900$_{\text{Heather}}$ + €800$_{\text{Pearl}}$ – €300$_{\text{cash paid}}$ = €1,400
Share capital: €500$_{\text{Heather share capital}}$ +100$_{\text{Heather new shares}}$ = €600

Consolidated balance sheet	€000
Net assets (900$_{\text{Heather}}$ +800$_{\text{Pearl}}$ – 300$_{\text{cash paid}}$)	1,400
Share capital (500$_{\text{Heather}}$ +100$_{\text{new shares}}$)	600
Share premium (on new shares)	400
Profit and loss account (Heather only)	400
	1,400

2.5 Megalith and Pebble (a)

Cost of control account

	€000		€000
Cost	3,000	Share capital (500 @ 80%$_{\text{group share}}$)	400
		Retained reserves (2,000 @ 80%$_{\text{group share}}$)	1,600
		Balance c/d	1,000
	3,000		3,000
Balance b/d	1,000	Goodwill written off	1,000

Revenue reserves

	€000		€000
Goodwill written off	1,000	Megalith	59,000
Balance c/d	59,200	Pebble ([3,500 – 2,000$_{\text{pre-acquisition}}$] @ 80%$_{\text{group share}}$)	1,200
	60,200		60,200

2.6 Aardvark and Bobbin (d)

Cost of control account

	€000		€000
Cost (10,000$_{\text{shares}}$ × €4 + 80,000$_{\text{cash}}$)	120	Share capital (100$_{\text{net assets}}$ @ 75%$_{\text{group share}}$)	75
		Balance c/d	45
	120		120

2.7 Monster and Minnow (d)

Share capital: €1,000,000 + 80,000 new shares = €1,080,000 share capital
Share premium: €50,000 + 160,000 premium on new issue = €210,000 share premium

2.8 Rasher Sausage and Burger (a)

Minority interest

	€		€
Burger reserves (15 @ 20%$_{\text{minority share}}$)	3,000	Sausage share capital (10 @ 20%$_{\text{minority share}}$)	2,000
		Burger share capital (10 @ 20%$_{\text{minority share}}$)	2,000
		Sausage reserves (15 @ 20%$_{\text{minority share}}$)	3,000
Balance c/d	4,000		
	7,000		7,000

2.9 Newbridge and Sheffield (d)

Minority interest

	€		€
		Ordinary share capital (8 @ 20%$_{\text{minority share}}$)	1,600
		Preference share capital (1 @ 70%$_{\text{minority share}}$)	700
Balance c/d	2,700	Reserves (2 @ 20%$_{\text{minority share}}$)	400
	2,700		2,700

2.10 Koala and Bear (c)

Consolidated revenue reserves

	€000		€000
Cost of control (15,000$_{\text{pre-acquisition}}$ @ 60%$_{\text{group share}}$)	9	Koala	40
Minority interest (25,000 @ 40%$_{\text{minority share}}$)	10	Bear	25
Balance c/d	46		
	65		65

2.11 Lion, Tiger and Cub (a)

Consolidated revenue reserves

	€m		€m
Tiger cost of control (10$_{\text{pre-acquisition}}$ @ 80%$_{\text{group share}}$)	8	Lion	20
Tiger minority interest (15 @ 20%$_{\text{minority interest}}$)	3	Tiger	15
Cub minority interest (10 @ 40%$_{\text{minority interest}}$)	4	Cub	10
Balance c/d	33	Cub cost of control (5$_{\text{pre-acquisition}}$ @ 60%$_{\text{group share}}$)	3
	48		48

2.12 Christmas and Tree (b)

Consolidated revenue reserves

	€		€
Cost of control (15$_{\text{pre-acquisition}}$ @ 90%$_{\text{group share}}$)	13,500	Christmas	60,000
Tiger minority interest (25 @ 10%$_{\text{minority interest}}$)	2,500	Tree	25,000
Goodwill amortised (2 @ 1,000)	2,000		
Balance c/d	67,000		
	85,000		85,000

3.1 Heron, Sparrow and Swift (d)

3.2 Bright and Cool (a)

Stock €60,000
Unrealised profit in stock €60,000 x50/150= €20,000
Value of stock in consolidated balance sheet €60,000$_{\text{stock}}$ – 20,000$_{\text{unrealised profit}}$ = €40,000

3.3 Clock and Watch (a)

Adjustment to Plant and machinery: Reduce plant to its original cost, i .e., (€20,000)
→ €356,200$_{\text{clock}}$ + 187,000$_{\text{watch}}$ – 20,000$_{\text{adjustment}}$ = €523,200
Adjustment to accumulated depreciation: Reduce by 20,000 × 10%, i.e., (€2,000)
→ €119,700$_{\text{clock}}$ + 78,870 – 2,000$_{\text{adjustment}}$ = €196,570

Question	Ans	Workings/explanation	€	€
3.4 Bee and Wasp	(a)	Cost of investment		100,000
		Land and buildings	40,000	
		Vehicles	23,000	
		Stock	30,000	
		Debtors	27,000	
		Creditors	(10,000)	
		Net assets at date of acquisition	110,000	
		Group share (110,000 @ $90\%_{\text{group share}}$)		99,000
		Goodwill		1,000

3.5 Amp and Bulb (a)

(i) Adjustment to plant and machinery: Increase plant to its original cost, i .e., 5,000 Dr
(ii) Adjustment to accumulated depreciation: Increase by 5,000 × 10%, i.e., 500 Cr for 20X4
(iii) Adjustment for 2 years' aggregate depreciation eliminated on disposal:
$10{,}000_{20X2} + 10{,}000_{20X3}$

$\rightarrow 1{,}565{,}000_{\text{Amp}} + 872{,}000_{\text{Bulb}} + 5{,}000_{\text{adjustment (i)}} - 500_{\text{adjustment (ii)}} - 20{,}000_{\text{adjustment (iii)}} = €2{,}421{,}500$

3.6 Holmes and Watson (c)

	Holmes €000	Watson €000	Adjustment		Consolidated balance sheet €000
Net assets	80	50	+ Investments $80_{\text{@ book value}}$ – unrealised profit 10_{stock}	=	200

4.1 Parrot and Hornbill (d)

Cost of control account

	€000		€000
Cost	160	Share capital	50
		Retained reserves (120 @ $5/6_{\text{group share}}$)	100
		Balance c/d	10
	160		160
Balance b/d	10	Goodwill amortised (1/5)	2
		Balance c/d	8
	10		10

Consolidated revenue reserves

	€000		€000
Cost of control ($120_{\text{pre-acquisition}}$ @ $5/6_{\text{group share}}$)	100	Parrott	300
Minority interest ($180+12_{\text{dividend proposed}}$ @ $1/6_{\text{minority interest}}$)	32	Hornbill	180
Goodwill amortised	2	Proposed dividend	12
Balance c/d	358		
	492		492

4.2 Vane and Wimsey (b)

	€	€
Gross cost of investment		125,000
Less: Pre-acquisition dividend		
Total dividend for year	60,000	
Dividend paid after acquisition	40,000	
Post-acquisition dividend ($6_{\text{months}}/12_{\text{months}}$)	(30,000)	
Pre-acquisition dividend paid in post-acquisition period	10,000	
Group share (90%)		(9,000)
Net cost of investment		116,000

4.3 Mozart and Schubert (b)

Consolidated revenue reserves

	€		€
Cost of control ([15–2]$_{\text{pre-acquisition}}$ @ 55%$_{\text{group share}}$)	7,150	Mozart	45,000
Minority interest (20 @ 45%$_{\text{minority interest}}$)	9,000	Schubert	20,000
Balance c/d	48,850		
	65,000		65,000

4.4 Pansey and Snowdrop (b)

	€
Total dividend for year	450,000
Post-acquisition dividend (5$_{\text{months}}$ /12$_{\text{months}}$)	187,500
Group share (80%)	150,000

5.1 Red and Black (d)

Date	**Piecemeal acquisition**	**% share**	**Reserves**	**Group share** €
1/4/20X2	Investment becomes an associate $_{(10+25)}$	35	150 @ 35%	52,500
1/7/20X3	Increase to become subsidiary	25	[240 + 25] @ 25%	66,250
		60		118,750

5.2 Robin and Hood (b)

	€000
Total dividend for year	600
Post-acquisition dividend (4$_{\text{months}}$ /12$_{\text{months}}$)	200
Group share (75%)	150

5.3 Doncaster and Wentworth (c)

	€
Total dividend for year	300,000
Post-acquisition dividend (3$_{\text{months}}$ /12$_{\text{months}}$)	75,000
Group share (62.5%)	46,875

6.1 Alleline, Tarr and William (c)

	Group %	**Minority** %	**Total** %
William – Direct	60	40	100
Tarr – Direct	40	20	
Tarr – Indirect	40% × 60% 24	40% × 40% 16	
	64	36	100

6.2 Fish, Cod and Trout (c)

Group structure

Fish
↓ 80% (20W9)
Cod
↓ 80% (20X0)
Trout

	Group %	**Minority** %	**Total** %
Cod – Direct	80	20	100
Trout – Direct	—	20	
Trout – Indirect	80% × 80% 64	80% × 20% 16	
	64	36	100

Minority interest

	€		€
Cost Cod in Trout (100,000 @ 20%$_{\text{minority share}}$)	20,000	Cod share capital (200 @ 20%$_{\text{minority share}}$)	40,000
		Trout share capital (80 @ 36%$_{\text{group share}}$)	28,800
		Cod reserves (400 @ 20%$_{\text{minority share}}$)	80,000
Balance c/d	172,000	Trout reserves (120 @ 36%$_{\text{minority share}}$)	43,200
	192,000		192,000

Question	Ans	Workings/explanation
6.3 Wig, Hair and Bald	(a)	*Group structure*

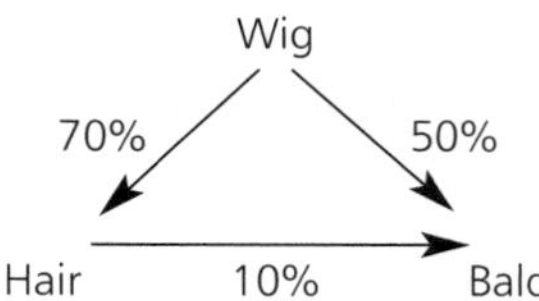

	Group %	Minority %	Total %
Hair – Direct	70	30	100
Bald – Direct	50	40	
Bald – Indirect	10% × 70% 7	10% × 30% 3	
	57	43	100

Minority interest

	€		€
Cost Hair in Bald (20,000 @ 30%$_{\text{minority share}}$)	6,000	Hair net assets (100 @ 30%$_{\text{minority share}}$)	30,000
Balance c/d	110,000	Bald net assets (200 @ 43%$_{\text{group share}}$)	86,000
	116,000		116,000

Question	Ans	Workings/explanation
6.4 Gandalf, Frodo and Sam	(c)	*Group structure*

Gandalf
↓80%
Frodo
↓75%
Sam

	Group %	Minority %	Total %
Frodo – Direct	80	20	100
Sam – Direct	—	25	
Sam – Indirect	75% × 80% 60	75% × 20% 15	
	60	40	100

Minority interest

	€		€
Cost Frodo in Sam (375,000 @ 20%$_{\text{minority share}}$)	75,000	Frodo share capital (1,000 @ 20%$_{\text{minority share}}$)	200,000
		Sam share capital (500 @ 40%$_{\text{group share}}$)	200,000
		Frodo reserves (300 @ 20%$_{\text{minority share}}$)	60,000
Balance c/d	465,000	Sam reserves (200 @ 40%$_{\text{minority share}}$)	80,000
	540,000		540,000

6.5 Grape, Wine and Vinegar (c) *Group structure*

Grape
↓80%
Wine
↓60%
Vinegar

	Group		Minority	Total
	%		%	%
Wine – Direct	80		20	100
Vinegar – Direct	–		40	
Vinegar – Indirect	60% × 80% 48		60% × 20% 12	
	48		52	100

Minority interest

	€		€
Cost Wine in Vinegar (110,000 @ 20%$_{\text{minority share}}$)	22,000	Wine share capital (100 @ 20%$_{\text{minority share}}$)	20,000
		Vinegar share capital (100 @ 52%$_{\text{group share}}$)	52,000
		Wine reserves (170 @ 20%$_{\text{minority share}}$)	34,000
Balance c/d	143,800	Vinegar reserves (115 @ 52%$_{\text{minority share}}$)	59,800
	165,800		165,800

6.6 Yeast, Beer and Bread (b) *Group structure*

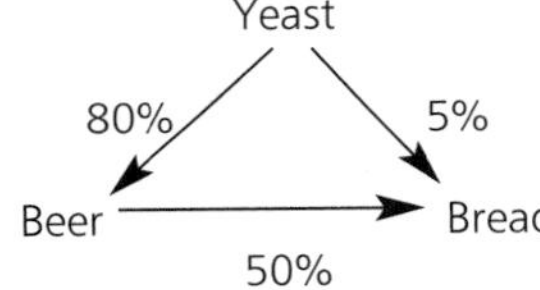

	Group	Minority	Total
	%	%	%
Beer – Direct	80	20	100
Bread – Direct	5	45	
Bread – Indirect	50% × 80% 40	50% × 20% 10	
	45	55	100

6.7 Milk, Cream and Butter (a) *Group structure*

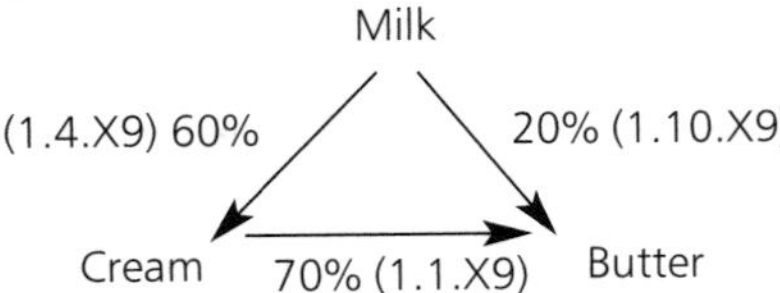

	Group	Minority	Total
	%	%	%
Cream – Direct	60	40	100
Butter – Direct	20	10	
Butter – Indirect	70% × 60% 42	70% × 40% 28	
	62	38	100

Pre-acquisition profits of Butter

Date	Pre-acquisition profits	Group share	€
1.4.X9	72,000 + [36,000 × 3/12=]9,000=81,000	81,000 @ 42%	34,020
1.10.X9	72,000 + [36,000 × 9/12=]27,000=99,000	99,000 @ 20%	19,800
			53,820

Question	Ans	Workings/explanation
6.8 Chicken, Egg and Mayonnaise	(d)	*Group structure*

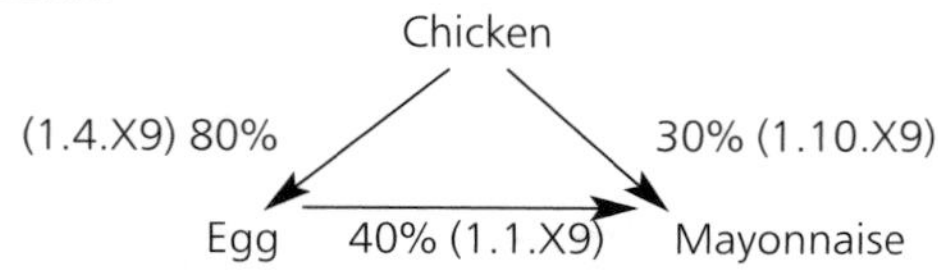

	Group	Minority	Total
	%	%	%
Egg – Direct	80	20	100
Mayonnaise – Direct	30	30	
Mayonnaise – Indirect	40% × 80% 32	40% × 20% 8	
	62	38	100

Pre-acquisition profits of Mayonnaise

Date	Pre-acquisition profits	Group share	€
1.4.X9	300,000 + [100,000 × 3/12=]25,000=325,000	325,000 @ 32%	104,000
1.10.X9	300,000 + [100,000 × 9/12=]75,000=375,000	375,000 @ 30%	112,500
			216,500

7.1 Eagle and Hawk — (c)

Investment in Hawk	€
Share of net assets at balance sheet date (2,390 @ $25\%_{\text{group share}}$)	597,500
Alternatively – investment in Hawk	
Cost of investment	640,000
Post-acquisition retained profits (1,140 – $720_{\text{pre-acquisition}}$ @ $25\%_{\text{group share}}$)	105,000
	745,000
Goodwill written-off (W_1)	(147,500)
	597,500

W_1: Goodwill on acquisition

Cost of investment	640,000
Net assets acquired ([$800_{\text{share capital}}$ + $450_{\text{share premium}}$ + 720_{reserves}] @ $25\%_{\text{group share}}$)	(492,500)
Goodwill	147,500

7.2 Blue, Black and Red — (c) *Group structure*

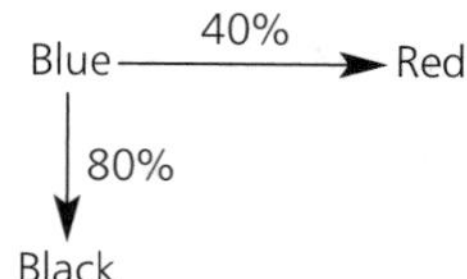

Revenue reserves

	€		€
Cost of control (150,000 @ $80\%_{\text{group share}}$)	120,000	Blue	450,000
Minority interest (250,000 @ $20\%_{\text{minority share}}$)	50,000	Black	250,000
Balance c/d	550,000	Red (150–100 @ $40\%_{\text{group share}}$)	20,000
	720,000		720,000

7.3 Laurent (c) *W_1: Group structure*

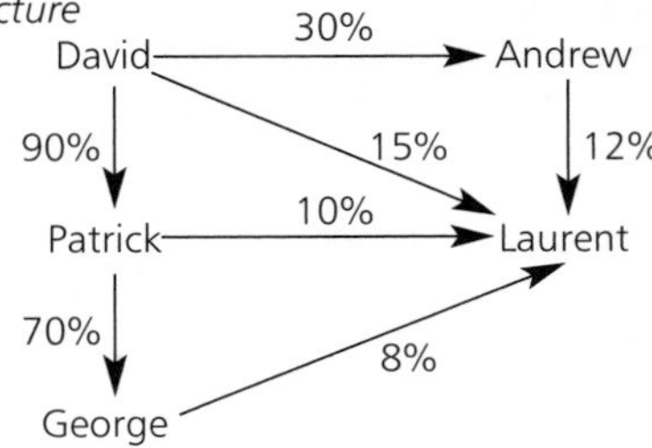

W_2: Determining associate relationship → Exercise of significant influence

There is a distinction between the proportion of the investee influenced by the parent and the effective rate of ownership. To calculate the proportion over which the investor has influence, the aggregate of the holdings of the parent and the *whole* of each subsidiary's holding (without deduction for any minority) in a potential associate is taken into account. However, the effective rate to determine how much of the associate's net assets and profits to include in the consolidated accounts allows for minority interests in the shareholdings

Company	**%**	**Laurent**
Andrew	Nil	Not a subsidiary, therefore holding in Laurent not taken into account in determining exercise of significant influence
David	15	
Patrick	10	
George	8	
	33	→ Associate

W_3: *Effective ownership in Laurent (not required for solution)*

Company		**Effective ownership**
		%
David	Direct holding	15.00
Patrick	$90\%_{\text{group share}} \times 10\%$	9.00
George	$90\% \times 70\%_{\text{group share}} \times 8\%$	5.04
		29.04

7.4 Darcy and Wickham (b)

Investment in Wickham	€
Share of net assets at balance sheet date (200 @ $49\%_{\text{group share}}$)	98,000
Unamortised goodwill	Nil
	98,000

Alternatively – investment in Wickham	
Cost of investment	250,000
Post-acquisition retained losses ((200) – $(100)_{\text{pre-acquisition}}$ @ $49\%_{\text{group share}}$)	(49,000)
Goodwill written off (W_1)	(103,000)
	98,000

(W_1) Goodwill on acquisition	
Cost of investment	250,000
Net assets acquired ([$400_{\text{share capital}}$ + $(100)_{\text{reserves}}$]@$49\%_{\text{group share}}$)	(147,000)
Goodwill	103,000

Question	Ans	Workings/explanation	
7.5 Fagan and Dodger	(c)	*Investment in Dodger*	€
		Share of net assets at balance sheet date (400 @ 30%$_{\text{group share}}$)	120,000
		Unamortised goodwill (W_1)	—
			120,000
		Alternatively – investment in Dodger	
		Cost of investment	200,000
		Post-acquisition retained profits (400 – 160$_{\text{pre-acquisition}}$@30%$_{\text{group share}}$)	72,000
		Goodwill written off (W_1)	(152,000)
			120,000
		(W_1): Goodwill on acquisition	
		Cost of investment	200,000
		Net assets acquired (160,000@30%$_{\text{group share}}$)	(48,000)
		Goodwill	152,000
7.6 Alex and Peter	(b)	*Investment in Peter*	€
		Share of net assets at balance sheet date (600 @ 30%$_{\text{group share}}$)	180,000
		Unamortised goodwill (W_1)	8,000
			188,000
		Alternatively – investment in Peter	
		Cost of investment	110,000
		Post-acquisition retained profits (600 – 300$_{\text{pre-acquisition}}$@30%$_{\text{group share}}$)	90,000
		Goodwill written off (W_1)	(12,000)
			188,000
		W_1: Goodwill on acquisition	
		Cost of investment	110,000
		Net assets acquired (300,000@30%$_{\text{group share}}$)	(90,000)
		Goodwill	20,000
		Amortised (3$_{\text{years}}$/5$_{\text{years}}$)	(12,000)
		Unamortised goodwill	8,000

7.7 Wine and Port — (c)

W_1: Group structure
Wine
↓30% (associate →exercises significant influence)
Port

W_2: Value of investment under equity method of accounting (in €000)
Goodwill on acquisition: 100 (1,000$_{\text{consideration}}$ – 900 [3,000$_{\text{net assets}}$ @ 30%$_{\text{group share}}$])
Amortisation per annum: 100 @ 5% = 5
Increase in net assets during 20X5: 200$_{\text{profit}}$–80$_{\text{dividends}}$=120$_{\text{retained profit}}$
Group share of net assets €936 (3,000$_{\text{opening net assets}}$ +120$_{\text{increase}}$ @ 30%$_{\text{group share}}$)
+ unamortised goodwill €95 (100 – 5$_{\text{goodwill amortised}}$)
= €1,031

Alternatively
(1,000$_{\text{cost}}$ + 36$_{\text{group share of post acquisition profits}}$ – 5$_{\text{goodwill amortised}}$) = €1,031

9.1 Using merger accounting — (c)

If the *investment in subsidiary* is less than the nominal value of the shares held in the subsidiary, then fewer Parent shares were issued in return for the *investment in subsidiary*. Under merger accounting, *investment in subsidiary* is recorded at the nominal value of the shares issued for the subsidiary

9.2 The merger method — (b)

9.3 Merger accounting (b)

9.4 Art Bog and Bacall (c) Under merger accounting, the investment should be recorded at the nominal value of the shares issued in consideration

$1{,}910{,}000_{\text{shares acquired}} \times 1_{\text{shares acquired}}/2_{\text{shares issued}} = 955{,}000_{\text{nominal value of shares issued}}$

9.5 John Group (b)

(W_1): Negative goodwill	€	€
Cost of investment		90,000
Net assets acquired		
Share capital (90%)	90,000	
Pre-acquisition reserves (90%)	90,000	180,000
Negative goodwill fully amortised		(90,000)

	Acquisition method	**Merger method**
John	290,000	290,000
Ann ([$400{,}000_{\text{Ann}} - 100{,}000_{\text{pre-acquisition profits}}$] @ $90\%_{\text{group share}}$)	270,000	
Ann ($400{,}000_{\text{Ann}}$ @ $90\%_{\text{group share}}$)		360,000
Negative goodwill amortised	90,000	
	650,000	650,000

9.6 Nigel and Georgia (a) Under merger accounting, all profits are distributable. However, dividends are not a dividend payable by the group until Nigel decides to declare the dividend.

$100{,}000_{\text{Nigel interim}} + 220{,}000_{\text{Nigel final}} =$ €320,000

9.7 Copse and Wood (c) Under merger accounting, where the nominal value of the shares issued is greater than the nominal value of the shares acquired, it is necessary to make an adjustment against reserves.

$3{,}000_{\text{Copse profit}} + 2{,}500_{\text{Wood profit}} - 1{,}000_{\text{difference on consolidation}}\ [2{,}000_{\text{shares issued}} - 1{,}000_{\text{shares acquired}}]$

10.1 Alpha and Beta (d) Profit on disposal ($95{,}000_{\text{proceeds}} - [100{,}000_{\text{original cost}} - 20{,}000_{\text{depreciation 2 years}}]$) = €15,000

Adjustment to depreciation charge: Increase by 5,000 × 10%, i.e., 500 Dr

Total adjustment: $15{,}000_{\text{profit on disposal eliminated}} + 500_{\text{depreciation charge increased}} = 15{,}500_{\text{reduction in profits}}$

10.2 Tom and Jerry (d)

Minority interest	€		**Minority share** €
Profit after tax × 9/12 (post-acquisition)	240,000		
10% preference dividend (10% × $800{,}000_{\text{preference shares}}$ x 9/12)	(60,000)	100%	60,000
Profit available to ordinary shareholders	180,000	20%	36,000
			96,000

10.3 Bridle and Horse (c)

Minority interest	€
Operating profit since acquisition	180,000
Exceptional item since acquisition	60,000
Available to ordinary shareholders	240,000
Minority share (20%)	48,000

Question	Ans	Workings/explanation
10.4 Roy and Paul	(d)	

Minority interest	€	Minority share €
Profit after tax	140,000	
10% preference dividend ($10\% \times 100{,}000_{\text{preference shares}}$)	(10,000)	100% 10,000
Profit available to ordinary shareholders	130,000	20% 26,000
		36,000

Question	Ans	
10.5 Hal and Sid	(c)	

Minority interest	€	Minority share €
Profit after tax	260,000	
Preference dividend	(10,000)	60% 6,000
Profit available to ordinary shareholders	250,000	20% 50,000
		56,000

10.6 Drum, Gold and King (d)

Group structure

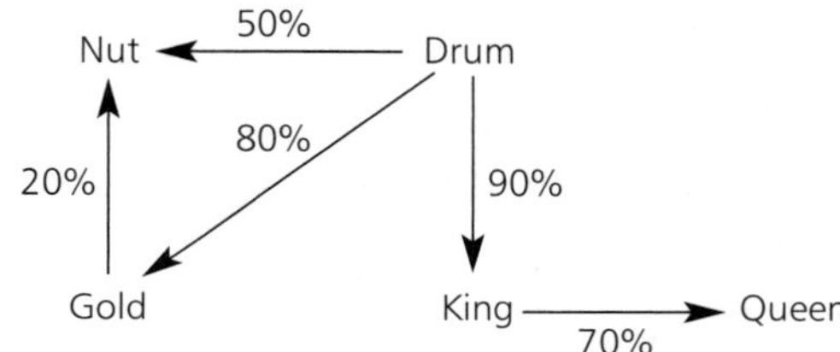

	Group %	Minority %	Total %
Gold – Direct	80	20	100
King – Direct	90	10	100
Nut – Direct	50	30	
Nut – Indirect	20% × 80% 16	20% × 20% 4	
	66	34	100
Queen – Direct	—	30	
Queen – Indirect	70% × 90% 63	70% × 10% 7	
	63	37	100

Minority interest in profit		€
Gold	€10,000 @ 20%	2,000
King	€10,000 @ 10%	1,000
Nut	€10,000 @ 34%	3,400
Queen	€10,000 @ 37%	3,700
		10,100

10.7 Acorn and Oak (c)

Cost of sales

$3_{\text{Oak}} + 2_{\text{Acorn}} - ([1.2_{\text{inter-company purchases}} - 0.4_{\text{closing stock}}] + 0.3_{\text{closing inter-company stock}}) = 3.9\text{m}$

10.8 Bill & Ben (1) (b)

(1) Turnover:

$2{,}400{,}000_{\text{Bill}} + 1{,}500{,}000_{\text{Ben}} - 200{,}000_{\text{inter-company sales}} = €3{,}700{,}000$

10.9 Bill and Ben (2) (b)

Cost of sales	**€000**
Bill	1,250.0
Ben	875.0
Duplicate cost of sales in Ben ($200_{\text{inter-company purchases}} - 50_{\text{closing stock}}$)	(150.0)
Cost of sales in Bill not sold externally	(37.5)
(25% @ [$200_{\text{inter-company}}$ – ($33.33\%_{\text{mark-up}}$/133.33% × 200)])	
or	
25% @ [$200_{\text{inter-company}}$ × 100%/133.33%]	
Opening provision	(10.0)
	1,927.5

10.10 Alba and Beba (1) (a)

Turnover: $4{,}650{,}000_{\text{Alba}}$ + [$2{,}865{,}000_{\text{Beba}}$ × ½] – $600{,}000_{\text{inter-company sales}}$ = €5,482,500

10.11 Alba and Beba (2) (b)

Cost of sales	**€000**
Alba	3,260.0
Beba – post-acquisition (1,980 @ 6/12)	990.0
Duplicate cost of sales in Alba ($600_{\text{inter-company purchases}} - 90_{\text{closing stock}}$)	(510.0)
Cost of sales in Alba not sold externally	
$90_{\text{remaining in stock}}/600_{\text{inter-company sales}}$ × ($600_{\text{inter-company sales}}$ × $100/133.33)_{\text{inter-company sales at cost}}$	(67.5)
	3,672.5

10.12 Knave and Ace (b)

Minority interest	**€**
Profit after tax post-acquisition period (120,000 @ 50%)	60,000
Minority share (60,000 @ 20%)	12,000

11.1 Leebase, Stringer and Temple (b)

Turnover

$100_{\text{Leebase}} + 120_{\text{Stringer}}$ = €220 (do not include turnover of associate)

11.2 Preserve, Jam, Marmalade and Honey (a)

Attributable profit

600_{Preserve} + [300_{Jam} @ 75%] + [$240_{\text{Marmalade}}$ @ 75%x 60%] + [540_{Honey} @ 45%]

$600_{\text{Preserve}} + 225_{\text{Jam}} + 108_{\text{Marmalade}} + 243_{\text{Honey}}$ = €1,176

11.3 Hop, Skip and Jump (1) (a)

Turnover: $840_{\text{Hop}} + 510_{\text{Skip}} - 200_{\text{inter-company}}$ =1,150,000

11.4 Hop, Skip and Jump (2) (b)

Cost of sales	**€000**
Hop	630
Skip	375
Duplicate cost of sales in Hop ($200_{\text{inter-company purchases}} - 80_{\text{closing stock}}$)	(120)
Cost of sales in Hop not sold externally	(60)
$80_{\text{remaining in stock}}/200_{\text{inter-company sales}}$ × ($200_{\text{inter-company sales}}$ × $100/133.33)_{\text{inter-company sales at cost}}$	
	825

11.5 Constable, Turner and Whistler (b)

Turnover: $400_{\text{Constable}} + 100_{\text{Turner}}$ = €500 (do not include turnover of associate)

Question	Ans	Workings/explanation
11.6 Stephen, Alison and Hugo	(c)	Transfer to reserves $450_{Stephen} + 270_{Alison\ (90\%)} + 50_{Hugo\ (20\%)} = €\underline{\underline{770}}$

12.1 Gutman and Wilmer (b)

	€000	€000
Proceeds of disposal		5,000
Cost of investment (@ $80\%_{share\ disposed}$)		(2,400)
Profit on disposal in individual accounts of Gutman		2,600
Proceeds of disposal		5,000
Net assets disposed of (6,000 @ $80\%_{share\ disposed}$)		4,800
Profit on disposal in individual accounts of Gutman		200
Reconciling the difference		
Profit in Gutman's individual accounts		2,600
Post-acquisition profits disposed of:		
($4{,}000_{closing\ reserves} - 900_{pre\text{-}acquisition}$)	3,100	
Goodwill amortised ($3{,}000_{cost} - 2{,}900_{net\ assets}$)	(100)	
	3,000	
Group share (@$80\%_{share\ disposed}$)		(2,400)
Group profit on disposal of investment		200

14.1 Colours (d) Blue is not a subsidiary as Colours does not (i) hold more than half of the voting shares (ii) appear to have the right to appoint or remove directors holding a majority of the voting rights at meetings of the board on all, or substantially all, matters

14.2 Easy (a) *W_1: Determining subsidiary relationship → Exercise of (voting) control*

$\frac{505}{1{,}000} = 50.5\%$ →Subsidiary

14.3 Cairo (d) *W_1: Group structure*

Under paragraph 21 FRS 2, a parent undertaking is exempt from preparing consolidated accounts where:

- the group is small or medium sized *and* is not ineligible as defined in Article 6 of the Seventh Directive
- the parent undertaking is wholly owned and its immediate parent is established under the law of an EU member state (provided the parent undertaking has no securities listed on an EU state stock exchange)
- the parent undertaking is a majority-owned subsidiary and meets all the conditions for exemption set out in Article 7 (and elaborated on in Article 8) of the Seventh Directive (i.e., the exempted undertaking and all of its subsidiary undertakings are consolidated in the accounts

of a larger body of undertakings, the parent undertaking of which is governed by the law of a member state; the notes on the annual accounts of the exempted undertaking must disclose the name and registered office of the parent undertaking that draws up the consolidated accounts and the exemption from the obligation to draw up consolidated accounts and a consolidated annual report)

- all the parent undertaking's subsidiary undertakings are permitted or required to be excluded from consolidation under the Seventh Directive

Card does not have to prepare group accounts, as it has no subsidiaries (it only has an investment in an associated undertaking). Cairo is a 100% owned subsidiary and is consolidated into a larger undertaking which prepares consolidated accounts in an EU state, so it does not have to prepare consolidated accounts

14.4 Subsidiary must be excluded (a) Exclusion on the grounds of severe long-term restrictions is *required* under paragraph 25 of FRS 2

14.5 Exclusion of a subsidiary (c) Under paragraph 24 of FRS 2, neither disproportionate expense nor undue delay in obtaining necessary information can justify excluding from consolidation a subsidiary that is material in the context of the group

14.6 Pheasant (c) Paragraph 27, FRS 2 specifies accounting treatment for subsidiaries excluded due to severe long-term restrictions. Such investments should be shown:

(i) at cost if the restrictions were in force when the investment was acquired
(ii) at the equity method on the date restrictions came into force, if after the date of acquisition
(iii) as an associated undertaking using the equity method, if the parent continues to exercise significant influence

14.7 Ant Pheas (d) Paragraph 31, FRS 2 specifies disclosures for excluded subsidiaries, which vary with the reason for exclusion. For all subsidiaries,(i) particulars of the balances between the excluded subsidiary and the rest of the group, (ii) the nature and extent of transactions between the excluded subsidiary and the rest of the group, should be disclosed. In addition, for excluded subsidiaries *not* accounted for using the equity method, (iii) dividends received and receivable from the subsidiary and (iv) particulars of any write-downs of the investment in the subsidiary should also be disclosed

14.8 Control is intended to be temporary (d) Paragraph 29 of FRS 2 specifies the accounting treatment for investments held exclusively with a view to subsequent resale (i.e., control is intended to be temporary) and therefore excluded from consolidation. The investment should be included as a current asset, at the lower of cost and net realisable value

14.9 Activities are so dissimilar (d) Paragraph 30 of FRS 2 specifies accounting treatment for subsidiaries excluded because of different activities and which are therefore incompatible. For different activities, the investment should be included in consolidated accounts using the equity method of accounting. Additional disclosure requirements under FRS 2 for excluded subsidiaries also vary with the reason for exclusion. For subsidiaries excluded because of dissimilar activities, disclosure of their separate financial statements (summarised financial information suffices in some cases) is required

15.1 Polka (d)

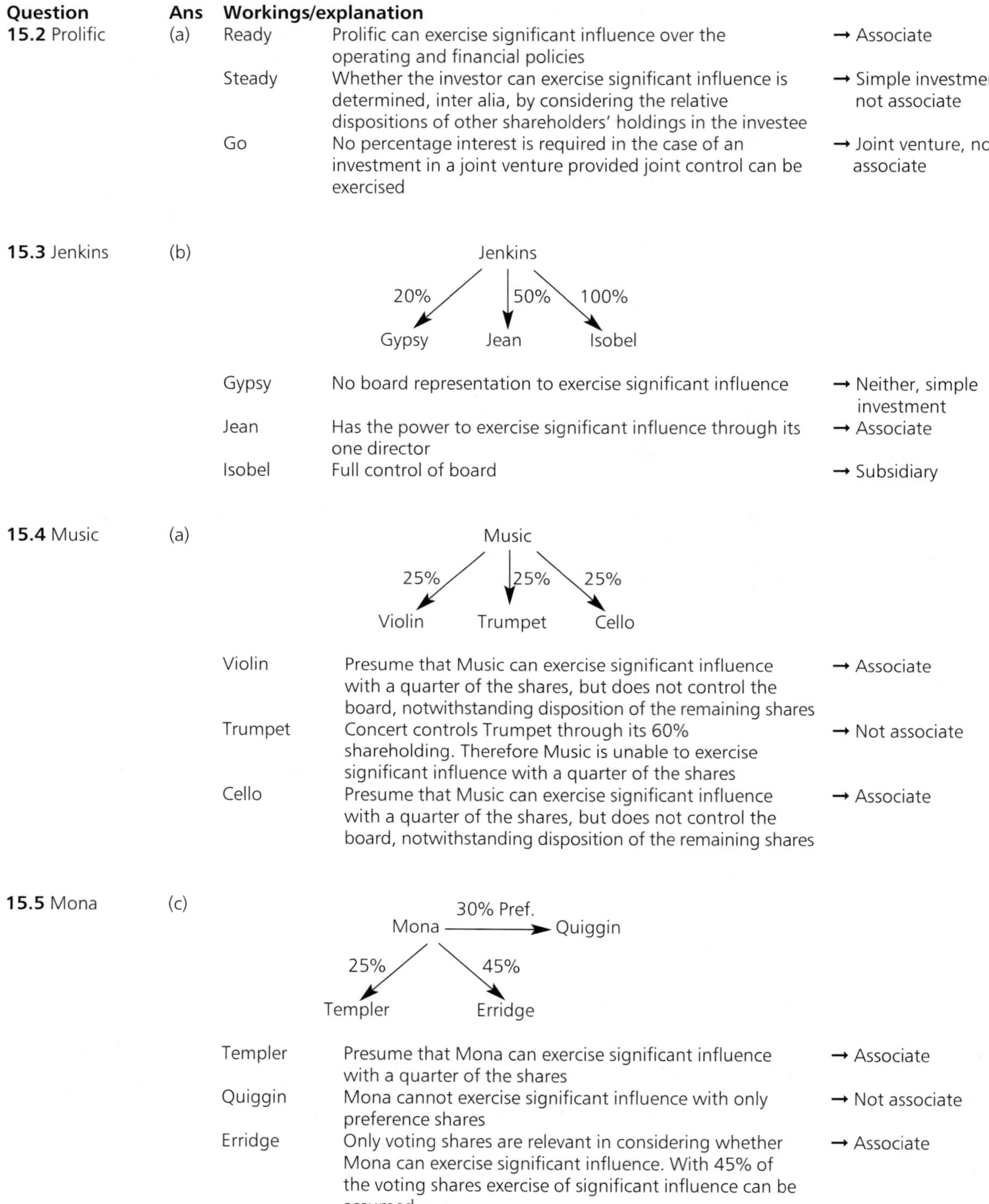

Question	Ans	Workings/explanation		
15.2 Prolific	(a)	Ready	Prolific can exercise significant influence over the operating and financial policies	→ Associate
		Steady	Whether the investor can exercise significant influence is determined, inter alia, by considering the relative dispositions of other shareholders' holdings in the investee	→ Simple investment, not associate
		Go	No percentage interest is required in the case of an investment in a joint venture provided joint control can be exercised	→ Joint venture, not associate

15.3 Jenkins (b)

Gypsy	No board representation to exercise significant influence	→ Neither, simple investment
Jean	Has the power to exercise significant influence through its one director	→ Associate
Isobel	Full control of board	→ Subsidiary

15.4 Music (a)

Violin	Presume that Music can exercise significant influence with a quarter of the shares, but does not control the board, notwithstanding disposition of the remaining shares	→ Associate
Trumpet	Concert controls Trumpet through its 60% shareholding. Therefore Music is unable to exercise significant influence with a quarter of the shares	→ Not associate
Cello	Presume that Music can exercise significant influence with a quarter of the shares, but does not control the board, notwithstanding disposition of the remaining shares	→ Associate

15.5 Mona (c)

Templer	Presume that Mona can exercise significant influence with a quarter of the shares	→ Associate
Quiggin	Mona cannot exercise significant influence with only preference shares	→ Not associate
Erridge	Only voting shares are relevant in considering whether Mona can exercise significant influence. With 45% of the voting shares exercise of significant influence can be assumed	→ Associate

16.1 Macrae (d)

16.2 EU Seventh Directive (a)

16.3 Jump, Hop and Skip (d)

One of the conditions of the Seventh Directive is that the cash value of any non-share consideration does not exceed 10% of the nominal value of the shares issued as part consideration.

Hop

Total consideration	
Equity	€
$300{,}000_{\text{shares}} \div 2_{\text{shares acquired}} \times 3_{\text{shares issued}}$ ($450{,}000_{\text{shares}} \times$ €$2.50_{\text{value per share}}$)	1,125,000
Non-equity (€$40_{\text{debentures}} \times 300{,}000/100$)	120,000
Total	1,245,000

Proportion non-equity to equity consideration:
€$120{,}000_{\text{debentures}}$/€$450{,}000_{\text{nominal value of shares issued}}$ = 26.7% → Condition not met

Skip

Total consideration = $150{,}000_{\text{shares}} \div 3_{\text{shares acquired}} \times 4_{\text{shares issued}}$ ($200{,}000_{\text{shares}} \times$ €$2.50_{\text{value per share}}$) = €500,000 + €60,000 (€$40_{\text{debentures}} \times 150{,}000/100$) = €$560{,}000_{\text{total consideration}}$
Non-equity element of total consideration: €$60{,}000_{\text{debentures}}$/€$100{,}000_{\text{nominal value shares consideration}}$ = 60% → Condition not met

16.4 Mason and Lockwood (a)

Lockwood acquired 92% (644,908/700,000) of the A non-voting restricted shares and 89% (6,231/7,000) of the B voting equity shares of Mason:

- *Seventh Directive*: Even though Lockwood took over 89% of the voting shares, the Seventh Directive rule is 90% of the relevant shares (i.e., equity shares → meaning participative rights to assets and liabilities)
- *FRS 6*: Size condition of FRS 6 appears not to be complied with. The original shareholders in Lockwood now hold 67% more shares in the combined entity than the former shareholders of Mason (Lockwood shareholders are 67% larger, exceeding the limit (which is rebuttable) set down in FRS 6 of 50%)

Voting shares	**000**	**%**
Lockwood	1,000	62.5
New shares issued	600	37.5
	1,600	100.0

16.5 Alleyn and Fox (b)

FRS 6 requires the following to be disclosed for mergers:

- Analysis of principal components of the profit and loss account and of total recognised gains and losses into:
  - post-merger period (combined)
  - period up to the date of merger for each party to the merger
  - previous period for each party to the merger

Applying these disclosure requirements to the question gives the following:

	Alleyn €000	**Fox €000**	**Group €000**	**Explanation**
Pre-merger	25	12	37	Period up to the date of merger for each party
Post-merger	35	28	63	Post-merger period (combined)
	60	40	100	

Question | **Ans** | **Workings/explanation**

16.6 Arm and Leg (a)

Under merger accounting, where the nominal value of the shares issued is greater than the nominal value of the shares acquired, it is necessary to make an adjustment against reserves $12{,}650_{\text{Arm profit}} + 14{,}250_{\text{Leg profit}}$ [$15{,}000$ @ $95\%_{\text{group share}}$] $- 16{,}625_{\text{difference on consolidation}}$ [$83{,}125_{\text{nominal value of shares issued}} - 66{,}500_{\text{nominal value of shares acquired}}$] = €10,275

16.7 Cart and Horse (c)

Under the merger method of accounting assets and liabilities are recorded in group accounts at their book values in the subsidiary undertaking's financial statements, i.e., €300,000

16.8 Matisse and Goldfish (b)

16.9 Orange and Peach (c)

Orange €400,000$_{\text{profit for year}}$ + Peach €342,000 [€360,000$_{\text{profit for year}}$ × 95%] = €742,000

16.10 Beef and Gravy (b)

Acquisition method: $132{,}000_{\text{Beef}}$ + [$90{,}000_{\text{Gravy}} \times 11_{\text{months}}/12_{\text{months}}$ =82,500] = €214,500
Merger method: $132{,}000_{\text{Beef}} + 90{,}000_{\text{Gravy}}$ = €222,000

17.1 Road and Street (b)

Fair value is 'the amount at which an asset or liability could be exchanged in an arm's length transaction between informed and willing parties, other than in a forced or liquidation sale'. (FRS 7, paragraph 2). In this case it is the realisable value of €350,000

17.2 FRS 10 (b)

17.3 Rook (d)

($110{,}000_{\text{purchase consideration}}$ – [$10{,}000_{\text{patents}} + 69{,}000_{\text{plant}} + 15{,}000_{\text{net current assets}}$] = €16,000)

18.1 Olive and Oil (a)

$200,000 ÷ 2.60 = €76,923

18.2 Diver and Shultz (c)

Shultz	**CHF**	**Rate**	**€**
Net assets	1,725	2.3	750
Ordinary share capital	720	2.4	300
Pre-acquisition profits	288	2.4	120
Post-acquisition profits	717	Bal	330
	1,725		750

Include $80\%_{\text{group share}}$ of post-acquisition reserves, i.e., 330 @ 80% = 264,000
Consolidated reserves: $540{,}000_{\text{Diver}} + 264{,}000_{\text{Shultz}}$ = €804,000

18.3 Pete and Schmidt (b)

Schmidt	**CHF**	**Rate**	**€**
Net assets	780	2.4	325
Ordinary share capital	500	2.5	200
Pre-acquisition profits	120	2.5	48
Post-acquisition profits	160	Bal	77
	780		325

Include $75\%_{\text{group share}}$ of post-acquisition reserves, i.e., 77 @ 75% = 57,750
Consolidated reserves: $570{,}000_{\text{Pete}} + 57{,}750_{\text{Schmidt}}$ = €627,750

18.4 Harold and Magath (c)

Difference on retranslating opening net assets [previously translated at opening rate] at closing rate

		€000
Net assets S80,960 translated at opening exchange rate	÷ 3.45	23,467
Net assets S80,960 translated at closing exchange rate	÷ 3.80	21,305
		(2,162)

Difference on retranslating retained profit [previously translated at average rate] at closing rate

Retained profit S3,230 translated at closing exchange rate*	÷ 3.80	850
Retained profit S3,230 translated at average exchange rate*	÷ 3.70	873
Total exchange loss in Harold's consolidated accounts = 1,748 ([2,162 + 23] @ $80\%_{\text{group share}}$)		(23)

* Dividends paid are usually translated at the actual rate applying when the dividends are paid by the parent – the model solution here assumes the dividends paid are translated at average rate

18.5 Jack and Cantona (c)

18.6 Wren and Bald Eagle (d)

18.7 Clark (c) *Closing rate/net investment method*: €77,000 (per Q)
Temporal method: $10{,}000_{\text{investments @ current rate}} + 14{,}000_{\text{stock@ historic rate}} + 62{,}000_{\text{plant @ historic rate}} =$ €86,000

19.1 Wood (d) (i) return on investment; (iii) investing activity; (iv) does not affect cash flow

19.2 Sceptre (d)
(i) Revaluation of tangible fixed assets is a non-cash item. However, it is a non-operating item and therefore would not affect the reconciliation of operating profit to net cash inflow/outflow
(ii) Changes in provisions for warranties affect operating profit but do not have cash flow implications, i.e. they are non-cash items. Consequently, they should be adjusted for in the reconciliation of operating profit to net cash inflow/outflow

19.3 Gough (d)

19.4 Newtown (d)

19.5 Dividends paid to minority (b) $€265{,}000_{\text{opening balance}} + €112{,}000_{\text{profit and loss}} - €284{,}000_{\text{closing balance}} = €93{,}000_{\text{dividends paid}}$
Or

Minority interest

Dividends paid (balance)	*93,000*	1 April 20X3 Bal b/d	265,000
31 March 20X4 Bal c/d	284,000	Profit and loss account 20X4	112,000
	377,000		377,000

19.6 Geoffrey (a) €9,000
$€220{,}000_{\text{opening balance}} + €20{,}000_{\text{profit and loss}} + €25{,}000_{\text{minority share of revaluation surplus}} - €6{,}000_{\text{minority share of exchange loss}} - €250{,}000_{\text{closing balance}} = €9{,}000_{\text{dividends paid}}$
Or

Minority interest

Dividends paid (balance)	*9,000*	1 Jan. 20X9 Bal b/d	220,000
Exchange loss ($9{,}000_{\text{group share}} \times 40_{\text{minority share}}/60_{\text{group share}}$)	6,000	Profit and loss account 20X9	20,000
31 Dec. 20X9 Bal c/d	250,000	Revaluation surplus	25,000
	265,000		265,000

Question	Ans	Workings/explanation
19.7 Tom and Harry	(b)	Acquisitions: $180{,}000_{\text{cash paid}} - 20{,}000_{\text{cash acquired}}$

Question	Ans	Workings/explanation	€000
19.8 Clare, Jim and Tim	(d)	Opening stock at 1.1.X9 ($1{,}800_{\text{Clare}} + 460_{\text{Tim}}$)	2,260
		Acquired with Jim (i.e., at 1.4.X9)	350
		Closing stock 31.12.X9 ($2{,}000_{\text{Clare}} + 360_{\text{Jim}} + 500_{\text{Tim}}$)	(2,860)
		Increase in stock	250

19.9 Elwin and Dunn (b) Under the merger method, the change in cash is for the whole year, irrespective of when the merger occurred

	€000
Closing cash at 1.10.X8 ($420_{\text{Elwin}} + 380_{\text{Dunn}}$)	800
Opening cash at 30.9.X9 ($250_{\text{Elwin}} + 240_{\text{Dunn}}$)	(490)
Increase in cash	310

19.10 Dividends received from associated undertaking (a) $96{,}000_{\text{opening balance}} + 82{,}000_{\text{share of associate's profit}} - 30{,}000_{\text{share of associate's tax}} - 120{,}000_{\text{closing balance}} = 28{,}000_{\text{dividends paid}}$

Investment in associate

	€		€
1 April 20X3 Bal b/d	96,000	Taxation of associate 20X4	30,000
Share of profit of associate 20X4	82,000	*Dividends paid (balance)*	*28,000*
		31 March 20X4 Bal c/d	120,000
	265,000		265,000

Question	Ans
20.1 Quasi-subsidiary	(c)
20.2 How quasi-subsidiaries are to be accounted for	(d)
20.3 Disclose which of the following	(c)
20.4 Disclosure requirements of SSAP 25	(a)
20.5 Disclosure requirements of IAS 14	(a)

Appendix 2

Professional accounting pronouncements at December 2002

UK GAAP

SSAPs in force

4 The Accounting Treatment of Government Grants
5 Accounting for Value Added Tax
9 Stocks and Long-term Contracts
13 Accounting for Research and Development
17 Accounting for Post-balance Sheet Events
19 Accounting for Investment Properties
20 Foreign Currency Translation
21 Accounting for Leases and Hire Purchase Contracts
25 Segmental Reporting

FRSs in force

Foreword to Accounting Standards
1 Cash Flow Statements
2 Accounting for Subsidiary Undertakings
3 Reporting Financial Performance
4 Capital Instruments
5 Reporting the Substance of Transactions
6 Acquisitions and Mergers
7 Fair Values in Acquisition Accounting
8 Related Party Disclosures
9 Associates and Joint Ventures
10 Goodwill and Intangible Assets
11 Impairment of Fixed Assets and Goodwill
12 Provisions, Contingent Liabilities and Contingent Assets
13 Derivatives and Other Financial Instruments: Disclosures
14 Earnings Per Share
15 Tangible Fixed Assets
16 Current Tax
17 Retirement Benefits
18 Accounting Policies
19 Deferred Tax

UITF Abstracts in force

Foreword to UITF Abstracts
4 Presentation of Long-term Debtors in Current Assets
5 Transfers from Current Assets to Fixed Assets

9 Accounting for Operations in Hyper-inflationary Economies
11 Capital Instruments: Issuer Call Options
13 Accounting for ESOP Trusts
15 Disclosure of Substantial Acquisitions
17 Employee Share Schemes
19 Tax on Gains and Losses on Foreign Currency Borrowings that Hedge an Investment in a Foreign Enterprise
21 Accounting Issues arising from the Proposed Introduction of the Euro
22 The Acquisition of a Lloyd's Business
23 Application of the Transitional Rules in FRS 15
24 Accounting for Start-up Costs
25 National Insurance Contributions on Share Option Gains
26 Barter Transactions for Advertising
27 Revisions to Estimates of the Useful Economic Life of Goodwill and Intangible Assets
28 Operating Lease Incentives
29 Website Development Costs
30 Date of Award to Employees of Shares or Rights to Shares
31 Exchanges of Businesses or Other Non-monetary Assets for an Interest in a Subsidiary, Joint Venture or Associate
32 Employee Benefit Trusts and Other Intermediate Payment Arrangements
33 Obligations in Capital Instruments
34 Pre-contract Costs
35 Death-in-service and Incapacity Benefits

(*Note*: UITF abstracts not listed have been withdrawn.)

IAS GAAP

IASs in force

1 Presentation of Financial Statements
2 Inventories
7 Cash Flow Statements
8 Net Profit or Loss for the Period, Fundamental Errors and Changes in Accounting Policies
10 Events after the Balance Sheet Date
11 Construction Contracts
12 Income Taxes
14 Segment Reporting
15 Information Reflecting the Effects of Changing Prices
16 Property, Plant and Equipment
17 Leases
18 Revenue
19 Employee Benefits
20 Accounting for Government Grants and Disclosure of Government Assistance
21 The Effects of Changes in Foreign Exchange Rates
22 Business Combinations
23 Borrowing Costs
24 Related Party Disclosures
26 Accounting and Reporting by Retirement Benefit Plans
27 Consolidated Financial Statements and Accounting for Investments in Subsidies
28 Accounting for Investments in Associates
29 Financial Reporting in Hyperinflationary Economies
30 Disclosures in the Financial Statements of Banks and Similar Financial Institutions
31 Financial Reporting of Interests in Joint Ventures
32 Financial Instruments: Disclosure and Presentation
33 Earnings Per Share
34 Interim Financial Reporting
35 Discontinuing Operations

36 Impairment of Assets
37 Provisions, Contingent Liabilities and Contingent Assets
38 Intangible Assets
39 Financial Instruments: Recognition and Measurement
40 Investment Property
41 Agriculture

SICs in force

1 Consistency – Different Cost Formulas for Inventories
2 Consistency – Capitalisation of Borrowing Costs
3 Elimination of Unrealised Profits and Losses on Transactions with Associates
5 Classification of Financial Instruments – Contingent Settlement Provisions
6 Costs of Modifying Existing Software
7 Introduction of the Euro
8 First-time Application of IASs as the Primary Basis of Accounting
9 Business Combinations – Classification either as Acquisitions or Unitings of Interests
10 Government Assistance – No Specific Relation to Operating Activities
11 Foreign Exchange – Capitalisation of Losses Resulting from Severe Currency Devaluations
12 Consolidation – Special Purpose Entities
13 Jointly Controlled Entities – Non-monetary Contributions by Venturers
14 Property, Plant and Equipment – Compensation for the Impairment or Loss of Items
15 Operating Leases – Incentives
16 Share Capital – Reacquired Own Equity Instruments (Treasury Shares)
17 Equity – Costs of an Equity Transaction
18 Consistency – Alternative Methods
19 Reporting Currency – Measurement and Presentation of Financial Statements under IAS 21 and IAS 29
20 Equity Accounting Method – Recognition of Losses
21 Income Taxes – Recovery of Revalued Non-depreciable Assets
22 Business Combinations – Subsequent Adjustment of Fair Values and Goodwill Initially Reported
23 Property, Plant and Equipment – Major Inspection or Overhaul Costs
24 Earnings Per Share – Financial Instruments and Other Contracts that may be Settled in Shares
25 Income Taxes – Changes in the Tax Status of an Enterprise or its Shareholders
27 Evaluating the Substance of Transactions in the Legal Form of a Lease
28 Business Combinations – 'Date of Exchange' and Fair Value of Equity Instruments
29 Disclosure – Service Concession Arrangements
30 Reporting Currency – Translation from Measurement Currency to Presentation Currency
31 Revenue – Barter Transactions Involving Advertising Services
32 Intangible Assets – Website Costs
33 Consolidation and Equity Method – Potential Voting Rights and Allocation of Ownership Interests

Bibliography

Alexander, D. and Archer, S. (eds.) *Miller European Accounting Guide*, Fourth Edition, Aspen Law & Business, New York.

Barker, P. and Ó hÓgartaigh, C. 1998. *Accounting for Groups: Theory and Practice*, Oak Tree Press, Dublin.

Cairns, D. and Nobes, C. 2000. *The Convergence Handbook: A Comparison between International Accounting Standards and UK Financial Reporting Requirements*, Institute of Chartered Accountants in England and Wales, London.

Chitty, D. 1998. *Model Group Financial Statements*, Accountancy Books, London.

Connor, L., Dekker, P., Davies, M., Robinson, P. and Wilson, A. 2001. *IAS/UK GAAP Comparison*, Ernst & Young, London.

Davies, M., Paterson, R. and Wilson, A. 1999. *UK GAAP*, 6th edition, Ernst & Young and Butterworths Tolley, London.

Dodge, R. 1996. *Group Financial Statements*, International Thompson Business Press, London.

European Commission. 1978. *Fourth Council Directive 78/660/EEC of 25 July 1978 based on Article 54 (3) (g) of the Treaty on the Annual Accounts of Certain Types of Companies*, European Commission, Brussels. Also available at http://forum.europa.eu.int/irc/dsis/bmethods/info/data/new/legislation/4th_directive.html

European Commission. 1983. *Seventh Council Directive 83/349/EEC of 13 June 1983 based on the Article 54 (3) (g) of the Treaty on Consolidated Accounts*, European Commission, Brussels. Also available at http://forum.europa.eu.int/irc/dsis/bmethods/info/data/new/legislation/7th_directive.html

European Commission. 2000. *EU Financial Reporting Strategy: The Way Forward*, European Commission, Brussels. Also available at http://europa.eu.int/comm/internal_market/en/company/account/news/ias.htm

Gray, S. J. and Needles, B. E. 1999. 'Intercompany investments, consolidated financial statements, and foreign currency accounting' in *Financial Accounting: A Global Approach*, Houghton Mifflin Company, Boston.

International Accounting Standards Board. 2002. *International Accounting Standards 2002*, International Accounting Standards Board, London.

Martindale, W. G. 1985. *Consolidated Accounts*, Jurispublications, London.

Nobes, C. 1996. 'EC group accounting – two zillion ways to do it', in Blake, J. and Hossain, M. (eds) *Readings in International Accounting*, International Thompson Business Press, London.

Nobes, C. (ed.) 2000. *GAAP 2000 – A Survey of National Accounting Rules in 53 Countries*, PricewaterhouseCoopers, London.

PricewaterhouseCoopers. 2000. *International Accounting Standards Similarities and Differences IAS, US GAAP and UK GAAP*, PricewaterhouseCoopers, London.

Swinson, C. 1993. *Group Accounting*, Butterworths, London.

Taylor, P. A. 1996. *Consolidated Financial Reporting*, Paul Chapman Publishing, London.

Index